Date Due

Latin American

Peasant Movements

LATIN AMERICAN
PEASANT MOVEMENTS

EDITED BY

Henry A. Landsberger

CORNELL UNIVERSITY PRESS

Ithaca and London

First published 1969

Standard Book Number 8014-0524-6

Library of Congress Catalog Card Number 74-87020

PRINTED IN THE UNITED STATES OF AMERICA
BY KINGSPORT PRESS, INC.

Preface

The important role played by the industrial working class since the end of the nineteenth century may well be assumed in this latter part of the twentieth century by the peasantry of some of the developing countries. The misery of their rural populations reflects the painfully slow growth of these countries in much the same way as the plight of the urban proletariat followed the perhaps too rapid transformations of western Europe and North America a century ago.

And like the factory worker of the past, the peasant of today shows an increasing readiness to organize or to be organized from the outside. For while Marx and other nineteenth-century intellectual revolutionaries looked to the industrial working class as the great motor of history which would end the capitalist era and give birth to the new socialist society, a substantial group of his followers now see the peasantry as fulfilling that function. Like Marx, and even more like Lenin, this particular group of latter-day Marxists envisages intellectuals as leaders in bringing the "revolutionary mass" to a conscious recognition of its mission. But as distinct from both Marx and Lenin, they do not regard the urban working classes to be that "revolutionary mass." Those who anticipate profound changes (and those who fear them) have ceased to look, as they did two generations ago, to the post-Napoleonic unrest in Britain's new industrial cities, or to the Paris Commune of 1870, or to the soldier-worker soviets of Leningrad in 1917, as harbingers of things to come. Today's precedents are the Chinese revolution and, for Latin America, the Cuban revolution, in which the peasantry had some role, although it is still being debated, while the industrial working class had practically none.

The rising importance of the peasantry is indeed most striking in Latin America, and it is not surprising that a species of peasant-oriented Marxism should be so much in vogue there. Throughout this century peasant unrest has been endemic in many parts of the region despite attempts to repress it. In fact, such unrest can in many cases—those of Mexico and Peru, for example—be traced back to the nineteenth century and even earlier, to times when economic protest was fused with a more general

v

resistance to the Spanish invader, who not only usurped economic rights but also imposed a foreign political and cultural system.

But in the nineteenth century the peasant was for the most part on the defensive, and generally unsuccessfully so. Particularly during the latter half of the century, with the triumph of liberal philosophies and of laissez-faire economics, vast areas of land held communally since pre-Columbian times were divided up. As the ownership of the land became concentrated in the hands of fewer and fewer private owners, cultivators who had previously been independent were forced to become landless laborers on the new haciendas.[1] This process naturally led to resistance, sometimes violent. But it was repressed with even greater violence.

The tide started to turn, as we realize in retrospect, with the beginning of the Mexican Revolution. Emiliano Zapata's Plan of Ayala of November, 1911, demanding the restitution of *ejido* land and also envisaging the expropriation of large haciendas per se in cases where villagers had no land, may well be regarded as the beginning of a new era. But it is not an era which has come either fast or easily. Even in Mexico, peasants did not win their battle for land on a large scale until the presidency of Lázaro Cárdenas in the 1930's, twenty-five years after the beginning of the revolution, and no other Latin American country followed suit until the Bolivian revolution of 1952.

From 1952 onward, however, organized peasant unrest—actual, threatened, or feared; successful or unsuccessful; spontaneous or provoked—has been a major factor in Latin American politics. While the Guatemalan coup by Castillo Armas was, among other things, a defeat for peasant aspirations, the 1958 overthrow of Pérez Jiménez in Venezuela initiated a period of great advancement, for which the Acción Democrática party had previously laid the groundwork during its "triennium" in power between 1945 and 1948. Then came the triumph of Castro's rural-based "guerrillas" in Cuba, followed by the inauguration of the Alliance for Progress through the Charter of Punta del Este, with its reference to "comprehensive agrarian reform" and the "transformation of unjust structures and systems of land tenure."[2] Finally, in the sixties, land reform

---

[1] In Mexico, for example, it was estimated that by the end of the Díaz dictatorship in 1910, about 1 per cent of the population owned about 70 per cent of the country's land. See International Labour Office, *Indigenous Peoples* (Studies and Reports, New Series, No. 35 [Geneva, 1953]), pp. 298–299.

[2] These quotations are from Title I, Section 6, of the Charter, which appears, together with the Declaration, in an anonymous article, "The American Republics Establish an Alliance for Progress," *Department of State Bulletin* (Washington, D.C.: U.S. Department of State), XLV, No. 1159 (Sept., 1961), 462–469.

programs have been formally adopted by Chile, Ecuador, Peru, Colombia, and Brazil, after a good deal of peasant unrest in the latter three countries. And where substantial peasant organizations did not exist before agrarian reform—as they did not, for example, in Chile—they established themselves, or were established, together with the reform program itself. Open or below the surface, threatening or repressed, before land reform or after, as members of the establishment or in opposition to it, peasant movements are part of the Latin American scene today.

Peasant movements are of great theoretical interest when seen as a special example of collective action by economically, politically, and culturally deprived groups attempting to improve their status. Approached from this point of view, peasant movements may be expected to share certain characteristics with the movements of other low-status groups— with industrial workers at the beginning of the industrial revolution, for example, or with Negroes in the United States today. At least, all three face some common dilemmas, even if each group solves them differently. Are outside leadership and alliances with other groups necessary, and what are their consequences? What happens when the peaceful use of legal means brings no results? Under what conditions do movements spring into life, since the underlying conditions of deprivation have presumably been present for some time?

Recognizing these intriguing similarities, Cornell University's Latin American program, its New York State School of Industrial and Labor Relations, and the program known as the Cornell Latin American Year generously supported the editor's plans to organize a seminar on Latin American peasant movements. The Land Tenure Center of the University of Wisconsin contributed by defraying the expenses of some participants. The conference was held on the Cornell campus between December 8 and 10, 1966. Apart from the contributors to this volume, the seminar was also attended by Mrs. Gelia Castillo of the University of the Philippines; Gennady Kuropiatnik, then a staff member of the Social Affairs Division, United Nations; Andrew Pearse of the Institute for Research and Training in Agrarian Reform, a United Nations Special Fund Project located in Santiago; and Rodolfo Stavenhagen of the National University of Mexico. Almost all the participants in the seminar had conducted research on a particular Latin American peasant movement.

This book contains the essays presented and discussed during the seminar. The authors were invited not only to describe the movements which they had studied but also to analyze them, using for this purpose a brief framework and a series of hypotheses formulated by the editor. The first chapter of this volume is an expanded version of the materials sent to the authors prior to the seminar. Further work on these hypotheses and their application to areas other than Latin America is in progress under the editorship of the author in cooperation with the International Institute for Labour and Social Studies in Geneva, Switzerland.

The chief purpose of the present volume on peasant movements is, therefore, to begin to remedy for at least one sociocultural area, Latin America, the almost total absence of literature on a topic both of current concern and of theoretical interest. Astonishing as it may seem, no major study of even one of the recent Latin American peasant movements, as distinct from books on peasant communities and societies or on agrarian and tenure problems, is easily available. Even articles on individual movements are quite scarce, at least in English.

By asking our contributors to adhere as closely as possible to a framework, we hope to have taken a step, beyond merely providing case materials, toward answering some basic questions that pertain to any movement of a low-status group: From what sectors of the peasantry—for example, lower strata or better-off sections—is the membership of peasant movements drawn? Who tend to be the leaders—are they peasants and, if so, what kind of peasants? If not peasants, who are they? What changes in general social structure, and specifically in agrarian structure, tend to precede peasant movements? What determines the means and methods adopted by peasant movements—for example, the choice of violence or petition? Who, if anyone, tends to be the ally of peasants, and who their enemy? How explicit and how radical are the ideologies sustained by peasant movements? Finally, under what circumstances are peasant movements successful in surviving as organizations and in achieving their goals?

A word, finally, on the sequence and coverage of the papers. Very roughly, they have been arranged from the most successful movement to the least successful. The book therefore begins with an analysis of the Federación Campesina de Venezuela, proceeds to essays on Mexico, Bolivia, and Chile, and ends with case studies of Guatemala and Brazil. There are two chapters on Peru: one describes the general situation of peasant organizations in that country today, and the other recounts the best-known case, that of La Convención Valley. Chapter 9 is a study of the manifold peasant organizations active in northeastern Brazil before the March, 1964, military takeover. The last paper does not deal with peasant movements as such, but rather with the great variety of mechanisms, both economic and political, which are used against them. While it is based principally on experiences in Brazil, the mechanisms discussed are quite common in many other regions of Latin America, and the paper is in that sense generic. Finally, a bibliography on peasant organization has been assembled which is intended to supplement rather than catalog the references made in the text.

Henry A. Landsberger

Chapel Hill, North Carolina
November 10, 1968

Contents

Latin American
Peasant Movements

1. The Role of Peasant Movements and Revolts in Development*

HENRY A. LANDSBERGER

Department of Sociology
University of North Carolina at Chapel Hill

Peasant Movements: The Problem of Their Definition

Truly important social phenomena are never easy to delimit empirically, nor is it easy to define theoretically the concepts which those interested in analyzing these phenomena have formulated around them. "Nation," "class," "authority," "values," "motives"—about all of these there is doubt. One who wished to undertake a cross-cultural study of "the middle class" would be faced with such questions of classification as whether a certain group of lower government bureaucrats in a country should be regarded as part of its middle class or not. At the level of theory, argument has never ceased over whether the concept of class should be based on ownership of property or whether it should be based on the control of power, whether resting on property or not. These and similar ambiguities both of classification and of meaning surround all

important concepts, but they can often be converted into fruitful empirical questions and hypotheses.

The Peasant

By tradition and usage there are certain areas of agreement on what a peasant is. The first characteristic most widely regarded as typical is that

---

* The material for this chapter was prepared in connection with a comparative study of peasant movements and revolts being undertaken by the International Institute for Labor Studies (IILS), Geneva, Switzerland. It is published here with the permission of the IILS. A somewhat shortened version is included in IILS *Bulletin*, No. 4, February, 1968.

In an earlier form, the chapter was helpfully criticized by participants in two seminars: one sponsored by the Agricultural Development Council at the University of Wisconsin in October 1966, and the other sponsored by the New York State School of Industrial and Labor Relations and the Latin American Program at Cornell University in December, 1966, at the latter of which earlier drafts of the other papers contained in this book were also presented.

the peasant is a "rural cultivator," someone who himself shares in the actual work on the land and is very close to it.[1]

A second characteristic, also widely agreed upon, is that the peasant has a dual orientation, to family and to market. He does not view his position merely from an economic point of view, as if he were running a business for maximum profit with all inputs and outputs valued at market prices. Rather, the peasant sees himself as, and in fact is, part of a familial household. This household affords him additional labor services which have no real market price. On the other hand, he must try to provide subsistence for his household at all costs; he cannot discharge its labor even when its retention is uneconomic.

Whenever man lives as a member of an extended family, the community—a geographic area consisting of several families who share many norms and institutions—is also likely to play an important role in his life. Hence many writers like to include a reference to the community in their definition of the concept "peasant." We might regard this as a third characteristic, albeit one less universally agreed upon.

A fourth characteristic of the peasant is his subordinate position in a hierarchical economic and political order. This point distinguishes him from members of primitive tribes. The peasant's subordinate position has the critically important result that a greater or lesser share of his effort is appropriated by others. This characteristic may be regarded either as part of the fourth or as separate. The particular form of the appropriation is unimportant at this general level. The essence is that the person who appropriates from the peasant does so beyond any service he or his class has performed, and that he is able to exact his appropriation through control of the political system—the state, the law, and ultimately force.

Some students of peasants and peasant movements have been concerned to set certain limits or make certain exclusions with respect to the term. Some prefer not to speak of "peasants" unless the group constitutes a substantial proportion of the total population of the society concerned, or in other words, unless the society as a whole can be characterized as being substantially a "peasant society." This does not imply that such a society may not include other groups of great importance—landowners most obviously, but perhaps also a rising urban commercial class, a growing state bureaucracy, clergy, a political or military elite, and others. The purpose of thus limiting the concept "peasant" is to avoid the simultaneous analysis of situations which are very dissimilar and

---

[1] Eric R. Wolf, *Peasants* (Englewood Cliffs, N.J.: Prentice-Hall, 1966), p. 1.

thus possibly noncomparable. In principle, this point is analogous to saying that a comparison may not be useful between the British Trade Union Congress, based on a work force which is almost 40 per cent industrial, and the labor movement of a Central American country whose industrial work force may not reach 8 per cent.

There have also been proposals to exclude hired labor from the category of "peasants," particularly labor on modern business- and market-oriented plantations. This exclusion is also based on an a priori impression that the position of such a group, and hence of any movement it is likely to establish, would be so different from that of peasants with substantial managerial responsibility or with more permanent links to a specific piece of land that comparisons are unlikely to yield profound insights.

Indeed, a more restricted definition of peasants would include only those rural cultivators who own the land on which they work, or at least a substantial part of it, thus excluding sharecroppers.[2] An even tighter restriction would limit peasants to those of medieval or early modern Europe, arguing once again that even present-day societies that are somewhat similar to feudal Europe and are often called "feudal," like those in parts of Latin America, differ so profoundly from the European feudal situation as to make the analogy misleading.

The criteria which should guide a student in formulating a conceptual definition in any field and in delimiting at the practical level the kinds of phenomena he wishes to study are themselves a subject of profound discussion in the field of epistemology.[3] Those of us who are not versed in this branch of philosophy but are nevertheless forced to make decisions about definitions often find it difficult even to know how to come to grips with the problem before us.

Those who incline toward a rather broad definition of the concept "peasant" and thus toward the inclusion of phenomena which may appear to be rather different are able to advance several arguments. First, a broad concept and wide coverage are useful when one prefers not to assert the existence of important differences on an a priori basis, but rather to leave the discovery of such differences to empirical research, after which the exclusions that seem reasonable can still be made. Whether or not move-

[2] Eric R. Wolf, in his "Types of Latin American Peasantry: A Preliminary Discussion" (*American Anthropologist*, LVII, No. 3 [1955], 452–471), was inclined to limit the term to those who owned the land they cultivated. In his latest work Wolf makes no such limitation; indeed, even rural laborers do not seem to be explicitly excluded.

[3] See, for example, Max Black's "Definition, Presupposition, and Assertion," in his *Problems of Analysis* (Ithaca, N.Y.: Cornell University Press, 1954), pp. 24–45.

ments of hired workers have, for example, different goals from the movements of smallholders is precisely what one might wish to clarify through empirical investigation, rather than assuming it to be true at the outset.

Second, it might be argued that even if important differences did exist, there is nothing wrong with uncovering them, thereby recognizing that there are subtypes within a rather broad category. Thus, even if it were true that laborers always ask for better wages and never for agrarian reform while tenants and smallholders always do ask for agrarian reform, why not establish and work with these differences?

A third argument is that the existence of important differences in one respect, for example in the relation of rural cultivators to land and its consequences, by no means precludes similarities in other important respects. Thus all peasants might have relatively little education and organizational ability, with the result that leadership often comes from outside the peasantry. In other words, perhaps we should not accept too readily the oft-repeated scientific adage that generalizations about very unlike phenomena are bound to be too general and therefore platitudinous. Let us find the generalization first and then weigh it.

A fourth argument is that even a reduced, supposedly homogeneous phenomenon (say, peasant movements limited to feudal Europe) may contain greater differences than those which distinguish it from excluded phenomena. Is English fourteenth-century feudalism really so much more similar to nineteenth-century Russian feudalism than to the present-day Andean systems? Is a sharecropper who is told exactly what to plant and when to plant it, who does not own his tools and has no security of tenure, really much more different from a hired laborer than he is from even a sharecropper with some security of tenure?

Finally, there is the problem that "laborer," "tenant," and "owner" are statuses which individuals may and do occupy simultaneously, making it impossible to place them in one or another category exclusively.[4] Indeed, this simultaneous occupancy of different statuses, all relatively low, may be critical to understanding the nature of the peasant movement which a group of such individuals establishes.

For all these rather practical reasons, we favor here a broad definition

[4] See, for example, Chapter 10, and Inter-American Committee for Agricultural Development (CIDA), *Land Tenure Conditions and Socio-economic Development of the Agricultural Sector: Brazil* (Washington, D.C.: Pan American Union, 1966), especially ch. 4, sec. C, "The Complexity and Polyvalent Nature of Farm Work," pp. 178–193.

of "peasant" as being a rural cultivator of low economic and political status. We shall regard even the matter of exploitation as something that should be empirically investigated. There is little doubt that exploitation is the natural consequence of low economic and political status, but it need not be built into the definition.

Altogether, instead of thinking in terms of whether certain persons are peasants or not, it is more convenient to think in terms of certain continuous characteristics, or "variables." These might include political status, security of land occupancy, managerial responsibility, family and community orientation, and exploitation. One would then investigate empirically the extent to which these variables or dimensions correlate with each other, the extent to which they are correlated with certain characteristics of the larger social structure, and what consequences they have for the characteristics of the resulting peasant movements.

In epistemological terms, we propose to move away from arguing what the essence of a certain holistic phenomenon, the peasant, "really" is. Instead we prefer to analyze the correlates of either one or, if we wish, of a group of variables which are relatively more easy to define conceptually and also easier to make operational, that is, to measure. The important ones are outlined in the following paragraphs. We do not assume and define from the outset that certain variables are positively correlated—for example, that low status and exploitation go together by definition. But we are perfectly ready to establish a correlation empirically. We propose to focus on the combination of the two variables "low economic and political status" and find out what their correlates are. The concept "peasant" thus becomes a quality—almost an adjective—which a certain individual or group may possess to a greater or lesser extent and which, logically at least, does not preclude its also possessing certain other qualities. Some of these will be highly related to each other while others will be little or not at all related, in the same way that a tall person is more likely to be heavy than light but is not more likely to be intelligent than stupid.

Economic Status

To assess the economic status of a rural cultivator, the following are the aspects to take into account:

1. Which of the resources (for example, land, water, tools) that the peasant needs as a cultivator does he own, and how much of each resource does he own?

2. How securely does he own these resources, particularly in the case of

land? Is it his for only a limited period after he clears it? Is his title dubious? Does he have an annual lease or a longer lease? We are thus recommending that the distinction between ownership and tenancy not be regarded as absolute, but as part of a single continuum of "security-insecurity" of control over a given resource.

3. To the extent that the peasant does not own the necessary resources, how much more difficult and expensive is it for him to acquire them than for higher-status individuals? Does he pay higher prices for food, land, fertilizers, credit, or hired labor than do others?

4. To what extent does the peasant control, that is, make decisions about and manage, the resources he owns or has acquired, deciding what crops to plant, how to organize his work and when to do it, and the like?

5. In selling his output, to what extent is the net price he receives made less favorable than that received by others, by his having to sell to the landowner or to the lender, by his having to pay taxes, and so on?

Points 1 to 3 concern inputs, 4 the transformation process of these inputs, and 5 the output of the productive unit. The total economic status of the peasant might then be conceived of as some kind of average of his standing on each of these aspects. But no doubt discrepancies or incongruities in status will often be important in accounting for some characteristic of a peasant movement, in which case the calculation of an "average" would obscure rather than clarify.[5]

This list of dimensions allows us to "scale" two important situations somewhat better than might appear at first glance. First, it does cover the situation of the agricultural laborer as someone who, in that capacity at least, neither owns any inputs (points 1 and 2) nor acquires or manages them (points 3 and 4). All these by definition imply a low status. But for various reasons, political or economic, the agricultural laborer may be well remunerated for his labor (point 5) and thus not be so low in status after all. This is the case on some modern plantations, where his status may not be extremely depressed. Secondly, the quasi serf, obliged to render labor services and also to have his family contribute personal labor, is appropriately placed low, since this implies that he does not control securely much of the labor services he needs (points 1 and 2), is not free to decide when to use the labor resources he supposedly does control

[5] John S. and Leatrice MacDonald, using a schema similar in purpose though different in kind to that proposed above, account for differences in the militancy of nineteenth-century and early twentieth-century Italian peasantry by analyzing the various status subdimensions separately. See their very suggestive "Institutional Economics and Rural Development: Two Italian Types," *Human Organization*, XXIII, No. 2 (Summer, 1964), 113–118.

(point 4), and probably pays an exorbitant price (via his labor services) for the land he is allowed to cultivate (point 3).[6] These dimensions, while they may not permit fine absolute measurement, should facilitate comparisons across time and space.

Political Status

In principle, it is no more difficult to design a series of relevant dimensions along which to locate the peasant's political status than it is to scale his economic status. Quite parallel to his status vis-à-vis the economic system it is possible, with Almond,[7] to think of the peasant's status relative to the following considerations:

1. *Political inputs.* Does he effectively, not only nominally, have the vote? Are there groups, organizations, and institutions specially concerned to receive his petitions and act on them?
2. *Political transformations.* Are peasants involved in the "interior" of the production process, where petitions become transformed into policies? Are peasants involved in decision-making bodies, in negotiations between pressure groups, and so on?
3. *Political outputs.* How many of the rules and decisions made by the political system actually favor him? Does the tax structure favor him? Are there politically determined prices which hurt him? Does he receive subsidies? Does he have access to the educational and social security systems?

These guidelines, as in the case of economic status, are too crude to permit actual metric treatment. They are merely intended to aid and make slightly less subjective the kinds of rough comparative judgments for which the framework proposed later in this chapter calls—judgments concerning the status of peasants who participate in movements compared with those who do not and judgments concerning changes in status over time.

There are, of course, statuses other than economic and political ones which are relevant in analyzing peasant movements. Particularly important in societies which are formally feudal is the legal status of the peasant. But much of this material in fact will be covered as part of economic and political status, since what is involved there are the legal aspects of that status. Also relevant is the peasant's religious status, or the

[6] The CIDA report on Brazil, previously cited, graphically illustrates various forms of exploitation based on a fusion of economic and political power by landowners (see *Land Tenure Conditions*, pp. 194–296: "Terms of Rural Employment").

[7] Gabriel Almond, James S. Coleman, *et al.*, *The Politics of Developing Areas* (Princeton, N.J.: Princeton University Press, 1960).

extent to which it differs from that of other groups in the religious
ideologies prevalent in the area; his social status (prestige), or the degree
of deference paid to him by others, particularly the elite; and his cultural
status, or the extent to which he participates on an equal footing with
others in educational, ritual, and other activities. These are discussed later
in this chapter, where the characteristics of people likely to become
involved in peasant movements are analyzed.

Movements and "Nonmovements"

As might be expected, we face the same two problems when attempting
to define and delimit the concept "movement" as we do in the case of
"peasant." First, shall we include phenomena which differ greatly from
each other, or shall we confine ourselves to movements in a narrow sense
so that we may deal with a relatively homogeneous phenomenon? Once
again, we argue for casting a wide net at this early stage of research.

Second, shall we think of a given historical movement categorically, as
either being or not being a peasant movement? Or shall we rather think of
"peasant movement" as being a quality or a series of qualities and characteristics which a movement may possess to varying degrees, without
precluding its possessing other characteristics to a greater or lesser extent
(and to some extent not even being a peasant movement at all)? Once
again we advocate the second position. We shall illustrate our positions
with five problems of classification and definition which anyone studying
the phenomenon of peasant movements must inevitably resolve.

Most students of peasant movements, including the author, are particularly interested in those collective peasant reactions which have the explicit objective of altering some important aspect of the existing economic
and political institutions to alleviate problems of low status, for example
those of the land tenure system. Let us regard this as constituting the
"core" of the phenomenon, which one would under all circumstances
wish to study. But logically and scientifically, the only way to clarify
why this kind of collective reaction occurs, rather than another, is to
study the negative instance—the conditions under which this kind of
institution-changing movement does not occur. Our "peasant movement"
must therefore be any collective reaction by rural cultivators to their low
status. The basic scientific questions then become the following:

1. Under what circumstances do people react at all to their low status?
2. Under what circumstances do their reactions become collective (defined
as a shared reaction influenced by the reaction of others who are in the same
situation)?

3. What circumstances determine whether the collective reaction takes one form rather than another?

4. What circumstances determine the success or failure of each of the different kinds of reactions?

We do not even claim, at this stage, to know all possible kinds of reactions to low status. Discovering them is an essential part of the program of research. But we do know, or can speculate, about some possible reactions, and doing so will help to illustrate the problem of scope of definition.

Less radical, for example, than aiming for a major institutional change such as the abolition of tenancy or wage labor is attempting to improve in a quantitative sense the terms of tenancy (lower rent, longer leases) or of wage labor (higher wages, written long-term contracts). Less radical still would be a collective reaction which did not even seek to change the terms on which outside resources are offered, but represented merely an organized attempt to utilize these resources on the terms on which they are offered—for instance, a credit society obtaining credit from a government institution established for that purpose. Finally, and least radical, are collective reactions which do not even look to the environment for resources, but seek to alleviate the problems of low status by purely internal redistribution, such as work-sharing or the internally rotating credit associations so well described by Clifford Geertz.[8]

The four collective reactions to low status listed above, while differing in degree of radicalism, are all oriented toward a goal external to the immediate act itself. The act is "instrumental,'" not in itself the end. This is one of the hallmarks of an organization.[9] But not all collective reactions have that characteristic, and not all are organizations. In some—for example, in hostile outbursts, where enjoyment of the destructive act is in part [10] or entirely the goal desired—no external goal exists. In the realm of peasant movements, this is the *jacquerie*. We include it in the broad concept of peasant movement, since the question, "Under what circumstances will peasants engage in destructive jacqueries rather than organize to achieve certain specific goals?" is pertinent. Obviously, this inclusion

[8] "The Rotating Credit Association: A 'Middle Rung' in Development," *Economic Development and Cultural Change*, X, No. 3 (1962), 241–263; also in Immanuel Wallerstein. *Social Change: The Colonial Situation* (New York: Wiley, 1966), pp. 420–446.

[9] Talcott Parsons, *The Social System* (Glencoe, Ill.: Free Press, 1951), p. 72.

[10] We say "in part" because the physical elimination of one's opponent, the burning of his house, which makes his continued presence impossible, or the burning of *cadastral* records, may be highly instrumental acts.

requires that the broad concept of "peasant movement" be clearly divided into "organizations," or movements with goals to the achievement of which an organization is instrumental, and "expressive" movements, which have no goals beyond their own activities.

A third deviation from the "core" meaning of "peasant movement" (a collective reaction oriented to institutional change that would be directly instrumental in raising economic-political status) is the movement that, while being a reaction to low economic and political status, does not have a direct bearing on economic and political institutions. An example would be those religious movements which have their origin in economic and political oppression, perhaps of the messianic and millenarian types discussed by Norman Cohn.[11] This kind of movement should also be included so that we may consider the question, "Under what circumstances do peasants react directly to their low status, and under what circumstances does their reaction take alternate channels, different in institutional content but functionally equivalent in the sense of being a reaction to the same problem?"

There are actually close parallels in the study of urban labor movements to the methods we are suggesting for the study of peasant movements. English social historians have approached the relation between religious nonconformism and political radicalism among the working classes in the early nineteenth century in the manner we are advocating.[12] Their hypothesis has been that religion and radicalism were alternative responses to low status. The existence of religion, then, to some extent weakened the possibility of radicalism. In other respects, nonconformism may ultimately have strengthened radicalism and espcially trade-unionism by producing self-assured, literate, and articulate leaders, much respected by their fellow workmen for their honesty. To understand this important web of reinforcement and incompatibility requires that both religious and overtly radical movements be studied.

A fourth deviation from the core concept of peasant movements consists of those reactions to low status which are progressively less collective. Most important here are—or appear to be at first sight—geographical migrations. They were a frequent type of reaction during the nineteenth and early twentieth centuries in practically all countries of Europe. Even

---

[11] See his *Pursuit of the Millennium* (New York: Harper, 1961). For late nineteenth-century Brazil, Euclides de Cunha describes very much the same phenomenon in his *Rebellion in the Backlands* (Chicago: University of Chicago Press, 1944).

[12] See, for example, E. P. Thompson, *The Making of the English Working Class* (New York: Pantheon, 1964).

migrations, however, may have a collective quality, at least at times. Sometimes whole villages left together, and certainly the action of each individual was substantially influenced by others. This partly collective, partly individual quality of a given reaction is even more apparent in the case of social banditry, small-scale millenarian movements, or other reactions by small groups or even lone individuals. They are labeled "social" not only because their cause and origin is in widely shared conditions of low status but because there is a certain amount of at least passive support from among that majority of peasants not directly involved in these quasi-revolutionary activities.[13] In that sense these reactions, too, have a collective quality. By the same token other reactions with a collective element, however passive, should be included in the field of study—for instance, refusal to pay rent or to send produce to the market, absenteeism, sabotage. We suggest, therefore, that these reactions be kept in sight even when they are not collective, because they constitute an alternative to collective action.

Fifth and last, in discussing the scope of the concept "peasant movement" we need to consider movements in which peasants participate collectively but which are not based on the low economic and political status of the peasant *as peasant.* The following are the most obvious examples:

1. Peasant-based nationalist movements against foreign and colonial conquerors, such as the Algerian FLN, guerrilla warfare against the Germans and Japanese in Yugoslavia and China respectively,[14] and the Tupac Amaru Rising in Peru.[15]

2. Rural clan warfare and feuds.

3. Religious strife in rural areas that is not based on peasant status considerations.

These movements may be substantially manned by peasants, but the opponent is perceived more in his national, kinship, or cultural capacity than as an economic oppressor.

Now it is most important to recognize that none of the five definitional problems and choices are exclusive. Concrete historical movements may not necessarily be either one or the other: they may be mixtures, and if

[13] These are the kinds of movements described in Eric J. Hobsbawm's *Primitive Rebels* (New York: Norton, 1965).

[14] See Chalmers Johnson, *Peasant Nationalism and Communist Power* (Stanford, Calif., Stanford University Press, 1962).

[15] See Lillian Estelle Fisher, *The Last Inca Rebellion, 1780–1783* (Norman: University of Oklahoma Press, 1966).

so, no true comprehension of them is possible without recognizing this fact. For example, the vigor of the Algerian nationalist independence movement and of the Inca uprising may not be explainable without realizing that there was also an economic, anticolonist element to reinforce the nationalist motivation; and as Johnson has pointed out, the vigor of the Chinese revolution may not be comprehensible unless it is realized that there was a nationalist (anti-Japanese) element to reinforce the economic motivation.[16] Similarly, movements may be both more radical and less radical (accept credit on present terms and press for better terms); both violent and goal-oriented; both indirect (religious) and direct (addressing themselves to economic and political problems explicitly). Certainly each of these characteristics is a matter of degree, of quantity. Movements have more or less of a religious element, are more or less collective, advocate more or less institutional change, are based to a greater or lesser extent on dissatisfaction with the peasant status as such (more so in China than in Yugoslavia vis-à-vis the Germans).

Thus, it is essential to distinguish between different analytic dimensions, to distinguish between the analytical dimensions and the concrete, historical phenomenon, and to view each dimension as a quantitative continuum. These three rules are necessary to avoid the famous "fallacy of misplaced concreteness." [17] Chart 1–1 is designed to make these ideas graphic.

Whereas anthropology and history have been the disciplines most concerned with the concept "peasant," sociology and social psychology have been most concerned with the concept "movement." There is no need to detail here the differences in definition which exist, since relatively recent reviews may be consulted by those who are interested.[18] More important from our point of view is a frequently-encountered similarity. Much of sociology seems rather perversely determined to emphasize the irrational and emotional elements in social movements and make them a defining characteristic, but for our purposes, we do not wish to do so.[19]

[16] *Op. cit.*

[17] A. N. Whitehead, *Science in the Modern World* (New York: Pelican-Mentor-Macmillan, 1948), p. 52.

[18] See Ralph Turner, "Collective Behavior," and Lewis M. Killian, "Social Movements," in Robert E. L. Faris (ed.), *Handbook of Modern Sociology* (Chicago: Rand McNally, 1964), pp. 382–425 and 426–455.

[19] It is interesting to note that others who are beginning to study rural movements in the setting of a modern society have likewise begun to question the utility of past emphases on the irrational. See Denton Morrison and Allan Steeves, "Who Joins the National Farmers' Organization and Why?: Accumulated Evidence in Relation to Theory on the Characteristics of Participants in Social Movements" (paper read at the annual meeting of the Rural Sociological Society, Miami, Fla., Aug., 1966).

Chart 1-1. Schematic representation of key dimensions of peasant movements

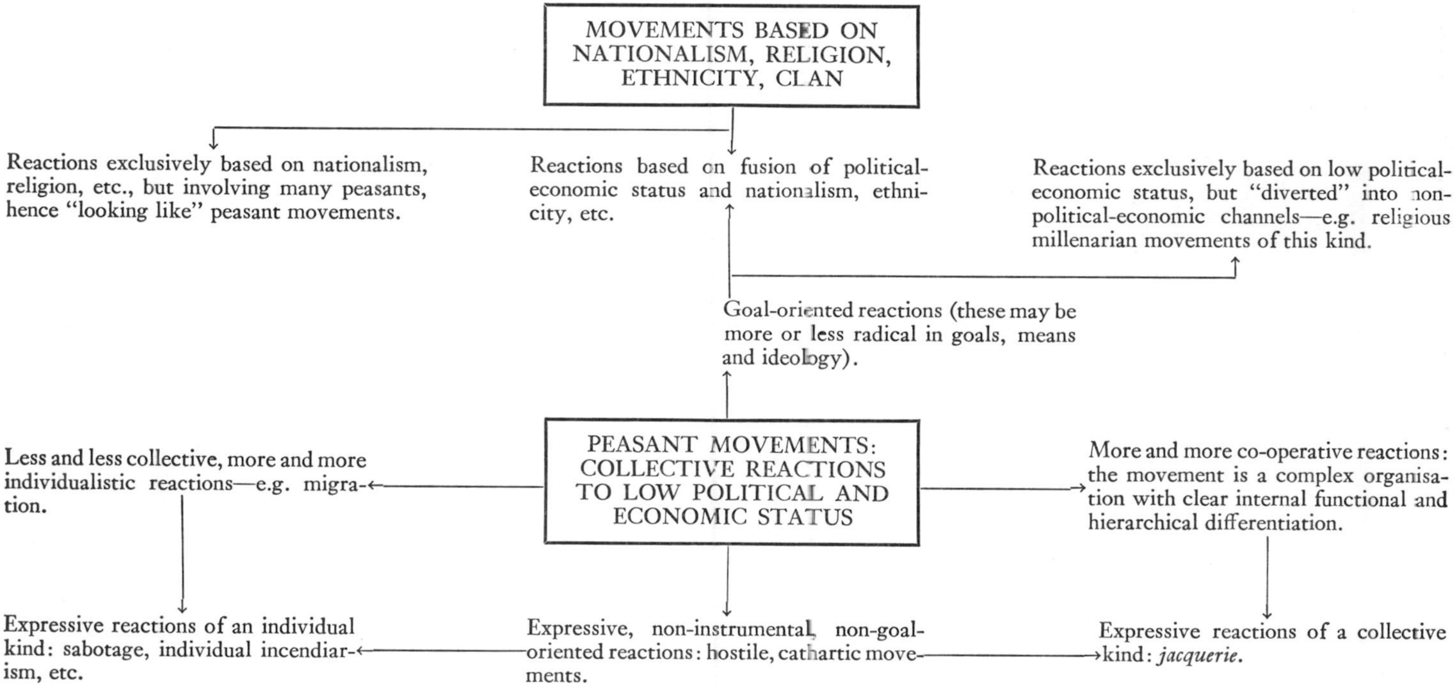

MOVEMENTS BASED ON NATIONALISM, RELIGION, ETHNICITY, CLAN

Reactions exclusively based on nationalism, religion, etc., but involving many peasants, hence "looking like" peasant movements.

Reactions based on fusion of political-economic status and nationalism, ethnicity, etc.

Reactions exclusively based on low political-economic status, but "diverted" into non-political-economic channels—e.g. religious millenarian movements of this kind.

Goal-oriented reactions (these may be more or less radical in goals, means and ideology).

PEASANT MOVEMENTS: COLLECTIVE REACTIONS TO LOW POLITICAL AND ECONOMIC STATUS

Less and less collective, more and more individualistic reactions—e.g. migration.

Expressive reactions of an individual kind: sabotage, individual incendiarism, etc.

Expressive, non-instrumental, non-goal-oriented reactions: hostile, cathartic movements.

More and more co-operative reactions: the movement is a complex organisation with clear internal functional and hierarchical differentiation.

Expressive reactions of a collective kind: *jacquerie.*

This chart is intended to portray the fact that, apart from fusion with movements not based on political-economic status, even "pure" peasant movements need to be described in terms of a three-dimensional space: (1) individualism versus co-operation, organisation; (2) goal-oriented, instrumental versus expressive; and (3) radicalism versus acceptance of status quo (as applied to the goals, means and ideology of the movement). It is the analyst's task to explain the movement's position in this three-dimensional space by drawing on causal variables such as the state of, and preceding changes in, the larger political and social structure, the peasant community, technological level and changes, etc.

Neil Smelser's *Theory of Collective Behavior*, a brilliant and creative work, illustrates this point. Some of what we shall shortly define as "peasant movements" he would regard as examples of a "norm-oriented movement," actually the most rational of the five kinds of "collective behavior" which Smelser describes. Nevertheless, for Smelser even norm-oriented movements share the general characteristics of collective behavior—a "belief in the existence of extraordinary forces . . . [and] beliefs . . . akin to magical beliefs." More specifically, Smelser defines norm-oriented movements as characterized by a "short circuiting" in the belief system and the perception of "unlimited bliss in the future" and general "exaggeration." [20] Another very recent example of the approach to social movements via the irrational is Hans Toch's *The Social Psychology of Social Movements*.[21] Despite the neutral tone of the original definition ("a social movement represents an effort by a large number of people to solve collectively a problem that they feel they have in common" [22]), the book's chapter headings convey its underlying tenor: "Illusions as Solutions," "The Psychology of 'Seeing the Light,' " and so on.

Let us repeat that we intend the words "peasant movement" not to be limited to collective behavior containing irrational elements but rather to be any collective reaction by rural cultivators to their low status. The reaction may under certain conditions consist in the formation of magical beliefs held in common. But under other conditions, peasants may band together in quite rational efforts to elevate their status and resolve their grievances. Or, both irrational and rational action and beliefs may exist side by side, and different conditions may account for the strength of each.

Peasant Movements, Development, and the Urban Labor Movement

Development

The words "development" and especially "modernization" are as fraught with emotion and ambiguity as the concepts we have already discussed. To avoid misunderstanding, it may be helpful at the very outset to make clear three things we do not intend to convey when we use them. First, no judgment is being made that a developed society is morally or ethically better than a less developed one. Second, no assumption is being made that underdeveloped societies are similar to each other in all im-

[20] Neil J. Smelser, *Theory of Collective Behavior* (New York: Free Press, 1962), pp. 270–312, 8, 109ff.
[21] Indianapolis, Ind.: Bobbs-Merrill, 1966.   [22] *Ibid.*, p. 5.

portant respects. In particular, no assumption is made that there is such a thing as a "traditional society," or that most nonmodern societies are traditional societies sharing very similar sets of norms, interpersonal relations, and the like. Third, no assumption is made that societies automatically evolve from less developed to more developed, or that any change that occurs in them is necessarily a sign of development.

While it will be demonstrated that societies can be ordered along two continua, one of which has frequently been given the label "development," there is really no particular need to use the word, since the continua will be adequately defined in themselves. In any case, such ordering does not imply that a society automatically "moves up" over time, nor does it imply that any change which it undergoes is necessarily toward "development" as defined. The two continua may be called horizontal differentiation and vertical assimilation.

Horizontal differentiation is the degree to which, in any society, there are separate institutions and organizations performing different functions: political, economic, religious, educational, familial, and others.[23] For our purposes the only assumption (and it could be investigated empirically) is that up to a certain point such institutional division of labor and specialization is a necessary condition to greater satisfaction of the basic human needs for material goods, culture, personal autonomy, creativity, new experiences, and so on.

This definition deliberately implies two qualifications. First, too much specialization may after a certain point create a new set of problems. Second, institutional division of labor may occur without greater satisfaction of needs; it is a necessary but not a sufficient condition for greater satisfaction. Moreover, specialization does not imply independence. It does not at all preclude the need to coordinate the separate institutions, perhaps through planning. All it implies is that societies in which only a single institution has "crystallized out" and in effect performs all functions and dominates them—for example, societies more or less entirely based on kinship—will have a rather low limit on the degree to which human needs of all kinds can be satisfied.

Horizontal differentiation, along which any society can be measured, might well be regarded as one aspect of "development," but such labeling is not important and may even be confusing. Among sociologists the idea that structural differentiations is an aspect of social development is, of

[23] Neil J. Smelser, among others, stresses this point in his "Mechanisms of Change and Adjustment to Change," in Bert F. Hoselitz and Wilbert E. Moore (eds.), *Industrialization and Society* (The Hague: UNESCO-Mouton, 1962), pp. 32–48.

course, at least as old as the work of Durkheim and particularly of L. T. Hobhouse in England at the beginning of this century.[24] Indeed, it merely generalizes to society as a whole what has been regarded as axiomatic in economics since Adam Smith (and in biology later): that specialization and division of labor are essential for high efficiency, but not themselves enough to ensure it, and that the process is subject to some limitations and disadvantages.

Of particular relevance for our purpose is the recent use of the concept of differentiation in political science by Almond and his collaborators.[25] Concerned with the internal development of the political subsystem of society, Almond and his collaborators have conceptualized its "modernization" (again perhaps an unnecessarily controversial term) precisely in terms of the growth of discrete, specialized structures to perform such functions as giving voice to the interests of different groups (for example, through the establishment of organized pressure groups and parties); making rules (through the growth of bodies specializing in legislation); adjudicating rules (through the establishment of a separate judicial system); and so on.

Parallel with this vision of development at the institutional, structural-functional level, Almond and his colleagues have been concerned with the changes in attitudes of individuals which need to accompany institutional development if the new system is to function optimally. Thus, the new discrete structures will not function well unless a "civic culture" exists, attitudes valuing highly the individual's participation in all aspects of political life from "putting in" his demands by being active in or supporting political parties to "consuming" the system's output of rules. The "civic culture" also includes attitudes which place a high value on supporting the system as such and as a whole, while the individual simultaneously retains strong ties to family and community, so that political cleavages do not become too stark and unrelieved. These, according to Almond and his collaborators, are the attitudes which help a differentiated political structure to function well, to neither atrophy nor explode.

Almond and Coleman describe ways of articulating group interests which differ in the degree to which they are "modern" and "developed." The most developed are called "associational" interest groups. These

---

[24] L. T. Hobhouse, *Social Development* (New York: Holt, Rinehart, 1924). Herbert Spencer and the Social Darwinians were, of course, those most interested in the concepts of differentiation and integration.

[25] Almond and Coleman, *op. cit.*; also Gabriel A. Almond and Sidney Verba, *The Civic Culture* (Princeton, N.J.: Princeton University Press, 1963).

consist of organizations with an explicit and continuous dedication to interest representation and with orderly internal procedures for policy formulation. Some peasant movements, including what we have called the "core" movements, are clearly of this kind. Less modern are the "institu tional" interest groups, whose members primarily have other missions— for instance, church dignitaries or state bureaucrats—and who engage in interest articulation only intermittently and informally. The sporadic concern of Indian communities (say, in Peru) with problems of land tenure fall into this category. "Nonassociational" interest groups, also typical of political underdevelopment, share with institutional interest groups the characteristic of intermittent and informal political activity, but unlike institutional groups, they do not operate from an organiza- tional base at all. Rather, individual members of ethnic, religious, and status groups, for example, articulate on occasion the group's interests. This would be equivalent to *ad hoc* groups of peasants—a delegation, perhaps—attempting to seek some specific objective. Fourth and finally, Almond and Coleman make allowance for "anomic" interest groups— mass action through riots, demonstrations, and crowds, roughly equiva- lent to the expressive noninstrumental jacquerie in the realm of peasant movements, which we have already discussed.

But while the four ways of articulating interests differ in degree of modernity, Almond regards them all as more developed than no articula- tion of interests at all. To at least this extent the political structure is "developed," though the word "differentiated" would be sufficient. There is no implication that the goals for which peasants are striving are "mod- ern" goals; they may be conservative. Only the fact of interest expression is considered.

The second continuum, vertical assimilation, has been less systemati- cally built into formal theories of development, though the idea of equality was, of course, a potent force in Western social philosophies right through the nineteenth century.[26] It is a measure of the gap between the richest and poorest, the most powerful and least powerful politically, those with most and least access to education and aesthetics, and so on. This continuum is a necessary complement of horizontal differentiation as a kind of arithmetical "weighting system." Many economists have long argued, though others do not accept the point, that a unit increase of a material good given to someone who has little of it will probably be more

[26] An exception is, once again, L. T. Hobhouse, who did build it systematically into his theory of social development. See his *Morals in Evolution* (London: Chapman & Hall, 1915), as well as his *Social Development*, cited previously.

appreciated than the same good given to someone who already has much. That is why the same per capita income may represent less real economic welfare in one state, where it is unequally distributed, than in another, where it is more equally distributed.

This idea can be generalized to other sectors of society, the political in particular, in the same way that the idea of horizontal division of labor has been generalized from the economic sector to others. A new organization to articulate the interests of those already powerful in the political system contributes less to political welfare than an organization for those who do not have other ways of articulating their demands. Likewise, at the level of individual attitudes, a greater increase in "civic culture" has taken place when a group previously without interest in political affairs voices a demand and seeks to influence events than when a group already involved in a "participant culture" does so.

If this "weighting," by a vertical factor, of the concept of horizontal differentiation is accepted, then at least those peasant movements which have the explicit objective of improving the conditions of their low-status members become even more integrally linked to the concept "development." Other reactions to low status—violence, messianic beliefs—are not by definition linked to the concept of development, although one may, of course, find empirically that there is a relationship (for instance, that messianic movements do not occur where the direct articulation of interests is possible).

There is a direct link between the existence of peasant movements and the structure of society measured by horizontal differentiation and vertical assimilation. In primitive societies, institutions and their roles are hardly differentiated. The economic sector is not sufficiently distinct from other institutions—particularly kinship—for a separate status of "peasant" to exist. Moreover, such societies are relatively small and poor, so that large vertical gaps are unlikely to exist. If any group is subjugated, it is more likely to be members of another society cast into slavery after it has been conquered. Consequently, any revolt will probably oppose all aspects of the superior alien society rather than just its economic and political institutions. Another kind of violence is feuding between different kinship and tribal groups, which may well include an economic element, but no vertical status distinction.

The kind of social structure that gives rise to peasant movements is more likely to be found in the ancient empires, and in feudal-manorial societies it will be found par excellence. In these societies the rural cultivator becomes particularly conscious of his low economic and political status. Feudal-manorial societies typically display a substantial status gap between rural cultivators and the rural elite, but this gap is neither "vacant" nor stable. There are growing sectors of urban commercial classes, clergy of different levels, some urban working classes, and government bureaucrats. Equally typical is a substantial but not complete horizontal differentiation between kinship, economic, political, and religious institutions. The difference between being a "rural cultivator" in the economic sector and being a "landowner" takes on real meaning. Yet the institutions are still very much interrelated; the church owns land, and at the level of individual role-occupancy, the landowner is often judge and politician.

Modern society is apt to show a trend toward greater equality of status, and while the rural cultivators, like every other group, have a series of highly specialized and technical problems (electricity, roads, tariffs), they are less likely to form a mass movement based on generalized low economic and political status. A later section discusses the importance of these facts, particularly how the feudal situation can lead to demands for substantial institutional change.

Peasant Movements and Urban Labor Movements

The many profound differences between urban industrial workers and peasants will surely be reflected in the kinds of movements they establish. Nevertheless, the two groups do have generalized low economic and political status in common, at least at certain stages of their developments, and this common characteristic might produce some similarities as well.

For this reason it may be fruitful to briefly compare the kinds of movements these two groups have established. Whether similarities outweigh differences, or whether there are any similarities at all, are matters for empirical investigation that should not be prejudged. An examination of the urban labor movement might at least stimulate interesting hypotheses for study in the rural field. Some broad similarities which we have found heuristically suggestive are the following:

1. Over the long run, the urban labor movement, in the United Kingdom and the United States at least, seems to have gone from a stage of isolated, geographically limited associations at the beginning of the nineteenth century, through a stage of trying a "general movement" (during the 1830's in both countries, and also later in the United States, at the time of the Knights of Labor), to a stage of separate unions for different interest groups, each systematically organized on a national basis, loosely working together at the top for a few purposes, largely political and

jurisdictional, that require coordination for success. Do peasant movements also go through these stages, beginning with isolated attempts at organization, followed by attempts to establish undifferentiated mass movements, and later recognizing that the problems of different groups (sharecroppers, small owners, and even the growers of different crops) are too diverse to make anything workable but a loose confederation at the top? May not at least the mere idea of stages in organization be worth pursuing, regardless of whether their nature or sequence is the same in both kinds of movements?

2. The industrial labor movement was aided by the existence of and help from classes higher in economic and political status and often was led in the first stages by people from higher classes. Is the same true of peasant movements?

3. The industrial labor movement has had three manifestations: the trade union, to further the interests of the worker as producer; the cooperative movement, to further his interest as a consumer; and the political party, to give him direct access to the state machinery, which—formally at least—has ultimate power over all other sectors. Producers' cooperatives, essentially a form of syndicalism, were also tried at times. Very complex and uneasy relationships have existed between these manifestations of the urban working class movement. This has been particularly true of the relationship between the trade union and political parties, in part because it has also involved the higher-status groups already referred to. Might there be a comparable situation in the case of peasant movements?

4. There is a close relationship between industrial structure and the structure of industrial trade unions, both at any one time and over a period of time. Construction craft unions differ from unions in mass production industries because of differences in the nature of the work, the market, and the structure of the employer's firm. Is this comparable to the differences between the trade unions of plantation workers, for example, and the movements of small farmers who have recently lost their land?

Over time, the nature of some professions, such as teaching and nursing, has changed so much that it is now difficult to know where trade unions end and professional associations begin; it has become a matter of degree, a continuum. Is the difference between peasants and farmers really an absolute, qualitative one, or may it not be useful to think of a long continuum, with similarities as well as differences?

5. The industrial trade union movement has always had internal divisions over radicalism versus gradualism in tactics and means, both at the

local level in dealing with one employer and at the national level in dealing with the system as a whole. These rival ideologies have had a powerful effect on the structure of the industrial workers' movement, often splitting it. Is there a parallel in the case of peasant movements?

Putting these points into their most general and most heretical form, it is not clear that the location of a movement in agriculture or in primary production, as distinct from industry and manufacturing, necessarily has any absolute theoretical or empirical significance. There are certain characteristics which are frequently, but even then not invariably, found in agriculture, and when present, they exert an important influence on the characteristics of the movement. But agriculture as such has theoretical similarities with industry as well as differences from it. The application to peasant movements of concepts elaborated in studying movements of urban low-status groups—that is, trade unions—seems entirely fruitful, provided adjustments of a perfectly normal, quantitative kind are made.[27]

Thus, the fact that peasants are often geographically scattered and isolated from each other may on occasion have hindered the process of organization.[28] But this factor is not always present, and anyway it has already been taken into account with regard to urban labor movements in Kerr and Siegel's famous article "On the Inter-Industry Propensity to Strike." [29] In any case, this is not a major conceptual distinction between agriculture and nonagriculture. Similarly, because vineyard workers live close to each other, and for other reasons, there is a tendency to say that winegrowing is not really "agriculture" but an "industry." This and other problems might be better resolved by questioning whether agriculture versus industry is in itself a useful categorical distinction.

A second quantitative characteristic which is frequently found in agriculture, but which, however weighty, cannot be said to define it, is that land is generally the power base of a traditional elite. The attempt to

[27] Indeed, there are many parallels even between urban industrial and peasant movements and the evolution of black-white relations in the United States. The Industrial Relations Research Association thought these parallels sufficiently suggestive to devote one of its spring meetings to them. See *Industrial Conflict and Race Conflict: Parallels between the 1930's and the 1960's* (Proceedings of the 1967 Annual Spring Meeting, Detroit, Mich., May 5–6, 1967) (Madison, Wis.: Industrial Relations Research Association, 1967).

[28] This fact was, of course, noted by Karl Marx in *The Eighteenth Brumaire of Louis Bonaparte* (New York: International Publishers, 1957), p. 109.

[29] Clark Kerr and Abraham Siegel, "On the Inter-Industry Propensity to Strike," in Arthur Kornhauser *et al., Industrial Conflict* (New York: McGraw-Hill, 1954), pp. 189–212.

narrow the economic, political, or social gap between a low-status group and the very elite of society is, by definition, a major change in the social structure. But conceptually and empirically this phenomenon is not confined to agriculture. It would blind us if we failed to keep the empirical activity "agriculture" separate from the concept "power base," because the latter helps us to explain why in the United States, resistance to unionization in the coal, steel, and metal manufacturing industries was so fierce at the beginning of this century. Coal and steel may be power bases as important as land. Nevertheless, to understand the fate of peasant movements it is indeed useful to bear in mind that in societies which are essentially feudal before modernization, as in late medieval Europe and some contemporary Latin American situations, the attempt to establish a peasant movement represents in and of itself a challenge to the existing social structure.

A Framework and Some Illustrative Hypotheses for the Analysis of Peasant Movements

The following framework strives to combine the approaches of two disciplines to the study of peasant movements. Since historians have written the most about peasant movements, we have tried to fashion the framework in terms that coincide with the way the historian traditionally tends to think. The major categories of the schema are ones he normally employs, perhaps made more explicit and more systematically subdivided and exhaustive. At the same time, parts of the framework are in the form of "variables" and "dimensions" more familiar to sociologists and economists than to historians. These variables are frequently linked by hypotheses, many of which are not original; writers on social movements, revolutions, and other forms of collective action have said much the same.

The approach typical of the historian is to emphasize the individual instance without making explicit the general rule of which it is an example. The theoretically-oriented sociologist may lack the specific example and de-emphasize the conditions that modify the general rule he likes to highlight. Both disciplines strive to explain more and more individual instances and also to formulate better general rules for doing so. They share the two goals, albeit with this difference in emphasis.

The framework is intended to act as a kind of checklist of points about which information needs to be gathered in order to understand the origins, structure, and outcome of a peasant movement. The topics it covers are as follows:

1. The long-run dynamics of the political and economic structure of the society in which the peasant movement takes place.
2. The events themselves.
3. The goals of the movement.
4. The mass base of the movement.
5. The allies and enemies of the movement.
6. The ideology of the movement.
7. The means of the movement.
8. The movement as organization.
9. Successes and failures of the movement.

The Dynamics of the Political and Economic Structure of the Society

Nothing is more important in understanding a peasant movement than to analyze the economic and political structure of the larger society in which it takes place. For since the reaction of peasants to their low economic and political status is the essence of a peasant movement, the entire economic and political structure needs to be understood. Moreover, all who have written on social movements, and particularly on revolutionary movements, have noted that the overt events occur only after some change has already taken place in the underlying position of those who engage in it or of those against whom they act. For this reason we must emphasize the "dynamics" of the society's political-economic structure, which requires that we analyze trends going back perhaps as much as a hundred years before the actual movement takes place.

What kind of change is most likely to be an original cause of a peasant movement? In order to have some intellectual target at which to aim, in part for heuristic reasons, we suggest the following hypothesis:

Hypothesis I.   Peasant movements are most likely to occur in societies where traditional elites have lost ground relative to newer elites through objective economic changes in the importance and structure of agriculture or objective political changes, such as war.

The hypothesis de-emphasizes the possibility that the starting point of a peasant movement is purely psychological, that it is, for example, an autonomous rise in the expectations of the peasants in relation to their economic or political status which makes them dissatisfied, or that the cause might be an autonomous diffusion of a new ideology. This theoretical position is defensible in the light of the widely accepted view that new political and economic norms generally do not begin to establish themselves at the very bottom of the social hierarchy.

The hypothesis also de-emphasizes the possibility that an autonomous rise in the psychological expectations of the high-status group might have led them to exploit the peasants more intensely, or that the starting point of a movement is an objective deterioration in the condition of the peasantry. Instead, it takes as the starting point the deterioration, either absolute or relative, of the economic position of the traditional elite.

In order to test the hypothesis, it is necessary to pay attention to long-term changes in both objective conditions and subjective aspirations, both the economic and the political realms; and for both the agricultural elites (particularly those affected by the movement) and the peasantry. Concerning, for example, the objective economic conditions of agricultural elites, possible changes in the prosperity of agriculture, particularly in the sector and geographical area affected by the movement, need to be investigated. Specifically, has there been a decline relative to other agricultural sectors, or relative to nonagricultural activities in general, which might have weakened the position of the elites? If so, what are the causes? Technological changes might have made some other crop, or the same crop in some other area, more attractive. Or perhaps the sector was particularly dependent on international trade, and for some reason its markets have failed or its prices have dropped.

Or perhaps—seemingly contrary to our hypothesis—a rise in economic aspirations has occurred among the agricultural elite, such as a desire to live in luxury in increasingly important cities. (We say "seemingly" because the rise of cities probably brought with it an objective deterioration in the relative, previously unchallenged, position of the agrarian elite.)

As a result of either the kinds of economic changes referred to above or of other kinds, such as war, changes may well have taken place over many years in the objective political status of the agrarian elites.[30] Studies of peasant movements need to take into account the possibility that the political power and influence of traditional agricultural elites as a whole, and particularly the power of the elites in the agricultural sector most affected by the movement, may have declined relative to that of other groups, urban or rural.

[30] Outstanding examples are the weakening of the Bolivian elite after the 1931–1935 Chaco War, of the English aristocracy during the Hundred Years' War with France, of Germany's lower aristocracy during the fifteenth-century as a result of the use of gunpowder, and of the Russian elite during World War I.

The fact that a deterioration in the objective situation of elites may frequently come first by no means denies the importance of subjective factors—rising aspirations within the peasantry and perhaps their frustration—at a later time, closer to the actual outbreak of the movement. Nor does it preclude the important role of improvements in the objective conditions of the peasantry, perhaps as a corollary to the weakening of the elite, and a later sharp, final deterioration in these conditions.

As the following examples show, a typical sequence is precisely that the traditional elites, objectively weakened and weakening also in "the will to govern" which so many writers have described,[31] permit some peasants to improve some aspects of their status. This whets aspirations, and the resulting incongruities—with some peasants better off, others not, or peasants better off in some parts of their lives but still subject to irksome restrictions in others—lead to discontent and the feelings of "relative deprivation" and frustration widely mentioned in the literature on social movements and collective behavior.[32]

At a later stage, just before the outbreak of the movement, the rural elite, even more hard pressed, may take a variety of steps that absolutely depress the level of some peasants by taking away newly won or long-established economic and political privileges. This relative deterioration vis-à-vis the recent past, the distant past, or the expected present may then lead to the establishment of peasant organizations.[33]

A few examples may make the preceding speculations more concrete.

In the case of La Convención Valley in Peru, the complete economic, political, and social domination of the *hacendados* (landlords) over the Indians working for them was first broken in 1881, when one of the more progressive *hacendados* founded what later became the provincial capital of Quillabamba precisely in order to lessen the Indians' dependence upon the *hacendados*. Over the years, especially during the 1940's, a commercial middle class grew in Quillabamba. Its livelihood depended on the fact that the Indians had begun to grow coffee on their rented plots. With the cash so

[31] See, for example, Crane Brinton, *Anatomy of Revolution* (Englewood Cliffs, N.J.: Prentice-Hall, 1965), pp. 50ff.

[32] For example, Killian, *op. cit.*, especially pp. 432–433.

[33] This is the kind of situation envisaged by J. C. Davies' "Toward a Theory of Revolution" (*American Sociological Review*, XXVII, No. 1 [1962], 5–19), which sees a sharp, unexpected downturn after a steady rise as fertile soil for protest movements. A distinction needs to be made, therefore, between absolute deterioration, deterioration relative to a recent rise, and falling short relative to an expected position. We visualize these three phenomena not in isolation but as a small part of much larger social changes in which the prior decline of other social strata may be equally or even more important.

earned, the Indians had been able to liberate themselves in part from their work obligations by hiring a second wave of Indians as replacements. Suddenly, however, the *hacendados* realized that their position was in jeopardy both locally and nationally through the rise of huge commercial plantations in Peru's coastal plains and of industry in Lima. They attempted to turn the clock back by growing coffee themselves (which would have required more work from Indians and would have made it impossible for the latter to cultivate their own coffee) and by evicting the Indians from the parcels of land which the latter by this time had substantially improved. To protect themselves, the Indians began to file grievances with the Ministry of Labor, and by 1958, eight peasant unions had established the Federación Provincial de Campesinos de la Convención y Lares.[34]

The story of the English peasant uprising of 1381 was in principle quite similar.[35] For more than a hundred years, the manorial system had been in slow decay because the labor services of villeins had been increasingly commuted for money, as in Peru. Landlords had been willing to do this for various reasons: it enabled them to live in the rapidly growing and attractive cities, and it enabled them to switch to sheep farming, which required permanently available labor which had to be remunerated in cash. But when the Black Plague threatened to tilt the scales altogether in the peasants' favor by making them scarce, the landlords took contradictory action. On the one hand, they attempted to restrain mobility, reimpose service obligations, control or prevent the rise in wages, and even make work obligatory (by the Statute of Labourers of 1350 and later Parliamentary acts). On the other hand, in their desperation and under duress, they had to concede higher wages, commute services, and employ or even lure away and abduct runaway serfs.[36] The resulting anomalies and incongruities, set against a basically declining lower nobility (which had been weakened by the war with France, among other causes), a feuding and divided upper nobility, and a basically rising peasantry and rising bourgeoisie were the setting for the revolt of 1381.

The French Jacquerie of 1358 was also the result of a declining and demoralized landed nobility. While the Hundred Years War, which had gone as badly for France before 1358 as it did for England afterwards, had spurred the process on, it was of much longer standing. The position of the lower German nobility was exactly the same in the early sixteenth century— declining, if Engels is to be believed. As military tactics changed, the need

[34] See Chapter 6.
[35] See George M. Trevelyan, *England in the Age of Wycliff* (London: Longmans, Green, 1909), pp. 186ff.
[36] R. H. Hilton and H. Fagan, *The English Rising of 1381* (London: Lawrence & Wishart, 1950), pp. 24ff.

for their services lessened and their objective decline was reinforced by the rising prosperity of the cities and their merchants. To obtain the increased revenues needed to keep their standard of living on a par with that of the new rising groups, they increased their pressure, often in highly arbitrary, nontraditional ways, on the entire peasantry. The results were a long series of uprisings during the fifteenth-century, and in the end, the Peasants' War of 1525.[37]

Finally we might draw attention to the Northeast of Brazil, where Francisco Julião established his famous peasant leagues and where many other groups, including the Roman Catholic Church, have also been active as organizers of peasants. This area, too, is one where landowners—in this case, sugar growers—have long been under economic pressure, losing out in relative and absolute prosperity to the more modern and productive sugar industry of São Paulo. As in the case of Germany and England, the smaller owners were under more pressure than the larger ones.[38]

There are, however, some examples which in one way or another contradict our hypothesis concerning the sequence "weakening of elite—improvement of peasant status—sudden downturn of peasant status." The French Jacquerie is a case in point. There is no evidence for a preceding long-term improvement in the peasants' position. It seems to have been a partly "anomic" interest group (in Almond's language; Smelser would call it a "hostile outburst") that formed when the peasantry could no longer bear the marauding bands of pillaging soldiers and French nobles, the arbitrary increases in taxes, seizures and ransomings, and the like. Movements to defend existing status in the face of absolute declines must also be allowed for. They too are instances of relative deprivation—relative to the past.

Second, in more modernized complex societies, our hypothesis emphasizing the decline of existing elites may not apply. Social structure becomes so complex that the status of no group, including that of peasants or farmers, depends in any simple way on changes in the status of a single other group. Hence, no deterioration in the status of a superior group is likely to affect a lower group directly. The relative decline of white cotton-growers in the South, an area which lags in modernization, may

---

[37] Siméon Luce, *Histoire de la Jacquerie d'après de documents inédits* (Nouv. éd.; Paris: H. Champion, 1894). Friedrich Engels, *The Peasant War in Germany* (Moscow: Foreign Language Publishing House, 1956), pp. 42–43. This picture is substantially borne out both by Gunther Franz, *Der Deutsche Bauernkrieg* (Darmstadt: H. Gentner, 1965), and by B. H. Slicher van Bath, *The Agrarian History of Western Europe*, A.D. *500–1850* (London: Edward Arnold, 1963).   [38] See Chapter 9.

perhaps be responsible in part for such receptivity to organization as the Negroes of the area show. But this model hardly seems true for the North and West, though it would be interesting to investigate the point. Certainly California's fruit pickers are threatened by mechanization; but are the owners, in turn, adopting mechanization because they are under pressure? A systematic study of many cases is needed to determine whether today, as distinct from the past, pressure always originates from a declining superior class. Study is also needed to determine the facts in the much more long-standing discussion of whether decline relative to previously improving status on the part of the inferior group is a precursor of organizations even in a modernized society where associating in interest groups is, by definition, a norm, regardless of past gains or losses in status and future expectations.

We shall cite one final example:

In the author's study of a Chilean agricultural workers' organization—the first massive one of its kind in Chile, involving a strike of over a thousand vineyard workers in 1953—no evidence was found that landowners imposed exceptionally harsh measures as a result of pressures on them. The employers had been reaping high profits for several years, and the vineyard workers in turn received remunerations superior to those of other agricultural workers. No indications could be found of a decline in their relative standing. The industry's prosperity, rather than its poverty, combined with the acceptance of collective bargaining as a norm, seemed to be at work.[39]

It may well turn out that our hypothesis is incorrect and that all causes —objective and subjective factors, improvements and deteriorations, changes in position of peasants and elites—are equally likely to stimulate the rise of a peasant movement. Particularly in explaining present-day movements, for example, the diffusion among the peasantry of rising expectations and of an egalitarian philosophy may be a more powerful force than in the past and may in itself be sufficient to produce a reaction against their low status. Chart 1–2 summarizes the possible factors affecting elites and peasants prior to the rise of peasant movements.

The Events Themselves

Once the stage for the occurrence of the movement has been set through an analysis of long-term economic and political trends, the movement itself can be described. Analytically, the flow of events might

[39] See Chapter 5.

Chart 1–2. Possible long-term changes in aspirations and in objective conditions, economic and political, of elites and peasants prior to the rise of peasant movements

	Elites	
Aspirations	*Economic status*	*Political status*
Rise	Possible: rural elite wishes to in-increase spending in new towns, courts, etc., and thus increases pressure on peasantry.	Possible: desire to initiate a process of feudalization, giving rise to peasant resistance.
Fall	Unlikely.	Spontaneous decline in political aspirations unlikely, but "loss in self-confidence" after wars, etc., possible as a phenomenon secondary to objective deterioration in political status.
Objective conditions		
Improvement	Possible: increased profitability of pasture or mechanization increases bargaining power and status of landlord, resulting in greater pressure on peasantry.	Grant of political privileges which strengthen economic position.
Deterioration	*Suggested as most likely:* change in prices, profitability of crops puts elites under pressure.	Likely as secondary phenomenon to objective economic deterioration or as primary phenomenon following growth of centralized bureaucracy; defeat in war, etc.

	Peasants	
Aspirations	*Economic status*	*Political status*
Rise	Possible: present-day spread of "rising aspirations."	Possible: present-day spread of political egalitarianism.
Fall	Unlikely: certainly would not cause a peasant movement.	Unlikely: certainly would not cause a peasant movement.
Objective conditions		
Improvement	Suggested as most likely as secondary phenomenon to deterioration of objective economic position of elite.	*Most likely* both as secondary phenomenon and as primary: spread of democracy.
Deterioration	Possible: population pressure weakens bargaining power.	Possible as a result of initial process of feudalism.

well be broken up and distributed under the different headings which they illustrate. But the reader unfamiliar with a particular movement will welcome a narrative account of the major events. This is equivalent to describing, before analyzing it, the French Revolution by referring to the hungry winter of 1788, the storming of the Bastille, the meeting of the Constituent Assembly, right through to the Terror, the fall of Robespierre and the establishment of the Directoire. Indeed, such a description might even constitute the first section of any study, rather than following the first analytical section dealing with preceding trends.

The Intermediate Period Preceding the Movement. Concerning the events leading up to the movement, there are not only long-run tendencies affecting economic and political structure. Often there are also critical events in the preceding period of, say, twenty or thirty years, such as the Black Death (1348–1349, 1361), which so much increased the bargaining power of the peasantry and weakened that of the landlords in the years before the 1381 revolt in England. In Latin America, the 1931–1935 Chaco War between Bolivia and Paraguay is a comparable example. A period of bad harvests or rapidly falling prices also fits into this general category of intermediate events.

In particular, it is quite likely that the peasant movement best known to nonspecialists and most likely to be written about is but one of a series of disturbances. The 1936 *sindicatos* of the Cochabamba valley of Bolivia are an example of relatively little known unrest preceding the much better known rising of 1952. The prolonged Bundschuh uprisings throughout the fifteenth century, preceding the 1525 German Peasant Wars, are another case in point.

Precipitating Events. The events actually igniting the movement are significant in diagnosing its nature. Rumors of land distribution and emancipation set in motion many eighteenth- and nineteenth-century Russian peasant movements,[40] and play a part in Peru today. The attempt to collect new taxes sparked off both the English Peasant Revolt and some of the German Peasant Wars and seems to have been a frequent precipitating event in Japan during the Tokugawa period.[41]

In other instances, an attempt to enclose land or otherwise to displace labor, to exact more labor, to change the marketing system for the agricultural products sold by peasants or for the urban products bought by them, or a change in landlords precipitated the outbreak. Such events are neither more nor less revealing of what the underlying problems might be than, for example, the fact that the assassination of an Austrian archduke by a Balkan nationalist precipitated World War I. There were many more causes of that war than the clash between Austrian and Balkan nationalism, but this was certainly one.

[40] See Jerome Blum, *Lord and Peasant in Russia from the Ninth to the Nineteenth Century* (Princeton, N.J.: Princeton University Press, 1961), p. 554.

[41] Hugh Borton, "Peasant Uprisings in Japan of the Tokugawa Period," *Transactions of the Asiatic Society of Japan*, Second Series, XVI (1938), 1–220.

Subsequent Events. Finally, in describing events subsequent to the movement (if it terminated) it is once again necessary to extend coverage beyond what might routinely be thought sufficient. Particularly if the movement met overt defeat, it is important to know whether the next period of unrest began five, ten, or a hundred years later. It is also necessary to know whether overt success, such as the inclusion of Articles 27 and 123 in Mexico's 1917 Constitution, resulted in substantive changes in land tenure or not. This point is treated further in the section "Successes and Failures of the Movement."

The Goals of the Movement

Any study of a peasant movement must, of course, describe the goals of the movement and relate them to the position in society of the participants. But apart from their content, goals can be compared to each other along what might be termed certain "formal" dimensions. These formal dimensions are breadth, depth, clarity, variability between subgroups, and variability over time.

Breadth of Goals. Movements differ in the variety and range of social institutions which they seek to affect. If a movement demanded only the lowering of rent—a single demand within a single institutional sphere, the economic—it would have a narrow goal. If it demanded also the right to buy land and buildings, and better credit and marketing facilities, its demands would be broader, covering almost the entire range of economic possibilities. If it also demanded better educational facilities and protection of the right to vote, it would have broader goals still, since the educational and political sectors are involved in addition to the economic.

Depth of Goals. This dimension concerns the profundity of an institutional change brought about by the achievement of any one goal, or in other words, how "revolutionary" the goal is. The task of assessing the depth of a goal is not simple, because a distinction must be made between the extent to which the peasants subjectively feel that a profound change is being sought in a certain institution and the objective fact of whether the change would really be revolutionary or not. Both the subjective and the objective facts need to be studied, but particularly the objective, since the subjective appreciations will in any case be analyzed in relation to "ideologies." The discrepancy may be considerable. Demanding the right to vote may be regarded as revolutionary but may in fact turn out to be far less so if the rural masses would not in any case use it, or if they would continue to follow the landlord's choice, as in the case of the rural South in the United States after recent voting rights legislation. On the other hand, a certain change may be intended as, and may seem to be, a modest, quantitative modification of some institution, but actually have a profound impact. Underestimation is perhaps less likely than overestimation, since at least those who are negatively affected by a certain demand would be likely to recognize its significance; indeed, the tendency would be to exaggerate its consequences. If a movement has different goals ("wide" rather than "narrow"), one would expect that some of these goals might be profound, others shallow.

Our hypothesis concerning the breadth and depth of goals of a peasant movement and the stage of development of the society in which the movement occurs is as follows:

Hypothesis II.   The goals of peasant organizations will become wider, or affect more sectors of society outside of the economic, the more the institutions performing noneconomic functions are also involved in the economic sector (church and government as landowners), and the more the economic institutions are involved in the noneconomic institutions (landlords as political decision makers and judges). Goals will become more narrow as society's institutions become more specialized and specific, more differentiated.

This phrasing intentionally suggests that the characteristics of a peasant organization—in this instance, its goal—are "dependent variables," affected by the nature of the surrounding institutional structure rather than determining it or being "spontaneous."

The "pure" peasant organization, one oriented toward change in many important institutions, is likely to appear at the end of an essentially feudal type of society. In its golden age such a society is characterized by relatively large and congruent vertical status differences between the strata. These differences are ultimately based on differences in the relations of the strata to land, the most important means of production. Those who are inferior economically (in landownership) will probably also be inferior legally, politically, and in terms of moral evaluation. There is a good deal of structural differentiation in a feudal society as compared with primitive society, but far less than in modern society. The church, the judiciary, the executive, and the economic production unit exist as distinct entities, but they overlap and there is a large amount of overlapping role-occupancy. Thus the church and the king are also big landholders, not only as individuals, but also as institutions. Landlords are judges or influence them; archbishops are often politically powerful. We refer to this deliberately as a feudal *type* of society because our definition of feudalism is broader than most of the many definitions acceptable to one or another historical school. For those wishing to confine the word "feudal" to obligations of military service, the word "manorial" might be more acceptable.

The congruity of statuses breaks down at the end of the golden age, for reasons that are treated later, but it is still essentially present. The lack of horizontal differentiation in the institutional structure and the great vertical differentiation tend to produce movements with profound and broad-ranging goals. They are profound in the sense that the quantity of change sought is substantial; their achievement would alter a major aspect of the social structure. Typically, the central demand of a peasant movement in a feudal society is that provisions be made for the confiscation, forcible purchase (expropriation), or renting of land. This would replace the system under which the peasant pays with days of labor service for the land he is allowed to cultivate, but not to own. The English peasants made this demand in 1381, and it was the root of the boycott by Peruvian peasants in La Convención Valley in 1962.[42] The peasants themselves may not have a vision of the feudal system as a whole. Perhaps they do not explicitly seek its destruction as such. Yet the change they ask is profound in the sense that if it were to occur, the landowning group, deprived of the monopoly of land, would also have lost the total local control over all other institutions (religious, familial, political) that accompanied it.

In considering the breadth of demands made, it is important to distinguish between the breadth of the leaders' demands and of the followers', lest the breadth of demands of the mass of peasants be exaggerated. Nevertheless, at least compared with peasant organizations in a modernized society, those in a feudal type of society are more likely to make a wide series of demands within and even outside the economic realm to reduce status differences in all sectors of society. We can say with greater certainty that even if such demands are not explicitly made, the achievement of the stated goals would affect the institutional order in other sectors and reduce the status gap.

Thus the first of the famous Twelve Articles, a series of demands widely presented by German peasants during the uprisings of 1525, was a claim to the right of each parish to elect and dismiss its own priest. The second article was a demand for the abolition of tithing. Clearly, these two demands involved major changes in religious institutions. The ninth article demanded

[42] See Chapter 6.

restrictions on the meting out of capriciously harsh (or mild) sentences, and that the landlord, who was also judge (as he often was in England), base his sentences on the long-established written code. Other articles dealt with the abolition of serfdom and personal services, the expansion of rights of hunting, fishing, and gathering of firewood and timber (that is, recovery of access to common land), and the abolition of certain highly irksome impositions such as death duties on widows.[43]

In the case of the English peasant revolt of 1381, it is certain that there was widespread demand for the abolition of serfdom. Since cries like "Hold ye with King Richard and the True Commons" (in contrast to the existing House of Commons) were widely heard in the County of Kent and other places, and on the basis of some other (not unambiguous) evidence, there is reason to suppose that the peasants were also close to asking for a major restructuring of political institutions.

The breadth of these demands and the profundity of the changes they would have wrought in society had they been realized are obvious. Moreover, even had there been no specific demands concerning church structure, the economic demands alone would have affected this and other institutional areas because of the lack of differentiation in the institutional structure typical of these societies.

It is unlikely that an organization based on economic roles in a modernized society would have such a wide range of goals. More likely, it would make highly specific demands, such as for subsidies, price supports, import duties, regulation of railroad tariffs, control of the length of leases, and compensation for improvements. Even when the economic demand is relatively substantial, other institutional areas would be less affected in a modernized than in a feudal type of society because political institutions, like the state, and pattern maintenance institutions, such as the church, are less directly involved in the economy.

In connection with this process of increasing functional specialization in the course of modernization, it is interesting to note that the Roman Catholic Church in one of Latin America's most modernized nations, Chile, holds relatively little land and is actively divesting itself of what it does hold.[44]

Very typically, too, in many Latin American countries the various governments are reducing their holdings. Government-owned land is being used to settle land-hungry peasants in Chile, Peru, and Colombia. This admittedly

[43] Gunther Franz, *Quellen zur Geschichte des Bauernkrieges* (Munich: Oldenbourg, 1963), pp. 174ff.

[44] See, for example, William C. Thiesenhusen, *Chile's Experiments in Agrarian Reform* (Land Economics Monographs No. 7 [Madison: University of Wisconsin Press, 1966]).

results more, however, from a desire not to make a frontal attack on private landholders, while still satisfying peasant claims, than (as in the case of the Church) from a desire to confine itself to the sector appropriate to it and thereby lessen a target for hostility. But the effect is the same; an economic claim no longer affects the government or the church directly as landholders.

Whereas peasant organizations in modern societies are likely to set goals more modest and more specifically confined to the economic sector than peasant movements in a feudal type of society, those in prefeudal societies are likely to set substantially noneconomic goals. Economic institutions are still embedded in other, particularly political institutions (that is, those which control the use of force), or in familial ones, so that the noneconomic institutions are the locus of the goal. In particular, conquest by one group of another frequently preceded or strongly reinforced the division into feudal strata. This was true of the Balkans, where Turks conquered Slavs; of Latin America, where Spaniards conquered Indians; of England, where Normans conquered Saxons; and of Spain, where Castilians reconquered the southern, Moorish-controlled provinces.[45] The uprisings of subjugated peoples are more accurately seen as revolts against a conqueror, in which the economic component is less crucial, or only coequal, with the political. The more recent the conquest, the more important the political element; the more the society has settled down into a postconquest feudal one, the more important the economic component. In any case, we are not dealing with "pure" peasant movements.

Clarity of Goals. It has already been noted that some movements may have no goals beyond their immediate activities, so to speak. The word "jacquerie" denotes peasant reactions to low economic and political status which appear to consist of no more than acts of violence and destruction expressive of frustration. The goal is reached in the act of destruction itself (catharsis takes place) and the act is not instrumental toward ends beyond itself. We might call this "primary violence."

While conceptually clear-cut and empirically possible, this kind of motivation may never in fact explain more than a part of any concerted peasant action, or that of any other low-status group, such as today's Negro violence in the United States. The permanent elimination of a dominant class which a successful jacquerie in fact achieves is, in all probability, at least a contributing motivation and clearly is a goal beyond the act itself. Violence thus becomes a means and is discussed below as "secondary violence." Wanton destructiveness of a cathartic kind is more

[45] J. H. Parry, *The Spanish Seaborne Empire* (New York: Knopf, 1966), pp. 28ff.

likely to be a subordinate element or an accompanying characteristic of a movement than central and exclusive. Nevertheless, it is of interest to take note when it occurs and to analyze both its causes and consequences.

Hypothesis III.   The causes of expressive, noninstrumental, "primary" violence lie in the absence of any other perceived solutions of problems caused by low political and economic status, together with the previous subjection of the peasant to violence and a weakening of the power of the dominant authority to coerce physically, giving rise to sporadic and uncertain suppression.

This describes, for example, the French Jacquerie of 1358. Peasants had been much abused by roaming bands of soldiers, often led by impoverished knights. The Hundred Years' War had disintegrated local authority, and the peasant simply had no other remedy. All three of the above conditions are met. It also describes violence in urban Negro ghettos on the part of youths who lose hope and are goaded by the brutality of a police force, which ultimately loses control of the ghettos so that military intervention is necessary to restore order.

Of greater practical importance than the absence of goals are the varying degrees of clarity, specificity, and concreteness in the goals proposed by different movements. "Land for those who work it" or "land and freedom" is clearly a cruder goal, not as well elaborated as a platform in which specific limits are set for landholdings according to the nature of the soil and in which different types of communal and individual landholding and management are envisaged.

Hypothesis IV.   It is likely that the clarity and sophistication of the goals of a peasant movement are a function of the general cultural level of the peasantry and of its leaders.
Hypothesis V.   Goals will be more specific when past institutional structures can serve as a reference point, for example, the restoration of communal lands in Mexico and Peru.

Great care must be taken, however, not to mistake the vagueness of propaganda slogans, perhaps deliberately adopted for good tactical reasons, as evidence that more concrete goals do not exist. Unfortunately it is particularly difficult in such situations to get evidence of more specific demands, precisely because they may be deliberately kept hidden. We are still not sure whether Premier Fidel Castro's failure to proclaim before 1959 a radical land reform program was a matter of tactics or whether he did not envisage such a program before then.[46]

[46] For the "Program of the 26th of July Movement," issued toward the end of 1956, see Enrique Gonzalez Pedrero, "La revolucion cubana" (Escuela Nacional de Cien-

Variations in Goals of Different Groups. The membership of peasant movements may well not be homogeneous, and this is likely to produce variations in the kinds of goals aspired to by different groups within the movement. At the very least there will be leaders on one side and followers on the other, and it is not to be expected that these two will have completely similar aims. For example, the establishment and maintenance of the movement as such is more likely to become the goal of leaders than members. At least as likely is some division along the dimensions of greater or less radicalism both of goals and of means. "Hawks" versus "doves," "hard line" versus "soft line," "revolutionaries" versus "reformists"—the words may vary, but the underlying division is the same and seems to occur in all movements. Finally, if peasants with different relationships to the means of production are included in the same movement (say, tenants and wage laborers), then differences in goals are likely to arise. This happened in Brazil's Northeast during the early 1960's, for example. It was also the case in Mexico, where the restoration of communal lands—a meaningful goal for Zapata's movement in southern Mexico—was less appropriate for the North, where fewer communities existed.

Changes in Goals over Time. Those familiar with the history of industrial labor movements in the North Atlantic countries know that in the course of the past hundred and fifty years a complex process of both change and invariance has characterized their goals. Job security and better wages were from the beginning desired by most labor groups, and they continue to be of great importance today. But alongside this kind of goal, there were in the early days frequent demands for a more general reconstruction of society, and such demands are far less frequent today. In other words, goals may become less profound and less broad over time.

Increased radicalization of goals is by no means excluded, however, and perhaps rather more likely in the case of peasant movements, particularly when no progress is made toward achieving more moderate goals. Quite frequently (for example, in Mexico and more recently, in Cuba), a demand that large landholdings be divided if illegitimately acquired or if needed by local landless peasants changes into a demand for the general and unconditional dissolution of large holdings. A third possibility would be a change in the content of goals in which greater or lesser radicalism,

cias Politicas y Sociales, 1959), cited in Loree Wilkerson, *Fidel Castro's Political Programs from Reformism to "Marxism-Leninism"* (Gainesville: University of Florida Press, 1965), p. 38n.

though perhaps evident to the observer, is fortuitous. No examples come to mind, however, and it seems likely that if goals change, the change will be significant after a time in terms of the radicalism-reformism dimension. We have two hypotheses in connection with this point:

Hypothesis VI.   Radicalization of goals will take place when originally narrow and shallow goals are frustrated; when they are achieved, goals will become more narrow and shallow.

Hypothesis VII.   Changes in the degree of radicalism of goals will occur in accord with more general changes in social ideology. If radicalization is occurring in social sectors of relevance to peasant movements (perhaps intellectuals), then the goals of peasant movements may be expected to follow suit, and vice versa.

The Mass Base of the Movement

Not all the peasants in a given society participate in a certain movement with equal intensity. Most obviously, different geographical areas are very unequally affected by peasant movements. The English Peasant Revolt of 1381 was chiefly confined to Kent and East Anglia. In Mexico the peasantry of Morelos, south of Mexico City, was by far the most active. In part, this kind of difference is due to differences between areas in long-term changes in political and economic structure. These points have already been discussed.

Here we are more concerned with the fact that even within an area similar in political and economic structure and history, some peasants, both individually and in groups, will participate while others will not; some individuals and groups, while participating, will be passive, perhaps even reluctant participants, while others will be "activists"; and most individuals will be followers, however active, while only a few will be leaders. What characteristics and background variables distinguish one kind of group and one kind of individual from their opposites?

The answer to questions of this kind is important because not only the quantity of participation but also the quality of a movement—its goals and ideology—are, to some extent likely to vary with the characteristics of its members. In this context, we use the word "characteristics" very broadly so that we may subdivide the concept with greater clarity. It refers to the peasant's economic situation; certain "modernizing" experiences or "acquired" characteristics, such as education, and their effect; the effects of demographic and ecological factors and of community structure, particularly the extent to which there exists a sense of community and experience in acting in concert; and certain basic psychological traits, and values and variations therein, such as the possibility, mentioned by many writers, that peasants throughout history and everywhere may be highly distrustful of others, fatalistic, and so on. These four types of characteristics may well influence each other. Thus, certain experiences, particularly education, may counteract otherwise prevalent psychological traits and values. It should also be noted that we have a dual problem of explaining group differences in such things as participation and activism, and of explaining individual differences within groups. Both types of differences are dealt with in this section because we believe their causes are frequently the same.

Economic Conditions. It has long been recognized that the first among industrial low-status groups to organize were the upper strata, those higher in income and occupational level. Thus, printers and other crafts-men were organized many decades before textile workers. Indeed, some of the craft unions trace their origin back to the medieval guilds. Later, it was still the more highly skilled groups, such as railway engineers and miners, who organized before the less skilled mass-production workers did.

One of the reasons for this phenomenon is that the organization of low-status groups, even of its better-off sectors, generally takes place against the desires of superior social strata. The kind of irreplaceability which goes with plying a skilled trade and the cushion of economic resources provided by a somewhat better income are necessary to over-come the resistance of these higher strata. Moreover, the better-off indi-vidual is more aware of what he has to lose as he looks "below" him, and his stake in preserving what he has is greater. Superior economic status is also likely to be associated with more modernizing experiences, more education, more experience with responsibility, and so on. However, these associated factors are dealt with under separate headings.

Hypothesis VIII.   It will be the better-off sectors of the peasantry who will be more likely to organize, and certainly the most depressed sectors who will be underrepresented. Within each group, the better-off individuals, certainly not the least well-off groups, will furnish proportionately more leadership and activists.

The author's study of a Chilean agricultural workers' movement (Chapter 5) revealed immediately that those involved were exclusively skilled vine-yard workers. We were amazed to find that the German Peasant Wars of 1525 were "entirely limited to areas engaged in wine production." [47] Moreover,

---

[47] Gunther Franz, *Der Deutsche Bauernkrieg*, p. 292.

the Chilean vineyard workers were, in all probability, in a better position economically than the average rural worker.

Similarly, concerning the German Peasant Wars and referring now to the determinants of individual participation, Franz says: "The carriers of the uprising were not the village poor, but on the contrary, practically without exception the village dignitaries: the mayors and judges, the innkeepers and smiths, the rich peasants who could later pay more than one hundred guilders in fines. Again and again we found proof that the richer peasants forced the poorer ones to join the movement after excluding them from all prior planning. Precisely the rich peasants wanted to gain for themselves a position in the political life of the nation congruent with their economic position." [48]

In England, too, the richest peasant who had come to depend most on hired laborers was most severely affected by the Statute of Laborers, which would have enabled the lord of the manor to monopolize available labor. [49]

Differences in "Modernizing" Influences. What have come to be called "modernized attitudes" or "values," such as activism (as contrasted with fatalism and passivity), a sense of efficacy, and future time orientation, are likely to be linked to the decision whether to become a member, to be active rather than passive, or to be a leader rather than a follower. (Being a leader is, of course, not only a decision on the part of the individual but also depends greatly on the response of others. But "followers" may find attractive in a leader precisely those experiences and attitudes which in fact fit him to be a leader.) In any case, certain external, relatively easily measured influences may well be among the causes of these "modernized attitudes." Some of these influences will affect entire groups and thus explain their greater participation as contrasted with that of other groups. Other influences which we shall cite are more suitable for explaining differences in participation between individuals, and still other factors may account for both kinds of differences.

Military service, for example, has often been regarded as a modernizing influence on peasants. Its psychological effect may be to give them greater confidence in themselves as they survive successfully in totally new environments and master new skills while becoming aware that their own upper classes may be unable to handle their share of crises and new situations. Military service may also make them realize that people live better in other areas, or at least that different social and economic arrangements are possible. Finally, military service may train peasants to cooperate and thereby encourage them to trust and have faith in each other. But

[48] *Ibid.*, p. 287.
[49] See Betty H. Landsberger and Henry A. Landsberger, "The English Peasant Uprising of 1381" (mimeo., 86 pp., 1966).

whatever the intervening psychological variables between military service and susceptibility to organization, the relationship has frequently been asserted to exist.

Education may also increase the skills needed to organize a peasant movement as well as change the personality of its recipients by making them more self-assured and increasing their aspirations. Since the better-off peasants are likely to have better access to education, the two factors reinforce each other in stimulating participation and leadership.

The effects of these and other variables have led to this hypothesis:

Hypothesis IX.   Individuals and groups most likely to participate in peasant organizations are those whose traditional values have been modified through education or through such circumstances as participation in military service and war, entry into an economic market, or closeness to towns and general accessibility to communications and transportation.

In the case of La Convención Valley in Peru, we have already noted that the peasants involved had begun to participate in the coffee market. It was the threat to push them back into serflike conditions laboring in the land owners' fields—that sparked the organization and the "rent-strike" of 1962–1963.

In Chile, the main road and the main railroad line south from the capital, Santiago, go through the community of Molina. Moreover, Molina had an extraordinarily developed infrastructure for a rural community: an agricultural school, a hospital, more private cars and trucks per head than even the provincial capital, two newspapers, up to seven times as many telephones as other rural communities, and so on.

The readiness of English peasants to revolt has also been related to the experience many of them had in the Hundred Years War.[50] The districts most affected were the counties closest to London.

In the case of Germany, all the modernizing agents which we have mentioned were present. The Southwest, which was the focal point of the uprisings (the North and East remained quiet), was where the heaviest recruiting of soldiers had traditionally been carried out so that many of its inhabitants had had military experience and had traveled far and wide. The whole cultural level of the region was far above that of the North and East, and not only did it have more universities, but there were enough "high schools" so that many individuals of village origin were attending them. The area was, of course, on the main routes of trade between Germany and the Mediterranean, and it was by far the most highly urbanized part of the country. It was in general highly politicized. The example of independent

[50] Petit Dutaillis and G. Lefebre, *Studies and Notes Supplementary to Stubbs' Constitutional History* (Manchester, England: University Press, 1930), pp. 272–274.

Switzerland was there; it was the area in which the Holy Roman Emperor resided, the area of the grand meetings of the Reichstag and of the Concilia. It was also the area in which religious controversy was fiercest and the area most involved in the vagaries of the market.[51]

The effect of military service has been noted also in connection with Bolivia and the Philippines.[52]

At the same time, the limitations in the modernizing effect of these factors need to be recognized. We shall emphasize in a later section that even at the lower, local level, leadership is frequently recruited from local intelligentsia, including teachers and priests, shopkeepers, village craftsmen and innkeepers. Franz puts it cryptically when he comments on the fact that Southwest Germany was the customary recruiting ground for many a king's or prince's army: "Hired soldiers might make good corporals: as field-marshals, they were bound to fail." [53] Our own experience in Mexico and Chile leaves us with very much the same impression.

Patterns of Community Relationships and Their Causes. While from a political point of view, a peasant organization is an "interest group," it represents from the sociological and administrative point of view precisely an "organization," a cooperative enterprise. It therefore requires communication, coordination, the assignment and acceptance of authority and responsibility, planning, and decision-making—all those administrative functions abundantly described in the literature on administrative and organization theory. As Reinhard Bendix—and in a somewhat different way Weber before him—pointed out, there are certain social and psychological prerequisites before an organization may be expected to function at all.[54] Put differently, organizations are likely to differ in the way they perform various functions, depending on the state of these prerequisites. In a culture which is generally authoritarian, specific organizations may also be more authoritarian, to give only one example of how environment affects organizational structure.

The readiness of peasants to perform the functions required by organizations may depend in part on whether their more general work and community experience with each other has provided them with comparable patterns of role experience. Nevertheless, traditional communities may also exert a restraining, conservative influence on peasant movements. Our

[51] Franz, *Der Deutsche Bauernkrieg*, p. 293.

[52] "The Peasant War in the Philippines," *Philippines Social Science and Humanities Review*, XXIII, Nos. 2–4 (June–Dec., 1958), 373–436 (reprint of an anonymous document dated 1946).

[53] Franz, *Der Deutsche Bauernkrieg*, p. 287.

[54] Bendix, "Bureaucracy, the Problem and its Setting," *American Sociological Review*, XII, No. 5 (Oct., 1947), 493–507.

task is to uncover the conditions under which the existence of a traditional community structure is a brake and under which it is an accelerator.[55]

For heuristic reasons, however, we propose the following hypothesis:

Hypothesis X.   The establishment of a peasant organization will be made easier by any experience peasants might have had in community life and work settings and in the performance of organizational functions and roles, such as cooperative planning and dividing responsibility.

While evidence is very scanty, it seems likely, for example, that the English peasant's experience in partial self-government had much to do with the complexity and advanced nature of the 1381 uprising. He not only voted on village bylaws and elected the committee to supervise their enforcement, but on occasion he also elected some of the personnel who supervised his work on behalf of the landlord, the reeve and the bailiff.[56]

Franz likewise draws attention to the fact that in the areas most affected by the Peasant Wars, not only the towns but also the villages had their *Rathaus* (town hall) and that there was more community activity around the church, local bathhouses, and inns than was the case in the North and East, where peasants lived much further apart.

In analyzing a much earlier peasant war—the resistance of Frisian peasants against feudal encroachment—Slicher van Bath puts great emphasis on the peasants' prolonged experience in such cooperative efforts as building and maintaining dikes, and he links this to their success in staving off defeat.[57]

In a more modern setting, one is tempted to link the organized restlessness of Peruvian peasants to their experience of some form of organized village life, the ayllu, though there clearly are severe doubts as to whether the highland village is or is not a "corporate community" accustomed to cooperation.[58]

Finally, in the case of the Chilean vineyard workers' strike (Chapter 5), we attempted to assess the degree to which Molina was an integrated community

[55] For an imaginative set of propositions concerning, among other topics, the relationship between community structure and peasant uprisings, see Mehmet Beqiraj, *Peasantry in Revolution* (Ithaca, N.Y.: Center for International Studies, Cornell University, 1966).

[56] George C. Homans, *English Villagers of the 13th Century* (Cambridge, Mass.: Harvard University Press, 1941).

[57] B. H. Slicher van Bath, *op. cit.*, pp. 189–194.

[58] See Eric R. Wolf, "Types of Latin American Peasantry," especially pp. 455ff., and William A. Mangin's excellent summary of contradictions in the literature concerning the characteristics of highland communities (and highland individuals!) in "A Classification of Highland Communities in Latin America" (paper presented at the Conference on the Development of Highland Communities in Latin America, March 21–25, 1966, at Cornell University, Ithaca, N.Y.).

by calculating various indices of *anomie:* rates for different kinds of crime (particularly against the person and against property), illegitimacy rates, and so on. This was of particular interest because the employers had, in effect, accused the union of breeding on "the general lawlessness of the zone." On illegitimacy, Molina had a rate per thousand live births barely half of any other area, rural or urban, with which we compared it; while on crime rates, Molina was always at the average or below it, never above.

Probably of equal significance to the social structure of the peasant community by itself is the relationship to it both of those who might be expected to oppose the movement, for instance the landlord, and those who might turn either way, such as rural craftsmen, merchants, priests, and teachers. For example, in the case of the Andalusian peasants described by Hobsbawm, the absence of the landlord might have been as important to their movement as the fact that they lived close together in barracks-like structures without their families.[59] In China, the relationship between the local peasant community and the larger political structure seems to have been even more important in affecting the existence—or, in this instance, nonexistence—of peasant movements. The linkage, based on familial relationships, between the local peasant family and some of the higher bureaucrats and intellectuals served to syphon off some of the dissatisfaction with the *status quo.*[60]

As in the case of economic and political structure, changes over time may be as important as any characteristic of community structure taken by itself. Thus it may not be the absence of the landowner, but the fact that at one time he lived with the peasants and then moved into town, perhaps into a glitteringly new capital or a royal court, which is significant for the peasant movement.

For the most part, community structure must be taken as "given," since no single investigation can trace causes further back than one or two steps. Nevertheless, there are two factors influencing community structure that may be "active" at the time of the movement itself and important in its establishment. These are agricultural techniques and their influence on the concentration and dispersion of the population, and demographic structure and trends. Vine cultivation, for example, not only requires skilled labor, but also a great deal of labor concentrated in one spot. Thus, demographic data for the Chilean community of Molina

[59] Eric J. Hobsbawm, *Primitive Rebels*, pp. 74ff.

[60] Barrington Moore, Jr., *Social Origins of Dictatorship and Democracy: Lord and Peasant in the Making of the Modern World* (Boston: Beacon, 1966), pp. 165–166 and 207–208.

revealed it to be a very densely populated community for its rural character. Sugar-cane growing also requires much intensive labor, and in Peru, Puerto Rico, Brazil, Mexico, and Argentina, cane workers have been among the most easily organized. The demographic factor, however, needs to be investigated not only for its effect on community structure but also as a generator of economic pressure.

Franz refers to the pressure of population in southwestern Germany once the great plagues of the fifteenth century had passed. Population pressure is known to have been a factor in Mexico and to be presently a factor in Peru; and Patch likewise refers to the fact that the valley of Cochabamba, heartland of the campesino movement, had "the highest ratio of Indian population to arable land." [61]

As in the case of traditional communities, whose effects on organizing potential were found to be ambiguous, the relationship between density of population or type of settlement pattern and susceptibility to organization, is evidently not a simple one. For example, the Riel Rebellion in Canada during the latter part of the nineteenth century, in part a peasant movement as well as having an ethnic and religious basis, occurred in a relatively sparsely settled area,[62] and peasant movements have occurred both where the population lived in villages and settlements and where it was dispersed. The relationship is perhaps a subtle, conditional one, and precisely because of this it should be studied. For example, the concentration of workers on a plantation may incline them to band together to defend their interests, but it may at the same time make it easier to prevent them from doing so, provided an efficient administration decided to block their efforts and had the resources necessary to do it. But such canceling out of two very different tendencies does not make the analysis of each any less worth while. It may help to explain, for example, the rapid spread of organization in modern sugar plantations in Peru once management for one reason or another had ceased to resist the organizing effort.

In sum, the following may be associated with greater or less susceptibil-

[61] Richard W. Patch, "Bolivia: U.S. Assistance in a Revolutionary Setting," in Richard N. Adams *et al.*, *Social Change in Latin America Today: Its Implications for United States Policy* (New York: Random House, 1960), pp. 108–176. Patch's description of the importance of the Chaco War in modernizing the peasant while weakening the ruling elite corroborates what we have said. So does his reference to an attempt by landowners to recover their lost position by buying from its owner the land rented by the *sindicato* (pp. 120ff.).

[62] Fred Wien, "The Riel Rebellion, 1869 and 1885" (unpublished paper, Cornell University, 1966).

ity to peasant organization: population density and growth rates; the spatial distribution of the population, for example whether or not it is concentrated in villages; and community structure—prior cooperation of peasants and experience in roles of authority, and the extent to which the landlord does not occupy important community roles. These three variables may be in part reflections of agricultural techniques and in part of purely cultural origin.

Psychological Factors Facilitating Participation. Some of the above factors, such as accessibility to communications, explain the differential involvement of areas, villages, and groups in peasant movements but cannot explain the differential involvement of one individual as compared with another. Other factors, such as education and military service, explain both: some communities are more affected by them than others, and within each community some individuals are more exposed to these experiences than others. Finally, however, allowance must be made for the purely individual incidence of the motivations, values, attitudes, and abilities making for greater participation and for leadership.

We know very little about leaders in particular and need to learn more about the kinds of motives—some altruistic and idealistic, others perhaps more egotistic—which induce some people to seek leadership positions. Nor do we know what kind of person peasants will accept as leaders. This surely varies somewhat from culture to culture, but there may also be some constants, such as a high energy level and at least average intelligence. These psychological variables are of great importance. For whatever their ultimate roots in unique individual or in shared economic and social circumstances, these motives are undoubtedly the proximate cause of being a member rather than a nonmember, active rather than inactive, and a leader rather than a follower.

The Allies and Enemies of the Movement

As important to the success of movements as the human resources within the peasantry may be the resources available to it, directly or indirectly, from other groups. Another section discusses the phenomenon of individuals from outside the peasantry who provide the leadership of the peasant movement. Here the concept of "ally" refers to the not infrequent situation in which nonpeasants support peasants partly because the peasant movement is congruent with their own aims. This includes the kind of situation in which some middle-class and intellectual groups support a peasant movement because they have an interest in seeing the traditional landholding elite weakened, even though they may have no real concern for the peasants' ultimate goal of owning their own land. The concept "interests" must also be defined broadly to include the realization by certain groups of whatever ideologies and moral values they have set as their goals. Some representatives of the Catholic Church, for example, may today support a peasant movement not only to maintain mass support for the Church but also because they see it as an instrumentality toward a more general value, such as the abolition of injustice, or as an "intermediate institution" perfectly exemplifying the principle of "subsidiarity" so strongly urged in the Social Encyclicals.[63] In any case, making conceptual provision for allies is related to our hypothesis that the establishment of a peasant movement is probably preceded by a period in which a traditional elite is losing status relative to some newer group but may be attempting to hold back this newer group to a status lower than is warranted by the situation. Such new groups, perhaps needing mass support as well as wanting to undermine the traditional elites, may turn to the peasantry for support.[64]

The groups and institutions most likely to offer some support are urban middle classes on the rise, institutions such as churches whose function is to maximize moral and ethical values, parts of the polity which are trying to gain independence and autonomy, such as state bureaucracies, and other oppressed classes.

Chile is a particularly good example of the importance of allies. In 1920, with the assumption of the presidency by Arturo Alessandri, the period of exclusive rule by the landed oligarchy came to an end. From then until the late 1940's there occurred *de facto*—and in part consciously and deliberately —a most fascinating phenomenon. Groups representing a newer, lower urban bourgeoisie were allowed to modernize the cities but had to leave the countryside untouched. Thus, the new labor code permitting trade unions and establishing, between 1925 and the late 1940's, one of the world's more comprehensive social security systems, applied only to the towns. But a new, genuinely modernized professional middle class was growing up apart from this bourgeoisie and growing increasingly restless in the 1930's. This was symbolized, in 1938, by the separation from the (Catholic, landlords') Conservative party of its urban, professional wing to found the Christian Demo-

---

[63] See Pius XI, "Quadragesimo Anno," par. 80 (published in *Seven Great Encyclicals* [Glen Rock, N.J.: Paulist Press, 1963], p. 147).

[64] This is a neo-Marxian kind of analysis which has a highly useful place in the understanding of peasant movements so long as it does not lead to a quest for orthodoxy. It is the kind of approach pervading not only Friedrich Engels' *The Peasant War in Germany*, but also the work of Gunther Franz, a far more orthodox historian.

cratic party. It was further symbolized by the break between the Marxist wing of this professional middle class and the Radical party, which it had supported in the Popular Front government in 1938. The point of interest to us is that there were many simultaneous symptoms of the erosion of the power of the traditional landowning class and of the reaching out of new urban classes toward the peasantry. In 1952 a new, inchoate middle group—but definitely not the old one—came to power, and social security as well as minimum wage laws were extended into the countryside. In 1957 voting laws were changed, enabling the peasant for the first time to vote without fear of coercion. It was in this period that the vineyard workers' strike occurred in Molina, impossible to conceive without the leadership and support not only of a local lawyer but of a group of Catholic laymen in Santiago, at the national level, and a small but not insignificant section of the Catholic Church, including the Bishop of Talca, other members of the secular clergy, and a group of Jesuits among the regular clergy.

In the Northeast of Brazil, the situation has been exactly the same: a distinctive section of the Church, including Archbishop Dom Helder Camera of Recife, has been eager to help the peasantry for various reasons, as have certain sectors both of the Catholic and the non-Catholic-oriented urban intelligentsia and middle class. The latter, as in Chile, had been held back by the lack of development of the area.

Concern among the radical intelligentsia over whether or not to seek at least a temporary ally in the peasantry dates back to an exchange between Marx and a young Russian admirer in the early 1880's, continues through Lenin, and has greatly come to the fore with the triumphs of Mao Tse-tung and Fidel Castro.[65]

During the peasant uprisings at the end of the Middle Ages, support from various urban groups who did not by any means identify their interests with that of the peasants came to be important. The support received by the unfortunate French Jacques from Etienne Marcel, the leader of the uprising against the French crown then going on among the Parisian burghers, is perhaps the best-known case. However, the English peasants in 1381—particularly those in Essex, who were not as politically conscious as those of Kent—had been subjected to special propaganda efforts by elements from London. These came from the established food-vending guilds (butchers, bakers, and fishmongers) who opposed the policies of the Crown and the newer groups surrounding it.[66]

[65] Books of relevance here are David Mitrany, *Marx against the Peasant* (New York: Collier Books, 1961); George D. Jackson, Jr., *Comintern and Peasant in East Europe, 1919–1939* (New York: Columbia University Press, 1966); and Johnson, *op. cit.*

[66] Andre Reville and Charles Petit-Dutaillis, *Le soulevement des travailleurs d'Angleterre en 1381* (Paris: A. Picard, 1898), p. 72.

Finally, one should not underestimate the fact that governmental institutions, though generally on the side of the elites, begin to show increased independence the more modernized the society becomes. Among the civil servants of Chile (the inspectors of the Ministry of Labor in 1953) there was an increasing awareness of and sympathy for the miserable conditions of the peasantry. These civil servants generally live in very reduced circumstances themselves and they become resentful of the fact that pride in their own work is frustrated both by the power of the landlords and the lack of facilities (transport, office space, and equipment) of a public administration system which is starved by the failure of the landlord to pay taxes. While this kind of civil servant generally is not willing to risk his job by pursuing infringement of the law by powerful landlords, he is not likely to resist the introduction of new governmental policies on behalf of the peasants, provided his own status is also raised.

Nevertheless, the following is our hypothesis:

Hypothesis XI.   The allies of low-status groups such as the peasantry tend not to endure except for those individuals who for various reasons of personality become, in effect, leaders of peasant organizations and cannot be regarded as representing a distinct group of allies.

Whether out of revulsion against the possible excesses which the peasantry might commit or has committed, or as a result of the more certain and immediate inducements held out by the peasants' opponents, or because ardor and courage cool with time, the peasants' allies disappear after the first setback, or at least they begin to counsel caution very vigorously. This was a very notable aspect of the author's study of the Chilean Vineyard Workers' Union, described in Chapter 5.

In the peasant movements of the late Middle Ages, for instance in Germany, there was some support even from the lower nobility. But when fear arose that the peasants were marching not only against the clergy or the great nobility (very attractive targets for the lower nobility) but against the lower nobility itself, their support soon evaporated.[67]

An interesting inversion of this "alliance-detente" pattern exists in some of the more modernized countries, where middle-class groups may come into power with the help of an urban working class, cool toward it, and then seek a new power base among the peasants to counterbalance an ever more demanding industrial working class. Such was the case of President Obregon's increasing reliance on peasants in the early 1920's in Mexico,[68] and of the MNR's increasing reliance on peasants in Bolivia for this same reason

[67] Franz, *Der Deutsche Bauernkrieg*, p. 186.
[68] Marjorie Ruth Clark, *Organized Labor in Mexico* (Chapel Hill: University of North Carolina Press, 1934), p. 103.

prior to 1964.[69] Urban workers are generally not aware enough of peasants' problems to concern themselves with alliances, and if anything there tends to be status rivalry and a conflict of economic interests between these two groups. The break between the Mexican Federation of Labor, supporting Calles, and the peasants, supporting Obregón, at the height of the former's power in the 1920's is a case in point. The increasing reliance of the Acción Democrática party of Venezuela on the peasantry is another.

It is clear already that one cannot think of whole classes as either supporting or opposing the peasants, but that it may be more accurate to think in terms of certain subclasses having a higher probability than others of producing individuals who ally themselves with peasants. Yet such individuals may constitute quite a low proportion within their group (for example, intellectuals or lower clergy). And the same group will have another probability—or even the same—of producing individuals who help their opponents.

The following matters need to be elucidated: what the motives are, both in terms of personal values and in terms of subgroup interests, that induce these outsiders to ally themselves with peasants; under what conditions such help becomes more massive and begins to involve parts of an institution (the Catholic Church in Brazil's Northeast) or the entire institution; what particular kinds of subgroup are liable to give such help; and whether, within the life cycle of a movement, there is a recurring sequence of alliances and detentes.

One model which should certainly be used to analyze these coalitions is some adaptation of the "exchange theory" elaborated in the past few years by George Homans, Peter Blau, and others.[70] It would have to focus on interorganizational and intergroup relations and exchanges, not only or even substantially on relations between individuals. A quasi-economic analysis, using concepts such as investments, marginal return, and marginal cost to explain why organizations may draw away from each other, is perfectly possible. Such an analysis would obviously have to be quite subtle, including in the elements being exchanged not only tangible but intangible resources. These might include peasant good will toward the Church. The analysis must also allow for the fact that groups may try to maximize not only institutional stability but certain altruistic values, and it

[69] Robert J. Alexander, "Labor and the Bolivian Revolution," in Everett M. Kassalow (ed.), *National Labor Movements in the Post-War World* (Evanston, Ill.: Northwestern University Press, 1963), pp. 181ff.

[70] Homans, *Social Behavior: Its Elementary Forms* (New York: Harcourt, Brace & World, 1961), and Blau, *Exchange and Power in Social Life* (New York: Wiley, 1964), particularly pp. 333ff.

must allow for the circularity of certain effects. For instance, a rise in peasant strength may lead other threatened groups to unite. But in one way or another, exchange, bargaining, coalition, and conflict theory are applicable in this context.

Concerning the enemies of the peasantry we need to elaborate less, because the situation is more obvious. Not only will a peasant movement be resisted by those who are directly asked to give up relative economic and political privileges, but its enemies will also include those who depend on and are allied with these directly threatened groups—the churches in some countries, or dependent politicians and bureaucrats. In all probability, the mere demand for a change in the *status quo* will arouse resistance from all those who, although neither directly nor even indirectly involved, vaguely sense that a change in one sector of society, however remote from their own, may ultimately damage their own position.

One aspect of the behavior of the peasant's enemies is perhaps worthy of comment. Throughout history, leaders of the peasantry have been eliminated from the contest by deceit and ruse of a brazenness which those who employed it probably would not have used on one of their own kind. Karle, the leader of the French Jacques in 1358; Wat Tyler in the English Peasant Revolt of 1381; Lorenzini in Molina, Chile, in 1953 (where, of course, there was no question of physical elimination, only of temporary apprehension by the police)—all were removed from their positions of leadership by the same tactic. They were invited to negotiate on neutral ground, and once separated from their followers, prevented from returning. There may well be some sociological significance to this curious uniformity, indicating not only the intensity of the threat these men and their movements represented, but also that all legitimacy and therefore all normative protection was denied them and their "deviant" ideals.

The Ideology of the Movement

By ideology we mean a person's social beliefs and values about the society in which he lives. This includes his views on social causality (fate? a ruling class?); his views on what society used to be like and where it is going; his ethical evaluation of these past, present, and future states; his perception of the roles of different institutions; and so on. Peasant movements may have ideologies to a greater or lesser extent, and much of what Smelser and others have said in general about ideologies and susceptibilities to them applies also to peasant movements.[71] It is not necessary to

[71] See Smelser, *op. cit.*, pp. 319–381.

summarize this extensive literature here, but certain points are worth highlighting.

The first of these is that many and perhaps most persons hold no clear or explicit beliefs of this kind, or at most, their beliefs are in the form of implicit assumptions which they would find difficult or impossible to verbalize and which can only be deduced by observing their behavior.[72] As with the goals of peasant movements, therefore, we find that ideologies have certain formal characteristics, such as their greater or lesser clarity and degree of explicitness, by which they can be judged and differentiated, quite apart from any differences in their content.

Like goals, the ideologies of peasant movements can be judged according to their depth, or the degree to which the vision of future society is similar to ("shallow") or different from ("deep") the existing society. In Mannheim's terminology, is a "utopia" which differs from the present envisaged? (A utopia may, of course, be a return to a past state, actual or imagined.) The kinds of views and interpretations of societies past, present, and future which are called "ideologies" also vary in breadth according to whether they include interpretations of many or of few sectors of society and whether they have more or less parochial points of view. The latter point is particularly important, for very often the first peasant movements in any society have little or no awareness of their society as a whole. There is no realization that their problem is shared, not only by the next community but by the next county, the entire province, and perhaps the nation as a whole and even beyond. This parochialism at an ideological level, paralleled by the perception of peasants living in other areas as different and perhaps not trustworthy, can play an important role in weakening a movement. This happened, for example, in the German Peasant War of 1525.

There is, of course, a close relationship between the goals of a peasant movement and its explicit or implicit ideology. Just as goals can vary between subgroups and over time, so can ideologies. In particular, the peasant seems even less likely than the average modernized citizen to think in ideological terms and to formulate ideologies.[73]

Hypothesis XII.   Its leadership, particularly its outside leadership, imparts to peasant movements such ideologies as they have, particularly in the case of radical ideologies.

[72] This is also true in the United States, as demonstrated by Philip E. Converse's "The Nature of Belief Systems in Mass Publics," in David E. Apter (ed.), *Ideology and Discontent* (Glencoe, Ill.: Free Press, 1964), pp. 206–261.   [73] See *ibid.*

Norman Cohn has pointed this out both in connection with the English and the German peasant uprisings.[74] The greater ideological involvement of leaders than of followers was noted also by Leeds and Galjart in Brazil and Quijano in Peru,[75] as well as by the present author in Chile.

Nevertheless, the role of ideologies in peasant movements must not be underrated. When a whole social structure is in process of change, ideologies are likely to arise and to become salient even among strata which are normally not susceptible to them. Certainly Franz's description of the various peasant uprisings in Germany right through the fifteenth century and up to 1525 make it clear that many of these movements, even when making strictly economic claims, sought to base them on a rather explicit social ideology that emphasized a widely understood framework of ancient Germanic rights, Christian society, and even a hazy vision of secular democracy and equality similar in some respects to that of the nineteenth and twentieth centuries.

The ideology of leaders from superior strata in movements of low-status persons is, however, by no means necessarily more extreme. It may be more moderate than the view of the average peasant. In other words, there are apt to be greater divergences of opinion among outside leaders as to tactics, ultimate goals, and the nature of present and future social arrangements than among the members themselves, who are not so ideologically sensitive. This phenomenon is well known to students of the socialist movement and was graphically described by a student of Robert Michels.[76] These differences are one of the causes of disunity and weakness in peasant movements, with some of the outsiders counseling moderation, others radicalism.

In sum, the formal characteristics of the ideologies of peasant movements to be considered are very much the same as the formal characteris-

[74] "Medieval Millenarianism and Its Bearing on the Comparative Study of Millenarian Movements" (paper delivered at the Conference on Religious Movements of a Millenarian Character under the auspices of the Editorial Committee of Comparative Studies in Society and History at the University of Chicago, April 8–9, 1960; cited by Smelser, *op. cit.*, p. 357).

[75] Anthony Leeds, "Brazil and the Myth of Francisco Julião," in Joseph Maier and R. W. Weatherhead (eds.), *Politics and Change in Latin America* (New York: Praeger, 1964), pp. 109–203; Benno Galjart, "Class and 'Following' in Rural Brazil," *América Latina*, VII, No. 3 (1964), 1–22; Aníbal Quijano, "El movimiento campesino del Perú y sus líderes," *América Latina*, VIII, No. 4 (1965), pp. 43–65.

[76] Hennoch Brin, "Zur Akademiker und Intellecktuellenfrage in der Arbeiterbewegung" *Nouveau Journal de Strasbourg*, 1928 (Inaugural-Dissertation zur Erlangung der Doktorwurde der Philologisch-Historischen Abteilung der Hohen Philosophischen Fakultat der Universitat Basel).

tics of their goals: clarity, radicalism, breadth, and variability, both across time and across subgroups.

There are, however, at least two points concerning the content of ideologies which are particularly relevant to peasant movements. The first concerns the kind of social, economic-technical, and political structure with which the ideology—particularly its utopian, future-oriented aspects —might be compatible. Is it basically an anarchistic vision politically, difficult to reconcile with developed governmental structures? Does it envisage plots owned and managed by individual families, difficult to reconcile with the large-scale farming methods technically required by some crops? Clearly, the less compatible the desired future state of affairs with the state of affairs which is realistically probable and required by the need for development, the greater the potential difficulties if the movement should triumph.

The second question concerns the roots of ideologies in the past. Of particular interest here is the extent to which the content of the ideology can be traced to problems faced by the peasants themselves and the extent to which it is merely an "import," manufactured by other groups, and also, if it is imported, from whom—the intellectuals? a church? certain commercial groups? The content of ideologies is more likely to come from outside the peasantry, but the possibility of an endogenous ideology must not be ignored and, if present, its sources should be established.

The Means of the Movement

Very much the same kind of analysis of formal dimensions applied to goals and ideologies can be applied to means. A movement may be more or less clear as to the methods it intends to employ. It may employ a wide or narrow range of methods—petitions, demonstrations, passive resistance of various kinds, influencing key figures in spheres other than the economic and political, such as the church. A peasant movement may propose to use means regarded as "legitimate" by one or more subgroup of society ("shallow" means), or it may use means not regarded as legitimate, particularly violence (radical, revolutionary, "deep" means). Means may also vary over time, becoming more or becoming less radical or revolutionary.

Finally, there may be differences between subgroups in the means envisaged. Here again, differences between the leaders and the rank and file are particularly important and often center on the question of violence. It is likely that a leader has the clearer view of the methods to be adopted, but he may or may not be more likely to advocate extreme means. A rather complicated hypothesis may be necessary with regard to the latter point:

Hypothesis XIII.   In "expressive" movements, the leader may be horrified at the excess of the rank and file, as was Guillaume Karle in the Jacquerie. But in goal-oriented organizations, the leader may be more prepared than his followers to use "secondary" violence as a premeditated means to vanquish the enemy, as was Thomas Muenzer in the Germany of 1525, or to unify and animate a divided and sagging movement. The deliberate provocation of incidents and even the production of martyrs is more likely to be contemplated by leaders than by the rank and file.

The Movement as Organization

The foregoing factors—the goals of the movement and the means it intends to and does utilize, its own human inputs and the allies on which it can count, its enemies and the changing social, political, and economic structure facing it—all tend to limit the organizational structure a movement can adopt if it is to be successful. Setting a wide range of goals and accepting an ideology envisaging the reconstruction of society as a whole requires, ideally, a correspondingly broad geographic basis for the movement. The adoption of violence as a means requires a paramilitary type of organization, fast and accurate channels of communication, discipline, and good security measures. In this sense, the internal organization of the movement is ideally a "dependent" variable, and only if the organization in fact meets the ideal is success likely.

The organizations we actually find are, of course, influenced less by these ideal functional requirements and more by the reality of the situation—the pre-existing social and community relations, the skill and vision of the members and leaders, and so on. What dimensions should be used to describe the organizational aspect of peasant movements?

The Extensiveness of the Movement over Space and Time. Regardless of whether they are well, poorly, or not at all organized, movements clearly differ in their geographical extension and in their temporal duration. There is a great difference, for example, between sporadic incidents occurring in scattered locations of a limited zone, a whole zone's being affected and perhaps a few others to a lesser extent (as in the case of the department of Cuzco in Peru in 1963), and a whole section of a country or the entire country's being affected, as in southwest Germany in 1525.

Degree of Organization. The degree to which the movement has at its disposal an internal, *de facto* equivalent of an administrative system should be assessed. Written statements specifying administrative procedures would of course be one source of evidence that such a system exists. But written documents are not likely to be common, nor are they necessary as proof. Much more important is the *de facto* functioning of such a system —that people act as if they were certain that it existed. In principle there could be two subsystems, a vertical one of authority and a horizontal one of division of administrative labor.

The vertical system might well have two separate flows, one upward from the membership, in which policy is formulated, and one downward, through which policy is implemented. Evidence of such a two-directional subsystem of authority would be regular consultation of membership in groups, through delegates or as individuals, and an executive hierarchy presumably based at least in part on geographical units. Are there, for example, local leaders whose authority is widely known and acknowledged?

Concerning the horizontal subsystem, one looks for routine methods to recruit members and obtain other needed resources, and to communicate and distribute information. Communication, often linked to the authority system, is necessarily difficult in a rural setting. Yet the task of establishing a functioning communication network has to be tackled before an organized movement can come into being. Sometimes, as in the case of the Bundschuh (a series of disturbances in southwest Germany in the fifteenth century), dissident religious sects and other out-groups such as beggars or youths have been used as communication links. It would be desirable to obtain a more systematic inventory of the methods used to solve the communication problem.

Apart from whether or not there are well-functioning authority and communication systems, two aspects of internal structure deserve separate discussion, however briefly. For when they are present, they indicate certain underlying sociological weaknesses frequently encountered in peasant movements, and are therefore diagnostically significant.

The Problem of Loyalty and Discipline. Many writers have noted both the frequency with which peasants have divulged conspiracies to higher authorities (in Catholic countries sometimes via confession) and the indiscipline and apathy which they have shown in battle or under the conditions of "social combat" represented by joining a protest organization. Are such treason and indiscipline, and the quick loss of interest and apathy, generally prevalent? Under what circumstances have they not occurred? Is there a connection with the fact that the peasant is organizing against "legitimate" authorities in ways which the peasant, having accepted the values of higher strata, cannot but regard as illegitimate, even though from other points of view they are justified? Or is such betrayal of peasant leaders caused simply by fear of the overwhelming power of the opposition?

Leadership. A second critical aspect of internal organization is the recruitment of its leadership. The discussion of the mass base of the movement hypothesized that among the peasantry, the most modernized, economically best-off elements would be more likely than other groups of peasants to provide leaders. However, it seems even more likely that substantial proportions of the leadership will not be drawn from the peasantry itself but will instead be recruited from the same groups which, when they act as groups, are the peasants' allies: the craftsmen and shopkeepers of market towns, urban intellectuals, lower clergy, lawyers, and the like.

Hypothesis XIV.   The less modernized the society, the lower the rung of the organizational ladder from which outside leadership is recruited. Insofar as there is a national leadership, it will be drawn, *de facto* and until a relatively late stage of societal development, from urban middle classes, particularly intellectuals. Insofar as there is regional and local leadership, it will be recruited from local bourgeoisie, craftsmen, shopkeepers, lawyers, and lower clergy.

In the English rising of 1381, the best-known leaders were Tyler, a tiler from either Essex or Kent, and John Ball, a priest.

In the German Peasant Wars of 1525, the outstanding figures were Thomas Muenzer, a defrocked priest; Michael Gaismair, a personal secretary to bishops and noblemen; Florian Geyer, a member of the lower nobility; Ulrich Schmied, a smith; Wendel Hipler, another personal secretary and aide to the counts of Hohenlohe; Matern Feuerbacher, an innkeeper; and so on.[77]

In Chile, the driving spirit behind the Molina Vineyard Workers' Union was a local lawyer (later a deputy for the Christian Democratic Party), Emilio Lorenzini, who had gone to Chile's best schools and universities, although his family were locally resident, well-to-do immigrants. They did not belong to the established, upper-middle, professional and middle middle-class families from which the rest of the Christian Democratic leadership came.

In Brazil, Francisco Julião was a landowning lawyer not of peasant origin, nor were the priests chiefly involved in organizing rival unions, Frs. Crespo and Mello, nor were the leaders of other organizations, Communist, Maoist, Trotzkyite, and others.[78]

[77] Franz, *Der Deutsche Bauernkrieg.*

[78] These facts are agreed upon both by skeptics who do not see these organizations as modernizing and as representing much of a departure, such as Anthony Leeds and

At levels below the top, even at the local level, particularly in the less modernized societies, leaders still tend not to be peasants but to be drawn from local craftsmen, merchants, teachers, and the like, though they are sometimes of peasant origin.

In England, one of the leaders of the rising in East Anglia was Lister, a dyer. Other well-known names are Wrawe and Grindcombe, priests in Cambridge and East Anglia, respectively.

In the vineyard workers' strike movement in Chile, the second-level figures were an individual whose father had drifted somewhat uneasily back and forth between working his own plot of land and being a construction worker; the leader himself, who had been to grade school and was attempting to push his way into lower white-collar status; an agricultural engineer; a person who drifted into the zone from the North of Chile, of uncertain background and education, but in all probability not a peasant by background and definitely not by previous occupation; two local pharmacists, one a woman; the wife of the local lawyer; and the local priest.

In Peru, in La Convención Valley, there was the same mixture of outside intellectuals (Hugo Blanco), lawyers from nearby towns, and local tradesmen, many of whom were cholo or mestizos, that is, halfway toward acculturation.[79]

This discussion of the internal structure of peasant movements completes our list of determining or independent variables. The determined or dependent variables are, of course, the successes and failures of the movement.

Successes and Failures of the Movement

In the case of organizations, "success" has two clearly separate meanings: survival as a movement and organization, and the reaching of its goals. Theoretically at least, either one is possible without the other. It is particularly important not to mistake the disappearance of a movement, perhaps after a severe defeat, as a sign that its goals have not been reached, though they may have been reached sometime after its demise.

It seems, however, that peasant movements were not very successful in either of these senses until modern times. In France and Germany, for example, so-called peasant organizations even in the late nineteenth cen-

Benno Galjart, and those like Gerrit Huizer who see them as definitely the beginning of a class-based movement. See Anthony Leeds, *op. cit.*; Benno Galjart, *op. cit.*; and the "Comentario" by G. Huizer, *Americana Latina*, VIII, No. 3 (1965), 127–144.

[79] This statement is based on both the chapter by Craig and the article by Anibal Quijano, *op. cit.*

tury were generally dominated by large landholders and served their interests, not those of the poorer peasant. Not until the twentieth century has there in France been any organization with a left-radical as well as right-radical orientation.[80] In the developing areas, like Latin America, it is only the more modernized societies such as Chile, Venezuela, and Mexico (and Colombia in part) that have made substantial provision for the articulation of peasant interests.

Bolivia is an exception. There, however, the movement established itself at an opportune moment of political dissolution and did not overcome a ruling elite by itself. The subsequent (urban) revolutionary government came to terms with the movement, as described by Patch.[81] The story of the Mexican Revolution seems strikingly similar in at least some very important respects. The original overthrow of Dictator Porfirio Díaz by Madero was the act of urban intellectuals of gently liberal persuasion and not of peasants. In the ensuing prolonged civil war, peasant action played an important part but did not fundamentally alter the control by urban middle-class elements, just as in Bolivia. The most radical peasant movement, that of Zapata, was vanquished. These urban elements granted many benefits to peasants, and in certain localities peasant organizations remained strong, as they did in Bolivia after 1952. But agrarian reform did not become massive until the presidency of General Cárdenas, and in any case the mere transfer of land, while it diminishes the power of the traditional elites, does not automatically bring with it an equal increase in the political power of the peasantry. The real growth in the political influence of the peasant and his organizations in Mexico has probably been steady, but it has been slow. Perhaps it has kept pace with the rate of modernization of Mexico as a whole, but it has not exceeded it.

There may be a more underlying regularity, which might be formulated as follows:

Hypothesis XV.   In societies which are basically still of the feudal type (wide distinctions in status, relatively poor differentiation in institutional sectors), peasant organizations are likely to be involved in revolutionary activities through no fault of their own, so to speak. They will fail in these activities unless the existing system is in any case ready to collapse, in which case peasants' organizations may help the process of collapse but will not be its leading agent.

Only in modernized societies will peasant organizations be successful,

[80] See Gordon Wright, *Rural Revolution in France: The Peasantry in the Twentieth Century* (Stanford, Calif.: Stanford University Press, 1964).   [81] *Op. cit.*

that is, in those societies where status differential has in any case already been reduced and where there is considerable institutional differentiation and specialization. In such societies, the basically rather limited demands of peasants will be accommodated and hence frustration sufficient to cause major outbreaks of violence will be averted.

This hypothesis postulates, implicitly but deliberately, a great similarity between rural and urban low-status organizations. Just as very little success accompanied the many "general unions" of "all working men" which abounded in both the United States and Britain at the beginning of their industrial revolutions, and which were sometimes more but usually less revolutionary, so early peasant organizations do not generally succeed. The old system is still too strong, and they too weak economically, culturally, and legally. But as they rise in status, as the traditional elites weaken, and as institutions arise which accommodate conflicting interests, peasants increasingly succeed, as did industrial workers before them, organized not on a general basis but on the basis of specific interests. As in the case of the American Federation of Labor unions, certain key, privileged peasant groups will establish themselves early. Their day has come not so much because they adopted more realistic goals and methods but because the situation strengthened their hand, and seeing this, they seized the opportunity. The mass of the less skilled does not become organized until later and typically only with the helping hand of an outside charismatic figure and a group surrounding him, and the most important help of the law. What Franklin D. Roosevelt and his New Deal supporters and, above all, the Wagner Act did for the industrial unions in the mid-thirties, Cárdenas did for Mexico's peasants, likewise creating a legal and administrative structure to shelter and foster peasant organizations. In this setting of strong leadership from the top plus legal protection and economic incentives, specific industry groups—for example, sugar-cane workers— are slowly gaining power.[82] In Chile too, peasant organizations have begun to flourish only now, after Eduardo Frei and his Christian Democrat supporters attracted a majority the size of which Chile had never seen before. Their administrative agencies are doing all in their power to implant and nurture peasant organizations which are basically still quite weak. It is almost inevitable that the hunt by urban groups for the support of the peasants will, under these circumstances, result in fierce political competition and divisions in the peasant movements.

Peasants thus succeed in raising their status by organized pressure only

[82] See Henry A. Landsberger and Cynthia N. Hewitt, "Preliminary Report on a Case Study of Mexican Peasant Organizations" (mimeo., 84 pp., 1966).

as their status is in any case becoming more equal and as resistance to their efforts is in any case becoming weaker, and as the environment—the legal framework, the economic situation, a charismatic leader, or benevolently inclined groups—are in any case ready to ally themselves with the low-status group of peasants. Obviously, their own efforts (and the potential threat) are a most important ingredient in raising the status of peasants, but their efforts alone are by no means enough, nor likely to be decisive.

These are some of the hypotheses which we hope to explore in the following pages.

2. Venezuela: The Peasant Union Movement*

JOHN DUNCAN POWELL

Center for International Affairs
Harvard University

The Federación Campesina de Venezuela (FCV) is undoubtedly one of the most important peasant movements to emerge in Latin America. Compared with other peasant movements it is relatively cohesive and highly structured. It nicely fits the definitional criteria established here for the study of a peasant movement—the incorporation of a wide range of social, economic, and political goals impinging upon (and implying profound changes in) major institutions and relationships within each of these realms, and their consequent collision with other social, economic, and political groupings whose established status is threatened by the changes manifest in the movement's demands. This clash of interests has been primarily worked out through adjustments in the political system, but on occasion it has exceeded the system's capacity for conflict management and has erupted into violence.

In many ways, the peasant union movement in Venezuela—the FCV is the formal, organizational representative of this movement—presents an ideal case for study and analysis. The movement has been intimately involved in the Venezuelan agrarian reform program, which since 1958 has been noted as the largest nonrevolutionary land reform program in the hemisphere. The social, economic, and political antecedents of the

* The research for this paper was financed by the Land Tenure Center at the University of Wisconsin. This multidisciplinary research and training center, established in 1962 under a contract with the Agency for International Development, focuses on Latin American land reform problems. During three months of the field work, I was a consultant for the Inter-American Development Bank in connection with the study and evaluation of the Venezuelan agrarian reform being carried out for the Comité Interamericano de Desarrollo Agrícola by Dr. Thomas F. Carroll, Dr. Michael Sund, and the Universidad Central de Venezuela. Data from the CONVEN project for peasant samples were generously furnished by John R. Mathiason, a principal data analyst on the Massachusetts Institute of Technology team. I am deeply indebted to Mathiason for his collaboration and assistance on my research. (CONVEN is a computer code for "Conflict and Consensus in Venezuela.")

reform are of relatively recent origin, dating back to around 1915. There-fore the body of documentary evidence for a case history is of managea-ble proportions, and many participants in the political events since 1935 are still available for interviews.[1]

Of particular interest are the organic links between the peasant union movement and the rudimentary political parties formed in Venezuela during the mid-1930's. These links, which have developed continuously since that time, provide the basis for the impact of the peasant union movement on the rest of society, and conversely, the basis for penetration of the campesino subculture by forces of modernization. The result of bringing the rural society into an interdependent relationship with the larger society has been an irreversible, accelerated process of integration. The Venezuelan experience may not be an entirely appropriate or appli-cable model from which others may learn, but it seems now to be a successful example of nation-building through the incorporation of the peasantry into the political process.

Historical Genesis

The pre-World War I economy of Venezuela was a rudimentary, plantation-based agricultural export system, dominated by sugar, coffee, and cacao. At that time the country was considered to be among the most backward in social, political, and economic development. Two closely related events then occurred which led to the stagnation of the agricul-tural sector and its replacement by the petroleum industry as the growing edge of the national economy.

The first of these events was the loss of Venezuela's primary market for its high-grade coffees—Germany—through the World War I blockade. Following the war, Germany's internal financial conditions precluded the re-establishment of a vigorous consumer's market. With the advent of the Great Depression, the foreign markets of other components of the agri-cultural sector were damaged. Before world trade had completely re-covered from the international financial crisis, World War II once again brought serious market dislocations to the primary product economies of Latin America.

While Venezuelan agriculture was thus experiencing difficulties, the petroleum industry, beginning about 1920, started to grow in attractive-ness as an opportunity for capital and entrepreneurial talent. This devel-

---

[1] The results of such an analytic case study, carried out from 1963 to 1966, are incorporated in John D. Powell, "The Politics of Agrarian Reform in Venezuela: History, System and Process" (Ph.D. thesis, University of Wisconsin, 1966).

opment compounded the problems in the agricultural sector. One result was a gradual dwindling of credit sources for commercial agricultural operations and a rise in the cost of credit where it was available. Agricultural operations were becoming marginal or submarginal, and the campesino population soon experienced the consequences.[2]

During this period the rural population of Venezuela was approximately two million. Of these, about one-third, or some 700,000, were considered "economically active." Among the economically active population, according to the 1937 agricultural census, only 32,324 persons were classified as landlords. It was among these persons, who were engaged in commercial agriculture, that the effects of the agricultural sector's problems were first felt. But by virtue of their function as employers of wage labor and their control of the land resources used by tenants, sharecroppers, and squatters, this small group was able to transmit the impact of the economic difficulties to the peasant masses. The peasants thus faced decreased employment opportunities for wage labor (essentially seasonal labor by subsistence farmers surrounding the commercial holdings), and diminished wages and longer working hours for those who could still find employment. In addition, fees and payments in kind were forced upward by landlords attempting to maintain marginal economic positions. Owing to their labor or land tenure dependence on the landowning class, therefore, some 75 per cent of the economically active rural population experienced a worsening of their own economic position—and that of the persons dependent upon them.[3]

The erosion of the rural economy from the 1920's onward was accompanied by a certain amount of rural unrest and occasionally violent outbursts. Surface indications of the tensions which resulted as the peasants were pushed closer to the margin of survival included violent as well as legal landlord-tenant conflicts, changes and resistance to changes in landlord-*colono* or landlord-sharecropper arrangements, scattered land invasions, and even isolated attempts at guerrilla warfare.[4]

In early 1936 peasant union organizers began to move into this situation of implicit and explicit conflict. These organizers primarily recruited local peasant influentials as leaders about whom a local *sindicato* could be formed. The organizers were political agents and local or regional adher-

---

[2] For a general analysis of the development of the Venezuelan economy, see International Bank for Reconstruction and Development (IBRD), *The Economic Development of Venezuela* (Baltimore, Md.: Johns Hopkins Press, 1961).

[3] For a detailed development of this and other arguments presented herein, see Powell, *op. cit.*   [4] *Ibid.*, pp. 33–37.

ents of the most important of the new political organizational movements, ORVE (Movimiento de Organización Venezolano). ORVE became a rudimentary political party, the Partido Democrático Nacional (PDN), late in 1936, and after being forced underground in 1937 it emerged legally in September 1941 as Acción Democrática (AD). Among the most important leaders of ORVE, later the PDN, and eventually AD, were Rómulo Betancourt and Raúl Leoni. These men and others of the famous Generation of '28 student leaders had settled during their formative years of exile on the strategy of forging a mass base of potential electoral support through the instrumentality of the labor movement. Betancourt was particularly committed to the syndicalization of the peasantry for this purpose, and from 1936 onward he directed a strenuous organizational drive to lay such a foundation. During the 1936–1939 period, the leadership cadre of ORVE–PDN numbered approximately six to eight hundred; of these, about two hundred were directly engaged in full-time organization of peasant unions.[5]

The incorporation of the leadership of Acción Democrática into the military coup d'état of October 18, 1945, accounts in large part for the blossoming of the peasant union movement. With Rómulo Betancourt as President of the Revolutionary Junta and Raúl Leoni as Minister of Labor, peasant and urban unions no longer had difficulties in securing legal registration and operating privileges. The underlying strategy of the party to build a base of mass support through organizing the labor force was rapidly implemented under a cooperative and benevolent AD government. By 1948 the peasant union movement had developed into a full-blown national industrial labor organization, emcompassing more than five hundred locals and approximately a hundred thousand peasant members.

At the same time, the AD government moved to restructure the political system to bring its primary political resource—its mass base—to bear on the electoral process. Prior to 1945 the electoral process had been quite marginal to the distribution and transfer of political power. Suffrage was restricted by property and tax requirements, and national elections were highly indirect—voters elected the state legislative assemblies, which elected the members of the national Congress, which in turn elected the President of the Republic. In fact, the mantle of presidential power was

[5] For excellent documentation and interpretation of these details (and of general political events from 1936 onward), see John D. Martz, III, *Acción Democrática: Evolution of a Modern Political Party* (Princeton, N.J.: Princeton University Press, 1966).

passed on from the incumbent to his chosen successor. The AD govern-ment legalized party activities, expanded suffrage by enfranchising all Venezuelan citizens over eighteen years of age regardless of sex, property, and tax qualifications or literacy, and made the election of the national Congress and the President direct, by secret ballot. Prior to these reforms less than 5 per cent of the population had participated in the electoral process. The post-reform ratio jumped to over 35 per cent; the bulk of the increase was accounted for by AD voters, especially in the rural areas. Based on this expanded electorate and operating under a new set of political "rules of the game," AD candidates were elected to a National Constituent Assembly, which legitimized the new suffrage criteria in the 1947 Constitution. A new Congress in which AD members were in the substantial majority and a new AD President, Rómulo Gallegos, were elected under the Constitution in late 1947.

At the same time, the Revolutionary Junta was taking far-reaching moves to solidify the AD-dominated peasant union movement in the rural areas. The impact of these developments was so great, one must conclude, that the real revolution in the control of land and political power oc-curred in Venezuela in the 1945–1948 period and not after 1958, as is popularly believed.[6] The little-known but highly significant *de facto* agrarian reform of 1945–1948 set forces in trajectory and established conditions which after a period of quiescence under the Pérez Jiménez dictatorship re-emerged to influence, if not determine, the nature of the post-1958 *de jure* agrarian reform. The 1945–1948 agrarian reform had two major aspects: the dramatic growth in the instrumental capabilities and powers associated with the role of peasant union leader, and the elevation and political consolidation of the peasant union leader vis-à-vis the rural landowner.

Prior to the October revolution, a peasant union leader, while an elite and influential figure among his campesino cohorts, had almost no instru-mental powers. Often he could not gain legal recognition for the local he had organized. What the peasant union leader lacked in ability to control instrumental pay-offs to his peasant followers, he had to try to make up

[6] Robert J. Alexander, in *The Venezuelan Democratic Revolution* (New Bruns-wick, N.J.: Rutgers University Press, 1964), presents the popular view that this revolution occurred after 1958, under President Betancourt. He considered the 1945–1948 period to be the "forerunner of the revolution" (ch. 2). The many facts which my research uncovered, however, are convincing evidence that the 1945–1948 period constituted the revolution, a consequence of which (following ten years of reaction under Pérez Jiménez) was the formal consolidation of the revolution under Betancourt.

for with affective pay-offs.[7] Beginning in December, 1945, however, the Revolutionary Junta began granting various instrumental powers to these leaders. That month the newly created Comisión de Tierras in the Instituto Téchnico de Inmigración y Colonización (ITIC) began accepting and acting on petitions for land submitted by local peasant union leaders. The Comisión was empowered to requisition public lands controlled by several government agencies (particularly the Agriculture Bank) or to lease suitable lands from private owners for subleasing to peasant unions. The ITIC provided technical advice in the form of plans for the best utilization of the leased lands, and the peasant union leaders contracted to organize and supervise their members in the execution of the plans. In May, 1946, ITIC was funded with ten million bolivars (one bolivar was equivalent to twenty-two cents in American currency) to administer as credit for the operation of these leased lands. The leaders of the local union were incorporated into the Junta Directiva, which disbursed these installment credits directly to the campesino tenants.

Thus, within the short period of seven months, the local peasant union leader, by virtue of his linkages with the Revolutionary Junta, had been granted the potential for exercise of enormously effective instrumental powers. He could determine which campesinos were included or excluded from the petition for land, he functioned as an administrator for the farm plan to which such a land grant was tied, and he was responsible for certifying that the individual member had complied with the tasks assigned him under the farm plan, thereby making the peasant eligible to receive his credit payment. The extent to which the authority, prestige, and status of peasant union leaders were enhanced through these instrumental powers may be inferred from the fact that by the time of its overthrow in November, 1948, the AD government had leased approximately 125,000 hectares of land to most of the more than 500 local peasant unions, granting access to land to more than 73,000 peasant union members and providing each member with an average of 332 bolivars in credits.[8]

The major instrumental power invested in peasant union leaders was influence in the granting of access to land. The rural landowner, whose traditional instrumental power was the denial of access to vast land and

[7] For the useful distinction between instrumental and affective leadership, see Sidney Verba, *Small Groups and Political Behavior: A Study of Leadership* (Princeton, N.J.: Princeton University Press, 1961).

[8] The data concerning ITIC were gathered in interviews and from confidential government and political party documents. They were carefully evaluated and were validated by other publicly available sources of information when possible.

water resources, still remained an obstacle to consolidation of political power in the rural areas by the AD-dominated labor-party alliance. By refusing to lease land to ITIC, landlords limited the amount of pay-off a peasant union leader could bring his followers. This obstacle was swept away by the Decreto de Arrendamiento de Prédios Rústicos of March 4, 1947. This decree required all owners of private lands not actively under cultivation to rent them to government agencies (ITIC) or directly to peasant unions. Article 11 placed all government lands—federal, state, and municipal—under a net of local Agrarian Commissions, which included an officer of the local peasant union. If the landowner objected to the terms offered by the commission or refused to come to terms, he could be fined; or he could carry his case to a three-man Board of Appeal, one member of which was a representative of the peasant union seeking the lease of his land.[9] Thus was the locus of local power—social, economic, and political —shifted from its traditional role matrix to a new one. The chief difference in performance lay in the fact that the landlord had traditionally exercised his powers for negative ends, while the peasant union leader exercised his for positive and dynamic purposes. The consequences of this shift, while dampened during the Pérez Jiménez regime, are still being felt in the rural areas of Venezuela.

On November 24, 1948, the government of AD President Gallegos was deposed by a military coup d'état. The newly installed junta referred to the effort of Acción Democrática to erect "a state within the state" through the party alliance with the labor movement as a justification for the coup.[10] Within three years Colonel Marcos Pérez Jiménez emerged as the dominant figure in the military cabal, and until 1958 he ruled Venezuela as a dictator.

The 1948–1958 regime suspended, but failed to eliminate, the operation of the new political process which had been structured under the AD regime. Thus, political parties, beginning with AD, were declared illegal and driven underground. A clandestine, multipartite resistance movement, spearheaded by AD, grew out of the experience of governmental suppression. The 1948–1958 regime did not reduce the expanded electorate, possibly because of the massive approval of the new formula for increased political participation. Instead the electoral process itself was compro-

[9] Junta Revolucionária de Gobierno, *Gaçeta Oficial* (Caracas), No. 22,327 (June 4, 1947). This is a complete copy of Decreto No. 557.

[10] See República de Venezuela, *Documentos oficiales relativos al movimiento militar del 24 de Noviembre de 1948* (Caracas: ONIP, 1949), especially pp. 17–23.

mised and manipulated in order to create a façade of electoral legitimacy for the Pérez Jiménez rule.

By Decree Number 56 of February 25, 1949, the entire Venezuelan Confederation of Labor, of which the Peasant Federation was a part, was dissolved because of its "political nature." Following a clash with the International Labour Organization over this suppression, the dictator took steps to establish his own labor movement, placing a communist labor leader at its head.[11] Until his overthrow in 1958, opposition labor leaders were unable to operate with the blessing of the state and functioned instead in clandestine alliance with their political colleagues.

The military government took immediate steps to halt the AD agrarian reform programs. Land and credit distributions were halted, and leases drawn up under the *prédios rústicos* decree were invalidated. Furthermore, peasants were evicted from private lands onto which they had just been moved, and eventually from most of the public lands as well. In a closely related development, large quantities of public lands were transferred to private hands. By 1958, over 96 per cent of the peasants who had been granted access to land under the AD government had been dislodged from their plots.[12]

Of the terror and suppression under Pérez Jiménez, we need note only two long-range consequences.[13] First, the assassination, torture, imprisonment, and exile of AD-affiliated peasant union leaders apparently had a profound impact on the campesino subculture, judging from the frequency with which this theme has been utilized in the oratory of peasant union leaders since their post-1958 emergence. Leaders set their claims to legitimate peasant leadership by virtue of their demonstrated willingness to make great sacrifices for the role.[14] Second, the suppression of the political parties and their labor movement affiliates coalesced diverse political tendencies into a common struggle against the dictatorship. This experience in the 1948–1958 crucible imparted considerable thrust to multiparty collaboration, establishing the conditions for a series of coalition governments following the dictator's overthrow and the rebirth of a labor movement with multiparty leadership.

Recent political developments in Venezuela are relatively well known.

[11] For a report on the suppression of labor under Pérez Jiménez, see International Labour Office, *Freedom of Association and Conditions of Work in Venezuela* (I.L.O. Studies and Reports, No. 21 [Geneva, 1950]).

[12] Powell, *op. cit.*, pp. 149–152.   [13] For details, see Martz, *op. cit.*

[14] See Powell, *op. cit.*, pp. 154–157 for details of the lot of present-day peasant union leaders under the Pérez Jiménez regime.

We shall confine our attention here to three relevant factors: the coalition tendency in government, the same tendency in the peasant union movement, and the agrarian reform program.

Elected in December, 1958, AD's leader, Rómulo Betancourt, became President and formed a coalition cabinet in early 1959. The Social Christian party (COPEI) and the Democratic Republican Union (URD) were both included in the original Betancourt coalition, but URD went to the opposition in November, 1960, over the issue of dealing with Fidel Castro. COPEI remained in coalition through the remainder of Betancourt's term of office. Raúl Leoni, elected President in December, 1963, became the third AD President. He failed to come to terms with COPEI and formed instead a new coalition, bringing URD back into the government along with a small personalist party, the Frente Nacional Democrática (FND). This coalition lasted until early 1966, when FND disintegrated, and the coalition majority was maintained by Leoni through the incorporation of independent splinters into the government.

The exit of URD from the coalition government in 1960 was paralleled by the exit of its labor union affiliates from the Confederation of Venezuelan Workers (CTV) and from the Peasant Federation (FCV). These same groups reaffiliated with the CTV and the FCV following the re-entry of URD into the 1964 governmental coalition. On the other hand, when COPEI left the governing coalition in 1964, its labor union affiliates continued to participate fully in the over-all labor movement, including the FCV. In short, while the peasant union movement continued to be dominated by AD leaders, since 1958 central authority and power within the organizational framework of the FCV have been shared with leaders from COPEI and URD.

Under the 1960 Agrarian Reform Law, Venezuela has pushed forward a rather massive public policy program aimed at the rural areas.[15] Emphasis has shifted from the 1945–1948 procedure of leasing land to peasants to the gradual establishment of a new class of peasant smallholders. As we shall see, the peasant union movement continues to play a critical role in the administration of the reform, although from 1945 to 1948 this role was formal, and since 1958 it has been informal. Budgetary support of the various coalition combinations for the agrarian reform program has been large and fairly stable. The Instituto Agrário Nacional (IAN), principal

---

[15] An evaluation of this extremely complex program is the purpose of the CIDA study mentioned in the first footnote to this chapter. It is expected to take approximately three years to complete and will be published by the Organization of American States.

governmental agency for the reform, received 1,358,100,000 bolivars from 1958 through 1966; the Banco Agrícola y Pecuária (BAP), which furnishes the campesino credits for the program, was allocated 888,800,000 bolivars in the same period. The Ministério de Agricultura y Cría (MAC), which furnishes the extension services, technological inputs, and other support services for the program, received 2,495,300,000 bolivars. The total was 4,742,200,000 bolivars for IAN, BAP, and MAC combined.[16]

By mid-1966, this massive program had established more than seven hundred *asentimientos,* or agrarian reform settlements, which furnished more than five million acres of land to more than one hundred thousand campesino families. The magnitude of this program of agrarian reform is closely related to the massive resurgence of the organized peasantry that began immediately after the flight of Pérez Jiménez into exile in the early morning of January 23, 1958.

The Movement as an Organization

Thirty years after the organization of the first peasant union of sixty-four members in 1936, the Federación Campesina de Venezuela had grown to include 3,476 local unions with some 550,000 campesino members. While the FCV as an organizational *form* has dominated the peasant movement, it has from its inception been a *movement—"el movimiento campesino"*—addressing itself to, and seeking to represent, the total peasant subculture. In spite of the elaboration and specialization of functions which has accompanied the growth of the FCV, its motto remains "The Social and Economic Emancipation of All Campesinos."

The Existence and Clarity of Organizational Goals

The motto of the Federación Campesina furnishes a clue to the initial organizational goals of the movement. It reflects the fact that beginning in 1936, a number of goals were fused into one. The goal formation inputs consisted of two basic types: broad, synthetic goals held by the professional organizers, and specific, situation-bound goals held by local campesino groups and their leaders. The broad goal of the original organizers was political in nature—the building of a mass base of potential electoral support—and had a logical, means-end relationship built into it. If the organizers could bring a mass base of support to bear, they could gain

---

[16] This summary data was furnished by Jorge R. Schuster, adviser to the Vice-Minister of Agriculture, who completed his Ph.D. in agricultural economics at the University of Wisconsin under the sponsorship of the Land Tenure Center. His dissertation was an actual-cost analysis of the reform program.

influence in the decision-making process of local, state, and national government. Then they could attempt to direct the outputs of the governmental system in response to the expressed needs of the campesinos comprising their support base. If successful, such a development would consolidate and augment the support of the peasantry for the instrumentality which served them.

The situational goals of the great number of peasant communities (which were the target of the organizational efforts of the ORVE and PDN professionals), on the other hand, were clear in terms of highly limited and specific ends, but were almost empty of content in terms of rational means-ends concepts. A local peasant group might want landlord X, who owns *finca* Y, to grant their animals access to his water supply, or to stop evicting *conuqueros* (slash-and-burn squatters) from his vast pasture lands, or to start buying cacao again and employ seasonal labor to process it. But they had little or no knowledge of what to do. The union organizers provided an attractive logic for "what to do," and the response of local campesino leaders and their followings provided the necessary mass base of support "to do it."

Viewed in historical perspective, the original macrogoals of the peasant movement were revolutionary in nature. We have seen, in fact, that a revolutionary restructuring of the political system was closely bound up in the process of agrarian reform from 1945 to 1948, and that many of the changes wrought during that period seem to have been permanent. Microgoals, on the other hand, while dependent on the establishment of certain far-reaching preconditions, were in themselves quite limited and modest in character. Local peasant goals evolved out of experience with an unsatisfactory social pattern—control by a few of land and water resources—and generated a basic desire for an emancipation from the land. Beyond that most basic and generally held goal, the microgoals with the highest specific content were focused on improvements in living conditions—housing, sanitation, health conditions and services, and transportation facilities. This battery of microgoals seems to have been held consistently throughout the development of the peasant movement in Venezuela. A survey of local peasant union leaders conducted in 1966, in an effort to get at the goal-seeking behavior of local syndicates, sought to identify the perceived problems which faced the membership of the local (Table 2–1).[17] The assumption was that "solutions" to perceived problems

---

[17] A survey based on a nationally drawn, randomly selected sample of 118 local peasant union leaders. For methodological details, see Powell, *op. cit.*, Appendix III. Columns of percentages in this and subsequent tables do not always total 100 owing to "don't know" responses or responses that could not be used because of errors.

constituted the instrumental goals of the local union. Following problem identification, the respondents were asked to characterize a list of postulated problems as "grave," "minor," or "nonexistent" in their local community.

Table 2–1. The identification and characterization of perceived problems in the rural areas of Venezuela

Problem	Percentage saying problem "greatest"	Percentage saying problem "grave"
Insufficient land	28.0	67.8
Agrarian reform inefficiencies	17.8	n.a.
Inadequate roads	11.9	61.0
Lack of potable water	11.0	61.0
Insufficient credit	6.8	64.4
Inadequate education	5.1	39.8
Unsanitary housing	5.1	67.8
Farm-related problems	4.2	35.6
Lack of medical facilities	3.4	68.6
$N = 118$		

While land ownership appears to be the most salient goal in a hierarchy of local objectives, lack of medical facilities and unsanitary housing appear to be equally painful local problems, and along with problems of providing sanitary water supplies and penetration roads, they generate a spectrum of social welfare goals. The low salience of "farm-related" problems, such as lack of fertilizers, hybrid seeds, fencing, farm machinery, and the like, emphasizes the nature of the Federación Campesina as a social movement rather than an exclusively occupationally-derived form of collective action.

The Environmental Ends-Means Continuum

The initial political goals of the organizers of the peasant union movement grew out of the political environment in which they were formulated. Similarly, the interaction of goal-seeking behavior with the changing political environment created the means—the people, strategies, and tactics—through which these goals were sought. As goal-seeking behavior through specific means affected the political environment, original goals were modified, updated, or otherwise related to the total march of surrounding events. Thus, from 1936 to 1945 the priority goal was to build an organizational base of political support. Once access to government was achieved through AD's participation in the coup dé'tat, this support base was utilized in the electoral process to legitimize and extend the role of the party in the governmental process. The peasant union sector of this base of support (original goal) was then utilized (as a means) for carrying out an extensive *de facto* agrarian reform program from 1945 to 1948. During the dictatorship of Pérez Jiménez, the same organizational form—the peasant union movement, operating clandestinely —was one means by which AD and the other parties survived governmental suppression. Their goal was to reestablish a claim to participation when the political process was reopened following the overthrow of the dictator. Once achieved, participation was exploited to direct a renewed, massive governmental effort toward the relief of problem conditions in the rural areas (agrarian reform). Thus a continuous flow of interdependent relationships was developed among the political environment, organizational goals, organizational means, and the rural environment.

On the local level, microgoals were likewise generated out of specific environmental situations. Land-related goals were dependent in part on the form of economic organization built into the local land-man-crop ecology and on the derivative land tenure status of the local campesinos: smallholders, renters, tenants, sharecroppers, or combination squatters and seasonal wage laborers. Local means, or goal-seeking activities, varied widely according to these differing situations. The living-condition goals, however, were shared so widely that certain generalized means, such as forming peasant unions to transmit demands for improvements to government, were widespread and persistent over time.

Means to specific local ends were determined by the interaction of trial-and-error goal-seeking behavior with the local political environment and the community power structure. From 1936 to 1945, lacking any legitimate channels of access to higher governmental sources of authority, local unions interacted directly with the local landowners to rectify conditions they found unsatisfactory. The resulting events were uncoordinated, disorganized efforts at direct problem-solving which produced some adjustments, but more often frictions and occasionally violence. From 1945 to 1948, channels of structured access to the governmental process became available to many local campesino organizations through the AD party, and local leaders began functioning as brokers for the interests of their campesino clients—petitioning for land, technical advice, and credits. Such access, originally a goal of local leaders, then became the means through which they sought to bring the organized resources of the government to bear on the resolution of their local, situation-bound problems. With the military coup of 1948, such access once again became merely a sought-after goal as the instrumental problem-solving capabilities of local union leaders were blocked by the return of the local landlord to a position of power and the eviction of the peasants from agrarian reform projects.

Immediately following the overthrow of Pérez Jiménez, but before a structural channel of multiparty access to the decision-making process was reestablished by the election of an AD-dominated coalition government, local leaders and peasant groups reverted to direct problem-solving activities by means of widespread land invasions. There is some evidence that many of the lands invaded were the same to which peasants had been granted access from 1945 to 1948, but other lands were invaded as well.[18] By 1961, when the Betancourt government was strenuously pushing the agrarian reform program thereby opening more legitimate channels for redress and goal-seeking activities by the peasantry, the widespread use and threat of land invasions were strengthening the hand of the opposition to total reform, and thus became a liability to the government. The peasant union movement was induced (although it required a purge of radical leadership to consolidate the decision) to renounce land invasion as a means to the solution of the land problem. Thereafter, local peasant union leaders concentrated on their brokerage and representational functions. Table 2–2 illustrates how their activities, undertaken to accomplish

Table 2–2. Local peasant union activities reported by leaders

Activity	Percentage of leaders reporting
Meetings to discuss community problems	80.5
Helping members obtain BAP credits	78.0
Petitioning Ministry of Education	69.5
Petitioning IAN for land	66.9
Petitioning for rural housing projects	66.1
Petitioning for penetration roads	65.3
Petitioning for public health projects	65.3
Organizing educational programs	37.3
Organizing social events	36.4
Sponsoring athletic activities	24.6

$N = 118$

[18] See Jorge F. Schuster, "La estructura económica en seis asentimientos campesinos," a manuscript prepared in the Ministerio de Agricultura y Cría (mimeo., 1965).

their microgoals, correspond to their perception of environmental problems (Table 2–1).

Certain generalizations can be made from the data in Table 2–2. First, leader-follower interactions are concentrated in union meetings, where the problems and prospects of the local community and its needs are discussed and where leaders report on their brokerage activities. The other two areas of leader-follower interaction are in the credit-seeking process and occasional social activities.[19] It appears from the data that peasant union leaders spend much of their time and energy in the performance of the brokerage function. Other data gathered in the survey show that petitioning a government agency for its services was not confined to the submission of a formal request but was followed up by extensive face-to-face contact with representatives, local or regional, of the appropriate agency. For example, concerning the three major agencies, IAN (land), BAP (credits), and MAC (extension services and roads), peasant union leaders reported high rates of intergroup contact.

Table 2–3. Local peasant union leader interaction with government officials

	Percentage of leaders reporting contact with:		
Frequency of face-to-face contact	IAN officials	BAP officials	MAC officials
Daily or weekly	21.2	16.1	13.5
Monthly or yearly	36.5	35.5	34.8
Infrequently	6.8	8.5	10.1
$N = 118$			

Factor analysis revealed that those leaders not accounted for in Table 2–3 (that is, those reporting "never" having had personal contact with such officials) were newly recruited leaders, especially those who had recently entered the peasant union movement through the vigorous organizational drive of the Social Christian party (COPEI).

Finally, other evidence indicates that when local leaders run into resistance or obstacles in the performance of their brokerage functions, they turn to the state and national leadership of the Federación Campesina for

[19] Only 16.4 per cent of the local leaders reported attempting to secure collective contracts for wage laborers doing seasonal work—a very common practice among peasant union members. Such an activity would seem to be a "traditional" type of union concern, and lack of attention to it by the FCV underscores the broader social and political nature of its concerns.

exertion of pressure from a higher level. The following sections show why the higher leadership strata of the peasant union movement are able effectively to transmit such pressures for action through appropriate communications channels to the responsive arena of authoritative decision-making within various government agencies.

The Internal Organization of the Movement

The size and complexity of the Federación Campesina must be perceived in order to properly appreciate its functions.[20] The almost four thousand local unions are represented at the regional level by executive committees called Seccionales. These committees, consisting of five or six officers supported by a small staff, are elected at regional conventions called approximately once every three years by the national executive committee. Their primary function seems to be communication. They either transmit local union brokerage demands to the appropriate regional governmental office or "buck" such demands up to the national level of the FCV, where the superior status and authority of its officers can be brought to bear. The Seccionales, of course, are two-way transmission links, passing information and instructions originating at the national level down to the local unions. There are currently twenty-two Seccionales; their jurisdictional boundaries coincide in most cases with the states.

The thirteen-member national executive committee of the Federación Campesina is the standing, supreme authoritative body of the organization. It is elected approximately every three years at a national Campesino Congress organized for this purpose. In addition to its primary function as a transmission link for local brokerage demands and as a more generalized representation of campesino interests, the national organization performs certain services for the membership. These include a vocational school program, the mass purchase of farm machinery for members, and the organization of campesino enterprises, such as a union-run rice processing operation at Calabozo. The FCV also recently began establishing direct-sale farmers' markets in urban centers for members.

The workings of such a complex form of collective action as the Venezuelan peasant union movement are not readily conveyed in simple terms. To facilitate the description and explanation of the internal organi-

[20] We are primarily interested here in organizational functions. For a detailed institutional description, see John D. Powell, "Preliminary Report on the Federación Campesina de Venezuela: Origins, Organization, Leadership and Role in the Agrarian Reform Program" (Research Paper No. 9 [Madison: University of Wisconsin Land Tenure Center, 1964]).

zation of the movement, it is convenient to break the analysis down into two broad areas: membership and leadership. The latter analysis can then be further refined according to position in the leadership hierarchy.

Membership. The 550,000 members of the Federación Campesina are drawn from a pool of over two million rural residents. Descriptive statistics for this pool indicate the prevalence of low income levels (the mean is $150 per person annually, in the lowest decile of Venezuelan incomes),[21] high rates of illiteracy (61.4 per cent), and high rates of affliction with gastrointestinal diseases (82 per cent).[22] Living in hazardous environmental circumstances without the financial and other material resources necessary to ameliorate them has created a distinctive subculture of rural poverty. The data in Tables 2–4 and 2–5 reflect the pessimistic attitudes which permeate this subculture.[23]

Such attitudes and perceptions, which spring in part from living in a difficult organism-environment situation, are characteristic of the total

Table 2–4. Perceptions of present life (in per cent)

	Campesino sample groups		
Personal life today	*Asentados* *	Non-*asentados*†	Farm laborers‡
Very happy	0.5	2.7	3.0
Happy	34.6	35.0	44.4
Not very happy	49.2	43.7	42.0
Unhappy	12.6	15.9	8.3
N =	*191*	*183*	*166*

Source: Based on recent survey research conducted by the CONVEN project of the Massachusetts Institute of Technology and the Universidad Central de Venezuela.

* *Asentados* are inhabitants of government agrarian reform settlements (*asentimientos*).

† Non-*astendados* are a dependent sample of nonsettled campesinos living in the same counties in which the sample *asentimientos* were located.

‡ Farm laborers are wage hands who were on commercial farm operations at the time of survey.

[21] See IBRD, *op. cit.*, p. 113, and Carl S. Shoup, *et al., The Fiscal System of Venezuela* (Baltimore, Md.: Johns Hopkins Press, 1959).

[22] U.S. Army Medical Health Service, *Health and Sanitary Data for Venezuela* (Washington, D.C.: Medical Information and Intelligence Agency, 1961).

[23] John R. Mathiason, who is currently working on the CIDA study of the Venezuelan agrarian reform, has made public a preliminary analysis of the peasant attitudinal data in his chapter in Frank Bonilla and Jose Silva Michelena (eds.), *Studying the Venezuelan Polity* (Cambridge: Massachusetts Institute of Technology Center for International Affairs, 1966).

Table 2–5. Perceptions of magnitude of personal problems (in per cent)

Problems are worse than one can bear	Campesino sample groups		
	Asentados	Non-*asentados*	Farm laborers
Frequently	22.5	15.3	8.9
Occasionally	14.7	14.8	26.0
Very rarely	32.5	34.4	28.4
Never	19.4	24.6	25.4
N =	*191*	*183*	*166*

Source: CONVEN.

peasant subculture. In addition to these shared attitudes, the members of the Federación Campesina bring into the peasant union movement special economic concerns that derive from their land tenure status. Different status types share certain common, environmental concerns, but in addition, each places emphasis on different status-derived interests.

The data in Table 2–6 indicate that the peasant union movement represents a wide variety of tenure-derived interests. Furthermore, the complexity of the data parallels studies which consistently show that there are few "pure" tenure types in Latin America; mixed-tenure types

Table 2–6. Land tenure status of peasant union members, as estimated by their union leaders

Tenure status of union members	Percentage of union leaders estimating many, few, or none of each tenure type among their membership		
	Many	Few	None
Squatters	46.6	13.6	9.3
Farm laborers	33.1	27.1	11.0
Sharecroppers	10.2	22.0	35.6
Tenants	13.6	12.7	39.8
Smallholders	14.4	23.7	27.1
Asentados *	22.0	20.4	36.4
N = 118			

* *Asentados* are estimated in a separate item and may therefore be double-counted as "smallholders," depending on whether they had final title or not and on the respondent's judgment about whether an *asentado* was in fact a landowner.

of peasants predominate.[24] The most prevalent mixture in Venezuela seems to be the *conuquero,* or squatter and seasonal farm laborer, who often utilizes slash-and-burn techniques on his subsistence plots.

Leadership. Significant differences in local, state, and national leadership characteristics have been brought to light through extensive research on the peasant union movement.[25] These are analyzed below on a topical basis, which facilitates comparison, rather than on a stratum-by-stratum basis.

In terms of age, there is little significant interstrata difference, nor is there a great difference in leader-follower characteristics. The three CONVEN peasant samples yielded a median age of 41 years. The median age of our local union leadership sample was 40; of state FCV leaders, 37; and of national FCV leaders, 38. In terms of the extreme youthfulness of the total Venezuelan population, the ages of members and leaders of the peasant union movement are well above national norms.

Important leader-follower and interstrata leadership differences show up in measures of education level. One would intuitively expect leader-follower differences, but the rather clear relationship between amount of education and position in the leadership hierarchy is somewhat startling. Considerably more sophisticated research would be required to draw causal inferences from the relationship between education and position in the leadership hierarchy. It is clear, however, from an understanding of the leadership functions which have been described so far (and which are further analyzed later), that the higher up one proceeds in the hierarchy, the greater are the role demands in terms of communications skills, both verbal and written; ability to analyze complex problem-situations, and the ability to function efficiently in ambiguous role situations, often under stress. All of these abilities may well depend on level of education (see Table 2-7).

On the important question of the social origins and identifications of the leadership of the movement, we find a complex situation. It was stated earlier that the original organization of the movement was catalyzed by "outside" change agents, oriented toward the accomplishment of national

[24] See, for instance, the analysis by Richard Adams in John J. Johnson (ed.), *Continuity and Change in Latin America* (Stanford, Calif.: Stanford University Press, 1964).

[25] Leadership interviews were conducted in 1961, 1964, and 1965–1966. All national leaders of the FCV who held office from 1964 through 1966 were interviewed; a 20 per cent sample (frankly, accidental) of state FCV leaders was obtained through interviews; and the local leadership sample survey was carried out through use of a questionnaire instrument, administered in an interview situation.

Table 2–7. Comparative education of campesinos and FCV leaders (in per cent)

Level of education	Campesino groups *			FCV leaders		
	Asentado	Non-*asentado*	Laborers	Local	State	National
No school	66.5	52.5	50.0	30.5	4.3	0.0
Some primary	23.6	32.1	31.3	45.7	17.4	4.1
Complete primary	1.4	3.6	4.0	18.6	52.1	61.5
Some secondary or more	0.5	0.7	2.0	4.2	21.7	32.8
N =	*191*	*183*	*166*	*118*	*23*	*24*

* CONVEN samples.

goals, who came in and recruited the local leadership of the peasant unions. By 1966, higher leadership strata still exhibited a greater tendency to have come from noncampesino backgrounds than local leaders (see Table 2–8).

Not only do local leaders come overwhelmingly from campesino family backgrounds, but when asked to identify their own profession, or calling, 86.4 per cent responded "farmer," while national and state leaders identified themselves as either "labor leaders," "political professionals," or other nonfarming professionals. These self-identifications may derive in part from differences in the amount of experience which each leadership stratum has had in the labor movement—an average of eight years for local leaders, fourteen years for state leaders, and sixteen years for national FCV leaders—and the different exposure each stratum has had to other branches of the labor movement.

Table 2–8. Father's occupation, as reported by local, state, and national leaders of the FCV (in per cent)

Father's occupation	Local	State	National
Campesino	83.9	56.5	45.8
Small business	5.9	21.7	8.3
Laborer	3.4	8.7	20.8
Professional	1.7	0.0	16.6
Large landowner	0.0	4.3	4.1
Other	0.0	4.3	4.1
N =	*118*	*23*	*24*

Table 2–9. Labor movement background reported by local, state, and national leaders of the FCV (in per cent)

Branch of labor movement first joined	Local	State	National
Agriculture	89.8	43.4	59.0
Transportation	1.7	13.0	4.5
Construction	2.5	26.0	0.0
Industry	0.0	13.0	22.7
Petroleum	1.7	4.2	9.0
Other	1.7	0.0	4.5
N =	*118*	*23*	*24*

From the data given in Table 2–9 we can see, then, that local leaders identify almost exclusively as campesinos, and their union experience has been dominated by the peasant union movement. The role of peasant union leader is apparently so diffuse and multifunctional that role incumbents identify more clearly with their roles as agriculturists. State and national leaders, on the other hand, emerging from somewhat different family environments, have by virtue of long and varied experiences in the labor movement structured specific identities for themselves as professionals.

In terms of role identity, one might be tempted to say that state and national leaders identify with nonpeasant roles, while local leaders identify with an indigenous role, and that therefore state and national leaders are "outsiders," but local leaders are not. But this would misread the complex reality of the situation in two ways. First, the role of union professional (as well as that of political professional) has been entangled with peasant constituencies since the founding of the labor movement in 1936. "Union leader" and "political professional," far from being nonpeasant roles, are often intimately related to peasant referents. Peasant unions represent over 70 per cent of the total number of unions in Venezuela, the FCV is the largest component of the Confederation of Venezuelan Workers, and the two most popular political parties, AD and COPEI, are largely rural-based.

Second, while local leaders strongly identify with agriculture, they also identify with the "outside" world—that is, the urban-based larger society. Local leaders do come from and live in the rural communities where their unions are located: 29.7 per cent were born there, an additional 12.7 per cent have lived there for more than twenty years, and another 21.2 per cent have lived there for from ten to twenty years. But at the same time there is a certain amount of the "outside world" built into their life experiences. At the time of interview, 34.5 per cent of these local leaders had previously lived in a city or cities for up to ten years, and 12.7 per cent had for more than ten years! The most plausible explanation for this is that they had moved to urban areas as young men and later returned to their places of origin. This factor of experience in the larger society enhances their ability to perform demanding "cultural brokerage" functions for their campesino neighbors, including representation before agrarian reform government agencies.[26] The fact that they are better equipped by experience to perform these functions increases their effectiveness in obtaining instrumental benefits and consolidates their leadership position in the local community. The explanation of why these men returned to the rural setting after exposure to urban life may be related to the process of recruiting leaders into the peasant union movement.

For each of the strata of peasant union leadership—local, state, and national—we find a common pattern of sequential associations, which logic indicates is a recruitment pattern (Table 2–10). From the data, it

Table 2–10. Sequential associations of peasant union leaders

Leadership level	Average number of years affiliated with:		
	Political party	Labor movement	Federación Campesina
Local (N = 118)	14	8	7
State (N = 23)	16	14	8
National (N = 24)	17	16	14

seems highly probable that today's peasant union leaders, with few exceptions, joined their particular political party first, later became involved in the labor movement, and still later became active in the Federación Campesina. A plausible explanation for this sequential pattern would be that it represents a recruitment process. Some local leaders may have been drawn into a political party during their youthful sojourns to urban centers. Others, never leaving the rural areas, joined during the early years of the movement before unions existed in great numbers. Some

[26] For an insightful treatment of the cultural broker concept, see Adams, *op. cit.*

years later, all became involved in the party's efforts to organize the peasantry into unions, and those who had been living in urban areas seized the opportunity to advance as party leaders by returning to their rural communities and helping to organize a local union. They could serve the party better in this way, and perhaps they felt more comfortable in a rural setting than when competing in the urban milieu with the better-educated and more widely experienced labor leaders who were their party colleagues.

There was considerable motivation for such a "return home" in 1958, following the overthrow of the dictator, when the parties threw themselves into a rebuilding effort after a decade of supression. Perhaps the motivation also had a personal dimension, since these local leaders were returning to rural areas where the peasantry had been cruelly evicted from the long-sought parcels of land obtained during the 1945–1948 period. In the meantime, other leaders steadily served the party needs in the hierarchy of the union movement, some of them exclusively in the peasant sector, some in other branches and moving relatively late in their careers into the Federación Campesina. This especially characterizes state leaders, many of whom were brought into the FCV in 1962 from other branches of the hierarchy to replace the radical leadership elements that were purged from the peasant union movement.

It should be clear by now that just as interactions among the political environment, organizational goals, organizational means, and the rural environment hold the explanatory key to the genesis of the peasant union movement, so they hold the key to understanding the internal organization and leadership characteristics of the Federación Campesina. It should also be clear by now that the Venezuelan peasant union movement is intimately involved in the national political process. We must now examine the exact nature of this involvement.

Linkages with the Political System

The relationship between the Federación Campesina and the political party system is more than an alliance of autonomous organizations. It is an amalgamation. Parties and the peasant union movement interpenetrate one another deeply. The mechanism for effecting this interpenetration is dual role-holding by the leaders of the FCV—that is, simultaneous incumbency in closely related party and peasant union roles.

A typical example would be a secretary general of a local union who holds the position of agrarian secretary on a party executive committee in his community; state officers might hold similar positions on the state executive committees. The president of the FCV from 1962 through 1966, Armando González, held the position of agrarian secretary on the national executive committee of the AD party for several years, then maintained a position on the committee as political secretary. National FCV leaders affiliated with other parties held similar positions. There are, then, a variety of party positions which FCV leaders might hold on party committees, although they tend to be related to the labor or peasant spheres of interest. Among the 118 local FCV leaders in our survey sample, 25.4 per cent held, or had held, at least one local party office. An additional 5.1 per cent had held more than one. Dual role-holding was found to be universal among state and national leaders, and as we have suggested, top national leaders sit in on the most important decision-making bodies in the parties. This was the case for leaders from each of the three major political parties participating in the peasant union movement in mid-1966—Acción Democrática, which dominates the movement and controls the loyalties of some 65 per cent of the local unions and their members; the Social Christians (COPEI), which controls about 30 per cent of the locals; and the Unión Republicana Democrática (URD), which accounts for the remainder of the local unions and members. Organizational positions and power in the state and national executive committees of the Federación Campesina are distributed to reflect the divisions of control indicated above. Competition to recruit new local leaders and form additional unions is carried on freely by each party, and shifts in the balance of organizational power, reflecting possible changes, normally occur at the state conventions and the Campesino Congress.

The holding of dual party–peasant union roles, then, is so common, and the nature of the roles is so diffuse and interdependent, that it might be more accurate to consider such leaders as participants in a fused political–labor union role system. Considerable efforts were made in the informal interviews with state and national leaders to identify possible situations in which an incumbent might feel forced to choose between conflicting roles. So fused were the roles, however, that such a possibility was perceived only in elaborately specified and unusual circumstances. The response of the national president of the Federación Campesina to such a question was typical: "We are loyal members of Acción Democrática . . . but as campesino leaders and syndicate directors we have a class orientation with which we try to make AD an instrument of the class, not the class an instrument of the party, or a springboard for the party." Class —that is, campesino—and party interests are so intertwined and mutually interdependent that a conflict of interest seems remote.

Through their party positions, peasant union leaders have gained access to the decision-making process in the coalition governments which have governed Venezuela since 1958. Many leaders gain more direct access to the government through the electoral process. Among the local leaders in our sample, 15.2 per cent had been elected or appointed to local government or law enforcement positions, thereby extending still further their knowledge of, and influence in, municipal and county governments. Of the state FCV officials interviewed, 39.1 per cent had been elected or appointed to public offices at the local or state level of government. The twenty-four national leaders interviewed included five who had been elected members of their state legislative assemblies. Four national leaders (two AD, one COPEI, and one URD) were, at the time of interview, elected members of the Chamber of Deputies in the national Congress.

Other channels of access for Federación Campesina leaders to important decision-making circles depend neither on party influence nor election to public office, but are legally structured role attributes. Under the terms of the Agrarian Reform Law, two members of the five-man Board of Directors of the National Agrarian Institute (IAN) are named by the Federación Campesina. Since 1962 one of these members has been named by AD and one by COPEI. The FCV has held a position on the Board of Directors of the Banco Agrícola y Pecuária (BAP) since the FCV rebirth in 1959. The BAP representative has customarily been an AD leader. The Federación Campesina is also represented in the third principal reform agency, the Ministry of Agriculture (MAC), on the advisory committees of a variety of agricultural product boards. These positions are filled by leaders from all three parties. Finally, the FCV is entitled to representation on the National Agrarian Reform Coordinating Committee, established by law to effect cooperation and combined planning among the many agencies concerned with portions of the agrarian reform.

The Rural Problem-Solving System

The political and governmental linkages of the leadership of the peasant union movement have bound together a number of substructures in the political system into a functionally specific problem-solving subsystem. This subsystem we shall call the rural problem-solving system. It functions as follows.

The human stresses and strains generated by the physical characteristics of the rural environment, interacting with the man-land rural ecology, produce a potential for goal-seeking mobilization among the peasantry. This potential is tapped by local leaders and tranformed into participation in peasant union activities. Leader-follower interactions produce specific information on local problems and specific demands for governmental goods and services to meet them.

Local leaders communicate these demands for problem-solving action. If relevant problem-solving resources are controlled by local government representatives, the leaders transmit them in person. If the required resources are of greater magnitude or if a satisfactory response is not forthcoming, the local leader transmits the demands via the state or national hierarchy of the Federación Campesina.

At all levels, peasant union leaders utilize their skills, experiences, and political resources to press campesino demands through whatever party or governmental channels of access they may enjoy. At the higher levels of leadership, these channels penetrate into the most powerful decision-making forums in the political system. In pressing these demands, peasant union leaders bargain from a position of influence in one of the most important elements of support for government since 1958—the peasant vote. Through the complex and sophisticated skills of the top national leadership of the peasant union movement, peasant-derived demands for governmental goods and services are interlaced with considerations of peasant voting support and converted into specific pressures for the agrarian reform program.

These pressures exert themselves in the budget-making process and in the planning and programing process of the agencies involved in agrarian reform. Finally they are converted into specific field projects. As field projects are undertaken, local peasant union leaders interact, following up their demands and filling their brokerage roles. The projects, as they proceed, affect environmental conditions in the rural areas, or some aspect of the man-land ecology. These environmental or ecological changes, in turn, are experienced by the peasantry and generate feedback through the forum of the peasant union.

In short, the problem-solving process is a self-sustaining interchange of influence, information, and goods and services. It is dynamic and adaptable to changing circumstances, in both the rural and the political environments. It ties together a number of substructures in the political system into a highly interdependent subsystem with clearly defined structural and functional boundaries. This is the rural problem-solving system. (See Chart 2–1).

Conclusion

Professor Landsberger has suggested that "peasant movements do not begin either to survive or to reach their goals until very slow-moving but profound changes in the economic, power, and value structure of the

Chart 2–1. The rural problem-solving system

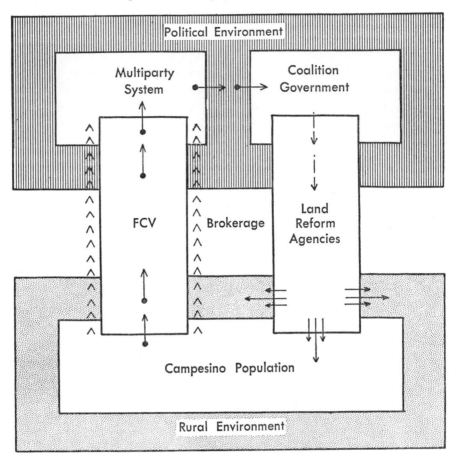

Major Transactional Flows:
Inputs:

●——→ ●——→ demands for goods and services

> > > > > voting support

Outputs:

·——→ ·——→ budget-making & programing

⇒——→ field projects

larger society take place. Thus, the success of peasants is basically a symptom of these underlying and larger structural changes, rather than being an independent event." [27]

The interdependence of peasant success and the political matrix is clear, but the exceptional nature of the peasant union movement in Venezuela lies in the fact that its success, rather than being a basic symptom of profound structural changes in the social and political systems, was an important contributory factor in that process of change. Knowing as we do the genesis of the peasant union movement, we recognize, in fact, that the structural changes in the Venezuelan polity were precisely the macro-goals of the original organizers of the movement. The basic transformation of the political system, then, from a closed-access, ascriptive-elite type to a competitive party, open-access, instrumental-elite type is in part a measurement of the success of the peasant union movement.

The critical question concerning the FCV, unlike other peasant movements in Latin America, is not whether it can be considered a success, but how successful it has been. This requires a careful analysis of the context of success, a search for empirical measurements of defined elements of success, and some judgments concerning the implications for future social, economic, and political development.

The context of success in the Venezuelan case is bound by the democratic regimes which governed from 1945 to 1948 and from 1958 to the present. It was within these regimes that the basic structural and functional changes in the political system occurred. During the first phase (1945–1948), a measurable degree of contributory credit (for the electoral and constitutional changes effected) can be attributed to the AD-organized peasant electorate. Rómulo Betancourt claimed that Acción Democrática won every election during this period because of "massive rural support." [28] A careful and more precise estimate has been made indicating that peasant votes accounted for over one-third of all AD votes in the 1946–1948 elections.[29] While AD's popularity during this period was urban as well as rural, the rural base was more stable and dependable and performed a major share of the important support function for the political system during this period.

During the decade of suppression under Pérez Jiménez, the peasant

[27] Henry A. Landsberger, unpublished manuscript, 1966.

[28] Rómulo Betancourt, *Venezuela: Política y petróleo* (Mexico City: Fondo de Cultura Económica, 1956), p. 355.

[29] Peter P. Lord, "The Peasantry as an Emerging Political Factor in Mexico, Bolivia and Venezuela" (M.A. thesis, Columbia University, 1965).

union movement was responsible for the survival of important elements in the democratic political system which had been structured during the 1945–1948 period. While difficult to relate to quantitative referents, the hypothesis that the activities of peasant union leaders and members played an important part in the clandestine resistance movement is compatible with available historic evidence—and also with applicable findings from studies of the role of peasants in "internal warfare." Gil Carl Alroy stated:

Unlike urban dwellers, peasants can provide foodstuffs for extended periods of time and can arrange information networks covering extensive areas. They can generally make whatever resources they possess available at the periphery of the incumbents' controls, at their weakest points. Urban dwellers, by contrast, can offer resources and skills rarely possessed by peasants, but must act under conditions of optimum control by the incumbents. . . . As a general proposition . . . active support by the peasantry should favor the insurgents, particularly by providing resources that facilitate the waging of protracted warfare. All that we know about guerrilla warfare seems to validate this proposition.[30]

Following the overthrow of the dictator, the contribution of the peasant union movement was again one of electoral support for AD and other democratic parties that formed part of the coalition governments from 1958 to 1966, especially the Social Christian party. It has been estimated that in the 1958 and 1963 elections, peasant voting support accounted for fully half the votes for Acción Democrática, and for over a third of the votes for the various parties which formed the coalitions under presidents Betancourt and Leoni.[31]

In short, the peasant union movement played an important role in changing the political system to benefit the Venezuelan citizenry in general. During the first phase of these changes, suffrage was expanded and regulated to give voters a direct role in the election of the Congress and the President. During the phase of clandestine resistance to Pérez Jiménez, the peasant union movement helped preserve important structural elements of the democratic party system which had been driven underground. Beginning in 1958, through its stable electoral support of the government, the peasant union movement contributed to the government's ability to reform and improve the political system's functional capacity for regulation and distribution. One of the most important

---

[30] *The Involvement of Peasants in Internal Wars* (Research Monograph No. 24 [Princeton, N.J.: Princeton University, Center of International Studies, 1966]), pp. 23–24.   [31] Lord, *op. cit.*

evidences of this enhanced capacity was the passage of the Agrarian Reform Law of 1960 (regulation) and the program which resulted from it (distribution). Peasant voting support in 1963 helped to perform the "system maintenance" function for the political system and its rural problem-solving subsystem.[32]

Although success in accomplishing the macrogoals of the peasant union movement is clear, success in the accomplishment of the host of microgoals is less so. This uncertainty about local successes springs in part from the difficulty of relating what was desired to what has been accomplished in any precise and systematic fashion. We do know that some one hundred thousand campesino families have been settled by the program, almost half of all campesino families classified as landless by the National Agrarian Institute in 1960.[33] We also know that considerable amounts of campesino credit have been granted and that there have been a variety of improvements in rural housing, public health conditions, school and road construction, and so forth. But many, if not all, of these improvements benefit nonmembers as well as members of the peasant union movement. To establish a quantitative measurement of the degree of local union success seems impossible without further systematic research in the local union environs.

There is some evidence, however, of satisfaction with the agrarian reform program, and of attitudinal changes related to participation in the rural problem-solving process in the peasantry, particularly in Federación Campesina members and leaders. These intangible measurements of success may well prove in the long run to be more important than measurements of material benefit, although the two seem closely related. Charles Erasmus, a sensitive social anthropologist, found in Venezuela—as Nathan Whetten had in Mexico—that peasants often felt the agrarian reform had brought them "personal freedom." [34] This general sense of liberation seems to be related to the elimination of the rural landlord's absolute control of vast land and water resources, upon which the peasantry depends for its livelihood. Escape from the consequences of arbitary use,

---

[32] For an attempt at systems analysis of the functions of the political system, see Gabriel Almond and G. Bingham Powell, *Comparative Politics: A Developmental Approach* (Boston: Little, Brown, 1966).

[33] Instituto Agrário Nacional, *Informe* (Caracas: The Instituto, 1961), Vol. II.

[34] Charles Erasmus, "Agrarian Reform: A Comparative Study of Venezuela, Bolivia and Mexico," in Dwight B. Heath, Charles J. Erasmus, and Hans C. Buechler, "Land Reform and Social Revolution in Bolivia" (mimeo.; Madison: University of Wisconsin Land Tenure Center, 1965); Nathan L. Whetten, *Rural Mexico* (Chicago: University of Chicago Press, 1948).

and possible abuse, of such power is one major result of an agrarian reform. The state becomes an active participant in the land tenure system, regulating and influencing access to land, its use in farming, and its distribution as a form of personal or family wealth. Thus the peasant feels "free"—and along with this feeling go higher hopes and expectations for the future. Here we find that peasant union membership seems to augment, or reinforce, such feelings, especially among those not yet granted the land benefits available under the agrarian reform but aspiring to them (see Tables 2–11, 2–12, and 2–13).

The significance of these quickening hopes and expectations lies in the fact that they are a consequence of a purposeful mobilization system in action. The rural problem-solving system is bringing the peasantry into a fruitful, interdependent relationship with the modernizing state. Furthermore, there are signs that many of the behavioral elements of this mobilization system are full of promise for stability—that is, a projection of the

Table 2–11. Relation between perception of improvement in personal economic situation and union participation (in per cent)

Personal economic situation in the last five years has	Attend union meetings?			
	Asentados		Non-*asentados*	
	Yes	No	Yes	No
Improved	45	36	40	23
Remained same or worsened	55	64	60	77
N =	*106*	*50*	*60*	*83*

Source: Adapted from CONVEN data supplied by John R. Mathiason of the Massachusetts Institute of Technology.

Table 2–12. Relation between perception of personal future and union participation (in per cent)

In the next five years personal situation will	Attend union meetings?			
	Asentados		Non-*asentados*	
	Yes	No	Yes	No
Improve	89	81	93	63
Be the same or worse	11	19	7	37
N =	*96*	*43*	*57*	*79*

Source: CONVEN data by Mathiason.

Table 2–13. Relation between perception of Venezuela's future and union participation (in per cent)

The Venezuelan situation in the next twenty years will	Attend union meetings?			
	Asentados		Non-*asentados*	
	Yes	No	Yes	No
Improve	95	89	93	74
Be the same or worse	5	11	7	26
N =	*99*	*44*	*54*	*74*

Source: CONVEN data by Mathiason.

system and its consequences into the future seems assured, barring disastrous complications in the national political situation.

The local peasant union leader is the key element of strength and stability in this march of events. We have already noted the highly indigenous character and the strength of the community roots demonstrated by local FCV leaders. We saw, too, that the local leader serves as a kind of general cultural broker for the peasant subculture in its dealings with the larger society. There is additional evidence, moreover, that the brokerage role is especially operative in relating the peasant to the political culture of the nation (see Table 2–14).

Union leaders have a high rate of intergroup contact with political leaders—much higher than the rates reported by the CONVEN peasant samples. The rate of contact of these peasant groups with union leaders, however, is of a very high order. For *asentados*, 25.8 per cent reported a low rate of contact, 32.4 per cent moderate, and 40.4 per cent high. For

Table 2–14. Comparative leader-follower contacts with political leaders (in per cent)

Rate of personal contact with political leaders *	Union leaders	Campesino Groups †		
		Asentados	Non-*asentados*	Farm labor
Low	27.9	68.3	68.5	69.5
Moderate	44.9	23.9	18.2	18.5
High	26.3	6.5	10.8	8.7
N =	*118*	*191*	*183*	*166*

* Low rate of contact includes never or a few times in life. Moderate rate of contact includes yearly and monthly. High rate of contact includes weekly and daily.

† CONVEN data.

non-*asentados* the rates were 35.5 per cent low, 23.3 per cent moderate, and 39.3 per cent high, and for farm laborers they were 45.9 per cent low, 28.4 per cent moderate, and 22.5 per cent high. This suggests that the peasant union leaders serve as the local community contacts for the political system in its communications with the peasant subculture. This hypothesis is strengthened when we recall the number of local union leaders who are at the same time local party officials and realize that the degree of role fusion may be so great that campesino union members may not even perceive that their union leader, with whom they have frequent contact, may at the same time be a political leader. For this reason, the contacts with political leaders in Table 2–14 may be underreported and show up instead under contacts with union leaders.

In summary, local leaders are well established in the communities where their unions operate but are better educated and have had more experience with the larger society than their campesino neighbors; they serve an important brokerage function for their union members in dealing with government agencies concerned with agrarian reform; many of them have had leadership experience in a political party; and all interact more frequently than the members of their unions with political leaders inside and outside their village communities. They are, therefore, in an extremely advantageous position to act as influential interpreters of the larger society in general and the national polity in particular. In communications theory, those who fill such roles are known as "opinion leaders," and their function in the "two-step flow" of information is well known to social scientists.[35] Research concerning the two-step flow hypothesis depends heavily on mass media exposure rates for evidence of it. If our local union leaders are claimed to be important opinion leaders, then they ought to exhibit higher rates of mass media exposure than their followers, as Table 2–15 indicates.

The conclusion is compelling. Local peasant union leaders are performing a socialization function in general, and a political socialization function in particular. They are inducting the peasantry into the political system in a widespread and fairly systematic fashion. We have seen much suggestive evidence of how they perform this function by mobilizing peasant participation in local union activities, and we know much about the specific problem-solving purposes toward which many of these activities are directed. Now we need to explore the implications of this kind of

[35] See, *inter alia*, Elihu Katz, "The Two-Step Flow of Communication: An Up-to-Date Report on an Hypothesis," *Public Opinion Quarterly*, XXI (Spring, 1957).

Table 2–15. Comparative mass media exposure of campesino followers and leaders (in per cent)

		Campesino groups *		
Rate of exposure	Union leaders	*Asentados*	Non-*asentados*	Farm labor
Radio				
None or infrequent	11	31	19	12
Weekly	17	23	28	24
Daily	70	46	53	61
Newspaper				
None	26	65	58	44
Infrequent	26	19	13	11
Frequent †	44	16	29	28
N =	*118*	*191*	*183*	*166*

* Data from CONVEN.

† Frequent newspaper exposure means weekly or daily.

political education for the peasantry in terms of the national political system.

A most important implication lies in the fact that the peasantry is learning rudimentary political participation in the context of a rough union democracy. Not only are there elections for local, state, and national officers of the unions, but there is interparty competition for peasant membership. Let us not obscure the facts that the Venezuelan campesino is relatively backward and unsophisticated, that his understanding of the intricacies of the political system and the problems with which it must cope on the national scale is incomplete, and that he may therefore be potentially exploitable by skilled leaders. But the peasant union leadership has demonstrated through the years a dedication to peasant interests and some degree of success in serving these interests on the national and local scene; there are individuals competing for local leadership within single party communities and interparty competition for peasant loyalties in others, both of which tend to generate choices for the peasantry in terms of people and programs; and the peasants do participate, through the internal union electoral process, in determining who governs.

The nature and quality of the local leadership generated by this rough democracy has important implications for the economic and political development of the nation. Local leaders possess the skills necessary to bridge the gap between the peasant subculture and the larger society. They are dedicated to work in the rural areas. We questioned local peasant union leaders about their desire to migrate—to other villages, towns, big cities, even foreign countries—and 88.1 per cent indicated satisfaction with their current situation. Such a finding suggests that in the absence of any radical change in the rural problem-solving system, these leaders (and similar successors) can be counted on to stay for the long pull necessary to effect fundamental changes in the peasant subculture.

The values into which these men are socializing the peasantry are of the utmost significance. Local peasant union leaders, farmers themselves, tend to be innovative and investment-oriented and to believe in hard work as the way to "get ahead." These characteristics, which set examples for the members of their unions, were established through two items, the first open-ended, in our questionnaire: "If your income increased considerably over the next five years, what is the first use you would put the extra money to? The second use?" (Table 2–16) and "Please tell me, in your opinion, which of the following characteristics is the most important in order to prosper in your work—make important friends; work hard; learn new things; introduce new techniques; be loyal to the organization to which you belong; belong to the party which your boss belongs to?" (Table 2–17).

Such characteristics should have an important bearing on the work attitudes, propensity to innovate and adopt new farming techniques, and willingness to learn of the peasant union members who associate with and follow these leaders. The importance of such attitudes for the potential of agricultural development in rural Venezuela seems fairly obvious.

Local leaders constitute the growing edge of the entry of the campesino into the life of the nation. As such, their attitudes toward broad

Table 2–16. Local union leaders' uses for extra income

Would use extra income to	Percentage	Rank
Invest in farming	48.3	1
Better housing	25.4	2
Buy food, clothing, furniture	11.9	3
Improve education	4.2	4
Charity or public service	2.5	5
Save	1.7	6.5
Help relatives or friends	1.7	6.5

$N = 118$

Table 2–17. Local union leaders' opinions of key to success

In order to prosper in your work	Percentage	Rank
Work hard	36.4	1
Learn new things	18.6	2
Make important friends	15.3	3
Be loyal to your organization	8.5	4
Introduce new techniques	5.9	5
Belong to boss's political party	5.1	6
$N = 118$		

policy alternatives in the nation-building process are quite important. When compared with peasant follower attitudes (Table 2–18), they assume a special importance as "leading sector" opinions, indicative of the direction in which peasant attitudes will be "pulled" through association and participation in conjoint activities.

These rankings indicate, among other things, that peasants may be less confident about maintaining their present influence in government and may therefore choose the preservation of this instrumental relationship before other alternatives. Leaders, on the other hand, seem more confident in this relationship and choose to proceed with utilizing it to accelerate economic growth. Survey data measuring the political efficacy of leaders and followers support this interpretation.[36] Concerning support for spe-

Table 2–18. Rankings of measures most important for Venezuela (forced choice)

Measure	Priority ranking by group *		
	Union leaders	*Asentados* †	Non-*asentados* †
Accelerate economic growth	1	2	2
Maintain democracy	2	1	1
Redistribute the wealth	3	3	3

* Ranking based on a weighted mean rank-score.
† CONVEN data furnished by John R. Mathiason.

[36] Furthermore, we found that the political efficacy measurements for local peasant union leaders were higher than those measured by CONVEN for local farm and ranch owners, a reflection of the power shift in the rural areas. See Powell, "Politics," pp. 360–367.

Table 2-19. Ranking of public policy priorities (forced choice)

| | Priority ranking by group * | | |
Policy	Union leaders	Asentados †	Non-asentados †
Improve education	1	4	3
Accelerate agrarian reform	2	1	1
Eliminate unemployment	3	3	4
Construct more houses	4	2	2

* Ranking based on a weighted mean rank-score.
† CONVEN data.

cific public policy priorities (Table 2-19), peasant union leaders and followers again demonstrate interesting differences, probably derived in large part from their differing educational levels.

As the educational system penetrates the rural areas and economic conditions improve sufficiently to allow children more time in school, it seems likely that the value of education will be more generally seen throughout the campesino population. Current peasant choices of agrarian reform benefits and housing over education are perfectly consistent with everything we know about the absence of deferred gratification behavior in backward peoples. Local peasant union leaders, however, do exhibit the capacity for deferred gratification which is often taken to indicate "modern" attitudinal orientation. Local union leaders, who have enjoyed superior educations themselves, advocate the highest priority for education. Perhaps they in some fashion understand the necessary (but insufficient) nature of education as a lever for progress in other realms of public policy and leadership effectiveness.

A note of caution is in order in this basically extremely optimistic interpretation of the Venezuelan peasant union movement. The bases for such optimism are, I think, fairly convincing—much of the data marshaled here supports it. The bases for caution are more speculative or conditional in nature, but none the less important. They primarily concern the political umbilical cord of the movement. Linkages with the multiparty system, which have proven invaluable in the accomplishments of the peasant union movement since 1958, may not always remain an asset in a variety of conceivable political circumstances. One such circumstance might be the occurrence of a military coup d'état. The 1948 coup was such an instance, and the political affiliation of the peasant movement with the AD party served as a spur to the reactionary government to suppress the movement as well as the party.

Other complications could occur in the vicissitudes of electoral politics in Venezuela, opening up or closing off access to government for peasant union leaders associated with political parties, which, after all, win and lose elections and enter and leave coalition governments. The more-or-less normal cyclical fortunes of such an organization as a political party have an important side effect on the peasant union movement because of their interdependent relationship. Such occurrences may well provoke, for instance, crises of primary loyalty and identification on the part of leaders who fill both party and union leadership roles. Many other possible complications might have an important impact on the peasant union movement—its leadership structure, the internal distribution of power and influence, the ability to control and influence followers, even its survival as an effective form of collective action.[37]

This note of caution should not, however, produce a pessimistic outlook for the future of the peasant union movement in Venezuela. The movement has experienced many of the potential problems just mentioned and has not only survived but prospered. The 1948 coup resulted in a suppression of the movement, but it emerged after ten years more solidly entrenched in peasant loyalties and better led than before. Major political parties, such as URD, have left the government coalition and the union movement over policy differences but have been reincorporated when these differences diminished; COPEI left the governing coalition in 1964 after six years, but its working relationships in the peasant union movement with peasant leaders of the government party seem unaffected.

Finally, the social and attitudinal changes in the peasantry that have already been set in motion by the peasant union movement seem relatively invulnerable to the shifting fortunes of the political party system. Similarly, the character and quality of the local peasant leadership structure seems immune even from governmental suppression. The direction of the peasant union movement is clearly upward, and the vehicle for progress will in all likelihood remain the Federación Campesina. Circumstances

[37] For a more thorough analysis of such problems, see *ibid.*, chs. 11 and 12. A political crisis of profound dimensions seemed to be developing within *Acción Democrática* during the winter of 1967–1968 over the nomination of a presidential candidate for the 1968 elections. Such a crisis would seem the most likely source of drastic—but impossible to predict—changes in the present rural problem-solving system.

may change the form and nature of the vehicle, but it is most improbable that they could change its direction. The Venezuelan campesino is established in the sometimes painful trajectory that characterizes the mobilization of backward peoples in an orderly and fruitful entry into the mainstream of modern national life.

3. Mexico: The Zapata Movement and the Revolution

ROBERT A. WHITE, S.J.

Department of Sociology,
St. Louis University

The Mexican Revolution of 1910 began under the leadership of Francisco Madero as an attempt to end the thirty-four-year dictatorship of Porfirio Díaz and to effect democratic political reforms, particularly free elections and limited presidential terms. Madero did include in the Plan of San Luis Potosí, which announced his revolution against Díaz, a paragraph which vaguely promised to restore lands illegally taken from small landholders, but he did not intend any immediate, sweeping land tenure reform.[1] Before 1910 there had been proposals to force the haciendas to cultivate or relinquish their large tracts of idle land, but almost no one, even among the young radical liberals, was demanding that the hacienda system, as a land tenure form, be ended entirely. There had been some discussion among Mexican elites of agrarian legislation to curb abuses of labor on the haciendas and to increase agricultural productivity. But there was little consensus regarding the kind of agrarian legislation Mexico needed and less understanding of the aspirations of the peasant cultivators themselves. Even among the masses of peasants the dissatisfaction was vague and ephemeral, with no articulate demands for expropriation of the haciendas.

When Emiliano Zapata and his peasant followers in Morelos rallied to Madero's call for a general rebellion against Díaz, they were only one relatively unknown rebel group among many in the revolution. And the Zapatista group was perhaps the only one that was explicitly fighting for the restoration of the communal village lands.[2] Yet by 1912 the Zapatista movement was causing the Madero government to consider far-reaching land reforms,[3] and when the revolutionary armies were triumphant over

---

[1] Charles C. Cumberland, *Mexican Revolution: Genesis under Madero* (Austin: University of Texas Press, 1952), pp. 208–211.   [2] *Ibid.,* p. 212.

[3] Jesus Silva-Herzog, *El agrarismo mexicano y la reforma agraria* (Mexico City: Fondo de Cultura Económica, 1959), p. 192.

the Huerta reaction in 1914, they accepted as their ideology Zapata's Plan of Ayala. The Mexican Constitution was revised in 1917 to provide a legal basis for the end of the system of great haciendas and the restoration of communal land tenure, the *ejido*. In the 1920's and 1930's the most tangible results of the Revolution were the large-scale expropriations of the haciendas, the establishment of a new rural social organization based on the ejido, new forms of rural education and farmer associations, and the growth of a national Indian-agrarian ideology.[4] And in this agrarian revolution Emiliano Zapata is considered the single most important influence.

The basic questions underlying the present analysis are these: Why did the Zapata movement happen when it did? Why did it acquire the ideological and organizational structure that eventually characterized it? Why did it have such momentous results? Mexico's previous great civil wars—the War for Independence in 1810 and the War of the Reform at midcentury—had sought changes in the feudal social structure with little success. There were many peasant uprisings in Mexico in the century before 1910. Why were these previous movements unsuccessful and that of Zapata eventually so influential? In short, this analysis is interested in isolating "causal factors" which influenced the origin and development of the Zapata movement. There is also the broader question which may be simplistically stated: "What causes peasant movements?" But this analysis of the Zapata movement can do little more than advance the evidence of one case in support of some general propositions.

Although it would be impossible to isolate literally all of the major and minor factors that contributed to the development of the Zapata movement, we will proceed under the assumption that there is a set of major factors which are both necessary and sufficient for explaining the occurrence of a given peasant movement.

The fact that movements are a historical process and that some of them make impressive beginnings and then fail of further achievement has prompted many to analyze social movements in terms of a life cycle or natural history approach.[5] Movements tend to pass through stages such that the conditions that facilitate the transition from the first stage to the second are not the same as those present in the transition from the second

[4] Moisés González Navarro describes the early phases of the Mexican Revolution of 1910 as primarily agrarian. The emphasis on organization of labor and industrialization came later. See "The Ideology of the Mexican Revolution" in Stanley Ross (ed.), *Is the Mexican Revolution Dead?* (New York: Knopf, 1966), pp. 177–197.

[5] For a comprehensive discussion of definitions of social movements, see Lewis M. Killian, "Social Movements," in Robert Faris (ed.), *Handbook of Modern Sociology* (Chicago: Rand McNally, 1964), pp. 430–431.

stage to the third. A society may be experiencing severe structural strains, but no movement will eventuate because there is no ideology present to guide vague frustrations into concrete channels of action or because there is no precipitating factor electrifying enough to push a discontented population to the point of mobilization.[6] Thus the Zapata movement may be explained as the intersection of successive factors, the presence of which caused the movement to proceed from a given stage to the next.

In the language of Smelser's theory of collective behavior,[7] the rise of the Zapata movement was influenced by six sets of factors combining in the appropriate sequence and manner: [8]

1. There were two principal factors of *structural conduciveness:* the hacienda system with its great disparity of wealth and status supported by a system of laws and legitimating values, and the intensive program of modernization of the Díaz government which set in motion many currents disturbing the organization of the traditional order.

[6] Ralph Turner, "Collective Behavior," in Faris, *op. cit.*, pp. 392–393.

[7] The distinctive feature of Smelser's developmental model is its economic analogy of "value added." In a simple "natural history" model a series of stages are delineated. But in the "value added" model the factors of later stages may be present but "dormant" and are not activated until the factors of earlier stages have combined in the appropriate manner. For example, an ideology may have been elaborated, but until social strains are present no one may be interested in it. See Neil Smelser, *Theory of Collective Behavior* (New York: Free Press of Glencoe, 1963), pp. 18–19.

[8] 1) A social structure is *conducive* to the formation of particular kinds of movements if it makes certain types of *structural strains* and *beliefs* likely or unlikely or allows strains to become accentuated. See *ibid.*, p. 15.

2) *Structural strain* "refers to the impairment of the relations among parts of a system and the consequent malfunctioning of the system" (*ibid.*, p. 384)'. "Strain . . . expresses a relationship between an event or situation and certain cultural and individual standards" (*ibid.*, p. 50).

3) A set of *beliefs* is important because, as *structural strains* begin to affect a social structure, the *beliefs* define the strains in terms of a particular problem, outline the causes and solutions to the problem, and focus vague frustrations upon specific objects of aggression and hostility. In short, the *beliefs* "create a 'common culture' within which leadership, mobilization, and concerted action can take place" (*ibid.*, p. 82). As a set of *beliefs* is incorporated by the social organization of a mobilized movement as a rationalization of its existence and a definition of its goals, beliefs may be referred to as an *ideology.*

4) A *precipitating factor* may be any event which focuses attention on the strains and convinces the aggrieved population that the strains are no longer to be tolerated and that collective action should be taken at once. See *ibid.*, p. 16.

5) *Mobilization* refers to that stage in which an explicit social organization is formed to realize more or less specific goals.

6) *Social controls* may be operating throughout all phases of the formation of a movement either to prevent the movement from reaching the mobilization stage (easing the tension of structural strains or instilling a set of beliefs which are tolerant of strains, and so forth) or to destroy the social organization of the movement once it is mobilized. See *ibid.*, pp. 17–18.

2. The long-standing *structural strains,* the centuries-old conflict of the Indian peasants with the large landholders in defense of their communal village lands, were greatly accentuated in the fifty years before 1910 by the exploitive land policies that Díaz permitted; at the same time the mainte-nance of low agricultural wages in the face of rising prices and the awareness of the better wages and living conditions of both the Mexican urban worker and the agricultural worker in the United States sharpened the *subjective perception* of discrepancy between aspirations and objective conditions.

3. A set of *beliefs* (ideology) which defined the solution to this situation in terms of armed revolt was part of the Mexican peasant tradition and was exalted in the peasant's folk literature, especially in the popular ballads, the *corridos.* Also, during the decade from 1900 to 1910 a radical movement developed among young Mexican activist intellectuals stimulated by interna-tional labor movements and various currents of socialist philosophies, and this movement was destined to provide a legal and philosophical dimension to the peasant expression of grievances.

4. The Madero phase of the revolution in 1911 and 1912, though primarily intended as a political coup d'état, was a *precipitating factor* of a profound social revolution because it not only enlisted the military help of the leaders of dissident peasants, industrial workers, and urban intellectuals who were suffering under the repression of the Díaz regime, but conceded to them a kind of political power and a new sense of political legitimacy.

5. As the Mexican agrarian movement entered its *mobilization phase* south of Mexico City, the charismatic personality of Emiliano Zapata welded local peasant bands into a large guerrilla army capable of great sacrifices over a period of nearly ten years, from 1911 to 1920.

6. The forces of *social control,* the Díaz government with its rural police force and standing army, had become weak and ineffectual and were rather easily toppled.

This theoretical framework is sketched briefly here at the outset in order to bring into sharper focus the set of necessary and sufficient factors which combined to push the Zapata-led movement toward the formation of a new Mexican society. But these factors have a historical as well as a theoretical relationship, and rather than follow rigidly any theoretical framework, we will discuss the rise of the Zapata movement in terms of its own historical stages of development. Thus it will be possible to see more clearly the various factors and stages of development peculiar to a Latin American peasant movement.[9]

[9] For a definition of "peasant" and "peasant movement" see "Peasant Movements: The Problem of Their Definition" in Chapter 1.

Structural Conduciveness: The Status System of Rural Mexico in the Nineteenth Century

The Development of Mexican Peasant Society

The institutional and legal framework of land tenure which developed in the early colonial period encouraged bitter conflict between the peasants and the elite classes. In the pre-Colombian era of Mexico, land in the central mesa was traditionally held communally in the name of the kinship group (the *calpulli*) and allotted to heads of families by a village leader (the *calpuleque*) elected for life. But even in this period a hereditary class of warrior-nobles, overlords, and priests was developing which did not cultivate the land but lived from the proceeds of land perpetually allotted to them and tilled by virtual serfs.[10]

The colonial laws of the Indies recognized and amply protected the communal land tenure of the Indian villages, though the Spanish called the village lands (the Indian *altepetlalli*) the ejido, a term traditionally used for the Spanish village commons[11] But the colonial system also allowed a conflicting pattern of land tenure to grow: the *encomienda*, the concession in trust by the Spanish Crown of one or more Indian villages for purposes of administration, collecting tribute, and Christianization of the Indian. Though the *encomienda* was considered a temporary arrangement, the access to wealth, prestige, and nobility for poor Spanish soldiers and immigrants was through acquisition of large tracts of land cultivated by the dispossessed Indians, and neither the Spanish Crown nor the protests of individuals like Bartolomé de las Casas could stop this institutional system. Colonial schools, hospitals, churches, and monastic establishments needed to be supported, and the only fairly large and stable sources of income were sizable land holdings. Almost inevitably the *encomienda* evolved into a large hacienda, a hereditary, feudalistic pattern of land tenure with Indians tied to the land as serfs.[12]

By the nineteenth century the hacienda was firmly established as a basic institution of Mexican society. Each hacienda constituted an almost self-

---

[10] George McBride, *The Land Systems of Mexico* (New York: American Geographical Society, 1923), p. 116; Eyler Simpson, *The Ejido: Mexico's Way Out* (Chapel Hill: University of North Carolina Press, 1937), p. 5.

[11] Eyler Simpson, *op. cit.*, pp. 11–14, gives an account of how the Spanish accommodated their peninsular land tenure system to the Indian land tenure system.

[12] François Chevalier, *Land and Society in Colonial Mexico* (Berkeley: University of California Press, 1963), pp. 7–49, 229–262, and *passim*.

sustaining social and economic unit, producing nearly all of its own food and equipment and satisfying practically all its other needs. It was sometimes incorporated as a unit of local government, the *municipio*, and it offered the services of a local community—a store, a church, a post office, a burial ground, a jail, and occasionally a school. The typical owner lived in the great hacienda residence only a few weeks or months of the year. The hacienda was left in the hands of an administrator who had almost unlimited authority over the hacienda community and rarely hesitated to use the whipping post, the saber, or even the pistol whenever the indolent or obstreperous peon needed discipline.

The *peones acasillados*, those who lived on the hacienda, were given a one-room adobe hut, a small plot of ground to plant corn for household use, a wage amounting to about 25 Mexican centavos a day (equivalent to 12.5 cents in United States currency),[13] a gallon or two of corn each week, and perhaps a little pulque. The peon could buy other simple necessities on credit at the hacienda store, the *tienda de raya*, so that almost all of the wages returned to the hacienda. The wages almost never sufficed even for simple necessities, and the hacienda was accustomed to advance to the peon small amounts of ready cash two or three times a year on national holidays. As a result, the peon was kept perpetually in debt to the hacienda store.[14]

Since according to the laws then in force, the peon could not leave the hacienda until his debt was paid, the worker was tied to the hacienda and unable to seek better opportunities elsewhere. Most administrators were careful to see that this debt mounted in order to ensure plentiful and cheap labor. Worst of all, this debt could be passed from father to son, tying families to a hacienda for generations. Since in many instances peons were forbidden under threat of fines to buy elsewhere than at the hacienda store, there was little to distinguish this life from slavery.[15]

The *peones alquilados*, laborers who lived in villages near the hacienda, were increasingly landless and, consequently, dependent on the hacienda for their livelihood. If they worked on the hacienda or were sharecroppers, they were usually tied by obligations at the *tienda de raya* also. Even the *rancheros*, the small, independent landholders, and small cultivators in those villages which were able to hold on to their communal lands had insufficient land or lacked equipment, animals for work or livestock,

---

[13] Nathan Whetten, *Rural Mexico* (Chicago: University of Chicago Press, 1948), pp. 90–107. The Mexican peso stood at approximately 2.00 per dollar from 1900 to 1929 (*La economía mexicana en cifras* [Mexico City: Nacional Financiera, 1965], p. 171).   [14] Whetten, *op. cit.*, pp. 103–104.   [15] Eyler Simpson, *op. cit.*, pp. 38–40.

technical training, credit, market facilities, and other requisites of a profit-able agricultural enterprise. They, too, found it necessary to seek at least part-time work on the haciendas.[16]

From the beginning of the colonial period the Indian peasants were engaged in a continual struggle to maintain clear title to their land and to prevent the encroachment of the haciendas. They fought desperately not only because without land they faced starvation or dependence on the haciendas but because their way of life was built around the cultivation of the village land. Among the more traditional peasants a system of religious rituals was connected with the planting of corn and the various phases of its growth. Social status was measured in terms of owning a small plot of land or having a regular plot in the communal land. Certain fiestas were tied in with the rhythm of the crops and harvesting.[17] To destroy this traditional pattern was to sap life of its meaning, and the tendency was to look on village agriculture as an idyllic form of life. As one of the peasants of Tepoztlán, Pedro Martínez, said to Oscar Lewis, "I love the country. . . . Man, when I go into the fields it even gives me an appetite . . . out in the fields. That's where I feel happy. Naturally, I love the country. I am a peasant!" [18]

Maintaining the corporate existence of the ancient kinship-based vil-lages was also an important consideration for the peasants. Zapata's own village of Anenecuilco possessed land titles, maps, and other documents—some carrying symbols in the indigenous Nahuatl language—handed down to the leaders which demonstrate the village's existence for seven centuries. As the haciendas engulfed these communities, kinship groups whose life and work together had been linked to a particular piece of communal land for centuries were dispersed and their villages obliterated.[19]

By the second half of the nineteenth century, Mexican society, still basically rural, had three important characteristics: a two-class system of Indian peasants and landed elite, largely of European descent, with an immense disparity of wealth, prestige, and power due to the elite's near monopoly of land and water resources and the lack of political organiza-tion among the peasants; a relationship of deep resentment and conflict

[16] Whetten, *op. cit.*, p. 105.
[17] Oscar Lewis, *Life in a Mexican Village: Tepoztlán Restudied* (Urbana: Univer-sity of Illinois Press, 1951), pp. 54–55, 135–141.
[18] Oscar Lewis, *Pedro Martínez: A Mexican Peasant and His Family* (New York: Random House, 1964), p. 446.
[19] Jesús Sotelo Inclán, *Raíz y razón de Zapata* (Mexico City: Editorial Etnos, 1943), chs. 1, 2, and 3, especially pp. 136–137.

between peasant and elite; and the focusing of this conflict on the issue of retention of village lands.

The Reinforcement of Peasant–Elite Status Differentiation by Race, Language, and Style of Life

The conflict between the peasant and the landed elite was centered on the allocation of wealth, that is, whether the peasants were to own land communally or work on the haciendas as landless laborers. But this conflict was greatly magnified by the fact that the hacendado was generally of European or light mestizo descent, lived an urbanized, cosmopolitan style of life, and was cast in the inherently superior role of *hidalgo* (hereditary nobility). The peasant, on the other hand, was generally of Indian or mostly Indian descent, lived the country or folk style of life, and was cast in the role of the peon, one who works with his hands. Furthermore, these racial and cultural differences were used to erect a belief and value system which defined the hacendado as inherently superior and thus tried to justify the allocation of wealth and power into his hands.

The most basic difference between the peasants and the elite was racial. During the colonial period a kind of caste system of Spanish, creoles, mestizos, and Indians developed. The Indian was considered a legal minor and subject to economic and social discrimination. Even the mestizo class was prevented from holding public office or other positions of power and influence because they suffered from "degeneration." [20] Among the elite the notion that the Indian was inherently inferior and incapable of betterment persisted.[21] Lesley Byrd Simpson encountered this attitude in the 1920's:

Thus in Mexico I have rarely talked with a member of the dying aristocracy without being met with a kind of ritual: "The Indians are an inferior race." "They will not work unless coerced." "They were better off under the old

[20] Whetten, *op. cit.*, pp. 50–53; Herbert I. Priestley, *The Mexican Nation* (New York: Macmillan, 1924), p. 120; Charles B. Parkes, *A History of Mexico* (Boston: Houghton Mifflin, 1960), p. 116.

[21] Curiously enough, the superiority of the European became a part of the general cultural tradition and was accepted in a subtle form even by the mestizo and the Indian. Some Mexican philosophers have diagnosed a national inferiority complex deriving from the fact that the Aztecs took the Spaniards for gods and placed themselves in the role of "children" toward their Spanish "fathers." The mestizo, according to this analysis, continued to attribute to the Spaniard superior qualities and in the nineteenth century replaced the Spaniard with the French, the English, and the Americans. See John Leddy Phelan, "México y lo Mexicano," *Hispanic American Historical Review*, XXXVI, No. 3 (1956), 313.

system." "They made better real wages, had more leisure, worked more efficiently, and were happier." "Education is bad for them, makes them discontented and 'uppity.' "[22]

On the other hand, resentment against the *gachupines*, as the Spanish have traditionally been called, was part of the culture of the Indian lower classes. The Mexican folk ballads, the *corridos*, frequently portray their heroes as hating the *gachupines* and battling with them. The Zapatista *corridos*, especially, bring out the hatred of the *gachupines* and charge Porfirio Díaz with having favored the Spaniards over Mexico's Indian population.[23]

Silva-Herzog states flatly that Mexican society at the turn of the nineteenth century was shot through with racial discrimination. "Any person with white skin was called decent (*gente decente*) and those with a brown skin, riff-raff (*pelados*)." Agustín Aragón, writing around 1900, noted that anyone who spoke out in favor of the Indian was called a socialist.[24]

The differences between city and country were always great in Mexico, but never greater than around the turn of the century. The Mexico City of Porfirio Díaz prided itself on being the Paris of America. The splendor of Mexico City was supported by the hacendado families, but the middle classes and even the working classes shared in the modernity of Mexico City and the larger towns. The urban worker could earn four or five times as much as the agricultural workers. He was much more likely to provide at least an elementary school education for his children, read a newspaper, have the services of a doctor and hospitals, and find better housing, and he was not subject to the completely arbitrary action of the hacienda administrators.[25] In the country the peasants were almost totally illiterate [26] and had a system of folk religion, folk medicine, and folk amusements which was quite different from that of the better-educated townspeople.[27]

For the townspeople the word "campesino" (country-dweller) was synonymous with simpleton, and the peasant was continually suspicious

[22] *Many Mexico's* (Berkeley: University of California Press, 1952), p. 234.

[23] Merle E. Simmons, *The Mexican Corrido as a Source for Interpretative Study of Modern Mexico (1870–1950)* (Bloomington: Indiana University Press, 1957), p. 291.

[24] Silva-Herzog, *op. cit.*, p. 132.   [25] Parkes, *op. cit.*, p. 308.

[26] Whetten, *op. cit.*, pp. 403–404. About 75 per cent of all Mexicans were illiterate in 1900 and 70 per cent in 1910, but nearly all schools were in the cities and larger towns.

[27] Robert Redfield, *Tepoztlán, A Mexican Village* (Chicago: University of Chicago Press, 1930), pp. 170–223.

of the sophisticated townsman as a sharper who was trying to cheat him.²⁸ The popular *corridos* frequently reflect the animosity which the country people felt toward the townspeople and the more affluent classes.

There exists among the *pueblo* of Mexico a long-standing tradition of social criticism, especially satire on the social mores of the upper classes. Inasmuch as attire characteristically distinguishes social classes in Mexico, it is not unnatural that the *pueblo* should single out styles of dress in particular as humorous material for satirical attacks upon the privileged classes. Because of their elegant clothes, the rich are referred to disparagingly as *catrines* (fops) or are castigated by even more uncomplimentary appellations. . . . Often not only dress but standards of morality as well become the subject of popular songs which censure the upper classes.²⁹

It is unlikely that Mexico City and other large cities were more than names to most of the peasants of Mexico. For them the townsmen were the more citified people who lived around the central plaza: the shop-keepers, teachers, lawyers, and wealthier landowners. Redfield, in his study of Tepoztlán, describes the class distinction between *los correctos,* who wore shoes and dark trousers and were literate, and *los tontos* (the ignorant), who wore sandals and white trousers and were generally illiterate laborers. *Los correctos* were citified people who had some con-tact with the urban centers, considered themselves cultured, and rejected many of the folk customs of the country people. *Los tontos* lived in the outlying *barrios* and villages, maintained the folk religious and medical practices, and were identified as *indios.*³⁰

---

²⁸ Carleton Beals cites a little street play he observed in Mexico City in which the qualities of the clever but shallow city-dweller were contrasted with the simple, credulous country Indian who, though easily duped, proves, at bottom, far wiser than his urban baiter—much to the delight of the street audience. Beals also recalls the typical themes of the *corridos,* nostalgic memories of the country. "Better, declares the singer, than the city pin-stripe trousers and spats are the tough country '*panta-lones de cuero*' [pants of leather]; better than tight shoes are the comfortable sandals (*guaraches*); better than autos are the slow-moving ox-carts creaking along with unhurried dreams under the lazy sun; better than new-fangled brilliantine to make the beloved's hair glisten is the dear smell of the country grease" (*Mexican Maze* [New York: B. W. Huebsch, 1931], pp. 252–253).   ²⁹ Simmons, *op. cit.,* pp. 57–58.

³⁰ Redfield, *op cit.,* pp. 205–216. Oscar Lewis, who studied Tepoztlán some twenty years after Redfield, questions whether the terms *los tontos* and *los correctos* were used in Tepoztlán to describe social class distinctions. But whatever the terms used, the social classes and the animosity between them do exist. As Oscar Lewis himself attests, even after twenty years of the leveling process of the Revolution there were distinctions in wealth and social class and a definite feeling of superiority among the townspeople toward the *indios* of the surrounding villages (Lewis, *Life in a Mexican Village,* pp. 430–431, 54–55).

When the Revolution came to Tepoztlán in 1911, the animosity of the *indios* against *los correctos* broke forth, and the cultured *correctos* fled to Mexico City to save their lives. The people of Tepoztlán learned to build their houses more modestly afterward because they remembered that those who showed off their urban culture had their houses destroyed and experienced other reprisals during the Revolution. There is a continuing envy and malice against those who show off wealth, and in the 1940's it was considered best to live simply because there was still fear of a recurrence of what had happened thirty years earlier.[31]

The role of *hidalgo* was brought to New Spain by the *conquistadores* and was the goal aspired to by most Spanish immigrants. The soldier of Castile had traditionally seen a high position in the feudal social system as the reward of war. Rodrigo de Albornoz, the *contador* of New Spain in the time of Cortés, complained to Charles V that all wanted to be nobles and none laborers.

If, in any of your dominions, Caesarian Majesty, it was ever necessary to prescribe the manner of life of your subjects and vassals, here it is even more necessary, for, since the land is rich in food and in mines of gold and silver, and everyone becomes swollen with the desire to spend and possess, by the end of a year and a half, he who is a miner, or farmer, or swineherd, no longer will be so, but wishes to be given Indians, and so he spends everything he has on ornaments and silks, and, if he has a wife, the same thing holds true for her. In like fashion other mechanics cease the pursuit of their trades and incur heavy expenses, and do not work or extract gold or silver from the mines, in the belief that they will be given Indians to serve them and support their families in gentility.[32]

The role of *hidalgo* gradually developed into that of the hacendado. For the hacienda had value not only as an economic enterprise but also as a source of prestige. The role of hacendado carried with it the pride of proprietorship, a minimum of toil, the leisurely oversight of an estate, and unlimited opportunity for the exercise of authority over humble servitors. "A large rural estate is the . . . ambition of every true Mexican," noted McBride in 1920, and "the *hacendado*, the 'man on horseback' . . . is the real hero of the nation." [33]

The superior status of the hacendado may have been achieved through military or economic effort, but in time it was attributed to inherent qualities that were passed on to offspring. Since those in higher positions had a monopoly on education and contact with the sources of higher

[31] Lewis, *Life in a Mexican Village*, p. 181; Redfield, *op. cit.*, pp. 207–216.
[32] Cited in Lesley Byrd Simpson, *op. cit.*, p. 227.   [33] *Op. cit.*, p. 40.

culture, the theory of hereditary superiority was backed by higher accomplishments. This was accompanied by a belief that only the elite
could really benefit by education or training in the fine arts. In the
ideology of paternalism, the lower classes were looked on as quite helpless
and in need of the *patrón* to think for them, care for them, and give them
moral and religious guidance.

Ultimately the Mexican status system was founded on a set of values
which exalted the person of European descent, the town culture, and the
landed proprietor who did not work with his hands. These values defined
the social institutions and the roles played by landed elite and peasant, and
directed the allocation of wealth, prestige, and power. Individuals might
be mobile within the system, so that an aggressive peasant might by good
fortune eventually become a hacendado. But once arrived he fitted into
the role of hacendado and continued the system. Hidalgo began the
Mexican War for Independence in 1810 leading a ragged army of eighty
thousand disinherited Indians and mestizos with the cry, "Will you make
the effort to recover from the hated Spanish the lands stolen from your
forefathers three hundred years ago." [34] But the War for Independence
only put the creoles in the place of the Spanish, and the War of Reform
in 1858 was Mexico's bourgeois revolution, which brought the mestizos to
power but did little to alleviate the oppression of the peasant masses.[35]
Unless the fundamental values and their connected ideology were challenged, Mexico would remain a simple, two-level society with immense
differences of wealth and prestige and endemic conflict between peasant
and landed elite.

Structural Strains: The Accentuation of Peasant–Elite Conflict During the Regime of Porfirio Díaz, 1876–1910

The Political Economy of the Porfiriato

The persistence of colonial stagnation and political chaos in spite of
Independence and the Mexican Reform Constitution of 1857 had convinced many Mexicans, including Díaz, that democracy was an expensive
luxury for Mexico. In 1876, therefore, Díaz set about the pacification,
industrialization, and economic modernization of Mexico through a policy of uninhibited power strategies. To groups with power or resources
—the hacendados, the generals, the clergy, the office-hunting middle
classes, the intelligentsia—he conceded basically what they wanted, in

[34] Quoted in Ernest Gruening, *Mexico and Its Heritage* (New York: Century,
1928), p. 30.   [35] Parkes, *op. cit.*, pp. 233ff.

return for toleration or support of his regime.[36] But in the game of political power concessions, those who had nothing to offer Díaz—the Indians, the peasants, and the working classes—were bound to lose.[37]

The Mexican brand of nineteenth-century liberalism, derived from the theories of social progress of Comte and Spencer, was most developed by a group called the *científicos*, the scientific planners. The *científicos* were men representing the new moneyed class coming into prominence around 1890 who systematically sought to control the Díaz government. Strong proponents of control by the "enlightened" creole upper class, they claimed that the native Mexicans were an inferior race, incapable of governing themselves. They maintained that economic development would be accomplished only by creole control and preventing any political participation by the illiterate masses. Above all, they were proponents of Anglo-Saxon economic virtues and the superiority of French scientific and humanistic culture. Foreign interests were favored in concessions for the exploitation of resources, and special treatment was given the foreigner in government decisions and court processes.[38]

The *científicos* took credit for much of Mexico's rapid economic development at the turn of the century. The value of exports went up from $27,318,788 in 1874–1875, to $45,133,111 in 1894, to $293,700,000 in 1910–1911.[39] But the overall economic policy tended to allocate the profits of Mexico's economic growth to a small clique of businessmen and financiers who dominated money and credit, controlled the most lucrative concessions, and in general monopolized production, foreign trade, and banking.[40] Without doubt the large investments in railroads, harbors, telegraph and telephone lines, cotton and sugar mills, and many other industries brought Mexico unprecedented prosperity. But the new schools, theaters, government buildings, and beautification programs were for the cities, and industrialization meant better standards of living for the urban middle and upper classes.[41] At the same time a number of Díaz policies deliberately kept low the standard of living of the laboring class, especially of the rural sector, which formed 80 per cent of the population.[42] The Porfiriato's arbitrary favoritism toward the powerful, the depreciation of the native Mexicans, and the industrialization program

---

[36] Parkes, *op. cit.*, p. 283.   [37] Cumberland, *op. cit.*, pp. 3–26.

[38] Parkes, *op. cit.*, pp. 299–303.

[39] Silva-Herzog, *op. cit.*, p. 105; *La economía mexicana en cifras*, p. 205.

[40] Cumberland, *op. cit.*, pp. 9–10.   [41] Parkes, *op. cit.*, pp. 301–302.

[42] Cumberland, *op. cit.*, pp. 9–10; cf. Eyler Simpson, *op. cit.*, p. 33, for a discussion of population distribution in 1910.

directly or indirectly inflamed the already strained peasant-elite relations to the explosion point.

The Díaz Land Policies

The *Ley de desamortización* (Law of Expropriations) incorporated into the Constitution of 1857, provided that the properties owned by corporations, civil or ecclesiastical, were to be sold to the tenants or usufructuaries occupying them and that properties not rented or leased would be sold at public auction.[43] The law was designed to disperse ecclesiastical holdings, but it also envisaged stimulation of the Indians' economic development by the incentive of individual proprietorship instead of communal tenure and a counterbalancing of the large landholders' power by creating a middle class composed of small farmers.[44]

The landholding villages were said to be civic corporations, and the law was interpreted to mean that all communal property was to be granted to the Indians holding the different plots. In the North and Northwest, where the mestizo was predominant, the law helped those who understood the institution of private property. But in the central mesa and in the South, where the Indian groups survived and where collectively held property was the only kind understood or appreciated, the measure had disastrous effects. The villages opposed and evaded the law in various ways, but as the Indians received individual titles, they were an easy prey to unscrupulous speculators and the hacendados. Many of the villages were still managing to maintain their communal holdings, but in 1889 and 1890, Díaz issued two circulars declaring that all village lands were to be divided and the titles allotted. He called upon governors and local officials to enforce these laws rigorously.[45] The landholding villages were thus deprived of any legal protection. It is estimated that at least 2,272,750 acres of communal land were allotted during the Díaz regime and that practically all of it passed directly or indirectly into the hands of the hacendados and land companies.[46]

There were also other ruses to gain control of village land. The Colonization Law of 1894 provided that anyone could denounce and file claim to land for which no legally registered titles existed. Since the villages were prohibited from possessing land, their titles were illegal, and the land was subject to denunciation. But even if the villages within the

[43] Eyler Simpson, *op. cit.*, pp. 22–25.   [44] McBride, *op. cit.*, p. 133.
[45] Eyler Simpson, *op. cit.*, pp. 24–25, 29.   [46] Whetten, *op. cit.*, p. 86.

large tracts opened up by surveying and colonization could not be deprived of land by denunciation, other means could force them to abandon their property or to pay rent for land they had held for generations. By laws passed in 1888, 1894, and 1896, the definition of federal waters was extended and the president was empowered to give exclusive water rights to individuals and companies. Without water resources, land was useless to the villages and would have to be abandoned.[47]

The Díaz regime was also making it possible for large tracts of virgin government land to pass into the hands of the great haciendas. In 1883 a law enabled the colonization companies to keep one-third of the land surveyed and buy the rest at special rates. In 1894 a still more liberal colonization law opened the way for Díaz to reward political favorites with outright grants. About 134,500,000 acres of government land, or about 27 per cent of the total area of the nation, passed into the hands of a relatively few individuals in this period.[48] By 1910 less than 1 per cent of the families of Mexico controlled 85 per cent of the land, and 90 per cent of the villages and towns on the central plateau had almost no communal land.[49]

Before the Revolution of 1910 the conflict between the villages and the haciendas over the retention of the communal lands was most acute in the state of Morelos and the adjacent areas—the very region in which the Zapata movement began and continued to find its principal support. In 1911 and 1912, when Zapata was vociferously asking that the Madero government restore the land to the villages, there were no echoes of his demands or significant armed uprisings over the land issue outside of Morelos.[50]

Several interrelated factors seem to lie behind the origin of the agrarian revolt in Morelos. As Table 3–1 shows, in the states of Morelos, Guerrero, México, Puebla, and Tlaxcala—later the area where the Zapatista movement was based—a very large percentage of the peasant population lived in free villages—that is, villages which were not actually on the property of the haciendas. In many cases these free villages had lost or were losing nearly all of the communal land, but as long as the village retained its juridical personality there was hope of recovering the land. In the states north and west of Mexico City the villages not only had lost their land

[47] Eyler Simpson, *op. cit.*, p. 30.   [48] Eyler Simpson, *op. cit.*, pp. 30, 28.
[49] Cumberland, *op. cit.*, p. 22; Eyler Simpson, *op. cit.*, p. 31.
[50] Cumberland, *op. cit.*, p. 62; Frank Tannenbaum, *Peace by Revolution* (New York: Columbia University Press, 1933), p. 193 (cited hereafter as *PBR*).

Table 3–1.   Percentage of rural population in free villages, by state

State	Per cent		
Oaxaca	84.9 *	Nuevo Leon	37.3
México	82.1 †	Chiapas	36.2
Hidalgo	78.2 *	Nayarit	34.7
Puebla	77.2 †	Aguascalientes	33.6
Veracruz	75.2	Jalisco	33.4
Morelos	74.1 †	Chihuahua	33.0
Tabasco	67.7	Querétero	33.0
Tlaxcala	65.0 *	Coahuila	30.4
Sonora	54.4	Durango	29.5
Yucatán	54.0	Sinaloa	26.4
Baja California	52.0	Tamaulipas	23.2
Guerrero	49.8 *	Zacatecas	21.1
Campeche	49.4	San Luis Potosí	17.8
Michoacán	39.4	Guanajuato	13.3
Colima	39.1		

Source: Tannenbaum, Frank, *MAR*, p. 56. Tannenbaum computed these percentages from the nomenclatures given in the census classifications of 1910 and 1921. All the communities referred to as *hacienda, rancho, labor, finca, campoagrícola,* and so on were taken as hacienda, non-free villages. Those referred to as *congregación, communidades,* and so on were taken as free villages. Tannenbaum, *MAR*, pp. 451–453.
* States with populations sympathizing with the Zapatistas.
† States with populations solidly supporting the Zapatistas.

but had become completely absorbed by the haciendas; in a sense, the struggle was over for these villages.[51]

Morelos had long been one of the principal zones of sugar production in Mexico. But in the late nineteenth century the extension of the railroads into the state and the development of new sugar refineries with the latest equipment made the export of sugar more lucrative than ever before. The "sugar barons" who dominated the politics and economy of

[51] Tannenbaum, *PBR*, p. 193; Tannenbaum, *The Mexican Agrarian Revolution* (Washington, D.C.: Brookings Institution, 1930), pp. 53–63 (cited hereafter as *MAR*). Although Eyler Simpson has questioned Tannenbaum's method of arriving at these statistics of free and hacienda settlements (Simpson, *op. cit.,* p. 36n), the fact that a very large number of villages in Morelos were "free" in the minimum sense described above and were contesting the loss of land is corroborated by John Womack, Jr., "Emiliano Zapata and the Revolution in Morelos, 1910–1920" (Ph.D. thesis, Harvard University, 1965), p. 104. Oscar Lewis, who investigated the historical background of land tenure in Tepoztlán and surrounding communities, is also inclined to accept Tannenbaum's findings (Lewis, *Life in a Mexican Village* pp. xxvin–xxviin). Allowing for a certain margin of error in Tannenbaum's statistics, they are still indicative of the status of free villages in 1910.

Morelos were embued with the philosophy of the *científicos*. They were convinced that the subsistence farming of the rancheros or the villages was a cause of economic stagnation and that the development of Mexico depended on large-scale, technically advanced plantations.[52] Consequently the haciendas were using every means to incorporate the village lands of Morelos and even to disperse the villages themselves. Of the approximately one hundred landholding villages in Morelos in 1910, there was probably not one which was not involved in some kind of litigation to protect or recover its land.[53] As long as the peasants had their own corn patches they were not interested in providing cheap labor for the haciendas. If the hacendados could not deprive the peasants of their land, they easily obtained the collaboration of the local political bosses to issue orders preventing the peasants from planting their *milpas* (cornfields).

One might be inclined to think that a Mexican peasant movement would find its greatest support among those who experienced the greatest oppression—the peons who lived on the haciendas under the complete control of the hacendados. The background of the Zapata movement suggests, however, that the most fertile ground for peasant movements is not among low-status cultivators who have lost everything, but among those who are in the process of losing the most.

The five states with high percentages of peasants in free villages also tended to define the agrarian problem differently than the rest of Mexico. The Indians of the central mesa and Yucatán had developed agriculture as the basis of their economy and had a communal land tenure system long before the Spanish conquest. But in the north of Mexico the Indians were originally nomadic groups living mostly by hunting and fishing, with little conception of land or property.[54] When northern Mexico was settled in the modern era, the hilly land less suitable for large scale cultivation was occupied by rancheros, and the rancho, not the communal village ejido, became the dominant type of small holding. After the triumph of the Revolution, when agrarian leaders deliberated land tenure reforms, those from the north continued to defend the ideal of small, property-owning cultivators against the ejido system.[55]

The rancheros, the small independent cultivators concentrated in the

[52] François Chevalier, "Le soulèvement de Zapata, 1911–1919," *Annales, Economies, Sociétés, Civilisations*, XVI, No. 1 (Jan.–Feb., 1961), 74–75.

[53] Womack, *op. cit.*, p. 104.   [54] Whetten, *op. cit.*, p. 76.

[55] McBride, *op. cit.*, pp. 88–89; Robert E. Quirk, *The Mexican Revolution, 1914–1915* (Bloomington: Indiana University Press, 1960), p. 213; Silva-Herzog, *op. cit.*, p. 241.

west central states of Jalisco, Guanajuato, and Michoacán, have little in common with the Indian *ejidatario*. These small farmers are today mestizos, descendants of peasant folk who immigrated from Spain to establish a peasant farming system in the new world.[56] They do not consider themselves Indian (they even look down on the Indian), speak only Spanish, and maintain Spanish traditions.

The attitude [toward the Revolution] of a typical ranchero in the State of México illustrates the political interests of his class. When asked if many of the young men from the neighboring ranchos had gone into the revolution, he replied that his fellows took no interest at all in the affair; that they were all right as they were and did not like such *revueltas;* all they wanted was to be let alone—the typical attitude of the property holder, large or small.[57]

Later in the 1930's the Sinarquista movement, which had as one of its principal battle cries the end of the government collectivistic ejido program and the distribution of small plots to independent property owners, found its greatest support among the rural population in the states with large numbers of rancheros.[58]

It is significant that such a large percentage of the peasant population in Morelos, Guerrero, México, Puebla, and Tlaxcala were in the free villages and shared a similar interest, the struggle to retain the village land, at the same time. When all the individuals in a given area are simultaneously roused by the same grievance, they tend to reinforce each other's perception of the problem. They are also much more likely to unite and to come rapidly to the point of action than if only scattered parts of the population are affected or if various sectors of the population define the grievance differently. It was precisely the population of these states that was able to define its ideology most clearly and to sustain the Zapatista movement for almost ten years.[59]

Another characteristic of these states in comparison with other parts of the nation was the very high population density in 1910.[60] Eyewitness accounts state that in Tepoztlán, Morelos, "the wealthy hired oxen and peones, but there was always an excess of people. They paid the oxen

[56] McBride, *op. cit.*, pp. 100–102, 88–89.   [57] *Ibid.*, p. 102.
[58] Whetten, *op. cit.*, pp. 484–522; Parkes, *op. cit.*, pp. 384–385, 427.
[59] Seymour M. Lipset, in his study of agrarian socialism in Saskatchewan, shows that the concentration in one area of a rural population who shared similar interests and similar grievances influenced the rise of a series of radical agrarian movements in the North American high plains (mostly a wheat-growing area). *Agrarian Socialism* (Berkeley: University of California Press, 1950), pp. 1–36.
[60] McBride, *op. cit.*, p. 12; see also Whetten, *op. cit.*, p. 30.

driver 25 centavos a day and the peones 18 centavos a day." [61] In the long run, too many people trying to extract a living from reduced land resources with inefficient methods was the basic problem of the central mesa. These problems remained even when the haciendas were given back to the villages in the 1920's and 1930's.

Widening the Status Gap between Peasant and Landed Elite

Although the Constitution of 1857 and even the colonization laws of the Díaz regime had envisaged a middle class of small independent land-holders, the favoritism shown the haciendas in practice not only nullified these hopes but put many small farmers out of business. Agricultural credit was extended on favorable terms only to the hacendados; the small farmers and the villages paid far more than their share of taxes and export-import duties; and government regulations favored the large farm-ing operation. There were no agricultural schools or extension programs which might have taught the small farmer better methods. Marketing facilities were primitive. Irrigation projects were constructed for the haciendas, not the small farmers or the villages. By 1910 nearly 95 per cent of the heads of all rural families were propertyless.[62]

The institution of the *tienda de raya* and debt bondage also impeded both vertical and horizontal mobility. In the period before 1910 half of the rural population was estimated to be bound by debt slavery. When American and other industrialists entered Mexico to build railroads and develop mining at the turn of the century, they could secure a labor supply only by "buying" peons from the haciendas—that is, by paying off the relatively small debts of the peons that might have been pending for generations.[63]

Even if the peons had been free to move into roles of greater economic or social power, they did not have the educational background or the skill to do so. Cheap labor was one of the principal inducements to foreign capitalists as well as the basis of profit in Mexico's growing export of primary products. It was in the interest of the state and the landed class to keep the workers unorganized, docile, and ignorant.[64] The Díaz regime was not distinguished for its efforts in education, and the rural population was almost totally overlooked. Only as his regime was collapsing in 1911

[61] Lewis, *Life in a Mexican Village*, p. 93.
[62] Tannenbaum, *MAR*, pp. 74–79; McBride, *op. cit.*, pp. 83–86.
[63] Parkes, *op. cit.*, pp. 305, 308.
[64] Marjorie Ruth Clark, *Organized Labor in Mexico* (Chapel Hill: University of North Carolina Press, 1934), pp. 4–5; Cumberland, *op. cit.*, p. 15.

did Díaz issue a decree establishing a system of rural schools, and then he dedicated only 160,000 pesos ($80,000) to the whole undertaking.[65] In 1910, 70 per cent of all persons ten years of age and over could neither read nor write, and nearly all the schools were in the cities and towns. Public policy tended to reflect the elite attitude that Indian and peasant masses were incapable of profiting from education and were perpetually relegated to the bottom of the social pyramid.[66]

The Squeeze of Inflationary Food Prices and Stationary Wage Levels

One of the most explosive policies of the period was to allow the prices of basic commodities to rise steadily while the wages of agricultural workers remained the same, thus lowering the real income of the agricultural population. The relatively rapid increase in the cost of living seems to have resulted from a combination of industrialization with increased demand for foodstuffs in the cities, the notorious inefficiency of the Mexican hacienda, and a protective tariff on imports of agricultural commodities.

With construction of the railroads and the deterioration of the interior roads, the cities actually had better contact with reliable supplies of foodstuffs from the exterior, especially from cheap sources in the United States, than from the interior. Though tariffs were imposed to slow imports and to protect producers, Mexicans did not raise enough to support the growing population and could not readily transport it to distribution centers. The net result was simply a rise in prices. Price increases from 1891 to 1908 on basic staples were significant: sugar, 32 per cent; flour, 101.4 per cent; corn, 95.6 per cent; wheat, 99.8 per cent; beans, 64 per cent; and chile, 113.6 per cent. The only sector that gained by this was the hacendados, whose prices were safely protected from the import of cheap grain. As one result, the value of land increased a great deal in this period.[67]

Wage statistics for nineteenth century Mexico are only approximate, but it seems clear that agricultural wages did not change substantially from 1792 to 1908. In 1792 the average daily wage varied between 25 and 30 centavos; in 1908 the minimum agricultural wage average throughout Mexico was about 23.5 centavos (about 12 cents) while the average agricultural wage stood at roughly 36 centavos. In the same period the price of corn rose 179 per cent; rice, 75 per cent; flour, 711 per cent;

[65] Eyler Simpson, *op. cit.*, p. 277.   [66] Whetten, *op. cit.*, p. 404.
[67] Tannenbaum, *MAR*, pp. 145–149.

wheat, 465 per cent; beans, 565 per cent; and chile, 123 per cent. The purchasing power of this 1908 wage was approximately one-fourteenth that of the corresponding American agricultural worker.[68]

One of the principal reasons why agricultural wages stayed so low was that the gradual taking over of the village lands and the land of the small independent farmers unloosed a growing mass of landless laborers competing for work on the haciendas. It was a simple result of the law of supply and demand, and there was no effective legislation setting minimum wages for agricultural workers.[69]

New Reference Groups: Mexican Industrial Workers and Agricultural Workers in the United States

For centuries Mexican peasants had experienced a life of toil and exploitation with incomes barely covering subsistence needs, and, although conditions were gradually becoming worse, the peasant tolerated enormous abuses because he knew no other lot for people of his status. But at the turn of the century the Mexican peasant became aware of two significant groups on his social level which enjoyed much better wages and conditions. This awareness tended to heighten the peasant's sense of deprivation just when his situation was becoming more intolerable in other respects.[70]

With the rapid extension of the railroads in the 1890's, transportation of cheap Mexican labor to the United States became feasible, and agricultural workers from as far south as Michoacán and Morelos discovered better wages, a higher standard of living, a modern industrial organization, and the procedures and advantages of American labor unions.[71] Gustavo Durán noted in a conference before the Mexican Scientific Society in 1911 that many Mexican agricultural workers were emigrating to the United States or trying to do so in the hope of better wages and to escape the oppression of the hacienda administrators. Workers with experience in the United States brought back "ideas that were, in essence, revolutionary in the Mexican environment. It is no accident that so many of the earlier leaders of the Revolution had had longer or shorter sojourns in the United States." [72]

[68] Eyler Simpson, *op. cit.*, pp. 37–38.

[69] Silva-Herzog, *op. cit.*, pp. 128–131; Clark, *op. cit.*, p. 134.

[70] Robert K. Merton, *Social Theory and Social Structure* (rev. ed.; New York: Free Press of Glencoe, 1963), pp. 227–260.

[71] Manuel Gamio, *Mexican Immigration to the United States* (Chicago: University of Chicago Press, 1930), pp. 30–50.

[72] Silva-Herzog, *op. cit.*, p. 131; Tannenbaum, *PBR*, p. 136.

Perhaps even more important than work experience in the United States was the creation of a free, mobile labor force in the textile mills, mining, and other industries, and especially in the construction and maintenance of the railroads. Andrés Molina Enríquez states that the "dynamite of the railways charged the mine which later the Revolution set off. . . . The construction of the railways . . . involved the employment of laborers who for the first time received real [i.e., cash] wages, wages which radically improved their economic condition. Along the whole length of the railway lines which traversed the country gathered laborers who had escaped the yoke of our great hacendados." [73] By 1910 industrial wages, while still relatively low, were frequently four or five times that of the rural worker.[74]

The railroads and industrialization also introduced a modern market economy into the hinterland regions and opened Mexico to a flood of new manufactured items both from Mexican industries and from the United States. The desire for the new goods whetted appetites for increased buying power and higher wages.[75]

Formation of an Ideology: Mexican Traditions of Agrarian Protest

The landed elite maintained their control of Mexico, and the cultural institutions of the country were still built upon the concept of the superiority and privilege of the elite. But there were also profound traditions of protest and rebellion in defense of the Indian peasant. The relations of peasant and elite were continually volatile and violent peasant uprisings were an ever present fear. We find, however, two distinct traditions of agrarian protest: the folk tradition of the illiterate peasant who saw protest in terms of direct, vindictive reprisals against concrete personalities, replete with the hatred and emotion stemming from the frustration of their daily lives; and the learned tradition of the educated —the lawyers, journalists, cultivated politicians, philosophers, and professors—who saw protest in terms of national politics and, especially, legal and philosophical reforms. These two traditions of protest correspond to the two halves of peasant society which Robert Redfield describes: the urban and the folk traditions, the "great" tradition of the centers of learning and wisdom and the "little" tradition of the countryside.[76] These

---

[73] Quoted in Eyler Simpson, *op. cit.*, p. 44n.   [74] Parkes, *op. cit.*, p. 308.

[75] Eyler Simpson, *op. cit.*, p. 44n.

[76] Robert Redfield, *Peasant Society and Culture* (Chicago: University of Chicago Press, 1956), pp. 67–104.

two have tended to develop autonomously in Mexico, with interchanges and mutual influences at various periods of history.

The Peasant Tradition of Protest

The Mexican peasants, like peasantry around the world, tended to be rather conservative, hesitant to take chances which would jeopardize the little they possessed, and fatalistic with regard to the adversities and injustices they suffered. Also the landed elite were often able subtly to convince the peasantry that elite beliefs about the peasants—their indolence, their lack of responsibility and aspirations, their ignorance and immorality—were true, and the peasants accepted this paternalism because they did not feel they could manage independently. In this manner the elite were able to exercise a quiet form of preventive social control over possible peasant movements.[77]

But the Mexican peasant was acquainted with many uprisings of the nineteenth century and these offered him models of action. He was also influenced by the folk songs and stories which painted an idealistic picture of protest and idolized the heroes who stood in open defiance of the social order which the peasant supported by his labor. To the Mexican peasant, used to the armed violence of his countryside, rebellion appeared not only possible and legitimate, but an avenue to higher status among his own people.[78]

Many of the continual peasant uprisings of nineteenth-century Mexico were little more than local disturbances, but others were important enough to gain mention in the historical record. In 1849 there was an agrarian uprising of more than 1,000 men in the State of San Luis Potosí led by Eluterio Quiroz. This "movimiento de Sierra Gorda" published a decree of agrarian reform and was able to hold out for more than six months against the government. In 1848 and 1849 there were various agrarian uprisings in the state of México. A certain Zavala proposed division of the haciendas and a plan to designate as Emperor an Indian of pure blood, descendant of Moctezuma, with the requirement that he marry a maiden of pure Indian descent. There was also an uprising of peons in Morelos in 1859.[79]

In 1869 the campesino Julio Chávez López, socialist and disciple of Rhodakanaty, launched an agrarian revolution in Puebla, but without

---

[77] Smelser, *op. cit.*, pp. 306–310.

[78] See Tannenbaum's discussion of the role of violence in Mexican life and politics (*PBR*, pp. 87–105).   [79] Silva-Herzog, *op. cit.*, p. 63; Chevalier, "Zapata," p. 69.

success. In 1877 the First Campesino Congress was held and from this there were formed campesino leagues that fomented uprisings in many states.[80] In 1879 a large group took up arms in the region of the Sierra de Alica, Guanajuato, and published the Plan de Tepic, çalling for revision of titles and the return of land to the Indians. In 1881 there was an uprising led by Patricio Rueda in the Huasteca Potosina calling for municipal government and an agrarian law. In 1882 a group in San Luis Potosí began guerrilla warfare and issued a plan stating that God gave the land to all men, but that the Spanish conquest, the Reform Laws, and the distribution of much of the communal lands had converted Mexico into a proletarian mass groaning under the tyranical government of the hacendados. In 1896 nearly a thousand Indians attacked Papantla because their land had been taken away from them.[81]

The state of Morelos in the late nineteenth century was the scene of continual violent struggles against the hacendados and local political bosses. The history of Tepoztlán in the fifty years before 1910 indicates why it quickly became a loyal Zapatista village in 1911. In the middle of the nineteenth century the Tepoztecans were carrying on a feud with the Hacienda de San Gaspar, which had taken over the titles of the communal land of Tepoztlán and was prohibiting the people from using their forest reserves. Agents of the hacienda were killed on sight in the village. About 1880 a Felipe Gómez was municipal president and was preventing the Tepoztecans from opening *tlacolol* (clearing the hillside for corn planting) and from producing charcoal for sale. Those who protested were recruited into the army or sent to the penitentiary. Finally the villagers rose up, and Gómez was murdered in his house. In 1893 a Tepoztecan, Roberto Ibarra, attempting to extend an abortive rebellion against Díaz organized in Guerrero, recruited twenty men from the area of Tepoztlán to overthrow their own dictatorial municipal president. In the 1890's the Reform Laws distributing communal land to individual owners were being applied to Tepoztlán and the Hacienda of San Gaspar was again trying to grab the village land. But individual owners secured their claims and backed up these claims by force. In the years before the Revolution of 1910 the local *caciques* were preventing the villagers from using their communal lands in order to provide a source of cheap labor for the surrounding haciendas.[82]

This milieu of continual violence and protest generated an "outlaw"

[80] Victor Alba, *Las ideas sociales contemporáneas en México* (Mexico City: Fondo de Cultura Económica, 1960), p. 11.   [81] Silva-Herzog, *op. cit.*, p. 106.

[82] Lewis, *Life in a Mexican Village*, pp. 114–115, 230–231.

subsociety and subculture. Those who took part in the protests were certain to be the object of the vengeance of the local *caciques,* and there was nothing to do but flee to the mountains or to another state where the "law," that is, the arbitrary machinations of the *caciques,* could not reach them.

Perhaps the best reflection of the popular heroes, grievances and sense of legitimacy in rural Mexico is the folk ballad called the *corrido.* The *corrido* often took the form of a narration of some event of special significance for the singers—a battle, the death of a local hero, or some scurrilous happening in the countryside. They were to be heard at every fiesta, at markets, cockpits, and *cantinas.* Traveling *cancioneros* often carried by *corridos* the news and tales of high romance from one isolated village to another.[83]

One of the most popular types of *corridos* in the sixty years before the Revolution of 1910 was that celebrating the deeds of bandit-heroes, men continually chased by the *federales* and the *rurales* (the federal troops and the mounted rural police), but protectors of the poor.

In 1882 Porfirio Díaz was still engaged in pacifying the country after having assumed power in the late 1870's. The process involved the capture and execution of many guerrilla leaders who had begun operations against the French during Maximilian's empire and had continued afterwards, some as out-and-out bandits, some as revolutionists attempting to overthrow the Díaz government who maintained themselves by looting and highway robbery. The first heroic *corridos* of Greater Mexico were composed about these outlaws.[84]

If one examines the *corridos* of these outlaws and guerrilla leaders one finds all the qualities of the social bandit described by Hobsbawm as typical of peasant societies.[85] Like Robin Hood in England, Diego Corrientes in Andalusia, Janosik in Poland and Slovakia, Stenka Razin in Russia, or the bandits glorified in Chinese peasant lore, such bandits are champions of their people; they exact revenge or redress wrongs; they claim land for the landless. The social bandit is the poor boy that has made good by remaining on the side of the oppressed.[86]

There are an especially large number of *corridos* telling of Heraclio

[83] Simmons, *op. cit.,* pp. 3–64; Edward Laroque Tinker, *Corridos & Calaveras* (Austin: University of Texas Press, 1961), pp. 3–16.   [84] Tinker, *op. cit.,* p. 29.

[85] E. J. Hobsbawm, *Social Bandits and Primitive Rebels* (Glencoe, Ill.: Free Press, 1959), pp. 13–29.

[86] Eric R. Wolf, *Peasants* (Englewood Cliffs, N.J.: Prentice-Hall, 1966), pp. 106–108.

Bernal, an outlaw and guerrilla leader who ranged over central and western Mexico. After he was killed in 1882, the balladeers made Bernal a hero of epic proportions. The *corridos* tell of his greatness, how he was captured and put to death, and how all lamented his absence. The songs about Bernal show typical qualities of the Mexican folk hero: protector of the poor who gave money to needy families; defender against the hacendados; always fearless; a favorite of the girls "from Altata to Mapimí"; feared by the rich, the *gachupines*, and the Americans; chased by the federal troops and the rural police; a picturesque horserider; and an excellent shot.[87] The ideal of manhood and peasant leadership portrayed in the heroic *corridos*, which Zapata heard so often as a youth, suggests the portrait of Emiliano Zapata himself as a peasant leader.[88]

The Learned Tradition of Protest

Mexico's learned tradition of agrarian protest stretches back to the conquest: the efforts of Bartolomé de las Casas and the Spanish Crown to defend the Indian; the suggestions of land reform made by Manuel Abad y Queipo at the beginning of the nineteenth century; Hidalgo and Morelos; Melchor Ocampo's attempts to bring about a new Mexico of small property holders at the time of the Reform.[89] In the Díaz period most of the lawyers, educators, and intellectuals were caught up in the enthusiasm for Spencerian positivism and laissez-faire liberalism. Those who chose to criticize the Díaz land policies openly did so with reserve; those who proposed outright expropriation were soon forced to go underground. Hardly anyone then saw Mexico's agrarian problems clearly enough to offer a concrete program to replace Díaz's own random, poorly planned efforts.[90] But from a few scattered protests in the 1890's the learned sector went on to reach agreement on certain general principles of agrarian reform by 1910 and in the heat of the Revolution these ideas would evolve into a new agrarian program.

Perhaps the best known of the more moderate critics of the Díaz land policies were Wistano Luis Orozco, a well known jurist and judge who had argued the cases of the campesinos against the haciendas, and Justo Sierra, writer, representative in the national congress, educator, one of the most independent and influential intellectuals of the Porfiriato. In his

[87] Armando María y Campos, *La revolución mexicana a través de los corridos populares* (Mexico City: Talleres Gráficos de la Nación, 1962), pp. 73–120.

[88] Díaz Soto y Gama, *La revolución agraria del sur y Emiliano Zapata, su caudillo* (Mexico City: N.pub., 1960), pp. 262, 272; Simmons, *op. cit.*, p. 292.

[89] Alba, *op. cit.*, pp. 15–17, 58–60.   [90] Eyler Simpson, *op. cit.*, pp. 375–376.

Legislación y jurisprudencia sobre terrenos baldíos, published in 1895, and in later writings, Orozco criticized strongly the Díaz land giveaways and proposed the creation of a modern agriculture based on small property holders, to be done by selling government land only to small landholders and distributing the great idle tracts of land held for speculative purposes. He would have reformed tax laws to curb the haciendas and protected wage earners on the haciendas, but he argued against large scale expropriation by the state and wanted land sold in small lots.[91] In 1876 Justo Sierra challenged the classical liberal emphasis on the sanctity of private property and justified "expropriation without previous indemnification," later one of the key issues of Mexican agrarian reform. Sierra continued through the 1880's and 1890's to point out the potentially explosive conditions of the peons, the excesses of the hacendados, and the necessity of splitting up the haciendas.[92] But neither Orozco nor Sierra, being essentially nineteenth-century liberals, seriously considered the restoration of the communal lands.

More radical agrarian reform action was being proposed in the decade from 1900 to 1910 by young students and activists who had contact with socialist and anarchist ideas and formed a loose movement called the Liberal Party. Among those most active were Antonio Díaz Soto y Gama, destined to be one of the greatest of the Zapatistas and Mexico's agrarian leader during the 1920's; Antonio Villareal, later to initiate the first steps of the ejido program as Obregón's minister of agriculture; the Flores Magón brothers, members of the IWW who fomented much of the labor agitation and the major strikes before the Revolution; and Juan Sarabia, later an important *agrarista*. Individuals like the Magaña brothers, leaders in the Zapatista movement, and Francisco Múgica, who gave the Constitutional Convention of 1917 its radical turn, were also in contact with the movement. After the Second Liberal Congress in 1902 the opposition of the Díaz regime drove the movement underground and its newspaper, *Regeneración*, was published by Ricardo Flores Magón in St. Louis, Missouri.[93]

In the Manifesto of the Liberal party published in *Regeneración* in 1906, there was a quite definite program of agrarian reform. Owners of haciendas would be required to put into production land not used; if the land remained unused, the state was to expropriate the land, and distribute

[91] Silva-Herzog, *op. cit.*, pp. 118–122; Alba, *op. cit.*, pp. 135–137.

[92] Silva-Herzog, *op. cit.*, pp. 100–103, 106–112.

[93] Gildardo Magaña, *Emiliano Zapata y el agrarismo en México* (Mexico City: Editorial Ruta, 1951–1952), IV, 31–42.

it without cost in small plots with the provision that the land be cultivated, not sold; the government would establish an agrarian bank to
provide long-term loans at low rates of interest so that the poor as well as
the larger farmers could benefit by credit programs; the debts of agricultural laborers to their employers were to be declared void and the *tienda
de raya* suppressed. An eight-hour day, a minimum wage, and measures to
insure decent housing were to be adopted for agricultural laborers.[94]

This was to be attained by nothing less than armed revolt against the
Díaz regime. This manifesto is considered one of the most important
ideological precursors of the Revolution and of the reform measures of
the Constitution of 1917.[95] But it makes no mention of restoring the ejido
nor does it explicitly propose that the land tenure system of the great
haciendas be ended.

A milder form of agrarian protest was the Christian Social Action
movement. Its principal spokesman was Trinidad Sánchez Santos, founder
of the newspaper, *El País,* and its program was propounded in numerous
semanas sociales ("social seminars"), agrarian congresses, and a series of
Mexican Catholic Social Congresses held from 1903 to 1909. In these
congresses proposals were made to establish rural savings banks and
production and consumption cooperatives for the benefit of small landholders, to form a committee of Catholic lawyers to defend the interests
of the Indian in court, to suppress the *tienda de raya,* to establish schools
on the haciendas and set up regional agricultural schools. But much of the
discussion of the Congress merely concerned means to bring about
changes in the personal attitudes and morality of the peasantry. There was
little disposition to propose the radical reform of institutions like the
system of land tenure.[96]

In 1909 Molina Enríquez published his book, *Los grandes problemas
nacionales,* which Luis Cabrera says was for the Mexican Revolution what
Rousseau's *Social Contract* was for the French Revolution. The scholarly
analysis of the exploitation of Indians and peasants and the disastrous
results of the Díaz agricultural policy was a revelation to many Mexican
thinkers. It showed the need for breaking up the large estates, providing
new systems of credit, regulating and developing the use of water resources, and reforming politics in the rural areas. But the indirect means
of land tenure reform suggested by Molina Enríquez would have greatly
delayed the distribution of land. The large estates were to be split up

[94] Silva-Herzog, *op. cit.,* p. 152–155.   [95] *Ibid.,* p. 155.
[96] Paul Murray, *The Catholic Church in Mexico* (Mexico City: Editorial EPM,
1964), pp. 334–368; Alba, *op. cit.,* pp. 111–118.

voluntarily by the hacendados, by limiting the amount of land any individual could inherit, and by special credit facilities for buying and cultivating parts of the haciendas.[97]

The village school teachers, priests, and lawyers—those individuals who were educated in the learned tradition and were in some contact with national intellectual currents, but resident in the villages—also played important roles in the Mexican tradition of agrarian protest. These were the cultural brokers of protest, to use Eric Wolf's term, and they operated as points of interchange for the thoughts and feelings of the two traditions. The local school teachers—such as Otilio Montaño of Tlatizapán, Morelos, who propagandized socialist ideals and the exaltation of the Indian,[98] and Pablo Torres Burgos of Ayala who helped to bring the local peasants into contact with Madero's campaign against Díaz's re-election —were important in giving local discontent a more general ideological content. School teachers as secretaries and adjutants of the half-literate revolutionary generals proved to be important influences in the development of revolutionary ideology.[99]

By 1910 there was a rising tide of protest among both the peasants and the young activist-intellectuals though as yet there was little communication among the many potentially revolutionary groups. Within the learned sector there was a new generation that had been educated abroad or had read widely and they were not ready to tolerate the Mexico of Porfirio Díaz. But the various movements were blindly ignored or suppressed. Briefly we will examine why the system found it so difficult to change.

The Monolithic Power Structure of the Porfiriato

In 1910 Mexico was still a relatively simple two-class society, for the various elites shared such similar backgrounds and interests that, in reality, they formed one elite. If the local politicians, the generals, the higher clergy, the intellectuals, and the press were tolerant of, if not openly cooperative with, the interests of the new industrialists and the hacenda-

[97] Andrés Molina Enríquez, *Los grandes problemas nacionales* (Mexico City: Ediciones del Instituto Nacional de la Juventud Mexicana, 1964); Alba, *op. cit.*, pp. 128–135; Silva-Herzog, *op. cit.*, pp. 142–146.   [98] Alba, *op. cit.*, p. 127.

[99] Gonzalez Navarro, *op. cit.*, pp. 179–180. For a more general discussion of the role of cultural brokers in a peasant society, cf. Eric R. Wolf, "Aspects of Group Relations in a Complex Society: Mexico," *American Anthropologist*, LVIII (Dec., 1956), p. 1072; Charles Wagley, "The Peasant," in John J. Johnson (ed.), *Continuity and Change in Latin America* (Stanford, Calif.: Stanford University Press, 1964), pp. 45–47.

dos, it was because they had a similar value system and perception of the world. And those who did consider the possibility of some concessions feared what would happen if the "barbarian masses" got a taste of power.

The Díaz governmental system operated through 27 appointed governors, 300 *jefes políticos* (local political bosses), and 1,800 municipal presidents, many of whom were the instruments of the hacendados if not hacendados themselves. If the peons were not docile they were inducted into the army or shipped off to work in Quintana Roo, Yucatán. The famous *rurales* were at hand to quell any rebellion.

It was almost impossible for the peasants to get a favorable ruling in court. As a typical case, in 1902 a group of some sixty, including Emiliano Zapata, led by Jovito Serrano from Yautepec, Morelos, went to Mexico City to protest the seizure of the Yautepec village lands by the Escandón hacienda. The case was carried to the Supreme Court of Mexico, and the noted attorney, Serralde, even arranged an interview with Porfirio Díaz who assured the villagers that justice would be done. After three years of litigation not only was the case lost but Serrano and his companion, Castillo, were apprehended by the police—presumedly bribed by the hacendado Pablo Escandón—and deported to Quintana Roo where Serrano died in 1905.[100]

Criticism of the Díaz regime might have been expected from the intellectuals and the educators or even from certain sectors of the church or the press. But this was generally not the case. The intelligentsia of the Díaz period were educated in the positivism of Comte, Spencer, and John Stewart Mill, and they enthusiastically gave the political and economic policies of Díaz a quasi-moral basis. With their Mexican version of Comte they looked on the Díaz regime as moving Mexico beyond the theological stage (the colonial period) and the metaphysical stage (Jacobin Liberalism) to the positive stage in which a rational, scientific order was established in place of the anarchic liberty that had characterized Mexico's first fifty years of independence. Not only did the laissez-faire policies evolve from the social Darwinian ideas of the key role of the naturally superior and the survival of the strongest, but they were viewed as the most equitable system in the long run.[101]

The relationship of the Church and the still officially anticlerical Díaz

[100] John H. McNeeley, "Origins of the Zapata Revolt in Morelos" *Hispanic American Historical Review*, XLVI, No. 1 (Feb., 1966), 155.
[101] Patrick Romanell, *Making of the Mexican Mind* (Lincoln: University of Nebraska Press, 1952), pp. 42–53; Alba, *op. cit.*, pp. 73–96.

government was one of mutual tolerance,[102] but in the Mexican social structure the Church hierarchy formed what Eric Wolf calls a peasant-elite coalition. Thus the potential conflict between the peasant and the landed elite is muted by peasant-elite kinship ties (or fictive kinship such as the *patrón-peón* relationship) or by special solidarity ceremonials linking together the peasant and his overlord.[103] In Mexico there existed on the one hand a fairly strong sense of identification by the peasants with the Church and the local pastor because of tradition and, in many instances, a pastor's very genuine concern for the personal problems of the peasants. On the other hand many pastors shared the hacendado view of the peon as a helpless, irresponsible creature and they sincerely thought that he needed the firm, paternalistic care of the elite. In 1923 the historian Gruening asked the peons on a hacienda in Guanajuato why they did not want to receive ejidos. "If we got them, we wouldn't be able to take care of them," they replied. When asked who had told them that, they answered, "The boss . . . [and] . . . the *padre*." Many local priests of humble origin supported the Zapatistas and the agrarian reforms, but Gruening's interviews with two archbishops and five bishops between 1923 and 1925 reveal that these clergymen still opposed agrarian legislation and felt the hacendados should be paid for the land unless it had been taken illegally.[104]

The Díaz government subsidized the press, even the opposition press which was used by Díaz to undermine members of his government who were becoming too popular. Editors who openly attacked the dictator could expect prison sentences since right of jury trials for press offenses had been abolished and journalists could be convicted of libel or sedition by the decision of a single magistrate. Nevertheless, a whole series of opposition papers, mostly prolabor and frequently socialist, anarchist, or syndicalist in tendency operated underground or in exile in the years before the Revolution.[105]

Thus in the Mexico of 1910, as in many peasant societies, we find the key institutional areas controlled by the same individuals holding multiple roles or by individuals from the same elite background linked by acquaintance or even by kinship. As the strains experienced by the peasants grew more acute, especially in Morelos, their protests were more insistent. But the peasant groups in presenting their protests met these same individuals in whatever institutional channels they approached and, since there was little flexibility or consideration for the peasants' complaints, they

[102] Murray, *op. cit.*, pp. 290–316.   [103] Wolf, *Peasants*, pp. 81–95.
[104] Gruening, *op. cit.*, pp. 215–219.   [105] Parkes, *op. cit.*, pp. 294–295.

were driven to the conclusion that only noninstitutionalized, violent means would resolve their grievances.

Mobilization, Part I: The Emergence of Emiliano Zapata as a Revolutionary Peasant Leader

The Selection of Zapata as *Calpuleque*, Defender of the Village Lands

Emiliano Zapata was born in 1879 in Anenecuilco near Cuautla in the central part of Morelos. His parents were mestizos and the family ranked in social class between the hacienda peon and the independent ranchero. His father farmed a little parcel of land in the village but due to the encroachments of the haciendas lived mainly by buying and selling horses. Zapata was an important and respected name and José Zapata (probably a great uncle of Emiliano's) was an important village leader and military figure in the area from 1865 to 1876.[106] Emiliano learned to read and write at a primary school in nearby Ayala, but he spent more time working on his father's farm and learned especially well how to handle his father's horses. As a boy one of his greatest delights was hearing his uncle, Don José Zapata, tell romantic stories of his campaigns as a soldier in the War of Reform and of fights with the bandits of La Plata who molested the villages of the area thirty years before.[107]

When his father died the sixteen-year-old Emiliano took over the small farm and continued raising melons and training horses.[108] He became particularly outstanding as a horseman and liked to dress in the slightly fastidious *charro* costume of southern Mexico: wide ornamented hat, short vest with neckerchief, and long tight pants ornamented with buttons down the side. He especially enjoyed the *jaripeo*, the local broncobusting rodeos. Díaz Soto y Gama describes him as having a very sharp intelligence, but speaking laconically in the fashion of Mexico's southern campesinos.[109] Young Zapata is pictured as a proud, independent villager, sober and hard-working, but with a bit of the restless and the sport about him.

The village of Anenecuilco straddles a small river and its fertile sandy soil is ideal for melons and other truck gardening. Records indicate that it paid tribute to the Aztec overlords and had a history of seven hundred years of fighting to keep its land and the little surplus it produced. Throughout colonial times and into the nineteenth century Anenecuilco

---

[106] Womack, *op. cit.*, pp. 9–10.   [107] Sotelo y Inclán, *op. cit.*, p. 171.
[108] *Ibid.*, p. 172.   [109] Chevalier, "Zapata," p. 75.

was involved in continual litigation with the Hacienda of the Hospital and the Hacienda of Mapastlán and had lost much of its land. Anenecuilco saw the neighboring villages of Olintepec and Ahuehuepán swallowed up and in 1887 the *junta de defensa* of the village took up arms to defend its land only to be forced to flee by federal troops.[110] By 1895 the Hacienda of the Hospital had taken over the fertile, irrigable land of the village and was charging a rent and a period of labor on the hacienda for the use of the lands. In addition the hacienda had taken over part of the pastures, and to recover any cattle or horses that wandered into the area the villagers had to pay five pesos.[111]

In 1897 when Emiliano was twenty he was arrested in Anenecuilco by the *rurales*, apparently for having spoken out too freely against the local hacendados. But his older brother Eufemio and a friend met the party taking Emiliano to the nearby town of Cuautla, managed to free the prisoner, and the two brothers were able to escape to the neighboring State of Puebla. Through Frumencio Palacios, a friend of the Zapata family in Cuautla, Emiliano got a job as caretaker of horses on the Hacienda of Jaltepec, Puebla.[112] After a year the Zapata family was able to straighten out the affair with the authorities sufficiently to allow the young outlaw to return to his native village.[113]

In 1904 the villagers decided to resolve the dispute with the Hacienda of the Hospital and the *jefes políticos;* they took the titles and maps to officials in Mexico City where, after two years of careful study, the lawyer Francisco Serralde declared that their claims were absolutely valid. In 1906 the governor of Morelos arranged a meeting between the administrator of the hacienda and the villagers of Anenecuilco and Ayala, and Emiliano Zapata is listed as attending. But the administrator would make no concessions and in 1907 the leaders of the villages again took the case to Governor Manuel Alarcón. The Governor wrote back abruptly that they had presented no solid proof of title to the land "possessed" by the Hacienda of the Hospital. The villagers then left their titles and maps with the governor's office, but time passed and by 1908 there still was no decision.[114]

Emiliano Zapata's name appears on several of the petitions the villagers made at that time.[115] In 1908, in the face of frustrating delays and because

---

[110] Sotelo y Inclán, *op. cit.*, pp. 24–28, 136–137, 171.   [111] *Ibid.*, pp. 158–159.

[112] This account is verified by Porfirio Palacios, son of Frumencio, in his biography of Zapata (*Emiliano Zapata, datos biográficos-históricos* [Mexico City: Libro Mex-Editores, 1960), pp. 20–21.   [113] Magaña, *op. cit.*, I, 94–95.

[114] Sotelo y Inclán, *op. cit.*, pp. 161–166.   [115] *Ibid.*, p. 173.

"justice" seemed to be imparted according to the whims of the powerful, Zapata called together the villagers and suggested that they defend the right to their land with arms.[116] This action alarmed the neighboring hacendados and the Governor, and Emiliano Zapata was inducted into the Ninth Cavalry Regiment which at that time was garrisoning Cuernavaca. Emiliano remained with the federal troops only six months, but the military experience proved to be valuable to him later and he came to know the weaknesses of the *federales* well.[117]

During his military service Zapata distinguished himself by breaking "unmanageable" horses and through his favor with Ignacio de la Torre y Mier, a wealthy hacendado who admired his horsemanship, he was released from the service. De la Torre y Mier brought Emiliano to Mexico City to manage his stables, but the farmer from Anenecuilco found life there disgusting. Years later he recounted to Gildardo Magaña how depressed he was to see the luxury of the life of the hacendados in Mexico City where even the horses in their elegant stables had more conveniences than the campesinos. This deep dislike of the city and its people would remain to the end of his life. When Zapata returned to Anenecuilco he found himself the target of the local hacienda administrators and the *jefes políticos*.[118]

In the election for governor of Morelos in February, 1909 the official candidate was Pablo Escandón, member of the wealthy hacendado family which had taken over the lands of Yautepec and staff officer of President Díaz. Since Díaz had announced that he was permitting opposition candidates, Patricio Leyva, a member of the recently organized national Democratic Party, became the opposition candidate against Escandón. Refugio Yañez and Pablo Torres Burgos formed a *Leyvista* group in Ayala and invited villagers in the area to join. Emiliano Zapata joined and became active in the campaign.[119]

When members of the Democratic party came from Mexico City to Cuernavaca to speak on behalf of Leyva, they found that the city was full of troops under General Juvencio Robles. One of the speakers, Gabriel Robles Domínguez, told his audience "that they were within their rights in preventing Colonel Escandón from carrying out his promise to plant sugar cane in the very atrium of the parish church at Yautepec. . . . The crowd responded by crying out against their relatives being forced into military service and against the spoilation of their little farms or water rights until they had not enough to eat or drink." Later that evening the

---

[116] Magaña, *op. cit.*, I, 95.   [117] Sotelo y Inclán, *op. cit.*, p. 173.
[118] Magaña, *op. cit.*, I, 95, 96.   [119] *Ibid.*, p. 96.

jefe político threatened to hang Robles Domínguez. On election day the polling places were manned largely by government employees protected by the armed forces and Pablo Escandón was victorious.[120] The frustrating Leyva campaign left the peasants of Morelos in a state of great unrest and with a new sense of political organization; Emiliano Zapata was now connected with a nucleus of political opposition to the unpopular Escandón.[121]

Meanwhile, in 1908 the *junta de defensa* of Anenecuilco had managed to take their claims directly to Porfirio Díaz hoping that he could exert pressure on the governor, but Governor Alarcón died and the officials of Governor Escandón paid little attention to their petitions. Then in the summer of 1909 a new crisis arose: the Hacienda of the Hospital, out of revenge for the villagers' action, refused to rent land to the Anenecuilcans and rented to Ayala instead. In September, 1909, the village elected Emiliano Zapata to the traditional post of *calpuleque*, head of the *junta de defensa*. Zapata was deeply impressed by a careful study of the sacred village documents, titles, and maps going back hundreds of years and he gave the Anenecuilcans his word that their land would be restored.[122]

When the governor continued to ignore their petitions, Zapata led eighty men out to the land of Anenecuilco and the Ayalans withdrew. Anenecuilco planted corn in 1910, but a bad harvest resulted and Zapata deepened the conflict with the hacienda by adamantly refusing to pay rent. Zapata's bold action so impressed the men of the area that he was chosen head of the *junta de defensa* of the three villages—Anenecuilco, Villa Ayala, and Moyotepec—and supervised the distribution of plots, defiantly ignoring the fence lines of the haciendas. The *jefe político* appeared on the scene with ten men announcing to Zapata, "They tell me that you have taken up arms." "No," answered Zapata, "We are simply distributing this land." The *jefe político*, seeing the hundred determined men behind Zapata and sensitive to the generally explosive situation in the entire state of Morelos, withdrew.[123]

Francisco Madero, Precipitating Factor of the Zapata Movement

In November, 1910, Emiliano Zapata was interested in little more than being a loyal leader to the peasants of his area and cultivating his watermelons in peace. But in early November Francisco Madero, who had been leading the campaign against Díaz's re-election, published his revolutionary Plan of San Luis Potosí. Since his participation in the Leyva campaign

[120] McNeeley, *op. cit.*, pp. 156–157. [121] Magaña, *op. cit.*, I, 96.
[122] Sotelo y Inclán, *op. cit.*, pp. 173–177. [123] *Ibid.*, pp. 184–185, 187–189.

Zapata had been drawn into close contact with more nationally-oriented local leaders such as Pablo Torres Burgos, a school teacher of Ayala who often helped the farmers in simple legal matters, and Gabriel Tepapa, leader in the Jojutla area and veteran of the War of the Reform.[124] Together they read the Plan of San Luis Potosí and noted especially the words in its third article:

As it is just to restore to their former owners the lands of which they were dispossessed in such an arbitrary manner, such rulings and decisions are declared subject to revision and those who have acquired them in such an immoral manner . . . will be required to restore them to their former owners.[125]

This combination of bold peasant leaders and local intelligentsia came to the conclusion that there was no turning back now that their conflict with the haciendas had become open. They saw that their only hope lay in a change of regime and they decided to answer Madero's call for a general uprising. In mid-December, using the money contributed by their villages to the *junta de defensa,* they sent Pablo Torres Burgos north to San Antonio, Texas, to establish contact with Madero and receive his orders for organizing the rebellion in Morelos.[126]

Certainly Madero was the precipitating factor which caused Zapata's local peasant organization to grow into a national agrarian movement. And the manner in which Madero set in motion the Revolution of 1910 was an important factor in preventing Zapata's uprising from being quickly stamped out as had all the other peasant uprisings in the previous hundred years.

Francisco Madero came from a wealthy hacendado family in the northern State of Coahuila, but he had studied in the United States and France and was indignant that in spite of its economic progress Mexico was so backward politically. His appearance was not that of a leader of men—he stood five foot three, had a high thin voice and a nervous air about him—but he more than made up for this by his determination to see democratic institutions restored in Mexico. As early as 1904 he began to devote his time and money to a campaign against Díaz's re-election. He had a wide but vague appeal: the radical young social reformers of the Liberal party, the old liberals of the War of the Reform, the masses of peasants and workers, the new middle class, even those of his own hacendado class—all looked on him as preferable to Díaz. Yet with his

---

[124] Womack, *op. cit.,* p. 49.   [125] Cumberland, *op. cit.,* p. 209.
[126] Magaña, *op. cit.,* I, 97.

rather ephemeral idealism he seemed to be the least threatening of opposition candidates. Whereas the movements initiated by Ricardo Flores Magón and the political campaign of Bernardo Reyes were quickly cut down, Díaz allowed Madero to spend three years traveling all over Mexico establishing a political organization. With blind tenacity and indefatigable zeal Madero argued for the return of democratic institutions to Mexico to any group that would listen. In the end Díaz and the *científicos* sidetracked Madero and won a controlled re-election. But when Madero reacted by calling for a revolution, he had already won widespread sympathy and there were uprisings in support of him in every part of the country. Díaz was forced to cope with dozens of rebellions, thus diverting from Morelos federal troops that might easily have crushed Zapata had he been alone in an uprising.[127]

Madero might have tried to topple Díaz by a single military force under his own command, or in conjunction with a military junta, or, conceivably, through disaffected sectors of Díaz's own government. Instead he chose to coordinate simultaneous popular uprisings all over the country.[128] The masses of people, most of them peasants and workers, seized the opportunity to remedy their diverse grievances and gain all that had been denied them by the elite. Once these popular uprisings had military power and a certain legitimacy, they did not intend to relinquish them until their aspirations were realized. Consequently, Madero precipitated not merely a political change, but a revolution which challenged the whole peasant-elite structure.

The Weakness of the Díaz Government

Pablo Torres Burgos returned to Morelos from San Antonio with Madero's authorization to establish a junta made up of Gabriel Tepepa, Rafael Merino, Emiliano Zapata, and Torres Burgos as leaders of the revolutionary force in Morelos.[129] Tepepa, Merino, and Zapata began recruiting peons from the villages and haciendas and on March 10, 1911, began guerrilla activity as three relatively independent bands operating throughout the state of Morelos. Within a month the revolutionary forces were occupying many of the outlying villages and within two months they had occupied the key town of Cuautla. The capital, Cuernavaca, was occupied on May 25 and on June 7 Zapata was one of the first to greet Madero at the railroad station on his triumphal entry into Mexico City.[130]

The rapidity of the collapse of the Díaz government is an indication of

[127] Cumberland, *op. cit.*, pp. 30–118.   [128] *Ibid.*, pp. 144–151.
[129] Womack, *op. cit.*, p. 125.   [130] McNeeley, *op. cit.*, p. 160.

another major factor in the initial success of the Zapata movement: the weakness of the forces of social control. Social movements, precisely because they are collective action to change institutionalized patterns, nearly always find themselves in conflict with those agencies responsible for the integration of society and the maintenance of the patterns of value —the government, the police, the courts, the press, licensing boards, and religious authorities.[131] The Díaz government by selective concessions to discontented peasant groups, alertness to potential rebellions, and the use of its military force might easily have prevented the Zapata movement from coming to full mobilization.

But Díaz had miscalculated by allowing a revival of serious political discussion in 1908. A flood of opposition and minor rebellions opened up, and when Díaz cracked down on them this only accentuated the feeling of oppression. Also, by 1910 Díaz and his advisors were literally weak with old age: many of his governors and cabinet members were between seventy and eighty, and Navarro, the general at Ciudad Juarez where Madero won his crucial victory, was a veteran of the War of the Reform. The Díaz policy of playing factions against each other had destroyed internal cohesion and trust, and in the end Díaz brushed aside his war minister and assumed control. The army, nominally a force of 30,000, actually contained only 18,000, and these unwilling conscripts were badly equipped by officials who always managed to put part of the army budget into their own pockets.[132]

Mobilization, Part II: Zapata Becomes the Leader of a National Agrarian Movement

The Leadership Qualities of Emiliano Zapata

When the Maderista revolution began in Morelos in early March, its rather tenuously recognized head was Pablo Torres Burgos with Rafael Merino, Gabriel Tepepa, and Emiliano Zapata commanding their own guerrilla bands. But Torres Burgos was treacherously shot in late March by federal forces under Dabadié, *jefe político* of Cuernavaca; Rafael Merino died fighting at the town of Izúcar de Matamoros on April 18; the elderly Tepepa was shot by conservative Maderistas under General Figueroa of Guerrero in late May. But the peasant armies had begun to recognize Zapata as their *de facto* leader soon after the fighting started, and in a conference of rebel chiefs on April 22, he was recognized as head

---

[131] Smelser, *op. cit.*, pp. 17, 364–379.   [132] Parkes, *op. cit.*, pp. 315–319, 320.

of the Madero Revolution in Morelos.[133] Almost from the outset the personality of Emiliano Zapata dominated and shaped the uprising in Morelos and surrounding states and the movement began to take on distinctively agrarian goals.

The personality and leadership ability of Zapata was probably the single most important factor in the success of Mexico's agrarian revolution. The forces of Zapata were made up of bands of 50 to 300 men representing various villages and haciendas under the leadership of the most energetic guerrillero of each group.[134] Mexico with its mountainous terrain and varied climates is a land of regional cultures and villages, each with its own folkways. Each guerrilla band saw the revolution in terms of revenge against the local hacendado or *cacique* and members were primarily loyal to their local leader, frequently a relative or close friend. From 1913 to 1916 Zapata had an army of at least 20,000 men;[135] only a *super-caudillo* with a charismatic personality like that of Zapata (or Francisco "Pancho" Villa) could bring together a large peasant army for concerted action over a long period of time. Emiliano Zapata had an irresistible charm that commanded both loyalty and discipline; his subordinates referred to him simply as *el hombre*. Díaz Soto y Gama recalls that his gaze was penetrating, disconcerting to those he did not trust completely, and the men were overheard saying, "You can never fool the Chief . . . the Chief knows what you are carrying inside of you." [136]

Zapata tended to be retiring and did not take others into confidence easily; yet he was perfectly self-possessed and every word was meaningful. He was always quite affable with subordinates, especially with the backward village Indians, but inflexible and terrifying to those who crossed him or were disloyal. When Otilio Montaño was suspected of betrayal, Zapata had that veteran, who had fought with him seven years and had helped write the Plan of Ayala, summarily shot.

Emiliano Zapata conceived of his own role as a kind of *calpuleque*, a defender and distributor of the land for all the Indian peasants of Morelos. He never forgot the charge that the people of his village put upon him when they elected him leader of the *junta de defensa* of Anenecuilco. When Madero offered Zapata a hacienda in Veracruz as a reward for his efforts in the Revolution, he replied:

Senor Madero, I did not enter the Revolution to make myself a hacendado. If I have any merit, it is for the confidence which the farmers who have faith in

[133] McNeeley, *op. cit.*, pp. 158–160.   [134] Chevalier, "Zapata," p. 169.
[135] Womack, *op. cit.*, p. 432.   [136] Díaz Soto y Gama, *op. cit.*, p. 256.

us have put in me because they believe that we are going to fulfill what was promised to them, and if we abandon this people who have accomplished the Revolution, they will be justified in returning to take up their guns against those who have forgotten their promises. . . . The only thing we want, Senor Madero, is that the *"cientificos"* hacendados return to us the land which they have stolen from us.[137]

Nor would he allow others in his movement to enrich themselves. When some Zapatista chiefs took possession of former haciendas, he ordered them distributed to the villages.[138]

Unlike many peasant leaders of the Revolution he was not interested in becoming a professional politician nor did he have the ambition that his movement become the government of Mexico. As Zapata told Judge Duval West, American representative of Secretary of State Bryan in 1915, he had no desire but to restore the village lands in Morelos and return to his life as a simple farmer.[139] Zapata may have been provincial in his views and almost obsessed with his dislike for the city, but he established his agrarian movement as a grass roots organization, articulating the interests of the peasant masses, and this dedication to the peasants remained the ideology if not always the actual practice of Mexico's agrarian movement in the 1920's and 1930's.

What lifted Emiliano Zapata above most peasant leaders was his reflectiveness and profundity. He saw the peasants' problems as expressions of human suffering and as a Mexican tragedy. "I am pursued as a bandit," he said to Díaz Soto y Gama on one occasion, "for the crime of making it possible for those who have always known hunger, those who never have eaten sufficiently to find food a little more easily." He had a deep sense of destiny and carried with him an air of impending sacrificial tragedy. "I know well," he said on several occasions, "that Hidalgo was right in saying that the authors of these enterprises never live to see the fruit of them. . . . In order for the Revolution to triumph, it is necessary that I die first. . . . I will fall through the work of betrayal . . . but I will die as the slave of principles, not of men." [140]

It would be a mistake to view Zapata as simply a rude outlaw chieftain, though the Mexican press and many of Mexico's educated elite continually portrayed him as such. He was a master tactician of peasant guerrilla warfare, and for nine years the Zapatista forces exerted great pressure on the Mexican government with few arms and munitions, taken largely

---

[137] Quoted in Magaña, *op. cit.*, I, 133.   [138] Díaz Soto y Gama, *op. cit.*, p. 261.
[139] Quirk, *op. cit.*, p. 230.   [140] Díaz Soto y Gama, *op. cit.*, p. 262.

from federal troops.[141] Above all Zapata realized that the success of his guerrilla activities depended on the support of the villages in the area where his troops operated. He guaranteed the security of the villagers and in turn could count on them for food and information regarding the enemy.[142]

In his dealings with Madero in the triumphant but uncertain days of the Maderista Revolution in the summer of 1911, Zapata showed the qualities of a statesman. Madero, who had led a revolution for free elections, was determined that he would assume the presidency only as a freely elected candidate. In the six months before elections were held, however, Madero accepted as interim president De la Barra, the man appointed by Díaz before he resigned and left for Europe, and with De la Barra an interim government containing many Porfiristas.[143] Madero did not suspect the strong reactionary tendencies of the elite and their immediate efforts to regain power. He did not see clearly that the real issue of the Revolution was not free elections but land and the rights of the laborer. With their sense of superiority and their belief in the right to rule, the elite were not ready to engage in democratic discussion and compromise regarding this issue.

Madero allowed the interim government to appoint as governor of Morelos Juan C. Carreón, the manager of the Bank of Morelos, and after Carreón, Ambrosio Figueroa, an enemy of Zapata's, both of whom sympathized with the hacendados. Meanwhile the hacendados, organized as the Sons of Morelos, were urging the disbanding of the Zapata troops, adamantly refusing to make concessions regarding land reform, vilifying Zapata and his men in the newspapers, and ordering reprisals against former revolutionaries. The government not only acceded to the demands that Zapata's army be completely demobilized, but allowed federal troops to continue harrassing the Zapatista revolutionaries.[144]

In his first meeting with Madero on June 8, 1911, Zapata told Madero that Figueroa was not to be trusted, that nothing progressive could be expected from Carreón, and that the peasants of Morelos had fought only for land reform and expected it to be carried out as soon as possible.[145] As the summer progressed, the federal troops moved to reoccupy Morelos and though Madero did not approve of this neither did he realize that vigorous action was needed to stop it. Zapata was aware that De la Barra was actually aiding the hacendados in their plotting and tried to inform

[141] Chevalier, "Zapata," pp. 69–70.
[142] Palacios, *op. cit.*, pp. 241–243.
[143] Cumberland, *op. cit.*, pp. 149–170.
[144] *Ibid.*, pp. 173–175.
[145] Magaña, *op. cit.*, I, 131–134.

Madero, but Madero remained unconvinced. Nevertheless Zapata tried to work out a peaceful solution with Madero, and restrained his followers in spite of the hostilities and reprisals inflicted against them. In late August the designs of the hacendados became clear when the federal army, in what was apparently an attempt to capture Emiliano Zapata, moved against Zapatista troops demobilizing near Cuautla. Fighting began, but even during September and October Zapata informed Madero that though he intended to go on fighting the hacendados until the village land was restored he was willing to come to terms. But the government would grant amnesty only if Zapata would accept legal responsibility for property and personal damages.[146] Under these conditions Zapata lost all hope in Madero and a month later announced he was continuing the Revolution under his own banner, the Plan of Ayala.

In December Zapata showed his political wisdom in a letter to Gildardo Magaña in Mexico City:

Since I am no politician, I do not understand these half-ways triumphs, those triumphs in which the defeated are those who win, these triumphs in which, as in my case, it is offered—demanded of me—after a triumphant revolution, that I leave not only my State but my Country. . . . I am resolved to fight against all odds and all [enemies] with no more defense than the confidence, the affection, and the support of my people.[147]

And so he continued his movement for the next nine years.

In Emiliano Zapata were all the qualities of the Indian and the peasant at their best: dogged determination, ability to sustain suffering, loyalty to his people, a quiet reflective wisdom, a directness and lack of pretense, a love of the countryside. He understood his people and they could communicate with him. His leadership kept Mexico's agrarian movement a truly indigenous peasant movement.

The Ideology of the Zapata Agrarian Movement

The uprisings that formed the Maderista phase of the Revolution of 1910 were not the result of any overall, guiding ideology; each had its own vague definition of certain problems and some notion of solutions. Madero's victory opened up the possibility of a freer interchange of ideas, especially between peasant and worker groups and the young radical intellectuals, and a great debate began in Mexico regarding the nature of the agrarian problem and its possible solutions. The agrarian ideology that developed was essentially a popular expression and grew up piecemeal, the

---

[146] Cumberland, *op. cit.*, pp. 174–179, 182.   [147] Magaña, *op. cit.*, II, 96.

result of speeches by half-literate generals, pamphlets and newspapers of liberal intellectuals, and debates in the Revolutionary caucuses and conventions. To a great extent this new agrarian ideology was simply the Zapatista ideology.[148]

When Emiliano Zapata and the other peasant leaders of Morelos led their bands into the Madero Revolution, the ideology that motivated them was furnished by the long tradition of Mexican peasant agrarian protest —complaints against haciendas, the local *caciques*, the storekeepers, and the *gachupines*—and, more explicitly, Article 3 of the Plan of San Luis Potosí, which guaranteed that land illegally occupied would be restored to the proper owners. But the experiences of the summer and fall of 1911 convinced Zapata that the aspirations of the peasants of Mexico were not going to be realized under Madero and on November 28, 1911, he published his own Plan of Ayala which stated clearly the ideals for which the revolutionary armies were fighting.

Zapata considered the Plan of Ayala to be an extension of Madero's Plan of San Luis Potosí, just as he considered his movement to be carrying on what Madero had started but betrayed into the hands of the hacendados and other monopolistic interests. The first five articles of the Plan of Ayala declared that Madero was no longer recognized as head of the insurgents, acclaimed in his stead General Pascual Orozco, at that time leading a rebellion in the north of Mexico, and declared that the revolutionary junta of Morelos would not make any agreements of a political nature until the former Porfiristas and now the Maderistas were defeated.[149]

Article 6 provided that lands which had been illegally taken from the villages or from individuals were to be immediately returned to the possession of those who held titles. Explicit provision is made, however, for appeals "by the usurpers, if they think they have a right to the lands, before special courts to be established upon the triumph of the revolution." Article 7 looks to the needs of the villagers and individuals who "are no longer owners of the land they tread"; one third of the large estates were to be expropriated on the basis of previous payment (*"se expropriarán, previa indemnización de la tercera parte de esos monopolios"*) and distributed to the landless "in order that villages and citizens might obtain *ejidos, colonias* [and] *fundos legales*." [150] The clause providing for prior payment was perhaps impractical since there would not

---

[148] Tannenbaum, *PBR*, p. 176.   [149] Cited in Magaña, *op. cit.*, II, 83–85.
[150] *Ibid.*, pp. 85–86.

have been funds available to pay cash for the land in large amounts, making difficult rapid, large scale expropriations.[151]

Article 8, somewhat vindictive, stated that all who opposed the plan directly or indirectly would have *all* their goods nationalized and two-thirds of these would be sold to provide indemnification of war expenses, pensions for widows of victims of the war, and so on. Article 9 invoked the Reform laws of *"desamortización y nacionalización"* as the basis of expropriation mentioned in Article 8. Articles 10 to 15 provided for an interim government upon the triumph of the revolution.

A first draft of the Plan of Ayala was dictated by Emiliano Zapata and written up by Otilio Montaño, acting as Zapata's secretary. Later Zapata personally revised the draft of the final copy. In spite of its practical and technical deficiencies, the Plan of Ayala embodied the aspirations of the peasants and gave them a concrete program for which to fight. It is also one of the first public proposals for large-scale expropriation as well as for the return of land illegally held.

One of the specific characteristics of the peasant ideology as expressed in the Plan of Ayala and elsewhere is its vindictiveness and direct hostility toward the responsible agents: the hacendados, *caciques*, and *científicos*. The learned tradition may have thought of reform in terms of changes in law and in technically complete programs, but for the peasant the "law" was the local *cacique* or *jefe político*, and a change meant an elimination of these local authorities at whose hands the peasant had suffered directly.[152]

Indianismo and hostility toward the *gachupines*, the Spaniards who were perceived as the wealthy exploiters of the poor Indian, were also a part of the ideology of the movement. The hated administrators of the local sugar mills were referred to as *gachupines* and when the campaign began in Morelos the stores of the Spanish in Jojutla were an object of looting.[153]

As in countless other agrarian movements [154] the ideology preached by Zapata was quite provincial in its outlook and exalted the virtues of the country dweller and the ideals of country life. Judge Duval West received an interesting picture of Zapata's agrarian ideology from his interview in April, 1915.

[151] Silva-Herzog, *op. cit.*, p. 179.   [152] Tannenbaum, *PBR*, pp. 90, 121.

[153] Tannenbaum argues that it was the ideology of the Zapata movement which was primarily responsible for injecting the strong current of Indianism into Mexican national ideology (*PBR*, pp. 176–181); Magaña, *op. cit.*, I, 100.

[154] Alvin Johnson, "Agrarian Movements," *Encyclopedia of the Social Sciences,* 1930, I, 489–490.

Zapata told West that justice lay in seizing the property of the rich and giving it to the poor. He conceded, though, that he had little education and no experience beyond those matters pertaining to his life in Morelos. Zapata said that he found it impossible to live in the city, that his home was among his people, on their farms and ranches. In the state of happy anarchy he envisioned for his Mexico, he saw no need for a government or a standing army. All men, he said, should carry their arms as they tilled the fields. If the enemy should come, then the men must leave their occupations to defeat him. Life to Zapata was the soil, the air, the mountains of Morelos. And for these ideals—land and liberty—he led his revolutionary movement. But his interest was only with Morelos. Let the rest of Mexico secure its freedom and happiness in the same way.[155]

Zapata refused to cloud his message with personal interests or the abstract ideals of a foreign ideology which he did not think answered the needs of his people. When one of his young chiefs encouraged him to look into a book describing communism, Zapata did so carefully. He replied that it contained many good ideas, but refused to swerve from the Plan of Ayala, "since I am convinced that what is contained in that Plan, if it is carefully carried out, will bring about the happiness of the Mexican people; so I don't have to get myself into the problems you propose." [156]

In contrast to the distinctly anticlerical ideology of the learned tradition of protest, the peasant movement in general showed respect and sympathy toward the Church, the clergy, and religion. The personal religiosity of Zapata is attested to by accounts of friends and the portrait drawn by the popular Zapatista *corridos*. He gave guarantees to the priests of the area and would not allow any infringement of religious liberties. Local pastors continued to exercise their ministry in Morelos during the fighting and sometimes showed their open favor of Zapata's cause. The final draft of the Plan of Ayala was typed up by the local pastor, who gave his warm assent to the document.[157] In general the Mexican peasant accepted the agrarian program, but not the antireligious or even, to any great extent, the anticlerical ideology of the official Revolutionary movement. In the most formally Catholic areas of Mexico,[158]—the States of Jalisco, Michoacán, and Querétaro—opposition to the

---

[155] Quirk, *op. cit.*, p. 230.   [156] Díaz Soto y Gama, *op. cit.*, p. 271.

[157] Chevalier, "Zapata," p. 72; Díaz Soto y Gama, *op. cit.*, p. 260; Simmons, *op. cit.*, pp. 291, 306; Baltasar Dromondo, *Emiliano Zapata* (Mexico City: Editorial Guarania, 1961), p. 118.

[158] Allen Spitzer's distinction between folk and formal religion as extreme points on a continuum is helpful in understanding the different cultural expressions of Catholicism one finds in Mexico ("Notes on a Mérida Parish," *Anthropological Quarterly*, XXXI [Jan., 1958]), pp. 3–20.

antireligious ideology of the Revolution caused resistance to the practical programs of agrarian reform.[159]

The Zapatista Movement Puts Pressure on Mexico City

When the victorious Madero entered Mexico City in June, 1911, there was a growing consensus among Mexico's leaders that a serious situation had developed among the landless Indian peasants and that something had to be done. In early April Luis Cabrera, the noted young politician who had had direct contact with the oppressive conditions of the peons as a young school teacher, published an open letter addressed to Madero, asking him to recognize that the people of Mexico had risen up to follow him not just for political reforms, but as a reaction against the repression of the peasants and the absorption of small properties by the haciendas. Even in the Díaz government in its dying moments the Secretary of Interior Development recommended that the government break up the large estates by buying tracts of land and selling them in small lots. The mistake of breaking up the ejidos was admitted as well as the illegal possession of land.[160] Zapata, in his first interview with Madero on June 8, 1911, demanded restoration of the village lands.

Among the victorious Maderistas, ideas concerning land reform had not advanced much beyond the vague conviction that somehow the rural masses ought to have access to arable land. When he was nominated Madero offered no agrarian program other than recommendations for the founding of agricultural and mortgage banks for irrigation and reclamation projects to encourage small farmers. Most of the revolutionary leaders surrounding Madero seemed to agree that there was no necessity for immediate action in distributing land and that with no more than a just, democratic administration the situation of rural poverty would be rectified.

Moreover, there was wide divergence of opinion regarding the steps to be taken. Madero himself believed that the development of small holdings would be the best means of reducing the economic and social degradation of the rural areas. He did not realize that the Indian had not developed a concept of private land ownership, and neither he nor his advisors had seriously considered the role of the ejido in an agrarian program. Article 3 in the Plan of San Luis Potosí, which so attracted Zapata, primarily referred to the restoration of the ranchos, not the ejidos. Nor had Madero

[159] Frank Brandenburg, *The Making of Modern Mexico* (Englewood Cliffs, N.J.: Prentice-Hall, 1964), pp. 169–177; Whetten, *op. cit.*, pp. 508–511.
[160] Silva-Herzog, *op. cit.*, pp. 161–164.

seriously considered the problem of aiding millions of landless peons, and none of the revolutionary leaders had proposed the possibility of expropriation or general redistribution of the haciendas. Madero's naïveté regarding the determination of the hacendados to hold on to what they possessed is reflected in his exhortation to the planters of Morelos to initiate land reform voluntarily.[161]

But the rising sentiment in favor of land reform began to bring forth various proposals. Pastor Rouaix, a young engineer who had worked in surveying the haciendas and knew at first hand the conditions of the peons, criticized strongly the proposal of the Díaz regime to sell eight hectares of land to peasants without considering whether there was sufficient water. Rouaix felt that proper planning of resources must precede any distribution of land. Like many professionals he was more cautious than the peasant armies themselves would be.[162]

In August of 1911 Andrés Molina Enríquez, thoroughly disgusted with Madero's compromises with the policies of the old Díaz regime, issued his own Plan of Texcoco and called for a new revolution. He proposed expropriation of large estates, at that time a much more radical step than most would contemplate, and general distribution of land to the peons. But most in the learned tradition were much more conservative than Molina Enríquez, and he attracted almost no adherents.[163]

By the fall of 1911 the discussion of the agrarian question was one of the most popular topics of the day. Wistano Luis Orozco wrote against Molina Enríquez, arguing that the state had no right to intervene directly in expropriation, but could only set up means for it to be done by private agencies. Molina Enríquez replied that an evolutionary kind of land reform would lead to compromises with the landed elite, and a thorough land reform demanded rapid, decisive action in which the power of the hacendados was challenged. Furthermore, society did not exist for the land, but land for society.[164]

Madero took the first slow steps in September by persuading the interim president, De la Barra, to appoint a commission to study agrarian needs. But most of the members of the commission shared many of the old Porfirista views and when their report was made in February, 1912, they had failed to conclude that expropriation was necessary, that the

[161] Cumberland, *op. cit.*, pp. 208–212.

[162] Silva-Herzog, *op. cit.*, pp. 165–168; Silvano Barba Gonzalez, *La lucha por la tierra* (Mexico City: Editorial del Magisterio, 1963), pp. 149–151.

[163] Barba Gonzalez, *op. cit.*, pp. 87–92; Cumberland, *op. cit.*, pp. 210–211; Silva-Herzog, *op. cit.*, p. 168.   [164] Silva-Herzog, *op. cit.*, pp. 168–173.

ejido should be restored as a viable institution, or that the government should bear any financial burdens in distributing land to the peons.[165]

Meanwhile, in October of 1911, the Zapatista guerrillas attacked Milpa Alta, a mountain village overlooking Mexico City, throwing the city and the government into panic and causing an immediate cabinet crisis.[166] In December, Zapata sent a copy of the Plan of Ayala to Gildardo Magaña in Mexico City for publication. The major newspapers which were publicizing Zapata as the "Attila of the South" and a threat to the safety of Mexico City would not publish the Plan of Ayala, but Enrique Bonilla, publisher of *El Diario del Hogar*, a leftist newspaper, got Madero's approval to publish it. "Sure, publish it," said Madero, "so that all can see what kind of a crazy man Zapata is." [167] There was apparently wide interest in the Plan from all parts of Mexico, and the issue ran several extra editions. Most important, the Zapatistas were steadily growing in military strength and beginning to control large parts of the state of Morelos and the mountains around Mexico City. Madero took office on November 6, 1911, and throughout 1912 one of the principal preoccupations of Madero's government and the Mexican congress was how either to control or to appease the Zapata rebellion. It was at this point that the learned tradition began to listen to what the peasant tradition had to say. Zapata, by presenting a clear goal which expressed the aspirations of millions of peasants and backing it up with force of arms, began to exert a powerful influence on the course of the Revolution.[168]

In 1912 newspaper articles, pamphlets, and books were pouring forth with solutions for quelling the Zapatista rebellion and proposals for agrarian reform, and much more radical legislative action was being discussed by the Mexican Congress. Antonio Díaz Soto y Gama and Juan Sarabia, representing the left wing of the liberal group, made a proposal for expropriation without previous indemnification. In December, 1912, Luis Cabrera—supported by Roque González Garza, José Macías, and fifty-nine others—introduced a bill for the restoration of the ejidos on a communal basis. Luis Cabrera's views were greatly influenced by Molina Enríquez's scholarly book, *Los grandes problemas de México*, and show a real advance in agrarian thinking. The restoration of the ejidos was to be made possible by the restitution of land illegally taken, and if villages did not have titles they would be endowed through expropriation without

[165] Cumberland, *op. cit.*, pp. 211–214; Silva-Herzog, *op. cit.*, pp. 185–192.
[166] Cumberland, *op. cit.*, p. 182.   [167] Magaña, *op. cit.*, II, 95–97.
[168] Silva-Herzog, *op. cit.*, p. 193.

previous indemnification. The government would retain legal title and allow the villagers to work the land free of charge.[169]

That Zapata's military activities were putting pressure on Mexico's politicians to introduce rapid expropriation is indicated by sections of Cabrera's speech before the legislature on December 3, 1912:

When we view Zapatismo as a phenomenon of poverty of our rural classes, then it will occur to us to look for remedies for the necessities of those classes. . . . Now we will no longer be able to continue the system of employing the political force of the Government to drive those classes to work the whole year on the haciendas at very low wages. . . . People will either take up their rifles and go out to fill the columns of the Zapatistas or they will find other licit means of utilizing their energies, making use of the pastures, woods, and lands of their ejidos.[170]

Madero and Manuel Bonilla, his minister in charge of agricultural development, expressed doubts about the practicality of the measures and the ability to finance them, but consideration of the bill continued until the overthrow of the Madero government by Huerta in February, 1913.

Zapata's Allies among the Young Radical Intellectuals

In February of 1913 came the inevitable reaction of the military, the hacendados, and other allies of the old order. The army under General Huerta forced Madero to resign; Madero was shortly after "accidentally" shot, and Huerta assumed the presidency. The brutal dictatorship of Huerta shocked the Mexican nation, and when Venustiano Carranza published his Plan of Guadalupe on March 26, 1913, announcing a military campaign to re-establish constitutional government, many of the young intellectuals joined either Carranza's Constitutionalist forces in the North of Mexico or Zapata in the South.

Zapata already had a group of very helpful allies in Mexico City among the young radicals affiliated with the Liberal party movement. In the spring of 1911, during the Madero phase of the Revolution, various groups who recognized the general leadership of Camilo Arriaga, one of the founders of the Liberal party in 1900, planned a concerted uprising which became known as the Conspiracy of Tacubaya. A "Political-Social Plan" was published which, in addition to announcing union with Madero, repeated many of the essential points of the Liberal Manifesto of

[169] *Ibid.,* pp. 198–208; Cumberland, *op. cit.,* pp. 217–218.

[170] Eduardo Luquín (ed.), *El pensamiento de Luis Cabrera* (Mexico City: Talleres Gráficos de la Nación, 1960), p. 201.

1906: the restoration of suppressed municipalities, protection of the Indians, the restitution of illegally held land, and the expropriation of the large estates.[171] Among the supporters of the Plan were Dolores Jiménez y Muro, Francisco J. Múgica, later the radical president of the Constitutional convention, and his brother Carlos, and Rodolfo and Gildardo Magaña. But the plot was discovered and Rodolfo Magaña, a rebel fleeing to Morelos, turned up in Zapata's camp. There he showed Zapata the "Political-Social Plan" and when Zapata saw the provisions for land reform he replied enthusiastically that they were both fighting for the same thing. Zapata asked Rodolfo Magaña to write to the rest of the group in Mexico City in his name and to invite them to join the Zapatista ranks.[172]

The Magaña brothers, Carlos Múgica, and Dolores Jiménez y Muro met with Zapata in Cuernavaca in June and agreed to act as his agents in Mexico City and to support him through the press. Rodolfo and Gildardo Magaña were most active in behalf of the Zapatistas and were Zapata's special envoys to Pascual Orozco, intending to establish relations with the rebellion in Chihuahua in July, 1912. Returning to the south with ammunition for Zapata, Gildardo Magaña was imprisoned in Mexico City. The imprisonment threw together many of the young radicals, various Zapatistas, Andrés Molina Enríquez, and Francisco "Pancho" Villa. Gildardo Magaña undertook to teach Villa the rudiments of reading and writing. Through Magaña, Villa learned of the Plan of Ayala and began to have a strong sympathy for Emiliano Zapata and his ideal of restoring the ejidos.[173]

In May of 1913 Huerta closed down Mexico City's recently founded coordinating center for the radical labor movement, the Casa del Obrero Mundial, and many of its leaders escaped south to the Zapatistas. Among them were Antonio Díaz Soto y Gama, who became the leading ideologue of the Zapatistas; Octavio Jahn, a French syndicalist; Rafael Pérez Taylor and Luis Méndez, both of vaguely Marxist background.[174] Paulino Martínez, radical politician and publisher of an underground newspaper during the Porfiriato, also joined Zapata. Ignacio Díaz Soto y Gama, brother of Antonio and professor at the National School of Agriculture,

[171] Magaña, *op. cit.,* I, 105, 106–108.

[172] Not only did the Magaña brothers, educated in the American Friends' School in Philadelphia, join the movement, but they brought to Zapata 10,000 pesos given to them by their father to support the Conspiracy of Tacubaya (cf. Womack, *op. cit.,* p. 134; Magaña, *op. cit.,* I, 109–110).   [173] Magaña, *op. cit.,* I, 138–139; II, 145–166.

[174] Clark, *op. cit.,* pp. 22–26; Womack, *op. cit.,* pp. 319–320.

led a large number of his students into the Zapatista camp. Between 1913 and 1915 many university students and others of radical revolutionary interest continued to join the agrarian movement of the South.[175]

When these newcomers from Mexico's urban, educated sector entered the Zapata movement, the separate worlds of the peasant and the learned traditions came together and an interesting division of labor developed. The young intellectuals deeply respected Zapata's charismatic leadership of the movement and they learned from him the kind of agrarian reform that Mexico's peasants wanted. They became Zapata's spokesmen: acting as his secretaries and aides, composing his occasional manifestoes, and carrying out his diplomatic missions. With their various talents they were able to translate Zapata's goals into proposals which were technically sound and congruent with the requirements of Mexico's legal traditions, agricultural science, and administrative organization. They perceived the agrarian problem not just in the provincial terms of Morelos, but from a national perspective, and through their personal contacts and their ability to use the various national communications media, they linked up the Zapatista movement with national politics. The genius of a true peasant leader had been needed to articulate the peasant interests and to mobilize an organization with enough power to be effective. But as the movement progressed to the stage of legislation, practical programs of implementation, and development of a new national ideology, the learned sector played an increasingly important role.

The Peasant Armies Come to Power in Mexico

This combination of peasant generals and liberal young intellectuals made the Constitutionalist phase of the Revolution much more radical than the Maderista phase. Zapata was now the chief of the Revolutionary Army of the South, and by 1914 he and chieftains allied with him controlled all the states south of Mexico City to the Isthmus of Tehuantepec.[176] Carranza was himself a landowner and imbued with the ideals of nineteenth-century individualist liberalism, but the majority of the *caudillos* who signed the Plan of Guadalupe were, in the words of Silva-Herzog, "men of the country or inhabitants of small villages who knew well the deficiencies of management in the great haciendas and the inhuman life of the rural proletariat." [177] The leading Constitutionalist generals were Alvaro Obregón, who was once a mechanic on a hacienda and a chickpea

[175] Díaz Soto y Gama, *op. cit.*, pp. 212–224; cf. Palacios, *op. cit.*, pp. 188–190.
[176] Magaña, *op. cit.*, IV, 152–175.   [177] *Op. cit.*, p. 219.

farmer on rented land,[178] and Francisco "Pancho" Villa, who was an escapee from a hacienda in Durango.

In Morelos the Huertista General Juvencio Robles realized that every peasant was a potential enemy of the federal army and attempted to terrorize the people into deserting the Zapatista forces. But when Robles began to burn every Morelos village suspected of being "a nest of Zapatistas" the people only turned to Zapata for help in defending their lives and possessions. And when Robles tried to recruit every able-bodied man for the federal army, the men flocked to the Zapatista ranks rather than be sent off to the north to die fighting Pancho Villa and Obregón.[179]

With the bravado of Villa and the strategy of Obregón the Constitutionalist armies moved down from the north toward Mexico City, capturing one important railroad junction after another. As the armies of Villa, Obregón, and the Zapatistas gained control of Mexico they swept away state governors, local chieftains, or local officials who were not of frankly revolutionary views. Generals and the young radicals took these local offices, and laws were immediately passed abolishing the *tienda de raya*, providing for land reform, minimum wages, and other reforms.[180] When the Constitutionalist forces took Durango, Pastor Rouaix was elected governor of Durango by plebiscite and one of his early acts was passage of the first official agrarian law in Mexico to expropriate and distribute land to the former peons.[181]

By July of 1914 victory over Huerta was in sight and plans were made at a meeting at Torreón to hold a Revolutionary Convention in Aguascalientes which would be a "preconstitutional" conference to discuss reforms. The delegates were to represent the fighting men of the Revolutionary armies, mostly peons led by peasant and young radical generals. At the insistence of Antonio Villareal, the former Magonista, and the followers of Villa, it was agreed that the Convention at Aguascalientes would take up agrarian reform as its principal topic. Article 8 of the Pact of Torreón "promised land division for the peasants and social legislation for the urban proletariat." [182]

Huerta submitted his resignation in July, 1914, and on August 15 Obregón occupied Mexico City for the Constitutionalists. But within the

[178] E. J. Dillon, *President Obregón, a World Reformer* (Boston: Small, Maynard, 1923), pp. 40–48.   [179] Womack, *op. cit.*, pp. 280–286; Magaña, *op. cit.*, III, 232–236.
[180] Silva-Herzog describes the agrarian reform activities of generals Lucio Blanco, Francisco J. Múgica, Eulalio Gutiérrez and others (*op. cit.*, pp. 219–229); Magaña, *op. cit.*, III, 276–289.   [181] Barba Gonzalez, *op. cit.*, pp. 150–151.
[182] Quirk, *op. cit.*, p. 42.

revolutionary armies there was a growing conflict between the more conservative Carranza, who looked on the revolution primarily as a means of re-establishing civilian, constitutional government, and those who wanted profound social reform—the peasant generals and the new generation of young radicals. The clash between Villa and Carranza was based on intense personal dislike, but between Zapata and Carranza it was a matter of principle. Although numerous attempts were made to have Carrancistas and Zapatistas come to an agreement, Zapata looked on Carranza as of the hacendado class and did not trust him. Moreover, Zapata had long determined that he would not cooperate with or make concessions to any government of Mexico unless the provisions of the Plan of Ayala were accepted.[183] But Carranza had never been favorable to legislated social reforms or the breaking up of the large estates, and he refused to make the concrete commitments which the Plan of Ayala involved.[184]

In late August of 1914 the Zapatistas issued "The Declaration of Objectives of Milpa Alta," making clear that they would not accede to the half-way measures of the Constitutionalists. The statement was written by Antonio Díaz Soto y Gama, one of the founders of the Socialist party of Mexico in 1911 and a disciple of Kropotkin's "creed of the good peasant." It reflected the directness of Zapata mingled with the socialist-syndicalist philosophy of the Casa del Obrero Mundial. The declaration of Milpa Alta denied that the Carrancistas were true revolutionaries or had any real concern for the people. The political reforms they proposed were, in reality, against the progress of the rural classes. The men of the South would not yield to the vague promises of the Constitutionalist leaders, but were determined to crush feudalism in Mexico once and for all. With this statement of policy the Zapatistas continued fighting against Carranza for the next five years.[185]

When the promised Convention convened, first briefly in Mexico City and then in Aguascalientes, it was quite apparent that the worker-peasant classes had come into power and intended to legislate according to their interests. Most of the delegates wore military uniforms or the simple dress of the peasant. "Eulalio Gutiérrez, soon to be president of the assembly, . . . reminded one observer of a peddler who traveled from door to door

---

[183] Dromondo, *op. cit.*, p. 192. Much of the Zapatista dealings with Carranza were being directed by Manuel Palafox, then Zapata's secretary, a man whose curious personality reinforced the provincialism and defensive attitude of the Zapatista forces at this time (cf. Womack, *op. cit.*, pp. 338–347). [184] Quirk, *op. cit.*, pp. 64–65.

[185] Womack, *op. cit.*, pp. 319–320, 65–66.

selling bedding on installments. He wore a Panama hat and the rude dress of a countryman, and he was thickly mustachioed 'like a Turk.' " Luis Cabrera was the temporary head of the meeting and one of the few who had any idea of parliamentary procedure. But when he tried to run the meeting and impose the Carranza list of "acceptable" delegates, the military members ignored Cabrera's list, took over the Convention themselves, and elected Eulalio Gutiérrez, a former foreman in a copper mine.[186]

The Convention of Aguascalientes Takes the Zapatista Ideology as Its Own

General Felipe Angeles, whom Zapata respected, persuaded him that it was in his interest to send delegates to the Convention. Twenty-six Zapatistas with Paulino Martínez as president and Antonio Díaz Soto y Gama as vice-president went first to Villa's headquarters one hundred miles north of Aguascalientes to establish strategies of cooperation with the "Centaur of the North." Then the delegates of the Army of the South —most of whom had never been out of Morelos before—ventured warily and timidly into the meeting with their wide sombreros, skintight britches, and peasant blouses.[187]

The following day the Zapatistas were invited to speak, and Paulino Martínez recounted for the assembly, most of them men of the North not entirely familiar with Zapatista goals, the history of the Revolution in the South (the real Revolution he thought) and he was scornful of the nineteenth-century Liberal faith in effective suffrage and no re-election as means for curing Mexico's ills. Land and Liberty! With these the Mexican people would have real economic freedom. These ideals could be achieved only by Villa and Zapata, "Indians, both of them," and only under the banner of the Plan of Ayala. The Army of the South was not interested in the presidential chair, only in land for all. He concluded by inviting the delegates to accept the Plan of Ayala as the standard of the Convention. Díaz Soto y Gama followed with an emotional speech stating that Mexico's Independence had benefited only the creoles; now had come a Revolution to free the native race.[188]

González Garza came as Villa's personal representative and said that, to a man, the Villistas were in complete agreement with Zapata and the Plan of Ayala. But Obregón, who personally took a more moderate position, challenged whether all of the Army of the North were in complete

---

[186] *Ibid.*, pp. 88–90.   [187] *Ibid.*, p. 107.   [188] *Ibid.*, pp. 108, 109–111.

agreement with Zapata. González Garza then asked all who did not support the Plan of Ayala to stand. Not a man from the North moved.[189] The Convention accepted the Plan and Eulalio Gutiérrez was elected provisional president of the Republic of Mexico.

The peasant uprising which started in Anenecuilco three years earlier now represented the aroused peasants of all Mexico, and the ideology which had grown out of the acute conflict in the villages of Morelos provided an agrarian ideology which crystallized and defined the aspirations of all Mexican peasants.

Mobilization, Part III: The Zapatistas Keep Alive the Hope for Social Revolution in Mexico

The Forces of the Convention Lose Control of Mexico

The Carrancistas angrily withdrew from the Convention, setting up their government in the eastern port of Vera Cruz, and in November, 1914, Obregón, who had a personal dislike for Villa, joined Carranza in declaring war on the forces of the Convention. Most of the generals, however, remained loyal to Villa and together the Villistas and Zapatistas occupied the Capital and most of the rest of Mexico. The Convention continued as the rather chaotic governing body of Mexico and developed out of the principles of the Plan of Ayala a detailed body of agrarian and labor reform.

Carranza now realized that he could not hope to rally support among the workers and the peasants of central and southern Mexico unless he offered programs that matched those of Zapata and the Convention. Therefore, in spite of his antipathy toward legislated labor reforms and land reform through expropriation, he published a series of detailed decrees dealing with labor and agrarian reforms. The decree on land reform was largely the work of Luis Cabrera, who, with Pastor Rouaix, formed an agrarian advisory group for Carranza. It provided for the establishment of ejidos by restitution of land illegally held or, if no titles could be shown, by expropriation of land contiguous with villages. Provision was also made for national, state, and local Agrarian Committees to initiate and supervise the process of land distribution. Carranza's agrarian decree of January 6, 1915, was important because it reversed the land tenure policies of the 1857 Reform Laws which had emphasized individual ownership, and it became the legal precedent for much subsequent

[189] *Ibid.*, pp. 112–113.

agrarian reform legislation. But it had four serious defects: it left the hacienda system largely intact because only villages with *categoría política* (political status), not the hacienda communities of *peones acasillados*, could petition for land; the burden of initiative was placed on the local villages, leaving them open to pressure; the injured parties could stop the procedure of restoration or expropriation of land by court injunction; military commanders had the right to distribute land in their areas, and this led to great abuses.[190] Subsequent events showed that Carranza had no real intention of large-scale land reform once he was securely in power. Between 1915 and 1920 only 190 villages received definitive possession of land and only 180,000 hectares were distributed. It was the power of Zapata and Villa in the winter of 1914 that made Carranza move as he did and Zapata was the real factor behind these reform measures.[191]

But the decrees gave the Constitutionalist generals something to hold out to their men and as the tide turned against Zapata's weary guerrillas, Otilio Montaño and others were tempted to think it was better to make peace with Carranza since he did offer some kind of agrarian program.[192] To attract urban workers into the Constitutionalist army Carranza authorized Obregón to enter into an agreement with the labor unions of Mexico City whereby favorable labor legislation was guaranteed and the unions were "permitted to proceed behind the lines to agitate and organize the workers in the districts that were reclaimed from the enemy." Although Villa and Zapata had many adherents among those associated with the Casa del Obrero Mundial, Dr. Atl (Gerado Murillo), the revolutionary painter, persuaded the workers that greater certainty of labor and agrarian reforms lay with Carranza, and the Casa provided six "red battalions" of workers.[193]

From the time of the reform decrees the tide bagan to turn in Carranza's favor. Obregón and his regrouped armies defeated Villa in a series of brilliant maneuvers, and the Zapatistas, who never cared to take the offensive in long-term campaigns outside Morelos, were left isolated in their southern mountains. In August, 1915, the Convention was forced by the advance of the Constitutionalist armies to retire from Mexico City to Toluca, and in October to retreat to Cuernavaca in Zapatista territory.[194] By the spring of 1916 the Villistas and Zapatistas had been reduced to guerrilla bands surrounded in the mountains of Chihuahua and Morelos.

[190] Eyler Simpson, *op. cit.*, pp. 56–62.
[191] *Ibid.*, p. 79; Silva-Herzog, *op. cit.*, p. 238.   [192] Womack, *op. cit.*, pp. 460–461.
[193] Tannenbaum, *MAR*, pp. 169–170; Alba, *op. cit.*, p. 175; Quirk, *op. cit.*, pp. 186–187.   [194] Quirk, *op. cit.*, pp. 270–293.

Throughout 1915 the Convention, dominated by Antonio Díaz Soto y Gama and other Zapatistas, formulated the most radical legislation yet considered by a national Mexican governing body,[195] and in October, 1915, issued its agrarian law. The system of great haciendas was to be destroyed and a new system of agriculture established on the basis of the small cultivator in the ejido and in private holdings. Land and water illegally taken from the villages were to be restored, and land was to be expropriated to satisfy all who needed it. A significant advance was the decision to evaluate the land to be expropriated on the basis of the last fiscal declaration of the land owner, an ironic measure since the declarations always greatly undervalued the land. Agriculture was to be developed by establishing credit facilities for the small farmer, irrigation projects, agricultural schools, agricultural experimental stations, and systems of instruction in better farming methods.[196]

Throughout 1914 and 1915 Professor Ignacio Díaz Soto y Gama and his students from the National School of Agriculture worked with Manuel Palafox, Zapata's Minister of Agriculture, and the Convention's Agrarian Commission supervising the distribution of haciendas and marking out the boundaries of village ejidos in the states of Morelos, Guerrero, and México.[197] Felipe Santibáñez, an experienced agronomer, directed the establishment of a credit system with credit unions (Asociaciones de Crédito) made up of farmers in each village, district credit unions (Sociedades de Asociaciones de Crédito) servicing the villages and providing crop insurance, and a rural loan bank in Morelos (Caja Rural de Préstamos del Estado de Morelos) which supplied credit for seeds and working animals.[198] With the retreat of the Zapatista armies and the disbanding of the Convention at Jojutla, Morelos, on May 16, 1916, the Morelos agrarian program collapsed, but the young agronomers and university students such as Marte R. Gómez and Felipe Carrillo Puerto continued their sympathy for Zapatista ideals and were leading agrarians in the 1920's and 1930's.[199]

By the spring of 1916 Carranza, not the peasant armies, ruled Mexico, but the peasants' experience in destroying the old hacendado power and

---

[195] *Ibid.,* p. 213.

[196] Silva-Herzog, *op. cit.,* pp. 240–241; Díaz Soto y Gama, *op. cit.,* pp. 208–212.

[197] Díaz Soto y Gama, *op. cit.,* pp. 212–224.

[198] Carleton Beals, *Mexico* (New York: B. W. Huebsch, 1923), pp. 110–111.

[199] Marte Gómez was president of the Farm Loan Bank in the mid-1920's and a leader in drafting the Agrarian Code of 1934 (Eyler Simpson, *op. cit.,* p. 456n). Carrillo Puerto was the socialist-agrarian governor of Yucatán in 1922–1923 (Gruening, *op. cit.,* p. 163).

ruling villages and states as they pleased was a victory never taken from them. As Oscar Lewis says of the Indian peasants of Tepoztlán, "The participation of the villagers in the ranks of the Zapatista forces, the revolutionary slogans of 'land and liberty' and 'down with the *caciques*' had left its imprint on the psychology of the people and acted as a distinct leveling influence." The Indian had a new sense of identity; the myths of the inherent superiority of the European, the sophisticated urbanite, and the hidalgo-hacendado were no longer believed; and *Mexicanismo, Indianismo,* and *agrarismo* were now introduced as value themes of Mexican culture.[200]

The Zapatistas Hold Out for a More Sympathetic Regime

Once Carranza was securely in power, he issued a resolution on June 19, 1916, which greatly increased the number of formalities the villages had to go through to get their land and simultaneously reduced the authority of the State Agrarian Commissions. And on September 19, 1916, the power originally given to local authorities to make provisional grants of land to villages was taken away so that only the National Agrarian Commission could sanction the distribution of ejidos. This, together with the confusion of communication at the time, stopped practically all land reform. (Later, in 1919, an official circular even required all villages to *pay* the nation for any lands they might receive by expropriation, a complete reversal of the idea of land reform.) [201]

On October 1, 1916, Zapata published *Exposición al pueblo mexicano y al cuerpo diplomático*, a document which attacked Carranza for having restored to the hacendados the land previously distributed to the peasants, for closing the Casa del Obrero Mundial, and for suspending the guarantees of workers in Mexico City.[202] In the hands of a reactionary regime, such as that of Carranza proved to be, the agrarian decree of 1915 and even Article 27 of the Constitution of 1917 meant nothing. The Zapatistas knew this, and they knew that there was rising sentiment against the Carranza government. The strategy of the Zapatistas from 1917 to 1920, inspired mainly by Gildardo Magaña who was playing an increasingly

---

[200] Lewis, *Life in a Mexican Village*, p. 51. Tannenbaum echoes many others when he says that "the chief by-product of the Revolution is . . . a discovery by the Mexican people of their own dignity. . . . The spiritual change is best seen in the new attitude toward the Indian . . . the sense of evaluation . . . appreciation of the Indian as a human being. . . . Coincident with this change . . . has been the discovery of the significance of the country as against the city" (*PBR*, pp. 181–182).

[201] Eyler Simpson, *op. cit.*, p. 78.

[202] Dromondo, *op. cit.*, p. 229; Parkes, *op. cit.*, p. 363.

important role in the movement, was to maintain a network of communication among potential revolutionaries and to foment guerrilla uprisings in other parts of the country wherever possible.[203]

In the autumn of 1916 Carranza called for the election of delegates for a convention to make certain changes in the Constitution of 1857 which seemed to be demanded by the recent Revolution. But he was planning only a few changes in the organization of the government and his original draft contained almost nothing of the radical social and economic doctrine which the delegates eventually incorporated.[204] The Villistas and Zapatistas were excluded, and many of the delegates were the professional lawyers and politicians of Mexico City who represented an older generation and the more moderate middle class. Nevertheless, the effective majority were the young Revolutionary generals and colonels who sympathized with Zapata's ideals even though they did not choose to follow him politically. Carranza tried to control the Constitutional Convention as he had tried to control the Convention of Aguascalientes. But the young General Francisco Múgica, backed by the powerful Obregón, led a parliamentary revolt of young radicals, and it was the spirit and political maneuvering of Francisco Múgica which dominated the convention and led it to adopt Articles 27 and 123.[205]

The delegates were generally dissatisfied with Carranza's first draft of Article 27 because it did not make clear the primary land-tenure rights of the nation nor did it provide a clear basis for expropriation without previous indemnification.[206] Article 27 of the Constitution of 1917 evolved in two weeks of intensive special sessions in which all delegates with agrarian interests met and aired their opinions. Although the Zapatistas had little or no direct influence on the formulation of Article 27, most of the aspirations of Zapata were vindicated in it.[207]

Article 27 of the Mexican Constitution has three general purposes: to

---

[203] Womack, *op. cit.*, pp. 464–465.   [204] Eyler Simpson, *op. cit.*, p. 62.

[205] Tannenbaum, *PBR*, pp. 164–167.   [206] Silva-Herzog, *op. cit.*, p. 249.

[207] The final draft of Article 27 was prepared by a special committee made up of José Macías, jurist of more moderate leanings, José Lugo, former Revolutionary general, Rafael de los Rios, young member of Carranza's Ministry of Agriculture, Andrés Molina Enríquez, the well known ethno-historian and expert in Mexican land tenure, and Pastor Rouaix, at the time Carranza's Minister of Interior Development. Andrés Molina Enríquez and Pastor Rouaix were probably the two individuals most directly influential in the final wording of this important piece of agrarian legislation (Rouaix, "Genesis de los articulos 27 y 123 de la constitución política de 1917," *Biblioteca del Instituto Nacional Estudios Históricos de la Revolución Mexicana*, XVI [1959]). For a quite detailed discussion of the provisions and implications of Article 27, see Eyler Simpson, *op. cit.*, pp. 62–74.

define and limit the nature of property, to define the persons and legal entities having the right to hold property, and to lay down the broad principles for the reformation of land tenure in Mexico. The ownership of lands and waters is vested originally in the nation, which has the right to transmit title to private persons and to place limitations on the distribution and right of property. The payment for expropriated property may be "after the act," according to the interpretation later followed by the government, and is to be based on evaluations made by the owner for fiscal purposes. The nation's ownership of waters and minerals is inalienable and only the right of exploitation may be conceded to private parties. Property held in common by settlements (*rancherías*), villages (*pueblos*), tribes and other bodies of population have the legal capacity to enjoy in common waters, woods, or lands belonging to them. Article 27 establishes the principle that the system of large estates is to be destroyed by placing limitations on the extent of private holdings; that the ejidos are to be restored or created by outright grant; and that lands or waters illegally taken or held in prejudice of the public interest are to be recovered.[208]

Zapata's answer to Carranza's Constitution of 1917 was to strengthen his ties with the villages of Morelos and to set in motion a program of education and municipal organization in the towns he controlled. Zapata insisted in a series of circulars that schools be established in all the communities under his control regardless of the obstacles caused by the fighting since, as he stated, "one of the ideals for which we are in this struggle is the development of public schools." [209]

In the winter of 1917 and in 1918, due to a temporary letup in General Pablo González's military campaign in Morelos, the feeling prevailed in the Zapatista camp that the Carranza regime was weakening. On January 20, 1917, a manifesto was issued encouraging the people of Mexico to desert Carranza who, it claimed, was an aristocrat who had tricked the people into supporting him with false promises.[210]

In August, 1917, the Zapatistas undertook to unite the growing Mexican opposition to Carranza. A further manifesto was issued declaring that Carranza had betrayed the Revolution, and that the authentic Revolutionaries were those who still fought under the banner of Ayala. Gildardo Magaña, who had an aptitude for conciliatory diplomacy and had wide

[208] Article 27 does not establish the socialization of property as a norm, but years later General Múgica told Frank Tannenbaum that "the soldiers wanted . . . to socialize property [but] they found all of the learned men in the Convention opposed to them. Article 27 was a compromise" (Tannenbaum, *PBR*, pp. 166–167).

[209] Womack, *op. cit.*, pp. 440–445; Palacios, *op. cit.*, p. 249.

[210] Womack, *op. cit.*, pp. 445–455; Dromondo, *op. cit.*, pp. 233–234.

personal contacts throughout the country, worked to persuade Pancho Villa, Vasquez Gómez, and other Revolutionary spirits inside and out of the Carranza government to sign the manifesto in a show of solidarity.[211] Manifestoes "To the people" and "To the Revolutionaries" appeared again in December, 1917, but no major revolt against Carranza could be provoked.

In 1918 deep divisions were appearing among the Constitutionalists, especially between Carranza and the Sonorans—Obregón, Calles, and Hill. Throughout 1918 Magaña systematically studied and cultivated relations with Obregón, Hill, and others then in exile.[212] On March 15, 1918, a manifesto was directed to the increasingly discontented workers inviting them to join the campesino opposition to Carranza. In August of 1918 Zapata, through Magaña, designated Doña Dolores Jiménez y Muro as a representative to ask Obregón to consider the unification of the revolutionary elements to bring about an overthrow of the Carranza government.[213]

In the winter of 1918 and 1919 the villages supporting Zapata's guerrilla bands were decimated by the Spanish influenza. At the same time General González stepped up the offensive, devastating what was left of the countryside, taking possession of nearly all of the towns of Morelos, and forcing the few remaining Zapatista troops into inactivity in their mountain hiding places. Defection of some of Zapata's foremost generals began: Manuel Palafox, once Zapata's secretary and his Minister of Agriculture in Morelos, started his own separatist movement; Otilio Montaño was discovered plotting against Zapata and was shot.[214] Only the hope that the forthcoming elections would turn out the Carranza government kept the Zapatista organization alive.

While the Zapatista military operations were failing, its manifestoes to the discontented factions continued to make the movement's presence felt. On March 17, 1919, Emiliano Zapata published a brilliant open letter in which he showed that in spite of all the blood that had been shed for greater liberty among the farmers and workers, Carranza's regime had become a dictatorship. Carranza was infuriated by the letter and, sensing that the Zapatistas were strengthening the resentment against him, decided that all efforts must be made to do away with Emiliano Zapata. On April 9, 1919, Zapata was lured into an elaborate trap and shot. However, Gildardo Magaña had been playing an increasingly important role in this diplomatic phase of the Zapatista movement and, since he was the main

[211] Womack, *op. cit.*, pp. 462–468.   [212] *Ibid.*, pp. 472–473.
[213] Dromondo, *op. cit.*, p. 243.   [214] Womack, *op. cit.*, pp. 459–461, 481, 541.

link of communication among the scattered guerrilla bands, his leadership was gradually recognized by most of the guerrilla chieftains.[215]

In June, 1919, when Obregón broke with the Carranza government and announced that he was a candidate for the presidency, Magaña quickly established ties with the Sonoran general. Obregón's campaign stirred the opposition to the president and in April, 1920, Carranza began a move to take Obregón into custody. The Sonorans under De la Huerta then began a revolt against Carranza with the Plan of Agua Prieta, and the Zapatistas coordinated their own guerrilla activities with this rebellion. On May 9, 1920, Obregón rode victoriously into Mexico City accompanied by Geneveo de la O, one of the principal Zapatista generals.[216] A few Zapatista chieftains still did not lay down their guns, and it was only after De la Huerta's interim government assured them that the villages could retain the permanent possession of their land that they made peace with Mexico City.

With the triumph of Obregón the Revolution had run its course.

In effect it totally swept away not only the political regime of Porfirio Díaz but all of Porfirian society, that is, the social classes or groups together with their ideas, tastes and manners. Not only the commanders-in-chief of the army but their officers and all the soldiers disappeared without exception. Landholders, urban and especially agricultural, were almost entirely replaced by new ones. Not one of the great newspapers survived. Only two out of fifty banks continued into the new regime. Official bureaucracy—federal, state, and municipal—was wholly reformed . . . in no other Latin American country has an event of such magnitude occurred in the last hundred years except now in Cuba.[217]

And in Morelos, Dr. Parrés, who had been the doctor serving the Zapata forces through the years of its rebellion, became governor of the state and Geneveo de la O was made military commander.[218]

The Results of the Zapatista Movement

The *Agraristas:* Successors to the Zapatistas

Given their legitimacy in the new power structure of Mexico and their favor with Obregón,[219] many of the former Zapatistas emerged as political

[215] *Ibid.*, pp. 459–460.

[216] *Ibid.*, pp. 541, 543; John W. P. Dulles, *Yesterday in Mexico* (Austin: University of Texas Press, 1961), p. 38.

[217] Daniel Cosío Villegas, "The Mexican Revolution Then and Now," in Stanley R. Ross (ed.), *Is the Mexican Revolution Dead?* (New York: Knopf, 1966), p. 117.

[218] Tannenbaum, *PBR*, p. 180.   [219] Womack, *op. cit.*, pp. 545–546.

leaders in deciding how agrarian reform would be carried out. Díaz Soto y Gama, long one of Zapata's chief spokesmen, founded in June, 1920, the National Agrarian party (Partido Nacional Agrarista) and the *agraristas* never failed to put forward Emiliano Zapata as the hero and, in a real sense, the founder of their movement. Shortly after the victorious Obregón arrived in Mexico City in May, 1920, Díaz Soto y Gama had an interview with him and was assured by the Sonoran general that the distribution of land to the poverty-stricken Indian peasants was of primary importance for his new government.[220] Even during the short interim government of De la Huerta the question of breaking up the large estates was brought up for discussion in the congress by the *agraristas*, and Obregón had not been in office more than a month when he signed the *Ley de Ejidos* (The Ejido Law) which lifted some of the restrictions placed on the law of January 6, 1915, by Carranza and attempted to lay down some procedures for land reform.[221]

Next, the *agraristas* managed to have a special six-month session of the congress convoked in 1921 to discuss a comprehensive agrarian reform law. Díaz Soto y Gama and his associates traveled throughout Mexico and fomented such popular pressure by peasant groups on both President Obregón and the Congress that in 1922 the Agrarian Regulatory Law was passed.[222] This law firmly established the ejido system as the framework within which Mexico's land reform would take place. Under the Agrarian Regulatory Law, settlements on abandoned haciendas, as well as villages with *categoría política* were eligible to receive land, but the resident laborers on haciendas were still excluded. The size of ejido plots and the minimum amount of land exempted from expropriation were fixed, and the legal process was established for initiating petitions for ejidos and for making decisions on definitive possession.[223]

The National Agrarian party met for its first national convention in 1923 and already had thousands of delegates representing hundreds of thousands of campesinos from all parts of Mexico. The speeches given and the resolutions voted at these meetings indicate the problems agrarian reform was facing then: the brutal practices of the hacendados to prevent the villagers from petitioning or holding on to ejidos; demands for a better market for Mexican agricultural products; petitions to rescind the use of court injunctions to hold up distribution of haciendas.[224]

In these years of hesitant, experimental steps in agrarian reform the

[220] Dulles, *op. cit.*, pp. 129, 93–94.   [221] Eyler Simpson, *op. cit.*, pp. 81–82.

[222] Díaz Soto y Gama, *op. cit.*, pp. 292–293.

[223] Eyler Simpson, *op. cit.*, pp. 82–85.   [224] Silva-Herzog, *op. cit.*, pp. 306–307.

National Agrarian party exerted enormous influence in the development of agrarian reform policies. The ejido program was its basic platform and a continuous battle was carried on against those who proposed that small individual property owners, not the ejido, should be the goal of land reform.[225] Obregón had doubts about the program, but he could not ignore the *agraristas* because he looked for political support from them against the powerful Labor party (Confederación Regional Obrera Mexicana) led by Morones. Silva-Herzog comments that "the National Agrarian Party was, during six or seven years, the genuine representative and defender of the Mexican campesinos. The brain of the party, the source of doctrine and ideology—we know by personal experience—was Antonio Díaz Soto y Gama." [226]

In 1924, however, the National Agrarian party came into conflict with President Calles, Obregón's successor, and during Calles' term from 1924 to 1928 the power of the *agraristas* waned. Calles was not sympathetic to the communal principle of the ejido system and looked on the program as only a stopgap remedy for the misery of traditionalistic, landless peasants. In line with this general policy, during Calles' term a new law (The Constitution of Ejido Patrimony) was enacted facilitating the distribution of ejido parcels to individual owners.[227]

In 1929 Calles and Portes Gil moved to coordinate the various contending interest groups into one large National Revolutionary party. The National Agrarian party was brought into this new coalition, but its founder and guiding light, Díaz Soto y Gama, was carefully excluded. It soon became apparent that Calles had gathered the power of the various parties into his own hands and that the campesinos had lost an autonomous party which was primarily responsive to their demands and which articulated their interests.[228] It is at this point, when the Agrarian party was absorbed into the official Revolutionary Party and lost the independence that Zapata had so tenaciously fought for, that the Zapatista movement can be said to have ceased to exist as an autonomous, collective force.

In June, 1930, Calles announced his personal opinion that the ejido program was a failure. At his behest as the political boss of Mexico, the president, Pascual Ortiz Rubio, decreed that in the state of Aguascalientes the villages were to present petitions for land within sixty days, after

[225] Alba, *op. cit.*, p. 315.   [226] *Op. cit.*, p. 313.
[227] Eyler Simpson, *op. cit.*, pp. 88–90.
[228] Robert E. Scott, *Mexican Government in Transition* (Urbana: University of Illinois Press, 1964), pp. 121–125; Parkes, *op. cit.*, p. 392.

which all restitution or donation of land was to cease. By the end of 1931 more than a dozen states had similar "stop" laws and the ejido program began rapidly to grind to a halt.[229]

The *agraristas* attempted to fight back at Calles and his group of *veteranos* (the old Revolutionaries) mainly through maneuvers in the legislative branch. A law was pushed through in 1931 (before the conservatives could gather their forces) which deprived the landowners of the right to stop expropriation by court injunctions (*amparo*). In the famous six-year plan announced in December, 1933, the *veteranos* drafting the agrarian sections put the ejido program in a subordinate role, but the *agraristas* fought back and were able to include a section which at last enabled the hacienda communities (the *acasillados*) to petition ejidos. The greatest victory of the *agraristas* of this period—Gilberto Fabila, Marte R. Gómez, Narciso Bassols, and Graciano Sánchez—was the comprehensive Agrarian Code of 1934. In addition to solidifying and clarifying previous gains for the ejido program, it greatly speeded up land distribution by making it possible to obtain definitive possession in 150 days.[230] These *agraristas*, some of them former Zapatistas, were a continuation of the Zapatista movement, though they acted as individuals and not in a separate organization. With many of the legal obstacles removed, the distribution of land in ejidos made its greatest progress from 1934 to 1940 during the presidency of Lázaro Cárdenas, a man who shared the *agrarista's* positive view of the ejido program.

The original impulse was given to the Mexican agrarian revolution by indigenous peasant leadership organized autonomously and loyal first of all to the campesino sector. But the grass-roots articulation of interests by peasant leaders in the peasant tradition gradually grew weaker as the Agrarian party lost power in the late 1920's and then was absorbed into the National Revolutionary party. On paper, the National Campesino Confederation is the largest mass organization in the Revolutionary party, and should, theoretically, exert a great deal of influence. But as time passed more and more of the decision-making has centered in the President and his immediate advisors, and policy decisions, rather than moving from the grass roots up, usually emanate from the bureaucracy and leadership of the agricultural sector of the party (carefully chosen and loyal to the President), filtering down through the hierarchy to the rank and file. "The ejido farmer and the small landowner have relatively little independent political experience, so they are easily manipulated by pro-

[229] Eyler Simpson, *op. cit.*, pp. 117–118.   [230] *Ibid.*, pp. 118–120, 455–462.

fessional farm leaders *who do not spring from or feel immediately responsible to their rural constituents* (italics added)." [231] Robert Scott suggests
that the agricultural sector's weakened political base gives them a poor
bargaining position in the allocation of national resources.

This shows up in the apportionment of services among the various factors in
Mexico's national life and economy. A great deal of money is being spent for
rural services—roads, schools, medical facilities, and the like—but compared
with relative needs, a much higher proportion is being spent in cities and on
industrial and business development. We find in rural Mexico an almost
classical example of the ineffectual position in the political process of large
numbers of unaware, unorganized and unintegrated people in competition
with much smaller, but politically acute and organized groups.[232]

The question arises, does Mexico need once more a contemporary version
of Emiliano Zapata?

But while the political and legislative victory won by 1920 with the
advent of Obregón and his "Revolutionary family" and the ratification of
Article 27 of the new Constitution may have been, in retrospect, more
apparent than real, a more substantial transformation was taking place in
the ideological sphere. In the 1920's and 1930's the novelists, painters,
philosophers, and educators began to reflect on the accomplished fact of
the new position of the Indian, the peasant, and the worker, and they
gradually elaborated a new Mexican ideology. From 1920 to 1940 Mexican painting, literature, and philosophical thought were filled with themes
of the Revolution, the exaltation of the rural masses, and Mexican nationalism. In part this was due to the spontaneous enthusiasm of the new
generation of intellectuals for the ideals of the Revolution. But also they
were quite ready to lend their talents to the attempts by the Revolutionary governments to refashion the basic value patterns of Mexican society.

In their work they attacked the old value premises which gave priority
to European descent, the urban culture, and the role of the *hidalgo*. The
myth of the superiority of the landed elite was destroyed by their positive
evaluation of manual labor, the Indian racial and cultural background, and
rural life. From these attempts to project a new value system came a new
system of social status and the possibility of a new allocation of power,
prestige, and wealth.

Conclusions

The best explanation of the occurrence of the Zapata agrarian movement may be found in the theoretical framework outlined at the begin-

[231] Scott, *op. cit.*, pp. 134–139, 70.   [232] *Ibid.*, p. 71.

ning of this chapter: 1) the *structural conduciveness* of Mexican society, based on the hacienda type of agriculture, and the forces set in
motion by the Díaz program of modernization, which not only upset the
integration of the old order, but strengthened the worst features of that
order (the exploitation of the peon, emphasis on European superiority,
and so on); 2) the growing *structural strains* in the accentuation of the
conflict over the retention of the village lands and the sharpening of the
subjective sense of deprivation by the appearance of new reference
groups; 3) a set of *beliefs* among Mexican peasants which idealized
armed revolt as a means of agrarian reform; 4) a *precipitating event*
which fomented widespread, simultaneous uprisings and gave those uprisings a sense of political legitimacy; 5) in the *mobilization phase* the ability
of Zapata to organize a peasant army and sustain that organization for
nearly ten years; and finally 6) the weakness of the factors of *social
control.*

However, the remarkable characteristic of the Mexican agrarian revolution was the completeness with which it overturned not only the land
tenure system and the power structure but the value premises supporting
the traditional Latin American plantation society. It was, in the terms of
Smelser, a value-oriented movement.[233] Fundamentally the structural
strains besetting the Mexican rural social structure were in the area of
values, but only a number of fortuitous circumstances led the Zapata
movement to generalize its focus until finally the value issues were made
explicit.

Zapata and his peasant followers originally saw the solution to their
economic problems in the restoration of the village lands to which Anenecuilco, Ayala, and other communities of the local area could prove title.
But the solution began to generalize almost immediately. In June, 1911,
when Emiliano Zapata talked with Francisco Madero after the collapse of
the Díaz government, the issue was not only the restoration of the land to
the villages of Morelos, but also the governorship of the state. Zapata saw
no hope of lasting agrarian reform unless the hierarchies of agents responsible for the courts and police were changed. Furthermore, beginning
with the decision to issue the Plan of Ayala and especially in the phase of
the Convention of Aguascalientes—when the movement was not only the
undisputed government of the state of Morelos but the dominant influence in the action of the Convention—the focus of the movement was
upon legislation and technical implementation. Until this point, the move-

---

[233] Smelser, *op. cit.*, pp. 313-381.

ment had very largely centered upon Emiliano Zapata himself and it was his tenacity and ability to weld the bands of peasant guerrillas into a threatening army that had generalized the movement. But soon "local intelligentsia," such as Otilio Montaño and Manuel Palafox, and the radical young politicians with an urban, educated background, such as Antonio Díaz Soto y Gama and Gildardo Magaña, began to share with Zapata important roles in the movement. Finally in the 1920's and 1930's the implementation of the educational and agrarian reforms on a national scale required a mobilization in which a new Mexican ideology was formed. In this phase another group of allies,—philosophers such as Vasconcelos, painters like Diego Rivera, the novelists Azuela and Lopez y Fuentes, and others—became, in a real sense, *agraristas* and made the implicit ideology of the Zapata movement part of the national cultural tradition.[234] In short, the Zapata movement was thoroughly peasant-based, but it was fortunate that the individuals connected with the radical Liberal Party movement, the Casa del Obrero Mundial and others in revolt against the politics and philosophy of the Porfiriato, chose to link themselves with the agrarian movement. Otherwise it seems unlikely that the Zapata movement would have broadened its original, regional focus to become so explicitly a society-wide, value-oriented movement.

Because of this happy coincidence of Emiliano Zapata's tenacity and leadership ability and the help of his allies in the learned sector, the movement generalized its "beliefs" in a series of stages approaching the model of value-oriented movements proposed by Smelser:[235] from 1) structural strains regarding the allocation of facilities, the restoration of the village lands; to 2) citation of the agents responsible for the problems, Zapata's demand for the removal of the *"científicos, hacendados, caciques"* mentioned in the Plan of Ayala; to 3) reconstitution of normative structures, the legislation directly influenced by the Zapatista movement in the Convention of Aguascalientes and indirectly the agrarian decree of January 6, 1915, and Article 27 of the Constitution of 1917; to 4) a reconstitution of basic values, the incorporation of the agrarian value themes of the revolutionary creed through educational and artistic efforts in the 1920's and 1930's.

The hopes of the Zapatistas for land distribution seem to have been

---

[234] During his period as Minister of Education in the government of Obregón, Vasconcelos was severely attacked by the "aristocracy" for his strong sympathy for the Zapatistas of Morelos (cf. Vasconcelos, *El desastre* [Autobiográphica], in *Obras completas* [Mexico City: Libreros Mexicanos Unidos], I, 1239–1245). Vasconcelos was at this time honorary vice-president of the National Agrarian Party (cf. Dulles, *op. cit.,* p. 121). [235] *Op. cit.,* pp. 67–78, 120–129.

realized today in Mexico. The 8,400 very large haciendas have been reduced to 500 and these are mostly in remote, semidesert regions or tropical jungles. More than 50 per cent of all the productive land of Mexico has been distributed to 2.2 million *ejidatarios* and, in addition, there are now more than a million privately owned holdings of smaller size.[236] But in many ways the Mexican peasant remains as relatively poor as he was in 1910, and to a certain extent peasant discontent rightly still exists. Gruening found in his travels in Mexico in 1923 that the farmers of Morelos were exultant with their new land and freedom; but in 1925 they were saying, "in the *hacienda* days at least you were paid regularly; now you weren't sure of anything." [237] Today Mexico's agrarian planners are talking of a reform of the agrarian reform; land and liberty are not enough to solve the problems of rural poverty. The real solution seems to be to make the small farm more productive and provide industrial jobs for the rural surplus population.[238]

The Zapatista movement began with the problem of poverty experienced by the villagers of Anenecuilco and Ayala; but the focus of the movement generalized to land reform legislation and a new national ideology. This generalization process short-circuited many of the long-term and intermediate reforms necessary to cure the backwardness of Mexican agriculture and the lack of a stable political culture.[239] The rather vague battle cry of "land and liberty" was important in mobilizing a national movement. But much remains to be done to fill in the gaps that were left, perhaps justifiably, between 1910 and 1940.

[236] Edmundo Flores, "The Agricultural Development of Mexico," in A. Curtis Wilgus (ed.), *The Carribean: Mexico Today* (Gainesville: University of Florida Press, 1964), pp. 68–69.   [237] *Op. cit.*, p. 162.
[238] Silva-Herzog, *op. cit.*, pp. 572–573; Ramón, Fernandez y Fernandez, "The Mexican Agrarian Reform: Backgrounds, Accomplishments, and Problems," in T. Lynn Smith (ed.), *Agrarian Reform in Latin America* (New York: Knopf, 1966), pp. 153–166.
[239] For a more extensive discussion of the concept of "short-circuiting" as a phenomenon characteristic of collective behavior, see Smelser, *op. cit.*, pp. 67–68.

4. Bolivia: Peasant Syndicates among the Aymara of the Yungas— A View from the Grass Roots

DWIGHT B. HEATH

Brown University

There are few countries in the world where peasant movements have had as profound and pervasive an impact as in Bolivia. The impact has been profound in the degree to which the way of life of the peasants themselves has been changed, and it has been pervasive in affecting other social institutions of the nation.

Although no social scientist has yet devoted his full time to making a long-term systematic study of the subject of political socialization in Bolivia, everyone who has worked there during the past fifteen years has found it necessary to devote part of his attention to it. In the course of conducting a variety of ethnographic research projects, under various auspices [1] among different tribal and peasant groups in Bolivia, I have frequently found the effects of agrarian syndicalism to be important, sometimes in unexpected ways. [2]

The anthropological approach to peasant movements has peculiar strengths as well as significant limitations in comparison with that of any other behavioral science. The traditional emphasis on field work, in the sense of close and sustained contact with the subject group, is no longer unique to the anthropological enterprise and its value is widely and increasingly recognized in economics, political science, sociology, and related disciplines. Just as some other social scientists are joining anthropologists in venturing to "the field," with all its confusion of uncontrolled variables, some anthropologists have begun in recent years to join our

[1] Research on a variety of historical and ethnographic topics in Bolivia has been sponsored by the Henry L. and Grace Doherty Charitable Foundation, the Social Science Research Council, Brown University, the University of Wisconsin Land Tenure Center, and the Research Institute for the Study of Man.

[2] For a discussion of agrarian syndicalism as a counter to alcoholism, see Dwight B. Heath, "Comments on David Mandelbaum's 'Alcohol and Culture,'" *Current Anthropology*, VI, No. 3 (1965), 289–290.

colleagues in other disciplines in addressing ourselves to the analysis of complex institutions in literate societies, and attempting to make meaningful statements about bureaucratic organizations, large-scale legal and administrative programs, and even nation-states.

Often the most valuable contribution we can make to understanding such complex systems is in providing a different perspective—a view from the grass roots. Everywhere—and perhaps especially in Latin America—neatly drawn tables of organization are often idealized representations of a loosely structured reality; the text of laws is notoriously discrepant with their application in specific cases; and official pronouncements in capital cities tend to tell more about the officials who are speaking than about actual events or attitudes in rural areas. An approach to national institutions from the top provides a breadth of perspective that can never be achieved from a lower level. But an approach from below provides an order of truth that is difficult if not impossible to grasp when working from above. Perhaps the most effective way to study this order of phenomena would be to coordinate these complementary approaches, but rarely does one individual have both the interest and the varied abilities to do both kinds of work, and large-scale team research has not yet, to my knowledge, been applied to any contemporary peasant movement, although it seems "a natural."

The Setting

For purposes of comparative analysis, this discussion is limited to such a view from the grass roots, specifically, a portion of the yungas region of Bolivia. The bulk of my data refer to the province [3] of Nor Yungas, a distinctive zone of montane jungle in rugged valleys east of the Andes in the department [4] of La Paz. From August, 1964, through July, 1965, I was engaged in ethnographic and epidemiological research in and around the provincial capital of Coroico. It was obvious from the outset that the numerous Aymara-speaking peasants in the surrounding countryside played a variety of important roles in the life of the town, and the peasant movement in the region commanded my attention, in part because the townspeople themselves consider it of immense historical, economic, and political importance.

As my research progressed, it was possible gradually to gain the confidence—and even friendship—of peasants as well as townspeople, and to

[3] A *provincia* is Bolivia's administrative counterpart to a county in the United States.

[4] The nine *departamentos* of Bolivia are analogous to states in the United States.

participate in a variety of syndical activities. Although I never achieved easy fluency in Aymara, I enjoyed the advantage of working through a skillful interpreter who had for years lived with the peasants and was well known and well liked by them. At the same time, I was able to maintain rapport with the townspeople, most of whom are whites or mestizos. As an outsider, I was able (in their own terms) "to be friends with God and the Devil at the same time," and feel confident that my data, based on observation, participation, open-ended interviewing, and a minimum of archival research, provide generally valid and reliable characterizations of the contrasting beliefs, attitudes, and behaviors of the several social groups, some of which were mutually antagonistic. I have no doubt that systematic documentary research would yield significantly different data, especially amplifying the historical perspective, but it was beyond the scope of my research. My data, then, represent primarily what is known and thought by the local people; my few interpretations, identified as such, are generally based on knowledge and concepts not shared by them.

The Physical Setting

The yungas is a rich region on the eastern slopes of the Andes, comprising warm, moist, steep-sided valleys separated by sharp parallel spurs running out from the main range, the Cordillera Real. With a subtropical climate, the natural vegetation is that of the montane rain forest and is spectacular on the steep hillsides that range from 10,000-foot peaks to rushing rivers at 2,000 feet. It is difficult to imagine two more different ecological situations than those where most of the Aymara live. The warm and humid yungas with its lush and varied vegetation is a world apart from the cold dry altiplano, and the yungas region has always been much less densely populated than the flat open plateau.

Most of the people of the yungas are Aymara-speaking peasants who have become small-scale freeholders since the traditional quasi-feudal order was overturned in the early 1950's. A few small settlements of Negroes are scattered through the countryside, and old mestizo towns serve as administrative and commercial centers.

The Temporal Setting

Unfortunately, there were no systematic studies made in the yungas before the revolution of 1952, so we are dependent on the oral tradition and fragmentary documentation for a reconstruction of the earlier way of life of the Aymara in that area. Whole communities of Aymara appear to have been sent from the altiplano into the yungas region by the Inca, displacing the indigenous Leco eastward late in the fifteenth century. Coca [5] and gold were the principal products of the region and continued to be throughout much of the Spanish colonial period. In the republican era, mining diminished markedly, but coca has remained a major product, linking the area economically with the more densely populated altiplano. In recent years, as trucks have begun to replace mules as principal means of transportation, coffee, plantain, and citrus fruits are other important crops in the market-oriented agriculture that occupies most of the population, using archaic methods.

There have been no peasant uprisings in the yungas region, as there were sporadically throughout both the colonial and republican periods on the altiplano. The Aymara of the yungas never attacked or besieged a town or a hacienda—militant activities that were episodic outbursts against intercaste abuses elsewhere. There was no rape, murder, pillaging, or cannibalism as is recounted by former landlords, many of whom still fear the Aymara in the altiplano area.

The Chaco War of the 1930's is seen by Bolivians as a turning point in their history; its effects were immediate and far-reaching. Both Bolivia and the nominal victor, Paraguay, suffered enormous losses of manpower and wealth. The process of spiraling inflation was started, and remained unchecked until 1956. More important, however, were the social consequences of the war. For the first time, the weakness of Bolivia's traditional leadership was dramatically exposed, and the feudal system proved inadequate to meet modern problems. Many Indians saw other parts of the country for the first time as draftees and became aware both of the existence of other groups of people within the country and of the meaning of the Bolivian nation as an entity. Many of the veterans of the Chaco War banded together in associations which sought not only redress of their specific grievances but also changes on the national level.

The period during World War II was one of ideological ferment, and several new political parties came into being. These included the Revolutionary Workers' party (Partido Obrero Revolucionario, POR), which held to Trotskyite principles, and the Party of the Revolutionary Left (Partido de la Izquierda Revolucionario, PIR), which was Marxist in

---

[5] The leaves of this plant, from which cocaine is derived, are dried and chewed, often with lime to heighten the effect, by Indians of the highlands. Coca-chewing seems to alleviate hunger, cold, pain, and fatigue; it also has occasional ritual significance. There is little support for widespread allegations that coca is physically or morally damaging. Light in weight and not apt to spoil easily once they are properly dried, coca leaves are an ideal crop for an area where transportation to distant markets is still costly and difficult.

orientation. The party which proved to be the most viable was the Nationalist Revolutionary Movement (Movimiento Nacionalista Revolucionario, MNR). The MNR emerged as a loose coalition of diverse individuals, and it still accommodates a wide variety of outlooks ranging toward the left of the political spectrum.

The MNR's first practical experience in government came in coalition with a short-lived military junta under Gualberto Villaroel. Víctor Paz Estenssoro, who subsequently headed the party, served as Minister of Finance, and other MNR cabinet members were influential in the accomplishment of a variety of social innovations during the early 1940's. At that time the trade-union movement was first officially favored, and it quickly became firmly established in the mining regions.

The Aymara of the yungas seem not to be aware of the fact, but townsmen recall that another important and unusual move of the Villaroel government was to make overtures to the Indian peasants who have always been a numerical majority of the population but who participated minimally in the nation's political, economic, and other social systems. In May, 1945, a National Indian Congress was called, the first time in many decades that any government of Bolivia had shown an active interest in the situation of the Indian masses. At the end of that meeting, four decrees were issued, officially abolishing the compulsory personal service (*pongueaje*) which Indian tenants had traditionally owed to their feudal landlords, fostering schools for peasants, and defining the mutual obligations of landlords and tenants.[6] There is no clear indication that the letter or the spirit of these laws was respected by landlords anywhere in Bolivia, but they may be related to a reduction of labor requirements—from four days weekly to three—which is generally remembered but unexplained by older peasants in the yungas.

When Villaroel's government fell at the hands of revolutionaries a year later, Víctor Paz went into exile in Argentina. Virtually all Bolivians were surprised when—still in exile—he gained a plurality in the presidential election of 1951, but the decision went to Congress since he did not have a true majority of the votes. A military junta intervened, until the MNR finally came to power in a bloody revolution April 9–11, 1952.

The accession to power of this party did not represent, as had many of Bolivia's previous revolutions, a mere changing of the palace guard and transfer of political incumbency from one upper-class clique to another.

[6] *Decretos leyes* 00318–00321 of May 15, 1945.

The turmoil of 1952 was the basis of a profound social revolution. It significantly altered the status of the former elite, and resulted in immediate and important modifications of political life and government policy which were subsequently codified in constitutional changes.[7] The formal organization of government continued much the same as before, although the locus of effective power was greatly altered. The oligarchy (locally called *rosca*) were generally exiled, impoverished, or otherwise rendered ineffectual. The army was emasculated, and its weapons distributed to miners and peasants, who formed local militias. Clearly the patterns of the old order were broken, and popular support for the revolutionary regime was assured when Paz enacted universal suffrage, enfranchising the Indian masses who had previously had no voice.

The new government strove quickly and fairly effectively to come to grips with one of the most serious problems facing the nation: how to incorporate the numerically predominant but hitherto passive Indians actively into a more open social system. A Ministry of Peasant Affairs (Asuntos Campesinos) was established with the task of defending the peasants and planning fundamental reforms in their economic, social, and political positions, which had been promised by the MNR. The very name of the new ministry reflects the zealous reformism of MNR officials who expunged the word *indio* (literally: "Indian," but with deprecatory connotations) from Bolivian Spanish, and substituted *campesino* ("peasant"), which is far less emotionally charged.

But social reform is not effected by semantic fiat. According to townsmen and peasants alike, in a rare instance of unanimous concurrence, it was itinerant agents of the MNR who brought the idea of syndicalism to the yungas shortly after the revolution of 1952. The fundamental question of how the peasant syndicates first came to be is one of the thorniest in recent Bolivian history. The emergence of agrarian syndicates in Cliza and Ucureña in the 1930's is historically important, but does not seem to have set a trend. That such a trend did sweep the country in the early 1950's is obvious; there is some difference of opinion about who served as messengers and organizers.

According to Robert J. Alexander, "during the first year it was in power, the MNR government carried out the policy of establishing peasants' unions and organizing the members of these unions simultane-

[7] Bolivia's fourteenth constitution, enacted July 31, 1961, incorporated many of the revolutionary changes instituted by the MNR. It was repealed by the military junta late in 1964.

ously into local units of the MNR. These local agrarian groups throughout the country formed their own peasant militias, also armed by the government." More specifically, he says that it was "under the direction of the Ministry of Peasant Affairs [that] peasant unions were established throughout the country, for the first time giving the Indians organizations which could defend their interests." [8] In the sole published history of syndicalism in Bolivia, Barcelli similarly states that Ñuflo Chávez as Minister of Peasant Affairs and Vicente Álvarez Plata as First Secretary of the Ministry devised a plan of syndical organization for peasants that would soon lead to their organization on a national scale. For that purpose, they sought the material cooperation of the directors of the FSTMB (Federación Sindical de Trabajadores Mineros Bolivianos, Syndical Federation of Bolivian Mine Workers) to carry out the projected plan. It can be said that they were the decisive factors in this primary organization of the agriculturalists. Those former leaders of the miners in the provinces, and Chávez Ortiz and Álvarez Plata from La Paz, had created a multitude of agrarian syndical organizations that were present at the June, 1953, national congress of labor unions. [9]

A strikingly different view, emphasizing the vigorous grass-roots basis for peasant syndicalism in one region, was vividly presented by Richard W. Patch and has been accepted by many nonspecialists as applying to the country as a whole. He stressed that this kind of organization, as well as agrarian reform, was accomplished "from the bottom" of the sociopolitical hierarchy and was not the outcome of enlightened direction "from the top." On the basis of long-term extensive and intensive research in the Cochabamba Valley region, he said:

The early meetings of the Sindicato Campesino de Ucureña del Valle organized task forces of campesinos and young MNR students from Cochabamba, dispatching them to the farthest reaches of Bolivia. Often these teams of organizers were the first to bring news of the revolution to Indian villages of remote valleys and lofty plateaus. The syndicate groups showed the campesinos how to organize new syndicates of their own. Most of these later syndicates remain personally loyal today to [Ucureña leader José] Rojas, for they believe that he and no one else was responsible for their being established in the first place. As the wild fire of revolt and hope raced through the villages, the entire campesino movement was completely outside the control

[8] Alexander, *The Bolivian National Revolution* (New Brunswick, N.J.: Rutgers University Press, 1958), pp. 148, 47.

[9] Agustín Barcelli, *Medio siglo de luchas sindicales revolucionarias en Bolivia* (La Paz, Bolivia: Editorial del Estado, 1956), p. 319.

of the national government or the MNR party leaders. The only center it recognized was Ucureña.[10]

In a subsequent paper Patch stressed that the early syndicates were not only independent of the government but actively opposed to it on many counts; he also emphasized that his discussion applies to the Quechua but not to the Aymara.[11]

However faulty such sources may be, it is striking that contemporary newspaper accounts and the recollections of peasants, townspeople, and government officials, including outspoken critics of the MNR as well as staunch supporters, overwhelmingly agree that most of the original organizers of the syndicates were MNR agents, often identified with the Ministry of Peasant Affairs. At least in the yungas region, there is no indication of the grass-roots action described by Patch.

In the simplest terms, it appears that different political forces were at work organizing the peasants in different parts of the country. In most areas, including the yungas, the MNR and a few more leftist groups seem to have been the prime movers in sending both miners and college students to arm and organize the peasants shortly after the old order was unseated by revolution in April of 1952.

The Cultural Setting

Regional variation in Aymara culture is recognized but not yet well documented in specific detail. LaBarre's survey made passing mention of the distinctive character of the yungas but offered no substantive evidence to distinguish Aymara life there from that in "the Lake Titicaca plateau," which was his focus of concern.[12] Tschopik clearly limited his analysis to the community of Chucuito on the Peruvian lakeshore, and Hickman dealt with the neighboring village of Chinchera.[13] By far the

[10] "Bolivia: U.S. Assistance in a Revolutionary Setting," in Richard N. Adams *et al.*, *Social Change in Latin America* (New York: Council on Foreign Relations, 1960), p. 122. See also Patch's unpublished Ph.D. thesis, "Social Implications of the Bolivian Agrarian Reform" (Cornell University, 1956).

[11] "Peasantry and National Revolution: Bolivia," in Kalman Silvert *et al.*, *Expectant Peoples* (New York: Random House, 1963), p. 111.

[12] Weston LaBarre, *The Aymara Indians of the Lake Titicaca Plateau, Bolivia* (American Anthropological Association Memoir 68 [Menasha, Wis.: The Association, 1948]).

[13] Harry S. Tschopik, *The Aymara of Chucuito, Peru*, Vol. I: *Magic* (Anthropological Papers of the American Museum of Natural History, XLIV, No. 2 [New York, 1951]); John M. Hickman, "The Aymara of Chinchera, Peru: Persistence and Change in a Bicultural Context" (Ph.D. thesis, Cornell University, 1963).

most detailed and sophisticated work on the Aymara to date is that of
Carter, with its focus in Irpa Chico, a free community just outside La
Paz.[14] He also collected some comparative data from former haciendas and
other communities on the northern altiplano but explicitly denies any
detailed familiarity with the situation in the yungas.[15]

There had been no systematic sociological or anthropological study in
the yungas before the revolution of 1952. In the late 1950's, some brief
studies were made in the vicinity of Coroico by Isabel Kelly, but none of
the results of her work have yet been published. In 1963, Buechler
conducted an extensive comparative survey of outcomes of agrarian reform which has just been published, and in 1965–1966 he expanded
this study to include economic and other relations between a few Aymara
who migrated to the yungas and the community on the northern altiplano from which they had come.[16] In 1964–1965, William and Barbara
Leons were engaged in a study of peasant social systems and the newly
formed community of Arapata.[17] During the same period, I was engaged
in collecting ethnographic and epidemiological data in and around
Coroico.

Sociopsychological Factors

Many Bolivians viewed Indians as subhuman beings, and there was little
communication at a meaningful level between the tiny, totally dominant
upper class and the silent mass of peasantry. Even an ardent *indigenista*
who rhapsodizes about his country's Inca heritage, and who has served as
Minister of Education to a populace of whom fewer than half speak
Spanish, confesses that he cannot deal with an Indian as an individual:

The Indian is a sphinx. He inhabits a hermetic world, inaccessible to the
white and the mestizo. We don't understand his forms of life, nor his mental
mechanism. . . . We speak of the Indian as a mass factor in the nation; in
truth we are ignorant of his individual psyche and his collective drama. The
Indian lives. The Indian acts and produces. The Indian does not allow himself

[14] William E. Carter, "The Ambiguity of Reform: Highland Bolivian Peasants and
Their Land" (Ph.D. thesis, Columbia University, 1963).
[15] *Aymara Communities and the Bolivian Agrarian Reform* (University of Florida
Monographs, Social Sciences, 24 [Gainesville: The University, 1964]).
[16] Hans C. Buechler, "Land Reform and Social Revolution in the Northern
Altiplano and Valleys," in Dwight B. Heath *et al., Land Reform and Social
Revolution in Bolivia* (New York: Frederick A. Praeger, 1969); Buechler, "Agrarian
Reform and Migration on the Bolivian Altiplano" (Ph.D. thesis, Columbia University,
1966).
[17] Barbara M. Leons, "Changing Patterns of Stratification in an Emergent Bolivian
Community" (Ph.D. thesis, University of California at Los Angeles, 1966).

to be understood, he doesn't desire communication. Retiring, silent, immutable, he inhabits a closed world. The Indian is an enigma.[18]

Foreign anthropologists, unlike most Bolivians, have tried to deal with Indians as human beings, and they have often succeeded. Transcultural contact does not always foster warm feelings, however, and characterizations of the Aymara by several observers before the 1950's were universally negative. A consistently dreary thesaurus of epithets was applied to the Aymara: anxious, apprehensive, brutal, careless, closed, cruel, depressed, dirty, dishonest, distrustful, doubtful, drunken, dull, fearful, filthy, gloomy, hostile, ignorant, insecure, irresponsible, jealous, malevolent, malicious, melancholic, morose, negative, pessimistic, pugnacious, quarrelsome, rancorous, reticent, sad, silent, sinister, slovenly, stolid, sullen, suspicious, tense, thieving, treacherous, truculent, uncommunicative, unimaginative, unsmiling, untrustworthy, violent, and vindictive.[19] The fact that such a list was compiled by different individuals, themselves from various cultural backgrounds, suggests that more was involved than personal prejudice. LaBarre and Tschopik offered a variety of explanations for why the Aymara demonstrated such negative personality traits.

But the picture is not altogether dismal. Anthropologists who have worked with the Aymara during the 1950's and 1960's have generally found some positive aspects as well.[20] It has recently been suggested that this apparent change may be in large part a function of different methods of field research and approaches to the Aymara.[21] The interrelation of culture and personality is generally accepted, and long-term changes have been noted throughout the world; although the time has been short, I personally wonder about the possible impact of the revolution of 1952 as a "liberating" force on Aymara character, in relation to its obviously deep and pervasive impact on many aspects of Aymara culture.

[18] Fernando Díez de Medina, *Thunupa* (La Paz, Bolivia: Gisbert, 1956), p. 253.

[19] David Forbes, "On the Aymara Indians of Bolivia and Peru," *Journal of the Ethnological Society of London*, II, No. 2 (1870), 193–305; E. George Squier, *Peru: Incidents of Travel and Exploration in the Land of the Incas* (New York: Harper and Bros., 1877); Adolph Bandelier, *The Islands of Titicaca and Coati* (New York: American Geographical Society, 1910); Emilio Romero, *Monografía del departamento de Puno* (Lima: Imprenta Torres Aguirre, 1928); LaBarre, *op. cit.*; LaBarre, "Aymara Folktales," *International Journal of American Linguistics*, XVI, No. 1 (1950), 40–45; Tschopik, *op. cit.*

[20] For example, Carter, *Aymara Communities*; Hickman, *op. cit.*; Dwight B. Heath, "The Aymara Indians and Bolivia's Revolutions," *Inter-American Economic Affairs*, XIX, No. 4 (1966), 31–40.

[21] John F. Plummer, "Another Look at Aymara Personality," *Behavioral Science Notes*, I, No. 1 (1966), 55–78.

Economic Factors

In striking contrast with the altiplano region where most of the Aymara live, the yungas region has long been marked by a beneficent climate, a surplus of land and a shortage of labor. Most of the sparse literature available on Aymara culture to date deals with very different problems, those of extreme pressure on limited land resources in a hostile environment, and associated overpopulation.

Haciendas in the yungas were administered by the landlord, by a permanent administrator, or by both. Absentee land ownership characterized only about half of the properties in prereform yungas (a considerably smaller proportion than in the altiplano), but the landlord was usually assisted by a permanent salaried foreman. Often, but not always, a *sutta* would be designated by the landlord as an Indian foreman. Like the *jilakata* of the altiplano, his job was to mediate between the Aymara peasants and the landlord or the *mayordomo*.

The classic *colono* system prevailed in this region, strikingly similar to that amply described in many other highland regions of Latin America. Specifically, a *colono* was required to work three days per week on the landlord's holdings, and to provide other kinds of unpaid labor, in exchange for usufruct rights to a *sayaña*, an allocation of 2½ to 8 *catos* of land (⅜ to 2 hectares).

Besides the *colonos*, there was another group of peasants called *yanaperos*, who worked only one or two days and enjoyed the use of proportionately less land (never more than one hectare). The number of peasant heads of households on a hacienda rarely exceeded fifty. Few haciendas in the region were larger than 100 hectares in area, and many had nearly half of their area uncultivated because of the shortage of peasant tenants.

A *sayaña*, the land allocated to a *colono*, was rarely a single plot; more often it comprised a number of tiny parcels. Although this distribution of holdings may sound inefficient, it was actually advantageous in allowing individuals to exploit a variety of growing conditions. Because of the range of altitudes in this steepily hilly area, even a small hacienda might include three ecological zones, suitable for coca, coffee, and citrus and plantain respectively. Usually each *colono* had a small plot of each of these crops, and the landlords' holdings were similarly scattered and diversified.

Agricultural methods were antiquated, emphasizing heavy labor without machinery, fertilizer, or other capital investments. Virtually the only tools used were the machete and the *chonta*, a short-handled pick-mattock, made in at least five different blade-shapes for various kinds of weeding, planting, digging, and terrace making. Tools usually were lent by the landlord, and peasants could use them on their *sayañas* as well as for assigned tasks on hacienda lands. Peasants were free to dispose of the entire harvest from their *sayañas;* although they cultivated primarily for their own subsistence, many also produced small surpluses for market. Clothing or raw wool were often provided by the landlord, and those few things that the Aymara wanted that were not locally produced (matches, salt, kerosene) were available at cost in the commissary of the hacienda.

Both *colonos* and *yanaperos* were required also to provide other kinds of unpaid service. Among these was the *faena*, group work on maintenance of trails or roads, walls, and other hacienda property, performed on Sunday mornings after the week's work assignments had been issued. Furthermore, *colonos* were required to serve occasionally as *pongos;* that is, a peasant would be a house servant at the beck and call of the landlord and his family for a week at a time, either in the manor house or in a town house if the landlord lived there. During this period, the *pongo's* wife would be their cook and maid as well. This work as *pongo* was done by turns, as was that as *mulero*, whereby each *colono* served a week or two at a time as mule-herder or as driver on the mule treks, which were the only means of getting produce to the nearest large market or (in the 1920's) to the distant railroad or (since 1935) to the sole all-weather road.

Labor obligations were usually for consecutive days (Monday through Wednesday), rather than being at the choice of the *colonos*. Not only the heads of households had to work; each was required to provide the labor of women and children as well—that is, the use of a *sayaña* "cost" about five man-days of work weekly. The workday lasted eight hours, including time for a cold luncheon and a couple of coca breaks, under close supervision.

The landlords dominated the market, both locally and in La Paz; they controlled the courts and all political and administrative offices; and they constituted a quasi-caste dominant in every respect over that of the Indians. In many ways, the context was similar to that in much of highland Latin America. However, the situation in the yungas was distinctive not only with respect to the beneficent climate and the lush tropical vegetation which present ecological problems diametrically opposed to those encountered by other Aymara on the barren altiplano; in the yungas, also, crops have long been cultivated for the market, so that commercial agriculture is an old and widespread supplement to subsistence farming on large estates. Demographically the yungas has been marked by sparse population and high seasonal demand for labor (both coffee and coca must be harvested in a few crucial weeks). These unusual aspects of the local situation account for the frequent necessity to supplement the unpaid *colono* system with wage labor in the yungas, unlike the highlands, where peasants were virtually never paid before the MNR revolution.

One aspect of wage work was the possibility for a *colono* to earn and save cash. In a large family it was sometimes possible (with pooled labor) to meet the unpaid obligations to the landlord, tend the *sayaña*, and still occasionally work for wages. Payments were small, but an exceptionally frugal and industrious peasant could sometimes save enough to move to town as a shopkeeper or artisan, and a few even became freeholders.

Most haciendas were also dependent, to some extent, on labor from outside. There is a long tradition of seasonal migration to the yungas by men from limited areas of the highlands. Some came from regions of extremely dense population and heavy pressure on the land (Santiago de Huata, Huatajata, and other settlements on the shore of Lake Titicaca). Others came from the northern part of the frontier with Chile (Turco, Curahuara de Carangas), or from southern Peru (Moho, Taraco), both areas where poor soil and severe climate yield extremely limited production. Cash wages were small (even today they are only about Bs. 4,000 per *jornal*, or thirty-three cents daily in U.S. currency), but for many of the migrant laborers they meant survival. And many of those who came to the yungas for the July–September dry season eventually stayed on to settle in the area as *colonos*.

Aymara peasants of the yungas resent what they call the "slavery" of the *colono* system, although their situation was far less oppressive than that of their counterparts on the altiplano. They still distinguish between "good" and "bad" landlords, primarily on the basis that frequent floggings used to be meted out by the "abusive" ones.

The situation where this peasant movement took hold, then, comprised an unusual combination of economic factors. The predominant unit of production was the hacienda, with its labor-intensive and paternalistic organization as characterized by Wolf and Mintz,[22] and yet some special crops were grown almost exclusively for the market. Contractual wage-labor was commonplace, coexisting with the feudal *patrón-peón* pattern —not only on the same property but sometimes exemplified in the same individual. Peasants constituted a low-status majority, with extremely

---

[22] Eric R. Wolf and Sidney W. Mintz, "Haciendas and Plantations in Middle America and the Antilles," *Social and Economic Studies*, VI, No. 3 (1957), 380–412.

limited access to goods and symbols of the small dominant group; upward mobility could be achieved by a few, however, only if accomplished by horizontal mobility.

Other Cultural Factors

A number of distinguishing features set the Aymara peasantry of the yungas apart from the local gentry and the dominant national culture of Bolivia. In some cases the distinctions were clear and objective; in others, they were relative, so that an outsider might not have agreed with locally accepted criteria. Unfamiliarity with Spanish was an insurmountable barrier to many peasants, and almost none of those who achieved some fluency was able to overcome the distinctive Aymara accent. The general *indio* physique still exists as an important stereotype, despite the fact that some adult Indians have been able to "become" mestizos for decades. Until the 1940's the peasants of this area also had a distinctive manner of dress: a heavy broad-brimmed straw hat with tiny round crown, short tight trousers of homespun wool and a tight waistcoat of the same material, bare feet and a bowl-type haircut are generally agreed on by peasants and townsmen alike as having been identifying features.

Indians normally lived in small thatched huts of adobe or wattle-and-daub, scattered through the countryside. They were generally thought to be "ignorant," and this was attributed as much to "Indian blood" as to the actual absence of schools. Nominally Catholic, they were more influenced by their indigenous religion. Occasional fiestas provided frenetic contrast with workaday drudgery, but they were not integrated with a socioreligious hierarchy as was the case among the highland Aymara. Class differences were constantly reinforced by the quasi-feudal tradition—a peasant of any age could be called *yocalla* ("boy," in demeaning, condescending sense) and sent on an errand by anyone of the landholding group; they in turn were addressed by peasants, with hat in hand, as *tata* ("father").

Kin ties among the peasants were important, emphasizing patrilineal descent, monogamy, systematic respect for elders, a preference for patrilocal residence. Because surnames were virtually all names of animals and natural objects, it is tempting to speculate about these as possible survivals of a pre-Columbian system of totemic patrilineages, but there is no indication that the ayllu, so important on the altiplano, was a meaningful social unit in this region in the twentieth century.

Division of labor by sex was marked, with women's only agricultural contribution being collaboration in the coca and coffee harvests. Nearly all Aymara were farmers; a few skillful *yatiris* (approximately, "medicine men") served as diviners and curers, combining herbal and magical techniques; others learned rudimentary masonry, carpentry, or tinsmithing, but few other occupational opportunities were open to them.

Conflicts between peasants were usually resolved by the landlord, autocrat of his hacienda; the foreman or administrator would adjudicate in his absence. The dominant whites and mestizos always mediated between the peasants and the world beyond the hacienda. In retrospect, this brokerage role is justified by the gentry as benevolent paternalism; it is roundly condemned by the peasants as having been a systematic limitation of their horizons.

In short, the Aymara peasants participated in a distinctive local sociocultural system which provided no direct access to regional or national institutions of education, government, or commerce. Even when the social reformers of the MNR acceded to power in 1952, no one would have been so bold as to predict the degree to which the sociocultural system of the peasantry was to be opened and the changes in ways of thinking and acting that have in fact occurred. One of the principal initial and continuing agencies of change has been the peasant syndicate.

Organization of the Movement

We have already touched on the controversy over who introduced syndicalism, the first peasant movement among the Aymara in the yungas. Although no one has yet dealt systematically with the wealth of available primary source material, it appears that the groundwork was laid in the early 1950's by representatives of the MNR, who toured the area under the auspices of the party and the newly created Ministry of Peasant Affairs. This conclusion is based on the remarkably consistent testimony of townspeople and former landlords, supported by two syndical leaders —the only peasants who admit to remembering the events; it is both plausible and consistent with secondary published material and statements by MNR officials.[23]

Ideology, Objectives, and Means

The labor organizers (called *agitadores* by the conservatives) in this region were mostly young middle-class university students, some of whom may have had deep altruistic motivations about liberating the peasants but all of whom found this work a steppingstone to positions of greater responsibility within the MNR. In a country like Bolivia, where

[23] Such detailed specification of sources is cumbersome, but it is necessary in order to allow evaluation of historical "data" from the oral tradition.

the incumbent party has traditionally monopolized government, such partisan "legwork," difficult as it was, paid high dividends. Miners sympathetic to the MNR and with union experience also served in this capacity. The few syndicates in the area that are said to have been founded by agents from POR still showed their more extreme leftist militancy in 1965.

But how were peasants actually organized into syndicates? If the Aymara were as closed and suspicious as they have been generally characterized, the outsiders must have had to offer significant inducements to enlist their cooperation. Eloquent visions of greater freedom, wealth, and progress, even if expressed in their own Indian language, were not enough reason for them to support a political party of which they knew nothing and to commit themselves to constituting a formal organization unlike anything in their previous social structure. Concrete and immediate rewards were used.

It is difficult to imagine more concrete and immediate rewards than *cupos,* coupons providing discounts of up to 93 per cent on certain price-supported goods or access to extremely scarce goods. For example, when sugar cost 800 Bs. per pound, it could be had at any store for only 50 Bs. and a *cupo;* for a while, meat was available only to those who had *cupos.* In the postrevolution period of chronic food shortage and galloping inflation, such perquisites were valuable to peasants whose own production had suffered (and whose small cash income had been cut off for reasons described in the concluding section), and who no longer held access to hacienda commissaries, which had been discontinued.

At the outset, firearms and ammunition that had been taken from the armed forces were given to the peasants. In the yungas, Indian–white relations had never been as strained as in the highlands, where intercaste resentment occasionally flared into open revolt even before the MNR revolution. Although the small group of landlords had been dominant, there was less deep antagonism, so peasants did not drive the landlords off the haciendas, raid and vandalize the towns, or systematically terrorize whites and mestizos, as did newly formed peasant militias in many other regions. Rifles were valued, however, for use in hunting deer, boar, and other game as a supplement to farming, and also as symbols of new status, since Indians had previously been forbidden to carry firearms.

Another significant contrast with the altiplano is the timing of syndical organization in the yungas. It is apparent in terms of dispersed settlement pattern, limited means of transportation, shortage of personnel, and a number of other factors, that the organizers—or agitators—could not effectively cover the country in less than several years. The first syndicates in the region around Coroico seem to have been organized early in 1954. By that time militant syndicalism had already been effective in the areas of denser peasant population. Peasant syndicates had driven out the landlords, supported the distribution of land among former *colonos,* and opened channels for partisan patronage on the altiplano and in the temperate valleys; therefore it was credible when a syndicate was proposed in the yungas as a sort of peasant land corporation—a corporate entity for the principal purpose of reallocating hacienda lands to members. The complicated procedures for administration of agrarian reform need not concern us in detail here,[24] but it is important to understand a few aspects of the cumbersome organization in relation to objectives and means of this peasant movement.

The legislative basis for peasant syndicates was not spelled out in the agrarian reform law or in related decrees. Actually, the section dealing with peasant syndicates says only: "The peasant syndical organization is recognized as a means of defending members' rights and conserving social conquests. Peasant syndicates should intervene in the execution of the agrarian reform. They may be independent or affiliated." [25]

What happened in practice was that the *colonos* of a hacienda would form a syndicate—following guidelines of the organizers from La Paz— and the secretary-general would file with the local agrarian judge a *demanda* ("petition") for reallocation of land. Under the agrarian reform law, all *latifundios* (defined in Article 12 as "extensive rural properties which remain unexploited or deficiently exploited by the extensive system, with antiquated instruments and methods which allow waste of human effort") were subject to total expropriation, and *colonos* were to receive title to their *sayañas* or equivalent areas. Provision was made for communal plots, commons for grazing livestock, school areas, and other details to be worked out on an *ad hoc* basis by the agrarian judge and topographer on the site, so that specifications for the disposition of each property were unique—and subject to revision at several stages in the progress of the claim. Peasants had to pay for mapping, preparation of the brief, transportation and per diem for the judge and his assistant, as well as miscellaneous fees, honoraria, bribes, and other costs, merely to get the case on the docket in La Paz. Then it still had to be shepherded through a

[24] Cf. Casto Ferragut, "La reforma agraria boliviana: Sus antecedentes, fundamentos, aplicación y resultados," *Revista interamericana de ciencias sociales,* II, No. 1 (1963), 78–151; Heath *et al., op. cit.*

[25] *Decreto ley* 03464 of August 2, 1953: Article 132.

long and complex process of successive hearings and reviews before they could lay any legal claim to the land. In such a situation, it would not have been easy to convince them of the feasibility of forming syndicates unless they already had considerable confidence in achieving success.

The earliest *demandas* for expropriation and reallocation of hacienda lands in the area of Nor Yungas were filed early in 1954, by which time a significant portion of the haciendas in more densely populated regions had already been effectively given over to the former *colonos*. This early land reform elsewhere was often accomplished by illegal or extralegal means; it was also possible under the law that provides for provisional reallocation by the local agrarian judge after a single hearing, although costly and time-consuming litigation has continued so that some cases are still not finally resolved more than twelve years later. In short, the Aymara of the yungas knew, even before the organizers arrived, that syndicates had actually secured land for Aymara in other areas. They got such information by radio, hearsay, and personal contacts.

Although the syndicates were constituted primarily as means of securing title to land, they gradually came to serve other functions as well. The syndicates were effective organizations for political socialization and indoctrination by a small cadre skilled in demagoguery and able to channel small-scale patronage.[26] In those rare instances when an unusually dynamic and effective peasant leader was encountered, he was often taken to La Paz for brief indoctrination in MNR partisanship, after which his syndicate would become also a political command post (*comando*), supporting the MNR and damaging the opposition in a variety of ways.

Such support was expressed in occasional demonstrations, especially at critical times when a show of force was requested. The Aymara peasants of the yungas were less called on for this than were peasants nearer the major cities, but even they would join demonstrations in La Paz on crucial occasions. A messenger from party headquarters would come (by public transportation, hitchhiking on trucks, or walking, as best he could, where other means were not available) and relay the request to a local leader. By sounding the *pututu*, the traditional Aymara animal-horn alarm trumpet, he would quickly summon his constituency and alert neighboring groups to whom runners would carry details. With weapons, flags,

[26] My discussion deals with the syndicates that are loyal to the MNR party, which comprise over 90 per cent of those in the region. The few syndicates that are generally considered communistic (none is avowedly so) have very few members and are virtually ostracized by the others. It is unfortunate that I was unable to get comparable data on the supposedly leftist minority.

and sometimes even signs they had been given but could not read, the peasants would crowd onto trucks—as soon as some could be hired—and race to La Paz where their "*Vivas*," weapons, and sheer numbers often intimidated the opposition. On such occasions, the leader would be reimbursed for the truck rental and given a standard sum (usually Bs. 12,000, or $1.00 in U.S. currency) per man; about half of this fee would be passed on to the individual peasant as per diem, and many complained (confidentially, but not publicly) about the cost to them in terms of lost working time.

Similar arrangements prevailed on partisan holidays, when truckloads of peasant syndicates loomed large in show-of-force parades. Most peasants in 1965 agreed with the man who told me:

It's a relief not to have to go to La Paz more than say, 4 or 5 times a year, one or two days at a time. In the early days of the revolution we went 2 and 3 times a month, sometimes staying a full week. The party was in danger and we had to defend the achievements of the revolution. But it was hard. Women can not do the work in the fields. There was no opportunity to cultivate our plots. There was no production. Too much politics! It's better now—we ought to attend to our work and not play politics. The soil is our politics.[27]

Sometimes demonstrations were called for at the local level, too. The only incident approaching intercaste violence in this region occurred long after the revolution and was directed not against mestizos or whites as such, but against a group of young townsmen who were supporters of FSB (Falange Socialista Boliviana), the principal rightist party opposing MNR and generally identified with the dispossessed oligarchy. While six Falangists were returning to Coroico after a secret meeting with the head of their party, their truck was ambushed by forty peasants using rifles, machine guns, mortars, and grenades. The fact that no one was killed suggests that this may have been a symbolic gesture of warning rather than an outright attack. Similarly, about thirty peasants from that syndicate also marched on the manor house of a neighboring former hacienda, headquarters of a leftist-dominated syndicate with which they still have an unresolved boundary dispute, but they retreated after a three-hour skirmish in which about one hundred rifle shots were exchanged but no one was injured. Less dramatic partisan demonstrations include putting up MNR posters, or tearing and smearing those of the opposition; painting

---

[27] This and subsequent unacknowledged quotations are sentiments expressed by the people of Nor Yungas.

"MNR" conspicuously on walls, or defacing the initials similarly posted by other parties; staging big receptions (with bowers of flowers and abundant food and drink) for visiting party leaders, and menacing opposition visitors to the region.

The amount of time, energy, and apparent affect invested in partisan political activities suggests that there may be a profound ideological commitment on the part of the peasants. On this point, the data are equivocal. Many peasant supporters of MNR still fervently proclaim their support of the party, their devotion to Victor Paz (who, they feel, gave them the land), and their undying gratitude for the social revolution that gave them the vote, land reform, greater access to education, and a sense of national participation that they had not had before. They say this usually in standard catch phrases that they have heard at every public demonstration; but sometimes they also say it, haltingly, in their own words, even though they have been critical of their local leaders. On the other hand, even the staunchest supporter of MNR sometimes complains about the extent to which politics can interfere with farming. Agriculture is not only a livelihood but also a highly valued activity for most of these Aymara peasants who still never drink anything without the *ch'alla*, a ritual spilling of a small quantity in honor of Pachamama, the bountiful earth mother. It is my impression, based on massive anecdotal data too fragmentary to recount in detail, that most of the peasants with whom I dealt have a profound appreciation for the libertarian stance of MNR, and are grateful that they are, in their own words, "becoming human beings" after years of discrimination as subhuman *"indios" or "indiobrutos."* These same peasants, however, are ignorant of the history of the party, and even the few who can read know nothing of the writings of party spokesmen. They are vehement in their opposition to FSB, but most cannot formulate their rationale for this any more explicitly than to identify the Falangists as the former landlords.

The actual activities of the syndicates are varied and include far more than land claims and political demonstrations. Often these activities overlap with the jurisdiction of pre-existing formal institutions. For example, the syndicates and not the courts have supplanted the landlord in resolving conflicts between peasants. This applies not only to informal accusations of petty theft or minor assault but even to such institutionalized differences as divorce. Such conflict resolutions do not have the legal force of orthodox court procedures, but they are often respected locally nevertheless. The syndicates also mediate in cases of inheritance, land exchange, and so forth, despite the fact that they have had no official legal jurisdiction since dissolution of the *Juntas Rurales,* short-lived rural land courts of the mid-1950's. Even the peasants acknowledge that formally structured courts in the provincial capital are already supplemented by a chief of police and a *subprefecto* (sheriff), who dispense Solomon-like justice quickly and more cheaply. Peasants believe, however, that within the formal official system "justice belongs to the rich," so they rarely subject themselves to its costs and delays, and hesitate to lay themselves open to the indignities and abuses that they still frequently suffer from white and mestizo townsmen, including judges and other public officials. More often they seek to resolve their conflicts within the extra-official and relatively informal system of the syndicate, which usually includes a secretary of justice.

Another important kind of syndical activity is public works projects. On many of the former haciendas peasants pool their labor to build schools, and often they even hire teachers paid by special assessments (*cuotas*) when the authorities decline to assign government-paid teachers. The self-conscious concern with education is deep and pervasive in contemporary peasant life; in the words of one articulate spokesman:

The landlords took advantage of our grandfathers, our fathers, and us because we were ignorant. Now our sons must never suffer the abuses of slavery, because they know enough. The accomplishments of the revolution of April [1952] are of the utmost importance—there are no more Indians; we are becoming human beings! But the *real* revolution—the establishment of a completely new order based on social justice—that must be based on the education of the masses.

Other public works projects include the installation of water systems, the building and maintenance of roads, bridges, and trails, the construction of football fields or of plazas, and occasionally the construction of a first aid station (*puesta sanitaria*).

Syndicates are involved not only in law, education, and public works, but also in economics. One of the most popular and inaccurate myths concerning Indians in highland Latin America is their supposed predilection for communal cooperation. It appears that urban nationals have accepted this as uncritically as have foreigners, and many ambitious development plans have failed because they were based on this unfounded assumption. Contrary to the expectation—and explicit intentions—of those who fostered the syndicates, few have become cooperatives in any meaningful way, although many have become so in name and thereby enjoy certain advantages with respect to taxation. Although they are by no means communalistic, as is often assumed, this is not to say that the Aymara of the yungas are totally uncooperative. The *aini*, the traditional pattern of reciprocal labor exchange that used to be restricted to the extended family, now sometimes involves most of the members of a syndicate. Similarly, cooperation of other kinds has been taught as a crucial tool in effecting the peasants' common goals. They early learned, from their organizers and from the dramatic example of miners and other unionized workers, that there is power in numbers when they stand united. One of the most dramatic illustrations of this power, without official authority, is the case of the 25-pound *arroba*. In Coroico, the provincial capital, most of the mestizos and whites are *rescatadores* whose income derives primarily from buying and selling coffee. Until recently, these middlemen enjoyed a dual profit—on weight as well as price. The *arroba* of coffee they bought from peasants weighed 32 pounds; the *arroba* they sold at a higher price to dealers in La Paz weighed only 29. Both peasants and *rescatadores* had long been aware of this, but at a provincial congress of syndicates in March of 1965 the peasants resolved to lessen profits for the brokers. In speeches which repeatedly and eloquently stressed the peasants' participation in world culture, several local leaders sounded an appeal for standard weights. "The *arroba* here should be 25 pounds, as it is everywhere else. We are human beings just as are the French, the Spaniards, the Peruvians, the Africans, and others all through the world," they said. Within two months, the 25-pound *arroba* was used throughout the countryside. Once members of the congress had adopted such a resolution, it was enforced by threat of a sellers' strike. Their rallying cry was, "In unity there is strength." To reinforce this moral imperative among themselves, an honor system was imposed whereby peasants selling "a heavy *arroba*" would be fined Bs. 30,000 (about $4.20) for the first offense and progressively more for successive offenses, with 10 per cent of the fine going to the informer. This extralegal system of sanctions served effectively throughout the 1965 harvest despite complaints by the middlemen. Instituting the 25-pound *arroba* constituted an enormous achievement for the peasants in symbolic terms; in economic terms, it was a hollow victory because the price paid by the *rescatadores* was lowered proportionately.

When former president Hernán Siles, then leader of the MNR, arrived at the same congress, he urged peasants to keep their weapons—contrary to national directives—and to prepare for defensive action against the threat of suppression by the military, who had just recently ousted the MNR. Local syndicate leaders then took the initiative in planning a chain-reaction display of white flags to signal mobilization, in which peasants were to take arms, block the sole highway, and await orders. An emergency table of organization was devised by the peasants, including succession through five levels of leadership. All of this was done quickly and completely indpendently, with no directives from outside. Clearly, these are not country bumpkins being manipulated by urban politicians, but clever fighters devising effective strategies in terms of realistic assessments of the opposition's likely tactics, strengths, and weaknesses.

A variety of other apolitical activities occur among the peasant syndicates. Among the most widespread is soccer, which is enjoyed as a spectator sport with frequent intersyndical competition. In a few syndicates, teachers offer night courses in Spanish and in reading and writing; such courses are well attended, by women as well as men. Occasionally, a first aid kit and some medicines are kept for use, at cost, by syndicate members. Although there is no formal program of social security, orphans and the aged are usually cared for by kinsmen, but in a few instances when there were no relatives on the former hacienda, such individuals were informally adopted by neighbors within the syndicate. Occasionally, an imaginative and energetic agricultural extension agent takes advantage of the syndical organization in order to reach peasants more efficiently with demonstrations, films, and other educational services. A program to foster credit unions for peasants was being initiated by Franciscan missionaries in 1965, and they felt hopeful of prospects for working through the syndical organization. At the same time USAID (U.S. Agency for International Development) had offered to support the establishment of a cooperative for processing and selling coffee, and both the English consultant and the Peace Corps volunteer who were trying to enlist peasant support felt it was appropriate to work through syndicates.

Other means by which peasant syndicates could serve their members are often discussed, more by leaders than by the rank and file. For example, not only outsiders talk about the potential value of cooperatives; an important aspect of MNR policy was to foster cooperatives, by exhortation and by preferential taxation. Syndical leaders throughout the yungas agree that the peasant economic situation could be strengthened by the introduction of cooperatives for buying staple goods and necessities, and for selling agricultural produce.[28] In no instance, however, had this ideal been translated into action.

---

[28] This "agreement" is spontaneous expression of the view in response to open-ended questioning about feasible new directions for syndical action. It is noteworthy that this is *not* a reflection of the investigator's opinion.

The Aymara, like all Bolivians, were given the vote early in the MNR incumbency. Electoral manipulation was so blatant that wry jokes were made about "one hundred and ten per cent democracy" because local returns were often unanimously in favor of MNR, with votes totaling more than the population. Nevertheless, the symbolic value of the vote, and of the associated campaigning by political candidates among peasant syndicates, cannot be overestimated.

To some extent, the ideology and objectives of peasant syndicates are uniform throughout Bolivia.[29] Although the means chosen for the expression of ideology and the realization of objectives vary among regions and even among individual syndicates, there is considerable uniformity in this respect among the MNR-oriented syndicates in the yungas. One of the factors contributing to this uniformity is the organizational structure of the syndical movement.

Organizational Structure

To effect even minimal reform in a quasi-feudal system, it is necessary to create new social institutions. After the revolution of 1952, the peasantry on the former haciendas were often linked to each other only as distant neighbors and as former coworkers of a dispossessed employer. The landlord and foreman who had been the coordinators, decision-makers, and brokers usually left the community, so that leadership and organization were minimal until the syndicates emerged as effective institutions, based on new kinds of authority and explicitly oriented toward a new set of goals that could be subsumed under the novel rubric of peasant welfare. Although the syndicates were unlike anything seen by most yungas peasants before, they were not a unique social invention. Their organizational structure is very similar to that of the miners' unions, lending further support to the majority view that miners familiar with patterns of industrial labor organization probably played an important role, together with students, in the founding of peasant syndicates.

There are several plausible reasons for the miners' involvement in the peasant movement. Many of the miners worked only occasionally in the mines and remained essentially peasants in outlook, hoping eventually to return to their homes in farming villages. Furthermore, the Bolivian Labor Federation (Central Obrera Boliviana, COB) was controlled by Juan Lechín, a former miner and one of the left-wing leaders in the MNR revolution. COB was at times allied with POR, and for a while even

[29] See note 26 above.

powerful in the unusual institution of *cogobierno,* a sharing of political offices by the MNR as incumbent party and COB as the constituency of labor. COB, like MNR, was also interested in organizing the masses, and the miner-peasants were a valuable link between syndically-oriented political leaders and the peasants in the countryside.

The legislative basis for peasant syndicates was not enacted by MNR, and the agrarian reform law made only passing mention of them.[30] Their ideological militancy is implied in Article 126 ("The peasant community differs from the syndicate as follows: the former is not involved in the class struggle beyond the locality . . ."), and their purposes are briefly stated in Article 132 ("a means of defending members' rights and preserving social conquests . . . should intervene in the Agrarian Reform.").

The organizational structure of peasant syndicates is apparently derived from the model offered by industrial labor unions. Regardless of size, each syndicate is supposed to have a directorate of about twelve named officers; there are instances of small syndicates in which each member holds an office and some have more than one.

The secretary-general (*secretario general*) is the head of the syndicate, and is usually the only individual empowered to act on behalf of the syndicate as a corporate entity. As such, he initiated and followed up claims for reallocation of hacienda lands under agrarian reform. In this connection, such officers often had to travel frequently to La Paz in order to lobby for expeditious processing of their claims, to oppose counter-claims by the landlord or by outsiders who wanted to usurp lands, and to carry out other duties. Transportation, per diem expenses while away from home, fees, and bribes to bureaucrats were immediate costs, apart from the loss of time that interfered with their normal economic activities. Even after the issuance of land titles, these men often continue to lobby on behalf of their constituents—asking USAID for water pipe, seeking a teacher from the Ministry of Peasant Affairs, soliciting establishment of a first-aid station or a road. They must also attend meetings of larger organizations with which their syndicate is affiliated, such as provincial and departmental federations. Secretaries-general unanimously protest that they accepted the office and perform the tasks from a sense of social duty, although it is costly to them. By contrast, townspeople unanimously decry the leaders' supposed exploitation of their membership, presuming that they get rich on dues, bribes, and occasional special assessments. Detailed cost accounting over a long period would be re-

---

[30] *Decreto ley* 03464.

quired in order to evaluate these conflicting views fully, but my impression—based on a greater familiarity with the actual situation than most local whites or mestizos have—is that the exploitative secretaries-general are slightly in the minority, although their abuses are sometimes gross enough to eclipse the quiet altruistic activities of a few others. The extent and quality of their service is as varied as the personalities of the several secretaries-general, but it is probably safe to say that nearly half seem to be profiting economically from their positions; almost as many break even; and only a few are losing money on the job (notably, they enjoy no special respect for not profiteering). What is perhaps more important is that the rank and file members generally feel they are getting their money's worth, and all agree that the secretary-general performs many valuable and difficult services.

Quite apart from representing the syndicate elsewhere, the secretary-general also has considerable responsibility on the former hacienda. On those extremely few properties where the landlord is still in residence (having lost to reallocation all *sayañas*, and some other land for a school, soccer fields, etc., but retaining a small area immediately adjoining the manor house), the secretary-general usually is nominal foreman on the landlord's property and so earns a small salary. In some instances, by contrast, the secretary-general has been able to drive out the landlord by forbidding peasants to work for him. The secretary-general also oversees public works projects. He keeps track of those who have fulfilled their *faena*, and serves as foreman throughout the work. He must also provide hospitality to visiting secretaries-general and to other distinguished visitors. And any outsider attempting to gain effective entree into the community would be impolitic not to explain his mission first to the secretary-general, whose local authority is so great that he is often called on to act as judge (although he has no legal power with the official judicial hierarchy).

In short, the secretary-general is a "broker," [31] playing a crucial role as intermediary between his constituents and other sociocultural systems. Ideally, therefore, he should speak Spanish; most of those in the yungas do. He should also be a fairly articulate and dynamic person; many of them are. Although the secretary-general has power in many domains, it is by no means unlimited. In sharp contrast with the townsmens' stereotyped idea of them, there are only a few peasant leaders who have become *caciques*, or despotic autocrats. On the contrary, major decisions are

[31] Eric R. Wolf, "Aspects of Group Relations in a Complex Society: Mexico," *American Anthropologist*, LVIII, No. 6 (1956), 1065–1078.

usually submitted to the rank and file, although support is often achieved through demagogic oratory rather than studied debate. The peasants and their leaders speak proudly of the new democratic processes exemplified in regular syndicate meetings and in occasional special open forums (*cabildos abiertos*), although the opposition was shouted down in most of the few occasions I witnessed in which there was not absolute unanimity.

In some instances, a secretary-general also plays an important political role beyond the syndicate. In the yungas, peasants have not been elected or appointed to public office as have a few peasants from other regions. Nevertheless, a secretary-general may also be head of the local unit of MNR and have influential contacts in the party and in various ministries. Usually he is also an officer in a larger regional association of syndicates, and an enterprising man can make political capital out of the fact that he can muster a large number of men and an even larger number of votes.

Second in rank within a syndicate is the secretary of relations (*secretario de relaciones*), who is like a vice secretary-general and stands in for his leader whenever directed to do so. He appears to have no specific duties, but is kept busy attending to varied syndical business during the secretary-general's frequent absences.

Other offices vary considerably from syndicate to syndicate. Usually a recording secretary (*secretario de actos*) is supposed to keep minutes of the meetings, but even when a literate person is available there is rarely anyone who is conscientious about what most peasants consider a meaningless exercise. A secretary of justice (*secretario de justicia*) may act as judge in resolving minor internal disputes. In some syndicates, he is kept busy; in others, this is essentially an honorific position and it is the secretary-general who adjudicates. If there is a secretary of roads (*secretario de vialidad*), he may be totally inactive, or he may work hard mustering labor, equipment, and outside aid in building or maintaining roads, trails, bridges, and other aids to transportation. Sports play a strikingly large role in the weekly lives of these peasants, and a *secretario de deportes* usually organizes and manages the local soccer team, gets and cares for equipment, and arranges matches with neighboring syndicates. Most syndicates also have a treasurer (*secretario de hacienda*) who collects dues and occasional special assessments, keeps the funds, and makes payments, through the secretary-general. Usually the man in this position, like the recording secretary, is literate.

The high value placed on education is sometimes in competition with the need for labor in the fields. If a former hacienda has a school and teacher it may also have a *secretario de educación* as combination truant officer and one-man PTA. An ideal *secretario de agricultura* would function as an agricultural extension agent; in reality, this is often only a title with little meaning. The status of *secretario de ganadería*, where it occurs, is similarly devoid of duties because peasants in this region have almost no livestock and give minimal care to those animals they do own. A *secretario de higiene*, where designated, should keep a stock of medicines, attend to minor ills, and get medical help for syndicate members who need it. Other kinds of welfare assistance are occasionally dispensed by a *secretario de beneficiencia*, although the office is more often meaningless or nonexistent. Similarly, even the most effective *secretario de propaganda* offers publicity in only the most limited sense—by notifying members in advance of a meeting.

Several such secretaries constitute the directorate of any syndicate. There is little competition for syndical office at the local level, and secretaries often serve until they ask to be relieved. Sometimes elections are held annually, and re-election for several successive terms is common. Positions within the syndicate are not ranged in any particular hierarchy of prestige, and there is no standard sequence of progression. It would be inappropriate to consider the syndical organization as comparable in any significant way to the civil and religious hierarchy traditionally so important in the social organization of many highland Indian communities.

Individual syndicates are often linked in increasingly large assemblies of syndicates. The peasants of each former hacienda comprise a syndicate, usually named after the hacienda, although in most instances they continue to live in their dispersed homesteads. Some neighboring syndicates are grouped into *subcentrales*, on the basis of proximity, mutual interests, and the organizational predilections of *unos cuantos vivos* ("a few sharp guys") who try to gain some personal political or economic advantages by virtue of their leadership over numbers of peasants. Each *cantón* (the smallest administrative unit in Bolivian government, approximately comparable to a U.S. township) is usually also the seat of a *central*, and the *centrales* are incorporated into a Federación Provincial de Sindicatos Campesinos de Nor Yungas. Beyond that, the provincial *federaciones* are, in turn, grouped into departmental *federaciones*, and ultimately into a *confederación nacional*.

This bureaucratic hierarchy looks simple, and there is, in fact, considerable congruity between the ideal pattern I have described and the real pattern I observed—but, as always, exceptions prove the rule. For example, the seat of the *federación provincial* is not in the provincial capital; it, together with the Central de Cruz Loma, is located in a new community that is not yet recognized as a legal political entity. Cruz Loma is a settlement that has grown up over the past five years around a *núcleo escolar,* a regional school built by the Ministry of Peasant Affairs. Although it has no official status, Cruz Loma is the richest and most powerful peasant community in the region. It is also the seat of peasant justice for the entire province, and its leaders could sometimes make their voices heard in the ministries in La Paz until the MNR was overthrown in November, 1964.

It would not be appropriate in this context to describe in detail the individuals who play key roles in the political and economic competition for status, power, and wealth that characterizes these large-scale systems. It is important, however, to note briefly a few of the general characteristics, in both positive and negative terms, that relate to some of the theoretic propositions set forth by Henry A. Landsberger.[32] For example, syndical leaders are local Aymara peasants—not people from outside the region or from the provincial town-dwelling artisan or commercial middle class. Most are men of little schooling, with only a rudimentary command of Spanish. Furthermore, many do not fit with the old stereotypes of leadership—they include an exceptionally high proportion of unmarried men (single and widowed); many are unusually young for leadership, in traditional Aymara terms (i.e., they are in their mid-30's); and they are outspoken and willing to "face up to" the white man on his own ground.

Allies and Enemies

The partisanship of the MNR-affiliated syndicates was vividly demonstrated in a provincial congress early in 1965, five months after that party had been deposed by a military junta. President Paz had gone into exile, and the popular press was active in discrediting both the party and its individual members for abuses of power and dishonesty. Almost every speaker at the meeting, however, prefaced his remarks with a statement such as this:

Peasant syndicalism must be apolitical. We are concerned with the land and with out work, and can't be bothered with politics. . . . But we must recognize that it was the MNR that gave us our land. It was the MNR that gave us syndicates as a means of fighting for our liberty, defending ourselves against oppression, abolishing serfdom, and making ourselves human beings.

With only minor variations, this became almost a litany.

[32] See Chapter 1.

It is noteworthy that former President Siles, successor to MNR leadership, joined the peasants later that weekend when they marched peacefully into the provincial capital and held a rally on the church steps, reaffirming their commitment to the MNR. Their gesture was defiant in a dual sense at that time. The incumbent government was a military junta, ostensibly apolitical, and the town was viewed (appropriately) as a center of Falangist sentiment. There was no violence, but the peasants came away feeling they had effectively intimidated the townspeople, who had listened quietly to the strongly anti-Falangist speeches and not replied. It was after this demonstration that Siles told the syndicate leaders to defy the junta's order to give up their arms, and plans were made for defense by guerrilla tactics if the peasants should be attacked.

Militant violence by peasant groups has remained relatively rare in the yungas, especially in comparison with the situation on the northern altiplano and the Cochabamba Valley. Nevertheless, it is clear that the peasants think of armed force as a reasonable and effective means of achieving just goals and as a necessary means of defense against expected aggression. A noisy but harmless skirmish may also be a dramatic way of expressing a group's dissatisfaction, as in the cases cited above, where an MNR syndicate ambushed a truckload of Falangists and the same syndicate attacked a neighboring supposedly Communist-dominated syndicate.

Political partisanship is relative, and support of MNR is linked with opposition to other parties. Although there were eighteen political parties in Bolivia in 1965 and MNR had been ousted from power, it still had majority support in most regions. Among the others, only the Falangists (FSB) commanded any significant number of followers. The aims and memberships of these parties are vastly different, and there is considerable justification for the peasant notion that "the Falange is the party of the oligarchy." Former landlords, merchants, and other members of the bourgeoisie appreciate the strong elitist bent of FSB, and decry MNR as having "given the country to the Indians," and fostered "a constant state of anarchy."

MNR lost the reins of national government in November, 1964, when the vice-president led a successful military coup and renounced his party affiliation. Following this so-called Revolution of Restoration (*Revolución Restauradora*), there was restiveness, without violence, in the countryside for about two months. The stir was a fear on the part of peasants —and a hope on the part of white and mestizo townsmen—that the junta's accession to office would result in a return to the old quasi-feudal order, undoing the agrarian reform and reversing the other major social changes of the MNR's revolution.[33] Many assumed that the *bota militar* ("military oppression") would again support the landed gentry as had been the case until 1952. This did not occur and a decree dissolving the directorates of syndicates has been universally ignored by peasants in the yungas (and apparently elsewhere as well), so things continued at the local level much as they had before the coup. Channels of communication to officials were blocked, and patterns of patronage will undoubtedly diminish markedly, but there had been little perceptible impact on organization, activities, or attitudes of peasants by the time I left eight months later.

General René Barrientos, leader of the coup (and subsequently elected President), has actively courted the peasants with frequent pronouncements to the effect that "the social conquests of the [1952] revolution are irreversible;" he has engaged in indefatigable "stumping" throughout rural areas, and a convincing show of solidarity with the peasants of his native Cochabamba, with whom he drinks *chicha* and converses in Quechua. To the extent that he has been successful, he has belied the traditional view of the military as an enemy bloc.

In some measure, too, he has attempted to reinforce the idea of the peasantry as a unified bloc. The diversity of the Bolivian population remains a real obstacle to national unity. Linguistic and cultural differences between the Quechua and Aymara are best known and most striking, but there is also appreciable regional variation within each of these groups. Furthermore, there are several other peasant groups throughout the country; even those who do not have distinctive languages and cultures are often intensely regionalistic in their orientations. We have already discussed competition between neighboring syndicates within a single *central;* actual civil war between syndicates around Cochabamba was a bloody fact of life for several years. In view of the profound diversity among local groups, and the enormous potential for conflict among leaders competing for power or wealth, it is surprising that there have not been more frequent and more violent rifts within the peasant class. At the level of rhetoric, there is general consensus that "the peasantry must stand united in defending the accomplishments of the [1952] revolution"; at the level of overt action, there is little effective collaboration beyond the level of the provincial federation.

Another bloc recurrently mentioned in Bolivian oratory is the *rosca* (the oligarchy; literally: "screw," or "thread," as of a drill). It includes the landlords, usurers, businessmen, and others who are said to have "lived

[33] Dwight B. Heath, "Revolution and Stability in Bolivia," *Current History*, XLIX, No. 292 (1965), 328ff.

well on the basis of feudal exploitation of the masses." Class antagonism
was explicit in the MNR revolution and remains important both in theory
and practice; because the dominant socioeconomic class were virtually all
mestizos and whites, and the oppressed peasantry were mostly Indians, the
interclass antagonism is sometimes also phrased in racial terms, with the
misti ("white man") cast as the villain by the Aymara.[34]

In contrast with many other Latin American countries, the Roman
Catholic Church has not been a dominant political or economic institution
in Bolivia for several decades. It is rarely mentioned by peasants in the
yungas, and their nominal Catholicism seems to have little importance.
Before the reform, each hacienda had its chapel and religious patron or
patroness, but priests came from the capital only for local fiestas. Since
the reform the chapels have generally been abandoned, although local
fiestas of both the Christian and the indigenous calendar are still cele-
brated. A few years ago this region became a diocese under the charge of
Franciscan missionaries from the United States; they are generally liked
but hold to some North American standards that are incomprehensible to
the peasants. What little ritual practice there was has almost disappeared
since the new priests refuse to attend fiestas unless they have been invited
for several days' teaching and preaching beforehand. Some of the priests
feel that the peasants are all communists, and cite as proof the fact that an
entire new community was founded at Cruz Loma with no concern for
construction of a church. The North American Franciscans also differ
from their Dutch and Bolivian predecessors in demonstrating a greater
orientation to social service: supporting schools and a health clinic, attempting to establish credit unions, and so forth.

"Foreigners" other than priests tend to be vaguely classed together, and
limited contacts with individuals do little to affect partisan stereotypes,
which are based mainly on charges of economic imperialism. USAID,
however, is viewed as a rich uncle which should provide money, or at
least materials, for a variety of public works projects on request. Similarly
"the authorities" are allies or enemies, more on the basis of party affiliation
than any realistic evaluation of the attitudes of the persons in positions of
authority.

This tendency to deal with blocs or classes of people is balanced by
occasional establishment of particularistic relations with specific individuals, sometimes in violation of the stereotyped relations. For example,

[34] The Negroes who occupy a few of the former haciendas in the yungas interact
little with the Aymara but identify with them as fellow peasants in terms of class
antagonism.

resentment of the *rosca*, former landlords, whites, merchants, and Falangists does not necessarily interfere with a peasant's establishing ties of *compadrazgo* (coparenthood) with a townsman who is all of these. Such cases are commonplace and reflect a fairly clear compartmentalization between relationships based on economic advantage and others where sentiments play a more dominant role. In fact, despite their cherished new freedom, many peasants retain ties with former landlords who are strikingly paternalistic in ways reminiscent of the classic *patrón-peón* relationship. Reasons for this are found in the successes and shortcomings of this peasant movement.

Successes and Shortcomings

No one would deny that Bolivia has undergone a profound transformation since the MNR took power in 1952. On the contrary, it is difficult to comprehend the breadth and depth of changes which have revolutionized the social order. Methods used by the party in effecting change were controversial, but there is no longer any doubt about pervasiveness of change in social structure, and the durability of many innovations seems assured. Whatever new directions may emerge, it is unthinkable that there might be a return to the previous quasi-feudal system. This is not to say that there is no continuity; some striking examples are cited below.

No social revolution can be unqualifiedly good or bad, although the Bolivian experiment has been characterized in both ways. Eager local protagonists of the revolution proclaim that "it has liberated an enormous potentially constructive force. The Indian population was a sleeping giant that only now has awakened and cast off its chains." Opponents lament that, "in order to gain the votes of ignorant Indians, the MNR utterly destroyed the economy of the nation. They offered demagogy, without principles or planning, and the revolution is a total calamity." There is some truth in each of these stands, and, as is so often the case, a fuller truth may lie somewhere between the extremes.

If we speak in terms of "social justice" for the majority, we must favor the MNR and credit it with breaking the back of the old feudal order by emancipating many peasants from traditional economic and social bondage. The peasant masses were not merely admitted to citizenship in 1952; that year marked virtually their induction into the status of human beings, and many have phrased it in just such terms. Peasants are generally proud to have the vote (however flagrant electoral fraud may be) and their own parcel of land (however tiny); even more important appears to be the cherished intangible *dignidad de la persona* ("individual dignity").

Such striking improvement in the status of one portion of the population has, of course, adversely affected that of the other. The "liberation" of the peasant majority could be achieved only at great cost to the landed gentry who had enjoyed the leisure afforded by control over peasant *colonos*. In other areas, long suppressed resentment broke out in physical aggression, murder, rape, and looting, but in the yungas most landlords merely abandoned their properties. In either case, the life-style of the small, formerly dominant group suffered in greater proportion as that of the larger, formerly subordinate group improved.

The power of the *rosca* has been virtually neutralized, and much of their wealth is gone. In fact, most of those individuals who could afford to leave the country did so long ago. In those few areas of militant peasant uprisings, many were fortunate to escape with their lives, and lost everything which had been on their haciendas. Others who salvaged goods or money found these reserves quickly dissipated by the rampant inflation of the early 1950's. Some have made difficult adjustments in merchandizing and other service enterprises; a few continue directing agricultural enterprises; but most have left Bolivia, with no intention of returning.

The redistribution of wealth has been more pervasive in Bolivia than many had expected. It is the urban MNR sympathizers who constitute a conspicuous class of *nouveaux riches*. Political turmoil, galloping inflation, and complex differential exchange rates created a context in which there were abundant opportunities for graft, embezzlement, and other profiteering from public funds on a grand scale. Even most peasants are relatively wealthier now than a decade ago. This is apparent in the prevalence of consumer goods such as bicycles, radios, and accordions, which were virtually unknown before, and in the increase in Western dress and more substantial houses. Furthermore, most peasants appear to be eating more of the produce which they cultivate, even if their diet is no more varied than before. In all of these respects, it is easy to understand why peasants are generally pleased with the 1952 revolution and still are militant in their support of the MNR. Although they are still abysmally poor—not only by North American standards, but in a world perspective—the life of Bolivia's peasants is immensely better than it was before.

The political complexion of Bolivia is still changing, especially since the MNR was unseated in the 1964 revolution. The national army, which had been emasculated early in the MNR revolution, was revitalized and equipped with new weapons and the armed forces assumed control in the Revolution of Restoration. The leader of the junta was elected President in March, 1966, but his rapidly changing cabinets still reflect his military affiliation and support. Within this broad national context, it is worthwhile to evaluate successes and shortcomings of the peasant syndical movement in the yungas both in terms of continuity and discontinuity in the traditional social order, and in economic terms.

It has recently become fashionable for wealthier yungas peasants to own houses in the towns. They buy lots, from individuals or from the town council, at prices ranging to over Bs. 200,000 ($16.70) per square meter. New houses line entire streets in Coripata and Arapata, and the mestizos who previously formed the great majority of the population in these towns complain that they are "being inundated" by peasants. Generally these new houses remain empty during the week; peasants continue to live in dispersed homesteads on the former haciendas and come to town only during weekends and fiestas. Such town houses are usually more modern than the rural ones; cement floors replace dirt; corrugated metal replaces palmleaf thatch as roofing; windows and a second story are commonplace; and even stucco and paint may decorate the outside, strikingly more colorful than the smaller, plain adobe or wattle-and-daub constructions that still predominate in rural areas.

Most of the landlords have also moved to the towns, in fear of peasant retribution for prereform abuses, or in frustration at being unable to get reliable help to continue working the portion of the land consigned to them. For this reason many of the manor houses which were once magnificent villas are falling into ruin; a few are used by the syndicates as school buildings or assembly halls, but even these are not maintained.

It is one of the many ironies of the Bolivian land reform that peasants in the yungas region now generally have access to less land than they did before the reform. Within a hacienda, although all land belonged in a formal sense to the landlord, *colonos* were assigned usufruct rights to *sayañas* (which, in effect, became their own). Such usufruct rights were inherited (usually by the oldest son), and *colonos* were free to dispose of the produce of those plots. Consolidation of dispersed *sayaña* holdings into a single tract—even one with a total area larger than the sum of the plots previously held—is not an advantage in this area of marked ecological variation.

Furthermore, a significant portion of most haciendas remained uncultivated in prereform times, and an enterprising *colono* was usually welcome to use such land if he chose. It is difficult to ascertain how many of them actually did so, but presumably there were a fair number since peasants as well as former landlords usually mention this as one of the fringe benefits of the prereform system. Since agrarian reform divided the haciendas and gave individual peasants title to specific areas, almost no such unclaimed areas are now available within easy access. The recent emergence of transportation as a large-scale industry relates to the degree of participation in the market by peasants, and also affects the value of land in outlying areas.

The yungas region is unusual in Bolivia for having a long history of agricultural production for commercial purposes as well as for subsistence. Coca and coffee continue to be products destined for the market, but new channels of distribution have had to be established. Landlords used to sell the produce from their haciendas to wholesalers and exporters in La Paz; peasants who have virtually monopolized production do not have either the personal contacts or the quantity of goods that would be meaningful to those merchants. It is not surprising, therefore, to find peasants selling their produce to middlemen in the provincial towns, and to find that many of these middlemen were, in fact, landlords. These middlemen call themselves *comerciantes*, but are generally called by others *rescatadores*, a somewhat deprecating term. They profit both from price differences and from wight differences, as described above, and justify this in terms of personalistic relations with their peasant suppliers (*casadores*). The economic differential between buying and selling is termed interest rather than profit; there is some justification for this because the middleman often makes sizable loans to his peasant suppliers during the lean months between harvests, and gets the option on buying their produce but deducts only the value of the loan, without added interest, when the goods are delivered. Middlemen also serve as *compadres* to their clients. When peasants come to town, their *rescatador* should provide the hospitality of food and a place to sleep; they should reciprocate by bringing a few eggs, some fresh fruit, or similar token gift. Occasionally, too, the townsman will provide counsel or some aid if a peasant runs afoul of the law.

In sum, the relationship between a peasant and his middleman is strikingly consistent with the pattern of benevolent paternalism that was the ideal in the days of the haciendas, when a "good" *patrón* did the same things for a "good" *peón*. It should not be surprising to find that, in many instances, former *colonos* are pleased to remain in just such a dependent, secure relationship with their own former landlords. In this respect, there is remarkable continuity in social *organization* (in terms of the roles, or functions of relationships), in spite of considerable change in social *structure* (in terms of the form of status networks within the social system).

In the discussion of ideology, objectives, and means above, the description of syndical activities may have appeared to emphasize social innovations of the peasant movement. It is enlightening, however, to consider some of those activities, too, in terms of new forms serving old functions, or as possible survivals of previous patterns under the jurisdiction of a new institution. For example, when the secretary of justice and/or the secretary-general takes the law into his own hands in adjudicating a case between members of a syndicate, he is not significantly encroaching on the sphere of influence of the sheriff, the police, or the courts, none of which ever really had effective jurisdiction on the haciendas in prereform days. Rather, he is filling the role of the landlord, who used to do the same thing, with no regard for the formal legal institutions of the state. By the same token, public works projects undertaken in the name of the syndicate are more than analogous to the prereform *faena;* they are often identical, called by the same name and performed jointly on Sunday mornings, but now on behalf of the syndicate rather than the hacienda. For that matter, the secretary-general acts very like a prereform *mayordomo* when he oversees the *faena,* or work on property retained by the former landlord. Furthermore, he acts like a benevolent landlord when he serves as broker for his constituents in lobbying for a teacher, a sanitarian, or other form of patronage.

In rare instances, a powerful secretary-general has institutionalized a labor draft whereby members of the syndicate take turns cultivating his crops while he is away, ostensibly on syndical business. Such a pattern of mandatory labor in the fields of another is reminiscent of the *colonos'* obligation to the landlord, which was the primary target of agrarian reform. Less compelling in its similarity to the prereform situation, but still related, is the more common pattern whereby a few syndicate members voluntarily help in the secretary's agricultural work. There is no clear-cut survival of *pongueaje,* the housekeeping obligation of *colonos,* but the role of members' wives in cooking for and serving "visiting firemen" on syndical business is required and unremunerated as was similar work performed for the landlord in prereform days. When secretaries-general speculate enthusiastically about the potential value of instituting buying cooperatives, they cite the very advantages that peasants used to enjoy in the hacienda commissaries.

In short, despite sweeping changes in the forms of social structure instituted by the MNR revolution, there are many instances in the yungas in which aspects of the *patrón-peón* relationship persist virtually unchanged, in functional terms, between former landlords and the peasants who had been their *colonos*. There are also many instances in which a new *patrón-peón* type of functional relationship has been established, with a new form, the syndicate or the secretary-general assuming the dominant paternalistic status formerly held by the landlord, and the peasant continuing in a relatively dependent servile role. But it would be grossly inaccurate to view the syndicates as nothing but new names for haciendas, with absentee landlords now living in the towns as middlemen, or with secretaries-general acting as Aymara-speaking landlords.

Another aspect of the role of syndicates is their serving new functions, some of which are not only discontinuous with prereform patterns but are distinctly and dramatically aggressive against the old order. It is noteworthy, for example, that political socialization is by no means limited to the few dynamic secretaries-general who are effective lobbyists for their own interests and those of constituents. Awareness of and concern for the active role of citizenship has pervaded the syndicates, reshaping the outlook and the lives of many members as well as those of the leaders. At periodic meetings of the syndicates, occasional special open forums, political rallies, and on other occasions, peasants are outspoken in a way that no one would have predicted on the basis of the old Aymara stereotype.

Apparently Luis Antezana was only a little melodramatic when he wrote:

A profound psychological transformation was produced in the peasants when the announcement of the [agrarian] reform was made; they began to walk on their own land and to feel free, as if they were standing on the top of a mountain. They learned to speak in a loud voice, with pride and without fear. . . . The worker of the countryside had been dignified by being given land and liberty in all of its aspects. "*Indio*," a feudal concept, was the serf of an epoch which had disappeared. Today the *campesino* is the equal of anyone. . . . The peasant is a human being capable of receiving instruction, of reaching the University, of being owner of the land he works and making it produce, since the land belongs to him who works it.[35]

Alexander agrees:

This change in the psychology of the Indian was noted by the officials of the Ministry of Peasant Affairs, which was more closely in touch with him than any other branch of the government. Although the peasants who came to present their problems and their requests to the Ministry continued to show

[35] Luis Antezana, *Resultados de la reforma agraria en Bolivia* (Cochabamba, Bolivia: Imprenta Cuenca, 1955), p. 18.

respect for the authorities, they tended to become increasingly insistent in demanding a solution for their difficulties, whatever they might be. They no longer were coming hat in hand to ask favors, but were coming to demand what they now had come to consider their rights.[36]

There are other indications, too, of increasingly sophisticated political activity on the part of peasants. They did and do vote—sometimes a bit too eagerly and too frequently. More important, they have learned to lobby effectively with their demands vis-à-vis those who can best dispense the requested favors. They have learned, that is, to operate within the national political structure, which is bureaucratic in formal terms, but which does not actually function at all according to the classic Weberian criteria of impersonality, specialization, hierarchy, universalism, and regulation.[37] In so doing, the peasants have often bypassed the local white and mestizo authorities in Coroico and gone "over their heads" to higher officials whom they could influence with promises of political support and threats of road blocks and other disturbances.

In mid-April of 1965, when former MNR vice-president Juan Lechín was exiled as leader of a supposed international Communist coup, and the miners bitterly opposed disciplinary measures imposed by the military junta, Aymara peasants remained aloof, although some Quechua threatened to fight on the side of the President, who comes from Cochabamba and literally speaks their language. Then the junta declared all syndicate directorates annulled, ostensibly to oust Communists who had achieved dominance in the mines, and probably also to weaken opposition in general. He appears never to have gotten around to scheduling the promised elections for new slates of officers, even though his position has since been consolidated by constitutional election. But this was a hollow gesture, and the decree—although universally known in the yungas—was universally ignored; when I left the area, there was still no sign that any peasant syndicate had been affected.

It remains to be seen whether—or, more accurately, to what extent— peasant syndicates will persist in years to come. Even if they are dissolved —and that seems highly unlikely—the Aymara of the yungas have already clearly reached a significant degree of political sophistication and participate effectively in social systems that were not only closed, but virtually unknown, to them until recently. Not only are they aware of the state, nation, and political parties as such, but they use their knowledge to

[36] Alexander, *op. cit.*, p. 76.

[37] Adrianne Aron, "Local Government in a Bolivian Community" (paper read at American Anthropological Association meeting, Pittsburgh, Pa., 1966).

achieve their advancement. Although they did not take an active role in any of Bolivia's revolutions to date, they have been significantly affected by the program of politicization which drastically overhauled the Bolivian social order. Increased education and participation in syndicates have produced a generation of politically aware peasants who choose effective home-grown leaders.

Within the discipline of anthropology there is a new school of "ethnoscience." Ethnoscientific investigators claim that their concern with microscopically precise analysis of the details of linguistic and behavioral events is intended to allow them gradually to achieve such a degree of understanding of an alien cultural system that they can operate in it in terms of its own cues, rules, and logic. It seems to me a telling measure of the sophistication of some Aymara peasants that they can do this in the national political system, in the distant city of La Paz, where they were not even allowed to walk on the sidewalks fifteen years ago.

The achievements of the social revolution in 1952 appear to be irreversible, so that land reform, universal suffrage, and political socialization will probably survive subsequent changes in national administration. It is true that some facets of the old social structure survived even such revolutionary upheaval as characterized the MNR incumbency, but they are generally performing new functions. It is also strikingly true that some of the new social institutions play roles virtually indistinguishable from those institutions they violently displaced or supplanted. Probably the greatest break with the past is psychological, and in terms of long range social and economic progress, the most important accomplishment of the peasant syndical movement may be in developing formerly neglected human capital.

5. Chile: A Vineyard Workers' Strike— A Case Study of the Relationship between Church, Intellectuals, and Peasants

HENRY A. LANDSBERGER

Department of Sociology
University of North Carolina at Chapel Hill

PART I: THE EVENTS *

The Strike

The Beginning

On the afternoon of Monday, November 30, 1953, attempts were made by the *inquilinos* [1] of some twenty vineyards surrounding the town of Molina [2] to hand a message to their employer or to his representative. The message advised them that a one day warning work stoppage (*paro de advertencia*) would be called for the following day. The "warning" was intended to force the employers to begin to negotiate seriously over

---

* A fuller description is to be found in chs. 1–5 of Henry A. Landsberger and Fernando Canitrot, *Iglesia, intelectuales y campesinos* (Santiago, Chile: Editorial del Pacífico, 1167). Warmest thanks are due Fernando Canitrot, who shared the field work with me and made drafts of the descriptive section of the book.

[1] *Inquilinos* are the permanent workers attached to farms (*fundos*) in Chile. Unlike day laborers (*jornaleros*), the *inquilino* lives on the *fundo*. He receives a part of his remuneration in kind: not only a more or less modest house but, in particular, a plot of land for his own cultivation and grazing rights for fodder. He works on a year-long contract or, in the case of winegrowing, on a somewhat shorter contract, excluding harvest time, which is paid on a different basis. *Fundos* may be managed by their owners, but more frequently, in the case of vineyards, the owner lives in Santiago and the *fundo* is managed by an *administrador* who usually has rather limited decision-making powers.

[2] Molina, a town of just over six thousand inhabitants in 1952, was and is the administrative center of the department of Lontué, one of three into which the province of Talca is divided. As a department, it had a *gobernador* while the chief representative of the central government for the province as a whole, the *intendente*, was resident in the capital city of the province, also called Talca.

contract demands which had been presented to them and to the official tripartite conciliation boards[3] one month earlier.[4] The farm workers claimed—and the record seems to substantiate—that the employers had, in effect, made the official conciliation and arbitration machinery grind to a halt by such tactics as questioning the signatures of those who had signed the contract demands, requesting postponements of scheduled meetings, not sending their representative to meetings of the conciliation board, and so forth. Impatient with these delaying tactics, the workers and their leaders had decided on a warning strike.

On Tuesday, December 1, the vineyards indeed went untended. That afternoon many of the employers and farm managers were handed a second circular, signed by five persons, including Emilio Lorenzini in his role of Provincial Executive Secretary of ASICH (Acción Sindical Chilean: Chilean Union Action—a Roman Catholic workers' federation). The letter stated that, while some employers had arrived at agreements with their workers, others were not even ready to begin negotiations. ASICH was therefore giving the employers until Monday, December 7, to arrive at a settlement, failing which a regional strike of indefinite duration would be declared by the workers of all *fundos* indicated in the letter.[5]

On Wednesday the workers attempted to return to work only to find themselves locked out by the employers, who claimed that the illegal walkout on the day before had automatically annulled their work contracts. The workers declared an indefinite strike immediately and the two

[3] The Chilean Labor Code in force at the time (Law No. 8811, completely changed in 1967 by Law No. 16,625) made provision for farm workers, whether unionized or not, to present contract demands (*pliegos de peticiones*), provided this was not done during either harvest or sowing, for each of which a minimum of sixty days was set aside. These demands, if not accepted by the employer in a short time, came officially to a tripartite conciliation board composed of a representative of the employers, a workers' representative, and a government nominee. If its attempts to bring the parties to agreement failed, the board was automatically converted into a compulsory arbitration board: that is, it made an award on the basis of agreement by two of its three members, and that award was legally binding on the parties. Agricultural workers did not have the right to strike under any circumstances at any time. See *Codigo del trabajo*, Book III, Titles IV, V, and VI. These titles were added to the *Codigo* by Law No. 8811, July 29, 1947.

[4] Material on dates of presentation of contract demands, nature of demands, workings of the official conciliation machinery, and so forth, were obtained from the archives of the Molina Labor Inspectorate (the local office of the Ministry of Labor).

[5] This and other material was obtained from the Court of Appeals in the city of Talca, filed under "Against Emilio Lorenzini and Others."

sides were openly at war with each other: a minimum of 1,100 vineyard workers in twenty vineyards were idle, perhaps as many as 2,000 *inquilinos* in thirty vineyards.[6]

Reaction in the Capital

The like had never happened before in Chile, and by Thursday the affair was front-page news in most morning and afternoon papers in Chile's capital, Santiago, and the event continued to be headline news for the next four or five days.

The employers did not confine their reaction to locking out their workers. On Wednesday one of their local spokesmen was in touch by telephone with the Minister of the Interior, General Osvaldo Koch, asking him to take steps against the strikers. In particular, the employers asked him to invoke the then famous—or infamous—LDD: The Law for the Permanent Defense of Democracy.[7] The Ministry, in a series of telephone calls and confirmatory telegrams, did indeed instruct the governor of the department to order the detention of the strike leaders and to begin legal proceedings against them. Four of the five leaders, including Lorenzini, were rounded up, held briefly in the police station in Molina, and transferred to Talca prison in the dead of night.[8]

On Thursday afternoon a sizable delegation of employers[9] and their representatives from the Lontué Agricultural Association personally vis-

[6] Minister of Labor, Sr. Oscar Herrera, speaking on the afternoon of Thursday, December 3, as quoted in the Communist newspaper *El Siglo*, Friday, December 4.

[7] Law No. 8987, enacted in 1948 and repealed ten years later. Passed on the initiative of a president who had been elected in 1946 with the help of Communist votes but soon grew tired of his allies, the "LDD" was one of those vaguely drawn statutes to be found in many Latin American countries. They enable the government to hold in custody, to banish or to exile, and to remove from posts of responsibility in trade-unions (as well as dissolve such associations) any individual whom the government considers to be "a threat to internal security," "involved in acts likely to harm the state and community," and so on.

[8] Information obtained from the archives of the Governor's Office in Molina.

[9] The connotation of the appropriate Spanish word "agricultores" cannot, unfortunately, be conveyed in English or American for excellent sociological reasons. "Agricultores" in present day Chile conveys, gently, the idea of generally superior status, in social and power as well as in economic terms, though it does not imply that the person is necessarily a "latifundista," a slightly pejorative term for (overly-) large landholders. The English "employer" conveys only the economic, contractual and not the prestige and power aspect of the role of "agricultor" and its superiority only in that limited sense. The English word "farmer" reaches down into the poorer strata. Precisely because the Spanish "agricultor" does not do so, and because these "agricultores" were politically powerful and not small, neither of these two English words is fully appropriate.

ited the Minister of the Interior [10] to inform him of what they deemed to be the growing climate of agitation and potential violence in the zone, and to request that he take steps to ensure the freedom to work and the personal and material safety of the farmers. The Minister gave instructions that a special detachment of Carabineros [11] be sent from the city of Talca to Molina, some twenty miles distant.

The Strikers

The strike had clearly not been totally unexpected by the local leadership and various contingency plans had been made, some of which were put into operation, others not. An abandoned adobe hall had been rented from a nunnery; during the day, the strikers were confined to it by their leaders, who had also obtained the cooperation of local saloonkeepers not to serve alcoholic beverages to any strikers: all this to avoid incidents and to maintain a good "image." Indeed, work details went to clean and restore the local cemetery to symbolize that laziness was not the cause of the strike.

When news of the strike reached the Santiago headquarters of the ASICH, two leaders with considerable experience in labor problems were immediately sent to Molina. One was Roberto León, an official of the Bank Employees' Union who became, in effect, the strikers' chief negotiator and was involved in all meetings and conversations in the governor's offices throughout Thursday and Friday. The other was Manuel Naranjo, a young but already retired Army captain. His functions were internal: to keep the strikers entertained and out of trouble, to keep Communists from infiltrating, and Carabineros from making arrests. Legally, no one could be arrested while in the temporary hall; hence the strikers were, in effect, prevented from leaving. Also present from Santiago was a Jesuit priest, Fr. Jaime Larrain, who was particularly active in organizing donations of food from local merchants and shopkeepers. He took care, however, to steer clear of the strikers and of the negotiations. Finally there appeared in Molina a young lawyer, Hernan Troncoso, who represented ASICH in Chile's third largest city, the coal and steel center of Concepción. Apart from keeping Santiago—and the Bishop of Talca—informed, which all the others did also, he had the special assignement, given him by the

---

[10] The president of the Sociedad Nacional de Agricultores (SNA) as well as a former member of the lower house of the Chilean Parliament, accompanied representatives of the local agricultural association.

[11] Chile's national, and generally highly respected, police force. There are no local police forces.

Archbishop of Santiago, to look into the facts surrounding a brawl which had recently taken place in the area and had ended in the murder of one peasant by another. The employers had propagated the interpretation that the man had been assasinated for not wishing to belong to the union.

These four individuals—a bank employee, a former military officer, a young lawyer, and a Jesuit priest—replaced the leaders who had been taken into custody and the assistant parish priest who, though nominally chaplain of the union, had in fact been second in importance and influence only to Emilio Lorenzini. On Wednesday evening the priest received orders from the Bishop of Talca to stay in the rectory and have no (further) contact with the strikers. But Bishop Manuel Larraín [12] also instructed him to tell the police, should they try to take him into custody, that the appropriate person to arrest would be the bishop himself since he accepted full responsibility for everything the priest had done up to then.

Several humorous minor incidents marked the strike, some symbolizing the underlying sense of national unity which prevents splits between classes, between police and workers, and between religious denominations, from becoming irreparable in Chile. One occurred when the evidently Catholic-inspired and Catholic-led movement called on a group of Seventh Day Adventists (a tiny band of very timid souls, renowned for their singing) to come and entertain the strikers, which they did. The strikers were asked not to applaud the performance of hymns; they obeyed, and showed their approval by screaming.

Another anecdote concerns a group of jeep-mounted, out-of-town Carabineros who wanted to arrest José X, the last of the five leaders, but did not know what he looked like. They hailed him in the street without being aware of his identity and asked him where they might find José X. Seeing the possibility of a ride home, José told them he would be glad to guide them to X's hamlet if they would let him get into the jeep. Thus he reached his home in record time and in unaccustomed splendor, and before his family could open their mouths, he asked them whether they had seen José X. They apparently grasped the situation and said he had left for town an hour ago. Thereupon the Carabineros let José X get off, turned around, and sped back to Molina. They never caught up with him.

At a more serious level, conversations had taken place in the governor's

[12] Bishop Larraín, for twenty-five years the symbol of progressivism among the higher clergy of Chile and later honored with the presidency of the Latin American Episcopal Commission (CELAM), was tragically killed in an auto accident in 1966. His death was mourned even by the Marxist Left.

offices on Thursday evening between representatives of the employers and the workers, in the presence of the governor and the labor inspector. But while agreement was not ruled out, it was not ultimately reached due to "the intransigent attitude of both sides," as the confidential telegram of the governor to the Minister of the Interior indicated.

It is worthy of note that reporting within the government was throughout quite accurate and undistorted. Earlier telegrams had correctly indicated that only a one-day stoppage had been declared and that the zone was absolutely calm. Later telegrams clearly reported that the employers were locking the workers out. Plainclothes detectives, who for the previous three or four years had been present at the rallies of peasants and at political assemblies and open-air meetings of the regional CUT,[13] had similarly written quite fair accounts including even such subtle interpretations as that lawyer Lorenzini, while using rather violent language, was not seriously attempting to arouse the peasants to acts of violence.

A Crucial Intervention

In Santiago, meanwhile, the top leadership of ASICH became increasingly apprehensive. Ramón Venegas, its President and one of its founders,[14] had known about the contract demands but not about the decision to strike. When the strike broke out he immediately travelled to Molina and became convinced that the strikers would not and could not hold out

[13] Central Única de Trabajadores de Chile: the (then) newly established central labor federation to which the Catholic-led peasants belonged in addition to belonging to ASICH and in which Lorenzini and other leaders held official positions. Being Catholic progressives, there was genuine ground in common between the local Catholic leaders and the essentially Marxist-controlled CUT (in Molina, the Communists were ascendant, in other areas the Socialists). At the same time there was considerable subterranean rivalry and friction which came to the surface during the strike. As soon as the local leaders had been arrested and before the Santiago ASICH leaders arrived to replace them, the local Communists tried to take over. They were foiled by the wife of one of the arrested leaders, herself a leader and temporarily in charge. There were also tales of Communists shutting off the water supply to the strikers and of their "planting" the cook, who then proceeded to spoil the communal beans. This latter story we take with a grain of salt, if we may be permitted an atrocious pun.

[14] ASICH was founded in 1947 by a group of Catholic laymen and a Jesuit priest, Fr. Alberto Hurtado. Its members were individuals and its purpose—except in this case—chiefly that of education and indoctrination of individuals. It was not at this time a trade-union federation in any sense rival to CUT, although it later attempted to become one.

for more than three days, and also that severe reprisals—expulsion from homes, and perhaps even a massacre—were possible.

On Friday morning, therefore, he asked for and was granted an interview with Chile's aging first cardinal, the Archbishop of Santiago, Msgr. José María Caro, with whom he had long been friendly. (Venegas, a highly trained architect, came from a distinguished family.) Propelled also by a telephone call from Bishop Larrain, the Cardinal and Venegas decided to ask for an interview with the President of the Republic, General Carlos Ibáñez. They were given an appointment for later that morning, together with the legal advisor of ASICH, William Thayer.[15]

General Ibáñez, as was his wont, received them rather gruffly and proceeded, in effect, to give them a "dressing down," telling them that law and order would have to be maintained; that the campesinos [16] ought not to have been led astray by agitators; that agricultural production was the life blood of the nation and could not be disturbed, and so on. The Archbishop, quite capable of forthright speech himself, replied in kind. He said that the President was prejudging the facts, that the employers as well as the workers had contravened the law, and that those involved were good Christians and practicing Catholics, not agitators and certainly not Communists.

With the arrival of the Ministers of the Interior, Agriculture, and Labor (with the latter of whom the ASICH counsel William Thayer had for several years maintained close professional and personal ties), the conversation began to take a much more friendly turn. The President ordered the Ministers of Agriculture and Labor to travel to Molina (some 140 miles south of Santiago) as soon as possible. He authorized them to suspend legal action against strike leaders if this seemed indicated. He also authorized them to threaten the employers with the withdrawal of the extra police forces from the zone, cancellation of tax exemptions, and other reprisals if the employers refused to accept the terms the ministers might propose.

The Agreement

The two ministers, accompanied by Venegas and Thayer, set out together and separated ten miles from Molina, using two cars to keep up

[15] Appointed Minister of Labor in 1964 by newly elected President Eduardo Frei.

[16] "Campesino," while also capable of covering a broad spectrum of rural dwellers, on the whole is used to refer to low-status individuals and is thus the opposite of "agricultor."

appearances. The ministers immediately closeted themselves with the employers. While our evidence is only second-hand, it seems clear that they proceeded, as planned, to bring the employers into line by conveying to them that the government was neutral at best and that they might find themselves subject to various economic sanctions by the government, as well as liable under the relevant sections of the "LDD" because of the lockout: an ironic twist indeed!

At 8 P.M. on Friday evening, in the presence of the governor, the labor inspector, the officer in charge of the Carabineros, and others, an act was signed by the two ministers, by representatives of the employers (including their lawyer, whose wife had been helping the strikers at no little cost to family harmony), and by the two senior ASICH officials as well as by Roberto León, the bank employee who had carried the main negotiating burden up to this point.

The agreement had an ambiguous air of simplicity about it. The first clause simply stated that the workers would return to work immediately, thereby canceling both the indefinite strike and the lockout. The second clause stated that the contract demands would "continue through the normal procedures as laid down in Title V of Book III of the Labor Code." Formally speaking, such a clause is redundant since it says only that the law will take its normal course, but behind it lay the understanding that the employers would cease their undue delaying tactics. The third clause stated that the governor of the department would supervise the return to work. The fourth and final clause, and a very important one, stated that no reprisals would be taken against the strikers, although employers retained the right to discharge employees for the normal reasons specified in the relevant articles and subsections of the law. Most important, but informal and not written, was the agreement that the strike leaders, including lawyer Lorenzini, would be released and would not be prosecuted.

The four leaders were indeed released from prison the following day, but not until they had been visited in their cells by the Bishop of Talca, who took no steps to keep his visit quiet. If the strike were not settled by Sunday, he had assured the leaders, he would issue a circular letter to be read from all pulpits in the diocese, asking the faithful to donate food to the strikers. Since the strike was settled on Friday, the circular was never read. But Msgr. Larraín later published the contents of the already written document.

And to cap this strange week a torchlight procession was held in the little plaza of Molina on Saturday with the returned leaders as heroes, and the assistant parish priest at the head of the procession.

The Aftermath

Local Events

Local events during the following weeks justified the campesinos' sense of satisfaction, yet there were also danger signals. The difficulties which arose are probably typical of those with which any newly established union must deal, but in this instance they turned out to be symptomatic of underlying problems which ultimately proved to be beyond the capacity of the movement to solve.

By mid-December employers and workers had arrived at direct agreements, before the stage of compulsory arbitration, in five of the twenty-three *fundos* in which contract demands had been presented. In nine additional cases, arbitration awards had to be made because the two sides could not agree. But at least the machinery now functioned, and in two of the nine cases the workers later received better conditions than the arbitration award gave them. In two other cases, the demands of the workers were rejected on legal grounds. This left seven of the twenty-three still pending, but for five of these, meetings had already been scheduled. Further work stoppages occurred in ten of the vineyards in the first months of 1954. These were prompted by the employers' attempts to divest themselves of union activists—despite the famous agreement of December 4 ruling out reprisals—and by their alleged refusal to comply with the terms of the individual contracts signed later.

If these problems were symptomatic of the weakness of the movement vis-à-vis its environment, other events were indicative of internal strains which were ultimately to be at least as important. On Saturday, December 5, the day of general rejoicing, the Molina Regional ASICH Directorate held a meeting in which two key figures from ASICH-Santiago also participated: President Venegas and Manuel Naranjo. The minutes of the meeting clearly indicate that the Santiago officials implicitly took Lorenzini to task for not having kept them adequately informed and for not being guided sufficiently by the wishes and agreements of the membership. In short, he was criticised for being too independent of both those lower down and those higher up. Quite explicitly, the Santiago officials recommended a policy of great caution, with no more strikes, if at all possible, and even no public meetings during the next few months.

The Battle of the Press

These local events were not, however, what caught the eye of the Santiago public in the weeks following the strike. What did receive a good deal of publicity in the Santiago press was a highly acrimonious debate about the strike. At least thirty-six articles, eighteen paid insertions, seven editorials, various letters, and the verbatim reports of several sessions of the lower and upper houses of the Chilean Parliament appeared in daily and weekly papers between December 5, 1953, and January 19, 1954.

Charges and countercharges between ASICH and the employers were to be expected and did in fact take place. The Lontué Agricultural Association was very sensitive to the charge that there had been large-scale evasion of the social security laws by their members. It was alledged that social security taxes were not being paid and that some employers even pocketed a part of the legal benefits due the workers, particularly the family allowances to which rural workers had very recently become entitled. Even while the strike was in progress the ministers were aware of these charges, and in declarations to the press they made it clear that they took the charges seriously.

Above all, the employers were aroused by the fact that "outside agitators" were active in the area, both misleading satisfied peasants and falsely informing the government. The tone of employers' statements, the calculated efforts to stall the legal conciliation and arbitration machinery, and the clearly concerted lockout indicate that the employers saw the issue basically as that of union recognition. It is our impression that their concern was only secondarily with the content of the contract demands that had been made. The employers felt, in November, 1953, that the time had come for a showdown with Lorenzini about the organizing efforts inspired by him and others.

While these accusations and counteraccusations were only to be expected, a second attack, directed at the activities of the clergy, was certainly novel, though perhaps not surprising under the circumstances. The campaign of the Catholic Right had gotten off to an awkward start with a long editorial in the *Diario Ilustrado* [17] which, among other points,

---

[17] At that time, as now, this newspaper was owned by a group of persons belonging to the Conservative party: a party which until a few years before had been explicitly confessional and is generally regarded as representative of Chile's "landed aristocracy."

attributed the strike to "communist agitators." This error prompted the Archbishop to go to the President of the Republic and request that the government "might inform itself adequately," as he was later to put it.

The next major declaration came from the Bishop of Talca, and was published on Thursday, December 10, in *La Voz*.[18] The significance of the declaration lay in Msgr. Larraín's insistence that the Church would defend justice and attack injustice in whatever setting it is to be found:

All that is justified in these demands—and there is much—the Church approves. And if Catholic workers who are involved in the conflict—and practically all of them are Catholics—consult a priest whether in good conscience they can make this or that demand, the priest not only may, but has the obligation to give the appropriate reply.

He stoutly defended the efforts of priests and lay Catholics to feed the strikers and insisted that "the policy of the Church shall be not only to preach the social doctrine, but to encourage that it be put into practice." The declaration ended by calling on both workers and employers to be just and charitable, but its support of the strikers was unmistakable. A week later *La Voz* returned to the issue with both an editorial and a lengthy article. Clearly unsympathetic to the employers' disregard of the social doctrines of the Church as explained in the encyclicals *Rerum Novarum* (1891) and *Quadragesimo Anno* (1931), *La Voz* ended by insisting that the Minister of the Interior had been deceived (the insinuation was that he had been deceived by the employers).

For the first time, Church authorities now came under direct attack. As befitted the target, the status of the attacker was of the highest order: a senator belonging to the Liberal party who represented the province of Talca and had important interests in the wine industry. Despite his Liberal[19] affiliation, he published his declaration in the Conservative *Diario Ilustrado* and stated that he was doing so as a Catholic and because he had read the Bishop's declaration and other articles in *La Voz*.

He insisted, as the employers' association had done before him, that the workers actually attempted to undermine the established order by their one-day stoppage and, even more, by threatening an illegal strike of

[18] "The Voice": a weekly which had recently begun to be published by the archidocese of Santiago and which was then, and continued to be until its demise in 1965, in the hands of progressive forces within the archdiocese.

[19] Although anticlerical in the nineteenth century, the Liberal party in the middle of the twentieth was practically indistinguishable from the Conservative party: almost equally aristocratic at the top, it was almost equally Catholic and almost equally representative of the large landholders. The two parties merged in 1966 to become the Partido Nacional.

indefinite duration if their demands were not negotiated. But his severest strictures were clearly directed at the outside Catholic element, both lay and clerical. He complained bitterly that the sectors interested in justifying ASICH had shown no scruples in presenting to the public an absolutely false image of events and that ASICH was in alliance with Communist elements and employed their tactics. The agitation carried out by ASICH itself had resulted in the burning of three *fundos,* and a campaign of lies and calumnies had been launched against the employers, even though many were Catholics and well-known defenders of the Church. Senator Opazo roundly attacked *La Voz* for suppressing crucial facts in its reports and giving them a slant "absolutely devoid of the truth, something which cannot be tolerated in any Catholic publication." The Jesuits were accused of arriving from Santiago in a light truck (that is, in considerable numbers) to take over leadership from those who had been imprisoned, and the involvement of the local assistant priest was clear from the fact that Carabineros had a warrant for his arrest.[20] Finally, pointing warily but unmistakably at the Cardinal, he declared that "the government desisted from judicial action, contrary to its obligation, only because high and most respectable influences were interposed, as all the world well knows."

Both ASICH and *La Voz* replied, the latter taking the Senator and the employers severely to task for their disrespectful attitude toward the Bishop of Talca. By far the most weighty of the replies was that which came last, published on January 16, 1954, in the *Diario Ilustrado.* It was both harsh and sarcastic and came from the Archbishop himself.

Cardinal Caro began by questioning whether the Senator had the right to say that he spoke with frankness and total truthfulness, since the Bishop of Talca had contradicted him on at least two points (Communist inspiration of the strike and local clerical leadership). He expressed amazement at the Senator's censure of the truncated form in which *La Voz* had quoted from the encyclicals, since encyclicals were never quoted in full but only sentence by sentence. After all, he said, they were long, and in any case, one part did not contradict another. He defended his own action in informing President Ibáñez correctly of the nature of ASICH, defended ASICH itself in the strongest terms as "the loyal and selfless execution of pontifical teachings" and with considerable irony applauded the Senator's appreciation for the encyclicals in their entirety, "which

---

[20] This statement was made repeatedly by the employers. We found no evidence in the documents that the order for detention included the priest.

makes one hope that he will become the apostle for their practice: in their entirety!"

The echoes of the controversy could be heard for a long time. In May, 1954, for example, when Cardinal Caro began a visit to the Vatican, the Papal *Nunciatura* in Santiago had to issue a formal statement denying rumors that he had been called to Rome because of his intervention in the strike. To refute the rumors, the *Nunciatura* quoted lengthily from an article which had appeared on April 3, 1954, in *L'Osservatore Romano*, summarizing Cardinal Caro's stand and that of ASICH in a clearly sympathetic manner. In a broader sense, the struggle between progressive and traditional laymen for the sympathy of the Chilean Catholic Church not only has continued up to this day, but the Molina incident was far from marking its beginning.

Other Repercussions

There were many other repercussions which we can only briefly summarize here. Two sessions of the lower house of the Chilean Parliament and one session of the Senate were devoted to the strike.[21] Of note was the position taken by the Minister of Agriculture, Alejandro Hales, chief spokesman for the government and one of the two ministers who had signed the Molina agreement. He referred to the incident itself only to criticize the employers for "not showing on Thursday the same good will which on Friday carried them forward to sign an agreement after less than ten minutes of negotiations." He also praised the workers for rejecting political interference from both the Communist party and the Christian Democrats (then called Falange).[22] But Minister Hales' main purpose was apparently to convince the agricultural sector to see the incident as but a symptom of much more profound and general problems of ignorance and bad conditions which could lead to the awakening of the rural proletariat, endangering not only the country's agricultural activities, "but the social peace and tranquility of the Republic." Senator Frei—elected President of Chile in 1964—took very much the same stand, but with sharper attacks on the landowners and on current legislation. Spokesmen for the Socialist and Communist parties were, for their own very understandable reasons, as disturbed as the Right over the backing

[21] Chamber of Deputies, Dec. 19 and 30, 1953; Senate, Dec. 23, 1953.

[22] The Christian Democratic party was founded under the name "Falange" in November, 1938, by a group of progressive young Catholics who broke away from the Conservative party after the presidential elections of that year. Many of the leaders of this strike were identified with Falange, especially Lorenzini who had been elected to the town council of Molina in 1950 on the party's ticket.

the strike leaders seemed to have obtained from the Church. They also attacked the narrow, sectarian character which they imputed to the movement as a result of its sponsorship.

A less noted but very revealing reaction was that of the National Agricultural Society (SNA). While fully behind the winegrowers at the moment of crisis, the Society was sufficiently open-minded and curious to schedule a debate between ASICH's legal and ecclesiastic counselors and its own president. In what must surely rank as one of the frankest and most charming cynicisms ever, SNA President Recaredo Ossa stated that ASICH had been overanxious to meet a need which did not yet exist. In thirty years, when there might be more intense Communist agitation, then would he regard the activities of ASICH as justified. Implicit in this sentiment was an element—however minute—of acceptance for the new movement. And in its turn, in private conversations, the top leadership of ASICH hinted that the local leadership of ASICH might have been guilty of hasty actions and inappropriate language.

The Sagrada Familia Incident

Finally, it is worth noting that a strike movement occurred in January, 1954, in Sagrada Familia, the township which adjoined Molina. With no outside or local support and a more explicit political goal in mind—that of binding the campesino to the Falange—Juan Cifuentes performed in the township of Sagrada Familia the functions which Lorenzini was performing in Molina, and also won his battle. The strike itself was not widely reported although it paralleled that of Molina even to the extent that government officials (though of lesser status) traveled to the zone and threatened the employers with official reprisals if they did not arrive at an agreement quickly, which they did.

Yet the strike of nine *fundos* was in itself of less significance than a tragic event which occurred there in the following year, symbolic of the deep rifts within Catholic upper strata over the issue of progressivism *vs.* traditionalism. Juan Cifuentes came from a family which had produced a long line of bishops and ministers of state. Two of his brothers, however, were well-known progressive priests, and he himself had been an early and fervent supporter of Falange. He had made history in 1949 by fighting a case of fraud at the polls up to Chile's highest electoral tribunal. This not only awarded him the eleven votes needed to give him a seat on the local board of supervisors, but threw out so many Conservative votes (the party of most of his family) that a second Falangist was seated, to the stunned surprise of all involved.

The anger of some members of his family was so deep that in November, 1955, he was physically attacked by his brother-in-law and the latter's son. Juan Cifuentes had to shoot once to keep from being beaten. When the brother-in-law returned to the fray, Juan Cifuentes, already gripped by his assailant fired a second time into his arm and killed him. The courts accepted the claim of self defense, but considered the means "disproportionate" despite the fact that Cifuentes was a slight man while his two assailants were quite massively built. He was found guilty on this count but, having been in prison during the pretrial investigation, he did not have to serve longer. The verdict did deprive him of his political rights (that is, he could not run for office), which many considered to be the basic aim of his opponents from the beginning. The bitterness of feeling surrounding the case may be gauged by the fact that his father and his sister (the wife of the deceased) were the accusers in the trial and sought the death penalty.

The Origins of the Movement

After the strike of December, 1953, the movement came more fully into the open, engaging in a great variety of activities. Before describing these, however, it may be useful to sketch briefly how the movement established itself since, obviously, it did not spring suddenly out of the ground in the latter part of 1953.

Precursors

The beginnings of the local movement can be traced back to the mid-forties, when the parish priest of Molina, Sr. Bawer, established the so-called Catholic Brotherly Aid (Fraterno Auxilio Católico). It dispensed charity to the indigent and its members were ladies belonging, essentially, to the little town's bourgeoisie. Sr. Bawer's successor, Sr. Quiroz, introduced the so-called Social Seminars: a series of week-long programs during which the social encyclicals were discussed and their implications for the Church and the laity pondered. The Bishop of Talca would often come to the religious services with which these weeks opened and closed. Since women—and men—from the poorer sections of the population also attended these seminars, they provided the first meeting ground in which members of several social strata could get to know each other personally. In particular, they enabled the comfortable local professionals to understand some of the problems faced by their poorer fellow believers.

At about this time—in the late forties—Emilio Lorenzini returned from his university studies in Santiago. He had completed his course work in the Law School of the Catholic University but not the thesis which would have allowed him to practice. Emilio, then in his early twenties, was the son of the local flour miller, an immigrant from Italy. Emilio Sr., after making and losing several small fortunes, had finally settled into a very comfortable style of life, though he was socially not too close to the winegrowers, many of whom lived in Santiago.

The younger Emilio had clearly inherited both his father's volatile temperament and boundless energy, though these were channeled toward political and social rather than economic concerns: a turn which Lorenzini *père* viewed both with saddened puzzlement and with a certain amount of surreptitious pride, at least in later years. In any case, the history of Lorenzini *fils* had been far from smooth even to this point. He had been expelled from Chile's elite Jesuit high school after, among other things, openly campaigning against the candidate of the Conservative party in the 1938 Presidential elections and praising the Popular Front candidate of the Communist, Socialist, and Radical parties, Pedro Aguirre. This was regarded by right-wing Catholics as tantamount to deliberate heresy, for they expected the immediate burning of churches to follow the election of Aguirre.

After entering the Law School of the Catholic University in 1942, Lorenzini's early contempt for the "sissy" and "striped-pants" Falangist students he found there soon turned to intense partisanship. He became notorious for his use of Santiago's public transportation system to make converts among the captive audience he could briefly address between stops and until expelled by the driver. But while many of his own generation admired him for these and other proofs of his zeal, he also began to be considered "slightly crazy." His returns to Molina during vacations were clearly no more restful. On one occasion he almost succeeded in organizing a walkout of the workers in his father's flour mill, which the latter forstalled only by a few concessions made at the right moment. On another occasion, together with a young agronomist, he organized a walkout of vineyard workers.

Upon his permanent return to Molina, he became a part of the group of progressively-oriented Catholics who had already found each other under the leadership of the parish priests, Sr. Bawer and then Sr. Quiroz. The first concrete step along the road to organization was soon taken: they formed a consumers' cooperative. The whole affair was very modest, particularly in its financial aspects, but it was an important symbol of the move from words to action. Moreover, it institutionalized contact between local rich and local poor and also attracted as its first (unpaid) "manager" a young man who was later to become one of Lorenzini's chief aids, Luis Navarro. His wife, Gladys Gutiérrez de Navarro, held the campesinos together during the 1953 strike after the local leaders had been arrested and before the Santiago leadership had arrived.

It was at this time, also, that the young and still struggling Falange [23] struck organizational roots in the community. Cooperative, study circles for the discussion of Catholic social doctrines, Falange: all had more or less the same clientele, and in 1950 they helped bring about Lorenzini's election to the Molina town council.

Lorenzini Organizes

Ever more conscious of the problems of the rural population—low salaries, atrocious housing and food, lack of education—Lorenzini now began the arduous labor of organizing the campesinos. He was helped not only by Navarro, but also by a person whom he picked up on the road one fine day, lying there dead drunk, penniless and rootless, without local connections of any kind. Manuel Silva's background was never fully elucidated. His occasional claim to have studied civil engineering was possibly not true, and no one was ever sure whether he did or did not have a wife and child in the North of Chile, whence he had recently arrived. But it is certain that he was an excellent and passionate chronicler who not only wrote those minutes, letters, and memoranda for which the action-oriented Lorenzini could never find time, but who also kept various diaries which we found in the early 1960's in a closet in the abandoned adobe union hall. He crawled through fences and brush with Lorenzini, counseled him in his approach to and in the selection of "persons of confidence" in each of the vineyards, and helped him in those "classes" in labor law, reading and writing, public speaking, and Catholic doctrine which Lorenzini gave to the campesinos he had surreptitiously assembled.

At first, this work could better be described as agitating than organizing. Lorenzini did not have the organization of formal unions as his aim. [24]

---

[23] As in the rest of the country, it attracted less than 5 per cent of the vote in Molina until 1957.

[24] The Labor Code made the organization of unions of farm workers extremely difficult and not really necessary, since contract demands could be presented by groups of nonunionized workers. Unions of farm workers could only be established where more than twenty workers were employed; they had to be established on a farm-by-farm basis and were not allowed to federate; there was no protection for union officers; there were subtle incentives to members to ask for the dissolution of

He presumably hoped that an aroused and more educated rural proletariat would, through exerting pressure in some way, improve its conditions. His own political position as Falangist town councilor would, of course, be strengthened in the meantime.

In 1952, two events moved Lorenzini to think more specifically about organized economic pressure along trade-union lines. First, easily outraged as he was, he became impatient with his party, or at least its Santiago leadership. He had become embroiled in the defense of a group of local campesinos who had been falsely accused of stealing oxen. Reportedly, they had nearly been drowned in the course of police interrogation designed to persuade them to confess. The party did not act speedily enough for Lorenzini's tastes when he asked them to protest to higher authorities. Lorenzini cooled toward the party as a result and looked seriously at alternative organizational approaches to the solution of the campesino problem. By temperament, he was not an "organization man" or one to respect hierarchical authority, especially if the superiors showed less forcefulness than he felt was indicated.

The second stimulus for a more explicit attempt at unionization was Lorenzini's increasing contact with ASICH when he visited Santiago. Independently, the Molina group and ASICH-Santiago had been invited to attend the constituent congress of the newly established Central Labor Federation (CUT), where fear of the dominant Marxist majority drew the two together. Moreover, Fr. Alberto Hurtado, S.J., who died in 1952 and had been one of the founders of ASICH in 1947, had been very close personally to the Bishop of Talca. Both these men from good families had gone together through the same elite Jesuit high school (San Ignacio: the same school to which Lorenzini went twenty years later) and through the Law School of the Catholic University. Both had been inspired by the same earlier generation of progressive Catholic priests. Thus, friendship as well as common social orientation bound the Bishop of Talca and the Jesuit priest together, and made Bishop Larraín view with even greater warmth the efforts of ASICH to establish itself and to flex its muscles by working in his own diocese. He encouraged closer relationships between ASICH and Lorenzini, to whom the financial resources of the former were a welcome bonus.[25]

---

unions once established, etc. (See articles 419 and following of the Chilean Labor Code).

[25] Fr. Hurtado, a genuinely saintly individual, combined immense personal warmth and charm with no little acumen. He demonstrated the latter by his success in extracting from an admiring contingent of wealthy ladies contributions sufficient in

ASICH Enters: 1953

Thus stimulated, and with yet another progressive priest appointed in Molina to replace Sr. Quiroz,[26] organization began with great seriousness early in 1953. The Ministry of the Interior in Santiago, not to mention the governor of the department of Lontué, began now with some frequency to receive complaints from the vineyard owners about the "climate of agitation" stimulated by Lorenzini. Efforts to organize the first legal union in one of the vineyards had begun in 1952, and the supposedly national, but *de facto* local, Federación Christiana de la Tierra was established in early 1953. Lorenzini, Navarro, and Silva were put on the ASICH payroll. A Regional Directorate of ASICH was named with these three men, Gladys Gutiérrez de Navarro, an agronomist, a local pharmacist, and one or two campesinos on the board and the assistant parish priest as its chaplain. Manuel Naranjo and Fr. Jaime Larrain, National Chaplain of ASICH, began to pay frequent visits from Santiago, the latter holding spiritual retreats. Campesinos were sent to the trade-union school run in Santiago for ASICH by another progressive clerical veteran, Sr. Santiago Tapia, who had organized textile and metal workers in the early 1940's. The Directorate held eight meetings between August 31 and November 24, and, in addition, its representatives began to participate systematically in the activities of the provincial and regional congresses and committees of the newly established CUT.

The movement also began to take its collective-bargaining activities seriously. As early as March, 1951, workers led by Lorenzini had asked for the intervention of the governor to reach agreement over wages at harvest time. His intervention had proved helpful, though various brief stoppages had been necessary to enforce the agreements reached. The 1952 harvest was again marked by stoppages and walkouts, but in March, 1953, the intervention of the governor had an aura of semi-institutionalization about it. On the fourteenth of that month, a substantial number of winegrowers and five representatives of the workers met in the governor's offices and signed a quite complicated agreement in which vineyards

---

amount to establish a foundation which financed not only an orphanage but a Catholic Workers' Federation, ASICH!

[26] Sr. Quiroz had been obliged to leave after accusing some of the local employers of "squeezing their workers like lemons." The new appointee, third in succession with progressive views, had had union experience before his ordination and had been an active member of Falange. All of this was, of course, known to Msgr. Larrain who, as Bishop, was responsible for the appointment.

were classified according to their productivity. Wages per volume of grapes picked were higher on the less productive vineyards. In late August, 1953, a strike occurred in one of the vineyards and forced the owners to discharge a supervisor the workers detested.

Finally, on October 11, 1953, in a climate which the employers had some right to call one of "increasing tension and agitation," there was held the First Union Congress of Rural Workers of Molina. Delegates from twenty vineyards representing perhaps 1,800 workers met in the parish hall of Molina and formulated some fifteen demands covering wages and how they were to be paid, wages in kind, hours of work, irregularities in employer compliance with laws covering minimum wages and payment for Sundays, vacations and holidays, and the formation of new legal unions and of consumer cooperatives. Item 14 promised to "mount an energetic campaign against the vice of alcoholism which is the worst enemy of the trade-unions of rural workers and of working-class unity," and Item 15 requested ASICH Santiago to put a troop of lawyers at the disposal of the Molina Regional Directorate.

The relevant sections of this list of demands were presented to the employers and to the conciliation board on October 30 and 31, 1953. The employers showed no willingness to negotiate, and in late November a huge assembly of vineyard workers heard Lorenzini state that he felt a walkout would have to be called if no progress were made soon.[27] The idea was received with approval and thus, on Monday, November 30, the owners or their representatives found themselves with notices of the warning stoppage to be held the next day.

The Movement Flourishes

The events of December, 1953, were, of course, a milestone in the history of the movement. They marked the end of its infancy. From then on, activities which had been performed haphazardly, had only been talked about, or had existed only in the form of prototypes were carried on more systematically, openly, and substantially.

Collective Bargaining: Harvest Contracts

The contract to cover the work during the six-week harvest period was signed in the offices of the governor of Lontué sometime between March

[27] Late November and early December is a time when the vineyard worker is in a highly strategic position. If certain work is not done at that time, the whole harvest (to be gathered in the following March) may be lost. Once this work is completed, however, the employer can more easily sit out a strike.

14 and March 24, 1954,[28] and might well be considered the high point of the movement. The resistance of the employers had by no means collapsed, and addresses by Lorenzini at meetings of campesinos before the agreement was signed make it clear that the workers felt it necessary to threaten a strike and that they were most concerned over victimization of union activists. Nevertheless, ASICH legal counsel William Thayer[29] was able to report to that body's National Executive on March 8 that the employers had accepted ASICH as the workers' bargaining representative and that they accepted in principle the procedure of signing an agreement in the governor's offices. Indeed, in the agreement itself, the governor was named—by name, not office—as the arbitrator of any disputes which might arise. The agreement, apart from complicated schedules of monetary and in-kind payments, once again attempted to protect union leaders from victimization. In return, it made ASICH responsible for the maintenance of good order at work.

Every major aspect of these negotiations and of the final agreement ran counter to the spirit and/or the letter of the law. On every point, the agreement was more favorable to the union than the law permitted. Negotiations at harvest time; any kind of strike threat, let alone at harvest time; an agreement covering several *fundos;* outside representation of workers; ignoring the official conciliation and arbitration machinery and using the governor as mediator and arbitrator: none of this was contemplated by the Labor Code and much ran counter to it. To interpret briefly: Latin American laws, often decried as too rigid, detailed, and oppressive to the weak, can clearly be made to function more flexibly if real power, from various sources, is suddenly thrown massively on the side of the weak and if the general culture is one in which compromise and progress are valued.

Only one year later, however, in 1955, the situation was ominously different. When Luis Navarro, one of the officials of the union, tried to get in touch with the vice-president of the Lontué Agricultural Association to begin negotiations, he seems to have been repulsed with considera-

---

[28] We were unable to establish the exact date, which is not given on the copy of the contract in our possession. We know that a mass meeting of campesinos was held on March 14, at which time the contract had clearly not been signed. On March 24, Navarro addressed a meeting in neighboring Sagrada Familia and pointed with pride to the new contract.

[29] William Thayer, highly intelligent, experienced in labor law, distinguished in appearance and dignified in bearing, had always been the person to whom the employers felt they could talk comfortably, though this in no sense implies that Thayer was untrue to his side.

ble rudeness. According to a memorandum Navarro later wrote to Bishop Larraín, he was told that "ASICH officials in Molina are a bunch of bums and good-for-nothings who live off the backs of workers and for that reason I'll have nothing to do with you." The employers were requested to appear before the governor but offered a mere 20 per cent increase over wage rates paid during the 1954 harvest, whereas prices had risen an incredible 75 per cent during the previous twelve months. More important, they refused to sign a contract with ASICH covering various employers, and insisted instead that each employer deal with his workers without outside intervention except that of the labor inspector as provided by law. ASICH officials reluctantly decided to accept this proposition and agreed to a sixty per cent wage increase which the governor said he would try to get for the union. They warned, however, that they could not be responsible for the consequences of the confusion and delay which would probably result from individual negotiations.

The last days of March were, indeed, days of great tension and confusion. The workers were asked repeatedly by government officials to postpone their strike deadline because ministers were not available in Santiago or employers could not be reached. Finally, on Friday, April 1, work stoppages began in sixteen vineyards and continued through Sunday, and, in some, through Monday. Isolated walkouts had already occurred before then in one or two *fundos*. Once again, officers from ASICH-Santiago and from Concepción arrived, accompanied by a government official. Once again, strikers and their families poured into the union hall, and food was collected and prepared.

The employers never ceded ground on the issue of refusing to sign a contract, as a group, with ASICH as a group. But individual contracts began to be signed within hours of the beginning of the walkout (the first one was signed at 2 P.M. on Friday) and by Monday seven of the sixteen conflicts had been settled and more were being negotiated. As usual, isolated stoppages occurred later: according to the workers, to force compliance with the contract terms.

For harvests after 1955 we found no reliable information. Union officials assured us in the early 1960's that there had been no more serious difficulties and that the employers had even accepted ASICH as the representative of the workers. In view of the steep decline beginning in 1955 in the power of ASICH, such formal acceptance may have meant less in reality than appears on the surface.

Officially, ASICH—though regretting the necessity of another strike, and regretting the hostility and dilatory tactics of the employers—

claimed that the 1955 negotiations had been a triumph. The claim was based on the fact that more than "twice the number of men" (ASICH *Bulletin,* April, 1955) went on strike than in December, 1953, although arithmetic becomes a little confused at this point, since, on both occasions, about 1,800 workers were claimed to have been idle. Our own assessment is that the acceptance of a 60 per cent wage increase in the light of a 75 per cent inflation and the acceptance of the employers' refusal to sign an agreement with ASICH, cannot be called a triumph. The acceptance of these terms is all the more puzzling when one considers the speed with which the employers entered into agreement once a strike had been declared; this seems to indicate that the workers were in a strong bargaining position and much could have been obtained.

Collective Bargaining: Annual Contracts

It is clear that the change in climate which occurred between the successful harvest settlements of March, 1954, and the much more difficult ones of March, 1955, must have taken place before the negotiations for the annual contract in December, 1954.[30] For these negotiations were long and ASICH seemed to have made no attempt to negotiate a regional master agreement, possibly because these annual contracts, as distinct from the harvest contracts, traditionally vary sufficiently from vineyard to vineyard to make a master contract impossible.

In any case, the presentation of contract demands for some twenty vineyards lasted from mid-November, 1954, to early January, 1955. By late January, only eleven had been adequately settled (two more had been rejected because of legal flaws). During 1954 many workers complained of dismissal for union activity (fifteen in one vineyard alone in June of 1954), and these complaints increased during negotiating time and went

---

[30] Although the agricultural year for vineyards begins in May or early June (i.e., soon after the March harvest), negotiations for the annual contract take place in November and December. This is not as anomalous as might appear, for the most important part of the workers' remuneration fixed in the contract is a lump sum per *cuadra* for which the worker contracts to take care of all necessary work until harvest time. A *cuadra* is an area of approximately 412 by 412 feet, and workers will contract for three or four *cuadras.* The worker is therefore essentially a contractor: if he needs more labor, he hires and pays it if it is not contributed gratis by his family. During the nine months between May and harvest time, the worker receives advances against the lump sum finally due him. Thus, if he receives advances on the basis of last year's contract, he simply has more due him at the time of the final settlement after the harvest is in, if in this year's contract the lump sum is higher than in last year's. The contract also makes provisions for a production bonus (which does not become operative until the harvest is gathered in April). Payments in kind generally do not vary from year to year.

on without pause in 1955. Attempts at conciliating contract demands dragged on into March, 1955; ASICH representatives complained to authorities in Santiago; these sent telegrams to the local inspector; the latter attempted to set up meetings but had to report that legal flaws in the workers' cases had stalled the conciliation machinery; and in the end ASICH representatives themselves had to recognize some of these flaws or concede that the contracts had expired so long ago that nothing could now be done about them.

In sum, the union seems never to have achieved that full control over the negotiation of annual contracts which it had for at least one season— March, 1954—in the case of the harvest contracts, and in December, 1953 for that year's annual contract.

Collective Bargaining: Grievance Handling

Perhaps the settlement of complaints under an existing contract, by means of a formal "grievance procedure" managed entirely by the parties themselves until the final arbitration process, is an invention of the U.S. system of collective bargaining. In a broader sense, however, systematic efforts by unions to take up their members' complaints are by no means limited to the U.S. This is amply demonstrated by this little peasants' union, centered in a town of 6,000 inhabitants some 140 miles from Santiago, Chile. We even found a notebook bearing the title "Book of Complaints Concerning Work," (*"Libro de reclames del trabajo"*) begun on October 28, 1953, with entries up to July 29, 1955. The Chilean Labor Code makes systematic provisions for the handling of grievances: theoretically, a complaint is brought to the local labor inspector, and if not adequately settled there, it is channeled into the system of Labor Courts. Study of the files of the local Labor Inspectorate revealed that the union had during this period concerned itself with far more than the 151 grievances [31] noted in the "Book of Complaints." Yet we may perhaps take these 151 as indicative of the kinds of grievances which had to be dealt with: 39 differences over amount of wages due; 28 supposed failures of the employer to pay family allowances; 20 failures to pay a discharged worker the cash equivalent for crops he had to leave standing on the plot of ground he had cultivated for his own use; 42 alleged failures to pay

---

[31] These 151 grievances arose in the course of 72 "contacts." Those who made entries in the book did so on the basis of "contacts," that is, visits to the union offices by one or more campesinos from a *fundo*, or a visit by a union officer to a *fundo*. On either occasion, more than one complaint would generally be raised. The names of 51 different *fundo*s figure in the book, an indication of the scope of the movement.

severance pay, bonuses, and holidays; 11 failures of the employer to sign a written contract of employment; 11 cases of physical mistreatment.

Physical assault of farm workers by employers or other employees was rare. One case involving employers—the brothers Bruce, known in the area as "the three devils"—was exceptional: a long list of complaints was finally presented to Parliament involving brutal beatings, threats with firearms, burning of the shacks of the campesinos with all their material belongings. More typical, and obviously infuriating to the workers, was the deliberate refusal of the employers to pay serious attention to complaints. The following quotation from a letter written to Lorenzini by the workers of the vineyard "Santa Elena" is an example of this attitude:

Mr. A. D. arrives on his fundo about 4:30 in the afternoon, staying there about two hours, employing his time making out time sheets. In view of the silence and indifference in which he shrouded himself, and upon hearing the motor of his truck start, we tried to talk with him, but we were unsuccessful because instead of stopping, he accellerated and sped away from the fundo in the direction of Talca.

We could arrive at no accurate assessment of precisely what happened to the grievances.[32] One's impression is that a union officer—generally Navarro—would try to speak to the employer after the workers had vainly sought to win their case by themselves. The union was sometimes successful and if not, would often lodge a complaint with the labor inspector. He in turn would try to do what he could, given his limited means (his area covered more than 100 *fundos*, he had neither transportation nor secretarial assistance, though for a time there was an assistant inspector). The inspector would sometimes obtain something for the workers: perhaps a more generous financial settlement for a discharged worker, but very rarely his reinstatement. It is also likely that some restraining influence was exerted on employers in the area by the knowledge that the union and the labor inspector were active. It is clear that the Labor Court system was, for all intents and purposes, inoperative.

The union was certainly very conscious of its role in handling grievances and was frequently criticized by ASICH-Santiago for devoting too much of its energy to the problems of individuals and small groups. Nevertheless, it requested that a lawyer be assigned to open a "legal

[32] The union's "Book of Complaints" only noted the raising of the grievance. The files of the Labor Inspectorate were, of course, ordered by date so that it was practically impossible to match up—even for those grievances in which the Inspectorate was involved—the lodging of a complaint in one month with a visit to the *fundo* by the inspector two months later.

consultancy" in the area to deal with this and other aspects of the union's work, and ASICH-Santiago financed such legal aid for a brief period after 1955.

Welfare Activities

Even before the 1953 strike the union had helped vineyard workers—newly covered by the social security system, especially the family allowance scheme—to obtain the various legal certificates needed to draw benefits. By acting as notary public at one-sixth of the price charged elsewhere, it performed a useful service for several years afterward. Nor did the union confine itself to notarizing documents. Its representatives would often accompany the applicant to the relevant offices, help him state his case, write letters on his behalf, and, through personal contact, smooth the path for him through the formidable forest of state bureaucracies.

The union also extended services to its members and their relatives in times of emergency. A certain part of the annual budget—in 1955 perhaps as much as 10 per cent of total annual expenditures (excluding salaries)—went into help of this kind: burial expenses, help to widows and to the families of sick campesinos, loans (most of them never repaid) to workers who had been discharged and were awaiting receipt of their first unemployment benefit. The union even made arrangements to get a discount from a local funeral home, in return for which it advertised the service in its little paper and its radio show.

Finally, the union—Gladys Gutierrez de Navarro in particular—organized home and hospital visits to the sick and classes in dressmaking. These and other aspects of the union's educational activities deserve separate treatment because of their broad scope and the amount of energy invested in them.

Education, Character-Building, and Indoctrination

Any conversation with leaders of rural workers anywhere soon touches on the low educational and cultural level of their followers. The reference may be to the obvious evil of illiteracy or to a more general and diffuse failure to grasp the institutional structure of the society. It may refer to an even vaguer, less intellectual, but no less important perceived lack of character: a lack of initiative, of restraint vis-à-vis the temptations of alcohol and bribes, or a failure to shake off a passive, fatalistic approach to problems. These deficiencies—whether real or partially imagined—make the peasant a poor member of an organization trying to survive in a hostile environment and make it almost impossible for him to become a leader. The use of the terms "animallike" and "not yet human" is never very far from the lips not only of those opposed to improving the peasant's status but of those who are trying to help him to do so.

Conscious of these deficiencies, Lorenzini and everyone else connected with the Molina movement early placed great emphasis on attempts to raise the educational and cultural level of their followers. Not only were selected individuals sent to the ASICH school in Santiago. Not only were literacy campaigns pushed by the union in organizing its own classes and later in pressing local education authorities to provide free classes in places and at times suitable to the peasants. Most important, the periodic regional meetings for the many five-man Fundo Directorates which ASICH had established in the different vineyards were not only dedicated to discussing current trade-union problems and how to handle them, but were extensively used for such purposes as: making listeners aware of the benefits they had obtained from ASICH and the local movement; instructing these local leaders in labor law and union administration; explaining why ASICH rejected communism; explaining reasons for believing in God; encouraging them to foster in themselves certain personal qualities: resistance to alcohol, the savings habit, and

To be prudent as a serpent in starting a conflict; simple as a dove in speech and action; firm as a rock by the sea in standing up against lies, threats and criticisms; invincible as a tank in advancing in our program of education, training and economic betterment; and not to use ASICH for personal benefits but as a help in collective conflicts.[33]

The meetings stressed the need for unity, paying dues, recruiting new members, meeting regularly, reading union literature, and being a good worker, so that any complaint against an employer brought to the attention of the authorities would not be weakened on that score.

In addition, spiritual retreats led both by the assistant parish priest and by Fr. Jaime Larrain were held under union auspices. If union meetings were sometimes used for spiritual matters, so were some of the spiritual retreats not entirely confined to their central objectives. Discussion of union problems were sandwiched between prayer meetings and devotions, and explanations of the social encyclicals would sometime reach quite practical levels.

The union also maintained a library. The 107 volumes whose titles we

[33] From an agenda drawn up by Luis Navarro for his personal use in guiding a meeting of Directivos de Fundos, May 22, 1955. Several such agenda are in our possession.

found listed seemed to be predominantly religious, inspirational, and of the character-building type. Twenty-five seemed to be novels with religious themes; thirty were religious outright, including the lives of saints, devotionals, and descriptions of Catholic Action; fourteen dealt with chastity and/or preparation for marriage; twenty-three concerned Christian or general character-building; and four dealt with communism. Only ten volumes seemed to be straight novels and two were histories. The names of ninety-one readers were found: more than two-thirds were from the town of Molina; almost half were women.

The union sponsored for at least nine months (May, 1955 to January, 1956) a half-hour radio program every Sunday afternoon, in which Church social doctrine and news of interest to workers was presented, as well as musical entertainment by the union's own band playing popular ballads and folk music.

Finally, the union published a six- to eight-page paper in Molina during a twelve-month period under the title *Tierra y Libertad* ("Land and Freedom") It appeared fortnightly three times in October and November, 1953, then not again until March, 1954, when another three numbers were published at fortnightly intervals. From May until November it appeared very irregularly, and its publication was then transferred to Santiago. Its content mirrored the ideology of the movement. It featured attacks on bad employers, and occasional praises for good ones.[34] It described changes in social security laws; and contained attacks on capitalism [35] and communism; gave advice on how to raise pigs; praised the governor of the department and the labor inspector; uttered dire warnings against the dangers of alcoholism; and encouraged members to participate in literacy programs.

The Movement as Organization

We have already referred to the fact that the union moved toward crystallization of its internal structure. Indeed, the geographical dispersion of its membership made the need for some kind of formal communication system a matter of concern from the very beginning. But instead of a few "persons of confidence," there were now Fundo Directorates which did not, however, have legal standing except in the case of three vineyards which by 1954 had managed to establish unions under the labor code. These Fundo Directorates were called to formal meetings on a regional

[34] Some of whom were later also seemingly involved in unfair labor practices.

[35] "Capitalism is a sin against nature, it's a cancer of the economy and the society. It is atheistic in its structure." *Tierra y Libertad*, March, second half, 1954.

basis perhaps once a month. There was, of course, also the Molina Regional Directorate which invariably included: (1) the assistant parish priest as spiritual advisor, (2) a local pharmacist—Elias Selman—as treasurer,[36] (3) a sympathetic agronomist—Alberto León—as technical advisor, (4) Manuel Silva, (5) Luis Navarro, (6) Gladys Gutierrez de Navarro (in such senior positions as president or secretary), perhaps (7) and (8) two campesinos as directors, and (9) Lorenzini in some highly unusual position such as "Inspector of Activists and Director of the Movement." Since a great deal of informality reigned, most of these titles meant little. Lorenzini's was presumably intended to give him maximum freedom from routine administrative work.

Superior to the Regional Directorate was, presumably, a national organization variously called "Federación Nacional Cristiana de la Tierra," "Federación Cristiana de la Tierra," and "Federación Sindical Chilena de Trabajadores Campesinos." It had no real existence but was an expression of (unrealized) hope that the Molina regional organization would be but the first of many other regional campesino groups. ASICH had set up a Department of Campesino Affairs through which relations with Molina were carried on. But ASICH was a rather small and informal affair at the top, and information about the situation in Molina might come from its national chaplain, Fr. Jaime Larrain, or from any one of its national officers after one of their frequent *ad hoc* visits to Molina. President Venegas, Manuel Naranjo, Hernan Troncoso and others all kept closely in touch with affairs in Molina.

Although there was a formally democratic process for selecting members of the Fundo Directorate, the choice was made by Lorenzini, Silva, and Navarro, obviously based on sentiment among the farm workers. The Regional Directorate, although also formally democratically elected, was basically self-perpetuating, presumably with ASICH-Santiago having a voice. The policies formulated by the Regional Directorate, such as general plans for the subsequent twelve months (which did not have great practical significance), and plans for the harvest contract demands (which did have practical significance) were worked out jointly by the Regional Directorate and ASICH-Santiago in the course of visits and exchange of correspondence, and in consultation with the membership. Certainly the affairs of Molina were a frequent subject of discussion at meetings of the National Executive of ASICH in Santiago.

At its peak, the union seems to have had directorates in between 30 and

---

[36] A mild but devoted man who kept books under the most difficult of circumstances but otherwise was not very active in formulating policy.

40 vineyards, and to have serviced on an occasional basis another 20, for a total of between 50 and 60 *fundos* in the area of Molina.

External Relations

With much acumen and assiduity, the union concerned itself with the well being of—the local labor inspector. As we have noted, the position was undersupported in Molina as elsewhere. The inspector had to depend for transport and lunch on the good will of the employers. The union recognized that such conditions were unlikely to produce inspectors who were heroes. The power and influence of many of the vineyard owners, who had contacts at high levels in the government, were likely to cut short the local tenure of any inspector who took his job too seriously. Within these limits, the union felt the inspectors were doing what they reasonably could. To keep the inspectors' good will, to increase it, and above all to strengthen their material independence from the employers, the union kept up a steady stream of letters to the Minister of Labor, to the Directorate General of Labor (a section of the Ministry) and even to the President of the Republic, praising the inspectors and asking the authorities to increase the resources available to them.

Another and much more complicated set of external relationships was maintained by the union and its leaders with the Regional CUT and the men who guided it. We deliberately refer separately to "the union" and "its leaders," and to "CUT" and *its* leaders, because it is difficult to decide when relationships were personal, when institutional. It is certain that Lorenzini, Silva, and Navarro held official positions in the Regional CUT organization. Lorenzini would also appear on the podium with CUT officials whose political affiliations were Communist and Socialist (as his was Falangist) in those many meetings held in 1954 and 1955 to denounce the government's failure to deal with inflation. Those meetings were sometimes sponsored by CUT, and sometimes by *ad hoc* and highly impermanent "*Comandos de trabajadores y campesinos*"; sometimes they seemed quite frankly to be political rallies of all opposition parties, and speakers participated in their role as party members. This participation in protest and overt political activities, among other aspects of Lorenzini's conduct, caused great uneasiness in ASICH-Santiago and among the few but important clergymen who were sympathetic to the Molina movement.

Underneath this public, and in some sense very real, cooperation, there was, of course, a continuous subterranean struggle between Marxists and Catholic elements over the allegiance of the farm workers. Judging by some of the letters of complaint received in the union offices from various groups of peasants, Marxist representatives often portrayed CUT as an alternative to ASICH, although the Molina union was in fact affiliated with CUT until 1956. Lorenzini himself, despite his emotionality in many respects, was capable of combining a profound personal distaste for Marxism and a perpetual suspicion of Marxist activities at the tactical level, with an appreciation for the dedication of many adherents of Marxism, and a recognition that he and they held in common many criticisms of the existing order.

Decay

The movement did not go on from success. It was moribund within three or four years of the famous strike of December, 1953. While it was vigorous once again in the mid-sixties, this revival is intimately connected with the victory of the Christian Democrats (formerly Falange) at the polls in 1964 and 1965. In the late 1950's and early 1960's, the movement was at a low ebb indeed. One minor indication of this was the cessation of the stream of letters sent and received, minutes of meetings and diaries of activities, budgets and annual balances which provided us with so much information about events in the mid-fifties.

An index of weakness much more central to the objectives of the movement was the precipitous decline in the number of vineyards in which annual contract demands were presented and the results—very different from earlier years—of those few demands which were presented. In 1952, the workers of 20 vineyards presented demands; in 1953 those of 30. In 1954, it fell back to 23, in 1955 to 12, and in 1956 to 5, rising in 1957 to 9. The number of workers affected by these contracts declined from 1,138 in 1953 to 415 in 1957.

Equally significant are the increases or decreases in the workers' real wages. It is impossible to enter into the details of the two sources of data we used and the kinds of calculations to which we subjected them. One source was data collected by Manuel Silva for the union, and found in its files. The other source was telegrams found in the Labor Inspectorate giving rather crude single percentages of what had been asked for and what had finally been settled for.[37]

[37] Since changes in many monetary items—and in some in-kind items—were asked for, a very complicated system of weighting would have to be employed before a single percentage could have been arrived at by the inspector. We are certain that he had no time for any such calculation but probably took the single most important item—the price per *cuadra*—as representative. Monetary figures were, of course, deflated by us according to the official consumer's price index.

Both sources reveal the same trend. In 1953, workers obtained a real increase over 1952; from then on they suffered ever increasing losses, probably somewhere between 13 and 23 per cent in 1956, somewhat less in 1957.

The financial situation of the union was equally discouraging insofar as we could piece it together from the books of the treasurer (for 1954 and 1955) and books found in the union hall (for 1955 and 1956).[38] Summarized briefly, income in real terms fell by almost three-fifths between 1954 and 1956. According to the 1962 standard, we calculated income to have been 5,800,000 pesos in 1954 (about $2,900 in U.S. currency) and 2,400,000 pesos in 1956 (about $1,200). Even more ominous: dues were well over a quarter of total income in 1954, but considerably less than a fifth in 1956. The dues collected in 1956, were, in fact, just over one-fourth of those collected in 1954.[39]

Let no one assume that rural workers are necessarily incapable of making substantial contributions to financing their movements. We have made various calculations based on different assumptions of what each worker might contribute: ½ per cent or 1 per cent of his monthly wages; that wages might include only monetary wages or total wages; that only the 2,000 vineyard workers who were affected by the December strike might contribute, or the total of 6,000 estimated to live in the zone. Under the most conservative estimates (½ per cent of money wages for 2,000 workers) enough dues could have been collected to hire three officials at the legal minimum for white-collar employees and pay their 50 per cent social security contributions. This would have been four times as much as was actually collected. Under more expansive assumptions (dues of 1 per cent of total remuneration for 6,000 men) enough money for the salaries and social security payments of thirty officials would have been collected. Or, more realistically, four or five officials could have been hired, plus

---

[38] The two sources could be compared for the year 1955 and agree reasonably well. The treasurer's books showed a substantially larger income and expenditure because he received from Santiago certain sums for the salaries of officials (Lorenzini, Navarro, Silva) and for the payment of bills connected with the maintenance of the union hall and other expenses which never went into or out of the union books but which he handled directly.

[39] We are probably overstating our case by attributing the decline in purchasing power of wages and the decline in union dues to the decay of the union. These were years of inflation and it is probably quite usual for real wages and for union dues in real terms to decline in an inflationary period. However, dues collected in 1956 amounted to only 51,000 pesos of that year, as compared with 66,000 pesos in 1955 (in 1955 pesos): that is, an absolute decline had taken place even before deflation, and this surely is an unmistakable sign of weakness.

legal and secretarial aid, and the remainder available for direct help to peasants individually or collectively, for administrative and other expenses.

By far the most important indication of the decay of the movement—indeed, one of its direct causes and symbolic of even deeper causes—was the disappearance of the group of leaders who had built the movement and led it to triumph. Manuel Silva was the first to leave. Already transferred to Santiago in March, 1954, he was active in the little headquarters of ASICH as a kind of expeditor, a liaison man for the union in Molina. His transfer was, however, not based on reasons of organizational efficiency, but designed to enable him to undergo treatment for his alcoholism, in which it failed. In any case, his transfer to Santiago was a severe net loss to the strength of the movement.

Next to go was the assistant parish priest, Sr. Hector Barrios. A year after the strike he was transferred to another parish in the diocese of the Bishop of Talca, and there made senior priest. Despite his transfer, he continued to be chaplain of the union in Molina. He attended meetings of the Regional Directorate regularly until October, 1955, and again from January to June, 1956, after approval of a resolution that he be urged to attend. In June he resigned as chaplain, feeling that his geographical separation from the movement made it impossible for him to perform his functions properly.

The transfer obviously was the subject of rumors: there were stories of pressure put by conservative laymen on the Archbishop in Santiago, who in turn was reported to have transmitted them to the Bishop of Talca; there were stories of direct pressure on the Bishop of Talca. It is our impression that such events, if they occurred, probably did not contribute very much to the decision taken by the late Msgr. Larrain. The fact that Sr. Barrios continued to be the chaplain of the movement until 1956, and that he attended its meetings regularly, indicates that the Bishop of Talca in no sense sought to separate himself or his priest from the movement. Sr. Barrios' removal from his role as parish priest—as distinct from his role as advisor to the movement—very likely was influenced by the fact that he had ceased to be acceptable as a priest to some of his parishioners. At least as important, however, was the desire to give him the advancement he deserved and to remove him from the supervision of his immediate superior with whom he had to share a house, and who did not approve of his activities.

But the fatal blow to the movement was undoubtedly the growing separation from it of Emilio Lorenzini. Personal reasons played a considerable part. Lorenzini had been quite ill in July and August, 1952, and in mid-1955 he went to Santiago for a very serious operation that, in effect, removed him from the scene for the remainder of 1955. Moreover, his family insisted that he write his thesis so he could practice law, and he also began to help out his father in the flour mill to augment the income of his own growing family. His wife, deeply socially conscious herself and devoted to Lorenzini, approved of his activities in one sense. Yet as an equally devoted mother, she could not but regret his failure to build a career (as well as permanently damaging his prospects of ever doing so locally) and his prolonged absences from home, the irregular hours, and the undermining of his health brought by this pattern of living.

At least as important as these personal factors was the growing rift between Lorenzini and ASICH-Santiago and the growing concern felt by Msgr. Larraín over the tone used by Lorenzini in leading the movement. The concern of the Bishop of Talca and that of the Jesuits present in ASICH was, however, clearly secondary to the concern of the laymen essentially in command of ASICH. Rifts of this kind generally have a number of causes, which not only accumulate, but reinforce each other; under such circumstances it becomes almost impossible to decide which is the "real" cause or even to put the different causes into an order of relative importance.

It is certain that there was divergence over what might be termed (1) *leadership style*, in the administrative rather than the more usual sociopsychological sense of that term. By rational conviction—though surely reinforced by temperament—Lorenzini was an activist, literally "outgoing" and always ready to leave the office to organize peasants or deal with their grievances. ASICH-Santiago leaned toward a more passive position: receiving complaints from those members who sought out its help by coming to the union offices in Molina from the surrounding countryside. This course of action would have enabled Lorenzini to keep up to date with monthly reports requested by Santiago, establishing a roster of dues-paying members and performing other administrative duties. But Lorenzini was not one to wait until business came to him. Nor did he approve of writing regular reports and keeping membership lists, which he deemed dangerous because of the possibility of police raids. Knowing by heart not only the names but even the nicknames of many of the peasants in the area, he would visit the different vineyards on his own initiative or because he had heard there was a problem. This pattern naturally gave rise to repeated employer charges of "agitation" and "trespassing." Moreover, Lorenzini would become involved with anyone's problems, whether a member of ASICH or not. Santiago disapproved of all aspects of this pattern.

Still within the realm of the administrative, there were divergencies over (2) *finances* and (3) the *locus of decision making.* ASICH-Santiago contributed one-third of the union's income and expenditure, excluding salaries. It contributed two-thirds of income and expenditure if salaries are included, since salaries were a large item and were entirely financed from Santiago. Nevertheless, there were perpetual complaints from Molina about shortages and delays in the arrival of sums promised. Santiago, in turn, was perpetually nervous about not knowing what was happening. In particular, it feared that it might be surprised by the outbreak of another strike: a *fait accompli* which would force its hand and oblige it to use up such good will as it had with cabinet ministers and other high level officials. Hence, there was some tension between Santiago and Lorenzini over who had the right to decide whether and when to go on strike.

This concern over the formal allocation of strike decisions was, of course, indicative of a more basic difference over (4) *radicalism in tactics.* Lorenzini was regarded as too ready to use stoppages and strikes, which ASICH-Santiago considered dangerous in view of their illegality. It is clear, however, that the differences appeared greater than they really were. This was due to further differences in (5) *personal styles of speech and behavior* and, we suspect, a tendency on Lorenzini's part to deliberately "get a rise out of" the Santiago group, whom he regarded as too strait-laced and, in any case, deficient in real organizing and negotiating experience.

A letter he wrote from his sickbed to a group of campesinos who had written wishing him a speedy recovery begins characteristically with the words "Greetings and revolution, comrades campesinos!" A letter written to one of the more conservative personalities among the Santiago leadership ends with the flourish "I remain at your orders, awaiting a little strike that might really be worthwhile and arouse us from our provincial routine." During the December strike and before being taken into custody, he is reported to have talked by phone (it was feared that phones were being tapped) to one of the senior ASICH leaders in Santiago and, among items of a more serious nature, to have asked him to "send down a few machine guns so that we can receive the Carabineros with the honors due them."

Lorenzini's public utterances, however, were what most irritated Santiago. In his speeches he not only made frequent references to the fact that "the only means which the workers have to triumph is the strike," but employed more colorful phrases such as "there's really only one solution for the employer problem: hang them from the lampposts." He often gave savory details of the private (amorous) lives of some of the employers (by name) to disprove the claim that they had no money to pay higher wages. In one instance he gave the address of the apartment where the employer kept his mistress and the time on Saturday afternoon when he visited her. This and other oratorical flights were, of course, reported both in Santiago and to the Bishop of Talca. The latter found himself in a particularly difficult position. The social encyclicals have clear injunctions against stimulating class warfare and require that an attitude of love and charity pervade relations between employers and workers. The Bishop felt sufficiently strongly about the matter of tone and language to write a long letter to ASICH-Santiago, asking it to request that a different style be adopted by Lorenzini (he referred to him as "Emilio" for there was a good deal of personal affection for him on the part of the Bishop and, indeed, on the part of everyone). The Bishop stated that he did not wish to approach Lorenzini directly, in order to avoid accusations that Lorenzini was controlled by the Bishop.

That we are dealing in part with appearances and style and not only with genuine differences over tactics is apparent from an examination of Lorenzini's behavior in critical situations and from the fact that both church dignitaries and the lay group in ASICH were, to some extent, aware of Lorenzini's capacity for more conservative behavior. During the December strike, a large and, for the first time, threatening crowd assembled outside the police station after Lorenzini had been taken into custody, ready to prevent his being removed to the city of Talca. Lorenzini received permission to address the crowd and calmed them down. He later helped the police to whisk him out of Molina without his supporters' being aware of it. Another incident, well known in the area, ended in his persuading a group of enraged campesinos *not* to burn down an owner's house. We have already mentioned that the police were likewise aware of the fact that Lorenzini had no serious intention to stir crowds to violence, and that his meetings were invariably peaceful.

Finally, Lorenzini's continuing (6) *involvement with politics* caused concern for a variety of interrelated reasons. It made it easy for the employers to attack the union's efforts as politically motivated, not really concerned with the betterment of the rural proletariat, and chiefly designed to gather votes for Falange in general and Lorenzini in particular. It genuinely weakened ASICH's leverage with the government, which was clearly not altogether hostile to the union but would naturally become so if it turned out to be nothing but one of the opposition parties in disguise.[40] Friendly Church representatives also found it embarrassing to be linked to a political party—especially when that party consisted of half of its own flock but was busy attacking the other half (the Conservative party). Finally, the top leadership of ASICH, while certainly Catholic, progressive, and not friendly to the Conservative party, and in that sense in sympathy with Falange, was not in fact Falangist in orientation: its top leaders were not activists. This was particularly true of the years 1955–1956, when precisely those who had resigned from ASICH were closest to Falange, had most trade union experience, and were more tolerant of radical trade union tactics.[41]

The irritations over Lorenzini's political activities came to a head early in 1956, when it was rumored that he might be willing to run as deputy in the parliamentary elections scheduled to take place that March. ASICH ordered the suspension of a number of local union mass meetings to avoid all suspicions and requested that Lorenzini clarify immediately what he proposed to do. Lorenzini did not run, but from then on he removed himself more and more from the leadership of the movement and the leadership in turn made his position more and more difficult. Be it also re-emphasized that reasons of health, family, and career propelled him in the same direction.

The loss of Lorenzini left only Navarro and his wife of those who had originally led the movement. They were devoted to the cause, yet they possessed neither the personal magnetism to gather up the enthusiastic loyalty of the peasants nor the knowledge and ability to conduct the union's business, not even with the aid of one of the more promising local campesinos which ASICH financed for them. Essentially very humble individuals, the Navarros did not have the self-confidence necessary to deal with a governor, a labor inspector, or an official in the social security system. ASICH-Santiago, itself in rapid decline from 1955 onwards and beset by financial problems and bitter divisions among its leaders, had little energy to spare for Molina. In the growing atmosphere of bitterness and disillusion pervading both Santiago and Molina, the Navarros became

---

[40] Falange was in opposition during the presidency of General Ibáñez.
[41] Manuel Naranjo and Roberto León resigned during these years, leaving Ramón Venegas in effective charge.

the subject of suspicions and controversy and were separated from the ASICH payroll in 1960.[42]

PART II: ANALYSIS

In this section, we shall first examine some economic and social characteristics of the zone of Molina and its population. These characteristics can never by themselves account for the occurrence of the movement. But they can reasonably be considered as facilitating conditions, making the ground receptive and fertile rather than sterile. We shall then go on to consider the goals, means, and ideology of this vineyard workers' union in order, finally, to address ourselves to certain long-term, very basic changes in Chilean economic, political, and social structure which can be traced back at least to the beginning of this century and certainly to the Presidency of Arturo Alessandri in 1920. We regard these developments as providing the underlying explanation of the Molina strike, converting it, as it were, into a specific, local symptom of more widespread political and social changes.

Economic and Social Characteristics of Peasant and Industry

Participation in a trade-union is a daring venture for a peasant living in a society with steeply graded, ascribed status differences: a quasi-feudal society in which economic and political power and social status are all "above" him. Such participation indicates that the peasant concerned may be exceptional in two ways. First, he may be relatively more modern than others in his values and attitudes: more ready to reject his ascribed inferiority; possessing more of a sense of competence and efficacy; less fatalistic; perhaps more educated. On the interpersonal, as distinct from the intrapsychic level, the existence of such movements may indicate more trust and more experience in cooperation.

[42] It is beyond the scope of this study to describe and analyze in detail the problems which beset ASICH at the national level. Briefly, conflict arose over whether ASICH should convert itself into a federation of trade-unions affiliated with the International Federation of Christian Trade Unions (IFCTU), a policy toward which the encyclicals seemingly pointed, or whether special local circumstances made it advisable for ASICH to continue to be what it had been from its first founding in 1947: an organization to which individuals, not groups, belonged and whose primary purpose was education and indoctrination. Those with most trade-union experience and most sympathy with Falange, as well as the clergy most involved, leaned toward the latter policy but lost and withdrew with tremendous cost in leadership resources. ASICH failed in its attempt to rival CUT.

Second, the peasant must possess not only the desire to establish a union, but also the physical and economic means of doing so. He must live close enough to other peasants to make it possible for them to get together. Ideally, he should enjoy a superior economic status: the resources necessary to withstand countermeasures by employers; a superior occupational level, which, in turn, implies that it might be difficult for employers to replace the workers concerned; and the kind of self-reliance fostered by pursuing a skilled trade. Certainly in what are now the most developed countries economically—the United States of America, the United Kingdom, and others—the union movement typically began with skilled, highly remunerated workers, such as printers. Our hypothesis was that this pattern would be repeated in the rural sector, and in today's developing countries.

We were able to collect much information to help us assess the position of Molina's *inquilinos* with respect to the economic, demographic, and social characteristics relevant to these hypotheses, and this information we now present.

The Economic Position of the Molina Vineyard Worker

Since we had a good deal of information from two sources—the Inspectorate of Labor and Manuel Silva's union records—on the remuneration of vineyard workers, we made the attempt to calculate their earnings and compare them with some relevant base lines. For the latter, we took, first, the then newly established agricultural minimum daily wage,[43] and calculated that the agricultural day laborer might work thirty days a month at the legal minimum. (This overestimates the casual laborer's income and thereby results in a conservative estimate of our vineyard workers' relative superiority.) As a second baseline, we used the legal minimum monthly salaries of white-collar employees in the province of Talca. (White-collar salaries in the mid-1950's tended to be between 50 and 100 per cent higher than the legal minimum for blue-collar industrial workers.) We put a monetary value on meals, fodder, and other payments-in-kind to the vineyard workers (the union or the contracts themselves often contained the relevant information), but we did not monetize their housing, thus imparting a further conservative bias to our estimate of the vineyard workers' relative superiority. We estimated that the vineyard worker would take on four *cuadras*, which we knew was

[43] Available from the Ministry of Labor.

most frequently the case. We could not, however, make allowances for the wages he might have to pay any laborers he hired or which he ought theoretically to be paying to his family. In this respect, therefore, we overestimated his earnings, thus, hopefully, balancing our previous underestimate. We were informed that such hiring is not frequent.

As a result of these rather hazardous estimates, we obtained the results presented in Table 5–1, in which the monthly earnings of vineyard workers are expressed as a ratio of the two baselines. It should be noted, first, that the agricultural legal minimum in Latin America, more so than in the richer countries, frequently represents an ardently desired, unattainable maximum. The fact that Molina's vineyard workers earned two

Table 5–1. Ratios of earnings of vineyard workers to agricultural wages and to white-collar salaries in the province of Talca, 1953 to 1956

Earnings	1953	1954	1955	1956
Vineyard * vs. agricultural minimum †	2.1	2.6	2.7	2.7
Vineyard * vs. white-collar minimum ‡	0.9	0.8	0.8	0.8

* Monthly earnings of vineyard workers, based on working four *cuadras* for ten months, and including in-kind (except housing) as well as monetary payments.

† Legal daily minimum agricultural wages, converted to monthly earnings on the basis of thirty working days.

‡ Legal monthly minimum white collar salary.

and a half times or more than this minimum (note the interesting jump after the December 1953 strike) is therefore once again a conservative estimate indeed of their relative superiority. Equally impressive is the fact that these vineyard workers earned within 20 per cent of a white-collar employee's salary: well above the minimum industrial blue-collar wage.

Apart from the skill level of the workers, two further factors may account for these relatively high wages. These are connected with the status of the wine industry in Molina, in relation both to the total local economy and to the rest of the wine industry. As concerns the former, we may note that 23 per cent of the arable land in the county [44] of Molina

[44] Provinces are divided into departments, the town of Molina being in the department of Lontué. Departments are in turn divided into *comunas* ("counties") and these into *distritos* ("townships"). The town of Molina is in the county of the same name.

was devoted to winegrowing.[45] For the province of Talca as a whole—which produced more wine at that time than any other province in Chile—the figure is only 6 per cent. In all of Chile, a mere 2 per cent of the acreage is given over to winegrowing; even in the province of Talca, no other county reached more than 11 per cent: less than half of Molina's percentage. Absorbing as much acreage as this and, we presume, the same or an even greater percentage of the labor force (since it is a fairly intensive user of labor) the industry would find it difficult to replace "recalcitrant" labor locally. This may well have been a factor in the unionization of the zone.

Concerning the place of the county of Molina in the Chilean wine industry, we know that in the mid-1950's, 10 per cent of national wine production came from this small area. It is noteworthy that only 5 per cent of national wine acreage was to be found in Molina, indicating that Molina had a very high productivity per acre: another factor favoring unionism.

We also know that, viewed historically, Molina was part of a geographical zone in which the wine industry was dynamic and expanding, while in others it was shrinking. We know that total acreage in Chile devoted to wine was relatively stable. Throughout the fifties, after recovering from a slump in the late forties, it was no greater than in the early forties. Yet *irrigated* acreage in the central valley of Chile (all of Molina is irrigated) in 1946 was only 92 per cent of the 1941 total; in 1951, 97 per cent; in 1953, 109 per cent (a jump of 12 per cent in the two years of interest to us!); and in 1956, 117 per cent.[46] In 1958, the province of Talca produced 75 million liters of wine against the 53 million liters of its nearest competitor province, Linares; in 1955 it had produced only 64 million liters against the 59 million of its competitor. Wine production in the province of Talca, then, was so dynamic in the early and middle fifties as to rapidly outdistance its competitors. Further, the "central irrigated zone" (of which Molina is a part) has relatively low labor cost per hectare (25 per cent of operating costs goes to labor as compared with 30 per cent in nonirrigated areas). Returns on capital in this zone are 7.7 per cent as compared with 5.4 per cent for the industry as a whole, or 50 per cent

[45] This and subsequent figures are taken from the Third National Agricultural Census, 1955. See also chapter 7 of the author's and Fernando Canitrot's *Iglesia, intelectuales y campesinos* (Santiago, Chile: Editorial del Pacifico, 1967).

[46] Jose Luis Pistono and Carlos Clavel, *Estudio economico de la vitivinicultura* (Santiago, Chile: Corporacion Vitivinicola de Chile, 1960), Table 4, p. 19.

higher than that for the country as a whole.[47] Finally, profit per acre is also double that for the country as a whole.

At this point, we are in danger of becoming involved in a lengthy and indeterminate argument over capacity to pay, over whether prosperity is due to labor or to management and hence who should reap the benefits, and other such questions. We do not need to enter this treacherous ground. We are content to have demonstrated that the Molina attempt at organizing—relatively successful, at least for a time—took place in a sector of the wine industry which was growing and prosperous, in which labor costs were relatively low even though wages were high, which supplied an important sector of the market, and which locally employed a substantial sector of the labor force. Labor economists will recognize these as characteristics favoring unionization.

The Social Conditions [48]

Social factors that might have favored organization in Molina include, but are not limited to, attitudes, and these social factors are as positive as were the economic ones.

We may note, first, that Molina is geographically accessible and open to communication. In a country almost 2,700 miles long, to be but 140 miles south of the capital is to be close to it. Molina is both on the country's main north-south arterial highway and on its main railway line from the capital to the South.

Second, Molina is a highly urbanized county: 31 per cent of its total population of about 25,000 was classified as urban in 1952,[49] exceeded in the Province of Talca only by the county of Talca (i.e., the large city of Talca itself) and followed by a county less than half as urbanized.

Third, the county is well supplied with means of communication quite apart from road and railway. Its 63 private vehicles and 90 trucks per 10,000 population exceed comparable figures even for the county of Talca (with only 56 and 58 respectively), and in buses and cars for hire it is second only to Talca.[50] In some of these categories Molina exceeds not only the average for the country but even Santiago! Molina was likewise

[47] *Ibid.*, tables 47, 49, and 50, pp. 90, 93, and 94.

[48] Two undergraduates from the School of Economics of the University of Chile helped us draw together from various official sources the information used in this section. We remember them with esteem and would like to thank them: Joel Pfeng and Luis Adduard.   [49] Twelfth General Population Census, 1952.

[50] *Comercio interior y comunicaciones: 1952* (Santiago, Chile: Servicio Nacional de Estadística y Censo, 1952), pp. 64 and 66.

far better supplied with telephones than any other county in the province except that of Talca, and well above the average for the neighboring province of Curicó, which includes the substantial town of the same name.[51]

Fourth, Molina had both a high number of resident professionals and an unusual number of institutions in which they worked. It had two of the province's six hospitals (the city of Talca, with more than 60,000 inhabitants, also had only two). Of the province's 25 medical professionals not resident in the city of Talca, 21 lived in the county of Molina.[52]

To some extent, of course, these high rates are simply a reflection of the fact that the county is a relatively urbanized one. However, we have seen that in some instances Molina exceeds even the county of Talca despite the fact that the latter was more urbanized. In any case we merely wish to demonstrate the presence of persons, institutions, and material means that could in one way or another have served to propagate modern ideas among the peasants. The reason for their presence is of no direct concern at the moment.

Finally, the population of even the rural areas of the township of Molina (1) lived close together (*high population density*), (2) was *increasing rapidly*, and (3) was relatively *highly educated*. Thus, analysis of the Twelfth General Population Census shows that the county of Molina was third out of eight in the province in population density and, if the districts of the inhospitable Andean Cordillera are subtracted (as well as the town of Molina) the remainder of the county moves further up still in density. Between 1930 and 1952, the population of the township increased by 43 per cent whereas the town of Molina increased by only 35 per cent. This indicates that the rural population of the township grew faster than the urban population at a time when, for Chile as a whole, the rural total fell considerably in proportion. In all probability, this was another indication of the dynamism of the wine industry. Immigration undoubtedly accounted for some of this increase and we know that persons migrating from the politically radical North during the thirties and forties were most important in carrying ideas of unionization into the zone. Some of them were active during the strike itself.

Concerning education, and considering the rural population only, we know that, excluding the county of Talca, the rural part of the county of

[51] Information obtained for the year 1952 from the Chilean Telephone Company (Form No. 1067-A).
[52] *Demografia y asistencia social, 1951* (Santiago, Chile: Servicio Nacional de Estadística y Censo, 1951) p. 96.

Molina was in third place out of eight both in degree of literacy of the population of 15 years and over (60.7 per cent) and in primary school attendance for children between six and fourteen years of age. The county as a whole had percentages of adults with secondary and university education which were exceeded only by the county of Talca.[53] While on some of these indices Molina is clearly not an exceptional rural area, it is so on others, and in no case is Molina below average or in any way particularly underprivileged.

Organizing Experience

While we had not time to assemble a detailed social history of the area (for which information would, in any case, not have been systematic and reliable), we became impressed early in our interviews and in our perusal of documents with the fact that ferment and attempts at organizing the vineyard workers went back well beyond the time when the local Catholic element first became active. Some informants remembered a massive strike as early as the middle twenties. All agree that Communist organizers were active in the mid-thirties and that there were frequent clashes between them, other leftist groups, and the so called "White Militia." After the victory of the Popular Front in 1938, twenty unions were organized in less than two years only to decay when the government ceased to recognize them. Yet in 1947, contract demands were presented by the workers of at least one vineyard and a strike took place, reputedly organized by Communists. We also know that during the middle forties, a union existed in one of the vineyards that was later to become very active in the Catholic movement. We also know that in the early fifties, the names of "outside" Communists appeared on contract demands processed by the labor inspector and they appeared as members of the conciliation board, much as did Lorenzini's name later. By 1952, twenty *fundos* had presented demands, eleven of which were helped by Communists.

Social Integration of the Zone

Clearly the zone had been organizable for a considerable period and by individuals other than the Catholic group about which we know most. The employers had spoken of the area as having long been in a state of "agitation" and "ferment." With additional hints of alcoholism and stories of murders and brawls, the employers conveyed the impression that the zone was in a state of moral dissolution or anomie. But there is an alternative view: this must have been a particularly well integrated zone

[53] Twelfth General Population Census, 1952.

to support organizing efforts of this kind; this hypothesis seems to be born out by the figures on social integration that we examined. These dealt with: (1) the extent of illegitimacy, that is, the efficacy of norms concerning the family; (2) the incidence of crimes against the person (in view of the employer's accusation of a "climate of violence"); (3) the incidence of crimes against property (because of its obvious relationship, at least in the employers' eyes, to unjustified claims for wages, and so forth); and (4) the incidence of crimes related to alcoholism.

The rate of illegitimacy in the county of Molina in 1951 was 76 per 1,000 live births. With the exception of one other county (Pelarco), this was the lowest rate for any county in Talca, where rates were otherwise above 100 per 1,000 births. The average for all rural areas of Talca was 135; for the province of Curicó it was 174; for the department of Santiago, 190; and for Chile as a whole, 196.[54] Without question, therefore, Molina gave every indication of not being "anomic" in this respect.

To obtain a relative crime rate for the county of Molina we had to engage in a lengthy series of calculations. Because the incidence is low of various crimes per 10,000 of population of age 15 or over (the manner in which the statistics are presented [55]), large percentage fluctuations occur from year to year, and one additional murder may represent an increase of 25 per cent. Therefore we took three years (1951–1953), not just one, as a base. We chose as comparison points with Molina the same base lines which we had used in other statistics: the country as a whole; the department of Talca; the province of Curicó; and two very rural counties in the province of Talca: Curepto and Mataquito. We then ranked these areas according to the incidence of specific crimes (homicide, bodily injury, and so forth), averaged these figures, and ranked the resulting averages to get each area's standing on groups of crimes. The county of Molina is in third place out of six in the relative incidence of crimes of violence; it has the lowest incidence of property crimes; and it is tied with Curepto and Mataquito for the highest incidence of crimes related to alcohol—surely not surprising in view of the area's chief product. If only crimes of violence and property were considered, Molina would be almost at the bottom of the list. Molina is tied for fourth place of these six when all three types of crimes have been added and averaged.

[54] *Demografía y asistencia social, 1951–1954* (Santiago, Chile: Servicio Nacional de Estadística y Censo).

[55] *Educación, justicia, politica y administracion, 1951–1953* (Santiago, Chile: Servicio Nacional de Estadística y Censo, n.d.)

The rise of the union movement cannot, therefore, be linked to an extreme degree of social disorganization and anomie. Rather, we are inclined to see it as a manifestation of social solidarity and cohesion, built on a dense, expanding and relatively prosperous population, stimulated by high education, the presence of professionals, and easy access to communications and mass media.

The Movement's Goals, Ideology, and Means

Goals

To judge the goals of the movement we must look at both what it explicitly demanded and what it did. So judged, it seems to have had two quite different types of goals: one in relation to its environment, the employers in particular; the other internal, directed towards its membership.

Environmental Goals. These consisted of a long series of highly specific demands that can surely be called "normal" for any job-oriented, bread-and-butter union movement. Central to this first type were, of course, demands for wage "increases": often little more than attempts to protect existing purchasing power against erosion by inflation. Many times, too, demands for payment in kind really represented requests that norms which were supposedly customary and some of which were even legally obligatory would in fact be complied with: that lunch be given on rainy days and holidays as well as on work days; that pieces of meat be put into soup provided by the employer at least twice a week; and that the meat in fact be meat, not fat and gristle. Demands were presented to the two chambers of Parliament that the Labor Code be reformed; these demands were channeled via ASICH-Santiago and, indeed, more than half originated there. Finally, there were demands that the employer comply with the law and pay social security taxes to the government and family allowances to the worker. These requests are unusual only because it should have been the obligation of the government to see that its law were obeyed. They do not, in essence, go beyond the scope of bread-and-butter goals.

Notable, then, is the absence of goals which implicitly or explicitly would have required major institutional changes—such as land reform— or which would have led to major changes in the balance of power between existing groups, intentionally or otherwise. Perhaps the payment of better wages and social security contributions and the improvement of rural housing would have absorbed so much of the owners' income and wealth as to weaken them and thus, in effect, set in train major social and political changes. But few, if any, of the union's leaders gave evidence of having such a goal explicitly in mind and it is most doubtful, given the modest nature of the demands, that their fulfillment would have had this effect unintentionally.

There were some very small indications that at times the movement considered the possibility of pushing for more profound changes, and these straws in the wind are not without symbolic importance. Thus, at the first national convention of ASICH in January, 1954, one of the approved resolutions called for the promotion of "worker-employer bodies" and an "agrarian reform according to Christian principles." [56] A slight but symbolically significant rise in the status and power of campesinos may also be seen in the fact that Manuel Silva and Luis Navarro, at the national and local levels respectively, became the campesino representatives on a Special Commission for Campesino Affairs set up by the Ministry of Labor. But these exceptions cannot alter the general impression that we are dealing with a movement which, in relation to its environment, had modest goals of the trade-union type.

Internal Goals. This second type of goal was much more unusual. The intensity with which it was pursued cannot fully be explained without reference to the ideology inspiring the union's leadership, although that ideology is not by itself a sufficient explanation. We refer to the prominence in the movement's roster of activities of education of all kinds: cooking and sewing, literacy classes and trade-union education, lessons in Catholic social doctrine and indoctrination against communism and capitalism. The attempt to indoctrinate and culturally "lift" its membership is an interesting goal for an organization of this kind, since it hints at differences in background between members and leaders; we shall go into this later. There is no evidence that the membership resented these educational efforts. Inded, our experience indicates that there was enthusiasm for much of it, especially since educational aspirations of all kinds are perhaps rising faster than aspirations for material goods in countries such as Chile.

Nevertheless, the drive behind this massive educational effort came undoubtedly from above the membership and, in part, from outside the

---

[56] Our evidence is a typewritten circular sent out by ASICH afterward, summarizing the conclusions of the convention.

organization: It can be fully explained only by considering the social function assigned to labor unions by Catholic doctrine (ideology).[57]

Ideology

The ideas which influenced the actions of progressive Catholics—lay and clergy—in Chile in the mid-fifties came first and foremost from the two great social encyclicals: Leo XIII's *Rerum Novarum* (1891) and Pius XI's *Quadragesimo Anno* (1931). In addition, interpretations and elaborations of the encyclicals and of other papal pronouncements by individuals regarded as authoritative—such as Fr. Jean Villain, S.J.[58]—came to be known rapidly in Chile. Finally, there was the oral teaching of those progressive priests who had studied and travelled in Europe—such as Fr. Alberto Hurtado—and of those who had been exiled there but allowed to return to Chile—such as Fr. Francisco Vives, a devoted and revered teacher who died in 1935 after arousing the social consciousness of upper-class youths since 1912.

There are two outstanding general characteristics of *Rerum Novarum* and *Quadragesimo Anno.* The first is the vigorous and forthright manner in which both Popes condemn socialism [59] (which was to be expected), in which Leo XIII attacks employers,[60] and in which Pius XI denounces laissez-faire capitalism and Manchester liberalism.[61] Indeed, the encyclicals give the impression that socialism's spurious attraction for workers is in large part due to the misery caused by the avariciousness of "grasping men." [62] The second characteristic of these social encyclicals is their vigorous affirmation that Christianity as a religion and the (Catholic)

---

[57] Our use of the word "ideology" has no negative denotations whatsoever. Most religions are "ideologies" in the sense that, among many other aspects, they generally have a comprehensive and interrelated view of man and society at present, and a similar view of an ideal state of man and society which may or may not be similar to the actual state. Only in this way are we using the word "ideology."

[58] See his *L'Enseignement social de l'Eglise* (Paris: Spes-Paris, 1953).

[59] *Seven Great Encyclicals* (Glen Rock, N.J.: Paulist Press, 1963); see the section "Socialism Rejected," paras. 11 and 12, pp. 7-8, as well as paras. 3, 40, and others. *Quadragesimo Anno* is much more detailed and lengthy on this point, but see particularly paras. 111ff., pp. 155ff.

[60] *Ibid.*, para. 2, p. 2, and the many criticisms implicit in the sections entitled "Employer and Employee" (paras. 15-17, pp. 8-10); "The Right Use of Money" paras. 18-19, pp. 10-11); and others dealing with "Hours of Labor," "Child Iabor," "Just Wages," and so forth.

[61] *Ibid.*, para. 27, p. 131, with its reference to "those tottering tenets of liberalism." See also the almost Marxist analysis of monopoly capitalism and economic imperialism contained in paras. 101-110, pp. 152-154.   [62] *Ibid.*, para. 2, p. 2.

Church as an institution have a right to concern themselves with the problems of social justice, poverty, and the misery of the working class [63] and to "intervene directly." [64]

Since the beginning of this century progressive Catholics in many parts of the world have based their efforts of social reform on statements of this kind. Sections of the Chilean clergy and laity seemed to have become aware with surprising speed of precisely these parts of the encyclicals and of the programs to which they gave rise in the Catholic areas of Europe. As early as 1910 we find mention of a First Social Catholic Congress during which a National Federation of Catholic Social Works was established and a savings and housing association, "Social Peace," founded. A newspaper said at the time that "Chile will be the Belgium of America which will offer the world the beautiful example of social renovation by Christianity." [65]

At about this time, Frs. Fernando Vives, S.J., and Jorge Fernandez Pradel, S.J., began teaching *Rerum Novarum* to well-to-do Catholic youths—such as Manuel Larraín and Alberto Hurtado—in San Ignacio and in other settings. Another priest, Sr. Guillermo Viviani, founded the first Catholic trade-unions in the needle trades, railways, and commerce. Resistance by conservative Catholics was, of course, strong, and several of those concerned were exiled from Chile for long periods or silenced in other ways. But in 1921, the Archbishop of Santiago, Dr. Crescente Errázuriz, issued a pastoral entitled "Social Action," equal to *Rerum Novarum* in its sympathy for the oppressed worker and considerably more explicit in its condemnation of employer greed and inhumanity. Dr. Crescente Errázuriz presided over the Church during its final separation from the Chilean State in 1925 and appalled traditionalists by stating that it was not the business of the Church to ally itself with any political party (i.e., the Conservative party) or to encourage the faithful to vote for it.

Rerum Novarum encouraged the development of what it called "workmen's associations," and stated that "it were greatly to be desired that they should multiply and become more effective." [66] The encyclical did not specify whether they should consist of workmen alone or of work-

[63] "We approach the subject with confidence, and in the exercise of the right which belongs to us" (*ibid.*, para. 13, p. 7).   [64] *Ibid.*, para. 24, p. 14.
[65] *La Union* of Valparaiso, as cited in Alejandro Magnet, *El Padre Hurtado* (Santiago, Chile: Editorial del Pacifico, 1954), p. 39. Much of the material which follows comes from this excellent book; much also from personal interviews with participants in these and later events, some of whom, like Sr. Clemente Perez Perez, have valuable collections of newspaper clippings, brochures, documents, and so forth, which they kindly allowed us to inspect.   [66] Ibid., para. 36, p. 23.

men and employers together,[67] but it did clearly indicate a preference for Christian workmen founding their own union lest "their religion . . . be exposed to peril." [68] And from this, in turn, flows the primary emphasis which the encyclicals put on the goals of encouraging "piety and morality" to which the associations "must pay special and principal attention." [69] "Let our associations, then, look first and before all to God; let religious instruction have therein a foremost place, each one being carefully taught what is his duty to God, what to believe." [70]

Pius XI's *Quadragesimo Anno* (1931) presents a more shaded and subtle picture of possible union structures and goals, as is to be expected after the accumulated experience of forty years. It recognizes the possibility of establishing organizations concerned exclusively with "the protection of the rights and legitimate interests of their members in the labor market." [71] But it makes clear that such exclusive emphasis on economic goals, at the expense of the moral regeneration of its members, is due to special circumstances or to the "lamentable dissension of minds and hearts." The earlier leaning toward confessional unions continues in *Quadragesimo Anno*, and Leo XIII's emphasis on education and moral teaching as the primary goal of unions is quoted approvingly.[72]

Chile once again followed Roman pronouncements with astonishing speed and, in many ways, exceeded them in progressiveness and specificity. Archbishop Errázuriz' 1921 pastoral, "Social Action," already cited, is likewise more explicit on trade-unions and their functions:

And as the unfortunate (worker) is ordinarily impotent to have his complaints heard therefore the Church, his natural protector, is pleased to favor the establishment of associations of workers, which put them in a position to help themselves, of helping each other mutually, and to defend themselves against the cruelty of heartless employers.

In 1932, a collective pastoral—the first pastoral signed by all Chilean bishops of which we have knowledge—is entitled, significantly, "The True and Only Solution of the Social Question." Once again, it refers favorably to workmen's associations. But like *Quadragesimo Anno* on which it is clearly based, the pastoral ultimately sees the solution of social

---

[67] The mere raising of the possibility of joint associations, or corporations, is from other points of view an unusual endorsement of the latter. The reader will recall that ASICH looked forward to the formation of bipartite bodies. *Quadragesimo Anno* seemed to incline toward monopolistic corporations—superorganizations including both labor unions and employers' associations (see paras. 92ff., pp. 150–151).

[68] *Ibid.*, para. 40, p. 25.   [69] *Ibid.*, para. 42, p. 27.   [70] *Ibid.*, para. 40.
[71] *Ibid.*, para. 34, p. 133.   [72] *Ibid.*, para. 32.

problems in a return to Christianity—a change in the hearts and minds of individual men, rather than in the institutions.

We cannot here describe in detail the ever increasing amount of contact in the 1930's between "the poor" and certain groups of youths from the more comfortable sections of Catholic society. Much of this contact consisted of propagating the Church's social doctrine, which we may interpret, perhaps a little riskily, as an unconscious and highly ambivalent attempt both to radicalize and to tranquilize the Chilean working class. But some of this contact went beyond theology to teach workers their rights under the law. Finally, in the late thirties and early forties, there was action as well as teaching. In particular, a storm of protest from the Catholic Right followed the help given in 1940 by a local priest and by clergy and laymen from the so-called National Economic and Social Secretariat of the archdiocese of Santiago to the *inquilinos* of the *fundo* "Huelquen" near Santiago, when they presented contract demands to a well known Conservative landowner.

New attempts in the early 1940's to establish Catholic unions in the textile, metal, and shoe and leather industries [73] aroused even greater resistance. The Catholic Right was now thoroughly alarmed since these organizing efforts came on top of the establishment of the left-wing Falange in 1938. As a result of this resistance, progressive social and economic action was brought almost to a halt in the mid-forties, and a like fate seemed about to overtake political action. In 1947, Falange was on the point of dissolving itself after what appeared to be a direct attack on it in a declaration by Chile's bishops. Only Bishop Larraín's timely intervention, clarifying the declaration as condemning not individuals and political parties or their doctrines, but only certain specific positions, stopped the leadership of Falange from dispersing.

In retrospect, 1947 seems to have been the turning point in the internal political and ideological struggle of Catholicism in Chile. In that year, Fr. Hurtado, after observing Catholic progressive action in France and Italy, was authorized by Pope Pius XII himself, after a visit to Rome, to establish ASICH: a Catholic workers' federation devoted to trade-union education and religious and moral indoctrination. In 1949, the bishops of Chile issued a joint pastoral entitled "Concerning Social Problems" in which they energetically called upon Catholics to "cease all opposition . . . to the establishment of labor unions and give all help in all possible ways in their formation." The right to strike was explicitly recognized. In

[73] The old ones, dating back to the 1910's, had long since died.

1950, Cardinal Caro, in the name of the Conference of Chilean Bishops, wrote Fr. Hurtado a letter congratulating him on his efforts in the union field, and called on all Catholics to help him. Catholic activities in the labor field, albeit with a strong—though not exclusive—educational emphasis, were firmly established.

Thus did papal doctrine and European Catholic experience become transferred to Chile: perhaps less radical than extreme left-wing Catholicism in France, but certainly no less radical, we feel, than the tone of papal pronouncements. This was the doctrine, and we know that all those involved in the Molina situation, clergy and laymen, national and local, had devoted themselves to its study over many years. Many of these individuals had participated in the historical events we have recorded in which doctrine had explicitly been put into practice. The goals of the Molina movement had precisely the characteristics we would have predicted from doctrine: (1) assertion of the right to organize, (2) a heavy emphasis on religious and moral education, (3) some ambivalence over the prominence of material goals, (4) even greater ambivalence about the use of "radical" means such as strikes to achieve such goals, and (5) some leaning toward confessionalism. Hence we feel justified in asserting that ideology clearly influenced the goals of action. Indeed, in the light of the extremely limited space generally devoted in the encyclicals and in related pronouncements to the union's role in improving the workers' material position, it is, if anything, surprising that so much of the Church's energies went into noneducational, "business union" activities. Perhaps it is less surprising when Chilean Catholic as distinct from Vatican ideological pronouncements are examined. It is probably fair to say that, for the campesinos themselves, these mundane goals were a *sine qua non* for support of the union, although they gladly accepted the union's educational and ideological activities. For the leadership, the motivation was possibly reversed: for some of the Santiago leaders in particular, educational and moral goals were at times equal in importance to bread-and-butter union goals.

Means

Ideology influenced not only the goals of the Molina movement. It also seems of great relevance to an understanding of the dispute over means between Lorenzini and ASICH-Santiago. *Rerum Novarum* had only an oblique reference to strikes; it placed on public authorities the responsibility for eliminating the inhuman conditions (long hours, low pay) which the encyclical regarded as frequently the underlying cause of strikes

Strikes were therefore seen as expressions of frustrations, and *Rerum Novarum* associated them with violence and disorder. They were not seen as rational bargaining tactics. *Quadragesimo Anno*, clearly with an eye on Fascist Italy, cited with seeming approval a social order in which strikes and lockouts are forbidden,[74] though a few sentences later the encyclical stated, "we feel bound to add that there are some who fear that the state is substituting itself for private initiative."

Later writers such as Villain [75] made it clear that the strike was in itself not illegitimate and may even have been a moral obligation if the defense of subsistence salaries were at stake. Nevertheless, much greater emphasis was invariably given to the certain cost of strikes: to the harm they can do; to the far greater uncertainty of the benefits which might be gained; to the need to explore alternatives; and to the dangerous possibility of employing illicit methods in the strike (such as lies, the arousal of class antagonism, and so forth), even though the strike itself is justified. The famous Charter of Labor (the letter of the Holy Congregation to the Bishop of Lile, Msgr. Lienart, 1929) admittedly mentioned the right of workers to defend their professional interests in all freedom and in all independence, but it did so only to say that this can never justify recourse to the class struggle.

The overall tone employed by these writers in discussing the strike, therefore, undermines moral confidence in its use by all but the hardiest of souls—such as Lorenzini—and in all but the most extreme situations. When one adds to this the frequent injunctions against arousing class antagonism, and statements such as "the Church wants that labor unions be instruments of peace and concord," contained in the letter to Bishop Lienart, it is apparent that unions attempting to conform to the spirit of these injunctions could find themselves severely hobbled in the means at their disposal. Let us now suppose (and it seems realistic to do so) that a certain amount of license to attack employers verbally (to show that "nothing happens") is necessary in order to bind to a new union a fearful membership in need of strong and encouraging words from its leaders. And let us also suppose that a new union needs to feel free to threaten strikes, and even to use them quickly on occasion in dealing with employers who are only too ready to exploit any timidity on the union's part and any reluctance to use the strike weapon when it is most effective. Then, if these assumptions are correct, failure to employ these organizing and bargaining tactics speedily may doom the union to failure. Since

[74] *Ibid.*, paras. 94–95, p. 151.   [75] *Op. cit.*, pp. 274ff.

Catholic doctrine prior to the 1960's seems to have been hostile to their speedy employment, this doctrine was, probably unintentionally, a real obstacle to the establishment of unions, despite its defense of the right to organize at a more general level.

We find again that the events in Molina with respect to means parallel with some exactness what was prescribed by general Catholic doctrine as understood by progressive Chilean Catholics at the time. The doctrine surrounded with much moral ambiguity and danger the use of those organizing and bargaining tactics which are regarded as normal and necessary by the labor movements of many countries, even movements which are not Marxist and have no basic commitment to furthering class warfare. We feel that this reluctance to employ freely all the means at its disposal weakened the Molina union at critical moments, for example, in not defending its right to organize when, in March, 1955, the employers refused to deal with ASICH.

Our conclusion is that Catholic ideology was both an indispensable source of strength to the movement and a serious source of weakness. It inspired the action of key personnel, nationally and locally, laymen and clergy, at all levels. But while it aroused them to arms, it stayed their hands at crucial moments. While by no means the only cause of the ultimate failure of the movement, its contribution was significant.

One further phenomenon should be noted at this point which we believe to be to some extent an effect of ideology. A part of the story which we were unable to develop sufficiently in the abbreviated description of events presented here was the tension within the entire leadership group, not only between Lorenzini and ASICH-Santiago. The division over whether or not to convert ASICH into a trade-union federation rivaling CUT lost the federation a substantial portion of its top leadership resources, both lay and clerical, because it found itself outmaneuvered and was unwilling to live with the victory of the minority. But personal frictions of various kinds had much earlier begun the process of decimating this highly motivated and capable leadership group. Manuel Naranjo, for example, left over other issues, and the Navarros were forced out later. What could account for this high degree of interpersonal tension and its eventuating in the permanent loss of personnel? One explanation is that this was an unusually independent group of individualists who found it difficult to give in gracefully. The fact that so many of them had chosen an independent profession—law—where they would not be under organizational constraints might well be seen as a subtle indication of their personality.

More important we believe to be the following factors. Helping low-status groups is likely to bring the individual no reward other than the satisfaction of his ideals, at least in the early period during which the movement is still struggling. Indeed, practically all his human needs are apt to be frustrated except some altruistic ones. There may be no immediate remuneration, and even more seriously, his career prospects may be damaged permanently through participation in the movement. Family life invariably suffers and even community reputation is adversely affected. His work is apt to be so arduous as to endanger his health, and more likely than not its result is failure, thereby continuously raising the question: "Is it really worth it?"

If fulfillment of ideological visions is his only gratification, frustration on this score is likely to result in his withdrawal from the movement since it does not, and cannot, offer him any other satisfaction. And since it is very likely that everyone's ideological commitments differ slightly from those of his neighbor, most leaders will be disappointed most of the time. Several early supporters of the movement left, for example, because they felt moral revulsion when some individuals began to be paid for their services. In almost explicitly Weberian terms, they expressed bitter regret at the growing routinization and bureaucratization and looked back to the days when a small band of dedicated individuals worked for nothing. Others left when power and influence began to crystallize around one or two individuals; a psychic blow they were unwilling to tolerate in addition to other deprivations and the frustration of their devotion to micro-democracy. Still others left over such issues as whether or not to cooperate with Marxist groups.

In short, these professionals showed, for various reasons, a "hypersensitivity" [76] to ideological and policy issues which was ruinous to the movement. We believe this hypersensitivity to be connected with the fact that these professionals had no possibility for substitute gratifications—the mundane ones of financial prosperity, job security, promotion possibilities, success in the task itself—so that the frustration of their

[76] The concept of "ideological sensitivity" was created by S. M. Lipset, Martin A. Trow, and J. S. Coleman in their *Union Democracy: The Internal Politics of the International Typographical Union* (Glencoe, Ill.: Free Press, 1956), p. 357. In the context of the ITU, fighting over ideological issues was less divisive than if struggles had taken place over more mundane matters. We employ the term "hypersensitivity" to convey our belief that, in this particular case at least, constant and intense concern with correct ideological positions (for example, whether or not the failure to establish a confessional union movement was contrary to papal wishes) was severely disfunctional to the organization's survival.

ideological aspirations removed the only *raison d'être* for their participation.

Leadership, Allies, and Long-Term Changes in Chilean Society

The Social Origins of Leadership and its Significance

It is clear from the description of the movement that at no time was an important position of leadership, even at the local level, held by anyone who at the time was earning his livelihood as a campesino. Except for Silva (whose parentage is unknown) and the Navarros (whose parents might have been peasants for part of their lives) none of the leaders even came from peasant stock. The ASICH-Santiago group were middle-class, generally upper middle-class with upper-class connections. For the most part, they were professionals with an intellectual bent. Ramón Venegas was an architect educated in Europe as well as in Chile; William Thayer and Hernan Troncoso were lawyers: all three taught or were later to teach at various universities. Naranjo—a former Army officer from an impoverished family of landowners—was a widely-read man despite his activist inclinations. Roberto León was perhaps the humblest: a bank employee, but of a bearing that leads one to suspect a white-collar rather than a blue-collar background (we failed to establish his class origin). Locally, we find in Lorenzini a young law school graduate who was the son of a well-to-do merchant; we find a priest, an agronomist, and the wives of local professionals. Bishop Manuel Larraín Errázuriz, at the provincial level, belonged on both his mother's and his father's side to the most aristocratic families in Chile.

From two points of view, the composition of this leadership is not accidental. First, the total absence of peasants probably bespeaks a lack of leadership potential within that large stratum, hard and sad though it is to say so. There is no indication that the earlier Marxist groups had managed better than the Catholics to attract peasant leaders. An alternative explanation is that, while the potential was there, the middle class, whether Marxist or Catholic, was reluctant to give up the perquisites of leadership. Perhaps this occurred at a psychological level too subtle for anyone, observers like ourselves or any of the participants, to have suspected. But we doubt that such was the case. Consciously, the desire to find campesinos on whom to devolve responsibility was intense and appeared sincere on the part of both Marxists and Catholics. But no one appeared.

The failure of these particular peasants (comparatively well-educated and modernized though they were) to produce leaders was, of course, symptomatic of a more general passivity on their part vis-à-vis middle-class professionals, a pattern of behavior which was probably reinforced by traditional feelings of deference and gratitude. But whatever its causes, and farfetched though it may seem, this passivity had an important bearing on a phenomenon with which we dealt earlier: the progressive disintegration of the leadership group. For the passivity on the part of the members meant that, despite the formal existence of democratic machinery for the election of officers and for determining policy and resolving disputes, in reality these democratic mechanisms did not function. Letting the membership ultimately resolve such policy differences as might exist within a leadership group has the excellent functional consequence of making the loser feel less embittered: on the one hand, he does not have to give in to his opponent; on the other, his ego is less involved because he recognizes that ultimate power resides not in him or his opponent, but in this larger, anonymous group known as "the membership." Both factors make defeat easier to accept, and therefore less likely to result in withdrawal by the loser. The fact that, in peasant organizations led by high-status individuals, the membership does not and cannot serve this face-saving function converts disputes into unresolvable, personal battles. It is, in our opinion, a major and inevitable cause of the decimation of leadership "cadres" in this type of organization.

Apart from the absence of peasants in the leadership group, and their general passivity, a second aspect of leadership was of sociological significance. The Molina situation seemed to pit urban professionals against landowners and that, surely, could not have been entirely accidental. A brief review of Chilean political history from 1920 onward, and of the changes in social power relationships which it symbolized, will confirm this view.

Changes in the Sociopolitical Balance of Power

The triumph of Arturo Alessandri in the presidential election of 1920 is generally regarded as the end of an epoch stretching back to the beginning of the republic some one hundred years earlier, during which a wealthy landed and commercial oligarchy had a complete and absolute monopoly of formal power. Presidents, cabinet ministers, and members of parliament originated in that class almost to a man, and they generally represented no one else. The social reforms which Alessandri was unable to get accepted between 1920 and 1924 by persuasion, the army (in its only major intervention in Chilean politics) established by threat of force in 1924 and 1925. An advanced body of social legislation, including the

Labor Code and the beginning of a social security system was imposed.[77] General Ibáñez—the same man who was visited by Cardinal Caro in 1953—saw to the implementation of this legislation during his first presidency in the latter half of the twenties.

During the late thirties and forties the urban bourgeoisie—represented by the Radical party—was able to achieve both relatively rapid industrialization and a substantial increase in the political power wielded both by itself and the better-off sections of the blue- and white-collar urban working classes. It could modernize the urban sector, however, only by, in effect, agreeing to leave the rural sector untouched. One fitting symbol of this collusive agreement with the Right [78] was the coalition cabinets of the late forties, in which Conservatives and Liberals presided over by Radical presidents replaced the Communists and Socialists who had earlier occupied these same places after the election of 1938, in which the Radicals had been allied with the Marxists in a French-style Popular Front.

But for our case, an even more telling symbol of this agreement to keep "hands off" the countryside was the passage of Law No. 8811 on July 29, 1947, which added Titles IV, V, and VI to Book III of the Chilean Labor Code: a law governing unionization and collective bargaining in agriculture. When the Radicals came to power in 1938, the new government interpreted the 1925 code for the first time as giving agricultural workers the same (relatively wide) organizing and bargaining rights as industrial workers. As a result, considerable unionization took place. In Molina, forty-eight legal unions were established between 1938 and 1940, and all of them presented contract demands. But some time before 1942 the National Agricultural Society (SNA) threatened to challenge the government in the courts on its interpretation of the law. As a result, President Aguirre instructed the Ministry of Labor to stop giving legal recognition to agricultural unions, and in 1947, the law was enacted. It systematically left the agricultural worker weaker than his urban counter-

[77] See the interesting and detailed account of these events in James O. Morris, *Elites, Intellectuals and Consensus: A Study of the Social Question and the Industrial Relations System in Chile* (Ithaca, N.Y.: New York State School of Industrial and Labor Relations, Cornell University, 1966), p. 312.

[78] Despite our somewhat pointed language, no criticism is intended. To criticize history is in any case futile and arrogant: in this instance, there is good reason for thinking that no more than was gained and modernized could have been gained and modernized at that time. Similar unstated agreements between urban bourgeoisie and landed Right were not unusual in Latin America between 1910 and 1960, depending on the country. Concerning Argentina, for example, see Robert J. Alexander, *Labor Relations in Argentina, Brazil, and Chile* (New York: McGraw-Hill, 1962), p. 149.

part and symbolized the fact that the fiat of the Radical party stopped at the border between town and countryside.

The law of 1947, however, was not only the symbol of an epoch: it was also to some extent its swan song. General Ibáñez' extraordinary electoral triumph in 1952 was due at least in part to support from the moderate and "middle" Left. Thus, a majority of the Socialist party supported his candidacy, while only the smaller, more extreme wing of the party split off and, with the Communists, supported their own candidate. In any case, General Ibáñez' victory represented a revulsion against the Center–Right alliance. This new and rather inchoate coalition of groups [79] soon broke up, as General Ibáñez moved toward the traditional Right. But in the beginning of his presidency, in 1952, the forces behind Ibáñez had few commitments to the traditional landowning interests. The government's posture in the Molina incident symbolized this relative independence of various urban sectors from rural elites, an independence new in Chilean history except for a brief period after the triumph of the Popular Front in 1938. Also symbolic of this weakening of the power of the traditional landed elite was a decree extending minimum wage legislation into the countryside for the first time [80] and another decree giving family allowances to agricultural workers as well as to urban workers.[81] At the very end of Ibáñez' presidency, perhaps the single most important blow against the political power of the landowners was struck: Law No. 12,891 of June 16, 1958, modified various details of the voting procedure in such a way as to make it impossible for landowners to control the votes of the rural population.

This gradual loss of political power was, of course, matched by a shrinkage in the economic base of the traditional landed elite. Space does not permit detailed documentation of this fact. Suffice it to say that between 1920 and 1953, the share of the national product originating in agriculture declined from 23 per cent to 15 per cent, while in the same period the percentage of the labor force engaged in agriculture dropped from 36.2 to 30.7.[82]

[79] It included some radical right-wing, fascistic elements which were, however, as opposed to the traditional oligarchy and the Conservative and Liberal parties representing it as they were to the Marxists.

[80] *Decreto con fuerza de ley* No. 244, as published in the *Diario Oficial,* Aug. 1, 1953.

[81] *Decreto con fuerza de ley* No. 245, as published in the *Diario Oficial,* July 31, 1953.

[82] Marto A. Ballesteros and Tom E. Davis, "The Growth of Output and Employment in Basic Sectors of the Chilean Economy, 1908–1957," *Economic Development and Cultural Change* I, (Jan., 1963), 152–175.

But the decline of an elite such as this is never rapid nor continuous. We see in the weak local administration of the new laws and in the ultimate failure of the farm workers' union itself a partial indication of the continuing strength of the landowners. They were able to resist the erosion of their power at least in part and for a time. But they were by no means able to resist it entirely, and, indeed, not at all when the central government put on a determined show of strength. This the government did briefly in Molina in 1953. It has done so even more forcefully in the mid-sixties, when the very same group of progressive Catholics who helped the Molina vineyard workers in 1953, while in political opposition to Ibáñez, won national political power and sponsored a large organizing drive as well as a substantial radical agrarian reform program.

Given this broader context of a long-term decline in the strength of the landowners, it should become more comprehensible that the President of Chile—particularly General Ibáñez at the beginning of his second term of office in 1952—was so ready to change his position as a result of the relatively light pressure which the Cardinal could put on him. A new sector of the urban middle class, many of them professionals and intellectuals, was replacing the older middle sectors, which over the years had compromised with the traditional elite. In part, this new group was surely moved by ideology, that is, out of conscience and religious conviction. In part, perhaps, they may have acted on the conscious or unconscious recognition that Chile's sluggish development limited their personal opportunities to exercise their professional skills, and to gain the economic, prestige, and power rewards to which they felt entitled. Moved both by conscience and by self-interest to weaken the traditional elite and to obtain for themselves a vast new reservoir of support previously outside the political system altogether—the support of the campesino—the new urban professionals allied themselves with the peasantry and struck out into the countryside to mobilize this source of support.

Other Allies

But these lay middle groups,[83] chiefly professionals and their wives, were not the only ones to evolve into leaders, or at least temporary allies,

[83] We use deliberately the term "middle groups," introduced by J. J. Johnson. While these groups may have had a certain common economic interest—development —thus justifying in a very loose way the use of the word "class," they were in most respects very heterogeneous. Some were firmly oriented toward a Catholic ideology, others—outside the purview of this particular study—were equally convinced Marxists. Some came from quasi-aristocratic backgrounds, others from immigrant homes, others from middle-middle and even lower-middle backgrounds.

of the peasantry. While these groups were the most important outside supporters, the Church and the civil service as institutions also helped to some extent, and these deserve brief comment.

The support of public servants—in this instance, inspectors from Chile's Ministry of Labor—is easily overlooked, because it was weak and wavering. But we believe this to be quite typical, and in that sense it merits mention as an important "social fact." No great acts of heroism in defense of the poor can be expected from bureaucrats at lower levels of a hierarchy, and none occurred. These functionaries are typically ill-paid, and therefore economically defenseless, and they know that a stand against the local rural power structure will not be backed up by their superiors, or that such support, should it occur, is a political accident and very unlikely to be permanent. In Chile specifically (although we regard events there as typical of what tends to occur elsewhere) such a reversal took place after the initially progressive period of the Popular Front government between 1938 and 1942, and it occurred again within a year or two of General Ibáñez' election in 1952. On both occasions, inspectors who had been too friendly to labor found their careers damaged. Moreover, by virtue of his education and social background, the typical civil servant is unlikely to be wholeheartedly on the side of peasants.

But despite all of the above, several labor inspectors involved in the Molina situation showed considerable sympathy for the vineyard workers. Through their investigation of individual grievances—arbitrary dismissals, failure to pay agreed-upon wages in their entirety, and so forth—they probably maintained a steady, if mild, pressure on the growers which may well have restrained some of them from more flagrant abuse. Our main point is to illustrate that those who are on the sidelines of the struggle between peasant and landowner cannot simply be classed as allies or enemies, but may be somewhere in between, wavering, but potentially a source of support for the peasant, given the appropriate political climate and the expectation that such a climate will continue.

The role of the Church as allies of these peasants is even more intriguing. Its original support of the peasantry not only received a great deal of attention, but was, in fact, crucial. Its later coolness toward the movement was of equal importance in weakening the latter's possibilities of survival.

Obviously, the motivation of the clergy involved was in part quite similar to that of the Catholic laymen with whom they were in close contact and whom they paralleled in social background and education: some coming from quite humble homes, others from the best-known families in Chile. In particular, both laymen and clergy were stimulated by the spirit of the social encyclicals, with their dual emphasis on seeing social justice done for its own sake and on saving the oppressed from the false allures of atheistic materialism: a strong defensive undercurrent in all progressive catholic thinking until the late fifties at least.

The theme of saving the poor from ideological error and sin shades into a more mundane desire to protect the Church as an institution in a changing society. This kind of "selfish" motive at the institutional level is something of a parallel to the "selfish" motivation of the professional middle classes to weaken old established oligarchies and spur development, not only because this would lessen misery, but also because it would provide professionals with greater opportunities. In any case, as the classes on whom the church had traditionally relied for support diminished in power and as new groups—such as a more independent peasantry—became a factor in Chilean society, it behooved the Church to concern itself with the welfare of this new potential clientele in the same way as it was logical for other institutions—the state, political parties, and the like—to do so.

In part, therefore, the relationship between Church and peasantry (and between lay middle class and peasantry) can be conceptualized as an exchange, in which the Church gains the fulfilment of its idealistic goals at the level of values and gains support at the level of institutional survival. The vineyard workers in their turn obtained returns of very much the same kind: legitimation at the level of values and support at the level of institutional survival.

But, as always, there is rising cost and diminishing benefit as the exchange continues. For the union, identification with the Church limits its appeal after all peasants who are reassured by such identification have been recruited and those less friendly to the Church remain to be recruited. And we have already drawn attention to the cost to the union of association with the Church in terms of limiting the means it can employ, and the goals it can pursue.

To the Church there is, likewise, a rising cost curve and falling "marginal utility." Outrage among the established elite over the Church's *volte-face* becomes more intense and priests find their work made difficult (as happened in Molina). Moreover, moral gains are offset when the Church finds itself in moral difficulties as its association with unions pulls it into the midst of specific controversies in which it simply does not feel it legitimately belongs (controversies over government price and import policies, specific wage settlements, and strikes). This was of the utmost importance in Chile in the mid-fifties, when the Church tended to move simultaneously toward the left *and* away from any kind of theocratic interference in daily affairs. Even when feuds among the Catholic laity were involved, clergy increasingly took a hands-off position. We know that, in several controversies in the trade-union field, laymen whose policies were opposed by key sectors of the clergy were triumphant precisely because the clergy no longer felt it appropriate to insist on their views where strictly temporal issues were at stake. This stance, while it may sound lukewarm and opportunistic, struck us as very sincerely held and, in a sense, as modernistic as the simultaneous move to the left.

For purposes of this case, however, it is of fundamental importance to note that institutions allied to the peasant cause have problems of their own and dynamics of their own, and these are likely to make such alliances—as all alliances between any groups in the world—temporary and contingent.

Summary

In 1953 and 1954 the landowning elite was still too strong, the new urban coalition too confused, and the chosen path—that of trade-union-ism—too vulnerable to resistance for this movement to achieve permanent success. The new middle class was divided (between Catholics and Marx-ists), and the locally dominant ideology (Catholicism) was somewhat debilitating. Hence Molina, after a quick and surprising success, is a story of failure in the short run.

But in 1964, ten years later, triumph by very much the same group was possible at the national level, and with national triumph came renewed local success. For the Molina movement was, in the mid-sixties, once again strong. The reasons are in line with what we have already indicated as the causes of success and failure of such movements. (1) The agricultural sector has weakened even further, and with it, the strength of the landowners. Their contribution to the national product declined from about 15 yer cent in 1954 to about 12 per cent in the early sixties.[84] (2) The path adopted was the vote, against which the elite was powerless after the electoral reforms of 1958. The Conservative and Liberal parties were in ruins by 1964. (3) Chilean Catholic ideology had become independent of religious pronouncements, and, hence, more lay, more radical, and less debilitating. (4) The coalition between the old urban middle class organized in the Radical party and the Right organized in the Conserva-

[84] *La economia de Chile en el periodo 1950–1963* (Santiago, Chile: Instituto de Economia, Universidad de Chile, 1963), II, 6.

tive and Liberal parties had definitely lost force. This was symbolized by a crushing defeat, six months before the 1964 presidential election, in the by-election which took place in Curicó. After that defeat the Radical-Conservative-Liberal coalition literally disintegrated and its presidential candidate, Julio Duran, withdrew. Finally, (5) while the ideological division within the new professional and intellectual class continued and is likely to continue, a number of fortuitous factors once again allowed Catholics to triumph over Marxists instead of producing a stalemate.[85] The rivalry between Marxist- and Catholic-oriented middle groups and the disintegration of the Right are resulting in substantial gains for the peasantry (though perhaps not as fast as is ideally desirable). But, as was the case a decade earlier, these gains are, for the most part, not being won by pressure and under peasant leadership but as the result of efforts of urban, middle-class groups.

[85] "Fortuitous" within the narrow Chilean context. Allende, the presidential candidate of the Marxist Left, was hurt by popular fears that his victory would result in a repressive dictatorship along Castro lines. We say "once again" because the victory of the Catholics in Molina in 1953 was greatly aided by the fortuitous fact that their Communist rivals had to work somewhat surreptitiously due to the "Law for the Permanent Defense of Democracy" (LDD). However, the importance of this factor should not be exaggerated. We know that, despite it, Communist organizers managed quite successfully to be involved in the presentation of contract demands in 11 *fundos* in 1951: in 1953, they were involved in none. The law had not changed; and the explanation is that they were for the first time challenged by an energetic and effective rival.

6. Peru: The Peasant
Movement of La Convención *

WESLEY W. CRAIG, JR.

Brigham Young University

Descriptive information on peasants and peasant life in Latin America has increased in recent years, along with attempts to bring some order to description through more refined typologies. Unfortunately, little attention has been given to analysis and research in the area of the dynamics of peasant movements or peasant labor organization. Increasing ferment among Latin American peasants, and the potential for much more to come, should challenge social scientists to more intensive research into the ways in which peasants strive to improve their relative position and power in society.[1]

Generally still unanswered are such relevant questions as: What are the preconditions necessary for successful peasant organization? How does organization begin? Who become the leaders? What are their goals? How do organizations relate to the existing local regional or national social system?

This study attempts to shed some light on these questions by an analysis of one peasant movement that took place from 1952 to 1965 in La Convención Valley, some ninety miles north of Cuzco in the mountainous southern region of Peru. The movement became particularly well known in Peru during 1961-62 as Peruvian newspapers gave considerable coverage to the emergence of a Fidel Castro type by the name of Hugo Blanco who, according to these reports, was the organizer and leader (in La Convención Valley) of a Communist peasant organization that was

* The research for this chapter was carried out in La Convención Valley from September, 1964, to May, 1965, with support of a National Defense Education Act fellowship and a research grant from the Latin American Program of Cornell University.

[1] Several recent studies on peasant organization in Peru include Edward M. Dew, Jr., "Politics in the Altiplano: A Study of Provincial Change in Peru" (Ph.D. thesis, University of California at Los Angeles, 1966), and F. La Mond Tullis, "Modernization and Political Change: Peasant Movements in Peru's High Central Sierra" (Ph.D. thesis, Harvard University, 1968).

threatening to sweep across Peru.[2] The reputation of Blanco was magnified to such legendary proportions as to obscure the important processes which contributed to the emergence of a peasant labor organization in La Convención years before the advent of Blanco. The challenge of bringing this peasant organizational development into a more comprehensible and balanced perspective is also an objective of this report.

In 1962 a sizable detachment of Peruvian soldiers was dispatched to La Convención and eventually captured Blanco. Simultaneously, the military junta then in power in Peru moved rapidly to initiate an "agrarian reform program" especially for this valley. However, before the arrival of the military units, the peasant tenant farmers (*campesinos*) carried out a general strike against the plantation owners (*hacendados*) of La Convención Valley, who had traditionally controlled virtually all of the land in the valley. Since that time (1962) the campesinos or former tenant laborers of the hacendados, have organized in peasant labor unions, have refused to work for the hacendados, and have dedicated themselves exclusively to the development of their own small piece of property (*parcela*). These peasant labor unions (*sindicatos*) have been organized on every hacienda in the valley (numbering over sixty), and are joined together on a regional basis by a valley federation of peasant unions (Federación de Sindicatos de Campesinos de La Convención y Lares). Virtually all of the ten to eleven thousand tenant farmers in the valley became members of a peasant union and, to varying degrees, participated in the struggle for land ownership and independence from the hacendados.[3]

In 1963 the Peruvian national government recognized the demands of these peasant unions and formally abolished the contractual relationships which had existed between the hacendado and the tenant farmers. Under the old system the campesino was to provide a certain number of days of labor on the hacienda in exchange for the use of a small piece of property, averaging between four and twenty acres, on which he could grow

[2] The two Peruvian newspapers giving greatest coverage of this development were *La Prensa*, which consistently portrayed the labor movement as an organized communist uprising led by Hugo Blanco, and *El Expreso*, whose correspondent, Hugo Neira, filed a number of stories which were later compiled into a book, *Cuzco: Tierra y muerte* (Lima: Populibros Peruanos, 1964)—an interesting but superficial account of developments in La Convención Valley and Cuzco during 1962–1963.

[3] In addition to the principal peasant organization, the Federación de Sindicatos de Campesinos de La Convención, there were several small competing unions in the valley organized by the APRA political party. These were known as the FENCAP (Rural Workers Federation of Peru) unions; they did not, however, play a significant role in the over-all labor organization of the valley.

whatever he liked for his own subsistence—the usufruct staying with the campesino. The government promised legal title to these small parcels on the basis that the campesinos pay the government the value of the lands and then the government would, in turn, reimburse the former owner, the hacendado.

From a traditional structure of hacienda social relations, the entire valley, through these events, was transformed into a new system of small landowners (*minifundistas*) who were completely independent of their former masters. In a period of ten years a three-hundred-year-old feudalistic system of social relationships was overthrown and supplanted by organized independent campesinos engaged in the growing of coffee as a cash crop. The hacendados, in the absence of the traditional cheap labor of the tenant farmers, have been forced to find new ways of developing their lands or be forced out of business.

What were the factors that contributed to such a radical change in the social structure of this valley? What forces were influential in organizing the peasants of the valley? How were these peasants able to achieve their objectives of increased economic freedom? To answer these questions the author spent nine months in La Convención Valley from September, 1964, to May, 1965, during which time he interviewed hacendados, peasant labor union leaders, educators, religious leaders, doctors, merchants, lawyers, urban labor leaders, and government officials. In addition, a questionnaire was applied to a campesino respondent in each of the thirty-six newly emergent peasant communities—on lands formerly owned by the hacendados. Personal observation of peasant organizational activity included attendance at peasant union and cooperative meetings. Archival information was secured from the various governmental agencies operating within the valley and included the field data of a census of campesinos carried out by the national Agrarian Reform Agency in La Convención Valley during 1964–65. Personal documents consulted included the Christian Bües collection in the Dominican Mission in Quillabamba.

The Hacienda System in La Convención Valley

The La Convención Valley is located on the northward-flowing Urubamba River some five miles downstream from the famous Inca ruins of Machu Picchu. The river drops 2,300 feet from the entrance to the narrow valley, near the railroad terminal of Huadquiña, to the juncture of the Urubamba and the Yanatile rivers (sixty miles downstream), near the town of Quellouno. The upper end of the valley floor is 5,100 feet above

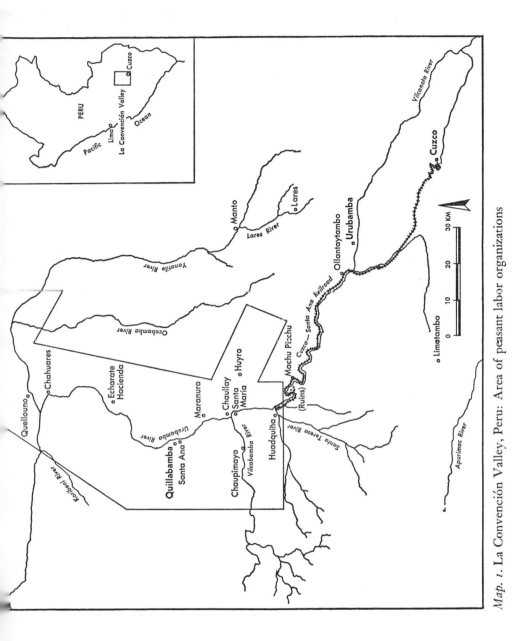

Map. 1. La Convención Valley, Peru: Area of peasant labor organizations

sea level, while the lower end, near Quellouno, is at 2,790 feet. The valley is quite narrow throughout most of its sixty-mile length with steep slopes rising from the valley floor to the mountains which range upward to 15,000 feet above the sea level. At several places along the river bottom the valley widens to nearly a mile. These areas, plus several narrow tributary valleys, constitute the bulk of the "flat" farmland on which cacao, sugar cane, tea, coca, and coffee are raised. The remainder of the farming is done along the steep slopes adjacent to the streams. Coffee, coca, and tea are the major commercial crops of these hillsides while bananas, yucca, and corn are raised for local consumption.

Most of the valley floor falls within the *ceja de la montaña* ("eyebrow of the mountain") region, alternately called "high jungle," which, while relatively humid, is not oppressively hot. There are extreme contrasts in vegetation for heavy rains fall at the higher elevations while the valley floor receives considerably less rain and undergoes a dry season that extends from May through August.

Relatively little is known of the precolonial settlements in the valley though it is generally believed that the Incas secured coca leaf from this area. Isaiah Bowman, who participated in the Yale expedition of 1911 to La Convención, states:

During the time of the Incas the value of the eastern valleys was already known inasmuch as rock-lined terraces and patios of the Incas can be seen today in Echarati and in Sahuayaco. . . . The tradition exists that these were Imperial plantations of coca worked by selvetic Indian slaves and that the coca leaves were sent to Cuzco by an Incan rock-finished road, now hidden by overgrowth.[4]

Spanish title to the lands in La Convención began as early as 1541 when the Huyro hacienda was ceded to the wife of the Corregidor of the Audiencia of Cuzco by Spanish royal decree—only eight years after the conquest of Cuzco by Pizarro.[5] From 1541 to 1650, Spanish grants were given to lands located on the higher tributaries of La Convención Valley but not until the latter date did settlement begin along the valley floor. As the large grantees (*hacendados*) moved further down into the valley floor and northward, the *naturales* (Machiguenga Indians) fled further downstream to escape the arduous work demands of the new settlers. This

---

[4] Isaiah Bowman, *Los Andes del sur del Perú* (Arequipa, Peru: Editorial La Colmena, 1938). (Translation of the English edition published in 1916; citations have been translated back into English by present author).

[5] Angel Menendez Rua, R. P., *Paso a la civilización* (Lima: San Martín y Cia., 1948), pp. 30–33.

resulted in a scarcity of labor which was only partially resolved by the importation of Negro slaves.[6]

The other source of labor, over the years, was to obtain Indians from their highland villages. Eventually this became the major means of resolving labor needs of the hacendados. Bowman indicates that, in 1911, "—there is a scarcity of labor. All of the hacendados have to have agents who contract laborers in the highland Indian villages." [7]

The lure held out by the hacendados to bring in Indians from the highlands was the promise of a small piece of the hacienda land—generally an undeveloped hillside—which the hacendado would lease to the Indian in exchange for a stipulated amount of labor on the hacienda each month. Referring to the period around 1911 Bowman says:

A great part of the labor of the haciendas is done at virtually no cost to the owners as they depend upon the so called *faenas* of these Indians. These are Quechuas who have built their huts along the steep hillsides and along the floors of the smallest valleys of the hacienda lands. . . . The Indian does not own the land that he works. He only has the right to live upon it and cultivate it for his immediate needs. In return he has to work a stipulated number of days each year on the hacienda of the owner.[8]

This obligation was only part of what became known as the *condiciones*, or demands of the hacendado. In addition to the stipulated number of workdays, the hacendado also required additional man-days of labor for working on his irrigation ditches, cleaning the church, providing domestic help for the hacienda (wives and daughters of the campesinos), cutting lumber, hauling goods to market, and other duties. There appears to have been a wide variation among the haciendas in the valley with regard to the total number of days per month that an Indian tenant would have to work for the hacendado. The average would appear to be between ten and fourteen days per month, but on occasion this rose to as high as twenty or twenty-five days.[9]

The only variation on this manner of securing labor, until recently, has

[6] Baltazar de Ocampo wrote in 1610 of an uprising of the Negroes employed on the sugar plantations in the Vilcabamba area (La Convención). See *Hakulyt Society Publications*, Ser. 2, XXII (1907), 203–247.

[7] Bowman, *op. cit.*, p. 64.   [8] *Ibid.*, p. 71.

[9] A study of some seventy contracts between the campesinos (*arrendires*) and hacendados of La Convención was made by a Cuzco law professor in the early 1930's, Carlos Ferdinand Cuadros y Villena ("El arriendo y la reforma agraria en la provincia de La Convención," *Revista Universitaria de la Universidad Nacional de Cuzco*, XXXVIII, No. 96 (1949), 77–154.

been a limited use of direct contractual labor (these workers are called *habilitados*) for restricted periods of one to three months for purposes of harvesting crops, planting, and so forth. Under this system Indians would be contracted in their villages in the highlands, or in one of the larger population centers such as Cuzco, to come down into the valley for a period of about three months and work for a stipulated wage. However, this form of contractual labor often appears to have merged into the pattern described by Bowman. At the end of the contractual period the Indian might decide to continue living on the hacienda and receive the right to till a small piece of land in exchange for future labor services to the hacendado (the *condiciones* described above). This alternative was often forced upon the Indian when the hacendado refused to honor his contractual commitment for wage payment and, instead, offered the use of the parcel to the Indian in payment for past and future services.

Through this system of land tenure all of the cultivable land in the valley was owned by hacendados and none by the small tenant farmers. As late as 1880 the settlement pattern in the entire area of La Convención consisted solely of the hacienda system. There were no independent communities in the entire valley, nor any small campesino-owned holdings. Rather, each hacienda was a semicommunity unto itself, with the Indian campesinos dependent upon the hacendado for contact with the outside—selling of any products, most of the transportation of any crops, legal transactions (of which there were few), and so forth. The haciendas even had their own small stores from which the Indians had to buy the few staple goods that they might be able to afford beyond the subsistence level.

The hacendados dealt directly with contacts in the departmental capital of Cuzco for buying of supplies and services and for labor contracting. In this manner the flow of services and supplies was from the individual hacendado in the valley directly to the commercial and political center of Cuzco—accessible (until 1933) only by mule transport out of the valley.

Emergence of Market Centers

The strangle hold of the hacienda system was so strong during the nineteenth and early twentieth centuries as to withstand several attempts by the national government to create independent communities by fiat.[10]

[10] Presidential decrees in 1887, 1893, and 1902 attempted to set up a taxing power within the valley to pay for expropriation of hacienda lands to be used for district capitals.

The first break in the solid front of the hacendado land monopoly occurred in 1881 when an owner of one of the smaller haciendas, at the site of the present provincial capital of Quillabamba, donated one-third of his hacienda for the creating of an independent town. Part of his expressed motivation for this action was this:

> There is another circumstance which has motivated this action and that is to help the multitude of indigent families and honorable merchants . . . who have no abode that they can call their own and who are vulnerable to expulsion at any moment by the hacendados on whose lands they dwell; they are thus forced to live in provisional huts without daring to provide themselves with the least conveniences enjoyed by the poorest citizens of other provinces.[11]

With this donation began the emergence of the first market center within the hacienda system. However, with the exception of Quillabamba, another fifty years were to pass before additional communities would begin to develop independently of the haciendas.

The construction of the railroad to Machu Picchu in 1928 provided a direct contact with the outside world and stimulated the growth of several small towns along the projected railroad line. (In the late 1960's this projected line down through the valley, from the northern terminal of Huadquiña, has still not been built.) The railroad builders set up their temporary campsites along the railroad right-of-way, and these gave rise to more permanent nuclei of population. However, the inhabitants of these campsites were unable to buy title to the land upon which they built their temporary business edifices and continued to pay rights of *sigiaje*, or rental, for occupying the lands of the hacendado.

Malarial Epidemic and Transportation Improvements

By 1928 the railroad had arrived at Machu Picchu, and in 1933 a penetration road had reached the provincial capital of Quillabamba. The traditional use of mules for transport out of the valley gave way to the truck and the train.[12] Nevertheless, the immediate impact of the new road into the valley in 1933 was effectively neutralized by a concurrent out-

[11] *Centenario de la Convención (año jubilar)* (Cuzco, Peru: Empresa Editorial, 1958), p. 3.
[12] Until late in 1965 there was still no direct road connection between La Convención Valley and the departmental capital of Cuzco; freight and passengers had to travel by road through the valley and then change to the narrow-gauge railroad from Huadquiña to Cuzco. The Peruvian government, using a company of military engineers, finally opened a passable road linking Cuzco with Quillabamba in December 1965.

break of malaria, which swept through the valley killing large numbers of the inhabitants [13] and causing many of the survivors to flee the valley. These refugees left unworked parcels behind them and the labor shortage increased the difficulty of working the fields of the hacendados. It was not until the late 1940's that malaria was finally brought under control and eradicated from the valley through the efforts of the United Nations health program in collaboration with the Peruvian Ministry of Public Health.[14]

With the elimination of malaria the highland Indians once again became interested in possible employment in the valley. The opportunity to secure a small parcel brought a large influx of migrants between 1940 and 1960, as evidenced by a dramatic increase in population. In 1940 the census counted 27,243 inhabitants in the province, in 1960 the number was 61,901.[15]

Data obtained during 1964–65 indicates that less than one-third of the campesinos living in La Convención in 1965 had been born in that province. The majority were born in the highland provinces of Urubamba, Calca, Anta, Acomayo and Apurímac—provinces contiguous with La Convención.[16]

Big Shift to Coffee

It appears that prior to 1933 the campesinos of the valley had been engaged mainly in a subsistence economy, raising just enough on their small parcels to feed themselves and their families. A few campesinos with larger parcels raised some coca for sale and export, but this most often had been included in the hacendado's shipments by mule from the valley. However, with the improvement of transportation by 1933, the eradication of malaria by the late 1940's, and the re-entry of the Indian migrants

[13] A public health physician who worked in the valley during the height of the epidemic estimated that eight to ten thousand people died of malaria in the valley during 1933–1935 (interview with Dr. Ramon Vallenas, Lima, May 13, 1966).

[14] Earlier attacks of malaria are recorded in La Convención during 1887 and 1897; these resulted in the abandonment of haciendas located downstream from Quellouno, according to the observations of a long-time German resident in the valley (Christian Bües, "Personal Papers," Quillabamba, 1937).

[15] Republica del Perú, Ministerio de Hacienda y Comercio, Dirección Nacional de Estadística, *Censo nacional de población de 1940*, VIII (Lima, n.d.); and Dirección Nacional de Estadística y Censos, Instituto Nacional de Planificación, *Sexto censo nacional de población—2 de julio de 1961—resultados de primera prioridad*. (Lima, n.d.) pp. 44, 45.

[16] Preliminary analysis of field data of campesino population census carried out on five haciendas in La Convención during 1963–1964 by the Oficina Nacional de la Reforma Agraria (ONRA).

to the valley, a new phenomenon of vital significance began to take place: the raising of coffee by the campesinos. Table 6–1 indicates the remarkable increase in coffee production for La Convención during the period 1945–1960.

Table 6–1. Coffee production, La Convención, 1945–1960 (in kilograms)

Year	Total production
1945	583,252
1950	772,000
1954	1,308,349
1960	3,820,116

Sources: Figures for 1945, 1950, and 1954 are reported in Isaac Tupayachi M., "Un ensayo de econometría en La Convención," *Revista Universitaria de la Universidad de Cuzco*, XLVIII, No. 117 (1959), 197; the figure for 1960 is from the yearly report of the Quillabamba office of the Caja de Depositos y Consignaciones.

This tremendous increase in coffee production during the decade of the 1950's took place concurrently with a corresponding rise in the price of coffee, as indicated in Table 6–2.

Table 6–2. Average annual price for coffee (in soles per kilogram)

Year	Price *
1945	1.21
1946	1.27
1948	3.97
1950	7.15
1952	9.01
1954	14.77

Source: Isaac Tupayachi M., "Un ensayo de econometría en La Convención," *Revista Universitaria de la Universidad de Cuzco*, XLVIII, No. 117 (1959), 197.
* Price index: 1945 = 100; 1954 = 1221.

Much of this increase in coffee production must be attributed to the returning campesino tenant farmers, rather than to the hacendados of the valley. The hacendados already had most of their developed lands planted with cacao, sugar cane and tea. As a result they were less willing (in the early stages of coffee production) to shift over to the new crop. Also, the valley floor, where most of the arable hacienda land was located, was climatically less adapted to the raising of coffee. The steep hillsides, at somewhat higher altitudes and with more rainfall, proved to be better suited to coffee raising, and this was precisely where the bulk of the tenant farmers were located.

Increasing Social Complexity

Concomitant with the increased production of coffee was the appearance of middlemen (*rescatistas*) in the newly emergent railroad centers and in Quillabamba. These businessmen were willing to extend credit to the campesinos in exchange for the promise of marketing their coffee. As output increased, the middlemen bypassed the hacendados and began dealing directly with individual campesinos.

With these new income possibilities the campesino began to think how he might increase production. One handicap was his *condiciones* to the hacendado for a certain number of days each month. Many campesinos decided to deal with this drain on their now valuable time by hiring another Indian from the highlands to work for the hacendado in their stead, or to have the Indian work the campesino's parcel while the campesino labored for the hacendado. To attract his village friend or relative down to the valley the established campesino would promise the newcomer the use of a small piece of his parcel with work obligations similar to those between himself and the hacendado. The original campesino who worked for the hacendado was called an *arrendire* while the newcomer who was to work for the *arrendire* was called an *allegado*. This system became even more differentiated as some of the *allegados* followed the same pattern and contracted with other Indians to be their tenant farmers; these sub-subtenants were called *suballegados*.

This increased complexity of the social structure and the increasing subdivision of existent lands into parcels of an increasingly smaller size, mostly dedicated to coffee production, finally caused the hacendados to react. Some began to convert part of their already cultivated lands to coffee production, thereby creating heavier demands on their *arrendires* at exactly those times of the year when the *arrendire* wanted to be free to harvest and tend his own coffee production. Other hacendados looked covetously upon the new coffee production on the parcels of their tenant farmers and began exerting pressure to reclaim these lands, along with the improvements (*mejoras*), for themselves.

Peasant Union Organization

Various external stimuli contributed to the emergence of the peasant union movement in La Convención during the early 1950's. With the election of Manuel Prado to the Peruvian presidency in 1956, a wave of strikes began throughout the southern half of the country, principally in Arequipa and Cuzco in the textile mills and the public transportation sectors.[17] It has been claimed that Prado restricted labor organization by the APRA political party (Alianza Popular Revolucionaria Americana) but allowed other labor groups to emerge during this period. These latter organizations were subsequently called "the Communist unions," particularly by the Apristas.

While there were several abortive attempts at peasant labor organization in La Convención, starting as early as the late 1930's and into the 1940's, it was not until 1952–1956 that labor organization began in earnest. With a cash income, good prospects for improving their economic condition, and a new-found commercial independence, the tenant farmers began to organize to protect themselves from the increased demands of the hacendados.

Organized protests (*reclamos*) by the campesinos began to be filed with the Ministry of Labor in Cuzco in 1952. In order to effect this protest the campesinos of an hacienda (*arrendires* and *allegados* together) combined to hire a lawyer who could formulate the protest and represent them to the labor office. An examination of all (thirty-three) protests filed between 1952 and 1962 [18] reveals a preponderant interest on the part of the campesinos in:

1. *The condiciones*—that the number of days worked per month for the hacendado was too onerous or beyond contractual agreements.
2. *Reduced working hours*—that the number of hours worked each day be reduced to the legal maximum required by national labor laws.
3. *Disposition of mejoras*—that the campesinos be allowed free sale and trade of their coffee and other crops without the intervention of the hacendado.

Once the campesinos of an individual hacienda had banded together to make the formal protest it was a short step to develop a more permanent organization. Simultaneous with the filing of their protests, the campesinos began to organize labor unions as a means of dealing more effectively with the increasing demands of the hacendados.

[17] A review of these events is summarized in Roberto Mac-Lean y Estenos, *Sociología del Perú* (Mexico City: Instituto de Investigaciones Sociales, Universidad Nacional Autónoma de México, 1959), pp. 169–238.
[18] From the files of the Cuzco Departmental Office of the Ministry of Labor (Ministerio de Trabajo); many of these protests were written on letterhead stationary of the peasant union and include the date of its founding, names of officers, and the name of the lawyer representing the union.

Interviews with early leaders of the movement revealed that the growth of a protest action—the filing of a protest and subsequent organization on one hacienda—provided a model for the campesinos of adjacent haciendas. The early-organizing unions were located in a tightly contiguous pattern near the southern end of the valley. By 1958, eight of these newly formed peasant organizations united themselves into a federation of peasant unions called the Federación Provincial de Campesinos de La Convención y Lares. The stimulus for organizing a federation was undoubtedly assisted by the more "open" policies of the Prado regime toward new unions during 1956–1958, as mentioned above.

The leaders of the new peasant unions included representatives from both the *arrendire* and *allegado* groups in the valley. Typical characteristics of a leader included having been a migrant to the valley from the highlands within five to fifteen years prior to his having become involved in the union movement. He devoted himself exclusively to farming, although several of the early leaders had prior experience as carpenters, shoe repairmen, or railroad laborers before settling down on their parcel. The men elected to leadership in individual unions were generally the most educated (which might mean as high as a fifth grade elementary education—in a few extreme cases even some high-schooling), could speak Spanish (as contrasted with monolingual, Quechua-speaking Indian migrants to the valley) and were, in general, the more acculturated of the peasants in the valley.

An unexpected finding about the union leaders was that a surprisingly large minority of the early officials were known to be *evangelicos* (Protestant fundamentalists). Interviews with several of these men revealed that each of them had seen in the labor movement an opportunity of bringing about the objectives of "social justice" which they claimed to have derived from the Scriptures. As one leader succinctly put it, "The Bible says that the meek shall inherit the earth—and we are the meek!" Another, who was secretary-general of the Federation for the entire valley (and later sent to prison as a "communist agitator") was the layleader for over a hundred *evangelico* believers on the hacienda prior to his election and participation in the union movement.

The early legal assistance of the lawyer in filing the protest with the labor office in Cuzco led to another significant development. While the study of the early lawyers reveals a wide range of known political affiliation (ranging from conservative lawyers through Apristas and radical left-wingers), nevertheless, the early contacts with various of these lawyers led to campesino contacts with the Federación de Trabajadores de Cuzco (FTC), an urban labor union consisting of textile laborers, railroad workers and construction employees. According to reports of early valley labor leaders, "the FTC was the only group to show any interest in our organizing efforts and who offered to help us." As a result of these contacts the peasant unions of the valley began to be called the "communist peasant unions." The help of the FTC initially consisted of legal assistance by various lawyers, closely allied with the FTC, who moved down into the valley and became the recognized legal advisors to the peasant Federation. In addition to advice and help with the filing of protests, these lawyers also advised on organizational procedures and, undoubtedly, strategy. For most of the lawyers that represented the peasant unions, legal assistance was not based solely on social considerations. The campesinos took up ample collections from among their ranks to pay for the services of these lawyers. Cynical observers have suggested that it was the relative wealth of the campesinos, rather than the achievement of the campesino's aspirations, that provided the real stimulus for so much legal assistance from Cuzco.

In addition to the lawyers, the FTC, at the request of the valley Federation, sent down various labor leaders for short periods to work with the campesino leaders. Several of the Cuzco labor representatives were of obvious Indian origin and found considerable acceptance among the rank and file of the emerging peasant unions. However, with but one major exception (Hugo Blanco) the leaders of the peasant unions in the valley were local men—bona fide campesino tenant farmers of the haciendas who had been chosen to positions of leadership from within their own hacienda, and not imported from outside the valley. Likewise, the Federation was apparently composed of legitimate representatives of the different hacienda peasant unions. Despite the outside advisory roles of the lawyers and various FTC representatives to the valley, the major part of the organization and development, particularly during the early phase from 1952 to 1960, was primarily an autonomous development within the valley and constituted an unusual Latin American phenomenon of a rural labor union organizing itself from the bottom up—rather than being organized and directed from outside.

Goal Fulfillment of the Movement

From 1952 until early 1960, the growth of the peasant labor organization was a relatively slow, deliberate process, primarily restricted to the southern part of La Convención Valley. In 1960 the tempo quickened and began to assume real "movement" proportions. Part of this was due to the natural momentum being developed by the original peasant unions who now began to flex their collective strength in more ambitious activities than mere legal protests. One such event was a "sympathy strike" carried out during June and July of 1960, in which the peasant unions of various haciendas refused to work for the hacendados on the grounds that fellow workers on another hacienda were being mistreated. This partial strike stirred the hacendados of the valley into contacting their congressmen in Lima with demands that the government take instant action against the strikers. Instead, the government sent an investigator from the Ministry of Labor to the valley to study the situation. However, when the commission reported back to Lima in September that the *condiciones* as a form of contractual labor arrangement should be abolished within La Convención, the report and recommendations were quickly shelved.[19]

Meanwhile, the euphoria of the Cuban Revolution proved a heady stimulant to Peruvian would-be Fidel Castros. Several of these were attracted to La Convención because of the "progressive" attitudes of the campesinos. Among many university students who came into the valley at this time was Hugo Blanco—a native of Cuzco who could speak Quechua and who had received advanced training in Argentina. His father-in-law, a Cuzco lawyer, had represented the campesinos of one of the hacienda unions in their protest to the Ministry of Labor office in Cuzco. Blanco went to the same hacienda in 1960 and began to work as an *allegado* to one of the *arrendires*. He was soon elected the representative of that particular peasant union to the Federation of the valley. Within the Federation he began to establish a reputation as an effective organizer of new unions, particularly in the northern section of the valley. However, he was but one of various Federation officials who were beginning to have unusual success in organizing haciendas. The "flash-point" for organizational success had been achieved through internal developments and such external factors as the recommendations of the Ministry's investigator. It had become obvious to the campesinos that the hacendados could no longer wield the power that they previously held.

Split in the Movement

By 1962 Blanco was able to bring considerable support to bear in the elections for secretary-general of the Federation, for which he was proposed as one of the candidates, backed mostly by the newly formed

---

[19] Virgilio Landázuri Carillo, "Informe sobre el problema de los arrendires del valle de La Convención (1960)." Landázuri, who was the chief investigator sent to La Convención by the Ministry of Labor, was interviewed in Lima in February, 1965.

peasant unions. However, the elections of May, 1962, brought into the open a basic cleavage in the peasant movement. Blanco, a confessed Trotskyite,[20] was an advocate of much stronger measures than those espoused by the earlier leaders of the peasant union movement. He felt that the campesinos, in the final analysis, would have to resort to violence and possibly guerrilla warfare in order to achieve the objective of land control. Ownership of the *parcelas* as a goal of the movement began to be publicly expressed in 1960 and was formulated into a slogan of *Tierra ó Muerte* ["Land or Death"] by the followers of Blanco.) In the elections Blanco was opposed by a group consisting of the older peasant union leaders of the valley—those who had been involved in its development over the past six to ten years and who wanted to sell coffee, not revolution.

The split between the early leaders and the Blancoites also brought into relief the underlying differences between the FTC, which had been advising the early union leaders, and Blanco's Trotskyite policies. The FTC was much more interested in getting political candidates of the Left elected to public office through the growing power of the labor unions, and Blanco's emphasis upon violence threatened the FTC's long-range objectives.

Blanco received a majority of the votes in the election. The results were heatedly disputed by the early-leader faction, who cried "fraud." Unwilling to accept the election of Blanco, the leaders of some twenty peasant unions, including most of the early union leaders, stomped out of the election meeting. Several days later, refusing to accept the legitimacy of the Blanco victory, they elected one of their own men to be the new secretary-general in a rump session.

Simultaneous with the holding of the first election, an order for the arrest of Blanco was issued by the police authorities of the valley. Blanco went into hiding for a period of nine months, during which time various killings of police and military officials took place, for which Blanco was held responsible. At the end of 1962, sick and dispirited, Blanco was captured and placed in prison.[21] During his period in hiding he had been unable to exert effective control over the Federation, now split between the FTC group and Blanco's followers.

Early in 1962, prior to Blanco's disputed election, the Federation had made an important decision which was to be decisive in the campesinos'

[20] Interview with Hugo Blanco, Arequipa prison, May 8, 1965.
[21] Blanco received a prison sentence of twenty years in 1967 and is currently serving out that sentence in the El Fronton prison at Callao.

bid for power. It had been decided to direct a complete boycott against the hacendados of the valley: no *arrendire* or *allegado* was to work for any hacendado in the valley, nor was any payment for rental of parcels to be paid. This policy was not universally implemented by all of the campesinos at one time; nevertheless, during 1962 and into 1963, union after union fell into line until, by early 1963, all of the campesinos in the valley, including both factions of the Federation, were supporting the policy. This boycott was still in effect as late as 1967.

On April 24, 1962, a presidential decree issued by the Prado government abolished the *condiciones* but stipulated that the campesinos must pay rent to the hacendados for their continued use of the parcels. The campesinos refused to make such payments.

A military junta toppled the Prado government in July, 1962, recognized the *de facto* control of the parcels by the campesinos, and, in a decree issued in November, indicated that the campesinos could keep their parcels; but in order to secure legal title, the campesinos must pay the government for the parcels and the government would then pay the hacendados the value of the lands claimed by the campesinos.[22]

The campesino movement had achieved its major early objective—abolition of the *condiciones*—and had secured for the campesinos a rightful claim to their parcels. The power of the hacendados in the valley had been broken and the pre-existent social structure of the valley radically altered, with the campesinos now completely independent of the hacendados.

With its major objectives achieved and the *raison d' etre* for its existence no longer an issue, the power and solidarity of the campesino movement began to wane. It would appear that the cohesiveness of a social movement is contingent upon the clarity and commonality of its goals. In this case the early goal of reduction, and later elimination, of the work obligations of the hacendado served to unite both *arrendire* and *allegado* in a common front against the hacendado. However, with the attainment of such commonly held goals and the disappearance of the focus of opposition the movement passed a critical high point and began to decline. Unless comparably defined and commonly held goals can be substituted for the original unifying goals, a movement begins to dissipate and become divided by latent divisions among its supporters. One such potential division (other than the political differences between Hugo

[22] Campesinos have yet to pay for this land, or hacendados to be reimbursed, as of August, 1967. This procedure is subject to Agrarian Reform regulations under which claims are still being processed.

Blanco and the FTC) was the existence of socioeconomic differences between the *arrendires* and the *allegados*.[23] An indication of such differences is revealed in Chart 6–1.

These differences were aggravated by the surveys of campesino land boundaries during 1964–1966. This activity resulted in considerable litigation between campesinos—often between an *allegado* and his *arrendire*. The animosity engendered by such litigation undoubtedly precipitated the decline in labor union solidarity.[24]

Chart 6–1. Characteristics of *arrendires* and *allegados* in La Convención

Characteristic	Arrendires	Allegados
Average size of parcel	21.7 acres	3.7 acres
Average age	42 years	35 years
Average years in zone	38	20
Percentage having voting certificate (*libreta*)	32%	16%
Percentage of illiterates	47%	57%
Number of children in family	3.3	2.2

Source: Representative samples from preliminary census field data of fifteen haciendas in La Convención obtained by the ONRA during 1964–1965.

In 1964 the conservative wing of the *sindicato* movement regained power in the Federation and began to cooperate with the agrarian reform program that was elaborated under the new Belaúnde government, elected in June, 1963. Attention of the campesinos was further diverted to the organization of producer cooperatives for the marketing of their coffee under the sponsorship of the Agrarian Reform Agency of the government. Though the unions were no longer the force which they had been, the government was compelled to recognize their continued existence and gingerly developed the new cooperatives over the framework of the existing peasant unions.

Early in 1965 a group of Cuban-trained guerrillas moved into the valley

[23] The possibility exists that differences between *arrendires* and *allegados* were also related to the support of Blanco or the FTC, with the *allegados* most in favor of Blanco's policies. However, the sensitive nature of research conditions in the valley precluded the obtaining of definite data on this subject without jeopardizing the entire research program.

[24] For a detailed analysis of solidarity in the emergent peasant communities in La Convención, see the author's *From Hacienda to Community: An Analysis of Solidarity and Social Change in Peru* (Latin American Studies Program Dissertation Series No. 6 [Ithaca, N.Y.: Cornell University, 1967]).

with intentions of inciting the campesinos of La Convención to new violence. Fatally misjudging the situation in the valley, the guerrillas obtained little support from the campesinos and were soon routed by government troops.[25]

Conclusions

What generalizations can be drawn from this case study that might apply to peasant movements elsewhere in Latin America? One factor is a basic recognition of the inhibitions placed upon the development or modernization of a peasant society by the power of the traditional land-owners. This power is manifested in limitations on the production, marketing, education, and mobility of the campesinos. The existence of such a repressive social system, obviously to the advantage of those holding power, is in itself a major impediment to change. Thus, the redistribution of power—the power to control one's own economic and social activities —becomes an early and most necessary objective of the peasants. While land reform programs are generally a rationalized effort in this direction, too often those holding power in such a system are unwilling to countenance any meaningful changes. To the extent that they exercise power in the broader national system, they can, and do, block significant changes in land tenure patterns and related power. One would expect to find that only as the hacendados' power in the national social system diminishes will there be any corresponding change in power relations in the smaller agricultural social systems, such as La Convención. That the national government of Peru did not heed the petitions of the hacendados in the early 1960's may be *prima facie* evidence that the power of the hacendados within the total structure of Peruvian society—at least those represented in La Convención—had been altered. It is not within the scope of this study to analyze such changes on the national scene, but to underscore the probable relationships. However, it is possible to speculate that the power of hacendados in the sierra regions of Peru had been undermined by technological improvements on the agricultural holdings in the coastal area. These highly commercial and increasingly competitive operations hold little similarity to the agricultural operations in the sierra. Further differentiation of Peruvian society might be traced to increased

[25] The guerrilla leaders could well have heeded the evaluation of Hugo Blanco regarding the basically conservative nature of the peasants of La Convención. Blanco said, "The campesinos of La Convención are too *petit bourgeoisie;* any future uprising of Indians will take place in the highlands, not in La Convención" (interview, Arequipa prison, May 8, 1965).

industrialization and the emergence of a middle sector having less and less in common with the objectives and interests of the sierra haciendas and plantations.

It should also be recalled that earlier efforts at labor organization had been recorded in La Convención. An explanation of why those efforts had not been successful is related to more than the unique nature of the preconditions within the valley. We propose that there had been an increasing interaction of the broader Peruvian social system on the changing social structure within La Convención Valley. Earlier efforts at peasant labor organization failed, not only because of internal resistances to change within the valley, but also because the broader social system of Peru had not differentiated sufficiently to provide the necessary linkage for potential change in La Convención.

Still, one must provide reasons why such radical changes took place in this particular, remote, rural valley of Peru and not elsewhere in the selva or highlands. Within the broader national framework it is necessary to analyze the unique developments in La Convención, including the requisite preconditions for land occupancy and development. Such conditions, as developed in the first half of this study, would include the rather obvious significance of changes in transportation, disease controls, world market prices, and heavy migration from contiguous areas. Somewhat less obvious is the impact of a coffee-raising technology.

The ease with which the small peasant can adapt to the raising of coffee has been noted by a nineteenth-century observer:

Few crops adapt themselves so well to both large and small-scale enterprise as coffee. If the first is profitable the second is more so, for without noticeable increase in the labor required by his maize and yuca each settler can convert a portion of his land into a cafetal. . . . All the effort required is the digging of holes and the setting out of the transplants at the time of seeding the maize and the yuca. The weedings that these crops demand will suffice for the coffee. After three years . . . the land will have been converted into a producing cafetal . . . which will give an income which could never be hoped for from a similar acreage of maize or yuca.[26]

Requiring little investment, technology or time, coffee raising spread quickly among the campesinos of La Convención, once the preconditions had paved the way. Once engaged in a commercially-oriented agriculture

[26] Mariano Ospina Rodríguez, "El cultivo de café" (a Colombian brochure of 1880), quoted in James J. Parson, *Antioqueño Colonization in Western Colombia* (Ibero-American series No. 32 [Berkeley: University of California Press, 1949]), p. 139.

the campesinos found themselves involved in a chainlike sequence of needs and demands.

That the hacendados initially allowed the campesinos to cultivate coffee was, in effect, to write *finis* to the very system they wished to perpetuate. One wonders whether the hacendados could not have anticipated the consequences of coffee raising on the part of their tenant farmers. A partial answer to this question is deduced from some very interesting parallel developments that occurred during the 1920's and 1930's in Colombia, where many families had begun to drift back into agriculture from the cities, thereby causing an increased pressure on the privately-owned large holdings. Hirschman reports that:

Engaging in other 'mutinous' practices, many peasants stopped rent payments on the ground that the land they cultivated did not legitimately belong to those who claimed it as their property. . . . Conflicts became particularly numerous and often violent in the coffee zone of Cundinamarca. . . . This area was the *only one in the country where most of the coffee lands were held in large plantations.* Work was carried out by peons in traditional semifeudal fashion: they were given a plot on which to live and grow subsistence crops and in lieu of paying rent they worked regularly on the plantations. Conflicts arose in the twenties *over the seemingly trivial demand of these peons to be allowed to plant coffee trees on their plots* in addition to the traditional corn, beans, yucca, plantain, etc. *This demand was strongly opposed by the plantation owners, who sensed that once the peons owned coffee trees they would cease to be peons.* With a cash income of their own they might turn into a less reliable labor force. As owners of coffee trees they could be fired or dislodged only after they were reimbursed for the value of the trees. *In general their bargaining power and status would vastly increase.*[27] (italics mine)

Several factors might account for the lack of initial resistance on the part of the hacendados in La Convención to campesino planting of coffee. Unlike the example cited by Hirschman, coffee was not the principal crop on the plantations at that time in La Convención. Also, the hacendados probably were relieved by the return of migrants to the valley after malaria controls were effected. Consequently, they were not prone to quibble over the choice of crops that the new *arrendires* might want to raise on the parcels. Any opposition to the coffee raising of the campesinos in La Convención appears to have been due more to the hacendado's attempts to retain control over the marketing of the tenant farmer's private production, rather than opposing initial production.[28]

[27] Albert O. Hirschman, *Journeys toward Progress* (Garden City, N.Y.: Doubleday, 1965), pp. 141–142; from ch. 2, "Land Use and Land Reform in Colombia."

[28] The reader will recall that *disposición de mejóras* was indicated to be one of the problem areas of the protesting campesinos.

Another startling parallel between La Convención and the coffeegrowing area of Cundinamarca in Colombia deserves consideration. In a footnote Hirschman indicates:

In some areas, the peons simply took the coveted right (planting coffee trees); after all, the planting of coffee tree seedlings is not readily detected. According to one document, *a peasant league—the apparent predecessor of the Communist-led organization which has dominated some coffee-growing areas near Viota for the past twenty-five or thirty years*—passed the word to all its members to plant coffee trees on their subsistence plots.[29] (italics mine)

That comparable conditions led to the early development of a peasant "league" emphasizes the relationship to coffeegrowing in Cundinamarca and La Convención.

In addition to the emergence of this peasant organization, Hirschman also calls attention to the role of the national government, and particularly to the message of President Alfonso López of Colombia to the protesting plantation owners:

The government . . . will try to protect the owners who are unjustly attacked . . . but it is not ready to choke off all aspirations of the campesino to economic improvements by the bloody application of such juridical concepts which permit the right to own land without developing it.[30]

There is one final factor which deserves comparison with the Colombian coffee development. As the peons of Colombia moved in on the long neglected holdings of the large hacendados or plantations, "new towns and villages were founded at a rapid rate in the area, the negotiations were often three cornered, with the public interest of the new municipios rather close to those of the settlers." [31] The identifying of the "new *municipios*" with the peons in Colombia recalls the growth of the middlemen and merchants in the newly forming communities in La Convención Valley, especially after the 1930's. With this increasing "urbanization" there was a concommitant increase in the complexity of the rural social system as the influx of migrants multiplied into divisions of *arrendires*, *allegados*, and *suballegados*, and as they divided the rural holdings into increasingly smaller plots. This increasing complexity of the social structure can also be conceived as a fundamental factor in rural change. The emergence of the peasant labor movement was the product of this increasingly differentiated society—both locally and nationally. Even the preconditions of improved transportation, public health controls, and community organization can be construed as the intromission of the na-

[29] Hirschman, *op. cit.*, p. 143.   [30] *Ibid.*, p. 147.   [31] *Ibid.*, pp. 137–138.

tional social system, and its increasing differentiation, into La Convención Valley. The increased pluralism of such a society creates new tolerance levels (as expressed so clearly by President Alfonso López of Colombia) which facilitate the changes in power relationships as implied in the emergence of the peasant unions. Given these interrelationships, the function of coffee raising by campesinos becomes a precipitating factor for change.

With these antecedents firmly established, the latency of leadership among the campesinos emerges among the more educated, aggressive, and frustrated. Connections with the changing national system find ready support, as in the case of the urban unions, and a more sympathetic ear from government.

And, nearly always, there waits in the wings the potential hero in history, the charismatic leader who can discern the appropriate milieu (though it may not be of his creation) for his talents and aspirations and who can capitalize on the currents of change for his particular objectives, if his discernment is sufficiently keen.

7. Peru: Peasant Organizations

JULIO COTLER and
FELIPE PORTOCARRERO

Instituto de Estudios Peruanos

Peasant organizations in Peru have typically assumed two forms: the highly institutionalized unions of agricultural workers of the coast and the much less institutionalized peasant movements of recent years in the more traditional areas of the sierra, or mountainous regions. A serious understanding of peasant organizations in Peru must begin with an appreciation of the differences between the regions in which these two types of organizations exist, for the socioeconomic differences between the coastal plain and the sierra are among the most salient characteristics of the Peruvian social situation.

Coast and Sierra in Peru

In 1961 the coast contained 47 per cent of Peru's population and contributed 61 per cent of the country's national income; the sierra contained 46 per cent of the population but contributed only 35 per cent of the national income. One major consequence of this difference was the fact that the average income per person in the coastal plain was 23 per cent greater than the national average, whereas in the sierra it was 29 per cent less.[1]

In 1961, 69 per cent of the coastal population lived in urban areas; in the sierra only 26 per cent of the population did so. Seventy-nine per cent of the coastal population over the age of 15 was literate, but only 41 per cent of the population in the sierra was literate within this age group.[2] Because Peru still has a literacy requirement for voting, this difference in the rate of literacy contributes to a sharp difference between the proportions of voters in each part of the country. In 1966, 69 per cent of the electorate lived in the coastal departments, whereas only 26 per cent lived in the sierra, even though the two areas have equal population.

[1] Banco Central de Reserva del Perú, *Cuentas Nacionales del Perú, 1950–1964* (Lima: The Banco, 1966).

[2] Dirección Nacional de Estadística y Censos, *Censo Nacional de Población, 1961* (6 vols.; Lima, 1966).

This striking difference is due to the fact that modernization was first stimulated in Peru, an underdeveloped and dependent country, through the demands of, and from impulses derived from, the international market. Thus the northern and central coast and the central sierra have achieved since the last decade of the nineteenth century a dynamism which, in different degrees, has broken the traditional system of rural domination. This has occurred through the introduction of enclave economies,[3] principally involving commercial sugar plantations and copper mines. Such economies favored the concentration of populations with proletarian characteristics; this, in turn, caused the rupture of bilateral relations based on personal obligations between the *patrón* and his *peón*.

The concentration of laborers in these enclave economies has favored the unionization of these new workers, their political participation, and their involvement in a more general process of modernization. Encouraged by the same external stimuli, the principal exports of the country were later concentrated in the same coastal region: cotton, and during the last ten years, fish meal and iron ore.

In contrast to what has occurred in the coast and central sierra, the traditional system still maintains its strength in the northern and southern parts of the sierra. This is particularly true in the south, where the largest concentration of Indian population is found. The traditional system is characterized in the most general terms by the domination of the peasantry by a group which is called "mestizo." [4] This group controls property and marketing systems; the mestizos are literate and therefore are voters and politically powerful at the local and regional levels. Access to such resources permits the mestizos to participate in the national institutions and social groups which direct the country, and thereby to exclude the peasants not only from obtaining the resources already possessed by mestizos, but even from being considered in national decisions of collective interest. Lacking these resources, the peasants, and especially the Indians, have no autonomous capacity to pursue their own interests.

This type of hierarchical relation encourages the development of a culture of dependence among the peasants with its concomitant passivity,

[3] "In an enclave situation, the economy is characterized by the formation of a highly dynamic and modern sector which is essentially an extension of the technological and financial development of the central economies" (Fernando Cardoso, "El proceso de desarrollo de América Latina" [mimeo., Santiago, Chile: Instituto Latinoamericano de Planificación Económica y Social, Nov. 1965], p. 24).

[4] Julio Cotler, *The Mechanics of Internal Domination and Social Change in Peru* (Studies in Comparative Industrial Development, III, No. 12 [St. Louis, Mo.: Washington University, Social Science Institute, 1968]).

fatalism, local identification, and social atomization. This dependence is reinforced, in turn, by the capacity of the mestizos to mobilize on their side the police, the courts, and the army on any occasion when they might be necessary to maintain the established order.[5]

Nevertheless, even in these traditional regions the process of social mobilization is now beginning, although under circumstances different from those already described for other parts of the country. Social mobilization in these areas is not the direct result, in fact, of the enclave or industrial economies. Rather, it is principally the result of the indirect impact which those ecomomic sectors and urban centers have had on the traditional regions. The expansion of Peru's economic relations with developed countries has brought a new style of life into some urban centers, which, in turn, is transmitted through new means of communication—such as the ubiquitous transistor radios—to the more traditional regions.[6] In this way the aspirations, identifications, and, on a lesser scale, the occupational structure of these regions are altered.

Thus, while the change which has occurred on the coast and in the central sierra has primarily involved economic activities and social relations, the current traditional regions are subject to modifications that initially involved cultural change, which in turn is leading to economic and social changes.

The contemporary process of urbanization in Peru has largely been stimulated by this cultural change. It is not the result of increased productivity of agriculture (which would have reduced the demand for agricultural labor) or of a significant increase in the demand for industrial labor. Rather, the migration seems to be the result of changing aspirations. Migrating populations settle with greatest frequency in the cities with the greatest signs of modernization. For example, in the last twenty-five years, the population of the seventeen coastal cities with more than twenty thousand inhabitants grew 240 per cent, while the eleven sierra cities of

[5] It is common in the literature of political science to characterize underdevelopment by the absence of organizations that articulate and aggregate the interests of distinct sectors of the population. The most widely accepted explanation of their absence traces it to the envy and the lack of confidence which are found within the context of poverty. In this respect see, for example, Edward Banfield, *The Moral Basis of a Backward Society* (Glencoe, Ill.: Free Press, 1965) On rare occasions, nevertheless, an attempt has been made to explain the incapacity to organize by reference to restrictions and repression which dominant groups exercise in order to impede the organization of the dominated groups, favoring as a consequence a socialization which tends toward dependence.

[6] Aníbal Quijano, "La urbanización en América Latina" (mimeo.; Santiago, Chile: United Nations Economic Commission for Latina America, June, 1966).

the same importance grew only 103 per cent in the same period. In other words, while these sierra cities had a growth rate similar to that in the rest of the country, the coastal cities doubled that rate.

The new urban population accelerated the political mobilization of urban centers because it required goods and services which the social order was not disposed to offer. This has led to a new political socialization that has had repercussions in the rural areas owing to the new forms of communication between the city and the countryside. As friends and relatives of country people migrate to the cities, they communicate their new experiences and ideas back to the country, causing a kind of "urbanization" of the countryside, in cultural terms.

Thus, different kinds of peasant organizations exist in Peru according to the conditions prevailing in these different areas. The peasant movements in areas of industrialized agriculture take the form of union organization. These unions are officially recognized by the government and are a regular part of the Peruvian political system. In the areas where low productivity is associated with the traditional system of domination, the Indians in the communities have organized themselves for the purpose of carrying out squatter invasions, in which they seize hacienda land for their own use. At the same time the Indian serfs have struggled for better conditions of work.

The present study attempts to sketch the outstanding characteristics of each kind of peasant articulation. It proposes to explore the topic with the hope of constituting a first step for later discussions. It is based upon an examination of documentary sources from the peasant organizations themselves, official information, newspaper reports, and interviews with peasant leaders. We will also examine the ecological and sociological variables which are associated with the different kinds of peasant mobilization. At the same time, observations on forms of recruitment, organization, programs, and relations with other institutions will be presented, as well as the historical context within which the organizations originated and have developed.

Coastal Unionism

Rural unionism on the coast of Peru has typically involved workers on sugar and cotton haciendas. This type of union has emerged as the most highly organized and institutionalized peasant organization in Peru—to such an extent that they have been recently officially recognized by the Ministry of Labor. Rural unionism in these zones emerged around the second decade of this century, as part of the same movement that produced the APRA party. APRA is the party that has traditionally shown the most interest in these unions, and its support is one of the basic reasons for their legitimacy and current development. Their legal recognition after 1956 was closely linked to APRA's own emergence as a legal political party. In addition to the benefits of their association with APRA, the unions' location in the most urbanized region of the country (the coast) and their involvement in the nation's most important agricultural sectors provide opportunities to press their demands upon public agencies and private enterprises.

Table 7–1. Number of unions by department and type of crop

Department	Cotton	Sugar	Other *	Total
Ica	39	0	25	64
La Libertad	1	13	18	32
Lambayeque	0	9	5	14
Lima	77	3	47	127
Piura	6	0	7	13
Total	123	25	102	250

Source: Peruvian Ministry of Labor, Employment and Human Resources Service, *Recognized Union Associations* (Lima, 1964) provided a list of recognized Peruvian unions; Carlos Malpica, *Los dueños del Perú* (Lima: Fondo de Cultura Popular, n.d.) provided a list of Peruvian haciendas; Peruvian Ministry of Agriculture, Service of Research and Agricultural Promotion, "Register of the Control Division" (official unpublished government document, 1966) provided data on the crops produced by each hacienda.

* Orchards, rice, market gardens, and unclassified.

There are 255 recognized rural unions in Peru, and all but five of these are found on the coast, strongly associated with the two most important export crops of the country: cotton and sugar. These two crops dominate large-scale industrial agriculture in Peru and contributed, in 1963, 35 per cent of the nation's gross agricultural product and 29 per cent of the total value of exports.

The geographical distribution of the unions for each type of crop is strongly associated with regional specialization by crop. As can be seen in Table 7–1, the cotton unions are concentrated in the departments of Lima and Ica and the sugar unions in La Libertad and Lambayeque. Correspondingly, in Lima and Ica 56 per cent of the nation's cotton is harvested, while 83 per cent of sugar production is concentrated in the departments of La Libertad and Lambayeque.

These coastal departments have Peru's highest index of agricultural mechanization. In 1957 there were 6,350 tractors in the country as a whole, of which 5,207 were to be found in the coastal area. In order of importance, the largest number of tractors were to be found in the departments of Lima, Ica, Piura, Lambayeque, and La Libertad, while in the entire sierra there were only about 1,000 tractors.[7]

Ownership of sugar-cane and cotton haciendas is in the hands of very few companies. Six businesses controlled about 90 per cent of the sugar production in Lambayeque and La Libertad, while 10 businesses controlled 41 per cent of the cotton production. However, the companies controlling cotton production do not have their lands geographically concentrated, as the sugar companies do. For example, one of the largest cotton-producing companies controls 10 haciendas, a total of 7,000 hectares, dispersed throughout the central coast.

Concentration of ownership in the sugar and cotton industries seems to be more convenient for the processing of these products than for their cultivation. In the 12 most important cotton-growing valleys, for example, there could be found 54 cotton gins; two companies, both foreign, controlled 14 of these, which processed 35 per cent of the national cotton production. The sugar industry is very similar:

Of 50 sugar mills which functioned in Peru in 1922, only 20 still existed at the end of 1932 and 16 in 1942. At present there are sugar mills only in Lambayeque, Zaña, Chicama, Santa Catalina, Pativilca, Huaura, Tambo and Huánuco. There has taken place, therefore, a considerable process of industrial concentration, and the present sugar mills serve vast areas of sugar plantations. This is the case of the Chicama and Santa Catalina Valley, where there exist only three great milling centers serving an area of 29,356 hectares: Casagrande, Cartavio and Laredo. The Lambayeque Valley is practically in the same situation since only four mills function there: Pomalca, Tumán, Cayaltí and Pucalá.[8]

Parallel to this concentration of industry and of land has been an increase in sugar production; but the cotton industry does not show such an increase. Between 1916 and 1959, sugar production increased by 56 per cent, whereas cotton production increased by only 1 per cent.[9]

[7] In 1955, 81 per cent of the cultivated land in Ica was worked with machines, 79 in Lima, 75 in Lambayeque, 62 in Pirra and 42 in La Libertad (Quentin M. West, "Demostración del uso del método de la encuesta en los estudios económicos en áreas agrícolas" [mimeo.; Lima: Instituto Interamericano de Ciencias Agrícolas, Zona Andina, 1955]).

[8] Carlos Moreyra and Carlos Derteano, "La Agricultura Peruana en el siglo XX," in José Pareja (ed.), *Visión del Perú* (Lima: Librería Studium, 1962) I, p. 156.

[9] *Ibid.*

Depending on the measure used, different conclusions may be drawn about whether the cotton or the sugar industry is more unionized. Data on the percentage of unionized workers are not available, but insofar as the absolute number of unions is concerned, the cotton haciendas may be considered more completely unionized (see Table 7–1). In terms of the actual area of land worked by unionized labor, however, more hectares of sugar (79,628) than of cotton (46,222) are unionized. The unionized sugar-growing hectares represent 50 per cent of all unionized land in Peru, while unionized cotton-growing land is only 29 per cent of the total.

Table 7–2. Average size of unionized haciendas by crop and tendency to strike

Crop	One or more strikes *	No strikes *
Cotton	496	441
Sugar	5130	710
Others	830	521

Source: Calculated from data in Peruvian Ministry of Labor, Employment and Human Resources Services, *Strikes in Peru, 1957–1965* (Lima, 1966); Malpica, *op. cit.;* Peruvian Ministry of Agriculture, *op. cit.*
* Average size is given in hectares.

Another way in which the problem of unionization on the coast can be approached is the propensity to strike. By this we mean the quotient which results from dividing the number of unions which have had one or more strikes by the number of those which have not had any strikes. The very high proportion of unions which did not have any strikes (73 per cent) between 1961 and 1965 is an indicator of the general passivity of the rural union movement. Nevertheless, substantial differences may be seen when the occurrence of strikes is examined in terms of the crops on the unionized haciendas. The ratio of the number of unions which have had strikes to those which have not is as follows: for sugar, 1.17; for cotton, 0.29; and for other crops, 0.18. Size, again, plays an important explanatory role in the propensity to strike. The large haciendas, which tend to be sugar haciendas, also appear to be more subject to strikes (See Table 7–2).

The Forms of Organization

The differences noted above between plantations devoted to sugar production and those specializing in cotton production are associated with different organizing forms of the workers involved. The sugar workers are grouped on an occupational basis, participating in unions of the Sugar Workers' Federation of Peru (FTAP). Unionized workers on haciendas that produce cotton and foodstuffs belong to the Rural Workers' Federation of Peru (FENCAP) without first belonging to a federation on the basis of industry. Both groups are separately affiliated with the Confederation of Peruvian Workers (CTP), an organization largely serving urban blue- and white-collar workers in industries and services.

FTAP. Because of its greater capacity for organization, the FTAP, in contrast with other groups of agricultural workers, has successfully demanded contracts that have improved and made more uniform the salaries and living conditions of its workers. These unions have also achieved a higher level of institutional consolidation. For instance, the sugar companies have a check-off system for union dues and grant leaves of absence to union leaders so that they may work full-time for the union.

Such a degree of bureaucratization reinforces the capacity of the FTAP to articulate the interests of its members and to negotiate with companies and the state. Between salaries and various payments in kind, such as food, living quarters, and utilities,[10] sugar workers receive an income which is roughly equivalent to that of construction workers in the city of Lima. For a rural worker this is a very good income. By way of contrast, the cotton workers in the department of Lima—who probably have the highest salaries in the cotton industry—earn less than half as much as the sugar workers.

Within the bureaucracy that has been established in the sugar workers' unions, fairly strong internal lines of communication exist which facilitate contact between the rank and file and the higher leadership. This system of communication favors the development of institutionalized recruitment and promotion procedures, which, in turn, facilitate a smooth flow of the union's affairs and the continuing socialization of its members. This successful communication has greatly strengthened the legitimacy of the union.

These internal characteristics of the FTAP and the history of fairly satisfactory relations between the union and the sugar industry during the

---

[10] A series of government decisions has permitted private firms to take the responsibility for providing the workers certain services that would otherwise be the responsibility of the state—such as medical care, education, and electricity. These decisions resulted from demands by the unions that these services be provided, yet paradoxically the result has been to make the workers and the unions even more dependent on the companies.

last decade,[11] suggest the growth of more institutionalized channels of communication between union and industry. At times both may pursue common interests, as was recently the case when unions and companies successfully demanded a rise in the price of internally consumed sugar from the government. But this does not preclude, as we will see later, the possibility that serious conflicts of interest can arise over the renewal of collective contracts.

The living conditions and salaries which sugar workers receive are substantially superior to those received by the rest of the rural workers in the country. This was made possible to a great extent by aggressive union demands, which forced the industry to initiate a process of mechanization that stimulated higher productivity in the cane industry.[12]

This process has had several serious consequences. It has required the specialization and occupational differentiation of workers, while simultaneously reducing the need for unskilled workers. Because of union pressure, however, the sugar firms have not been able to reduce the underemployed work force that resulted from mechanization without incurring serious conflicts.[13] This has led to an attempt by the industries to convert plants into real industrial centers, producing paper, alcohol, and plastics from the sugar cane, and thus provide employment for some of the workers displaced by mechanization.

The sugar enterprises include a numerous population residing in centers within the plantation and lacking other possibilities for employment or other services except those provided by the company. This leads to the development of typical company towns,[14] and, combined with the dimin-

[11] As will be made clear later, this situation of satisfactory relations was very much dependent on the cooperation during this period between leading agricultural interests and APRA, the political party most closely associated with these unions.

[12] Collin Delavaud, "Consecuencias de la modernización de la agricultura en las haciendas de la costa norte del Perú," in *La Hacienda en el Perú* (Lima: Instituto de Estudios Peruanos, 1967) pp. 259–280.

[13] "The FTAP agreed today to alert the masses of the entire country to be prepared to engage in an indefinite general strike in the case that the threat of massive firing should persist. . . . [The] vice president of this organization said that because of the automation of that industry no less than 1,500 workers are about to be fired" (*La Prensa*, Jan. 21, 1968, p. 11).

[14] Paramonga in the department of Lima and Cartavio and Casagrande in La Libertad had in 1961 populations of twelve, sixteen, and twelve thousand respectively, but none of them had legal recognition as a city. They are classified as plantations in the census. None of them has a local government, nor state institutions, with the exception of the civil guard. But, as in the great mining centers, even the civil guard receives food and lodging from the company. In addition the guards stationed in these centers receive a supplement to their salaries from the company.

ishing need for a work force in the sugar industry, means that the workers support a very heavy load in maintaining a family, including children of working age who cannot find employment near their homes.

The sugar enterprise, then, finds itself doubly pressured by its workers, because, although their absolute income is relatively high, it is, in effect, considerably reduced by family obligations. The workers thus demand not only higher wages but also an increase in the employment of their children and relatives. Periods of negotiation for collective contracts are frequently accompanied by bloody conflicts and strikes that have an average duration of three to four weeks.

Another consequence of the combined process of unionization, increments in salaries, industrialization, and occupational specialization is that the sugar workers have drawn away from other peasant sectors, especially those which are not organized, and tend to identify themselves with the urban working population. This situation is reflected in the fact that FTAP is not linked with FENCAP, even though it involves rural workers. The sugar workers' unions are concerned with achieving immediate social and economic benefits for their members and are not interested in promoting a general redistributive process among classes at a regional or national level. In this regard, their behavior is very much like that of the urban unions. Thus, for instance, they feel no interest in programs of agrarian reform.

It is true that APRA has been the promoter of unionization among sugar workers and has made it possible for union leaders to participate, although on a minor scale, in the direction of the party. Nevertheless, the FTAP seems to maintain a position of relative autonomy, which gives it strong bargaining power with respect to the employers, the government, and the political parties—even APRA. This autonomy is due to a number of factors: the unions' large membership—around 40,000—its cohesion, and the crucial place of sugar production in the national economy.

The autonomy and strong bargaining position of FTAP may be observed in the intensity of the conflicts in which workers engage before each period of negotiation for collective contracts. This degree of intensity may even violate the best interests of APRA in its present phase of collaboration with the traditional sectors of Peru. It is this collaboration that is the basis for the recent incorporation of APRA and the unions into the political system.

FENCAP. The Rural Workers' Federation of Peru (FENCAP) has been formed in the last decade by Aprista (APRA) leaders who organized and united various types of peasant groups: unions on haciendas and associations of small farmers, sharecroppers, and indigenous communities.[15] The unions of agricultural workers and the sharecroppers are found on the coast and are generally associated with the cultivation of cotton; the indigenous communities are found in the most modern areas of the Mantaro Valley, in the central sierra.

These types of organization are not recent. In 1945, the first unions of sharecroppers were begun in a serious way when the APRA promoted the passage of legislation that, paradoxically, legally recognized the subordinate status of sharecroppers. In the same period, the party sponsored the formation of peasant leagues in some areas with a high concentration of indigenous population in order to eradicate the use of coca, illiteracy and the abuses of the landlords.

The organizational pattern of FENCAP is characterized by a great geographical dispersion and a lack of homogeneity in the objective social situations and interests of its members. These factors limit the capacity of FENCAP to mobilize its own resources and form the basis for its dependence on its mentor, the APRA. The level of bureaucratization in FENCAP is very much lower than that of FTAP, and its professional staff consists of delegates from the APRA, whose salaries are paid by APRA and by the international organizations with which FENCAP is related.

The activities of FENCAP vary according to the different groups involved. In dealing with the cotton haciendas, the union promotes the organization of permanent workers, neglecting that of the part-time workers recruited for the harvest. FENCAP also encourages the establishment of a limit for the number of workers employed in each hacienda, based on the extent of its cultivated area—a policy which, in fact, reduces the opportunities for work of a temporary nature.[16] The union follows the new political lines established by the APRA and limits itself to demands for higher salaries, compliance with the hours established by law, and better working conditions. Like FTAP, it also has no interest in broader redistributive measures such as agrarian reform.

When dealing with sharecroppers and indigenous communities, the principal activity of FENCAP is the processing of the interminable legal

[15] The indigenous communities are corporative organizations based on kinship ties which use lands and/or water in common and maintain politico-religious functions and ties of internal solidarity. The large majority of the communities are found in the sierra, and the government has until now recognized about 1,500 of them. It is supposed that approximately 3,000 more exist which have not been recognized, with a population of about one million inhabitants.

[16] Cesar Fonseca, "Sindicatos agrarios del valle de Chancay" (B.A. thesis, Department of Anthropology, San Marcos University [Lima], 1966).

conflicts between them and the haciendas. These legal conflicts seem to
have substantially increased in the last few years. The Agrarian Reform
Law of 1964 stipulates that the sharecroppers are to receive as property
the plots of land which they have been working. A great many of the
coastal haciendas, especially those dedicated to the cultivation of cotton,
are worked, at least in part, through the sharecropping system. Hence, if
the Agrarian Reform Law is actually followed, a considerable number of
these haciendas will be divided up. To protect their properties, the
landowners often try to expel the sharecroppers from their land. But since
the law contains clauses which forbid such expulsions, the landowners
often resort to a variety of legal subterfuges to reach their goals. One of
the principal goals of FENCAP's legal services has been to aid sharecroppers who are faced with expulsion.

In addition, FENCAP processes petitions for the installation of public
services in the indigenous communities. This is done through the deputies
of the APRA, by means of their power to introduce parliamentary
initiatives in the Congress.[17] FENCAP also obtains assistance for the
communities from international sources, such as U.S.A.I.D.

After 1956, the unions controlled by the APRA obtained official recognition as representatives of the workers. Such recognition has permitted
them to integrate themselves into various governmental commissions and
to create ties with international organizations like the International Labor
Organization (ILO). They rely upon the technical and economic assistance of the Organization of American States, as well as being favored by
economic provisions of the national government and of foreign unions.

FENCAP and FTAP are also affiliated through the Confederation
of Peruvian Workers with the Inter-American Regional Organization of
Workers (ORIT), which is, in turn, intimately tied to the AFL-CIO of
the United States. Through that relationship, FENCAP and FTAP participate in the American Institute for Free Labor Development, which
sponsors the Center for Peruvian Labor Studies. These connections permit FENCAP and FTAP to obtain fellowships for leaders of their local
organizations to travel and study, principally in the United States.

The History of Coastal Unions

Rural unionism began in the sugar plantations of the northern coast of
Peru during the second decade of this century, at a time when the entire

---

[17] The "parliamentary initiatives" consist of the right of each representative to make
use of a determined amount of the budget as patronage for his constituents.

country was passing through a process of reorganization.[18] The government of Augusto Leguía (1919–1930) had succeeded in shifting its base of support from the traditional oligarchy to new sectors connected with foreign trade. During this period British investors were gradually displaced by North American concerns. The American investments were largely in the extractive industries—agriculture and mining—and favored the development of concentrations of workers in northern and central Peru, while the British investments had generally been concentrated in finance and public services, centered in the coastal cities.

This process was paralleled by the beginning of the development of unions on the plantations and in the mining centers, as well as by demands for the eight-hour working day in Lima. These ultimately resulted in the formation of the General Confederation of Peruvian Workers. In the universities, fights were waged at the same time for university reform. This agitation was the initial manifestation of interests of groups of the middle class, whose demands led to the formation of the APRA and Communist parties—the two political groups that grew out of this mobilization of the popular sectors of the country. The ideologies of these groups stressed the role of the state as a national institution and the necessity for complete participation of the marginal social sectors in the political system.

This period of ferment had an impact in all parts of the country. In such regions as Puno, Cuzco, and Ica, the peasantry began to revolt violently against the traditional order. In the Mantaro Valley, a reorganization of the social structure along communal lines was achieved. In other words, the northern peasant mobilization formed part of a process characterized by the emergence of new social sectors in the political life of the country, sectors which tried to create new institutions and new standards of values. The university professors, intellectuals, urban workers, miners, and peasants found themselves in a joint process of political mobilization, although fragmented and without institutional coordination until the emergence of the APRA and Communist parties.

The recruitment of leaders for the APRA party was carried out principally in the North, and for a long time APRA helped the union

[18] Joaquin Diaz Ahumada, *Historia de las luchas sindicales en el valle de Chicama* (Trujillo, Peru: Editorial Bolivariana, n.d.); Martinez de la Torre, *Apuntes para una interpretación marxista de la historia del Perú* (4 vols.; Lima: Editora Peruana, 1947); Peter Klaren, "*Origins of the Peruvian Aprista Party: A Study of Social and Economic Changes in La Libertad, 1870–1932*" (Ph.D. thesis, Department of History, University of California at Los Angeles, 1968).

movement in matters of organization, legal advice, and information-gathering. Thus party leaders were able to organize, both politically and socially, the working population of the plantations and to recruit from among that population their followers and militants, a pattern which eventually converted the North into a bastion of the APRA.

A strong tie began to develop between the party and the unions, a tie by which the fortunes of one were heavily linked to the fortunes of the other. The constant and repeated persecutions which the APRA suffered during the next thirty years also hurt the position of the union movement and reinforced the ties between the two: imprisonment and deportation were common experiences for leaders of both groups, as well as for their rank-and-file members and militants. On the other hand, to the extent that the APRA was granted legal standing, the movement of sugar workers was able to obtain legal recognition as well and to press successfully for certain demands with the support of the party. Between 1945 and 1948—its first period of participation in national politics as a legal party—the APRA organized several hundred unions on the coast, as well as sharecropper associations. Those groups later formed the basis for organizing FENCAP.

The ideological orientation of the APRA determined to a large extent the orientation of the labor unions. The necessity to eradicate feudalism and to develop state capitalism was the ideological pillar of *aprismo* in its classical form. Since internal forces capable of stimulating modernization did not exist in Peru, the APRA believed that the stimulus would have to come through foreign investment—to such an extent that (to paraphrase Lenin) imperialism would be the first and not the last stage of capitalism in Latin America. Foreign capital was thought to be the agent that would destroy existing feudalism in the country and would favor the formation of an entrepreneurial mentality, of industries, and, therefore, the development of labor organizations. These labor organizations and the APRA would be the groups charged with replacing the oligarchy of Lima and thus incorporating the peasant population in modern life, which foreign investments would at the same time be bringing to the country.[19]

During the last ten years, APRA has recognized that its legal existence as a party requires greater cooperation with the traditional sectors, and it no longer champions far-reaching changes. Syndical activity has been

[19] Víctor Raúl Haya de la Torre, *Discurso-Programa 1931* (Serie Documentos; [Lima: Partido Aprista Peruano, 1963]). See also: *Plan Agrario* (Documentos del II Congreso Nacional del Partido del Pueblo; [Lima: Partido Aprista Peruano, 1948]); Alfredo Saco, *Programa agrario del aprismo* (Lima: Ediciones Populares, 1946).

limited to the task of raising the standard of living of the organized working sector. Thus, at the moment, although it is true that the basic political resource of the party continues to be its union sector, APRA policy is oriented toward obtaining limited economic advantages for its members and in that way retaining their electoral support.

Peasant Movements in the Sierra

Peasant organizations in the traditional areas of the sierra have developed very recently, with a very different organizational form and very different political consequences for all of Peru. These organizations grew out of the peasant mobilization in the sierra that began in the last years of the 1950's and obtained its maximum expression between 1962 and 1964. That mobilization has particularly affected the peasant population that is in a state of servitude and the indigenous communities of central and southern Peru.[20] At the moment the process continues, but its rate of expansion has lessened substantially.

With the exception of the case of La Convención, it seems that the Indian serfs (*colonos*) have reacted differently to mobilization than have members of indigenous communities. The *colonos* formed unions to demand higher salaries and, above all, the elimination of personal and gratuitous obligations. The indigenous communities have sought the return of lands taken from them by the traditional haciendas through the very direct means of simply reoccupying these lands. Between 1959 and 1966, newspapers in the capital city reported one hundred and three invasions of haciendas in the whole country, with an exceptionally heavy concentration between August and December, 1963.[21] These months coincide with the first "hundred days" of the Belaúnde government, a period when the strong expectation of land reform provided a great stimulus for such invasions.

These new forms of peasant behavior took place within a context of

[20] Aníbal Quijano, "Contemporary Peasant Movements," in S. M. Lipset and A. Solari (eds.), *Elites in Latin America* (New York: Oxford University Press, 1967), pp. 301–340.

[21] These figures are based on a tally of reports of invasions in the major Lima papers. Since several of these papers were actively campaigning for heavy repression of the invasions between August and December, 1963, and were giving the invasions very full coverage, it seems likely that compared to these five months there was underreporting for the rest of the seven-year period. This supposition is confirmed by the work of Roberto MacLean, who found that in Cuzco alone there were 114 invasions during this seven-year period. See his "La Reforma Agraria en el Peru" (Cuadernos de Sociología, Biblioteca de Ensayos Sociológicos, [Mexico City: Instituto de Investigaciones Sociales, Universidad Nacional, 1965]), pp. 137–138.

social and political mobilization that began after World War II. One aspect of this mobilization is the process of migration discussed previously which brought to the principal cities of the country a dense population concentrated in the *barriadas* (poor neighborhoods, often formed through the squatter invasions of unused land). For example, it is estimated that a quarter of the population of Lima is found in the *barriadas* and that one-half of the total population of that city is made up of migrants. The mere presence of these migrants puts enormous pressure on the supply of public services and employment in the coastal cities. The family and institutional relationships which these migrants maintain with their places of origin have been increased by a notable expansion of modern means of communication in rural areas. Thus each new wave of migration feeds new ideas and aspirations back to the countryside and stimulates additional social change and further migration.

A second aspect of this mobilization is the expansion in the occupations characteristic of the middle class that took place at the same time, occupations linked with education and the increase in public services and private industrial activities. With this expansion, the new middle class began to create a new ideology oriented toward the organization of new mass parties, which were in active competition with APRA and which stressed the necessity of realizing "structural changes," including agrarian reform, as a means of easing the pressures that hastened rural migration.

A third aspect of this mobilization has been the radicalization of groups with leftist tendencies, especially under the influence of the Cuban revolution and the newly dominant role of more radical, Peking-oriented Communists. This radicalization has occurred especially in the university population, which is now recruited more and more from the migrant groups.

The very active campaigning and discussion of issues of reform that preceded the two elections of 1962 and 1963 further stimulated this mobilization. When the new Belaúnde government was finally installed in 1963, it further stimulated this trend by initiating a broad program of activities at the level of rural communities, such as the Popular Cooperation Program which got thousands of university students involved with the peasant population in community action programs. Through the students, the peasant movements have become associated with student organizations, urban unions, political and religious groups, which sought in different ways to institutionalize the peasant movement. In order to do that, these social sectors founded unions and peasant federations at the national level, thus bestowing legitimacy upon the movement and at the same time seeking support for their own goals.

Thus urban groups have organized, channelled, directed, and represented the movement with various degrees of success. They have actively participated as propagandists, organizers, legal advisers and processors of peasant demands. Nevertheless, these urban groups have not dominated the peasant movement, whose leadership is still clearly in the hands of peasants.

In contrast to this support from more radical groups, these peasant organizations do not receive support from any of the major political parties. They have not received the legal recognition and the accompanying political patronage that is only possible if they are "sponsored" by a major party. This lack of interest on the part of the major parties can be traced to two related causes. On the one hand, these illiterate Indians cannot vote and are therefore not worth cultivating as a source of electoral support. On the other hand, the established parties consider a serious popular mobilization that involves an expansion of the electorate to be illegitimate and dangerous, a threat to the present political system. As one high official put it recently, "What will become of us if all the Indians organized!"

Nevertheless, the peasant unions are receiving support from the more radical sectors, and are, to some degree, developing successfully. The growth of a collective perception of group interests has meant that the Indian communities have not only demanded the ownership of land, but also their rights as citizens, thus rejecting their traditional, subordinate role. The emergence of these organizations constitutes an essential step in the modification of the existing situation. They form the basis for a collective confrontation of the peasant population with the mestizos and therefore with national institutions. They are creating a crisis for the national political system.

The traditional sectors, which support the mestizos, have reacted violently to the present mobilization. In 1963 the majority of the Congress demanded that the government put an end to the invasions and peasant strikes. Some of the representatives even shouted at the government minister then present, "Fill them with lead!" Indeed, police killed a large number of peasants during the period 1962–1964 and imprisoned thousands of persons committed to the new peasant activities. Under the pressure of these land invasions the government did pass a minimal agrarian reform law. However, in order to discourage land invasions, an article was added which stipulated that peasants who invaded and occupied land could not become the owners under the land-redistribution terms of the law.

Even with this setback, the peasant mobilization and various attempts to organize guerrillas in the southern and central regions of the country did stimulate the government to carry out a few expropriations and community development projects. In addition, the army initiated a program that built new roads and provided some medical and educational services. The departments where the largest number of invasions had occurred and where the greatest peasant articulation had been achieved were declared by the government zones of agrarian reform. In the departments of Junín and Pasco a property of about three hundred thousand hectares was expropiated, and plans for another expropiation of this size were developed. In La Convención, department of Cuzco, a process of division of land was begun. The government also obtained an international loan to aid community development in rural areas, in order to try to satisfy some of the demands of the peasants.

Types of Organizations

The spontaneous character of peasant mobilization and its institutional precariousness, as well as a lack of available information, make its evaluation difficult. However, it seems clear that the principal organizations in the sierra are groups affiliated, on the one hand, with the Federation of Workers of La Convención and Lares and the Confederation of Peruvian Peasants (CCP), and on the other hand, with the Union Front of Puno (FSC) and the Christian Union Movement of Peru (MOSICP).

Although it is true that the Federation of Workers of La Convención forms a part of the CCP and, in fact, constitutes its bulwark, nevertheless the autonomy of the former, its dynamism, initiative, and special development demand that it be considered separately.[22]

Peasant mobilization in La Convención was much more radical than in the majority of other cases. Its special character seems to be due to two fundamental causes. One is related to the extensive migration *into* La Convención that has taken place recently. Because there has been a scarcity of labor in the area, the landowners have tried to encourage

[22] See Chapter 6; also Eric J. Hobsbawm, *Problemes agraires a La Convención (Pérou)*, Communication presentée au Colloque International du Centre National de la Recherche Scientifique. Paris, Oct., 1965; MacLean, *op. cit.*, pp. 29–39; Virgilio Landázuri, "Informe sobre el problema de los arriendos del valle de La Convención" Ministerio de Trabajo, 1960. Hugo Neira, *Cuzco: Tierra y muerte* (Lima: Populibros Peruanos, 1964).

production and a new settlement by granting more land than usual to the workers, particularly lands on mountain slopes, and by permitting them to raise coffee for sale. Paradoxically, the mountain slopes are most convenient for the cultivation of coffee, whereas the lower parts of the valley are more appropriate for crops of lesser commercial value. The considerable income derived from the sale of coffee stimulated in the 1950's an abrupt growth in the city of Quillabamba, capital of the province. The rapid expansion of population and prosperity of the settlers threatened to change the traditional character of social relations in the area and led the large landowners to try to reinforce the traditional system by withdrawing some of the specific benefits. This was resisted by the settlers, and as early as 1953 this resistance led to the formation of the first peasant groups in the valley—which later grew into the Peasant Federation of La Convención and Lares.

This history of rapid settlement, prosperity, and attempted reassertion of the traditional order was one of the two factors that led to the special character of peasant mobilization in this area. The second was the presence in the valley of Hugo Blanco and the Leftist Revolutionary Front (FIR), a group made up of the Leninist-Communist party, a splinter group from the Peruvian Communist party, and of elements coming from different parts of the independent Left. The activities of the FIR, under the direction of Hugo Blanco, included the creation of a Revolutionary Workers' School on the Chaupimayo Hacienda after they had seized control of that hacienda. That school diffused a new ideology and promoted massive invasions of the haciendas, which eventually led to the control of the entire valley by the FIR.

The first strike that the Federation unleashed against the plantations centered around the settlers' refusal to continue to provide gratuitous services to the hacienda owners—services which were not different from those paid to landlords in other parts of the country. Thanks principally to Blanco and his group, this activity lead eventually to the transformation of the land-tenure structure of La Convención through the direct participation of the peasants. Invasions were accompanied by demonstrations of peasants in the cities of Quillabamba and Cuzco, the capital of the department, where elements of the workers, students, and interested civil servants participated. This type of behavior on the part of the peasants had very important repercussions in the whole country, promoting the process of peasant mobilization that had been occurring spontaneously in other areas since the 1950's and leading to a wave of invasions and peasant strikes with a clearly radical tint.

At the same time, the movement served to change the conservative orientation which the traditional Peruvian Left had maintained in the cities of the southern part of the country.[23] In addition, the Cuban revolution and the increased importance of Peking-oriented Communists stimulated the creation of various leftist groups with revolutionary propensities, thus encouraging in other parts of the country the same kind of action which the peasants of La Convención had taken.

Owing to the radical character of the Federation of Workers of La Convención and Lares and the supposed inactivity of the current government, the military junta which took power in 1962 imprisoned Hugo Blanco as well as various other peasant leaders, dismantled the organization, and persecuted the groups which had supported it. Nevertheless, because of the great intensity of Federation activity, La Convención was the zone chosen for agrarian reform by the junta, though at the same time it remained under rigid military control. More recently, the Federation has been able to restructure itself, but because of the imprisonment of its leaders and the division of land now in progress in the zone, the objectives of the organization have been modified, as has its original cohesion, resulting in the limiting of its objectives to the cooperative sale of coffee, the procurement of higher export quotas, and the demand for more and more public services. But a militant spirit still exists, as shown in the massive demonstration of 1967, in which the Federation demanded more active land reform.

The Confederation of Peruvian Peasants (CCP) was begun in 1956 by the Peruvian Communist party, which hoped thereby to increase its base of support. Like FENCAP, the CCP did not limit its activities to one sector of the rural population but diversified its assistance to include the workers in cotton plantations on the central coast, indigenous communities, sharecroppers, and sierra hacienda workers. This dispersion and the lack of sufficient organizers created a situation similar to that which we have mentioned in the case of FENCAP. But, in addition, the CCP lacked an important political organization that could offer support, since the Communist party of Peru has little political strength.

After obtaining some organizing successes on the cotton plantations— similar to the growth of FENCAP's organizing activity—members of the CCP were violently repressed by the police, who, with the concurrence of FENCAP, accused them of instigating peasants to take over the

<hr>

[23] Silvestre Condoruna, "Las experiencias de la última etapa de las luchas revolucionarias en el Perú," *Vanguardia Revolucionaria* (Lima), No. 5, 1966, pp. 1–37.

plantations.[24] In the case of indigenous communities and sharecroppers, the CCP tried, as FENCAP did, to promote their legal recognition and to present their numerous complaints.

As a result of the actions of Hugo Blanco and his group in La Convención and the dissidence, caused by questions of an international nature, within the Peruvian Communist party, the CCP fell under the control of the Peking faction. From that time on, the CCP has maintained an ambiguous line: it continues to petition and to use legal channels, but at the same time it promotes radical conduct within the communities and among workers on the traditional haciendas. This resorting to radical tactics is due in part to the lack of means to pressure official institutions to gain minimum benefits for its members. For this reason also the peasants are often frustrated by the inability of the CCP to channel their demands. Thus the CCP at times loses its original legitimacy.

The CCP is made up of unions of Indian serfs and of indigenous communities, united to form provincial and departmental federations, with headquarters in the traditional regions of the sierra of the country. But in spite of this formal organization, the actual structure of the CCP is precarious. The current conflict among various factions of the Left which prescribe different strategies and organizing tactics are continuing to weaken the institutional basis of the CCP.

The Peasant Union Front (Frente Sindical Campesino, FSC) was formed in 1960 in the city of Juliaca (department of Puno), under the auspices of the Christian Democratic party and the direction of Néstor and Roger Cáceres.[25] The latter, besides being a deputy at that time, was also the secretary-general of the youth section of the Christian Democratic party. He was re-elected deputy in 1963, along with his brother.

Juliaca is at the junction of the highways which connect Arequipa, the second most important city in the country, with Cuzco and Puno. The city has succeeded in establishing itself as the commercial center of the zone, competing with the city of Puno, capital of the department, forty kilometers away. The growing importance of Juliaca can be seen in the 237 per cent growth in its population between 1949 and 1961. The city of Puno during the same period had an increase in population of only 77 per cent. Juliaca has become the center of diffusion in the process of moderni-

[24] Fonseca, *op. cit.*

[25] Edward McMillan Dew, Jr., "Politics in the Altiplano: A Study of Provincial Political Change in Perú" (Ph.D. thesis, University of California at Los Angeles, 1966), especially pp. 187 ff.

zation in the department, while Puno continues to be the headquarters of the traditional political apparatus.

In the process of urban differentiation, the Cáceres family has played an important role. The father amassed a small fortune during World War II in the retailing of groceries and the exporting of wool, and on the basis of his wealth his sons have obtained political control in the region. Presently, two of the Cáceres brothers are deputies in the Congress and bosses of the FSC; another is the mayor of Juliaca and administrator of the commercial establishment of the family (which is one of the most important in the zone); another is the editor of a local newspaper, and the fifth brother is the head of the radio station of the city. Their control of this radio station is the most important aspect of their political power. Transistor radios that can be turned only to this station have been distributed through the commercial activities of the family. The radio station transmits at key hours programs in Quechua and Aymara (the two languages of the peasants of this region), with heavy emphasis on regional and class struggles for a better life.

Serious differences arose between the Cáceres brothers and the Christian Democratic party when one of the brothers declared himself a candidate for the position of deputy; the Cáceres split from the party and organized the Independent Peasant party (Partido Independiente de Campesinos, PIC). That party was constructed on the base of the FSC and has served the Cáceres as an electoral basis for their positions in the National Congress.

The FSC depends upon the political and economic resources of the Cáceres family, and especially upon their radio and newspaper as means of communication. The support of the Cáceres deputies at least neutralizes the possible reprisals against the FSC of political and police authorities in the zone. The Cáceres family has trained its close supporters, who are fluent in the three languages of the region (Spanish, Quechua, and Aymará), to be professional promoters of the FSC, weaving an organizational net which has permitted the vigorous construction of a political base for the family. In the last municipal elections, supporters of the Cáceres family won in many of the districts of the department. This occurred in spite of the fact that illiterates, who constitute the immense majority of the adult population and of the new constituency that the Cáceres are trying to develop, cannot vote.

The FSC is thus of a mixed political-syndical character, based upon the resources and the support of the Cáceres family. The objectives of the FSC include regional development, which the Cáceres deputies have charged themselves with promoting, as well as other goals more strictly related to the peasantry, which seem to have less importance in the opinion of the family.

In regional terms, the FSC seeks the consolidation of Juliaca as a center of departmental development and the resulting displacement of power from Puno to Juliaca. Development would be promoted through the concentration of state services and resources in the city, which would modify the productive structure of the region. An example of this is the way in which, in 1965, the Cáceres family and their group consolidated public opinion to oppose the construction of a new airport in Puno, which would have displaced the existing airport in Juliaca. Similar reactions were prompted by the installation of a new public university in Puno and by a growing tendency, at one point, to devote most of the resources of the Puno Corporation, a state institution dedicated to developing the department, to the city of Puno. Finally, the insistence of the family on the creation of an industrial park in Juliaca suggests once again the emphasis that they place on regional objectives.

Demands of a strictly peasant nature are very restricted and have definitely secondary importance in the FSC. These include the lessening of obligations rendered by servile labor to landlords, the extension of the national social security program to the peasants, and agrarian reform. The right to vote for illiterates is the fourth objective of the FSC. However, none of this is seriously intended to mobilize the peasant masses. Rather, it is a part of the more general effort to promote the region.

It is very difficult to estimate the number of peasants affiliated with the FSC. In 1963, as a result of a peasant congress in Puno, the FSC was said to contain 650 unions and 200,000 members. That total is undoubtedly inflated, because it would include almost a third of the population of the department. The list of the unions that have processed petitions for official recognition in Puno totals 241, of which 117 are unions of indigenous communities and 113 are unions of Indian serfs. The information we have obtained concerning the size of fifty of these indicates that an average union has fifty members. If that sample is representative, and if the FSC contained 650 unions, the total membership would be about 32,500.

The Christian Union Movement of Peru (Movimiento Sindical Cristiano del Perú, MOSICP) was founded as a result of the Eucharistic Congress of 1954, for which the archbishopric of Lima formed an urban workers' committee with the support of the Catholic Youth Workers. From the beginning, the new organization was interested in instructing the workers, some of whom were union leaders, in the social doctrine of the Church. In order to do that, a Union School was constructed with the support of Catholic Youth Workers, Catholic Action, and the National Union of Catholic Students. From 1954 on, MOSICP, under the leadership of a priest, tried to establish ties with similar groups in other areas of the country, and it succeeded in joining together not only urban workers in Lima, but also in Arequipa, Tacna, and other cities of the North.

The involvement of MOSICP in rural areas of the country began in 1956 in the areas bordering Lima and was based on personal contact between the urban workers affiliated with the organization and the peasantry. In Arequipa and in the mining center of Toquepala, contacts were established with temporary workers who had come from Puno and who had been associated with MOSICP through the first organizing centers established by the Cáceres brothers. It was through those contacts that the Federation of Latin American Peasants was eventually formed. In 1963, MOSICP and the Cáceres brothers led a peasant congress in Puno, attended by six hundred delegates, as well as invited guests from other countries. At that time, because of disagreements within the Christian Democratic party, the Cáceres separated themselves from MOSICP and formed the Peasant Union Front, supported by the Quechua-speaking population in the south of the department. After that rupture, MOSICP found itself confined to the province of Ayaviri, in northern Puno.

The branch of MOSICP in Ayaviri was begun by students of Christian Democratic affiliation who had the decided support of foreign priests resident in the area. They hoped to organize Indian serfs and indigenous communities as a way of limiting expansion of the more radical Confederation of Peruvian Peasants (CCP) and the Peasant Union Front of Puno.

Starting from some short courses in the catechism which the foreign priests offered to peasant leaders, an Institute for Rural Education developed, at which a select number of peasants are taught agricultural techniques, religion, and unionism for an entire semester. These activities are supported by international financing, which church authorities of the area have managed to obtain. With the aid of such church and foreign assistance, MOSICP was able to persuade large landowners to pay the minimum wage established for the zone ($.33 daily in U.S. currency) and to obey the law which prohibits the expulsion of peasants from their plot of land. In addition, thanks to the support of international organizations like CARITAS, MOSICP offers economic assistance to its affiliates and thus reinforces its regional power.

In spite of the protection which MOSICP enjoyed during the period of repression between 1962 and 1964, its local leaders were nonetheless accused of being Communists—that is, followers of Hugo Blanco. They received treatment similar to leaders of the Federation of La Convención or the CCP. Some religious "advisers" of MOSICP have even been branded as Communists, but the protection offered them by regional Church authorities has saved them from being thrown out of the country. In Ayaviri, MOSICP has more than one hundred peasant unions with an average affiliation similar to that which was found in the Peasant Union Front. In other words, MOSICP has a membership of about 5,000 peasants in the department.

Some Final Observations

As we have said, regional variation in the phenomenon of modernization experienced in Peru during this century has produced peasant organizations with different structures and goals according to their different locations. The "modern" establishments, those in which agricultural workers are concentrated in semi-industrial patterns, tend to have highly institutionalized labor unions that, since the emergence of APRA in 1956 as a legal and more conservative party, have emphasized segmentary demands for gains and not class conflicts—that is to say, their demands are limited to immediate benefits for themselves and do not attack the entire existing social order.

In the "traditional" areas, on the other hand, where the peasants still live in a condition of extreme subordination, conflicts tend to break institutional canons, thereby redistributing resources and modifying social structure and social relations to a degree that has impact even at the national level. The demands of these peasants are inherently more radical than the demands of the coastal workers. Though higher wages and better hours for workers on a highly mechanized hacienda may cut into profits, they do not undermine the existing order in the way that the demand for land does. The essence of the traditional system in the sierra is the control of land by mestizos. If that is gone, the traditional system is gone. Similarly, the traditional system is so unproductive that it is hard for it to meet any demands at all. These factors account for the great strain imposed on the system by this more recent peasant mobilization.

The immediate stimulus for radicalism in these "traditional" regions is that the peasants have had their cultural references changed without accompanying changes in the structure of production, occupation, or income. This encourages their identification with revolutionary ideologies that focus on the problem of the control of agricultural land. This is a particularly important development in the Peruvian case because the parties have not been very interested in encouraging the political participation of these peasant sectors. Therefore, the radical transformation of the traditional agricultural sector unleashed the inconsistencies that can be observed at the moment in the traditional regions, in order to bring about political and cultural mobilization.

As distinct from earlier peasant movements in the sierra, the present movement has important ties to political organizations and developments in the cities. This linkage with the cities offers the possibility of overcoming the isolation which has traditionally characterized the peasantry. Thus, peasant organizations now find themselves for the first time involved in the national political process and at the same time challenging its institutional legitimacy.

8. Guatemala: The Peasant Union Movement, 1944–1954 *

NEALE J. PEARSON
Texas Technological University

Introduction

Guatemala was a traditional agricultural country in 1944. A small group of plantation owners or *finqueros*—2.1 per cent of the population—owned 72.2 per cent of the known arable land; they controlled the great mass of *Ladino* and Indian agricultural workers and tenant farmers.[1] The levels of living of the overwhelming mass of the population were low. Per capita income was among the lowest in the Americas. Foreign enterprise was important because it was a principal source of employment and foreign exchange. Over-all, the economy was stagnant. Labor-management relations in both rural and urban areas were oriented to "keeping the worker in his place," not toward increasing productivity. The country was under the rule of one of a long line of dictators, General Jorge Ubico (1931–1944). It was ruled primarily for the benefit of this small group of *finqueros* and army officers. The Roman Catholic Church and Protestant groups had little political influence. Law and order reigned.

A break with the past came in a series of events which have come to be known as the October 1944 Revolution. Free elections were held and Juan José Arévalo, who had spent many years in exile in Argentina, was elected President. The parties and groups supporting Arévalo were made up of young nationalists "interested in the physical betterment of the country and parliamentary in their solution of political problems."[2] Although most of these "revolutionaries" had a clear idea of the reforms they wanted to carry out, they were naïve and unsophisticated concerning the

---

* This chapter was prepared while the author was a member of the Department of Political Science, Miami University, Oxford, Ohio.

[1] *Ladino* is a corruption of the term *latino* (latin) which originally described individuals of European ancestry but which now includes those who have adopted Western cultural habits and dress. The distinction is primarily a cultural rather than a racial one.

[2] Kalman H. Silvert, *A Study in Government: Guatemala* (Middle American Research Institute, Publication No. 21 [New Orleans, La.: Tulane University, 1954]), pp. 6–8.

basic differences between indigenous revolutionary movements and the international communist movement and its objectives.[3] Marxist ideology provided a dialectical explanation of "imperialism" and a cause dedicated to overcoming both "imperialism" and "backwardness." The eventual contradictions between nationalism and Marxism remained imperceptible to most of Guatemala's radical politicians, intellectuals, and labor and peasant leaders for much of the period 1944–1954.

Peasants occupied a vulnerable position in Guatemalan society; they had no political power or influence to speak of before 1944 and only a little before 1950. But within this period, the young nationalist reformists and revolutionaries in the National Congress passed laws establishing a social security system, a statistical office (Dirección General de Estadística), an elaborate Labor Code, an electoral law, a central bank, a Production and Development Institute known as INFOP, a national airline, and such other institutional arrangements as increased autonomy for the governments of the *municipio* (an area similar in size and functions to the American county) and department (similar to the state).[4] Communists exercised a great influence in the labor movement that developed after the October 1944 revolution because of the lack of interest of democratic trade-union movements and governments in other countries in the reforms of the Arévalo period. The Labor Code of 1947 made organization easier for urban workers but almost impossible for rural workers and independent peasants because of high literacy requirements, the hostility of farm owners and administrators, the inadequacy of communications, and the lack of a trained corps of labor inspectors dedicated to enforcing the Labor Code. The two principal labor organizations which grew up during the Arévalo period—the Confederation of Workers of Guatemala or CTG, and the Guatemalan Trade-Union Federation or FSG—tried to organize some peasant groups. But their urban-oriented organizers and intellectuals failed to understand the peasant mind and the methods of arousing it on behalf of a peasant movement.

In 1950, the National Peasant Confederation of Guatemala (Confederación Nacional Campesina de Guatemala or CNCG) was organized by a small group of noncommunists as an organization which would raise the problems of the peasants "before the public and struggle for their solutions."[5] Agrarian reform—meaning redistribution of the land, rural

[3] Robert Alexander, *Communism in Latin America* (New Brunswick, N.J.: Rutgers University Press, 1957), p. 354.

[4] Leo A. Suslow, "Aspects of Social Reform in Guatemala, 1944–1949" (mimeo., M.A. thesis, Colgate University, 1949) discusses these reforms in detail.

[5] "Confederación Nacional del Campesino Fundase," *El Imparcial* (Guatemala City), May 30, 1950, p. 1, cols. 3–4.

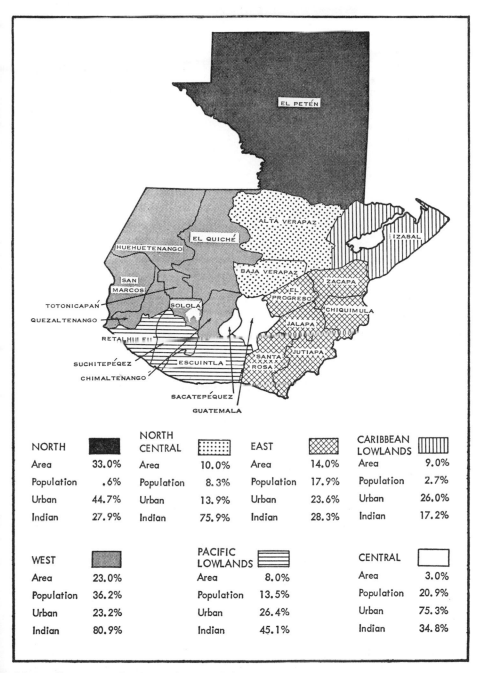

NORTH		NORTH CENTRAL		EAST		CARIBBEAN LOWLANDS	
Area	33.0%	Area	10.0%	Area	14.0%	Area	9.0%
Population	.6%	Population	8.3%	Population	17.9%	Population	2.7%
Urban	44.7%	Urban	13.9%	Urban	23.6%	Urban	26.0%
Indian	27.9%	Indian	75.9%	Indian	28.3%	Indian	17.2%

WEST		PACIFIC LOWLANDS		CENTRAL	
Area	23.0%	Area	8.0%	Area	3.0%
Population	36.2%	Population	13.5%	Population	20.9%
Urban	23.2%	Urban	26.4%	Urban	75.3%
Indian	80.9%	Indian	45.1%	Indian	34.8%

Map 2. Guatemala: Regional characteristics

Source: Institute for the Comparative Study of Political Systems, *Guatemala Election Factbook, March 6, 1966* (Washington, D.C., Jan., 1966), p. 2.

credits, and aid to the peasant in the cultivation of crops—was recognized as a "legitimate aspiration of the peasants." In short, the CNCG specifically sought a series of economic changes which would raise the economic, social, and political status and well-being of the peasants.

The changes brought about by the establishment of the CNCG and the Agrarian Reform Law of 1952 set off further demands for the correction of old ills and the creation of a new order. Since conditions were ripe for the rise of a political movement embracing the peasants, Leonardo Castillo Flores, Amor Velasco de León, and other young revolutionary activists took advantage of an opportunity to further their own political careers while also meeting the aspiration of many peasants. In the course of its growth, the CNCG acquired an organizational apparatus and recruited a small bureaucracy. However, the CNCG leadership failed to develop an ideology and a position of power strong enough to resist the maneuvers of the Communist-dominated General Confederation of Guatemalan Workers or CGTG (successor to the CTG) and the Guatemalan Labor party or PGT in a power struggle which took place in the fall of 1953.

The CNCG hierarchy at first adopted a nonpartisan doctrine of rewarding its friends and punishing its enemies with the votes it could deliver at the polls. This doctrine fitted the political facts of life in local congressional and municipal elections. The CNCG had friends and enemies in all of the political parties. However, the national leadership of the CNCG entered into a working alliance in 1952 with probably the strongest political party, the Revolutionary Action party or PAR, and its nonpartisan stance no longer fitted the facts. Once it entered into this political alliance and established political relationships with the CGTG leadership, the CNCG did not restrict itself to domestic political and economic matters but ventured forth on political crusades for ends which had no immediate bearing on the status of the peasant or the economic issues of land distribution, wages, and working conditions, such as peasant signatures on the Stockholm Peace Proposal and denunciation of NATO and United States participation in the Korean War.

Other threats to the status and income of the landowning *finquero* class were brought about by the Agrarian Reform Law of 1952. Increased production of corn, coffee, bananas, cotton, and rice seem to be directly related to the increased distribution of land. Many thousands of peasant families lived much better than ever before. Ownership or lifetime access to land—even with political strings attached and participation of many young educated Ladinos and Indians in peasant unions and politics—contributed greatly to improve the status and prestige of peasants as individuals and as a class.

The success of the CNCG was reflected in its rapid growth from 28 unions in June, 1950, to over 1,700 by February, 1954, and in the heated attacks made upon it by the *finqueros* and others whose power in the countryside was threatened by the CNCG and agrarian reform.

The Communists failed to create their own peasant movement; most peasants showed little comprehension of communist ideology. On the other hand, membership in Roman Catholic or Protestant churches did not deter peasants from participating in Communist-supported activities. While contributing little to the social revolution, the Communists were able to identify this revolution with themselves in the eyes of many persons within and without Guatemala. The inability of Arévalo and Jacobo Arbenz Guzmán, president from 1950–1954, to form a unified party or movement of the "Democratic Left" gave the CNCG no practical alternatives other than to follow the Communists after the power plays of November, 1953.

When Guatemalan Army officers forced Arbenz out of the presidency in 1954 because of his refusal to end his increasing dependence on the PGT, the *finqueros* quickly reasserted their control over the peasants and the countryside. Although no more than a handful of people lost their lives during the so-called "invasion" by Colonel Castillo Armas' "Liberation Army," many more were killed by Arbenz supporters on the way out and by fancied or real supporters of the Liberation Army on the way in. A majority of the executions against so-called communists took place in small towns and villages; an unknown number of CNCG leaders and peasants did not escape this mob justice. The CNCG and peasant unionism as active forces in Guatemala were destroyed. Not until 1965–1966 were there signs that peasant unionism was a force once again to be dealt with locally—if not nationally—but the new movement was still a shadow of the former CNCG.

The Environment

Population Characteristics

A majority of the population is descended from the country's earliest known inhabitants—the Mayan Indians. The nation's first census in 1950 said 53.4 per cent of the population of 2,790,868 was Indian. Other sources estimate the Indian population as high as 85 per cent.[6]

[6] Antonio Guerra, *El problema del analfabetismo en Guatemala* (publishing data unknown although it appears to have been written in the late 1940's), p. 12. Guerra claimed, "85% . . . speak their own dialects, occupy distinct regions, and, in the majority, do not understand Spanish."

Most Indians lived in the countryside. All but a small fraction were illiterate, had low levels of living, consumed little beyond what they produced, and, until the October Revolution, were almost untouched by government activities, except for meeting several well-defined obligations toward the national elite administered by the local village elders or *caciques:* these included the supply of labor for plantations and public works projects, respect for the wishes of national government leaders in voting on election day, and disclosure of the presence of labor organizers,

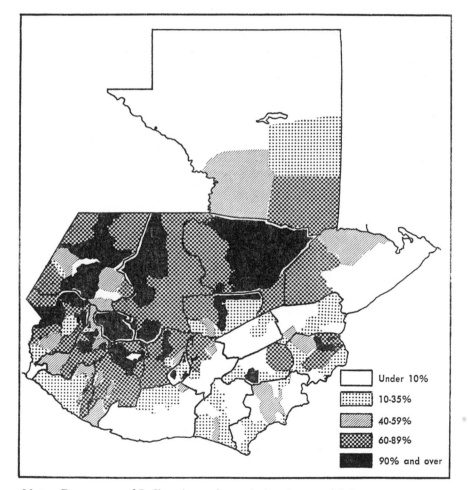

	Under 10%
	10-35%
	40-59%
	60-89%
	90% and over

Map 3. Percentage of Indians in total population, by *municipios,* 1950

Source: Whetten, *Guatemala: The Land and the People,* p. 52 (from *Sexto Censo de Población,* 1950).

political "agitators," and other outside "undesirables" who might disturb the traditional *status quo*.[7]

Indian communities are generally found in the cool, high, mountainous area of the country while Ladino groups are found in the temperate and warmer parts of the country (*la tierra templada* and *la tierra caliente*, respectively). Pockets of Ladinos are found in the western mountains as well as in many of the arid and semiarid parts of the Petén. In the eastern part of the country, there are two gatherings of Indian groups: the Pocománes in Jalapa, and the Chortís in Chiquimula and Zacapa. Between these two Indian groups is a Ladino corridor running from Zacapa south through Chiquimula to Jutiapa. This corridor corresponds to the Motagua River valley cutting across Central America from one ocean to the other.

Indian communities may be divided into three groups culturally and regionally.[8]

(1) The traditional or recent Indian who has retained Indian customs most strongly and who usually comes from an Indian community in which much, if not most, of the population is still monolingual (speaking only an Indian language) and in which men and women retain certain distinctive articles of clothing which set them apart as Indians. These groups are to be found mostly in the western and northwestern mountain areas although there is also a group of Chorti-speaking Indians on the Honduran border in the departments of Chiquimula and Zacapa.

(2) The modified or transitional Indian who has for some years adopted various Ladino customs. He may have come from an Indian community in which most of the population is bilingual (speaking some

[7] Representative works describing various Indian or mixed communities include Ruth Bunzel, *Chichicastenango* (Seattle: University of Washington Press, 1952); John Gillin, " 'Race Relations' without Conflict: A Guatemalan Town," *American Journal of Sociology*, LIII (March, 1948), 337–343; George McCutcheon McBride and Merle McBride, "Highland Guatemala and Its Maya Communities," *Geographic Review*, XXXII (April, 1942), 252–268; and Sol Tax, "The Municipio of the Midwestern Highlands of Guatemala," *American Anthropologist*, XXXIX, Part 1 (July–Sept., 1937), 423–444.

[8] These groups, their geographic distribution, and the process of ladinoization are discussed in the following works: Richard N. Adams, "Social Change in Guatemala and U.S. Policy," in Richard N. Adams, John I. Gillin, *et al.*, *Social Change in Latin America Today: A Collection of Essays by the Council on Foreign Relations* (New York: Harper, 1961), pp. 246–253; Nathan L. Whetten, *Guatemala: The Land and the People* (New Haven, Conn.: Yale University Press, 1961), pp. 44–81; and Stokes Newbold [pseud.], *A Study of Receptivity to Communism in Rural Guatemala* (Department of State, Office of Intelligence Research, External Research Paper, No. 116 [Washington, D.C.: Dec. 15, 1954]), p. 4.

Spanish in addition to an Indian language) and in which the women, but not the men, still retain a distinctive Indian costume. This group is to be found living in the piedmont regions of the Southeast and the Pacific Coast departments of Jutiapa, Santa Rosa, Escuintla, Suchitepéquez, and Retalhuleu, and in some towns in the West and Northwest. The process is an ongoing one and one may find communities within the same *municipio* at different stages of the process.

(3) The ladinoized Indian or Indian who has replaced most of his Indian culture with Ladino traits. This ladinoized Indian would be difficult to distinguish, on sight, from poor rural *Ladinos*. He would be monolingual, professing to speak only Spanish, and neither he nor his wife would retain any very distinctive articles of clothing associated with Indian groups. To identify him as a Ladino, one need only ask him or a neighboring Ladino what he calls himself. Both would say he was a Ladino and not an Indian. These groups are found principally along the Pacific Coast and the Motagua River Valley. They are usually found at the bottom of the social structure in a Ladino area; very few are found in the heavily Indian areas of the country. The ladinoized Indians usually live in a community other than a town; in towns they live in separate districts (*barrios*) away from other Indians.

The Indian communities play different political roles depending on whether they are traditional, modified, or ladinoized groups, and whether or not they are made up primarily of laborers or independent peasant farmers.

Politically, the traditional communities were of little significance prior to 1944 because they insulated themselves rather successfully against incursions of the *Ladino* culture. In voting for a particular candidate or party, they usually have been controlled in a Tammany Hall-like sense, but the traditional groups looked on politics with a certain amount of indifference because politics focused on Guatemala City and the outside world, while their psychic orientation was toward their own community and gods. However, even the traditional Indian communities were undermined psychologically and socially in many ways during the post–World War II period. As Indian communities became more transitional or modified, they came to be politically more important and to develop many of the political characteristics of Ladino villages in making demands upon governmental and political authorities.[9]

Rural laborers, whether Indian or Ladino, are more important in poli-

[9] Adams, *et al, op. cit.*, pp. 254–255. On the other hand, Roland H. Ebel ("Political Change in Guatemalan Indian Communities," *Journal of Inter-American Studies*, VI

tics than independent farmers because they can be reached more easily by political propaganda and marched or trucked more readily to the polls.

Regional Variations among Ladinos

Regional characteristics vary among the Ladinos, depending upon whether or not there are Indians living nearby. In the predominantly Indian departments of western Guatemala, there are few Ladinos who could be classified as peasants or campesinos. In that region, most Ladinos belong to a local upper class of landowners and tradesmen, economically dependent upon the lower-class Indian. In non-Indian regions, however, this agricultural lower class is made up of Ladino peasants. Elsewhere, the

Table 8-1. Literacy among the population seven years of age and above by ethnic group and by place of residence, Guatemala, 1950 (in per cent)

| | Residence | | |
Ethnic group	Urban	Rural	All
Republic	58.8	17.3	28.1
Ladino	73.1	32.9	49.1
Indian	20.6	8.4	9.7

Source: Guatemala, Dirección General de Estadística, *Sexto Censo de la Población*, 1957, p. xxxix.

recent Ladinos, that is, those who have arrived at Ladino status only within a generation or two as a result of the demand for labor or because of overpopulation in their areas of birth, are a mobile population. In predominantly Ladino regions, it was—and is—not uncommon to hear middle- and upper-class Ladinos refer to their country neighbors as "Indians," thereby indicating that the former groups still identify the new arrivals with their former Indian ancestors.[10] In any case, the idea that all peasants and/or rural inhabitants are Indians is a myth, for 60 per cent of the total Ladino population lived in rural areas according to the 1950 census results. Their levels of living were often little better than those for the Indian although their chances for an education were somewhat better, as shown in Table 8-1. Only in the departments of Guatemala (59.6 per cent), El Petén (50.7 per cent), Sacatepéquez (42.9 per

[Jan., 1964], pp. 91–104), found that no political changes may have occurred despite surface appearances based on his studies in San Juan Ostuncalco and Concepción Chiquiricuapa, two communities close to Quezaltenango.

[10] Richard N. Adams, *Encuesta sobre la cultura de los ladinos en Guatemala* (Guatemala City: Editorial del Ministerio de Educación, 1955), pp. 78–79.

cent), and Izabal (41.7 per cent) was over 40 per cent of the population literate. In these departments, the larger proportion of the literate population was found in urban areas.

Ladino Subgroups

As was the case with the Indian groups, there are no statistics on the numbers of Ladinos belonging to the seven subgroups which Adams identified in the late 1940's and 1950's. These groups included:

(1) The small and exclusive group which includes the "old families" and the *nouveaux riches* who followed European values, living standards, and customs. Coffeegrowing was the source of much of their wealth. Most of them tended to live in Guatemala City rather than on their plantations (*fincas*). Linked closely to them were the managers of the foreign corporations and the senior members of the army officer corps.

(2) The local upper class which lived in the department capitals or towns and which engaged in farming, commerce, and transportation. They hire both Ladino and Indian labor. Until the 1940's, this group, working with the national elite, exercised political control in the rural areas mainly through local officials called *jefes políticos* who enjoyed the support and resources of local planters and other notables.

(3) The emergent middle classes, primarily concentrated in Guatemala City and the department capitals, especially Quezaltenango. Although it was nearly unheard of for a *finquero* to do his own field work or to directly supervise this work, it was not unknown for a middle-sector farmer living in a department capital or small town to do some of his own field work while also supervising hired laborers. This group furnished most of the leadership for the innovations of the Arévalo-Arbenz period although other members of this group were also among those opposed to change in the social and political structure.

(4) The small independent farmers or peasants who worked their own lands. Many small owner-operators in eastern Guatemala where there was population pressure on the land and widespread distribution of small plots, (*minifundia*), joined the CNCG. Many others did not for reason which will be discussed later in this study.

(5) The mobile rural workers who were day laborers, sharecroppers, tenants, and renters in the upland areas but migrated to the coastal areas to work in the sugar and coffee harvests after planting their own small plots or leaving their families behind. To the writer's knowledge, there are no studies of the types of individuals contracting community work groups to go to the coastal harvest, but his subjective impression is that the labor contractors were recent Ladinos or ladinoized Indians who maintained

some ties with former areas of residence. These labor contractors were, and are, among the most active opponents of peasant union and agrarian reform legislation.

(6) The stable or permanent rural laborers who fitted the stereotype of what a peasant was for most urban Guatemalans. They generally rented land for cash or a share of the crop and may have owned a small amount of land which they farmed while working as *colonos* on plantation or local upper-class lands. Men from the last two groups joined the CNCG and the CTG or its successor, the CGTG.

During the 1944–1954 period, new networks of influence and control were established which affected both the Ladino and Indian communities. At the local level, new loci or foci of power were created with the organization of local branches of the national parties, peasant and urban workers' *sindicatos* which bypassed the older political controls and communication systems. In the traditional Indian communities which were dominated by a hierarchy based on age and respect for the elders who achieved office through a fairly stable series of steps upward, many young men were placed in newer channels of political power which forced the older patterns of authority to give way. Similarly, within many Ladino communities, the local upper class lost its former dominance of the channels of communication to higher authorities at the departmental or national level. Needless to say, a current of opposition built up at the local level as well as in Guatemala City among traditional power-holders who perceived their status was being threatened as long-established status gaps narrowed.[11]

Patterns of Landholding

Land has been concentrated in an extraordinarily small number of hands in the twentieth century. In 1926, an incomplete survey showed only 146,379 persons owning property out of an estimated two million population.[12] Much of this land was uncultivated. In 1935, only one-sev-

---

[11] Adams, *et al, op. cit.,* p. 270. In addition, in August and September of 1966, this writer observed carry-overs of traditional political views in several modest homes in Chichicastenango and Sololá. Pictures of strong-man presidents General Jorge Ubico (1931–1944) and General Miguel Ydígoras Fuentes (1958–1963) were hung on the inside of homes made of adobe brick and with tile or straw roofs. One of these homes, about a mile outside of Chichicastenango, also had 1966 campaign posters for Colonel Juan de Diós Aguilar de León, candidate of the Institutional Democratic Party (PID), the electoral organization created for the 1966 election by outgoing Colonel Enrique Peralta Azurdia and several big planters.

[12] Chester Lloyd Jones, *Guatemala, Past and Present* (Minneapolis: University of Minnesota Press, 1940), pp. 172, 175.

enth of the privately-owned land was under cultivation. The rest was pasture, forest, or idle.

The first comprehensive agricultural census held in Guatemala, that of April 18, 1950, showed 33.7 per cent of total land surface of Guatemala devoted to farms.[13] Only 55 per cent of this farmland was cultivated; the remainder was idle.

Table 8-2. Farm operators by size of holdings, 1950

Size of farms (in acres)	No. of farm operators	Percentage of farm operators	Percentage of total farm land
Under 3.5	165,850	47.6	3.3
3.5–17.2	142,223	40.8	11.0
17.3–111.4	33,041	9.5	13.5
111.5–1,114	6,488	1.8	21.9
Over 1,115	1,085	0.3	50.3
Total	348,687	100.0	100.0

Source: Richard N. Adams, *Encuesta sobre la cultura de los ladinos en Guatemala* (Guatemala City: Editorial del Ministerio de Educacion, 1955), pp. 64–65.

Some 7,573 persons, or 2.1 per cent of the landowning population, owned 72.2 per cent of the total land in farms. On the other hand, 47.6 per cent of the landowning population owned only 3.3 per cent of the total farm land, while 88.4 per cent of the landowning population owned only 14.4 per cent of the total land in farms. Half of the farms in the entire country were no larger than 3.9 acres in size. The average size per farm of 26.3 acres reflects the influence of large plantation holdings.[14]

The proportions of owner-operated farms varied from one region and department to another. The highest percentage of farm ownership in any region was in the West (72.5 per cent), a region which is highly Indian and whose small farms are operated on a subsistence basis (see Table 8-3). The high proportion of squatters reflected the inability or disinterest of both government and private owners in effectively administering their land.

Of the 2,512 farms operated by administrators, most were operated for absentee landowners. The national government expropriated between 120 and 130 farms from German nationals during World War II and organized them in the National Farms Department. Administrator-operated farms produced most of the coffee and other agricultural products enter-

---

[13] Adams, *Encuesta,* pp. 64–65.   [14] Whetten, *op. cit.,* pp. 93–94.

Table 8-3. Tenure statuses of farm operators, Guatemala, 1950

Tenure status	Percentage
Owner	54.9
Renter	17.0
Colono-laborer *	12.4
Squatter	10.0
Administrator	0.7
Others	5.0

Source: Guatemala, Dirección General de Estadística, *Guatemala en Cifras* (Guatemala City, 1959), p. 52.

* *Colono* is a term closely akin to sharecropper—someone working a determined amount of land for his own use while furnishing labor for the plantation.

ing foreign markets. According to the 1950 Agricultural Census, 1,744 farms—most of which were administrator-operated—produced 87 per cent of the coffee.[15] The 120 to 130 national farms produced about 25 per cent of the coffee crop.[16]

Size, Makeup, and Wages of the Labor Force

In 1950, 967,814 persons made up the labor force. Some 651,802 persons were in agriculture, fishing, and hunting—67.5 per cent.[17] Census officials estimated the number would run to around 750,000 in agriculture if children under fifteen and women who engaged in the seasonal coffee harvest were also included. In contrast, only 16 per cent of the population of the United States was engaged in agriculture in 1950.[18]

Per capita annual income in 1950 was 135.6 quetzals, or dollars, since the two currencies are equal. One estimate placed per capita annual income at 89.15 quetzals in rural areas and at 236.33 quetzals for urban areas.[19] The rural population of 1,906,889 persons (68.4 per cent) was estimated to have received only 45 per cent of total personal income in

[15] "Censo cafetalero arroja importantes datos sobre la produción en el país," *El Imparcial*, Dec. 18, 1953, p. 1, cols. 7–8.

[16] A half-page advertisement of the Department of National Farms, "Estado financiero de fincas nacionales," in *El Imparcial*, May 7, 1952, indicated that the national farms had turned over Q9,555,899.89 to the Guatemalan government in fiscal years 1946–1950.

[17] Guatemala, Dirección General de Estadística, *Sexto Censo de la Población*, 1957, p. lxiii.

[18] *The World Almanac*, 1959 (New York: New York World Telegram, 1959), pp. 263–268.

[19] José Antonio Palacios, "Formas de redistribución del ingreso de Guatemala," *Trimestre Económico* (Mexico City), XIX (July–Sept., 1952), 429–430.

1950. The urban population of 880,141 (31.6 per cent), however, received 55 per cent of total personal income in 1950. In contrast, farm operators in the United States earned an average income of $2,540; skilled and semi-skilled workers earned an average of $4,200, and professional and semiprofessional groups earned an average of $6,670 in 1950.[20]

As for daily rates, few statistics are available but the following are representative. In the late 1930's in Panajachel, department of Sololá (on the shores of Lake Atitlán), wages were 12.7 cents per day; in Chichicastenango, department of El Quiché, the day-labor rate was 13 cents in 1935 and as low as 10 cents per day in 1940.[21] Wage scales went up slightly during World War II in some places. In the late 1940's, *jornaleros* (day laborers) in the department of Sololá earned 25 to 30 cents a day without rations; with rations the wage rate was 20 cents per day for *colonos* (permanent workers).[22] In 1949, the minimum wage in effect on the national farms was 30 cents per day, but this was not always paid fully or in cash. As a result of payments in kind, 57 per cent of the workers on the national farms in 1949 earned less than $7.50 and 77 per cent earned less than $10.00 per month.[23] In mid-1966, prevailing wages ran to 80 cents a day or less.

Plantation Attitudes and Productivity

An examination of the 1950 Census data shows 431,014 persons living on 1,408 large *fincas* of over 100 persons each.[24] Average population on these large *fincas* was 306 persons, although some had more than 2,000 individuals living and working on them. In theory, these plantations were under the *municipio* and department governments. In practice, all of the inhabitants were employees of either a private owner or the National Farms Department. Government was thus no more than what the *patrón* (owner) or his administrator said it would be. Participation by *finca* inhabitants in community affairs was minimal, since the owner or his administrator directed most local affairs of other than a religious nature.

Although Guatemalan *finqueros* were required by law to furnish their workers and tenants with housing, food, schooling, and medical services,

[20] K. William Kapp and Lore L. Kapp, *A Graphic Approach to Economics* (New York: Henry Holt, 1954), pp. 77, 80.

[21] Sol Tax, *Penny Capitalism: A Guatemalan Indian Economy* (Institute of Social Anthropology Publication No. 16 [Washington, D.C.: Smithsonian Institution, 1953]), pp. 101, 188.   [22] Suslow, *op. cit.*, p. 46.

[23] Archer Corbin Bush, "Organized Labor in Guatemala, 1944–1949" (mimeo., M.A. thesis, Colgate University, 1950), Part II, p. 44.   [24] Whetten, *op. cit.*, pp. 39–40.

there were no standards as to what these services entailed. The available evidence indicates that their quality was minimal and that these services were sometimes withheld during the 1944–1954 period as a means of preventing workers or peasants from organizing into unions or to inhibit peasant union activity.

Although there was often a strong personal bond between some land-owners *(patrones)* and their workers or tenants, many *finqueros* followed a traditional pattern of making only one yearly inspection of their planta-tions and were interested only in the maximum amount of immediate cash income, however ruinous the production methods used. Land was seldom farmed intensively with modern technical and scientific methods other than by such foreign firms as the United Fruit Company.[25] Incompetent ownership and management as well as poor labor relations were problems for both the privately-owned plantations and the national farms. Few attempts were made to educate and improve the skills of the rural labor force.[26]

Agriculture was the principal economic activity. Coffee and bananas were the two main export crops, coffee making up about 75 per cent of exports through the years and bananas declining somewhat after World War II to between 5 and 12 per cent in the late 1950's and early 1960's. Coffee and banana production alone accounted for 13.2 per cent of GNP in 1947–1948, compared to the 13.8 per cent of the GNP accounted for by manufacturing and mining—including Indian handicrafts and lumber-ing.[27]

Precise figures are unavailable for prices paid for various agricultural products. Nevertheless, available statistics show a rise in the average price per *quintal* (110-pound bag) of coffee from around $9.00 in 1938–1939 to about $25.00 per *quintal* in 1946–1947; prices continued to rise through-

[25] International Bank for Reconstruction and Development, *The Economic Devel-opment of Guatemala* (Baltimore, Md.: Johns Hopkins Press, 1951), pp. 23–26 and 36–37. A map between pages 24 and 25 illustrates agricultural land use by region. Adams estimates that United Fruit owned 325 of the estimated 550 tractors in Guatemala in 1950 (*Encuesta*, pp. 27–28). In comparison, Mexico had 17,000; Cuba, 8,000; Chile, 4,143; and Uruguay, 2,890. Edward C. Higbe has discussed the pre–World War II fixation of the *finqueros* on low wages rather than high agricultural productivity ("The Agricultural Regions of Guatemala," *Geographical Review*, XXXVII [April, 1957], 190–200).

[26] *Labor Law and Practice in Guatemala* (Bureau of Labor Statistics Report No. 223 [Washington, D.C.: Government Printing Office, Dec., 1962]) covers this matter extensively, as does Bush, *op. cit.*

[27] International Bank for Reconstruction and Development, *op. cit.,* pp. 10–12.

out the 1950's until they reached a high of around $67.00 per quintal in 1956–1957. During this period, there was also an accompanying increase in total production and exports of coffee. Banana exports fluctuated considerably as shown in Table 8-4.

Table 8-4. Value of coffee and banana exports, Guatemala, for selected years, 1935-1961 (in thousands of dollars)

Year	Coffee	Bananas
1935	*	2,785
1938	10,000 †	5,481
1945	25,000 †	5,919
1947	30,000 †	8,687
1948	30,916	10,319
1949	37,367	7,585
1950	47,000 †	7,648
1951	56,000 †	6,010
1952	71,562	4,695
1953	68,229	12,580
1954	71,562	11,203
1955	70,582	9,417
1956	84,729	9,266
1957	90,000 †	*
1958	83,000 †	9,478
1959	*	8,595
1960	78,836	15,247
1961	69,161	11,645

Sources: IBRD, *Economic Development of Guatemala*, p. 12; Guatemala; *Anuario de comercio exterior, 1952*, pp. 328–329; *1953*, pp. 4–6; *1960*, pp. 4–18; *1961*, pp. 6–10; Franz Nowotny, *Recent Economic Developments*, p. 51; Guatemala, Oficina Central del Café, *Café, 1er centenario, 1859–1959*, unnumbered p. 15.

* Not available.

† Estimated by the author on the basis of available data.

Goals and Provisions of the Agrarian Reform Law

Numerous writers have commented on the agrarian reform program of the Arbenz government, but that program remains one of the least analyzed aspects of his regime.[28] Basically, it aimed at putting idle land

[28] One of the more dramatic and incorrect summarizations of the law's contents and application is to be found in Daniel James, *Red Design for the Americas: Guatemalan Prelude* (New York: John Day, 1954), p. 142. Ronald Schneider (*Communism in Guatemala, 1944–1954* [New York: Praeger, 1959]) discusses briefly the law's application and Communist infiltration into the machinery of the National

into use, at increasing production and productivity, and at spreading the loci of power in Guatemala through distribution of the national farms (in usufruct or lifetime use) and of private lands which were not being worked under certain conditions.[29] It provided for participation in the law's administration by the peasants and other groups at the local, departmental, and national levels rather than providing for administration from the top alone. The formal structure provided for participation at various levels by the *finqueros* and the Association of Guatemalan Agriculturalists (AGA), the interest group of the largest *finqueros*, but both individual plantation owners and the AGA largely ignored this machinery and tried to influence it at the presidential or National Agrarian Department (DAN) level. Limits on Expropriation (Article 9) included the following:

1. Holdings of less than ninety hectares;
2. Private farms of 90–300 hectares, two-thirds of which was cultivated;
3. Properties which were completely cultivated regardless of their size.
4. Forest reserves;
5. Communal lands of Indian or Peasant Communities; and
6. Land from agricultural enterprises whose products were destined for the domestic or international market such as coffee, cotton, citronela, lemon oil, bananas, sugar cane, tobacco, rubber, quinine, and cereals.

Land which was not being directly used for these crops or which was rented out in payment for personal services, or as a substitute in part or whole for cash salaries was not covered by this exemption.

Compensation for Expropriated Lands
(Articles 5, 6, 43)

Expropriation will be consummated by indemnification in the form of Agrarian Reform Bonds.

Indemnification will be based upon the property values registered as of May 9, 1952, and will be paid in proportion to the amount of land expropri-

---

Agrarian Department (DAN). The writer knows of no published English translation of the law, although he has translated parts of the law in "The Confederación Nacional Campesina de Guatemala (CNCG) and Peasant Unionism in Guatemala, 1944–1954" (M.A. thesis, Georgetown University, 1964), pp. 149–153. The text of the law in Spanish is found in the appendix of *Trimestre Económico* (Mexico City), XIX, No. 3 (1952), 540–563. Further references to the law or quotations are from this text.

[29] Whetten (*op. cit.*, pp. 164–165) compares the Guatemalan Agrarian Reform Law and program with that of Mexico, on which it was modeled. Robert A. Naylor, "Guatemalan Indian Attitudes toward Land Tenure," *Journal of Inter-American Studies*, IX (Oct., 1967), 619–639, is an important article to consider when examining the controversy over land granted in usufruct (lifetime use) or title by the law.

ated. In case there is no registered value for a property, a value will be set based on the value of surrounding properties.

Agrarian Bonds will pay 3 per cent interest annually in installments of up to twenty-five years maximum. Shorter terms for payment are possible. The amount of Agrarian Reform Bonds to be issued will amount to Q10,000,000 bearing 3 per cent annual interest, to be paid in installments of up to twenty-five years with payment guaranteed by the State.

In accordance with Guatemalan and Latin American tradition, Article 54 gave the President the ultimate authority in determining how the law was to be applied. The biggest landowners and the AGA wanted judicial review in addition to administrative appeal to the president, not to preserve the principle of separation of powers but in order to obstruct and delay the application of this legislation. It was one of the few times in the 1944–1954 period when landowners and lawyers were interested in the principle of separation of powers as a desirable end.

CNCG and Communist Participation in Agrarian Reform Machinery

Probably no piece of proposed legislation in Guatemalan history received as widespread attention and public discussion as the Agrarian Reform Law or Decree 900 of 1952.[30] The CNCG and other groups were given copies of the proposed law and asked to suggest amendments, some of which were incorporated by the Congress prior to final passage.[31] It was one of the first occasions in recent Guatemalan history when peasants or their leaders were consulted in the decision-making process, thus posing a threat to the established power elites.

Agrarian reform was supported by both the noncommunist and Com-

[30] The New York *Times* and *El Imparcial*, May 25–June 20, 1952, discuss the bill's passage, including rallies organized in Guatemala City by the CNCG and the Arbenz government between May 28 and June 1 which were designed to influence congressional votes. Although thousands of peasants participated in these rallies, it is difficult to know the extent of voluntary participation and the extent to which they understood their participation in these events.

[31] "Informe del secretario general III Congreso Nacional," a memorandum found in folder "CNCG Congress 1954," in the Guatemalan Transcripts (cited hereafter as GT), Box 11, Manuscripts Division, Library of Congress, Washington, D.C. The Guatemalan Transcripts are a collection of sixty reels of microfilmed documents and 35,000 prints, mimeographed and dittoed documents, and other material available for scholarly use. Schneider used these materials for his *Communism in Guatemala, 1944–1954*, as did Edwin Warren Bishop ("The Guatemalan Labor Movement, 1944–1959" [Ph.D. thesis, University of Wisconsin, 1958]) and the writer. But few other scholars have used these valuable materials, which range from correspondence between Arbenz and the military to laboriously written petitions from peasants to Castillo Flores.

munist reformists and revolutionaries who had lost faith in more gradual measures as a means of bringing about a fundamental transformation of the nation's economy in order to achieve higher levels of production and living. While the progressive landowners and industrialists who formed the right wing of Arbenz' support had to be pressured into rendering reluctant support for agrarian reform legislation, the CNCG and the Communists did not hesitate to support these proposals wholeheartedly.

Once again, the writer feels it is important to emphasize that Decree 900 set up a structure of agrarian committees at the department level (CAD) and *municipio* level (CAL) which any organization, including the AGA, could use to achieve or nullify the ends of the law. Schneider feels that the Communists "sought and received virtual control of the machinery set up for . . . administration of the . . . Law." [32] A department-by-department survey by the author indicates, however, that Communist control of the Department Agrarian Committees (CAD's), which were a key point of decision-making, did not exist although they placed some of their members on the committees in Chimaltenango, Escuintla, and Chiquimula. The Communists, however, did place members in the DAN, another key point in the decision-making process, as agrarian inspectors.

Table 8-5 shows the distribution of agricultural land used by departments and the expropriations which took place. Table 8-6 shows the percentages of land expropriated and distributed, while Table 8-7 shows the distribution of land by type.

The persons losing land were among the largest and most powerful landowners in Guatemala. The total amount of private land expropriated outside of the United Fruit Company properties comprised only 3.9 per cent of the total land in agriculture as Table 8-6 indicates. The average amount of land expropriated outside of the UFCO properties was 2,085 acres—another illustration of the large size of some plantations. In any case, the expropriation of landed properties increased the hostility of the *finqueros* and other property-holders toward the Arbenz government and the peasants because it transferred economic power to the peasants.

During the first six months in which the law was in effect, the CNCG and the CGTG frequently met with government officials to discuss the organization of Agrarian Committees in the departments (CAD's) and *municipios* (CAL's).[33] Although the CNCG and CGTG each claimed to

[32] Schneider, *op. cit.*, p. 215.
[33] Letter from Manuel Monroy Flores to Castillo Flores, June 12, 1952 (folder "CNCG Reserve Material," GT Box 10).

Table 8-5. Agricultural land use and expropriation, 1950–1954

Department	Fincas 1950	Fincas w/over 100 inhab.	Fincas producing over 200 quintales * of coffee annually	Fincas in which land was exprop.	Area of all fincas (in manzanas) † 1950	Manzanas † exprop.
Alta Verapaz	28,187	166	108	17	702,352	128,563
Baja Verapaz	11,761	25	19	14	222,541	23,356
Chimaltenango	18,054	88	80	51	176,800	30,376
Chiquimula	15,008	0	6	1	121,174	1,047
El Progreso	5,619	1	3	9	125,304	14,995
Escuintla	10,648	165	70	102	249,361	209,330
Guatemala	18,331	97	114	92	252,297	33,213
Huehuetenango	32,025	40	51	12	342,722	48,048
Izabal	4,739	30	1	5	200,058	118,097
Jalapa	11,807	6	5	11	162,624	4,509
Jutiapa	21,464	4	20	21	289,113	17,353
El Petén	2,162	0	0	0	20,538	0
Quezaltenango	19,540	162	214	14	179,691	7,125
El Quiché	25,642	54	10	21	270,914	73,764
Retalhuleu	8,542	106	91	0	192,473	18,336
Sacatepéquez	9,024	19	70	19	51,178	6,227
San Marcos	33,724	149	312	49	316,237	13,669
Santa Rosa	15,321	81	274	30	370,141	38,953
Sololá	13,559	11	41	6	46,248	2,063
Suchitepéquez	12,420	197	233	6	236,938	43,301
Totonicapán	17,620	0	0	0	28,513	0
Zacapa	5,973	7	14	5	164,153	2,759
Total	341,170	1,408	1,736	485	5,235,370	835,083

Sources: Data for fincas in 1950, area of all fincas in manzanas, and manzanas expropriated are from Adams, Encuesta, p. 65; data for fincas with over 100 inhabitants are from Nathan L. Whetten, Guatemala; The Land and the People (New Haven, Conn.: Yale University Press, 1961) p. 39; data for fincas producing over 200 quintales of coffee annually are from Dirección General de Estadística, Censo cafetalero, p. 26; data for fincas in which land was expropriated are from Oficina de Registro y Estadística del DAN, Fincas expropriades y entregadas a los campesinos de la republica hasta el 15 de Abril de 1954. ([May, 1954], Folder "Agrarian Reform Laws-Reports," GT Box 14); the document lists the names of the fincas in each department which had land expropriated but not the amount of land expropriated.

* One quintal is a 110-pound bag of coffee. A finca producing over 200 quintales per year would be producing more than eleven tons of dried coffee beans per year.

† One manzana equals 1.73 acres.

Table 8-6. Percentages of land expropriated and distributed, Guatemala, 1952–1954

Item	Acres or percentage
1. Agricultural land in *fincas*, 1950	9,057,200
2. Croplands, fallow, coffee and fruit trees	3,577,400
3. Highest known figure used by anyone for land expropriated	1,434,691
4. UFCO lands expropriated at Tiquisate and Bananera	653,197
5. Known quantity of national farm land distributed	430,000
6. Subtotal of items 4 and 5	1,083,197
7. Estimated private *finca* land expropriated, outside of United Fruit Company (UFCO) lands (Item 3 minus Item 6)	351,494
8. Percentage of total private, non-UFCO agricultural land expropriated (Item 7 divided by Item 1)	3.9%
9. Percentage of private, non-UFCO land in crops, fallow, coffee, and fruit trees expropriated (Item 7 divided by Item 2)	9.8%

Sources: Items 1 and 3: Adams, *Encuesta*, p. 65; Item 2: Whetten, *Guatemala*, p. 361.

Table 8–7. Land distributed by type under the agrarian program

Source of land	Number of acres			Number of recipients		
	Total	Lifetime	Title	Total	Lifetime	Title
Total Republic	917,659	780,851(*85.1%*)	136,808(*14.9%*)	87,569	75,522(*86.2%*)	12,047(*13.8%*)
Private *fincas*	555,098	418,290(*75.4%*)	136,808(*24.6%*)	47,832	35,785(*74.8%*)	12,047(*25.2%*)
National farms	235,647	235,647(*100.0%*)	—	23,222	23,222	—
State or *municipio* land	126,914	126,914(*100.0%*)	—	16,515	16,515	—

Source: Whetten, *Guatemala*, p. 163, based on data of the Dirección General de Asuntos Agrarios, May, 1958.

have organized the most agrarian committees in the first six months after promulgation of Decree 900, most committees actually did not start functioning until November or December, 1952.[34] Many agrarian committees were organized only on paper and even the CNCG recognized that formation of a CAD or CAL was not tantamount to appropriation and distribution of land.[35] There is little published evidence to indicate that the peasants were told to occupy the land by the CNCG, although there is evidence that Amor Velasco de León, one of the few extremist "fireat-

[34] "300 comites agrarios CGTG," *El Imparcial*, July 18, 1952, p. 1, col. 2; "1,100 comités agrarios en acción," *El Imparcial*, Aug. 1, 1952, p. 1, cols. 7–8. Castillo Flores announced on the latter date that "the majority of the committees had been founded in Izabal, the west and south of the Republic."

[35] Letter from Castillo Flores to Emilio Aguilar G., y demas compañeros firmantes, *El Rodeo Sansurate*, Jalapa, Nov., 1952 (folder "CNCG Other Material," GT Box 10).

ers" in the CNCG, did urge peasants to seize land they needed.[36] In many
cases, the CNCG representatives on the CAD or CAL were criticized by
the peasant unions and leaders for "not defending the interests of the
CNCG but those of foreign and private companies." [37]

No really thorough studies have been made of agricultural productivity
during the Arévalo or Arbenz period. But the data shown in Table 8-8 for
1946–1960 indicates that Guatemala had export surpluses in her balance of
payments in only the three years, 1952 to 1954, when the Agrarian
Reform Law was in effect. One cannot make a direct correlation between
such data, but, the available data do not show that Guatemalan agricultural production or exports suffered from the Agrarian Reform Law.[38]

As for subjective interpretations of the effects of the Agrarian Reform
Law on Guatemalan rural society, we have the following from Paul
Burgess, a North American Presbyterian missionary long resident in
Guatemala:

Things really began to hum, economically and ecclesiastically. . . . The
coffee crop was in, the cash advances and interest charges on the same, the
cooperative fees and all other expenses cancelled, and each family had from
$400.00 to $600.00 clear in cold cash, more than any of them had ever
possessed at one time before. . . . I think I can safely say that the agrarian law
has not done any more damage spiritually than a few "gushers" would do a
similar group of Presbyterians in a Texas town.[39]

Another revealing commmentary on the changed order of rural life was
disclosed inadvertently by *El Imparcial* August 2, 1954, in what was the
first—and last—of a series of articles which it said would discuss "the

[36] The writer found no telegrams or letters to indicate CNCG involvement in
peasant "invasions," although many *finqueros* and *El Imparcial* labeled as an "invasion
the continued presence of peasants on farm land which an owner refused to rent or
sell, as he had in the past. Information on Amor Velasco León came from an interview in September 1966 with a Guatemalan deputy who was active in politics in
the Arbenz period and who was an adviser to the CNCG at that time.

[37] "Informe" of Victor Segundo Carillo (folder "CNCG and Land Reform," GT
Box 12). It is undated, but it speaks of events in the fall of 1952.

[38] See Guatemala, Oficina Central del Café (Central Coffee House, an official
agency of the government) *Café 1er centenario, 1859–1959*, unnumbered p. 15; and
Guatemala, Ministry of Finance, *Anuario de comercio exterior, 1960*, pp. vii–viii, for
data on the total value and average price per *quintal* (110-pound bag) of coffee
exports from 1938–1953 and for data on the balance of foreign trade, 1946–1960.

[39] Paul Burgess, "Presbyterian Agrarians," *Guatemala News* (organ of the Guatemala Mission of the Presbyterian Church in the United States), XLIV, No. 6 (1953),
119. President Arbenz reported on the results in his Annual Report on the State of
the Nation, March 1, 1954, "Democracia, progreso y paz en Guatemala," *El Imparcial*,
March 1, 1954, p. 2.

Table 8-8. Foreign trade balance of Guatemala, 1946–1960 (in thousands of dollars)

Year	Exports FOB	Imports CIF	Credit (+) or debt (−) of Guatemala in foreign exchange
1946	36,679.1	36,203.6	+ 475.5
1947	52,032.9	57,319.3	− 5,286.4
1948	50,165.5	68,349.9	−18,184.4
1949	52,226.7	67,983.8	−15,757.1
1950	67,605.3	71,220.9	− 3,615.6
1951	76,085.0	80,846.5	− 4,761.5
1952	87,462.6	75,721.4	+11,741.2
1953	88,922.4	79,538.1	+ 9,384.3
1954	95,660.4	86,311.0	+ 9,349.4
1955	98,699.9	104,316.1 *	− 5,616.2
1956	116,291.2	137,709.2	−21,418.0
1957	108,820.1	147,354.4	−38,534.3
1958	102,459.0	149,696.5	−47,237.5
1959	102,065.4	134,002.6	−31,937.2
1960	112,674.1	137,864.5	−25,190.4

Source: Guatemala, Ministry of Finance, *Anuario de comercio exterior* (Guatemala City, 1960), p. vii.

* Not included is the sum of $2,332,000 in gifts of corn which Guatemala received from the United States of America in 1955. However, the costs of shipping, insurance, and other items, which amounted to $579,980, are included.

disastrous effects of agrarian reform." On the national farm of "La Concepción," Escuintla—which was sold or turned over to private enterprise by 1959—coffee and sugar production allegedly went down while peasants grew corn for themselves.[40] But equally, if not more important,

[40] Bush (*op. cit.,* Part II, pp. 45–48) and Suslow (*op. cit.,* pp. 88–89) discuss the farm and its peasant leader Gabriel Camey during the years 1948–1949. Neither writer detected any of the "Communist" tendencies attributed to him in 1954 by Daniel James and others. The plantation was one of the few *fincas* which still had a union in the summer of 1961 or 1966. *Café, ler centenario,* mentions on unnumbered page 11 that the "Brothers Baron Xavier Du Teil and Oscar Du Teil . . . had sown 110,000 new coffee trees." In 1966, most of the land occupied by this plantation in the lowlands northwest of Escuintla was planted in sugar, although the writer did not walk or ride to its northernmost limits, which might include the Pacific coastal slopes. The writer did not talk to Gabriel Camey, who was still working there, because of warnings by other workers of tension resulting from the shooting one day earlier of the plantation's administrator, an Army colonel. The shooting reportedly was carried out by left-wing guerilla terrorists of the Fuerzas Armadas Rebeldes (FAR) headed

the writer thinks, was disclosure of the fact that one peasant "hired another to work his plot at a salary of 80 cents a day, while the former slept in his hammock. . . . This was the new peasant aristocracy." [41] In reviewing copies of *El Imparcial* published since 1945, the writer has found no recorded instance in which rural workers, other than those who worked for United Fruit Company, were paid the minimum wage called for by the 1947 Labor Code. Once again, this is evidence of an improved level of living and status which irritated occupants of higher positions in Guatemalan society.

CNCG Leadership and Ideology

We noted earlier that the CTG and the Guatemala Labor Federation (Federación Sindical de Guatemala or FSG) had very little success in organizing agricultural workers and peasants between 1945 and 1950. By the spring of 1950, many peasants were dissatisfied with what the CTG was doing—or rather, not doing—for them.[42] Within the ranks of the CTG and in several departments, there were middle-ranking leaders and peasants who saw that the peasants were a mass group that needed to be organized if the labor movement were to succeed and who saw such an organization as a means of advancing and sustaining their own well-being as well as that of the peasants. Leonardo Castillo Flores, Amor Velasco de León, and Isaias Ruíz Robles were the CTG leaders who brought together four regional federations and twenty-five peasant unions in May, 1950, to form the National Peasant Federation of Guatemala (CNCG). Ronald Schneider has an excellent description of Castillo Flores at that time.

Tall, thin, mustachioed Leonard Castillo Flores was a twenty-eight year old school teacher earning $65 a month when he joined the newly-formed teachers' union, STEG, in 1945. Along with Víctor Manuel Gutiérrez, five

---

by Luis Augusto Turcios Lima. This shooting was one of a continuing series of kidnappings and attempted assassinations by the FAR, the left-wing 13th of November Movement headed by Marcos Yon Sosa, and the right-wing White Hand (Mano Blanco) Movement. In 1968, the left-wing groups were responsible for the assassination of two American military attaches on January 16 and of John Gordon Mein, the American Ambassador, on August 16.   [41] *El Imparcial*, Aug. 2, 1954, p. 1.

[42] Letter from Julio Emilio Arna Sanchez to Victor Manuel Gutiérrez, Nov. 22, 1949 (folder "CTG III," GT Box 15). Arana, apparently a CTG peasant organizer at that time, forwarded pleas from agricultural workers on *fincas* "La Concepción" and "El Tempisque" in the department of Escuintla for help in seeking increases in salary and in organizing a union. Arana Sanchez became CNCG Representative to the CAD for the department of Santa Rosa in Cuilapa in July, 1952, and was held under arrest by the Civil Guard as a "Leader of communist elements," according to *El Espectador* (Guatemala City), July 3, 1954.

years his junior, but a much abler leader in almost every respect, Castillo Flores rose to become Secretary of Records for the CTG, and in January 1947, was elected to Congress as a PAR deputy from Chiquimula. Apparently tiring of living in the shadow of Gutiérrez, Castillo Flores turned to the nearly virgin field of organizing the *campesino* masses. Since he did this without their sanction, the CTG leaders criticized Castillo Flores as an opportunist and divisionist, and threatened him with expulsion.[43]

Amor Velasco de León was an agricultural worker (*peón* has been used by some to describe him) from Huehuetenango, a heavily Indian department (73.3 per cent of the population) in the western highlands. Velasco de León went to Mexico early in his life and learned about unionism (*sindicalismo*) there. When he returned to Guatemala, he began working for the CTG and later joined Castillo Flores and Ruíz Robles, of whom little more is known, in forming the CNCG.

The CTG tried to forestall creation of the Peasant Congress called for by Castillo Flores by scheduling one of its own, May 12–14, 1950.[44] When the CTG Congress met, its leaders—Gutiérrez, José Manuel Fortuny, José Luís Ramos, and Bernardo Alvarado Monzón, all Communists—denounced creation of the proposed Castillo Flores organization in the following terms:

The bourgeoisie are afraid to let the peasants associate with the working class because the working class would then tell the peasants how the working class in Eastern Europe, with the solid aid of the peasants, had obtained power and divided the land for the peasants. . . . The working class was the best and most loyal defender of the peasantry, the vanguard of the working-class movement, and the only one that could instantly direct the battle of the peasants for the conquest of their goals: bread and land. Because of this, the peasants ought to align themselves with the working class and be the great ally and reserve of the proletariat. The working class of Guatemala has the role of guiding the movement for liberation of the peasants and snatching it away from the bourgeoisie who only want to deceive the peasants. The peasants should understand that only the working class will assist them in their struggle for the rights of both.[45]

[43] Schneider, *op. cit.*, pp. 158–159. "Victor Manuel Gutiérrez y Leonardo Castillo Flores (Dirigentes del PGT) muertos?" (*Gráfico*, March 7, 1966, p. 3) indicates Gutiérrez and Castillo Flores probably were killed while under detention by the National Police following their capture Saturday, March 5, 1966, the day before elections were held in Guatemala for the presidency, National Congress, and municipal offices.

[44] "Circular urgente de la CTG a las comunidades campesinas de Chiquimula," April, 1950 (folder "CTG & Founding of CNCG," GT Box 15).

[45] "Materias del Congreso General de la Confederación de Trabajadores de Guatemala, a celebrarse los Dias 12, 13 y 14 de Mayo de 1950" (folder "CTG & Founding of CNCG," GT Box 15).

The "bourgeoisie" were probably the ambitious Augústo Charnaud Mac-Donald and other leaders of the Revolutionary Action party (Partido Acción Revolucionaria or PAR) who supported the initial efforts to form the CNCG.

The actions of the CTG had little effect. On May 28, 1950, 200 delegates representing federations in the departments of Chiquimula, Guatemala, Jalapa, Jutiapa, and Zacapa, plus delegations from the departments of Alta Verapaz, San Marcos, Chimaltenango, El Progreso, and Sacatepéquez, met to found the CNCG.

The CNCG declared its basic principles to be the following:

I. The CNCG is an organization that functions democratically.
II. The CNCG recognizes Agrarian Reform as a legitimate aspiration of the peasants.
III. The CNCG recognizes that the peasantry need their own instrument to raise their problems before the public and to struggle for the solution of these in agreement with its class aspirations.
IV. The CNCG recognizes that as a class organ it is a functional ally of the proletariat in the struggle for the economic liberation of the people and for the maintenance of democracy as well as the current regime of the government.[46]

In seeking to implement these principles, it would demand more justice and more attention to the problems of the peasants such as rural credits, the distribution and easier rental of land, and aid in the cultivation of crops.[47]

In the beginning, the Executive Committee and the Consultative Council were made up of noncommunists and mildly anti-Communist reformists and revolutionaries of an urban and small-town middle-class background, particularly lawyers and politicians. The first officers of the Executive Committee were the following:

Secretary-General—Leonardo Castillo Flores, 33 years old, ex-schoolteacher, official in the STEG, and Secretary of Records for the CTG; later deputy from Chiquimula, 1947–1951. Killed March 5–7, 1966.
Secretary of Records and Communications—Alejandro Silva Falla, lawyer; politician who was successively member of the PAR, Socialists (PS), and the Guatemalan Revolutionary party (PRG); PRG deputy from El Progreso, 1953–1954.

[46] "Confederación Nacional del Campesino fundase," *El Imparcial*, May 30, 1950, p. 1, cols. 3–4.
[47] "Emplazamiento de los dirigentes de la CTG," *El Imparcial*, June 3, 1950, p. 1, col. 6; p. 3, col. 4.

Secretary of Organization and Propaganda—Amor Velasco de León, apparently of peasant background; worked in Mexico and became a self-taught peasant intellectual and spokesman in Chiquimula soon after the October 1944 Revolution; Secretary of Peasant Affairs, CTG, October 31, 1946–May 15, 1948; member, Political Commission, PS, 1952; PAR deputy from San Marcos, 1952; organized peasant groups for PRG after breaking with Castillo Flores in 1953; an agitator who was frequently credited in the press with "inciting the peasants to violence."

Secretary of Finance—Marco Antonio Soto Beteta, lawyer; administrator of the national farm "Santo Tomas"; PAR official, 1953–1954; CNCG Secretary of Labor Union Relations, 1954; textile industrialist, 1966.

Secretary of Conflicts—Manuel Marroquín Prado, no background information available; died July 24, 1950.

Secretary of Culture and Social Welfare—Clodoveo Torres Moss, student of law in 1950 from Quezaltepeque and Chiquimula; Secretary of Labor Affairs in the PS, 1951–1952; CNCG Secretary of Records and Communications, 1953; PAR Secretary of Agricultural Affairs, 1953; anti-Communist; farming and out of politics in 1966.

The Consultative Council was made up of noncommunist, left-of-center persons:

Augústo Charnaud MacDonald—politician; PAR Secretary of Propaganda, 1946; PAR Secretary of Organization, 1947–1948; Minister of Economy and Labor, 1947–1948; PS Secretary-General, 1951–1952; PRG Secretary-General, 1952–1954; Minister of Government (Interior), 1953–1954; opportunist *extraordinaire*.

Joaquín Carcía Manzo—lawyer, politician; right-hand assistant of Charnaud MacDonald in government posts; characterized by a 1966 Revolutionary party (PR) Deputy as a "gifted action man" who complemented Charnaud's expansive personality.

Miguel Angel Flores—lawyer, deputy from Izabal for Constituent Assembly, 1945.

Federico Bonilla Padilla—certified public accountant, 1945; CNCG Secretary of Training and Propaganda, 1951; PAR Training Secretary, 1952–1953; member PAR Commission on Discipline, 1954; noncommunist.

René Sánchez Fajardo—agronomist.

Staffing the CNCG at National, Departmental, and Local Levels

All of the names of Executive Committee members appear to be Ladino names; there were no Indians at the national level of leadership. All of the Secretaries-General of the Departmental Federations had Ladino names but various Secretaries of Organization, Records and Communications,

Rural Education, and so forth, in the heavily Indian departments, especially El Quiché, Alta Verapaz, and San Marcos had Indian names, such as Alfredo Tzi Cucul, President of the Peasant Community of San Pedro Carchá, Alta Verapaz, or Rafaél Tum, PAR Secretary of Peasant Affairs for the department of Suchitepéquez. At the local level, many unions had officers with Indian names. There is no evidence that foreigners ever joined, associated, or affiliated with the CNCG. On the other hand, foreigners participated in the work of the CTG, CGTG, the Communist party and several government offices, including the DAN.

Of thirty-one occupants of CNCG Executive Committee posts for whom the writer has data, the following is a list of occupations held before or during time of occupancy: DAN or National Agrarian Bank employee, or deputy, 9; university student of law, 1; practicing politicians, 1; lawyer, 4; agronomist or farm administrator, 5; rural school teacher, 1; certified public accountant, 1; radio announcer in small town, 1; peasant, 2; and unknown, 6. It is obvious that the bulk of national leadership was recruited largely from the urban middle classes, particularly men with an intellectual or legal background, who had a type of job security which enabled them to devote time to CNCG tasks. Peasants played a minor role in the highest leadership positions.

Size of the CNCG, Federations, and Local Unions

As shown in Table 8–9, peasant federations were formed in every department except the sparsely populated and underdeveloped El Petén. In his report to the Third National Peasant Congress in February, 1954, Castillo Flores claimed that 256,426 peasants were associated with the CNCG.[48] This is undoubtedly an exaggerated figure, but it is probably not unreasonable to assume there were at least 1,500 active unions in the CNCG based principally on the 1,408 large plantations with over 100 inhabitants on them or the 1,736 plantations producing over 200 bags of coffee per year. It is also reasonable to assume there were about 180,000 to 190,000 members in various stages of activity based on an average membership per union of from 100 to 125 members, a figure based also on

[48] "Informe," undated, pp. 1–2 (folder "CNCG III Congress, 1954," GT Box 11). In another part of the speech, he said that "80 per cent" of the peasants in the Republic were associated with the CNCG. This seems unrealistic unless one were to consider as peasants only rural male farm laborers seven years of age and over, of which the 1950 census counted 336,024. And the CNCG counted many members in the western and northern central parts of the Republic who were owners of farms, albeit small ones.

Table 8–9. Peasant federations, peasant unions, and *fincas* with over 100 inhabitants or producing over 200 *quintales* of coffee per year, by department, 1954

Department	Federations	Unions *	Number of *fincas* w/over 100 inhab. *or* 200 *quintales* coffee whichever is higher †
Alta Verapaz	1	195	166
Baja Verapaz	1	45	25
Chimaltenango	1	125	88
Chiquimula	1	28	6
El Progreso	1	22	3
Escuintla	2	170	165
Guatemala	1	84	114
Huehuetenango	1	123	51
Izabal	1	42	30
Jalapa	1	54	6
Jutiapa	2	35	20
El Petén	0	4	0
Quezaltenango	2	63	214
El Quiché	1	57	54
Retalhuleu	1	25	106
Sacatepéquez	1	53	70
San Marcos	2	212	312
Santa Rosa	1	86	274
Sololá	1	23	41
Suchitepéquez	1	48	233
Totonicapán	1	24	0
Zacapa	1	32	14
Total peasant unions		1,541	

* *Nomina de las Personerias Tramitadas de los Departamentos,* Folder "Unions II CNCG," GT Box 13, and data compiled by the writer.

† Table 8–5.

federation reports and membership rolls in the Guatemalan Transcripts.[49] Membership totals, of course, are not particularly useful except in relation to other data. Since about 450,000 persons voted in the 1950 presidential elections, the CNCG could virtually assure the success of any party it

[49] A letter from Jesus Casimiro Reyes to Secretarios de Organización, department of Sololá, no date, probably 1953 (folder "Unions II Campesino," GT Box 20), listed 34 unions in the Federation, 18 of whose members were listed by name, ranging from 25 to 307, and totaling 1,816. "Informe, secretario-tesorero," Carlos Sánchez, Federación de la zona sur de Quezaltenango, probably late 1952 (folder "CNCG Miscellaneous," GT Box 11), indicates 25 organizations with 3,040 members awaiting legal recognition.

supported if it could deliver a bloc of 150,000 votes. At the same time, the figures underscore the fact that a political party could succeed in Guatemala if it were supported by either the organized peasantry or organized labor in general.[50]

Factors in the Growth of CNCG Leadership

The various statistics on peasant unions within each federation and department do not show any correlation with the departmental statistics on literacy, numbers of *fincas* with over 100 inhabitants or producing more than 200 *quintales* of coffee per year, per cent of the population which is Ladino or Indian, or distance from the national or department capitals.

The key factors appear to have been highly motivated and able department and local leaders who were able to organize and maintain peasant unions in various places under a variety of circumstances, including situations in which there was opposition from the Communists or government agencies and officials. Arbenz' support for peasant unionism also aided these organizers.

On a more particularistic level, there is evidence that this local leadership was marked by higher levels of literacy, economic well-being, and participation in organized group activity. This view is supported by a study of 267 rural dwellers out of 1,600 men who were imprisoned in the two principal Guatemala city jails following the downfall of Arbenz.[51] This study will be discussed in the following sections.

Peasant Characteristics and Membership/Leadership in Organized Groups

There was no significant variation in the distribution of Indians and Ladinos in age groups nor in the amount of leadership exercised by

[50] United States Department of State, *Penetration of the Political Institutions of Guatemala by the International Communist Movement: Threat to the Peace and Security of America and to the Sovereignty and Political Independence of Guatemala* (usually known as the *State Department White Paper*), released Aug. 7, 1954, (published by Department of State and found in the Department of State Library, Annex B), p. 25, reported a hundred thousand registered members in both the CGTG and CNCG in April, 1953.

[51] Newbold, *op. cit.* The other 1,300 persons were urban political prisoners and ex-ministers and chiefs of government offices who were excluded from the study. The rural prisoners who were interviewed intensively came from Guatemala (58), Santa Rosa (54), Jutiapa (43), Jalapa (20), Escuintla (36), Chimaltenango (17), and San Marcos (30), and eight other departments (9). Only 97 Indians (36.3 per cent) were included in the sample, although they make up 54 per cent of the national population.

different age groups or ethnic groups in political or politically oriented organizations included in the study, such as labor unions, peasant unions, agrarian committees, and political parties. Neither was there a statistically

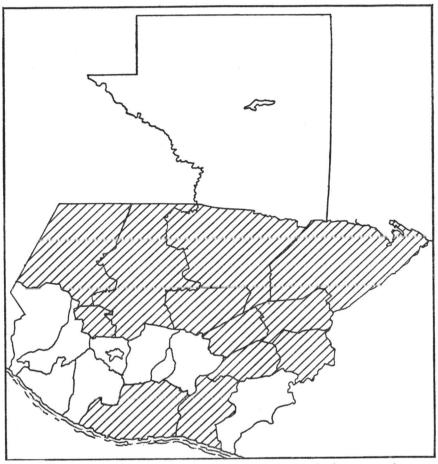

Map. 4. Departments in Guatemala that had *fincas* producing more than 200 *quintales* of coffee per year and more peasant unions than *fincas* with over 100 inhabitants

Source: Revised from Whetten, *Guatemala: The Land and the People,* p. 41, which shows the location of *fincas* with 100 or more inhabitants.

significant correlation between "economic inadequacy" and membership in a labor union, the peasant unions, or in agrarian committees.[52] There

[52] An individual was considered "economically adequate" if he had "access to five *manzanas* of agricultural land or more, or if he earned Q1 a day or Q30 per month or more"; if he did not meet the above criteria, or if he did not earn 40 cents or more a day as a day laborer while having access to three manzanas of agricultural land, he was considered "economically inadequate" by Guatemalan standards.

was a strong correlation, at the 99 per cent level of probability according to Newbold, between "economic adequacy" and membership in the political parties. In landholding, almost the same results were found, with an additional correlation (at the 95 per cent level of probability) between landlessness and membership on an agrarian committee. Since the agrarian committees were specifically concerned with getting land, such a correlation would not be surprising. There is also some correlation between landowning status and membership in a peasant union. Slightly higher percentages of the landless were members, compared to those who were not members (Table 8–10).

Table 8–10. Membership status of groups of differing economic adequacy and landholding status (in per cent)

	Economic status		Landholding status	
Affiliation	Adequate (N = 115)	Inadequate (N = 152)	Landowners (N = 60)	Landless (N = 190)
Union status				
Member	29.6	40.7	33.33	40.0
Not member	70.4	59.3	66.67	60.0
Agrarian committee status				
Member	26.0	32.9	21.7	35.3
Not member	74.0	67.1	78.3	64.7

Source: Newbold, *A Study of Receptivity*, pp. 27–29, provided the raw data from which these calculations were made.

The statistics in Table 8–10 support the propositions that "the better-off sectors of the peasantry . . . are more likely to organize and . . . the most depressed sectors . . . will be under-represented. . . . Within each group, the better-off individuals . . . will furnish proportionately more leadership and 'activists.' " [53] Newbold's data also strongly support a hypothesis that "leaders" from the sample would be more literate than "followers" [54] (see Table 8–11). Seventy per cent of all officeholders were literate while only 25 per cent of the "followers" in the sample were literate.

There was no statistically significant difference in literacy between the 96 persons who belonged to peasant unions, the 80 members of agrarian committees, and those who did not belong to these organizations. Accord-

[53] Henry A. Landsberger, Chapter 1.
[54] Newbold, *op cit.*, p. 22. A "leader" is defined as an "office- or post-holder" in Newbold's study.

ing to the 1950 census, the national average for literacy was 27.8 per cent; the percentage of literacy of peasants in the sample who were members of political parties and labor unions was higher; the percentage of literacy of peasants in the sample who were only members of peasant unions was about the same as the national average.[55]

During the Arbenz period, the number of radios possessed by peasants increased greatly, especially after the National Agrarian Bank (BNA) began making loans for this purpose. But even the radio did not necessarily bring an understanding of complex political issues into peasant groups. The radio served as audible support for those who already believed what was being said; much of what the radio said appears to have been

Table 8–11. Officeholding and literacy among peasants,
Newbold Study (in per cent)

	Literate (*N* = 90)	Illiterate (*N* = 177)	Total (*N* = 267)
Officeholders	30.9	8.5	18.7
Nonofficeholders	61.1	91.5	81.3

Source: Newbold, *A Study of Receptivity*, p. 22, provided the raw data from which these calculations were made.

meaningless to the greater proportion of the rural population if we accept as typical the reaction of members of the sample to an extensive recognition test involving twenty names and organizations:

The illiterate portion of the sample (66% as compared with the national average of 72.2%) showed very little comprehension of Communist ideology or terminology. They were generally uninformed, but where they did manifest knowledge, it concerned specifically Guatemalan and not foreign persons and events. However, there was a relatively high (in view of the lack of response in general) number of people who had opinions about the importance of the Labor Code and the Agrarian Reform. In the particular population it seems that the ideological propaganda had not settled beyond the local literate leaders and, for the most part, people who were not agriculturalists. If they heard Communist propaganda, which seems a reasonable supposition, phrases of foreign character did not stick.[56]

This is not to say that the peasants were confused but that ideological propaganda would have had to play up real needs and not the classical Communist needs if it were to have meaning to Guatemalan peasants in

[55] *Ibid.*, pp. 25–26.   [56] *Ibid.*, p. v.

this period. The fact that peasants understand the terms "Agrarian Reform" and "Labor Code" would lend support to this thesis. Two hundred members of the sample group of 267 were active in political, labor, peasant, and agrarian organizations, as follows:

200 or 75%   were members of political parties, labor *sindicatos*, peasant unions, or agrarian committees;

50 or 25%   held posts in one or more of the above organizations;

82 or 33%   were members of political parties;

90 or 35%   were members of peasant unions;

80 or 30%   were members of agrarian committees; and

25 or 8%   were members of labor unions

One might expect that this political activism would be reflected in a high level of knowledge of political affairs. This was not the case. Using

Table 8-12. Political knowledge of peasant union and agrarian committee members and nonmembers (in per cent)

Status	Peasant unions		Agrarian committees	
	Members ($N = 96$)	Non-members ($N = 171$)	Members ($N = 80$)	Non-members ($N = 187$)
Informed	14.5	12.2	11.2	13.9
Poorly informed	36.5	34.5	43.8	31.6
Totally uninformed	49.0	53.3	45.0	54.5

Source: Newbold, *A Study of Receptivity*, p. 31, provided the raw data from which these calculations were made.

Newbold's data, we find the 267 members of the sample distributed as follows: 138 or 51 per cent were completely ignorant; 94 or 34 per cent were poorly informed; 21 or 8 per cent were moderately well informed; and 14 or 5 per cent were really well informed.[57]

It was thought that the politically active would show a significantly greater amount of political knowledge than those who were not members of any political, labor, or peasant organizations. The data, however, support this hypothesis only with respect to membership in the political

[57] *Ibid.*, p. 16.

parties. Statistically, there was no significant correlation between being informed and membership in any of the organizations (see Table 8–12).

Political Indoctrination and Lack of Knowledge of Peasants

Newbold did not think that much could be learned concerning the degree of political indoctrination from short interviews under jail conditions.

Nevertheless, in the hope that some index or idea might be had of the amount and kind of political indoctrination which the interviewee had received, a number of questions were asked concerning the identification of people, organizations and ideas, and concerning opinions on political matters. In the majority of the interviews, the interviewees expressed almost complete ignorance concerning the matters mentioned. At first, the interviewers felt quite sure that the *"no sé"* ["I don't know"] which kept overwhelming [them] was principally a manner of defense on the part of the individual. In order to check this to some degree, the [questions were varied, along with issues and angles of approach] . . . [Newbold then came] to the conclusion [that many of his interviewees] who claimed ignorance knew little or nothing of the things mentioned. Support for this is to be found in the fact that a person who claimed not to recognize the name of Victor Manuel Gutiérrez also did not recognize the name of the Archbishop of Guatemala, Mariano Rossell y Arrellano, who had been in the public eye for many years, nor did they recognize the names of Winston Churchill, Karl Marx, or Joseph Stalin. It was also quite apparent that many had not actually heard of the "struggle between the classes," the "dictatorship of the proletariat," the "Communist Manifesto," and various other ideas and organizations. In a question requiring the interviewee to classify certain organizations and groups as "imperialist," "reactionary," "progressive," or "communist," there was little doubt but that most of them did not know what "imperialist" and "reactionary" meant. The term "progressive," it seemed, meant something good to many, so if they wished to indicate that they felt a particular individual, institution, or group to be good, they would usually say it was "progressive." [58]

There was some evidence that certain ideas sponsored by both the Arévalo and Arbenz regimes received some acceptance. Specifically, these were the ideas that a democratic government is selected by the people (70 persons), that there should be a distribution of land among those who did not have it (as a characteristic of a democratic country, 40 persons mentioned it), and that there should be laws controlling working condi-

[58] *Ibid.*, p. 32.

tions. Twenty-nine mentioned agrarian reform and twenty mentioned the labor code of 1947 as being the best works of the Arbenz and Arévalo administrations. Twenty-five persons mentioned the forced labor on highways and eleven mentioned the work control books as the most disliked characteristics of the Ubico regime.[59]

As might be expected, those who held posts of leadership in the organizations manifested a higher degree of knowledge than did the followers.

This seems to suggest one or both of the following possibilities: the political parties tended to draw indoctrinated people more strongly than did other organizations . . . and/or, the members of political parties were more effectively indoctrinated than were the members of the other organizations.[60]

The study hypothesized that leaders in general would be found among Ladinos except in those areas in which the population was overwhelmingly Indian. The data supported this hypothesis for the eastern departments of Jutiapa (Ladino) and Jalapa (mixed) but there was no significant difference among the eighteen officeholders from the coastal department of Escuintla. Of the sixty-six persons from the central part of the country, only six had held office; four were Indians and the other two were Ladinos, but this is not statistically meaningful.[61]

The hypothesis that leaders in general should come from *municipio* capitals (*cabeceras*) and followers more from the surrounding countryside was not sustained by the sample of 267 persons; in fact, a slight tendency to the contrary manifested itself (see Table 8–13).

When Newbold made his study, he heard many comments that the people in jail and the peasants "were being led like sheep." In his opinion, there was no basis for this statement. It was clear that the population interviewed was in general interested in some phase of the Arbenz government's activities.

In some cases, it was the possibility of acquiring land under the agrarian reform; in some it was getting higher wages; and in some it was simply the

[59] *Ibid.*, pp. 34–35. The work control books were similar to but not necessarily modeled after the labor passport system of the Soviet Union. Peasants—meaning Indians in most cases—had to prove they had worked so many days for the government during the year. This was not a problem for peasants living on the national farms but it created a system of *corvée* for independent peasants and sharecroppers. The writer was also aware in 1966 and 1968 of local military officials and *comisionados* acting as labor contractors for plantations having difficulty recruiting workers: a detachment of troops or reservists visited nearby hamlets and "persuaded" Indians to climb aboard trucks going to the fields.

[60] *Ibid.*, p. 37.   [61] *Ibid.*

exercise of power. It may be said that these people were being led like sheep in that they did what the Communists wanted; on the other hand, they were doing things which they too wished to do. The Communists were successful in identifying their goals with those of certain portions of the rural population; this can be laid to the cleverness of the Communists, but not necessarily to the "sheep-like" qualities of the population.[62]

Differences Among Regions and Work Groups and Receptivity to Agitation and Ideology

Data are lacking which would give us a complete understanding of the impact of various organizational or agitation techniques among different

Table 8–13. Officeholding and place of residence (in per cent)

	Cabecera dwellers (N = 139)	Rural dwellers (N = 128)	Total (N = 267)
Officeholders	14.4	23.9	18.7
Nonofficeholders	85.6	76.1	81.3

Source: Newbold, *A Study of Receptivity*, p. 22, provided the raw data from which these calculations were made.

ethnic groups and their impact on permanent as opposed to mobile laborers or landowners. However, some data are available for a number of departments which show the differential impact among various groups.

In the Pacific Coast department of Escuintla, various Ladino groups felt a need for land. A significant portion of the population was mobile and working on national farms as well as private *fincas*. The region was "ripe," so to speak, for professional agitators who could appeal to the felt needs of these peasants. And from these segments, local leaders such as Gabriel Camey of the national farm "La Concepción," and the PGT "firebrand" Carlos Manuel Pellecer (elected deputy for Escuintla in 1953) formed local groups whose leaders were given experience in agitation and leadership. On a moment's notice, Camey and Pellecer could mobilize several thousand agricultural laborers at "La Concepción" and another national farm, "Salta," who could walk or ride into the city of Escuintla on buses or trucks within 15 to 30 minutes. Guatemala City was only an hour away by bus or truck.

On the other hand, there were relatively few rural Ladinos with high mobility in Quezaltenango on the Pacific Coast or San Marcos in the

[62] *Ibid.*, p. 7.

western highlands. The Indians in these regions either lived as farm laborers on coffee *fincas* or owned small pieces of land on the coast. Communist "agitators" worked among the "modified" or "transitional" Indians of these two regions, but constant efforts by urban "outsiders" were necessary to keep these peasants "politically active." On the whole, no group appeared among the local population which could or would maintain political organizations at an active level once the outsiders left. Also, since most of the population was permanent and not mobile, it was not easy to maintain a constant barrage of criticisms downgrading local traditions and habits. Pellecer visited Quezaltenango on several occasions but he could neither sufficiently activate people to support the PGT or CGTG rural groups nor find a mobile population in which to initiate his agitation. In San Marcos, Amor Velasco de León had built an organization, but when he broke with the CNCG leadership of Castillo Flores and joined or stayed with the Guatemalan Revolutionary party, he was unable to maintain his leadership in that department. Very little land was expropriated as is seen in Table 8–5 in both Quezaltenango and San Marcos.[63]

In the Motagua Valley, there were politically active groups in the towns and populations with felt needs, but the Communists were not very successful in establishing their groups there; the noncommunist CNCG leadership managed to sustain itself in office for this reason. Of the persons from this region sampled by Newbold, there were few or none with an ability that demonstrated the presence of a group able to break traditional local customs and relationships. He also suggested that the old Ladinos in this region probably exercised a stronger than usual social control over elements who wished to disrupt tradition.

In other departments such as Alta Verapaz, Chiquimula, El Quiché, Sacatepéquez, Santa Rosa, and Suchitepéquez, noncommunist or anti-Communist peasant or nonpeasant leaders dominated the peasant federations. In each of these there was an undercover battle between the noncommunist elements and Communist or pro-CGTG (e.g., Gutiérrez) elements which either removed the noncommunists or seriously circumscribed their activities after the summer and fall of 1953.[64]

---

[63] See *Ibid.*, pp. 47–48, for comments by Newbold on these departments. See also a letter from Castillo Flores to Dionision Chun R., Malacatán, San Marcos, Oct. 1, 1953, which says Milagro Velasco—possibly a relative of Amor Velasco de León—was removed from his position as secretary-general of the coastal zone (*zona calida*) of the San Marcos Socialist Party "for political maneuvers and not processing requests for land." (Folder "CNCG Pol Relationships," GT Box 12).

[64] Pearson, *op. cit.*, pp. 135–141, covers these battles in detail. See also folders "CNCG" (GT Box 11) and "CNCG Relations with CGTG" (GT Box 13) for federation reports (*informes*) describing these events.

Religious Activism and Participation in Peasant and Political Organizations

Newbold's data showed some support for the hypothesis that active members and leaders of organized peasant and political groups would be less active in religious affairs. However, certain reservations or qualifications need to be made.

There was no correlation between membership in political parties and attendance at Roman Catholic Mass, but there was a statistically signifi-

Table 8–14. Membership in peasant unions, attendance at agrarian committee meetings, and religious activism (in per cent)

	Peasant union status			Attendance at agrarian committee meetings		
	Members (N=94)	Non-members (N=166)	Total (N=260)	Attend (N=75)	Did not attend (N=185)	Total (N=260)
Attend Mass often	48.9	52.4	51.2	42.7	54.6	51.2
Attend Mass sometimes	42.6	41.6	41.9	54.7	36.8	41.9
Attend Mass seldom	8.5	6.0	6.9	2.6	8.6	5.9
	(N=96)	(N=164)	(N=260)	(N=80)	(N=185)	(N=265)
Member of a *cofradía*	42.7	26.2	32.3	27.5	36.2	33.6
Do not belong to a *cofradía*	57.3	73.8	67.7	72.5	63.8	66.4

Source: Newbold, *A Study of Receptivity*, pp. 29–30, provided the raw data from which these calculations were made.

Note: Unfortunately, Newbold does not explain the discrepancy in sample sizes for *cofradía* membership and peasant union and agrarian committee activism.

cant correlation between membership in either labor unions (*sindicatos*) or agrarian committees and low attendance at Mass. There was a high correlation (95 per cent of probability) between membership in the political parties or peasant unions and membership in the *cofradías*, religious societies for the laymen. On the other hand, there was no significant correlation between membership in the labor unions or agrarian committees and membership in the *cofradías*.

There is little statistical support for the belief that the politically active were not religiously active. Table 8–14 shows these statistics.

The results of the study showed that political leaders participated less in religious affairs than did the general population. With respect to attendance at church, there was a significant correlation between the followers and high attendance at church. Only 33 per cent of the officeholders reported they attended church daily or weekly; 56 per cent of the nonofficeholders participated at least this often in church activities.[65] Approximately one-third of the officeholders and the nonofficeholders alike participated in activities of the *cofradías*.

In general, while there was some tendency for members of some of the organizations not to participate quite so actively in religious affairs as the nonmembers, the tendency was not very strong. It is not possible to say, on the basis of the sample data, that strong participation by individuals in the activities of the Roman Catholic Church meant weak political participation in various organizations extant during the Arbenz regime.

Newbold learned that religious participation did not conflict with political action. Among the leaders, there might have been a tendency for political activities to push religious activities aside. But this was also a condition found in the countryside prior to the June, 1944, Revolution when one commonly heard "so-and-so is a Communist and a Catholic." About the only comparative fact shedding light was a significant correlation between high religious attendance and high residential continuity. Seventy-two per cent of those who went to Mass daily had a high residential continuity but so did the 54 per cent who said they went monthly or to fiestas only. This suggests that other factors contribute to weakening religious attendance.[66]

Opponents and Allies: CNCG-CTG (CGTG) Relations

Any newly organized or emerging group faces different problems in seeking power in society than does a group which wants to maintain the status quo or prevent a decline in its status or prestige. The CNCG, as a new group, met resistance from groups already on the scene who did not want to share their power and influence with it.

As we have already noted, the CTG was hostile to the CNCG in May, 1950. In September, 1950, José Luís Ramos, then Secretary of Peasant Action of the CTG, charged Castillo Flores and Velasco de León with manipulating the peasants so that the PAR could stay in power.[67] The CNCG, he charged, had placed itself "at the service of the bourgeoisie" and could not solve any of the problems of the peasants nor help them learn "how to struggle for their rights"—rights which Ramos never specified.

The CTG maintained this air of hostility for more than a year. But by

[65] Newbold, *op. cit.*, p. 23.   [66] *Ibid.*, pp. 38–39.
[67] "Informe de la secretaria de Acción Campesina de CTG" (date unknown) (folder "CTG," GT Box 15).

February, 1951, the CTG apparently recognized the need to develop other means of combatting the influence and growing size of the CNCG. In a February 17, 1951, report (*Informe*) to the CTG, Gutiérrez said the labor movement (that is, the CTG) should extend a "fraternal hand" to the peasant movement. He admitted there were differences over agrarian reform despite conferences between the two centrals.[68] The open friction was thereafter modified into one of public cooperation accompanied by a behind-the-scenes maneuvering for power and influence within the Arbenz government and the countryside.

The CTG and its successor, the General Confederation of Guatemalan Workers or CGTG, had certain advantages in this maneuvering. They had Víctor Manuel Gutiérrez and José Luís Ramos. Gutiérrez was "the most valuable human asset of Communism in Guatemala."[69] He was hard-working, ascetic, and devoted to the interests of the working class. José Luís Ramos was equally active if not as brilliant. In addition to being CTG Peasant Secretary in 1950–1951, he was also, for a brief time in 1952, CNCG Secretary of Training—a position whose functions are not clear and head of the Peasant Affairs Commission of the Guatemala Labor party (PGT), 1953–1954.[70] The CTG and CGTG wanted to dominate the whole labor and peasant movement while the CNCG wanted to control only the peasant sector. The advantage of tactics, therefore, seemed to lie with the CTG and the CGTG.

Although economic developments in Guatemala during World War II and the Arévalo period created a large new class of urban wage earners, the conditions under which they emerged were such that a relatively feeble class consciousness developed among this group. The frailty of this class consciousness was reflected in the slow growth of the urban labor movement and in the fact that many urban workers remained unorganized. The CTG (CGTG) was the strongest labor group in terms of numbers and the closest ideologically to the CNCG oligarchy, or leadership elite.[71] But the CNCG's concern with land reform, education, and

[68] "Informe de secretario general de la X asamblea confederal," Feb. 17, 1951 (folder "CTG III," GT Box 15).   [69] Schneider, *op. cit.*, p. 94.

[70] Schneider, *op. cit.*, pp. 158–170, notes that Castillo Flores eliminated the founders and early leaders in carrying the CNCG "toward a closer cooperation with the Communists." The brief tenure and dismissal of Ramos, however, *may* be an indication that Castillo Flores dismissed him after using his talents and network of CTG acquaintances to build up the CNCG. In effect, one might infer that Castillo Flores turned the tables on the Communists at this time.

[71] The reader will remember that the FSG remained independent of the CGTG while the Railroad Workers' Union (SAMF) was often hostile to both groups and is still one of the strongest democratic trade-union groups in the country.

health measures for the peasants, introduced a range of activity alien to CTG (CGTG) members and leaders. Soviet Communist doctrine assigned a clearly subordinate role to the peasants in any alliance with the working class or proletariat.[72] Maoism, of course, did not triumph on the mainland of China until late 1949 and Chinese Communist doctrines were not exported to Guatemala in any meaningful amount during the Arévalo-Arbenz period. The relative lack of success of the CTG in organizing peasant unions prior to 1950 may have resulted also from the fact that CTG organizers—most of whom came from urban areas and were intellectually inclined—failed to achieve or maintain the "common touch" with the peasants. The CNCG, on the other hand, was able to muster peasant organizers in large numbers who worked for little or no salary and who understood the thinking and wishes of their peer group.

Thus burdened with their own theory and the backwardness or traditional nature of both the Guatemalan economy and the peasants who wanted to be their own landed proprietors and not salaried agricultural laborers,[73] the Communists and the CTG (CGTG) found it necessary and useful to achieve an accommodation with the CNCG. The big landowners still possessed considerable power and influence in 1951. The CTG and the Communist party had a small corps of domestic and foreign professional revolutionaries and labor organizers but they did not have the manpower necessary to create an extensive, integrated network of organizations in the countryside. It was in the interest of the CTG and the Communists to destroy the power of the landowners. If the CNCG could act as an instrument to that immediate end, the CTG would accept the fiction of an "alliance of workers and peasants." It was to the CNCG's

[72] M. A. Arshenev, S. F. Kochskin, B. S. Makiovsky, and M. S. Strogovich, *Teoria Gosadarstva i Prava* (Moscow: Institute of Law of the Academy of Science of the U.S.S.R., 1949), p. 244, quoted in W. W. Kulski, *The Soviet Regime* (Syracuse, N.Y.: Syracuse University Press, 1956), p. 548: "The proletarian State represents an alliance between the working class and the other toiling masses, with the hegemony or leading role in this alliance residing with the proletariat." Joseph Stalin, *Voprosy Leninisma* (Moscow: Foreign Language Publishing House, 1949), p. 234, quoted in Kulski, *op. cit.*, p. 548, also left no doubt in this matter: "Leninism stands unconditionally for a firm alliance with the substantial masses of the peasantry—for an alliance with the middle peasants, but not for just any alliance—only such alliance . . . which assures the leading role to the working class, strengthening the dictatorship of the proletariat, and hastens the destruction of classes."

[73] "Federación campesina en Coban," *El Imparcial*, Sept. 8, 1952, p. 1, col. 8, notes that the founding congress of the Peasant Federation of Coban adopted a statement that "workers from Alta Verapaz who ask for land under [the Agrarian Reform Law] will do so by asking for it in parcels and not the cooperatives," which the CTG wanted.

advantage to use the CTG and CGTG in establishing contacts with international labor organizations, although they were Communist-dominated, in the hope that these contacts might prove fruitful because there were no alternative sources of assistance from democratic trade or peasant unions or governments.[74]

Throughout its four-year existence, there were differences on the local level ranging from problems of CTG *sindicatos* wanting to join the CNCG, to competing claims for land and cases involving political matters.[75] Although the CNCG and CGTG generally maintained an air of unruffled "unity" in public, angry words often passed between the two

[74] Although Gutiérrez and the Communist-dominated International Union of Agricultural and Forestry Workers (UISTAF) tried to influence the CNCG to join the UISTAF as early as November, 1951, Castillo Flores and the CNCG ignored these overtures or stalled for time until August, 1953, when the CNCG Executive Council agreed to affiliate with the CTAL and the Communist-dominated World Federation of Trade Unions (WFTU). The Council stalled until February, 1954, when the Third National CNCG Congress agreed to affiliate with the Latin American Confederation of Workers (CTAL) and the WFTU. There was no formal exchange of correspondence and the affiliation was never mentioned in the publications of the WFTU, CTAL, and the Cominform. Although Castillo Flores and other peasant and worker leaders accompanied Gutiérrez and Ramos to the WFTU Congress in Vienna, Austria, in October, 1953, and later to the Soviet Union, this was never mentioned in WFTU or Cominform publications. The only Guatemalan organizations mentioned in these publications were *sindicatos* affiliated with the CGTG and with Carlos Manuel Pellecer's PGT organization in Escuintla.

The CNCG exchanged letters with the National Agricultural Workers Union (NAWU), affiliated with the AFL-CIO, but nothing developed from these contacts. The International Federation of Plantation, Agricultural and Allied Workers (IFP-AAW) did not exist at this time. The Inter-American Confederation of Labor (CIT) and its successor, the Inter-American Regional Organization of Workers (ORIT) were weak organizations and could offer little more than "moral solidarity." The Department of State did not formally assign anyone in Guatemala to establish contact with the Guatemalan labor or peasant movements until late 1957. USIA did not have any policies aimed at winning the support of workers, peasants, reformist intellectuals, or their leaders. Serafino Romualdi, the AFL-CIO representative in Latin America was unwelcome in both United Fruit Company and American Embassy offices as well as the CGTG and the PGT. Nevertheless, the AFL-CIO Executive Council commended Arbenz in February, 1954, for bringing "social justice to the Indians and peasants," and for raising "the standard of living of the workers" while also seeking to warn him that the Communists had no real concern with improving labor conditions. Further details and sources of information may be found in Pearson, *op. cit.*, pp. 86–99.

[75] Letter from Sindicato San José to Compañero Secretario de Trabajo y Conflictos de la CTG, no date (folder "CNCG Relations with CGTG," GT Box 13), has a penciled notation by Gutiérrez (translated): "Don't do it. The CTG is separate from the CNCG in spite of what Castillo Flores might say about the three great unified centrals." This CTG Sindicato of "non-salaried workers," probably renters, wanted to join the CNCG. Other letters could be cited on this point.

groups in correspondence.[76] Because this friction inhibited the work of both Centrals, there was a recognition in 1952 that coordination of certain activities was necessary. The CGTG made the first formal overtures in August, 1952, when it asked the CNCG to appoint three delegates to cooperate on a preparatory committee organizing a National Congress on Social Security.[77] However, despite offers by the CNCG to set up formal machinery to handle complaints and disputes, there is no evidence that this happened or that the CNCG really wanted to "coordinate" the activities of both groups on a long-range basis. *Ad hoc* arrangements were the usual manner in which problems were solved, if at all.[78]

CNCG Participation in CGTG and PGT Propaganda Campaigns

The CNCG never was able to build enough political power of its own to enable it to follow an independent or apolitical line.[79] Participation in the chorus of slogans and statements supporting the Arbenz government brought access to the government and its services.[80] The CNCG probably would have gained little by fighting the CGTG and the Communists in printed words or public speeches. This would have antagonized the government and the Communists who were interested in preserving a symbolic unity and a "united front." [81] Arbenz never appeared willing to

[76] Letters from Gutiérrez to Castillo Flores, and from Castillo Flores to Gutiérrez, April 24, 1954 (folder "CNCG Relations with CGTG," GT Box 13). Peasants in Chimaltenango charged that the CGTG and PGT were cooperating with a landowner to break up the CNCG union in San Martin Jilotepeque. Gutiérrez called the charges "calumnies." The peasants, he said, were threatening Max Salazar, a PGT Central Committee member and CGTG official, with "death." Castillo Flores rejected the "unjust charges made against leaders of the CNCG."

[77] Letter from Executive Committee, CGTG, to Castillo Flores, Aug. 10, 1952 (folder "CNCG Relations with CGTG," GT Box 13).

[78] The folder "CNCG Reserve Mat," GT Box 10, contains a number of letters of complaint by CNCG members of CGTG conduct and vice versa which CNCG and CGTG leaders exchanged. See also a letter from Castillo Flores to Gutiérrez, Dec. 26, 1952, and a letter from Gutiérrez to Castillo Flores, Jan. 2, 1953 (folder "CNCG Relations with CGTG," GT Box 13); Gutiérrez ignored a request for joint consultations, although he answered other questions and complaints from Castillo Flores.

[79] Pearson, *op. cit.*, pp. 100–120, discusses the CNCG's relationships with the various noncommunist revolutionary parties and its membership in the leadership of the PAR, PS, and PRG.

[80] *Ibid.*, pp. 54–63, discusses strike, collective bargaining, agricultural extension, literacy, rural health, and welfare programs of the CNCG in which it acted as a broker with government agencies in self-help programs of individual peasants or peasant communities as well as one-way aid programs.

[81] *Ibid.*, pp. 121–149, discusses the CNCG's relationship with the Communist revolutionary parties, the underground Communist Party of Guatemala (PCG), and the Guatemalan Labor Party (PGT), including the purges of noncommunists from

repudiate the Communist influence in the labor or peasant movements.[82] The CNCG faced two alternatives: (1) follow an independent political and economic line which would engender opposition and no hope of financial or other support, or (2) follow the CGTG, PGT, and the noncommunist revolutionary parties in a coalition of support for the Arbenz government.

The CNCG chose the second alternative as the one which would bring the most benefits and the fewest risks in the short run to its leaders and members. In the long run, the CNCG leadership may have hoped that Guatemalan society would be changed enough while the CNCG itself could strengthen its own structure for a more independent course.[83]

The CNCG sought political alliances with the noncommunist revolutionary parties and the Arévalo-Arbenz governments to insure its legitimacy and gain protection and support for growth. By adept maneuvering, the CNCG leadership managed to stay with the political party or coalition which offered the greatest political patronage and support.[84] But after February 1954, the party system had splintered so much that the CNCG's ability to deliver a large bloc of peasant votes meant little. The CNCG leadership itself had been so weakened or compromised by the Communists that it no longer had the bargaining strength of 1952. By 1954, the noncommunist revolutionary political parties had lost their cohesiveness with one another and amongst themselves. Policy initiative lay completely with the President and the PGT-dominated National Democratic Front (FDN).[85]

The CNCG and the Churches

Although the Roman Catholic and Protestant Churches in Guatemala did not openly act as a pressure group, they did act as important influences upon the attitudes of individual Guatemalans.

---

several peasant federations and from the CNCG Executive Council while Castillo Flores attended the WFTU Congress in October, 1953. The "myth of a united front" and alleged "peasant participation in rallies to form a democratic front" are discussed on pp. 129–131.

[82] *Ibid.*, pp. 127–128, discusses Arbenz and the Communists. CNCG support for Arbenz in 1954 is discussed on pp. 192–215.

[83] *Ibid.*, pp. 64–70, discusses CNCG attempts to start a peasant youth movement in 1954 and CNCG publicity media. Both were inadequately financed, inadequately organized, and had little impact on the urban or rural population.

[84] It should be remembered that Castillo Flores served as a PAR deputy from 1947 to 1951, that Guillermo Ovando Arriola served as a PAR deputy from 1953 to 1954, and that Amor Velasco de León served as a PSG deputy in 1952.

[85] Pearson, *op. cit.*, p. 132; Schneider, *op. cit.*, p. 296; and "Caja de sorpresa en el Congreso," *El Imparcial,* Feb. 16, 1954, p. 1, cols. 6–8, discuss the FDN.

CNCG's dedication to changing the status of the peasant antagonized many Roman Catholic clergymen. In the summer of 1951, the CNCG became so concerned about the "Communist" label placed upon it by Roman Catholic priests that Castillo Flores sent out many letters like the following to peasants:

We, as all of us know, are not Communist, but neither are we going to be steered and deceived by the reactionaries. We are not going to give ourselves a false propaganda that we are anti-Communists so that the reactionaries may wave a banner which would go against the revolutionary movement and against Guatemalan liberty.[86]

In the spring of 1953, many peasants were told by parish priests to make a choice between "Christianity" and the CNCG, which the priests called "communism." The CNCG issued a *Manifesto to the Guatemalan People* which said, in part:

The National Peasant Confederation, aware of the religious faith of the majority of Guatemalans and respectful of the freedom of thought and religion, never would ask for the extinction of the Catholic Church in Guatemala and considers itself obliged to always be the best defender of the Christian faith in our country.[87]

Nevertheless, CNCG members had continued trouble with the Roman Catholic clergy. In September, 1953, an Indian peasant in San Pedro Carcha, Alta Verapaz, wrote the following:

The reactionaries held an anti-Communist meeting on September 9 that was headed by priest José Diní, the *Alcalde* (mayor) of the *Municipio*, José Guay . . . and other reactionaries, and it dealt with the members [of the movement or brothers] (*compañeros*) as if they were Communists. [The sister of the Mayor] said the government was going to destroy the churches and that it was going to take away the land and even their wives [*mujeres*] . . . and that they were going to give the women to unknown men who were Communists. . . . When the President of the Indian Community [of Pocolá] died, [the priest] did not wish to give the *doble* [probably a local type of mass] because [he said] the President of the Indian Community was a "Communist." [88]

[86] Letter from Castillo Flores to Clemente Ramírez, July 26, 1951, and other letters in folder "CNCG Denials of Communism," GT Box 12.

[87] "Manifiesto al pueblo de Guatemala," March, 1953 (folder "CNCG 1953," GT Box 11).

[88] Unsigned letter, some pages of which are missing, addressed to Compañero Alfredo Tsi Cucul, Presidente de la Com. Camp. de San Pedro Carcha, Sept. 16, 1953 (folder "CNCG Collaboration in Defense of Regime," GT Box 11).

Guatemalan Protestant groups did not involve themselves in politics although the attitude of a North American missionary, Paul Burgess, on agrarian reform is noted above.

The CNCG and the Armed Forces

President Arbenz, a former career officer and Chief of Staff, retained the loyalty of his former subordinates and colleagues until late 1953 and early 1954.[89] CNCG leaders were aware of the army's importance in politics [90] and sought to ingratiate themselves with the army. When the Agrarian Reform Bill was under discussion in the Guatemalan Congress, Castillo Flores wrote the Chief of the Armed Forces proposing that all agricultural workers and peasants discharged from military service be given "the land necessary to dedicate themselves to agriculture." [91] There is no record of a reply. After the Agrarian Reform Law went into effect, several CNCG unions complained to Castillo Flores that army officers, not enlisted men, were given land under the legislation.

The officer corps was not unhappy over the arms shipped on the "Alfheim" from Eastern Europe which arrived at Puerto Barrios on May 15, 1954. However, discontent among the *finquero* group with Arbenz and agrarian reform, the increasing sense of Guatemala's isolation from the other Central American states and the United States, and Arbenz' ambiguity on the increasing role of the Communists in his government all led to dissatisfaction within significant portions of the officer corps. Arbenz' campaign to convince the country that the United Fruit Company and the United States government were conspiring against Guatemala had a boomerang effect: many people began worrying about a real plot and the armed forces did not want to fight a war with the United States or United States–supported forces.[92]

After many internal disputes, a small group of Guatemalan exiles formed an invasion force under the leadership of Colonel Carlos Castillo

[89] Sydney Gruson, "Guatemalan Army Apathetic to Reds," New York *Times,* Aug. 5, 1953, p. 5, cols. 4–5.

[90] The Guatemalan army is top-heavy with officers and promotion is often slow; hence plotting within the officer corps to take over the government is not uncommon. In 1966, the officer corps totaled 1,020; 370 colonels were on the active list out of a total of 470 colonels. Since World War II the army has also had about 8,000 enlisted men, of whom 4,000 are conscripts.

[91] Letter from Castillo Flores to Sr. Jefe de las Fuerzas Armadas, June 4, 1952 (folder "CNCG Other Materials," GT Box 10).

[92] Thomas W. Palmer, *Search for a Latin American Policy* (Gainesville: University of Florida Press, 1957), pp. 139–146, is probably the soberest analysis of United States policy in Guatemala during 1953–1954.

Armas, who obtained arms from sources in the United States and Europe. As early as May, 1954, the CNCG and the Arbenz government knew that Castillo Armas might return. Castillo Flores asked member unions to be "ready, waiting [and] vigilant . . . to combat the enemies of our Revolution." [93] This created a series of outcries in several newspapers—*El Impacto* and *El Espectador* were two—that the CNCG was forming a people's militia similar to the Guatemala City urban labor militia formed by Arbenz to defend the Arévalo regime in 1950 following the assassination of Colonel Arana or the armed terrorists who helped install a Communist regime in Czechoslovakia in 1948. The CNCG denied this and said that "the peasants are not trying to occupy the honored position of our military institutions nor much less that 'they wish to form another army within the nation.' " [94]

After the invasion on June 18, 1954, the CNCG thought the Guatemalan Army would easily defeat the force of 200 to 300 invaders. In a June 20 telegram, Castillo Flores said:

We must obey the orders of the Chief of the Armed Forces. . . . The National Army has beaten the enemy. Victory approaches. Struggle with those who would sell our dear fatherland. Maintain yourselves united for an open conflict with the traitors of Guatemala.[95]

In the end, Communist and newspaper propaganda and rumors about a worker-peasant militia frightened the officer corps sufficiently to bring about its defection from Arbenz.[96] If, in theory, Arbenz hoped to arm the workers and peasants, he was stymied by the refusal of the army officer corps to distribute arms or train worker and peasant forces. Arbenz resigned on June 27, 1954, and sought asylum in the Mexican Embassy.

Dissolution of the CNCG and Agrarian Reform

Shortly after he came into power, Castillo Armas said a new Agrarian Reform Law would be passed which would "give land to the peasant as

[93] "Los instigadores de la tragedia," *El Espectador*, June 5, 1964, p. 3, cols. 1–2.

[94] "Manifesto of CNCG Executive Committee," June 8, 1954 (folder "CNCG 1954," GT Box 11). This manifesto was not published by the Guatemala City press.

[95] Telegram from Castillo Flores to Luis M. Juarez, Santa Ana Hista, Huehuetenango, June 20, 1954 (folder "CNCG Collaboration in Defense of Regime," GT Box 11).

[96] On June 5, 1954, high-ranking officers presented Arbenz with a series of questions about his relationships with the Communists and about their influence in the government, the labor movement, and the peasant movement. See xerographic copies of manuscript of letter from Estado Mayor del Ejército, illegible signature, to President of the Republic and Commander in Chief of the Army, June 5, 1954 (folder "Armed Forces & Defense." GT Box 1).

his property" rather than as a "ward of the State"—a reference to the practice of giving titles for lifetime use only.[97] This statement and a July 27, 1954, decree opening up inaccessible national lands to the peasants were never implemented.[98]

Castillo Armas asked the *finqueros* to allow peasants who benefited from land distribution to harvest their crops as a matter of "social justice, sustenance, . . . and respect for the human being." [99] He was ignored. Workers were fired, wages reduced, and peasants expelled from the land.[100]

On July 24, 1954, the Guatemalan government abolished the legal status of 533 unions.[101] On February 1, 1955, the government rescinded amendments to the Labor Code which allowed peasants and farm workers to organize unions with less than fifty members and less than sixty per cent of the membership literate.[102] Rural unions were effectively blocked by law and the CNCG liquidated.

Status of the Peasants in 1968

Until 1966, all post-Arbenz governments discouraged organizational activities among the peasantry. At that time, the newly-inaugurated government of Júlio Cesar Mendes Montenegro began turning over 375,000 acres of land to 12,000 families living on 45 national farms. Predictably, the move was belittled by the extreme left as "meaningless and demagogic while the extreme right has talked ominously of a first step toward Communism." [103] Although no privately-owned land was

[97] Paul P. Kennedy, "Castillo Pledges Guatemala Gains," New York *Times*, July 13, 1954, p. 12, col. 3; "Crímenes contra la libertad son crímenes contra la patria," *El Imparcial*, July 13, 1954, p. 1, cols. 1–8.
[98] "Guatemala Gets New Land Decree," New York *Times*, July 23, 1954, p. 6, cols. 3–4.
[99] "Cooperación efectiva ofrecen a los campesinos las autoridades," *El Espectador*, Aug. 24, 1954, p. 8, cols. 4–5.
[100] "107 trabajadores despedida la frutera por ser agitadores rojos," *El Espectador*, Aug. 5, 1954, p. 5, cols. 4–5; "15,000 trabajadores sin empleo en el pais," *El Imparcial*, Aug. 19, 1954, p. 1, cols. 2–3.
[101] "Personería juridica de 533 organizaciones laborales se cancela por el DAT," *El Imparcial*, July 29, 1954, p. 1, cols. 2–3. This was the only article published during the first six months of the regime about cancellation of union or *sindicato* registrations. The CNCG or member unions were not listed but were probably included in unpublished portions of the decree. [102] Bishop, *op. cit.*, p. 170.
[103] "2 Battles Waged by Guatemalans," New York *Times*, Oct. 15, 1966, p. 8, col. 3. In July, 1961, Edwin A. Lahey reported "about 4,000 families have been settled on farms averaging 50 acres each" since 1954. More than 40,000 applications for farms were on file, while the total number of landless people desiring farms was 500,000

touched, the National Institute for Agrarian Transformation (INTA) also noted that more than 68,000 families were without land while 75,000 were trying to live on two and a half acres or less.

In December, 1962, Christian Democrats founded the Social Christian Peasant Movement in Guatemala. It had organized twenty functioning peasant leagues by mid-1966. Its nineteen to twenty thousand members were linked to the Latin American Confederation of Christian Trade Unionists (CLASC) with headquarters in Santiago, Chile. About ten other peasant *sindicatos* were functioning in 1966 and linked in a variety of ways with the Inter-American Regional Labor Organization (ORIT) with headquarters in Mexico City. Leaders of both groups have been fired upon by hired gunmen or local police linked to big landowners.[104]

Attempts have also been made to create rural cooperatives by local Christian Democratic activists, individual priests and ministers, United States Peace Corpsmen, and an occasional agricultural extension officer. The United States Aid Mission in Guatemala City has made loans and technicians available to rural communities interested in self-help projects. In mid-1966, these cooperatives numbered about 12,000 individuals, a very small number compared to the total rural population.

It is doubtful that the Mendes Montenegro government will sponsor the creation of peasant *sindicatos* similar to those which flourished during the Arbenz regime because of the hostility of most rich landowners and senior military officers. However, the Mendes Montenegro government will probably distribute additional amounts of government-owned national farm land and provide new roads, marketing, and medical facilities in the Petén region in order to ease the nation's chronic food shortage. Even the conservative political parties now give nominal support—as they

---

(Lahey, "Guatemala Offers Preview of Latin Aid Plan," Washington *Post*, July 30, 1961, p. E-1). See Department of State, *A Case History of Communist Penetration, Guatemala* (Department of State Publication No. 6465 [Washington, D.C.: Government Printing Office April, 1957]), p. 64, which claimed, "as of February 1, 1957, 10,751 farm families had been resettled on Government farms or on land made available to the Government by private planters." Obviously there are discrepancies between these figures. Apparently, both Guatemalan and American officials were trying to give the impression in 1957 and 1961 that land distribution was taking place. It is probably not accidental that neither the *Times* or *Post* articles nor the State Department publication noted the distribution of land to some 87,569 families during the Arbenz regime (see Table 8–7 in this chapter).

[104] *América Rural* (Mexico City), October, 1965, p. 8, discusses the July 29, 1963, shooting of Tereso de Jesús Oliva, by Guatemalan Judicial Police. *América Rural*, July, 1966, p. 2, discusses the work of José Lino Mundo Alvarez and the Social Christian Peasant Movement.

did not between 1950 and 1954—to agrarian reform in a country whose population has increased more than 65 per cent since 1950; Guatemala now has about 4.6 million people, at least half of whom are less than twenty years old.

We cannot know whether Guatemala's traditional civilian and military elites will permit peasant pressure groups to develop, or even if it will permit peaceful land distribution schemes similar to those of Italy, Japan, and Taiwan, or if the more militant ways of Mexico, Bolivia, and Venezuela will be followed. In any case, organization of Guatemala's peasants into an effective pressure group similar in size to the CNCG is not likely because there is little chance that the nation's rural education system will be changed to provide the necessary leadership for such a group.

9. Brazil: The Peasant Movement of Pernambuco, 1961–1964*

CYNTHIA N. HEWITT

University of Leiden
Holland

"Pernambuco is, at this moment," wrote the journalist Antônio Callado in late 1963, "the best laboratory for social experiments and the best producer of ideas in Brazil." [1] The attention of the rest of the nation, and of interested segments of the population of other American states (including the United States), was at the time focused on the progress of a rural labor movement which had been developing in Pernambuco for several years. The roots of the drive to organize Pernambucan peasants could be found in the work of Francisco Julião, who established the first peasant league in the state—and in the nation—as early as 1955. Nevertheless, the period of most intense activity in the field of peasant organization in Pernambuco began in 1961, when a segment of the Roman Catholic clergy decided to challenge the *ligas* through the promotion of rural labor unions. By April 1, 1964, when the military overthrew the national government of João Goulart and intervened in rural labor organization throughout Brazil, more than 100 peasant associations (leagues and Catholic unions) existed in Pernambuco. Their combined membership was estimated to be about 280,000. [2] Direction of peasant organization was no longer solely in the hands of Julião or the Catholic Church. Between 1962 and 1964, representatives of the Brazilian Communist Party (PCB, the Moscow-oriented group), the Communist Party of Brazil (PC do B, influenced by the Chinese doctrinal position), the Leninist Vanguard (Trotskyite), the administration of the state's Governor, Miguel Arraes,

* The author wishes to acknowledge that funds for field work during the summer of 1965 were granted by the Ford Foundation through the Latin American Institute of Columbia University.

[1] *Tempo de Arraes* (Rio de Janeiro: José Álvaro, 1965), p. 20. Translations mine.

[2] Estimated from figures provided by Mary Wilkie for late 1963: Church-sponsored Federation, 200,000 members; Ligas, 30,000; Communist unions, 50,000 (Wilkie, "A Report on Rural Syndicates in Pernambuco" [Rio de Janeiro: Latin American Center for Research in the Social Sciences, April, 1964], p. 7).

and the administration of President João Goulart also competed for the privilege of organizing Pernambucan peasants. The result was an extraordinarily complex movement in which leaders of markedly different ideological persuasions sometimes found themselves allies. At the base of the movement were hundreds of thousands of rural salaried workers, sharecroppers, and small farmers who may have had little understanding of the ideological premises of various leaders but who nevertheless received concrete benefits from participation in the movement.

The Environment

The state of Pernambuco is divided into three geographical zones: the *mata*, the *agreste*, and the *sertão*. The relationship between man and land is quite different in each region, and that fact obviously influenced the tactics, as well as the degree of success, of rural labor organizers.

The *Sertão*

The largest geographical unit of the state is the *sertão*, which includes more than 70 per cent of the land and 15 per cent of the population of Pernambuco. More than 735,000 people live in this "backland," where rainfall is light and vegetation sparse (except along the banks of the São Francisco and smaller rivers). The principal products of the region are cotton, agave, and cattle, as well as subsistence crops such as corn and beans. In the river valleys of the *sertão*, sugar cane and rice are also grown.

As Tables 9–1 and 9–2 show, large holdings are characteristic of the *sertão;* 70.2 per cent of the land is held in parcels of 100 hectares or more, and those holdings constitute only 7.4 per cent of all registered holdings.

Table 9–1. Distribution of agricultural establishments of various sizes and area covered by each size group in each zone of the state (N = number of establishments; A = area, in hectares, covered by the establishments in each size group)

Size group	Mata		Agreste		Sertão		Total	
(hectares)	N	A	N	A	N	A	N	A
0–9	21,007	54,063	137,845	365,260	41,251	168,525	200,103	587,848
10–99	2,387	61,744	18,423	474,647	30,040	991,969	50,850	1,528,360
100–999	1,729	665,698	1,756	432,855	6,059	1,621,646	9,544	2,720,199
1,000 or more	151	239,861	46	93,735	370	1,110,904	567	1,444,500
Total	25,274	1,021,366	158,070	1,366,497	77,720	3,893,044	261,064	6,280,907

Source: Mary Wilkie, "A Report on Rural Syndicates in Pernambuco" (Rio de Janeiro: Latin American Center for Research in the Social Sciences, 1964), p. 4, which used the preliminary summary of the 1960 census.

Table 9–2. Number of establishments in each size group expressed as a percentage of the total number of establishments for zone and state, and area of land (in hectares) covered by all the establishments in each size group as a percentage of the total land area in establishments for zone and state (N = number of establishments; A = area, in hectares, covered by the establishments in each size group)

Size group (hectares)	Mata		Agreste		Sertão		Total	
	N	A	N	A	N	A	N	A
0–9	84.0	5.3	87.2	26.8	53.4	4.4	76.7	9.2
10–99	9.0	6.0	11.4	34.7	39.2	25.4	19.3	24.4
100–999	6.5	65.0	1.1	31.7	6.9	41.8	3.7	43.5
1,000 or more	0.5	23.7	0.3	6.8	0.5	28.4	0.3	22.9
Total	100.0	100.0	100.0	100.0	100.0	100.0	100.0	100.0

Source: Same as Table 9–1.

Cattle raising is the predominant activity on such land. Correia de Andrade notes: "This cattle raising neither produces great profits nor demands great investments. Landowners live, in general, in the cities of the interior closest to their *fazenda* (ranch), where they dedicate themselves to other economic activities—above all, commerce." [3] Cattle are tended by *vaqueiros*, who receive one animal out of every four born in the herd under their care during each year. Other land on the *fazenda* is often given to sharecroppers or renters, who raise cotton and subsistence crops. Aside from payment in money or crops for the use of the land, tenants may also be required to give a day's free labor per week to the *fazendeiro* —an institution known as *cambão* (reminiscent of the medieval corvée), which is found more frequently in the *agreste* and the *mata* of the state. [4]

The great majority of the peasants in the *sertão* are small farmers. More than half of the registered agricultural establishments of the region in fact contain ten hectares or less. Few small landowners can support a family on such a plot unless it is near a river or has access to irrigation water. The occupational patterns of smallholders are therefore complex. Most of them are also salaried workers on more extensive holdings, and a large number migrate to the *agreste*, the *mata*, or outside the state altogether during part of the year, leaving their families to care for their plots while they search for work. During the periodic droughts which strike the *sertão*, migration reaches extremely high proportions.

Despite the fact that the economic situation of the majority of the

[3] Manoel Correia de Andrade, *A terra e o homem no Nordeste* (São Paulo: Editôra Brasiliense, 1963), p. 192.   [4] *Ibid.*, p. 200.

sertanejos of Pernambuco is very bad and their level of education is extremely low, it should be noted that peasants of the *sertão* exhibit an independence of spirit which is almost impossible to find among the peasants of the sugar region. Perhaps this is because the former, poor as they are, are likely to have some land of their own, unlike a majority of the peasants of the *mata*. Similarly, despite the fact that *sertanejos* are far more physically isolated from one another than their counterparts nearer the coast, they seem to have developed a much more cooperative spirit. Correia de Andrade notes that the *mutirão*, or cooperative planting of cotton by small farmers, has historically been a characteristic institution of the *sertão*.[5]

The ecological conditions of the *sertão* presented special problems for rural labor organizations. The *sertão* was simply too far away from the coast, the center of population of Pernambuco, to be reached easily by organizers from various groups. In addition, the wide dispersal of its population and the frequency of migration there made organization difficult. A few *ligas* seem to have been established in the region,[6] but apparently they were not very active. Several unions were also established in the *sertão* by the Church, and efforts were made to encourage the formation of cooperatives. Those efforts also seem to have met with little success. But it seems unwarranted to conclude that cooperative efforts in the *sertão* are impossible. In fact, the existence of some cooperative traditions and of a mentality less shaped by complete subservience to a landlord suggests that some organizations, once established, might function rather well in that region.

The *Agreste*

Several important characteristics differentiate the *agreste*, or transitional zone, from the *sertão* and the coastal region of Pernambuco. First, the *agreste* has more rainfall and better soil than the *sertão;* productivity per hectare is therefore greater. Second, land in the region is used for a wide variety of purposes, including cattle raising, coffee and cotton production, and the cultivation of many crops consumed in the coastal region, as well as for subsistence farming.

Differences in man-land relationships between the *agreste* and the *sertão* are more of degree than of kind. There are fewer large cattle ranches in the *agreste*, and their employees are more likely to be simple salaried

---

[5] *Ibid.,* p. 188.

[6] Antônio Callado, lists only one in 1960 (*Os industriais da sêca e os 'Galileus' de Pernambuco* [Rio de Janeiro: Editôra Civilização Brasileira, 1960], p. 45).

workers than the *vaqueiros* of the *sertão*.[7] Land on large holdings in the *agreste* is given to sharecroppers or renters, who face the same problems as those in other parts of the state. Often they can obtain credit only from their landlord at very high rates of interest, they suffer from a complete lack of technical assistance, they sometimes must work several days a week for the landlord at very low wages (*dias de sujeição*), and they very rarely enjoy any guarantee of stability. In addition, most are not allowed to make any permanent improvements in the land surrounding their houses, since they would then have to be indemnified for them if evicted.

The greatest difference in landholding patterns between the *agreste* and the other two regions of the state can be found by glancing once more at Tables 9–1 and 9–2. Only 38.5 per cent of the land area of the *agreste* is contained in agricultural establishments of 100 hectares or more, and 87.2 per cent of all landholdings are of less than ten hectares. The *agreste* is thus the region of Pernambuco which contains the largest number of *minifundistas*—holders of very small plots who often rent land on larger holdings or migrate to the coast to work in the cane harvest to support their families. At the same time more than a third of the land of the region is held in parcels of ten to ninety-nine hectares, providing the economic basis for what Correia de Andrade calls "a rural middle class, which has a standard of living noticeably inferior to that of the large and middle-sized proprietors, but an economic and social situation noticeably superior to that of landless workers." [8]

Francisco Julião explains in a book written in 1962 that organization should be easiest among sharecroppers, renters, small farmers, and "tributaries"—a term which presumably includes any peasant who receives a parcel of land in return for payment either in cash, crops, or labor.[9] Conversely, organization would be more difficult among salaried workers of the sugar zone. His reasons for such a statement are cogent. First, since sharecroppers, renters, and small farmers occupy parcels of land, they control more resources in a battle with landlords than a salaried worker; they can at least grow subsistence crops to keep from starving during a long legal battle, and they may be able to contribute financially to their legal representation. Moreover, sharecroppers, renters, and small farmers may process their legal claims through Brazil's Civil Code, which in 1962 was much more likely to be administered impartially than the labor laws applied to salaried workers.

[7] Correia de Andrade, *op. cit.*, p. 160.   [8] *Ibid.*, p. 152.
[9] Julião, *¿Qué son las Ligas Campesinas?* (Montevideo, Uruguay: Ediciones ARCA, 1962), p. 63.

If the tactics just described had been completely followed by Julião, the organization of peasant leagues during the period under discussion should have been more effective in the *agreste* than in the *mata*. The *agreste*, moreover, is linked by excellent roads with Recife and other urban centers and is fairly densely populated. Nevertheless the *ligas* of the *agreste* were fewer, smaller, and less active than those of the *mata*.

Several considerations may perhaps explain the situation. The most important seems to be that the peasant movement in Pernambuco was in large part "expressive"—a movement based on agitation for change. This statement is explored more fully below and should not be taken to mean that important concrete gains were not won in the process. Nevertheless, agitation proved more fruitful among the salaried workers of the *mata* than among the tenants of the *agreste*.

A second reason why Julião's analysis of necessary prerequisites for peasant organization could not in fact be put into practice was simply that legal changes under the Goulart administration modified the situation on which Julião's original premises were based. The Rural Labor Law, enacted in March, 1963, required each employer to deduct 2 per cent of his salaried workers' pay for their rural union. Goulart also enforced labor laws more strictly, aided in Pernambuco by the police force of Governor Arraes. Thus the salaried cane workers in fact had more financial and juridical resources than sharecroppers, tenants, and small farmers.

Organization of peasants in the *agreste* seems to have been largely in the hands of the Church-sponsored unions from their founding in late 1961 until the coup of 1964.[10] The demands of sharecroppers, renters, and small farmers in the region were for the abolition of the obligation to give a day's free labor per week to the landlord, assurance of stability of tenure through written contracts and adequate legal protection, payment for the use of land in cash rather than crops and the freedom to sell crops on the open market, adequate credit at reasonable rates of interest, technical assistance and schools, and, in at least a few cases, the sale or donation of land to tenants.[11]

[10] Respondents interviewed in 1965 noted that a few peasant leagues (organized by Julião) did exist in the *agreste*, but that they were generally not active.

[11] The question of the extent of pressure for the division of land in the *agreste* is an interesting one, especially related to one of the hypotheses in Chapter 1—namely that the goals of laborers, as distinct from tenants, small proprietors, sharecroppers, etc., are less likely to be "profound" (involving changes in the ownership or administration of the stock of capital [land]). All available information seems to indicate that there was little pressure for the direct ownership of land in the *agreste*. Nevertheless, isolated cases of invasions have been reported there. The *Jornal*

Some of those demands were met by organized pressure against land-lords—a collective refusal to pay rents or to furnish free labor, for example—accompanied by legal representation. An effort was also made by Church-sponsored groups to establish cooperatives in a few areas. But some demands, such as schools and technical assistance, could only be met by governmental assistance, and that was not forthcoming.

The *Mata*

It was in the *mata*, or coastal sugar zone, of Pernambuco that the most intensive efforts to organize peasants were made. The reasons are not hard to find. Although the region includes only a ninth of the area of the state, it contains almost half its population. And 88.7 per cent of all the land of the *mata* is held in parcels of 100 hectares or more, while 84 per cent of all registered agricultural establishments in the region contain less than ten hectares. The landholding pattern of the *mata* is thus a classic example of *latifundia* and *minifundia*.[12] Sugar cane dominates the region. A glance at the history of the sugar industry will therefore contribute to an under-standing of the social structure of the area.

Sugar plantations have occupied the best land of the *mata* since the sixteenth century; in fact the first cane in the new world was planted in Pernambuco. Until the late nineteenth century, both the cultivation and the processing of cane were carried out on individual plantations, or *engenhos*. The traditional society of Pernambuco, which Gilberto Freyre described so vividly in *Casa grande e senzala*, was based upon the *engenho* as the producer, refiner, and marketer of sugar products. By the 1880's, however, *engenhos* were being incorporated into much larger holdings, formed to supply cane to newly established sugar mills with complex machinery and high capital investment. These mills are called *usinas*. Owners of old plantations gradually closed their antiquated ox-powered mills and preserved only their function as suppliers (*fornecedores*) of

---

do Comercio of Nov. 6, 1963, described an invasion of public lands near Pesqueira by a group of which 98 per cent were members of the Church-sponsored syndicate and 5% (*sic*) were members of the *Liga*. The publication *Liga*, Feb. 5, 1964, reported that a peasant league of small farmers was being organized in Caruarú and that its demands included schools, credit, and "agrarian reform."

[12] It would be interesting to know approximately what percentage of all members of peasant organizations in the *mata* were *minifundistas*. It is my impression that the number was not large. Nevertheless, more exact information would allow a compari-son of the behavior of *minifundistas* in the *mata* with those of the *agreste*. The average size of small holdings in both areas is roughly equal: 2.5 hectares in the *mata* and 2.6 hectares in the *agreste*. Did the fact that *minifundistas* in the *mata* were much more likely to be surrounded by very large holdings than their counterparts in the *agreste* predispose them to more radical demands?

cane to the *usinas*. In 1962, over 46 per cent of the total harvest of cane of Pernambuco was on land directly owned by *usinas*. The remaining cane was raised on the property of 2,870 *senhores de engenho* or *fornecedores* —independent cane growers who enter into contracts with nearby *usinas* for the processing of their cane.

The sugar industry in Pernambuco is now directed by forty-six *usinas*, scattered throughout the *mata*. These mills, although they may be organized as corporations, are in fact the property of particular families that constitute the economic, social, and political elite of the state. Two of the three federal senators from Pernambuco own two or more *usinas*, and one of the senators also controls the largest newspaper and radio enterprise in Pernambuco. Many *usineiros* also seem to invest heavily in industrial ventures in the South of Brazil.

While great industrialists have gained increasing power in Pernambuco, the traditional landed elite (*senhores de engenho*) have been placed in a precarious position. In effect, the *senhores de engenho* have become little more than middlemen between workers in the fields and *usinas*. They are now completely dependent upon the *usineiros* for processing their cane and selling the sugar through the Cooperativa dos Usineiros de Pernambuco. Some no longer even own their land but rent it from a *usina*. Therefore they are frightened when *usinas* such as Tiriri experiment with cooperative programs in which peasants supply them with cane directly. The implication is obvious; *senhores de engenho* may no longer be needed in the sugar industry in Pernambuco.

The overwhelming majority of the peasants of the *mata* are salaried workers on land owned either by *senhores de engenho* or directly by *usinas*. Many are *moradores:* they live in scattered areas of the cane fields in houses supplied by the landowner. At times they receive the right to use the land surrounding their house for subsistence crops, but some do not. It should be noted that the land given to *moradores* for their own use is generally of very poor quality, and that no permanent crops or improvements are allowed by most landlords in order to avoid the payment of indemnity if the *morador* is discharged. Each *morador* has been required in the past to furnish the *patrão*, as payment for his house and perhaps for his subsistence plot, a certain amount of labor (usually three days a week) at a very low wage. He has then been paid a higher wage for any additional work provided. The Rural Labor Law of March, 1963, altered those arrangements in law if not always in fact. The rural worker is now to be paid a minimum wage for all days worked, and the *patrão* is allowed to deduct up to 20 per cent of his total wages as payment for his house as well as to make deductions for furnishing a subsistence plot. At times, *moradores* receive medical service or other forms of aid from their employers.

Two other kinds of salaried workers may be found in the *mata*. One of those does not live on the property of the *patrão*, nor does he receive any benefits such as medical assistance. He goes to the field every day from his home in one of the small towns scattered throughout the *mata*. A second kind of salaried worker migrates to the *mata* during the harvest season from the *agreste* or the *sertão* and lives during that period in barracks (often the old slave quarters of *engenhos*) provided by his employer. Both kinds of worker are as subject as the *morador* to several common abuses. One is the payment of wages in *vales*, or IOU's, which can often be redeemed only at the *barracão*—a kind of "company store" where prices are likely to be as much as two times higher than those found in the market place. A second abuse is simply the refusal to pay workers the minimum wage established for each zone of the state.

Despite the high density of population in the *mata* and the large labor forces required to harvest cane, there seems to be little evidence that any cooperative spirit has developed among the *moradores* and salaried workers of the region. The situation seems similar to that of Bahian cacao plantations described by Semenzato in the CIDA study of Brazil: "All in all, it does not seem to us that there exists among the workers a deeper solidarity nor a feeling for mutual aid." He notes "a certain individualistic attitude" which may be explained by the continuous turnover of men and the complete paternalism of the plantation.[13]

Uncertainty and instability are characteristic of the sugar industry. When world sugar prices are high, cane is planted on every available piece of land in the *mata*. The *morador* on land owned by *usineiros* or *senhores de engenho* may find that even the half-hectare formerly allotted him for subsistence crops is withdrawn by the *patrão* to be planted in cane. Conversely, if world sugar prices are low, *moradores* may be allowed to have a larger subsistence plot or to rent land from the *patrão*. Such was the case in Pernambuco during World War II. Correia de Andrade describes a situation in which "*engenhos*, divided into a large number of small establishments, became famous for the supply [of food] to continuously growing cities, which consumed the production of the small plots and made possible the development of a small rural middle class in the countryside." [14] At the end of the war, however, sugar prices

[13] Inter-American Committee for Agricultural Development (CIDA), *Land Tenure Conditions and Socio-economic Development of the Agricultural Sector: Brazil* (Washington, D.C.: Pan American Union, 1966), p. 256.

[14] Correia de Andrade, *op. cit.*, p. 108.

rose and *senhores de engenho* withdrew the privilege of renting land in order to plant cane on every available hectare. It was precisely such an attempt to withdraw land from renters which prompted the establishment of the first peasant league in the Engenho Galileia of Vitoria de Santo Antão in 1955.

Another consideration promotes uncertainty among elites as well as peasants in the sugar region of Pernambuco. The Northeastern sugar industry has experienced a long decline in its competitive position both within Brazil and on the world market. The sugar industry of the Northeast is more than 400 years old and for that reason alone suffers certain disabilities when it must deal with competitors in São Paulo established only thirty years ago. The machinery in many of the *usinas* of Pernambuco is old. Profits which should have been reinvested by *usineiros* of the state have often found their way into other industries instead. The Northeast is also hindered by tired soil and very hilly terrain. Unlike the São Paulo region, Pernambuco finds it very difficult to mechanize the planting or harvesting of cane. Therefore, while the cost of labor represents only 40 per cent of the total cost of producing a ton of cane in the South, the figure for the Northeast is more than 80 per cent.[15]

For many years, the Brazilian government has tried to protect the *usinas* and *engenhos* of the Northeast by charging a tax on each sack of sugar produced in the South. The price of sugar is in that way kept uniform throughout Brazil. This program is implemented by the Sugar and Alcohol Institute (Instituto do Açúcar e do Álcool, or IAA), which exercises complete control over the internal sale and export of sugar through a complicated system of regional quotas. The Brazilian government explains its protection of the sugar industries of the Northeast as an attempt to diminish the regional disparities within the nation and as a stopgap measure against unemployment and social unrest in the Northeast. Nevertheless, southern sugar producers are increasingly unwilling to pay the special taxes demanded of them in order to subsidize their less efficient competitors. It is a fact often stressed by those with an interest in agrarian reform in Pernambuco that only one-fourth of the *usinas* of the state could continue to operate if current governmental subsidies were withdrawn.

Goals and Ideology

It has been suggested above that the social structure of the sugar zone of Pernambuco is in the process of change from an almost feudal relationship between *senhores de engenho* and *moradores* to a modern capitalist

---

[15] Figures obtained from the Instituto do Açúcar e do Álcool.

system based upon the supply of cane to large industrial complexes using salaried labor in the fields. The roles performed by the elite are not yet well differentiated. There is no doubt that the economic elite (large landowners, whether *usineiros* or *senhores de engenho*) also control the politics and, to a lesser degree, the judicial system of the state. In some cases they also control local priests. It should be pointed out, however, that the Catholic Church and the federal government of Brazil, as institutions, do not participate to a marked degree in the economic sector of Pernambucan society. Neither owns large amounts of land, and both are rather clearly independent of the direct control of landholders in the state.

This complex blending of feudal and modern patterns in the society of the *mata* is perhaps one reason why the goals of the peasant movement there were both very specific and very diffuse. Another more readily apparent reason for the mixture of concrete proposals and vague, expressive demands was the nature of the Pernambucan peasant leaders themselves. A number of groups were active in promoting peasant organization: the Catholic Church, the followers of Francisco Julião, members of the Chinese- and Russian-oriented Brazilian Communist Parties, a few Trotskyites, and representatives of the state government of Miguel Arraes and the national government of João Goulart. Each group had its own explanation for the causes of peasant misery and its own plan for the construction of a new society. Ideology therefore played an important part in the stated goals of various groups that at the same time pursued concrete and highly practical goals.

The most basic goal of all groups was identical. As Julião put it in 1962, the greatest problem faced by any peasant organizer was that the *camponês* (peasant) did "not act like a human being, but like a vegetable. . . . The great task which we undertake is to make him live life like a human being." [16] That goal—to *awaken* peasants, to make them aware of their own possibilities—was also shared by Catholic leaders and Communists. Differences among groups arose primarily over the means by which the goal could best be attained and to some extent perhaps over the kind of society in which an "awakened" peasant class would live, but not over the issue of making the peasant into a "human being."

The goal implied profound changes; it was a challenge to the whole sugar society of Pernambuco. An "awakened" peasantry would have weakened the control of the landed elite in the economic and political sectors as well as in the judicial system. [17] It would have meant raising the

[16] Julião, *op. cit.*, p. 9.
[17] It should be noted, however, that a challenge to the landed elites was far more likely to hurt the *senhores de engenho* than the *usineiros*. The political and economic

status of peasants in all sectors of society—giving them dignity, not just better wages. Implicitly, then, all peasant organizers in Pernambuco thought in terms of goals which were both extensive and profound.

Explicitly, the demands of some groups were presented in language which made clearer reference to the depth of change desired than those of other groups. A small band of Trotskyites, with headquarters in the northern *município* of També, issued the most explicit denunciations of the existing social system. Their newspaper, *Frente Operário*, published in São Paulo, spoke of the need for a popular tribunal to try those associated with "capitalism and the latifundio." [18]

The demands of Communist and *liga* leaders were presented in a declaration drawn up after the Belo Horizonte Conference of 1961: "It is more and more urgent and imperative that an agrarian reform be realized which will radically modify the existing structure of our agrarian economy and the existing social relations in the countryside." They demanded "the most complete liquidation of the monopoly of land . . . and the consequent establishment of free and easy access to land by those who want to work it." [19] The leaders of the Church-sponsored *sindicatos* at the highest level also insisted on the need for "agrarian reform," but they did not phrase their demand in terms of class struggle.

The question of what specific kind of agrarian reform each group had in mind is not easily answered. The Declaration of Belo Horizonte, for example, stated only that Communist and *liga* organizers foresaw the holding of land "in individual or associated form, or through state-owned property." [20] The Church probably foresaw the establishment of peasant cooperatives which would supply cane to *usinas*—also operating as cooperatives after expropriation by the government.[21] No group seems to have had a clear blueprint for a functioning agrarian reform program. This is not difficult to understand, given the complexity of the problems faced in the *mata*.

Aside from rather vague demands for structural change of the sugar society, all peasant organizers in Pernambuco (with the exception of the Trotskyite faction) presented a series of specific demands. Most of those were limited to changes in the economic sector, although some also involved concessions in the political sphere. It is interesting to note that, despite the obvious ideological differences of Church and Communist

---

power of the former would have been seriously curtailed by eliminating their control over land. The power of *usineiros*, on the other hand, seems to be based on manufacturing interests as well as land.

[18] Sept. 16, 1963.   [19] Julião, *op. cit.*, p. 91.   [20] *Ibid.*, p. 93.
[21] *A Hora* (Pôrto Alegre, Rio Grande do Sul) June 15, 1963.

leaders, all of them agreed on the need for certain immediate improvements in the peasants' lot. Their common goals were undoubtedly dictated by confrontation with similar problems and can be briefly summarized: (1) an increase in the minimum wage of salaried workers; (2) an area-wide collective contract between rural syndicates and representatives of *fornecedores* and *usineiros;* (3) agreements on *tarefas,* or the amount of work to be accomplished in one day by any worker in the sugar zone; (4) the extension of social security to rural workers; (5) a *salário família* by which each child of a rural worker under fourteen years of age would receive 5 per cent of the minimum wage from the *proprietário;* (6) a thirteenth-month bonus every year; and a weekly day of rest and certain holidays; (7) a system of *carteiras profissionais,* or personal work records of each rural laborer, to be verified by the landowner; (8) the election of a delegate from each *engenho* to represent the interests of his fellow workers in the *sindicato rural;* the delegate was to be immune from discharge without trial; (9) the recognition of existing rural syndicates by the national Ministry of Labor; (10) the abolition of *cambão;* (11) guarantee of the right to rent land at a just price and to enjoy stability of tenure; (12) the improvement of technical services and educational facilities; (13) the extension of the right to vote to illiterates; (14) modification of the Constitution to allow indemnization for expropriated land in bonds rather than cash; (15) the encouragement of cooperatives; and (16) the carrying out of an accurate census and cadastral survey, as well as the formulation of a national plan for the encouragement of agricultural production.

These goals were presented by the leaders of various groups active in organizing the peasantry of Pernambuco. The extent of peasant participation in the formulation of those demands is unclear. Similarly, it is difficult to know how well the majority of the peasants of the state, and particularly of the *mata,* understood the programs outlined by their leaders. It does seem clear that few peasants understood the ideological differences between, say, the Church and the *ligas.* Peasants often participated in the activities of several groups at the same time.[22] And in many cases, they may have agreed with one *liga* member interviewed in Paraiba during the CIDA study of 1963: "We don't know what to do. One becomes crazy: one [person] says [we] must pay the landlord, the other [says we] must pay the judge, the third [says] not to pay it at all because land reform is coming and everyone will have some land. . . . It does not matter if we pay rent or work one day a week, but we'd like to have a solution." [23]

[22] This observation is based on field interviews.   [23] CIDA, *op. cit.,* p. 240.

Leadership

The highest leadership of all factions involved in the Pernambucan movement came from outside the peasant class. Francisco Julião, for example, was the son of a *senhor de engenho*, a lawyer and state deputy. The leaders of the Church-sponsored efforts were Padres Crespo and Melo,[24] assisted by a group of lawyers who worked with the Federation of Rural Workers of Pernambuco. The Trotskyite group was led by a twenty-three-year-old Uruguayan student. Communist efforts were directed by men like Gregorio Bezerra who, at the age of sixty-three, had long experience in organizational drives for the Brazilian Communist party. And the interests of both the state and national governments were represented by professional labor organizers, one of whom was also a member of the Moscow-oriented Brazilian Communist party.

These leaders were aided on a lower level by students, who seem to have played an important role in the orientation of local peasant groups. Segments of the Catholic University Youth and Catholic Agrarian Youth movements (generally known as JUC and JAC) worked with the Serviço de Orientação Rural (SORPE) of Padres Crespo and Melo. And the Pernambucan affiliate of the government-controlled National Students' Union seems to have contributed volunteers for organizing drives of both the *ligas* and the Communist party of Brazil.

It was the policy of all groups to encourage peasant leadership at the local level. The direction of unions by members themselves was particularly stressed by the Church, which had, from the founding of the Serviço de Orientação Rural in 1961, conducted leadership training courses for members of its rural unions. The directorate of the Church-sponsored Federation of Rural Workers of Pernambuco was in fact entirely composed of peasants.

The local leadership of the *ligas* seemed to vary. Some presidents were peasants, a few were rather large landowners,[25] and one—the leader of the largest *liga*, in Goiana—was a fisherman. Carneiro, writing about the *ligas* in the neighboring state of Paraiba, reported that most of the original leaders there had experience in urban labor organizations but that later leaders were peasants.[26]

---

[24] Padre Melo is also the son of a *senhor de engenho*.

[25] Three such incidences have been recorded: one in Buique, one in Cortês (where the president of the Liga had 320 hectares of land), and one in Sapé, Paraiba (where the president owned 50 hectares). See Callado, *Os industriais*, p. 50, and CIDA, *ob. cit.*, p. 313.   [26] CIDA, *op. cit.*, p. 312.

The leadership of communist unions remains something of a mystery. The president of the enormous Palmares union (including 21 *municípios*) was apparently a peasant who was once an active member of the *ligas* and had visited Cuba with Julião.[27] The president of the Barreiros organization, on the other hand, was Julio Santana, once described by Callado as "a mixture of political leader and bandit . . . an anarchist of the first class." [28] Whatever the exact number of peasants in positions of leadership may have been within any of the factions competing for control of the Pernambucan movement, however, it seems likely that they depended quite heavily on the advice and orientation of nonpeasants.

Tactics

Organization and Alliances

There was a wide difference in the tactics which various groups said they were willing to employ in promoting socioeconomic change in Pernambuco during the period 1961–1964. However, a closer examination of the actual methods used by each faction discloses marked similarities of approach to the problems at hand. It is quite possible that if the movement had been allowed to continue longer, increasingly radical methods would have been used; and some groups might then have distinguished themselves from others by completely rejecting those methods. It is unlikely, for instance, that many Church-sponsored organizations would have participated in the guerrilla war for which Julião was apparently preparing.[29] During the short life of the movement, however, various groups distinguished themselves less by absolute differences in tactics than by relative preferences for one means over another.

The most basic question of tactics within the movement was the form of organization to be adopted by each group. Was it better, for instance, to include many kinds of peasants—sharecroppers, salaried workers, renters—within the same organization, or should they be kept separate? Julião first thought in terms of organizing sharecroppers, tenants, and small farmers, but not salaried workers in the sugar zone. He later changed his mind, however, and entered the struggle for control of unions of salaried workers. The Church, on the other hand, had from the beginning included all kinds of peasants within its rural unions. And

---

[27] Wilkie, *op. cit.*, p. 12.   [28] *Tempo de Arraes*, pp. 97–98.
[29] Both Callado, *Tempo de Arraes*, p. 19, and Wilkie, *op. cit.*, p. 14, report that Julião believed in the necessity for guerrilla warfare in the Northeast.

Communist Party organizers seem to have concentrated solely on the organization of salaried workers in the *mata*. They gave as their reason for refusing to join the Federation of Rural Workers of Pernambuco (sponsored by the Church) the fact that it erred in representing more than one group of peasants.[30]

It was also necessary to decide which form of organization would be most effective. Julião's reasons for originally choosing to establish agrarian societies, or *ligas camponesas*, have already been explained, as well as the fact that his premises were sound in 1955 but less so after the Goulart government began to take a protective interest in the rural labor movement.

Catholic priests decided in 1961 to challenge Julião's leadership of the peasants through the establishment of a different kind of organization— rural labor unions, rather than agrarian societies. The advantages of the Church's choice became obvious as time passed. Unlike agrarian societies, the unions, combined under labor law into the Federation of Rural Workers, had the right to strike and to negotiate collective contracts with *senhores de engenho* and *usineiros*. Unions also received substantial funds after March, 1963, which were required by law to be discounted from rural workers' wages.

It is not surprising, therefore, that both Julião and the Communist Party organizers had decided by the end of 1962 to compete with the Church in the establishment of unions of rural workers. And since Brazilian labor law allows only one legally recognized union in each local administrative unit (*município*) of the state, that choice meant the initiation of struggles among various groups for the control of the single union in each *município*. The competition was increasingly bitter. The *liga* faction demolished the headquarters of the Church union in Pesqueira. A representative of the Goulart government assisted in the overthrow of the president of the Barreiros union, controlled by the *ligas* (the *liga* president had himself just gained his position after mobilizing a demonstration of 8,000 peasants against the former president of the union). The directorate of the union in Jaboatão, home of Father Crespo, was changed by a representative of Goulart despite a court order forbidding the action. A long list of clashes among competing groups would not be difficult to compile.

The peasant movement of Pernambuco thus consisted, after early 1963, of a series of temporary alliances among competing groups of organizers. The state government of Miguel Arraes worked with a representative of

[30] Wilkie, *op. cit.*, p. 12.

João Goulart, and both offered assistance to the *ligas* and communist unions. Funds from the union discount, for example, were generally channeled through communist and *liga* organizations, not through Church-sponsored groups. Similarly, funds provided by the federal government for the rural unionization drive of the newly established Superintendência da Reforma Agrária (SUPRA) were given to the former, not the latter.

Nevertheless, it would be wrong to assume that the *ligas*, the communist unions, and representatives of the state and federal governments always supported each other. A reporter from *Política Operária*, a publication of the Brazilian Communist party, described relations between Julião and the PCB as follows: "Initially, the Communist Party attempted to play a double role: on the one hand it founded its own associations that remained totally under its control, and, on the other, infiltrated elements into the work of the Leagues, hoping to bring them under their guidance. Nevertheless, quarrels and disputes were inevitable and, in general, what occurred was a division of the waters in most states." [31] Julião reportedly feared that Goulart, who supported the communist unions in Pernambuco, wanted to make him nothing more than a subordinate: as a member of the Chinese-oriented PC do B put it, "Julião has a fear of becoming a mere 'staff' member." [32]

Governor Miguel Arraes seems to have made a serious effort to promote the development of the Pernambucan peasant movement by supporting the *ligas* and the communist unions while not completely estranging some factions of the Catholic Church. Julião said of his relationship with the Governor: "Regarding my view of Arraes, it is one of support, although not unconditional, because he, like all human beings, makes mistakes at times." [33] After the coup of April 1, 1964, the Fourth Army in Recife reported that the Arraes government gave the largest *liga* in Pernambuco (Goiana) more than 80 million cruzeiros in 1963. Nevertheless, some *liga* officers criticized Arraes for trying to serve the Communist party and the bourgeoisie at the same time.[34]

According to Callado, Gregorio Bezerra—the organizer of the largest communist union in Pernambuco (Palmares)—"had nothing but praise for Arraes." [35] And Father Crespo sent the following telegram to the governor in February, 1964: [36]

[31] Robert E. Price, *Rural Unionization in Brazil* (Madison: University of Wisconsin Land Tenure Center, Aug., 1964), p. 46.

[32] *Ibid.* Callado also noted the same fear in *Tempo de Arraes*, p. 60.

[33] *Última Hora*, Dec. 1, 1963.   [34] *Diário de Pernambuco*, Dec. 12, 1963.

[35] Callado, *Tempo de Arraes*, p. 78.   [36] *Última Hora*, Feb. 2, 1964.

First year of your government positive. Congratulations. I wish you new gains in benefit of the people of Pernambuco, especially for the socio-economic liberation of the tillers of land (*agricultores*). Man of the *agreste* and the *sertão* still completely unaided. Lacks all agricultural production on a rational basis. We trust in the Government of Pernambuco for the solution of these problems. Count on the collaboration of this humble Pernambucan, for the real benefit of the people.

Goulart, on the other hand, seems to have been worried that Arraes would use the support of various factions in the movement to build independent political support. Callado notes that "Jango [Goulart] presented . . . more opposition to Arraes than to Lacerda, for fear of Arraes' influence in the circles of the left." [37]

As the movement gained momentum, splits were definitely visible within the Church. Father Crespo of the Serviço de Orientacação Rural (SORPE) was willing to continue an attempt at collaboration with Arraes long after Father Melo had denounced the Governor. Also, by late 1963 part of the directorate of the Church-sponsored Federation of Rural Workers of Pernambuco had joined Ação Popular, a movement which described itself as "an ideological political group of revolutionary action which proposes, side by side with other forces of the left, to radically modify the economic, political, and social structure of the country." [38] Finally, strains were visible between the Church-sponsored Movimento de Educação de Base (MEB), which was associated with Ação Popular, and less leftist segments of the Church.

The complexity of the system of alliances and enmities within the Pernambucan peasant movement was heightened by the fact that policies established at the highest levels of various organizations might not always be carried out on the local level. A whole subsystem of alliances seems to have existed. In Pesqueira, for example, the treasurer of the Church-sponsored union was also the president of the *liga*. And the Church-sponsored Escada union "maintain [ed] friendly relations with the independent [i.e., communist] syndicates and the Peasant Leagues, sometimes acting in conjunction with these latter as opposed to the Federation." [39] The law that allows only one union in each *município* forced priests and rival groups to work together at times. And more basically, many antagonistic groups seem to have worked together because each believed that it could win in the end. As Father Caricio of Quipapá put it, "If the situation of

[37] *Tempo de Arraes*, p. 154. [38] *Última Hora*, Feb. 2, 1964.
[39] Wilkie, *op. cit.*, p. 10.

the peasants continues to improve as it is now, they [the peasants] won't follow the Communist Party." [40]

Alliances across class lines also existed. By March 4, 1964, a General Strike Command had been formed in Recife by the *ligas,* the communist syndicates, some factions of the Church-sponsored movement, the state students' union, and several urban workers' unions. A union of urban and rural labor had always been the goal of the communist groups, supported by the Goulart government. Father Crespo's view was printed in the *Diario de Pernambuco* on August 14, 1963: "Peasants should be led by peasants. I don't believe that the worker of the city understands or can integrate himself into the dynamics of the agrarian problem."

Teaching, Agitation, and Negotiation

One of the principal means used by every faction of the peasant movement to strengthen its organization was instruction. This approach is well illustrated in Julião's open letter to peasants in 1961: "Listen to what I tell you: the person who needs to change, *camponês,* is you. . . . I will teach you the roads [to change]." [41] In simple language, Julião then explained that the most basic enemy of all peasants is fear and that fear can be conquered through unity. The same message was presented at meetings of communist unions. Callado recorded a talk given by Gregorio Bezerra at Palmares: "All of you now have two families: your own family and a collective one, which is the union." [42] SORPE, directed by Padre Crespo, also conducted a large number of discussion sessions among union members, using dialogue to make the peasants aware of their collective strength.

The line between teaching and agitation was not always clear, nor could it be. The Church, nevertheless, specifically intended to do the former and Julião the latter. In ¿*Qué son las Ligas Campesinas?*, Julião stated:

the only title which we desire to receive, if we deserve it, is that of simple social agitator—in the patriotic sense of placing before the people a fundamental problem for frank debate and the encounter of an adequate solution. . . . [T]he best way to reach the proper goal will not be dictated by us, but by the people, the mass, rich in teachings, inexhaustible in wisdom accumulated over generations. [43]

It was that philosophy which led the Church and many other observers to conclude that Julião intended only to "awaken" the peasantry without

[40] Callado, *Tempo de Arraes,* p. 74.   [41] Julião, *op. cit.,* pp. 75, 78.
[42] *Tempo de Arraes,* p. 77.   [43] *Op. cit.,* pp. 7, 8.

taking any responsibility for organizing it so that concrete gains could be won. Julião himself reinforced that impression when he commented to Antônio Callado in 1963: "Oh, Callado! Agitating is a joy. It's organizing that's so difficult." [44]

Julião used flamboyant speeches and peasant demonstrations to impress landowners with the need for change. He championed "radical agrarian reform, with the Law or with the masses. With flowers or with blood." [45] And he told newsmen (in 1959), "If I should have the idea to burn rural land, I guarantee that there would not be one remaining cane field in Pernambuco. I am able to eliminate them all within twenty-four hours." [46] To prove his strength, Julião led various marches of peasants on the state assembly building in Recife.

The Church, represented by Padre Crespo's SORPE, specifically entered the field of peasant organization in order to counteract what it considered to be irresponsibility on the part of the *ligas camponesas*. SORPE's program originally included the establishment of cooperatives, responsible negotiation with landowners, and a period of intensive training for peasants who would become leaders of Church-sponsored unions. Wilkie reports the advice of Federation lawyers to members of Church-sponsored unions as follows:

Now about strikes, if there is trouble on a plantation you must tell the syndicate delegate there. He must then discuss the matter with the employer and see if between them they can resolve the difficulty. If they can't, then the delegate comes to the syndicate to tell the president, and the president goes to the plantation to discuss the problem with the employer. If they fail to reach agreement, then the president can order a strike, only he. You mustn't stop work for any little reason, only after an attempt by the president to reach agreement, and only if this attempt fails can you strike.[47]

It is interesting to note, however, that, although the Church always stressed the importance of negotiation more than any of the other factions in the movement, the tactics of Church-sponsored groups became more "expressive" as time passed. When representatives of the Goulart government intervened in the union of Father Crespo's parish, Jaboatão, peasants loyal to Crespo staged an impressive march on Recife and were turned back by state police at the entrance of the city. Similarly, it was the Church-sponsored Federation of Rural Workers of Pernambuco which initiated a massive strike of all workers in the sugar fields of the *mata* in

[44] Callado, *Tempo de Arraes*, p. 58. [45] *Op. cit.*, p. 53.
[46] Callado, *Os industriais*, p. 104. [47] *Op. cit.*, p. 9.

October, 1963. And even SORPE's careful plans for the training of peasant leaders had to be virtually discarded after the race among competing factions for the control of rural unions throughout the state made a long training period an impossible luxury.

The increasingly "expressive" nature of the tactics employed by Church-sponsored groups can be explained in several ways. First, the nature of the political system with which the entire peasant movement had to deal probably forced such a trend. Marches and demonstrations in front of public buildings were a much more effective way of articulating demands than attempting to work through a party system which was notoriously lacking in vigor or organization. Second, *senhores de engenho* and *usineiros* proved over and over again that they were more likely to concede to groups which threatened than to groups which negotiated. (Church-sponsored unions in several *municípios* suffered when landowners broke contracts negotiated with them but yielded to threats of violence by a *liga*.) And finally, the leaders of SORPE were not always able to determine the tactics which would be used by individual union presidents.

The Pernambucan movement was, then, above all agitational. But it should not be forgotten that negotiation was never renounced by any group, including the *ligas* and the communist unions.[48] It is conceivable, of course, that some factions might have chosen to refuse to negotiate at a future date. But within the period under discussion, the *ligas* and communist unions joined the Church-sponsored Federation in a strike which was ended with the signing of a collective contract containing not a single demagogic phrase. The provisions of that contract are discussed below. It should also be noted that all groups engaged in organizing the peasantry of the *mata* made an effort to provide medical and dental services, as well as juridical assistance, for their members.

Success and Failure

The question of the success or failure of the Pernambucan rural labor movement must be considered in two parts: first, the extent of gains won for (and in some cases by) peasants before the military coup of April, 1964, as well as the relative strength of each faction in the movement before that time; and second, the condition of the movement after the coup.

[48] Negotiation was renounced by the Trotskyites, but they were jailed by Arraes in October, 1963. Callado called them the "mosquitoes of the revolution."

Before the Coup

There can be no doubt that throughout the period before the coup, a very large part of the resources of each faction—Church, *ligas,* and Communists—had to be devoted to maintaining that faction against attacks by other groups of organizers. It may, in fact, be stated that peasant leaders often fought other leaders within the movement at least as vigorously as they fought the landlords. That situation obviously lessened the number of gains which could be won from landowners for the peasants.

By April, 1964, however, the movement seemed to be on the way to unification under the control of organizers of the Communist Party, supported monetarily and legally by Goulart. The original leadership of the Church-sponsored Federation of Rural Workers of Pernambuco had joined Ação Popular and formed alliances in October, 1963, with Goulart and the communists at the convention in Rio de Janeiro which founded a national confederation of agricultural workers (CONTAG). In addition, the Church was weakened by Goulart's decision in late 1963 to divide the Federation into three parts: one for salaried workers, one for sharecroppers, and one for small farmers. The salaried workers of the *mata* provided most of the monetary resources of the Federation, but the small farmers and sharecroppers of the *agreste* furnished the voting strength necessary to keep the Federation under Church control. Therefore when the Federation was divided, the Church lost substantial ground to Goulart and the communist unions of the *mata.*

Similarly, the strength of the *ligas* was declining by the time of the coup. Several scandals were uncovered within the state leadership of the organization and were, of course, exploited by rivals. In addition, Julião was elected to the federal House of Deputies in 1962 and seems to have spent an increasing amount of time in Brasilia. The *ligas* suffered from his absence.[49]

If unification of the movement is chosen as a criterion of success, then the rural labor movement of Pernambuco was very close to it in March, 1964. If, however, success is judged on the basis of the independence of peasant organizations from governmental control, the Pernambucan peasant movement was increasingly less successful as time passed. The Goulart government commanded both the monetary and the legal resources to inhibit independent action within the rural labor movement and to force

[49] This impression was gained both from interviews in Pernambuco and from comments by Callado in *Tempo de Arraes,* p. 59.

unions into a national confederation fully controlled by the government.

The salaried workers of the sugar region received important benefits during the course of the movement. Most of those gains were granted by Goulart with little participation in their formulation by peasant leaders.[50] The fact that they were gifts from above, not projects worked out from below, does not, however, negate the value of those gains to rural workers. And it is certainly obvious that once benefits were extended by the national government to the peasants, the existence of peasant organizations made it easier for the government to enforce its program against the opposition of large landholders.

The following decrees and laws were promulgated between 1962 and the coup of 1964: payment of the thirteenth-month bonus was made mandatory in December, 1962; social security was extended to rural workers by a decree of November, 1963; and the Rural Labor Law, first presented to the Brazilian congress by Fernando Ferrari in 1951, was finally passed on March 2, 1963. Included in the Estatuto are the guarantee of a weekly day of rest and payment for certain holidays; the establishment of *carteiras profissionais,* or work records; the creation of the *impôsto sindical,* or payment of the equivalent of one day's wages per worker per year by each employer to the government, to be divided among various welfare funds, the national confederation of agricultural workers, and state labor federations; and the guarantee of stability to rural workers who have served the same employer for more than ten years, unless it can be proved at a trial that a particular worker has been guilty of serious misconduct. Landowners employing more than fifty working families are also to provide a school for children of their workers, and the allowable deduction by landowners who furnish a house to their workers is limited to 20 per cent of the minimum wage.

In addition to the benefits received by rural workers from the laws and decrees of the national government, peasants of the *mata* of Pernambuco gained concessions from landowners by means of a general strike in November, 1963. During October, the Church-sponsored Federation of Rural Workers began a drive to increase the minimum wage of rural

[50] The CIDA study quotes Caio Prado, Jr., as having said that "it is truly astounding to encounter the lack of interest for [the Rural Labor Law] revealed during the passage of the project in Congress, on the part of the political forces of the left and the progressives. If they had given due attention to the potential which it contains to renovate our economic and social agrarian structure, if the debate and study of the project had been more prolonged, it would have avoided the grave defects which the law unfortunately contains" (CIDA, *op. cit.,* p. 308).

workers by 80 per cent. The Federation also demanded a collective contract with employers and fulfillment of the obligations imposed by the labor law. The president of the Federation, who by that time had become associated with Ação Popular, issued an invitation to the *ligas* and the communist unions to join the campaign, because "only if we are united can we defeat the forces of reaction." [51]

After a month of fruitless negotiation among representatives of the workers, the *senhores de engenho*, and *usineiros*, a general strike of salaried workers in the *mata* began on November 18, 1963. More than 90 per cent of the sugar industry of the state was paralyzed, at an alleged loss of a billion cruzeiros (roughly a million and a half dollars) per day.[52] The strike lasted only three days, and ended with the promise of the employers to increase the minimum wage by 80 per cent, to pay the thirteenth-month bonus, and to pay for the days of the strike. There was to be no retaliation against workers who participated in the strike. The agreement was signed with the understanding that the compliance of the *usineiros* with their promises to rural workers depended upon the agreement of the Instituto do Açúcar e do Álcool to raise the price of sugar. Otherwise, *usineiros* declared that they did not have the financial resources to comply with their obligations. The price of sugar was in fact soon raised.

The salaried workers of the *mata* had thus received before April, 1964, important benefits from participation in the Pernambucan peasant movement. It should be stressed, however, that sharecroppers, renters, and small farmers were not so fortunate. Their problems were different from those of salaried workers and could not be settled by a strike. They needed credit, cooperatives, security of tenure—none of which were provided by the Estatuto do Trabalhador Rural or by the collective contract of November, 1963.

One final measure of the success or failure of the Pernambucan movement before the coup must be considered: the extent to which peasants were made aware of their collective strength. The stated purpose of the leaders of all factions was, after all, to "awaken" peasants, to explain their own capabilities, and to mobilize them for action. Such a task is extremely difficult, as the fate of the Pernambucan movement illustrated. Peasants were without doubt "awakened" and they were mobilized in support of various leaders. There was apparently not sufficient time, however, to develop independent initiative among them. When their leaders were

[51] *Última Hora*, Oct. 24, 1963.
[52] The Statistical Yearbook of the United Nations for 1964, p. 553, gives the average free rate of exchange of the Brazilian cruzeiro in 1963 as 620 to the dollar.

jailed or exiled or restrained in more subtle ways after the coup, the Pernambucan peasant movement collapsed.

After the Coup

Despite pronouncements by the new military government that no arbitrary actions by landlords against peasants would be permitted and that "legitimate" rural labor unions could continue to function, the fall of the Goulart and Arraes governments was the signal for a series of acts of **vengeance on the part** of large landowners against peasants who had taken part in rural unions before the coup. April 1, 1964, also marked the end of observance by many employers of the legal gains won by peasants in the preceding two years. Very few *usinas* in 1965 were paying the stipulated minimum wage, and some were paying their workers in *vales* or IOU's. Many employers had not paid the thirteenth-month bonus, nor were they paying a weekly day of rest.

All peasant organizations except those of the Church were closed and their leaders exiled or imprisoned after the coup. Many priests were also asked to appear before military tribunals and found their ability to act severely curtailed by the new government. And the military intervened in thirty of the thirty-one unions of the *mata* (most of which had been Church-sponsored), replacing their directorates with men chosen by the regional labor delegate of the federal government.

The Federation of Rural Workers of Pernambuco continues to exist, and is advised by Padre Crespo of SORPE. Nevertheless, the strength of the organization has been severely curtailed by the military intervention and by a split between its two original founders, Padre Melo and Padre Crespo. There is no doubt that the Federation is a captive of the Brazilian governmment, no matter how repugnant that idea may be to its founders.

Despite the fact that the Federation is extremely limited in its ability to win concessions from either landlords or the government, however, the local unions affiliated with the organization do provide important services to their members. Most unions offer medical and dental services to their members, as well as legal aid. Many also conduct literacy programs. And Father Crespo's Serviço de Orientação Rural continues to carry out leadership training seminars and to promote the formation of cooperatives throughout the state. It remains to be seen whether peasants who were frightened away from rural unions by the April coup can be encouraged to regain confidence in the effectiveness of collective action.

10. Societal Opposition to Peasant Movements and Its Effects on Farm People in Latin America *

ERNEST FEDER

*United Nations Economic Commission
for Latin America*

Villain Landlords or Institutional Villainy?

For the man who ekes out a living by working for others or for the self-employed who is denied access to income and wealth-producing resources, progress consists in society's adoption of institutions which

---

* The opinions expressed here are those of the author and do not necessarily represent those of the organization with which he is connected. The material presented in this chapter is based in part on the following publications: CIDA, *Land Tenure Conditions and Socio-economic Development of the Agricultural Sector in Argentina, Brazil, Chile, Colombia, Ecuador, Guatemala and Peru,* seven individual reports published in 1965 and 1966–1967; and CIDA, *Land Tenure Conditions and Socio-economic Development of the Agricultural Sector in Seven Latin American countries,* a Regional Report with Appendices. CIDA, the Inter-American Committee for Agricultural Development, is an agency of the Alliance for Progress, composed of the Economic Commission for Latin America (United Nations), the Food and Agriculture Organization (United Nations), The Inter-American Development Bank, The Organization of American States, and the Inter-American Institute of Agricultural Sciences. The reports have been published by the Pan American Union (PAU) and are available through the PAU office in Washington, D.C. The Regional Report and Appendices carry the following PAU documentation numbers: UP-G5/058, Rev. 3, Feb., 1968 (*Regional Report*); UP-G5/058-A, April, 1966 (Appendix I, *Some General Comments on Land Tenure and Development in Latin America;* Appendix II, *The Origins of Present Tenure System;* Appendix VIII, *Peasant Organizations, Community Development and Agrarian Reform;* Appendix IX, *Changes in Land Tenure and World Markets*); UP-G5/058-B Rev., April, 1968 (Appendix IV, *Inequalities in the Distribution of Wealth, Incomes and Levels of Living*); UP-G5/058-C, March 8, 1968, (Appendix V *Agricultural Labor in a Latifundio Agriculture*); and UP-G5/058-D, March 8, 1968 (Appendix VI, *Land Use and Farming Practices in a Latifundio Agriculture*). The Regional Reports and Appendices will be published in one volume in 1969.

The reports contain the most up-to-date information, on an almost continent-wide basis, about conditions under which peasants live and work. Tables in this chapter are based on statistical information elaborated by CIDA and published in these reports. The country reports will be cited as CIDA, *op. cit.,* Country; the Regional Report will be cited as CIDA, Regional Report, *op. cit.*

allow them this access or a voice in determining their own status so that they can share more fully in the benefits which accrue to society. From this point of view, the peasants in Latin America have achieved little, if any, progress. The *latifundio* agriculture of the hemisphere is built upon, and continues to function on the basis of, the economic, social, and political weakness of the farm people.[1] Their situation is characterized by lack of bargaining power as individuals or as a group. Incomes at the subsistence level, combined with strong social and political pressures originating from the rural power elite to prevent peasants from organizing, have so far proven to be almost unsurmountable obstacles to raising individual and collective bargaining power. Traditionally, the weak position of farm people has been a by-product of a permanent rural labor surplus. This surplus now appears to be rising as, for one reason or another, despite the steady migration of peasants to the cities, less and less labor seems to be used in agriculture in the face of an ever increasing rural labor force. The small rural power elite that is the main beneficiary of the existing agricultural structure is obviously vitally interested in maintaining farm people in their weak status, even at the risk of steadily increasing conflicts. A whole set of institutions and mechanisms has been developed which seek to serve this end.

Farm people do not only face landlords, merchants, police chiefs, mayors, the military, local or national politicians, and others who defend the status quo as individuals or single agencies hostile to farm people's organizations. This would be too simple a view. On the contrary, the entire social structure seems to turn against them when they seek to exercise the freedom to organize, which seems the only way of gaining increased bargaining power under conditions of surplus labor. Peasants face an entire environment hostile to collective action. In practical terms, this results from the efforts of the rural power elite to isolate farm people from the remainder of society and to atomize their efforts. When farm people try to gain additional rights and privileges for themselves, this must be viewed as an attempt to close the gap between themselves and the outside, nonfarm world. In this sense, the "integration" of farm people into the economy implies the breakdown of the economic, political, and social barriers which have been erected to keep them in isolation.[2]

---

[1] The terms "farm people" or "peasants" include all low-income producers on nonviable farms and all hired workers in agriculture. In the seven countries studied by CIDA they numbered approximately thirteen million or 64 per cent of the active work force.

[2] Peasant movements or organizations are often criticized because they are led by "outsiders" or are subject to "outside interference." At times the activities of leaders who "have no roots in the farm communities" are used as a pretext to repress peasant

If this theory is correct it has far-reaching implications. One of these concerns the problematic role of the exceptionally "decent" as opposed to the average "harsh" landlord or local political leader elected by the landlords. It is sometimes argued that the position of farm people in *latifundio* agricultures is not entirely hopeless because not all landlords are "villains" or that not all estate owners are poor farm managers because an exceptional, progressive owner uses his land intensively for his own and the national benefit. This argument, it would seem, is no more relevant than if one were to claim that all landlords are "villains." The crucial point is not whether they are villains or not, but that a "decent" landlord can reverse his attitude and become a "villain" without incurring risks of punishment or damage to his status.[3] For example, an owner who manages part of his estate intensively, employing hundreds of workers, could dismiss his entire labor force on short notice after having decided to shift his entire estate to an extensive livestock operation and retain only a handful of cowboys.

A *latifundio* agriculture also provides that estate owners, employers of farm labor, usually will not and cannot step outside the established norms of treatment of farm people. Employer-worker relationships are culturally determined, and an employer would violate the "rules of the game" were he to treat his workers in a manner which would deviate fundamentally from the accepted pattern. He would bring upon himself the scorn of his fellow landlords. The rules are, of course, established by the landlords themselves and in the rural society with which we are dealing, the harsh landlord, with his insistence on having the rules adhered to faithfully, sets the ultimate tone in the employer-worker relationship.[4]

---

movements. But the nature of the farm problem is such that assistance from "outside" sources is crucial to bridge the gap between farm and nonfarm people.

[3] The distinctions between decent and harsh, good and bad landlords have political connotations. A Chilean employers' delegate to the International Labour Organization (I.L.O.) stated, for example, that "a clear discrimination should be made between the good and the bad agricultural employer, with a view to supporting the former and to taking energetic action against the latter" (I.L.O., International Labour Conference, Provisional Record, 49th Session, Geneva, XLIX, No. 43 [1965], 421). But if the implementation of labor legislation or land reform were to depend on the interpretation of what a good or bad landlord is—about which there could be many differences of opinion—they could hardly be carried out.

[4] This explains why the landlords' reaction as a whole to any, even the mildest, questioning of their authority tends to be violent and out of proportion to the actual challenge to this authority. In the Southern United States prior to the Civil War, the ideological support of slavery became more far-fetched and radical as the break with tradition became more inevitable (see for example Gunnar Myrdal, *An American Dilemma* [New York: Harper & Row, 1962] I, 442f.). The similarity between the slave issue and the problem of farm people in Latin America is unmistakable.

Although there may exist, on the part of the estate owners, a limited range in the quality of treatment of their workers, this is not really relevant to the problem of the structural weakness of the bargaining power of the peasantry.

The tyranny of the rules of the game was described recently in two related interviews, one with a progressive landlord (a politician) and the other with members of the *ligas camponesas* in Northeast Brazil, in conflict-ridden Sapé (Paraíba). Discussing the cheating and terrorizing of workers by their employers, the landlord stated:

the mistake of the owners is not to deign to meet the problem of the workers, but always wait until the latter make a request. They are passive. I believe that the owners must . . . meet the problems of the workers and solve them. I am a politician and I am sharp." [5]

Although many farm people are unaware of the social significance of the "villain" landlord, the politically more astute members of the *liga* were not, as the following indicates:

In Areia, the opposition [to the *ligas*] stems from the owners of the sugar and aquavit plants. They are slaveholders; the farm workers cannot claim any rights. In Itabaiana and Pilar, the family Y. represents the most backward reaction, which understands relations with the farm workers only in terms of violence and impudence. . . . [One of the Y.'s] was sentenced to prison by the Judge of Sapé . . . as one of the instigators of the death of João Pedro Teixeira [a popular labor leader]. He did not go to jail because he is a deputy. . . . The great reaction in Itabaiana began when they surrounded the home of the workers, took their membership cards and beat them up. It was an armed group led by Y. who operated the land of his family and of owner-friends. After the death of J. P. T., [one of the Y.'s] organized the Farm Owners' Association of Paraíba with other owners in order to create pressure to be acquitted and he tried thus to share his problem with the other owners. [6]

Finally it is to be noted that the institutional wall facing farm people in their search for greater bargaining power has direct effects not only on the economic, social, and political status, but also on the attitudes and values of the farm people. Having themselves become institutionalized over time, these often represent a significant internal obstacle to the processes of collective action—being, of course, also part of the total cultural pattern. The net effect, then, is that farm people have to over-

[5] CIDA, *op. cit.*, Brazil, p. 317. This and the following conversation took place in early 1963.   [6] *Ibid.*, p. 311.

come not only the external obstacles set up by the environment as formed by the power elite, but also the internal difficulties inherent in the world of the farm people themselves.

Environmental Arrangements as Disincentives to Collective Action

Rural Autocracy

One of the fundamental aspects of rural life in Latin America, which explains many of the other phenomena mentioned later, is the autocratic character of *latifundismo*, which dominates agriculture.[7] *Latifundismo* is a system of power. *Latifundios* are generally autocratic enterprises, even if the number of people working on them is small and whether the owner lives there, nearby, or far away. The owner may not be directly responsible for the day-to-day operation of the farm, which may be left to a tenant or an administrator (farm manager). But the final decisions on important issues such as what and how much to plant, or what, when, and where to sell, as well as on minor issues, rests with him. Minor matters may be those regarding the life and welfare of his workers, that is, matters which in advanced rural societies and even in industrialized sectors of less developed countries have been taken over by public authorities or are resolved through cooperative and collective action. Hence the power of the landlord extends over the farming activities, as well as over the individuals who participate in these activities, and very often even over those who are not directly affected by his farm business.[8]

What makes this power distinctive is its virtual absoluteness and vastness. An estate owner's decisions are orders. Hence the organization of a *latifundio* is not unlike that of a military organization in which the top command retains the exclusive privilege of making decisions on all matters

---

[7] In Latin America the large-scale multifamily farms (*latifundios*) alone control the bulk of the land and other resources (see CIDA, *Land Tenure Conditions and Socio-economic Development of the Agricultural Sector in Seven Latin American Countries* (Preliminary Regional Report) (CIDA UP-65/058 Rev., May, 1966 [Washington D.C.: Pan American Union] pp. 6ff.). The available statistics underestimate the concentration of farm ownership and farm wealth because they do not account for a widespread pattern of large estate owners owning more than one estate and because owners of large farms underreport the size of their properties and the value of their capital, particularly of land.

[8] In Ecuador, for example, the Indian residents of small villages surrounded by large estates have to pay tolls for the privilege of passing through the estate on their way to town or they are forced to work for the estate owners in return for other small concessions (see CIDA, *op. cit.*, Ecuador, pp. 75, 238ff., 303f.).

concerning the soldiers' activities and where delegation of power exists only within certain narrow limits—qualified always by the right to intervene, even arbitrarily.

Administrative Hierarchy and the Sociopolitical Function of Administrators

Since large estates—except when they are left idle or are devoted exclusively to livestock—normally employ many workers, their social organization is likely to be complex, sometimes with a considerable number of "layers" of workers and supervisors, each with specific functions and a range of activities on which to make decisions (except for the lowest layer of workers, who cannot make any decisions). The higher the layer, the greater, normally, is the decision-making power of its members, although this power is always narrowly circumscribed and subject to sanction by the top command. A typical traditional hacienda of 630 hectares in the sierra of Ecuador, with a dairy enterprise and cultivated crops, had, for example, the following organization in approximate order of decision-making power. At least five or six levels of authority can be distinguished in this list of positions.[9]

Administration
Owner, living outside of the country
Administrator (manager), son of the owner, living 8 months on the estate
General (including domestic) services: 5 persons
Manager-supervisor
Supervisor for livestock
Supervisor for crops
Clerk

Productive Work Force
Practicing veterinary (without degree)
12 milkers (females), mostly members of *huasipungeros'* families
12 *huasipungeros*—rural workers residing on a hacienda who have to perform
    farm work or domestic duties under feudal conditions
9 permanent workers without land
48 *yanaperos*, living in small village, obliged to work for landlord in return
    for right to use the estate's roads, water, and other installations
8 temporary workers without land
1 tractor driver

[9] *Ibid.*, p. 227.

Similarly in Chile, a large *fundo* of 235 hectares (all irrigated), was organized as follows:[10]

Administration and Auxiliary
Owner
Accountant
Administrator (manager)
2 managing supervisors
Person responsible for keys and warehouses
Night guard
Gardener
Caretaker
2 overseers

Productive Work Force
Person in charge of barn
5 workers on horseback
Herdsman
4 tractor drivers
10 workers with plots (inquilinos)
10 wage workers
3 milkers

Of particular interest is the role of the administrator (manager) of estates. Contrary to a widespread belief, he is generally not skilled and experienced, with the latest knowledge in good farming methods, but merely a worker who has been on the landlord's payroll for some years and who distinguishes himself by his thorough knowledge of local customs, which he respects, and his greater loyalty to his employer. Although he normally receives a slightly higher remuneration, he is, from the point of view of the owner, a mere low-wage worker.[11] The relevant fact is however that from the landlord's point of view the administrator is "his man."

The administrator's most decisive function lies in the day-to-day handling of the farm workers. He can assign the daily work, pay out wages, punish, fire a worker, and hire a replacement—but only within the

[10] CIDA, *op. cit.*, Chile, p. 51.

[11] For examples on the role and functions of administrators, see CIDA, *op. cit.* Brazil, pp. 150ff. The sociologist Geraldo Semenzato reports that in one case the administrator of a wealthy cacao producer received a Christmas gift in kind worth less than three dollars in 1962, which is indicative of his subordinate, but still privileged, status. The workers received no such gifts (*ibid.*, p. 152).

framework set by the landlord. This implies that decisions regarding the number or type of workers to be hired and their remuneration rest exclusively with the owner. He may receive a request for more workers from his administrator and dispose of it as he sees fit, and he may consult his fellow landlords in setting the terms of their employment without resorting to his administrator's advice.

Since practically all large farms have administrators, the workers do not normally enter into direct contact with the employer, and any complaints or sentiments the workers may harbor with respect to the treatment received or the "system" as such is first directed against the administrator.[12] The administrator is, then, their first object of respect or, more frequently, of resentment. In the sociology of rural Latin America, the interposition of administrators as a "sponge" absorbing the immediate reactions of farm people fulfills an important function: it contributes to the stabilization and fortification of the existing power structure. Since the ruling class remains, in daily life, outside of the reach of the farm people, it can appear in the constant role of moderators, even benefactors, as actual or potential conciliators when conflicts come to their personal attention directly or via their administrator. It is the latter who absorbs the blame for any harsh treatment. Hence absentee management through administrators is both a convenience for the landlord, whose main interests normally lie outside agriculture and whose incomes from nonfarm sources often exceed his farm income, and a method to maintain the existing power structure.

When farm workers are victims of unduly harsh treatment, the owners' ephemeral presence results in their remaining the innocent-appearing element. In Brazil, for example, the following typical case arose: A farm worker, having resided on a large estate for eleven years, had requested permission from the landlord eight years before to build a new house to replace the old leaky shed in which he lived with his family. Recently the landlord had personally allowed its construction, but had asked the worker to sign a paper according to which he (the worker) would pay

[12] The sociologist Semenzato says: "The administrator . . . is the only tie between the worker and the owner. . . . Only with difficulty, has the worker direct access to the landlord and it is necessary to maintain good relationships with the administrator who, according to the worker's conception, is the 'strong man' besides the owner" (*ibid.*, p. 155). There are exceptions. In one instance, a rich landlord, seated at a large table and accompanied by his administrative assistants, listened at regular intervals to "complaints" of his workers, with the workers standing 20 feet apart so that they could not converse. But these circumstances are rather intimidating for the workers (*ibid.*, p. 153).

for the building material but property of the building would remain with the estate owner. According to the worker's wife:

My husband accepted this. He purchased the poles and the brick and began building the house. At that time the owner was sick and left for João Pessoa [capital of Paraíba]. The administrator and the son of the owner said to my husband that he cannot build this house because the owner had not given the order. My husband continued to build. The rains came and the water came right into the house, and had already killed the youngest son who could not stand the cold. Then I saw many people, the administrator, the son of the owner and his friends and they tore down the framework of the house. My husband said to me that we could not do anything more. He did not have money to purchase other lumber and bricks.[13]

The opportune disappearance of the landlord seems to be a deliberate policy. In another case, a worker had been ceded a plot of land as a tenant, but was later told to look for another one, at a location which was pointed out to him:

But there was no space there. All had already been occupied by workers. . . . Since we did not find any plots, we went to Mr. P. [the owner] and asked him to continue to work the plots previously occupied by us. *He gave us permission to do so.* We went and prepared the terrain to wait for the rain and to plant. But some people went to Mr. P. with stories that we wanted to remain on that land, and that he was going to lose it. At the end of January, three days after it rained and we planted, *a son of the owner arrived and said that his father did not want to cede any more land to his workers,* that he needed it for his livestock and that the pasture was poor. We showed him our plantings and he said that it was all right and that he was going to speak with his father about withdrawing the order. At that point several capangas [privately employed strong-arm men] appeared on the scene to throw out the people by force. It was Capa de Aço and others. They began with threats. We were already ready to leave, but only on the condition that they evaluated our expenditures with respect to the work carried out, in order to receive an

---

[13] *Ibid.*, pp. 230ff. The interview took place after a violent incident in which the husband was apparently killed when a group of armed members of the *liga* clashed with a group of armed vigilantes, members of the landowners' protective association. To understand the full significance of this occurrence, it is necessary to add that the landlords in that area prohibited the construction of new homes in order to rid themselves of permanent, resident workers and shift to wage workers living off the farm. This policy in turn was a "defense" against the rightful demands of the workers, supported by the labor unions, for enforcement of legal provisions regulating the relations between employers and tenants, such as the provision that landlords should reimburse tenants for "improvements" they made during the period of the lease or for crops they had planted when the contracts were broken by the landlords.

indemnification. The capangas arrived one day, asked why so and so was planting and fired three shots, which put an end to him. Afterwards, they came to my house in order to throw me out. Capa de Aço took out a gun and pointed it at me. I said nothing but turned to one side. My wife who was expecting asked not to shoot me. Thanks to God, they became less aggressive. Shortly afterwards my wife lost her baby. Another day they returned to the house and there was a fight. They entered with a rifle and a gun and the people from here arrived with knives and sickles. Three died; Capa de Aço was cut into pieces. What we want is to pay our rent and live in peace. We only want to produce for the market and live. But they don't want to accept our rent.[14] (italics mine)

In this manner, conflicts arising out of the "class struggle" [15] in the rural society often materialize at a level well below that of the power elite and serve to strengthen the latter or—no less important—leave it unmolested.

The social structure of the estate, besides being complex, tends to be rigid. For farm people dependent upon estate owners, this can have serious consequences. An autocratic organization is well adapted to having orders from above carried out efficiently and efficiency is highest when matters procede in a routine manner. But it can be quickly diluted, in terms of the management of the farm and particularly of its people, when emergency situations or major changes arise. For example, demands of workers have little or no chance of being heard quickly by the top command so that the organization of a *latifundio* is clumsy and inflexible from the point of view of the low-level worker. This tends to aggravate discontent and precipitate social conflicts. Since administrators can solve conflicts only within a narrowly defined framework—narrowly defined both by tradition and by the owner's orders, which are in most cases synonymous—and within the basic limitations of their power, situations often arise which cannot be handled by them on the spot or can be handled only by exceeding the power vested in them. This, in turn, can result in further sharpening the tensions. The rigidity of the social organization of *latifundismo*, then, does not allow—or allows only in exceptional cases—a gradual improvement in the conditions under which the peasants live, and unless strong concessions are wrought from the power elite

[14] *Ibid.*, pp. 142f.
[15] The nature of the conflicts in rural society is in dispute. See, for example, Benno Galjart, "Class and 'Following' in Rural Brazil," *América Latina*, VII, No. 3 (1964) pp. 3ff.; Gerrit Huizer, "Some Notes on Community Development and Rural Social Research," *América Latina*, VIII, No. 3 (1965) pp. 128ff.; and Galjart's reply (*ibid.*, pp. 145ff.).

through a systematic reduction of their bargaining power, it is the peasants who are the victims of this rigidity.

The Social Gap between Estate Owners and Farm People

To this must be added what appears to be a lack of understanding by the power elite of the ambitions, desires, and aims of the peasants. This, too, is a consequence of the autocratic nature of *latifundismo*. In industrialized countries, the power elite has learned through years of experience to know the demands of the working class and even to respect them, although it may resist them. The press and literature as well as education tend to decrease the area of misunderstanding or ignorance between classes. But in Latin America, there still exists an almost unbridgeable gap between the world of the rural power elite and that of the peasants, reinforced by the elite's seemingly strong wish to perpetuate this gap. The rural elite shows great ignorance of the world of the peasant and a mental block with regard to a (for the peasants) more favorable evaluation of the peasants' living conditions. Obviously power can afford ignorance, at least in the shorter run.[16]

Ignorance seems to be matched by lack of interest. The estate owner, whether or not he is an absentee landlord, is not part of the rural community in which he owns property: in a sense, nearly every landlord is an absentee, no matter where his residence. He does not share its institutions, nor its moods and ambitions. The schools are not for his children, the homes not for his entertainment, the hospital not for his care and the roads not for his travel unless they lead to his urban residence or are useful for his pleasure. The sociologist Julio Barbosa (Brazil) stated this succinctly as follows:

Notwithstanding the partial physical participation in the social structure where their properties are located, the large property owners are characterized sociologically by the large distance from this structure, in terms of integration and effective participation. Conditioned as this social structure is by their activities, and subject to their decision, they are removed from it, as far as their inputs and outputs are concerned and to a certain extent repudiate it through their indifference and omission and by staying at its margin.[17]

The relevant implication of the dichotomy of rural society is that the power elite is probably least in a position to help solve the problems of the

---

[16] Ignorance does not mean necessarily a complete lack of knowledge. For example, landlords may "know" how many children are in their workers' families, what their incomes are, and so forth, but they do not relate these facts to standards applicable to their own conditions.   [17] CIDA, *op. cit.*, Brazil, p. 165.

campesinato. These, it would seem, have to be solved by the campesinos themselves with the assistance of those who have a fuller appreciation of the meaning of social justice. If this conclusion is correct, then a policy aimed at "enlisting the aid of the landlords" to solve the economic, social, and political problems of the farm people lacks realism.[18]

The Subsistence Level of Wages and Incomes and Its Enforcement

The autocratic nature of *latifundismo* has an important and direct bearing on the incomes earned by farm people and on the conditions under which these incomes are earned. The landed elite apparently attempts to drive the incomes of farm people towards a subsistence level through a variety of methods which have pure economic as well as sociopolitical effects. The scores of methods by which estate owners deprive peasants of the ability to earn an adequate living reveal almost a greater ingenuity in finding ways and means to shortchange them than in finding methods to put the many physical resources which are at the disposal of the landlords to better and more productive uses. Taken together they make it difficult to deny that farm people are confronted with a conscious wage-income policy on the part of the landlords. Wages and incomes do in fact remain at the subsistence level. It would seem more plausible, therefore, to seek the reason for this phenomenon in the elite's search (well-anchored in tradition) to preserve in excess supply an inexpensive and obedient labor force that has no alternative but to accept what is being offered, rather than in some natural law according to which part of humanity is always destined to live in poverty and misery. Our thesis, then, is that an iron law of subsistence wages and incomes is promulgated and enforced by the rural power elite.

Low labor returns have, in turn, a significant effect on the organizability of peasants. They are not an absolute deterrent, but in combination

---

[18] In this connection, the following remarks by Allan Holmberg about the Vicos Indian serfs are significant: "Like other subordinated groups they have worked out a feigned behavior to confound authority figures. Although possessed of an earthy sense of humor and great conversational ability, the Vicos serf forgot his picaresque good humor, his conversational sparkle and courtesy when he found himself before his patron or other Mestizos. Serfs presented themselves as the most foolish and incapable of beings" ("Some Relations between Psychobiological Deprivation and Culture Change in the Andes" [mimeo., Cornell Latin American Year, 1966], p. 8). This feigned behavior is largely attributable to fear and suspicion, a defense mechanism against the superior power of the landlords built up over centuries of harsh treatment. Landlords are also suspicious and even afraid of the peasants, although their reaction to any questioning of the daily routine is more likely to be a show of force. No need for feigned behavior in their case.

with other factors, such as unfavorable terms of employment for farm workers or severely limited possibilities for small producers to make a living on nonviable farms, they are a serious obstacle to peasant organization.

Subsistence Incomes and Peasant Organizations

The bulk of Latin American campesinos have extremely low incomes. Their economic situation is more precarious than is normally believed to be the case, and some sociologists have stated that the available statistical information is inadequate to reflect the squalor in which they live.

The analysis of their economic situation is complicated by the fact that in contrast to urban workers the campesinos may secure incomes from a variety of sources, some of which can only be imputed at arbitrary values: wages, the sale of crops, consumption of home-produced foods, and perquisites furnished by the employers (such as a home, firewood, and so forth). The imputed incomes, if there are any, normally tend to raise the total earnings, but it is important to note that given the peasants' low total income, it is the cash from the sale of crops or from wages which counts most of all. This is the consequence of the fact that even in the remotest areas in Latin America farm people need cash to buy the necessities of life and equipment for the house or for farming (and there are other reasons for the importance of cash earnings which shall be noted below). Also significant is that the total incomes from *all* sources is generally not sufficient to put the farm families beyond the subsistence level. Even if family incomes appear at a first glance to be more adequate, per capita incomes are still very low because farm families are large. (In some cases a numerous family is a prerequisite of employment, as in the case of sharecroppers—a vicious circle of poverty engendering poverty.) A few examples from scattered areas are indicative.

In the rich valley of the Cauca (Colombia), it was estimated that in one small community, on units up to 10 hectares, the average annual income of farmers from the products of the farm (exclusive of any wages earned) was less than $170.[19] In the same area, very small farms (20 per cent of all farms) averaged about $57 annually, and slightly larger farms (46 per cent of all farms), about $120.[20] In the altiplano of Guatemala, average gross product (which is a rough approximation of farm income) on *microfincas* (tiny plots which are smaller than *minifundios*) was esti-

[19] E. Feder and A. J. Posada, "Análisis socio-económico de dos zonas de recuperación de tierras en el Valle del Cauca," *Economía Colombiana* (Bogotá), Nov.-Dec. 1964.   [20] CIDA, *op. cit.*, Colombia, pp. 202ff., 371ff.

mated at $9 per capita annually and on *minifundios* at $54, excluding very small amounts from other sources. On the coast, the average incomes of *minifundios* studied was $967, but in that area the *minifundios* are much less numerous than in the altiplano. Thirty-five families of workers earned an average of $396 including perquisites, but one-half of these workers earned less than $400.[21] In Brazil in 1962, eight out of nine farmers interviewed in a community in Pernambuco on units up to 12 hectares had per capita incomes which ranged from about $ −20 to $80 per year, with four farmers showing a per capita return below $25. Ten sharecroppers' families (all large families) on four large estates in the state of Ceará earned in the same year $15 per capita excluding (or $24 including) imputed incomes. Resident workers interviewed in the famous cacao plantation area of Bahia in Brazil earned cash wages of about $75 annually, or about $100 if the rental of the house and plot on which they lived is included.[22] In Peru, in some parts of the sierra, annual per capita income of the population was estimated by a United Nations team at about $15 or $20—one of the lowest living standards of the whole world. And according to 273 case studies of producers on *minifundios*, members of indigenous communities and wage workers, average cash family incomes per year from all sources ranged from a high of $529 (coast), $269 (sierra), and $443 (selva) on *minifundios* to a low of $333, $117, and $241 in the same regions for either hired workers or other groups. The families usually had between five and six members.[23]

It can be concluded that the modal campesino family income in Latin America is the equivalent of $300 annually except in the few regions where economic opportunities and tenure conditions are unusually good. Cash family incomes are much smaller and in large portions of rural Latin America they are typically far below $100 annually. These are the incomes earned not by a few but by several million farm families. Obviously small producers and rural workers would have to work many decades, in some cases up to several hundred years, to earn the yearly income of an estate owner derived from only one of his estates (see Table 10–1).[24]

The income figures we have cited still do not fully reveal the precarious situation of farm people: many small producers and workers have a

[21] CIDA, *op. cit.*, Guatemala, pp. 85ff.

[22] CIDA, *op. cit.*, Brazil, pp. 463ff., 434ff., 408ff.   [23] CIDA, *op. cit.*, Peru, p. 274.

[24] In Guatemala, an Indian family in the altiplano living on a *microfinca* would have to work almost a millennium to earn the annual average income of a *latifundista* from his one farm (not including therefore the latter's other farm and nonfarm income).

Table 10–1. Estimated number of years needed by a producer on a *minifundio* to earn an income equivalent to that earned by a *latifundista* in one single year from one estate, in six countries *

Country	Number of years
Argentina	66
Brazil	61
Chile	72
Colombia	36
Ecuador	165
Guatemala	399

Source: CIDA, Regional Report, Appendix VI.

* Estimated on the basis of gross value of farm production per farm, as an approximate measure of income.

negative cash balance at the end of the year as the result of cash expenditures for the most urgent necessities of life, such as food, exceeding cash earnings. Their indebtedness towards employers, merchants, or moneylenders for advances made tends to be permanent. This is evidence that noncash incomes, such as those derived from little plots for subsistence crops or the perquisites given by landlords, are inadequate to provide for a sufficient level of living.[25] According to available evidence the incidence of indebtedness is high, and debts often represent a high proportion of the annual income. For example, in Brazil's famous cacao area (Bahia), the average net cash balance (i.e., indebtedness) of about a dozen typical resident wage workers on large cacao plantations was well over half of the annual cash income of about $75. Ten of these workers had a negative cash balance, and in nine cases expenditures for food alone exceeded the cash income from all sources, although in eight of these cases the worker counted on a garden plot.[26] These eight workers with garden plots had estimated cash incomes from wages and from sales of produce which were only two-thirds of their expenditures for cash food purchases, most of which are of staple foods. In the state of Ceará, ten sharecroppers also had on the average a negative cash balance (after omitting off-farm incomes

[25] Landlords often pretend that farm people do not take care of their plots and would rather be idle than grow more food for themselves. This may be correct in isolated cases. But normally workers receive plots of land on completely exhausted soils because the landlords preserve for themselves the best areas; the landlord's farm work always takes precedence and the workers' duties with respect to the employer clash with the necessity of caring for their plots; and workers receive no technical and financial assistance whatever for the management of their subsistence food crops.

[26] CIDA, *op. cit.*, Brazil, pp. 413f.

of two croppers) with two of the ten croppers having a negative cash balance and practically all of the remaining men just breaking even.[27] Their expenditures for food averaged about two-thirds of their total farm and off-farm income. In Ecuador, as in other countries in Latin America, indebtedness is "used" (that is, planned) to tie workers to the farm.[28] Here are two interesting, typical cases involving one male and one female worker:

Debts of Antonio S., in sucres		*Debts of Mariana Y., in sucres*	
Previous year's unpaid debt	237	Deceased father's debt	108
Feb. 22: barrel of ocas	25	Feb. 23: cash. adv.	23
July 16: barley	40	Feb. 28: barley	40
Note: for stealing 10 potato plants	50	May 5: cash adv.	5
		July 16: one barrel of ocas	25
		Dec. 9: cash adv.	10
		Dec. 22: cash adv.	80
Total debt	352	Total debt	291

At the going wage rate, working full-time, the yearly earnings would have been insufficient to pay off these debts and debts would be carried over from one year to the next.[29]

Obviously one can find certain variations in incomes, with some families earning more, others less. But on the whole, the range within which incomes move appears to be narrow in absolute terms and provides only for variations in poverty, not for the difference between poverty and well-being. This area has, however, been explored little until now. For example, some sharecroppers receive larger or better plots of land than others for reasons that are not always clear.[30] Or some workers earn higher wages than others. It would appear that landlords discriminate among their workers on the basis of family size, length of employment, loyalty, or obedience to traditions. If so, this would demonstrate that except where workers are hired "in bulk" (such as through labor contractors) each contract of employment is, so to speak, individualized. This does not mean that employers ignore the iron law of subsistence wages or incomes; on the contrary, it tends to show that a more or less careful

[27] *Ibid.*, p. 437. The sharecroppers selected for interview had larger plots, and hence larger incomes, than other croppers on the farms studied. In addition to the croppers there were also serfs who earned much less than sharecroppers and worked several days a week free of charge, or at sharply reduced wage rates, for the landlord.

[28] The accounts are always kept by the employer, and the workers have no way of checking their accuracy.   [29] CIDA, *op. cit.*, Ecuador, pp. 143f.

[30] See CIDA, *op. cit.*, Brazil, pp. 434f.

calculation is made in each case by the employer with respect to the quantity of work which can be obtained from a given (low) pay. This would closely resemble the calculation which employers appear to make with respect to the type or form of wage payments which, regardless of circumstances, always seem to give about the same income.

Some variation may also be caused intentionally by employers as an incentive or disincentive for other workers. Thus some employers select "pet" workers whom they pay a higher remuneration or grant special privileges. For example, in Ecuador a young member of an Indian community was assigned duties as a "veterinarian" (*practico veterinario*) on a large estate although the other Indians were all serfs;[31] in the state of Matosinhos (Brazil) a father and son cut wood in a little community, earning substantially more than other workers.[32] Or a small producer may be singled out for special treatment, as recipient of credit and advantages denied other small farmers. The selection of "pets" is no doubt often made carefully by the landlords in an attempt to raise in the other peasants greater hopes in the possibilities of advancement—a useful maneuver in the face of the stark reality which affords farm people practically no outlook for betterment.

But all these variations cannot obscure the fact that the bulk of the farm people's incomes hover around a level which just barely permits them to subsist and allows for no savings and accumulation of wealth.[33]

The precarious financial situation of the many millions of farm people, living at or near a hunger level, is a nearly unsurmountable obstacle to peasant organization. Extremely low incomes mean that farm families are often, if not normally, on the brink of having or not having adequate amounts of food to eat in the house. One small Brazilian producer, on the day he was interviewed did not have any food to eat in the house. Another declared: if there is not much food, the children eat, while the parents go hungry. Diets of 1200, 1300, 1400 calories per person per day—inadequate even in favorable tropical climates—seem to be the norm. Even if the monthly contribution to a peasant organization were to represent only one day's wage of one of the members of the worker's family, it would represent a significant item in the family's budget, because under the circumstances the financial contribution to an organiza-

[31] CIDA, *op. cit.*, Ecuador, p. 224. Slaveholders in the United States also had pet slaves.

[32] CIDA, *op. cit.*, Brazil (Summary of Country Report), p. 39 (to be published).

[33] Variations in wage rates and annual incomes are by and large not due to changes in climate (good or poor harvests) or long-run changes in productivity. Wages are always low, regardless of harvest or improvements in output.

tion can mean the difference between eating and not eating for one or several days. In many cases this sacrifice simply cannot be made. This explains why peasant organizations often originate first among small tenants or workers with a slightly higher level of income,[34] and why many peasant organizations seem to contain a large number of non-dues-paying members, so that the burden of carrying on organizational activities is shouldered by a small minority. Without outside support, therefore, peasant organizations are under great financial strain, and often too weak to survive.

Institutions Facilitating the Enforcement of the Iron Law of Subsistence Incomes

The iron law of subsistence wages and incomes could not be enforced by the estate owners unless they controlled the largest portion of the

Table 10-2. Distribution of the rural labor force by class of farm in seven Latin American countries*

Class of farm	Total labor force (in thousands)	Family labor (in thousands)	Hired labor (in thousands)	Percentage hired labor
Minifundios	5,278.5	4,427.5	851.0	16
Family	5,262.5	3,875.3	1,387.2	26
Multifamily (medium)	5,980.1	2,548.8	3,431.3	57
Multifamily (large) (*Latifundios*)	3,716.6	381.7	3,334.9	90
Total	20,237.7	11,233.3	9,004.4	44

Source: CIDA.
* Argentina, Brazil, Chile, Colombia, Ecuador, Guatemala, Peru.

available supply of rural manpower or controlled the smaller producers' and farm workers' access to agricultural resources. That this appears to be the case is borne out by the available information, although statistical data are incomplete. For example, in seven Latin American countries the large multifamily farms (*latifundios*) alone reported having about 37 per cent of all rural hired workers (see Table 10-2). Most of the remainder is accounted for by medium-sized multifamily farms. Family farms and

[34] See, for example, CIDA, *op. cit.*, Brazil, pp. 323f. (quoting Manoel Correia de Andrade, *A terra e o homem no Nordeste* [Rio de Janeiro: Editôra Brasiliense, 1963], p. 246, with respect to the *ligas camponesas*).

minifundios employ principally family labor. The 37 per cent figure is probably conservative as it does not include, for example, all the farm people living on *minifundios* who work on the estates as hired workers. The mere statistics, of course, do not reveal the full degree of control by estate owners over farm people. It must also be analyzed in qualitative terms through the examination of the institutional arrangements surrounding employer-worker relationships. Still, the figures indicate that the few large estates, by employing the bulk of the rural manpower, are in a unique position to determine wage levels and terms of employment. It is also obvious that farm workers are looking towards the multifamily farms, which control most of the farm land as their main source of employment. That this expectation is not fulfilled will be explained shortly.

On the other hand, large owners also prevent farm people's access to land (or more land) and capital and hence to larger incomes. Land is sold normally to wealthy investors in large blocks which farm people cannot afford to buy, and even if it is sold in small parcels its price is prohibitive for all but a few exceptional peasants with savings or access to credit.[35] Moreover, estate owners are themselves constantly in the market for more land in small or large units and offer effective competition to any would-be peasant-purchaser because of their financial standing. Credit and other farm inputs are also channeled to the few large landlords.[36] In many cases, the shortage of capital handicaps even those producers whose land is large enough for a fair income if it could be adequately used. Even in pioneering areas, access to land is easy only for potent urban and rural investors. The climate, the absence of roads, schools, hospitals and other facilities in addition to the expansion of the sociopolitical power structure (*latifundismo*) from the older into the new communities, prevent farm people from seeing in the public lands a promising alternative to life in their home community.

The lack of access to land for farm people is difficult to show statistically. Brazil's preliminary census of 1960 allows the tentative conclusions that between 1950 and 1960 perhaps as much as 60 per cent of the total

[35] There are a few instances in which an estate owner may sell his land to, say, his tenants (see CIDA, *op. cit.*, Brazil, pp. 95f.). In Peru some land is reported to have been sold recently to tenants, even in apparent contravention of the land reform law. Although in most of these cases sales prices are very high, some peasants are eager to own a plot of land and prefer paying exorbitant sales prices to the insecurity of being a tenant.

[36] See, for example, E. Feder, "El crédito agrícola en Chile" (Instituto de Economía, Universidad de Chile, Monograph No. 29 [Santiago, Chile, 1960]).

new farm labor force was added to the underprivileged (poor) labor force and that on the whole, the living conditions for the smaller farmers became more precarious as most of the new farm land added during the decade went into large estates and as the amount of land in smaller farms increased less rapidly than the farm population on them.[37] The lack of access to agricultural resources implies for the power elite that keeping more and more farm people in an only slightly enlarged rural ghetto serves the function of maintaining a cheap supply of manpower, which even a massive migration to urban areas has not been able to dry up.

Another institution with far-reaching effects on the bargaining position of farm people and which deprives them of higher incomes is the under-utilization of the land on large estates. It affects the aggregate incomes of farm people adversely by lowering employment. Underutilization of land is part and parcel of *latifundismo* and has two specific aspects which are but the faces of the same coin: the small proportion of land in intensive (or labor-intensive crops)[38] and the large proportion of land in extensive land uses, such as livestock, requiring almost no labor, or of land left entirely unused.[39] The tradition of underutilization of land makes present-day *latifundismo* in Latin America particularly ill-adapted to the growing employment needs of a rapidly increasing, active farm labor force.

To get an approximate idea of the impact of the predominantly extensive land uses on farm employment, the following data are considered helpful. Large estates in seven Latin American countries have consistently the smallest proportion of land in intensive uses. (Table 10–3 shows this

[37] CIDA, *op. cit.*, Brazil, pp. 392ff.

[38] Intensive land uses are not necessarily labor-intensive. For example, large coconut plantations employ relatively little labor, although they represent a fairly intensive use of the land. Intensive land uses which require relatively little labor are more predominant on large than on small farms.

[39] The underutilization of land is obvious and easily demonstrated. It comes therefore as somewhat of a surprise to discover the obstinacy with which some observers see in a few isolated cases of "well-managed farm enterprises" the rule (according to which large size and efficiency are synonymous) confirmed by the exceptions of poor farming. For example, it was recently suggested on the basis of a productivity study of 99 farms in Brazil that Brazil owes a substantial debt to those large landowners who are active in settling, developing and improving the nation's agricultural resources; that land reform should protect these landlords, and that agrarian reform should begin with a reconstruction of the Ministry of Agriculture (W. H. Nicholls and R. Miller Paiva, "The Structure and Productivity of Brazilian Agriculture," *Journal of Farm Economics*, XLVII, No. 2 [1965], 347–361). The implication of these incongruous suggestions is that Brazil's poor peasants can be saved by better estate management. It is equivalent to suggesting that the problem of slavery ought to have been solved by improving the prices and markets for slaves.

Table 10–3. Relation of intensive land use and number of farm workers to size (class) of farm, seven countries * (in million hectares and million workers)

Farm class	Cultivated land †	All farm land	Farm workers (family and hired)
Subfamily	6.3	11.4	5.3
Family	29.4	102.1	5.3
Multifamily (medium)	39.5	118.1	6.0
Latifundios	40.7	257.9	3.7
Total	115.9	489.5	20.3

Source: CIDA.

* Argentina, Brazil, Chile, Colombia, Ecuador, Guatemala, Peru.

† Cropland, artificial or improved pasture, and fallow or idle land.

for the seven nations combined). As a result they have only slightly more cultivated hectares (40.7 million) than both *minifundios* and family farms together (35.7 million), although they control about 2.3 times more land than the latter.[40] Cultivated land includes cropland, improved or artificial pasture, and idle (fallow) land. If only cropland were used, the gap would be still larger because the proportion of cropland of all cultivated land decreases with the size of the farm. In terms of employment this also means that the *minifundios* and family farms combined gave employment to almost three times more farm people than the *latifundios* with over half of all the farm land. Obviously then, intensity of land use and employment are closely related.

The extent of underemployment can be estimated in a rough manner in terms of the number of additional workers who could find "employment" on *latifundios* if the latter were farmed as intensively as, say, the family farms.[41] If this is calculated for six of the seven countries shown in Table 10–3 (omitting Peru), an enormous deficit of approximately 34.5 million potentially employable workers exists (see Table 10–4). If medium-sized multifamily farms, which in many countries are also farmed less intensively than family farms, are added, the total number of additional work-

[40] The rates vary from country to country, however. In some countries *latifundios* have less land in intensive uses than family farms.

[41] The assumption that *latifundios* can devote the same proportion of their land to intensive cropping as family farms cannot be verified without very detailed soil surveys. The assumption is not unrealistic, however, given the fact that the large estates normally control the best land. Generally speaking, there is little evidence to support the hypothesis that size of farm is inversely related to quality of land and much evidence that some of the best land on the large estate is in extensive uses or unused.

Table 10–4. Estimated employment gap for agricultural workers on *latifundios* in six Latin American countries

Country	Number of additional workers theoretically employable on *latifundios* when farmed at a level of intensity equal to that of family farms * (in thousands)
Argentina	493
Brazil	30,227
Chile	1,849
Colombia	1,669
Ecuador	57
Guatemala	212
Total	34,507

Source: CIDA.

* Intensity is measured by the proportion of cultivated land. The number of additional workers who could find employment on *latifundios* has been estimated by dividing the number of hectares of cultivated land on *latifundios* (now representing the same percentage of the total farm land as on family farms, for each country) by the ratio of cultivated land to workers on family farms, and subtracting the number of workers actually employed on the *latifundios*. This estimating procedure does not imply of course that the land/worker ratio on family farms is recommended. It is the ratio that exists at present levels of technology.

ers would rise to 49.0 million. Inasmuch as actual hired employment was only 9.2 million on all multifamily farms, employment could theoretically be expanded more than five times [42] without increasing the total area in farms.[43]

The figures in Table 10–4 are of course not presented as an accurate measure of effectively existing employment opportunities; these could be larger or smaller. But they convey the idea that if the rural labor force—which is traditionally underemployed in an agriculture carried on at low levels of technology and management—expands even at a rate which is no greater than that of the expansion of the area under cultivation, landlords

[42] It is to be noted, however, that there is an excess of workers on *minifundios* of about 3,700,000 (estimated by using the same procedure as that used in Table 10–4). It is obvious that the *latifundios* alone could easily absorb this surplus.

[43] Actually the area in farm land is expanding primarily through the incorporation of previously unsettled areas. These new areas are also farmed extensively by owners of large estates and hence do not increase employment commensurate with needs. In other words, the expansion of the frontier implies an unproportionately small increase in rural employment.

find it relatively easy to enforce the law of subsistence wages and incomes.

The effects of the underutilization of land resources are magnified by a level of farm management that results in the rapid exhaustion of soils and forces agriculture to migrate constantly in search of new farming areas or encourages estate owners to shift from intensive to extensive farming operations. The generally low level of farm management on large crop and livestock enterprises throughout Latin America is now well documented. It is all the more astounding as the large estate owners have an almost exclusive access to other farm inputs and the sources of technical knowledge. In Brazil, for example, the shift to livestock operations in older, traditional farming areas is taking place on a broad scale and some estate owners even see in it "a solution to the labor problem." Take the case of the *município* Itabuna (Bahia), one of Brazil's richest cacao plantation areas where cacao growers form the landed aristocracy, which now has the state's largest cattle population.[44] Furthermore many, if not most, large estate owners do not have a strong economic incentive to intensify the use of their land either through improving farm management or through expanding the area in crops. They derive their total incomes not only from one or many estates but also from nonagricultural sources, such as business, the professions, and domestic or foreign investments. Even at a low level of intensity of land use and soils management, their total earnings are quite adequate for comfortable levels of living and large savings. The sociologist Semenzato noted, for example, that in the cacao area of Brazil:

it is invariably the same men who are in the cacao production, who are in the directorates of the banks, in the top organs of the cooperatives . . . and at times in the export houses. On the other side these very firms are also owners of the cacao plantations. There are banker–cacao farmers and livestock farmers. There are members of the directorate of the cooperatives who are influential politicians, large cacao growers, livestock men and great merchants. . . . Besides, these are the same men who are tied, directly or indirectly, by reason of their prestige and social position, to the industry of cacao by-products. And so forth. The greatest portion of the economic sectors is in the hands of the large producers.[45]

The sociologist Maria Brandão (Brazil), in describing the mode of acquisition and reasons for holding farm property, stated of one estate in Bahia located near Salvador that it had belonged to

[44] CIDA, *op. cit.*, Brazil, pp. 496ff.   [45] *Ibid.*, p. 171.

a businessman from Salvador, considered to be one of the wealthiest men who derived his fortune from the sugar business, [and] bought the first property of 1,089 hectares, part of an old sugarmill. Afterwards the other properties were purchased. Another owner in the area explained the reasons for these purchases: the vanity of the newly rich merchant who needed to "ratify" his social status through the ownership of land. . . . At present the property belongs to a member of the family of the old owner to whom it was given, a member of a liberal profession in government service and who justifies his interest in the property as "being a distraction." [46]

And Manuel Diégues Jr. stated in his well-known book on population and land in Brazil:

The large property owner continues to maintain a distinctive position on the social ladder. . . . Not rarely, he is also more merchant than farmer, that is, he takes more care of his commercial activities than of his property.[47]

This phenomenon is common throughout the hemisphere. Table 10–5, for example, shows the residence of the owners of several haciendas in Ecuador and their apparent lack of connection with the communities in which their property is located.

Table 10–5. Residence of owners on nine large haciendas, Ecuador, 1962–1963

Size of hacienda (in hectares)	Comments
1. 610	Owner, a foreigner, lives in Paris. In past 7 years, 3 different administrators. Present administrator distant relative of owner who comes from Quito. Lives 11 months on farm. The *mayordomo* lives in nearest town.
2. 2,955	Owner resides there 8 months with his family, is important politician.
3. 690	Lady owner, lives outside of Ecuador, owns other farms. Son is administrator, lives 8 months on farm and is only white person.
4. 2,441	Owner is government (Asistencia Social). Administrator has little contact with local community.
5. 1,298	Owned by church, rented to Jesuit foundation. Administrator is owner of neighboring farm.
6. 264	Livestock enterprise near Quito, operated by tenant and brother of tenant. Residence not given.
7. 12,000	Owner stays 2 weeks every month and lives in Quito.
8. 444	Owner lives 36 kilometers away in provincial capital.
9. 12,711	Owned by Swedish corporation in Stockholm.

Note: The first 8 haciendas are located in the sierra, the 9th on the coast.

[46] *Ibid.,* p. 175.   [47] Quoted in *ibid.,* p. 176.

The very manner of land utilization in combination with the divided interests of estate owners carries with it the seed of permanently low wages and incomes for farm workers; the progressive exhaustion of the soils, due to poor management, exerts a continuous downward pressure on wages and income levels. This furnishes the landlords with an apparently convincing argument that they cannot afford to raise wages. Thus the very socioeconomic structure of Latin American agriculture affords the estate owners a vested interest in low wages.

The Terms of Employment at Subsistence Levels: (1) Violations of Labor and Other Laws

One of the mechanisms by which wages can be kept at a low level [48] and which allows an accurate measurement of the extent to which incomes remain at subsistence levels [49] is a systematic violation of legal minimum wages and of other wage provisions as well as of laws on sharecropping and tenancy. A large proportion, if not most, of the rural workers in Latin America are protected by legislation which gives them, in addition to a minimum wage rate, rights to overtime pay, paid vacations, and other benefits. For example, in Brazil a statute of 1963 increased the rights already previously granted all wage workers, including a social assistance fund for sickness and survivors' benefits.[50] There is copious evidence that laws are violated not in isolated cases by individual offenders but in a wholesale manner, testifying to a broad contempt for the law and practically no law enforcement. For instance, according to a study of the Brazilian Ministry of Agriculture, wages paid various types of farm workers in 1957 were consistently and significantly below the legal wages, and rental deductions for housing furnished resident workers were considerably larger than those authorized by law in seven out of eight important agricultural states (see Table 10–6). Only in the state of Paraná were wages slightly in excess of the minimum because of the state's sharp expansion of agriculture during that period which required a heavy influx

[48] The term "mechanism" is used here to indicate a deliberate policy of estate owners.

[49] Minimum wages are theoretically set at levels which provide wage earners and their family with an income just about adequate for sufficient food, clothing, and other necessities of life. This could be called the "official" subsistence level. Since peasant incomes are normally well below this official level, it would be appropriate to define them as incomes-at-less-than-subsistence levels. However for the economist or sociologist this term would not be acceptable, inasmuch as incomes-at-less-than-subsistence would not allow their earners to survive.

[50] CIDA, *op. cit.*, Brazil, pp. 302ff.

Table 10–6. Estimated extent of wage violations in eight important agricultural states in eastern Brazil, 1957 (in per cent)

State	Difference between legal wages and wages actually paid		Rental deduction from wages for housing furnished workers Male field (hoe) workers	
	Male field (hoe) workers	Cane cutters	Authorized by law	Actual deduction
Ceará	−31	−29	30	48
Paraíba	−31	−26	27	42
Pernambuco	−36	−27	27	43
Minas Gerais	−42	−41	28	51
Espírito Santo	−31	−26	31	44
Sao Paulo	−23	−18	33	37
Paraná	+ 6	+ 9	24	16
Rio Grande do Sul	− 8	− 5	24	36

Source: CIDA, *op. cit.*, Brazil, p. 299.

Note: Minimum legal wages vary from *município* to *município* in each state. The above estimates are computed from the lowest prevailing wage rate in each state. Hence the wage violations are underestimated and the payments in excess of the legal rate (Paraná) overestimated. With respect to wages in Rio Grande do Sul, the type of workers whose wages are reported in the table (hoe workers and cane cutters) are relatively scarce in that state.

of men—a situation that probably has not been repeated since. This nationwide disregard for the provisions of the law demonstrates that in the best of cases the minimum rates become for all practical purposes maximum rates. In São Paulo, according to a study undertaken by the Secretary of Agriculture of that state, the average daily wage rate varied from 111 to 115 cruzeiros in 1959–1960—the legal rate being 170 cruzeiros —and the average monthly income was calculated at 2,250 cruzeiros when it should have been between 5,100 and 5,800 cruzeiros.[51]

It is noteworthy that the extent of the violations varies from farm **to farm** and that variations are even found on individual estates for identical types of workers. This is apparently the result of the previously-mentioned individual "bargaining process" between employers and workers.[52]

[51] *Ibid.*, p. 282.

[52] See for example, CIDA, *op. cit.*, Brazil, pp. 261–297. Minimum wage legislation, though applicable to farm workers, is not particularly well suited to farm workers. Normally it is focused on urban workers and is useful under urban conditions. For example, in Brazil the daily wage is computed by dividing the minimum monthly wage (the basic figure) by thirty. In most cases rural workers do not work thirty

In countries where the costs of food and other essential items increases in absolute or relative terms, cash wages rise usually as a result of increases in the legal minimum wage rates. Here, hired workers often lose out on two accounts: first, the legal increases are promulgated a long time after real wages have declined significantly, and second, rural employers violate the law by adjusting their wage payments some time after the new legal minimum rates have gone into effect. In this manner, there is a constant downward pressure on real wages.

The most serious violations of the wage laws occur in areas where feudal traditions are still very strong or where racial prejudices prevail. In northeastern Brazil, for example, sharecroppers or resident workers have to work one or more days per week either free of charge or at rates well below the going wages as a "homage" (i.e., personal obligation) to the landlord. In the state of Ceará, workers in bondage (*sujeição*) had to work for 50 per cent of the going rate.[53] In Ecuador's sierra, it was reported that the wage is "more a fiction than a reality." Not only are Indians' wages not paid out punctually but they are also not paid at the agreed rate. Or wages are not paid out in cash but in kind.[54] In Peru's sierra many workers in more outlying areas are still paid a tiny fraction of the going wage rates, amounting to only a few cents per day. Free or nearly free labor is a great advantage many estate owners are unwilling to give up.

Another abuse exists with respect to overtime. Although the legal minimum wages refer always to an eight-hour day, overtime is almost never paid. During the planting or harvesting seasons, workers have to put in normally a ten- or twelve-hour day. If this overtime were included in the calculation of the wage law violations, the gap between the legal and the effective wage rate would increase astronomically. In some areas, like the vast pasture regions of the Andes, shepherds are on duty twenty-four hours a day but receive only a token wage.

Many workers are not paid by the day or week but receive wages which are measured "by the piece." Workers often prefer this type of remuneration because they nurse the hope that they can then earn a higher total income. This may be true in isolated instances but usually

---

days. They get paid for the number of days worked (say, sixteen per month), whereas urban workers are more usually paid by the month. For the shortcomings of Brazil's labor legislation, see *ibid.*, pp. 302ff. Inadequacies of legislation are no justification for the violations of the law, however. Loopholes in the law are one thing, violations another. For example, in Brazil the employers do not pay the daily wage rate, as computed by dividing the monthly rate by thirty.

[53] *Ibid.*, p. 443.   [54] CIDA, *op. cit.*, Ecuador, p. 144.

their hope is false, as it is only based on the fact that during a short time period (say, a day) they may be earning more. Normally a piecework contract is subject to completing a certain quantity of output and in order to achieve it the worker must use the labor of members of his family or even hired men. Thus the wage may be higher in the short run, but it can only be earned at a higher cost to the worker. Employers probably make a fairly careful calculation, the end result of which seems to be that workers receive (more or less) about the same total income over the longer period as if they were paid by the day or week. One estate owner–politician in Brazil made some revealing remarks on this point:

The workers follow my orders and plant what I decide. There are 28 of them and they don't pay rent for the land. They are obliged to work when I need them for 300 cruzeiros daily. But in reality, it is more common for me to pay them by the piece, by unit produced. There are tasks which go better with a daily wage payment, others with payment by the piece. The following are paid on a daily basis: house repairs, opening of canals, constructions of fences, fertilizing. When fertilization is done on a piece basis, the worker goes too fast and there remains less fertilizer than is needed. When I was not a deputy and could remain here to control the work, I used to plant sugar cane on a daily basis. Not now. Where I continue to pay a daily wage is on the preparation of the seed. If I would pay it on a piece basis, the worker spoils the seed and would even cut the "eyes" to produce more. The following are paid by the piece: seeding, covering, cultivating, harvesting, and transportation. For an owner who is absent, it is preferable to pay by the piece to avoid being cheated by the workers or the administrator.[55]

The sociologist Semenzato (Brazil) also stated with respect to employment in the cacao plantation zone that

the so-called best period for piece work is the harvest and processing of cacao, but it happens that generally during this period there is a major influx of workers (though at present, the intensity of this influx has been reduced) which results in a decrease in the rate paid for (say) a box of cacao. The work paid on a production basis is intense and highly supervised, and requires from the worker an enormous effort. In fixing the payment, the producer takes into account the salary normally paid the worker per day of work, the production in terms of quality and quantity, requiring always a high production. It is the quantity of production and the efficiency which are important. . . . It is relatively common for the worker to be confronted with a fall in the rate of pay per unit to be produced when the landlord can count on a larger number of workers and hence on the same quantity of work (in less time).[56]

[55] CIDA, *op. cit.*, Brazil, p. 237.   [56] *Ibid.*, pp. 276ff.

It could be objected that not each employer carries out the wage arithmetic and that therefore the theory that employers make a conscious attempt to set wages at the subsistence level, no matter how it is paid out, does not hold. But this would underestimate the existing cooperation and close association between estate owners, about which further comments will be made later. It is actually sufficient for one or a few large employers to make the careful wage computations as they will be followed by fellow estate owners.

The assignment of work by the piece and piece-rate wages appear to lend themselves to a variety of methods of "cheating" on the part of the employers or their administrators against which the workers have little defense. For example the sociologist Carneiro (Brazil) reports with respect to disputes on sugar cane and other farms as follows:

When the work is on a production basis, the supervisors [in charge of assigning the specific tasks] who measure the amount of land to be cultivated or worked, sometimes use measures which are incorrect by jumping after having measured one length before measuring the next. Thus they pay the worker less than what they receive from the landlord for a certain area to be worked. When purchasing cotton, the administrators sometimes use false weights . . . and pocket the difference. The owners normally close their eyes to these malpractices since they are more in need of their supervisors than of the workers.[57]

At times the owners use these malpractices themselves. One landlord-politician stated in an interview:

The workers were bound to sell their products, mainly cotton, to the owner whose employees—to flatter him or to gain some personal advantages—used fictitious weights to harm the workers. They took a stone weight of 8 kilos and said it was 5, and so forth.[58]

More subtle than wage violations seems to be the disregard of the norms governing payment in kind. Sharecroppers or tenants normally receive their earnings in kind, as a share of the product they grow. Inas-

---

[57] *Ibid.,* p. 264.

[58] *Ibid.,* p. 236; see also pp. 316f. This appears to be one of several ways of "cheating" small producers out of part of their share. Of course tenants or sharecroppers also cheat their landlords at times. But this is made difficult by the permanent supervision of the administrator or the presence of the owner and his administrator during the actual sharing of the production. The owner may be absent from the farm during the entire year, but at harvest and crop-sharing he normally puts in an appearance. Under the conditions which prevail in a *latifundio* agriculture, the croppers or tenants, have no control over the activities of their landlords.

much as the terms of employment under which sharecroppers and small tenants work are much akin to those of wage workers, the "share" of the product earned by them is in reality a disguised wage, payable at harvest. One would suspect that these small "producers" would benefit or suffer like the landlords from the hazards of climate: if the harvest is good, their income would rise; if bad, it would fall. But here again, the institutional arrangements often disadvantage the peasants more than the owners: the share of the peasant is not always specified at the time of assigning him a plot of land. It is not uncommon for the landlord to inspect the plots prior to harvest and then to decide upon the share to be paid, naming a larger share if the harvest is good. Since the rental or sharecropping agreements are almost always oral, a peasant has no recourse against his landlord. The end result is that the final "take-home pay" remains about the same regardless of harvest: at the subsistence level.[59]

The inferior bargaining position of the peasants prompted the sociologist Maria Brandão (Brazil) to conclude:

The entire system [of work relations] is an instrument to drain the excess. *From the point of view of the worker, under whatever form he participates in the system, his ability to retain [part of] his income is systematically undermined.* If he requests some one else's land the returns from it depend on the productivity of his labor and of the land. *A greater productivity of the land calls forth a request for a greater rent from the owner. If the worker is a wage earner a rise in wages or the unit-price [for piece work] is counterbalanced by the intensive control exercised over the worker and the expansion or intensification of the workday.*[60]

The Terms of Employment at Subsistence Levels: (2) Preventing Peasant Savings

There are other economic methods by which landlords, with their vastly superior bargaining power, prevent peasants from earning higher incomes and from accumulating savings. Some of these are also in contravention of the law. The practices include the following: [61]

(a) Forbidding resident workers to plant permanent crops or make "improvements" on the plots assigned to them to grow subsistence foods. In some cases, when improvements have been authorized, they are not

[59] When harvests are very bad, landlords often assist their croppers or tenants in order not to lose their labor force. This is part of the feudal tradition. However, this assistance implies greater dependence for the workers, as advances made to them for food and other necessities are deducted from the next year's income or must be worked off by them.   [60] *Ibid.*, p. 272.

[61] For more details consult the seven country reports, CIDA, *op. cit.*

reimbursed. (This last practice was objected to by the *ligas camponesas* in Brazil and was one of the reasons for their organization.)

(b) Forbidding workers to plant those permanent or annual crops which earn relatively good cash returns in well organized-markets and which the landlord raises as commercial crops (except when grown under a share agreement).

(c) Preventing resident workers, croppers, or tenants from harvesting their crops when this conflicts with the employer's interests. For example, the landlord may request that the workers' plots be opened for pasture for his livestock before the workers' crops are brought in. At times livestock may enter the workers' plots because the workers cannot afford to build fences or are forbidden to do so.

(d) Shifting to new, less favorable arrangements when arrangements between producers and workers turn out to be favorable to the latter as the result of technological changes. In Brazil, for example, the cattle growers abandoned the system of sharing the offspring of livestock with the herdsmen in favor of a wage contract when better livestock was raised on the farms. This prevented the herdsmen from accumulating enough stock of their own to go into business for themselves.

(e) Forbidding resident workers, croppers or tenants to maintain livestock on their plots except small animals, such as chickens or hogs, in small numbers. It is not unusual for the landlord to request that part of the increase in the animals authorized be turned over to him in exchange for the authorization. In some cases the prohibition is absolute.

(f) Advancing money at usury rates of interest or merchandise at higher than market prices in landlord-owned stores. This forces croppers or tenants, obliged to liquidate their indebtedness at harvest time, to "sell" their share of the product to the landlord at prices well below the market. In many instances croppers or tenants have to "sell" their crop to the owner anyway under the original contract.[62]

(g) Using labor contractors when nonresident workers are numerous, often accompanied by bribery and high fees paid by the workers. Added to the violations of the minimum wage law, they increase the gap between the legal wage rates and the effective "take-home" pay.

(h) Charging workers high fees for minor services performed by the landlords, exorbitant rentals for the use of a house, or heavy compensation for any losses in crops or livestock under their care.

This last item deserves a more detailed comment because the practices

---

[62] For examples from Ecuador, see CIDA, *op. cit.*, Ecuador, pp. 254f.; see also pp. 97–105.

falling under this group reflect better than any other the submissive position in which Latin American peasants find themselves still in the 1960's. Fees for minor services or privileges often arise out of the hemmed-in position of the peasants which the estate owners exploit to the fullest.[63] For example, in Ecuador, on one large hacienda of 690 hectares, forty-five *yanaperos* residing in a nearby small community completely surrounded by large estates are obligated to work on the hacienda in return for the right to use its roads and other facilities. They form the estate's largest labor force. The circumstances force them to collect firewood and use the water and the grass growing along the sides of the roads to pasture their animals. Their obligation is to work two days per week without pay, furnishing the estate with a total of approximately 4,700 days of free labor, as a minimum, annually. However, the overseer assigns the worker more land than he can handle by himself so that he has to call on the able-bodied members of his family to assist him. Thus the total free labor furnished no doubt exceeds 5,000 days by a substantial margin. The value of the "privilege" accorded the workers is a fraction of the labor furnished even if this is valued at the minimum legal wage rate.

On another hacienda of 2,441 hectares, property of the state and managed by an agency of the government, sixteen sharecroppers are obligated to work two days per week for the landlord, for the right to collect firewood. On this estate *huasipungeros* receive $.12 per day (U.S.) four days per week all year round but in addition must furnish labor free of charge.

In the province of Cotopaxi the inhabitants of one indigenous community also have to pay with labor (three days per year) the right to use the roads of the estates (*pago de los pasos*). In addition they must turn over their sheep to the landowner for a week to help fertilize his land (*majadeo*). Without previous notice, the employees of the landlord collect the workers' animals by going from house to house and in this manner unite some three to four thousand animals without cost to the landlord, and at times with considerable cost to the owners if the animals are returned damaged or poorly fed. The members of the community also have to work for the estate owners in return for alleged violations, for example if an animal trespasses on the landlord's estate. In that case the animal is retained until the worker has completed his task. Usually this takes from four to five days and the worker may have to hire extra labor to pay off his "debt."

[63] The following examples are taken from CIDA, *op. cit.*, Ecuador.

Since peasants cannot accumulate savings or form cooperatives, landlords are often in a singularly favorable position to extort fees from the peasants for the use of equipment which the latter cannot afford to buy. An example is the use of small mills—a relatively low-cost investment—to grind meal for the consumption of the peasants, as in the case of yucca in Brazil. It is not uncommon for the landlord to derive pure profits from this type of investment. One recent study found that an estate owner in the state of Maranhõe (Brazil) charged his tenants one-fourth of their home-grown yucca for the privilege of using a mill. On the basis of data presented in the study it could be estimated that after about two years the landlord had recuperated his investment.[64]

The house and plot furnished resident workers or tenants is also a source of extra income for the owner when he deducts a rental from the peasants' wages (or shares). In the case of Brazil the rental income can be calculated fairly accurately. Until 1963, deductions from wages for a house averaged around 30 per cent of the wages as authorized by law; after 1963 the deductions were reduced to 20 per cent for "adequate" housing. (Presumably less is deducted if housing is not adequate, but the provision is nearly unenforceable under present conditions.) Under the circumstances the owners' housing facilities are normally paid off after a brief period of profit. It has been estimated in one case that the annual "rental income" of a landlord with 30 resident workers equals 10 times the

---

[64] W. H. Nicholls and R. Miller Paiva, *Ninety-nine Fazendas: The Structure and Productivity of Brazilian Agriculture, 1963* (preliminary ed.; Nashville, Tenn.: Vanderbilt University, Graduate Center for Latin American Studies, July, 1966), ch. 2, "The Itapecuru Valley of Maranhõe: Caxias," p. 65. It is important to note that the authors of this study, designed to uphold the merits of feudal agriculture in Brazil (see their article, *op. cit.*, particularly pp. 360f.), do not make the simple calculation in the text above. On the contrary, they conclude that the milling charge is "insignificant" as it is only 1.2 per cent of *all* the crops produced by the tenant, including, of course, those crops that he cannot eat. This and their statistical production functions convince the authors that there is no "exploitation" of peasants by estate owners in Maranhõe agriculture (where, incidentally, rural poverty is greater than in any other state of Brazil). This analysis is an example of how economists for whom the manipulation of statistical data has become an end in itself can, by the use of a simple—but the wrong—set of statistics, become impervious to the stark realities of life and fail to see the forest for the trees.
The calculation in the text reveals that after two years the estate owner earns a pure profit on his small capital investment of about $300 and that this profit equals approximately one annual tenant-income. To this pure profit one must add any additional returns arising out of the tenants' repurchase of the same yucca at market prices when, as customarily occurs, their supply of yucca remaining after paying the milling charges is inadequate for a year's consumption, plus profits from yucca sales on the open market, and from the landlord's own home consumption of yucca.

annual average income of a single worker.[65] Only in few cases is a deduction of 20 or 30 per cent justified, however, because the quality of the shacks in which Brazilian peasants live is poor, and costs of construction are low. The prevailing practice of paying workers daily rather than monthly represents an additional burden for the workers inasmuch as the total rental charge at the end of a month is higher the larger the number of days worked, although there is no additional cost for the landlord. Furthermore if several members of the worker's family work for the landlord, each member pays the rental; and the deductions apply whether the worker occupies a house, a room, or part of a room (as in the cases of barracks for single workers). If two families live in one house, each pays the rental.

These examples show that—as the sociologist Medina (Brazil) observed —the owner makes his greatest profit from his workers, who, besides being the labor force, become his borrowers, buyers, sellers, and tenants.

Many peasants suffer heavy economic losses through the imposition of punishment for real or alleged misdeeds. On one of the Ecuadorian estates mentioned earlier the workers must work off free of charge any penalties imposed upon them for alleged violations. The penalties are enforced by the employees of the estate by taking from them personal belongings as pawns (hats, ponchos, utensils, and so forth), a practice which is followed generally on this enterprise in order to enforce the work obligations. There are also twelve female workers who in addition to milking twice a day must perform other farm duties, mostly at harvest time. They are members of the families of the *huasipungeros*. Their wage is US$ .16 per day plus half a liter of milk per day. The *huasipungeros*, who cultivate about one hectare of land each, must work at least 4 days per week for the landlord, but during 2 months of the year they must work with their wife and oldest daughter. They receive daily US$ .06. In view of the abundance of labor on this farm, these workers all live in a very precarious condition. They are obligated to use their own tools when working for the landlord. The control is extremely severe and punishments are meted out freely by suppressing the wage payment for alleged violations or failure to work. The men are often abused by the foremen and overseers and their livestock damaged if it trespasses on the (unfenced) land of the landlord. The loss of an animal belonging to the owner and in care of the worker is counted against his salary at its market value. Since he cannot pay it off in cash, his belongings are taken from him (including his own livestock) and the value of these pawns is estimated at a low price.

[65] CIDA, *op. cit.*, Brazil, pp. 274ff. and 411.

The Terms of Employment at Subsistence Levels: (3) The Climate of Uncertainty and Insecurity

One of the tools of power is the deliberate creation of a climate of uncertainty and insecurity in others as a means of maintaining this power. So it occurs in agricultures dominated by large estates, as in Latin America. Farm people face continuously not only the uncertainties of harvests, plagues, or diseases, but also those imposed on them by the rural power elite.

There are a number of institutional arrangements which instill in peasants the certain knowledge that—to paraphrase a well known saying—their only certainty is with regard to the uncertainty of where the next day's piece of bread is to come from and whether they will still have a job. The effect of this uncertainty and insecurity—occurring as they do at the margin of subsistence—is intimidation of the peasants. They are restrained from making demands, even when entirely justified, for fear of losing their slim livelihood. Centuries of intimidation are one of the most serious obstacles to peasant organization.

One of the most effective mechanisms to keep campesinos on their toes is what the sociologist Julio Barbosa (Brazil) referred to as the "polyvalency" of rural labor. Polyvalency appears to be the opposite of specialization of labor (usually considered to be an index of modernization). It implies that workers do not work under one simple contract, but under a variety of arrangements with respect to the tasks to be carried out by them and with different norms as to remuneration and other elements. This characteristic of rural employment in Latin America is not mirrored in any available statistics. It is closely related to, and apparently increases with, the growing importance of cash wage payments during the transitional stages, but it is already inherent in the traditional landlord-worker relationships. The constant shifts in the types of contracts under which workers work for their employer or employers and from which they derive their various incomes are a common phenomenon in Latin American agriculture.

The multiplicity of functions comes about in part from the initiative of the workers who, faced with the impossibility of making an adequate living under one contract and being underemployed, are obliged to seek other types of work—although, as we have seen, the sum total of the contracts still does not give them an adequate income nor full employment. Viewed in this manner, polyvalency is a by-product of the excess supply of manpower. On the other hand, polyvalency has some economic implications also for the employers when they shift workers from one contract to another in order to reduce the costs of labor—in search of that combination of contracts which will result in a minimum wage outlay. But the more important consequence for the employers seems to lie in the scattering of the laborers' efforts, which leaves the workers in suspense and uncertainty since none of the contracts implies any security of tenure. This practice prevents the workers from resorting to collective action to protect their own interests. Theoretically, polyvalency could lead to greater ease in organizing when the peasants have a variety of sources of incomes and could pick off their various problems one by one. But in practice peasants are simply overwhelmed by the multiplicity of difficulties. Since solving any one of them would make little difference to the remainder of their problems, they become disheartened. They are never quite sure whether they wish to improve their situation, for example, with respect to the share to which they are entitled under a share-cropping contract, or with respect to the daily wage, housing, or any other employment condition which needs improvement. The polyvalency introduces in the rural communities a great deal of restlessness and social tension as farm workers try to get into the various job markets and compete with each other for the sparse job opportunities. It enhances their lack of solidarity.

One type of case arises when a small owner, tenant, or sharecropper seeks additional work as day laborer or as seasonal worker, leaving his family in care of his plot. Or he may seek employment as a farm manager, or as a sharecropper on another farm. At times he may fill three or four functions. A second case may arise when a sharecropper, *huasipungero*, *inquilino*, or other worker with land is obliged by the landlord to work a certain number of days for wages on the landlord's crops, or when he also has to work one or more days free of charge on the farm or in some domestic task. Or a sharecropper may work one plot of land on half-shares and another plot on thirds or fourths. Or a resident worker receiving daily wages may work on a piece-work basis part of the time. There are cases—like the "bonded workers" in Brazil's Northeast—where workers with small plots of land obtain a certain wage rate for part of the week and another, lower rate for the rest of the week or where they work gratis. (Chart 10–1 is an illustration of the multiplicity of functions of various types of farm workers in the state of Espírito Santo in Brazil.) [66]

The need to seek additional sources of employment is also the cause of

[66] *Ibid.*, pp. 186ff.

the immense migration throughout the continent which probably involves several million peasants every year. For example in Guatemala permanent workers traditionally form part of the coffee plantations in the coastal areas. In addition temporary workers from the altiplano, most of them *minifundistas,* arrive during harvest time, sometimes bringing their entire families. It is estimated that 160,000 or 200,000 persons participate yearly in this migration. Thus the number of temporary workers exceeds the

Chart 10–1. Scheme of polyvalent nature of farm work in Espirito Santo

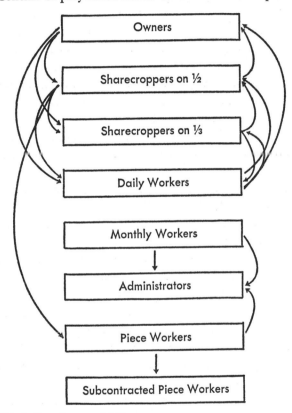

Source: CIDA, Brazil, pp. 186 ff.

permanent workers during part of the year. The *minifundistas* in the altiplano practically all work in a combination of many different occupations, of which the seasonal work on coffee plantations is, of course, one.[67] In Colombia, on 28 large farms studied, two-thirds of the labor force was composed of occasional workers, and in the case of two large farms

[67] CIDA, *op. cit.,* Guatemala, pp. 101f.

totalling 1,700 hectares, there were only 45 permanent laborers.[68] This implies a high rate of interfarm, seasonal migration, in many cases from other regions.

Polyvalency, then, is a distinct characteristic of much of Latin America's poor farm labor with an insecure land tenure status and a low level of living. It is most common on farms which produce crops and least common on livestock enterprises. It makes, where it exists, collective action of the workers nearly impossible. Hence it is not evidence of an inherent, oncoming disintegration of the agricultural structure. On the contrary, it is an integral part of the *latifundio-minifundio* complex as it exists today.

The insecurity of tenure of farm people also comes about in part as a result of a purposeful vagueness of the wage employment, sharecropping, or tenancy contracts which has been well institutionalized. The majority of contracts are oral and concluded informally. Important elements of the contract may be left unspecified, such as the length of time or the share of the crop. Even when specified, the employer has sufficient bargaining power in most cases to go back on his word and modify the contract terms. The employer normally also has the power to cancel the contract at any moment of his chosing, even if law or custom dictate that a contract ought to run for a definite period of time (such as throughout the growing season until harvest). A worker can be fired in most instances for a real or supposed misdeed or for no apparent reason whatever. A further element of insecurity is introduced by the fact that normally the landlord does not give receipts for any payments made by the workers and the bookkeeping of advances in cash or in kind is in his hands. For example, the purchases of a worker in an estate-owned foodstore may be registered by the owner's daughter or wife. The precarious tenure of farm workers can be exemplified by the following case from the State of São Paulo in Brazil. It was cited by the sociologist Medina on the basis of workers' demands presented to the labor court located in Ribeirão Preto against an estate owner reputed to be the wealthiest man of the region:

The farm in question . . . has 786 hectares and held 160,000 coffee trees. Since the time of purchase . . . the old coffee trees were eliminated and 300,000 new trees were planted so that [in 1963] 60,000 were only 3 years old, and the remainder 8 years. . . . [In October 1961] just when the owner did not need the workers anymore, since the coffee plantation was ready, he dismissed

[68] CIDA, *op. cit.*, Colombia, p. 157 and pp. 146ff; see also CIDA, *op. cit.*, Argentina (in English) pp. 48f.

them all. . . . In the labor court 31 suits were brought by 74 petitioners. Of these 56 were adults (42 males and 14 females) and 18 were less than 20 years old (5 males and 13 females). Of the adult petitioners, 9 were over 50 years old, and of these 3 over 70. 64 of the petitioners had 4 years or less of work on the farm . . . 61 were daily workers and 3 monthly workers. Their demands centered around the following rights granted under the labor laws: difference in salaries in relation to the legal minimum wage, payment of vacation and advance notice. With respect to the latter, the following declaration is found in the court proceedings: "The petitioners were dismissed without grounds by the clerk of the farm because they refused to sign a paper in blank." Though this was not proven in court the possibility of this having happened exists, given the passive attitude of the workers towards the employer.[69]

One student of land tenure conditions in Brazil stated:

One can see that in the work relations described there is a great harm which befalls the worker who does not possess land when he is obliged to subject himself to conditions of contracts which are truly treacherous. . . . The arbitrariness of the landlord also functions like a true sword of Damocles over the head of the worker since he has no written contract and does not have any guarantee that he will remain on the land, can be dismissed at any time and must look for another plot where he will work under identical conditions as in the first property.[70]

Vagueness may even be part of written contracts occasionally found on large estates. It tends to protect the landlord against his workers rather than the workers against the landlord. The well-known historian Clovis Caldeira (Brazil) observed after a study of written sharecropping contracts in the state of São Paulo:

The omission of the mention of the size of the area ceded to the cropper and even the failure to be more specific in some cases enable one to have only a partial insight into this phase of the arrangement. The fact that the "rent" paid to the landlord has no relation to the area explains the indeterminateness of many contracts. In such cases, it is usual to declare only that the landlord cedes "a site or a piece of land." [71]

It is also common practice for written contracts to be executed in one single copy only, which always remains in the possession of the landlord. All these arrangements imply that in case of conflict the workers have no

[69] CIDA, *op. cit.*, Brazil, p. 284.
[70] M. Correia de Andrade, *op. cit.*, p. 200, quoted in CIDA, *op. cit.*, Brazil, p. 227.
[71] CIDA, *op. cit.*, Brazil, p. 198.

recourse against their employers and no way of proving their case before higher authorities.

The imbalance of bargaining power has been summarized succinctly by the sociologist J. Ferreira de Alencar (Brazil) who stated with respect to a sharecropper's simple wish to use his own rather than his landlord's seed:

If one makes the assumption that the sharecropper would insist on planting his own seed, given the existing values, nothing would be more logical for the owner of the enterprise or his agent to conclude than that this sharecropper wishes to obtain in the future some additional right beyond those commonly established by the contract of sharecropping. If such a proposal would come from the worker not yet admitted to the farm, but candidate to a parcel, it would be only with difficulty that he would become a sharecropper. If he is already a sharecropper on halves in the enterprise, he would not receive another parcel to begin his plantings. If he were to insist, he would be dismissed from the farm for breach of the original contract and without receiving any indemnification that is [in the words of the owner] "since he left of his own will, that is he created the situation to leave." And the cotton which he had was already in the soil and came from the owner's seed.[72] This problem can only arise in the realm of hypothesis since the producer who is well integrated in the social organization of the community . . . makes a careful selection before admitting any workers with a view to avoiding conflicts and tensions on his property.[73]

The insecurity and uncertainty of farm people with respect to their jobs and incomes is not generally shared by the power elite where it concerns the constancy of their supply of labor or the low level of their wage bill. Notwithstanding the incessant migration of farm people from rural to urban areas, rural employers continue to be faced with a plentiful supply of manpower—an almost ironclad guarantee for low wages—to which they have been accustomed as a matter of tradition and in the maintenance of which they have a vested interest. However it must not be overlooked that changing socioeconomic and political conditions force the landowning class from time to time to make a number of adjustments in their relationships with the farm people, bowing to the inevitable. In the past, landowners have shown a remarkable ability and agility to make these adjustments come out in their favor, that is, without significant losses (if any) to the steadiness of their labor supply. By and large, estate

[72] Implying that the landlord sees no reason to pay any indemnification.
[73] *Ibid.*, p. 206.

owners continue to be successful in their policy to tie their workers to the farming enterprises without tying them to the land.

On the local level, there may appear temporary shortages of labor, although in some cases rural employers complain of shortages simply when they are not confronted with an inexhaustible supply of low-cost and obedient workers at all times. Normally such shortages are not important enough to cause employers to raise wages in order to attract more workers. Furthermore, shortages can be and often are overcome by transporting workers from areas of surplus labor. In Peru it was reported, for example, that workers were transported from more distant regions into the conflict-ridden valley of La Convención where the local farm people refused to work for the estate owners at any wage. (This is obviously a strike-breaking technique.) Or owners who own several large estates may transport their workers from one enterprise to the other, at times against the preference of the workers who are being uprooted. From one region it is even reported that there exists still a "slave market" for rural workers who are being "hired" for other regions, particularly for newly opened frontier areas.

On a broader level, adjustments have to be made to meet long-run changes in the terms of employment. In practically all of Latin America a massive shift has occurred from resident workers to wage workers living off the farms, as political pressures to abolish feudal and semifeudal practices have mounted. This shift has a "pull" and a "push" element. The pull consists in the massive migration of farm people to urban communities to flee oppressive conditions on the estates. The push consists in the landowners' policy to slowly rid themselves of their resident workers by not building houses for them, by not repairing those that are occupied, or by actually tearing them down. Here the estate owners appear to act "in self-defense" against the real or imagined danger that resident workers may claim possession of the plot of land that they occupy and reimbursements for improvements paid for by them or for unharvested crops—possession or claims to which they may be entitled under the law for the very conditions under which they occupy the plot. As a consequence, the power elite now relies partly on the plentiful and cheap pool of labor available in the towns or villages where rural workers live, usually in suburbs under miserable conditions but in apparent freedom, dependent as before on farm employment to make a living.

If political conditions were to become more favorable for the hiring of resident workers, the trend towards wage workers could be reversed if this were to prove more convenient and profitable for the estate owners.

The Terms of Employment at Subsistence Levels: (4) Strong-Arm Methods

The climate of uncertainty and insecurity in which farm people live is greatly enhanced by what appears to be a constant threat of violence or by actual violence itself. This is the result of the power that estate owners have as individuals or as a group to mete out not only economic but also physical punishment for real or alleged misdeeds. Punishment can be given by the landlords themselves, by their subordinates, or by local public officials whose jobs normally depend on the landlords. Even in more advanced agricultural regions of Latin America, the "right" of large estate owners to act in the capacity of jury, judge, and law enforcement agent is still normally taken for granted. Violence is most likely to occur when the rural power elite is—or claims to be—threatened by any questioning of its authority. The most severe action can be expected to arise as a countermeasure to peasants' efforts to organize.

An incisive method to "enforce discipline" on an estate is the use of a private police force of which brief mention was made in earlier quotations. The use of *capangas* (strong-arm men) is widespread in the northeastern sugar plantations of Brazil, and it is they who make the workers "toe the line," who intimidate or terrorize them, who give them corporal punishment. At times they kill. The tension existing in the sugar cane areas is well characterized by the following quotations of members of the *liga:*

"Notwithstanding the constant violence of the owners and the *capangas*, the *ligas* are growing stronger constantly. The death of each worker is so much more strength for the *ligas*. . . . The workers don't expect anything to happen immediately, they know that from their unity and patience depend future conquests. . . . Our leader is Assis Lemos. . . . Notwithstanding his pacifist attitude, he was attacked violently by the *latifundistas* and their *capangas*, who crushed his intestines and his testicles. He escaped from death one does not know how but stayed a long time in the hospital. . . . The political situation here is very tense. Whoever speaks in favor of the *liga* can expect to be shot at any moment. None of us who are here in this shed are safe. A shot can come out of the dark from one of the *capangas* who must be watching us now. U., the greatest political hope from Paraíba, prefect of Itabaiana, was assassinated 2 months ago by a nephew of [one of the Y.'s]. The vicar . . . of Sapé was obliged to leave because he was opposed, in some instances, to the owners. He was labeled a communist. They threw a paving-stone into the church. A woman cheered the *liga*, was undressed and cut up in the square of Sapé. When the elections come, the M.'s announce that there is a climate of insecurity in Sapé and ask for the state police to guarantee the outcome of the elections. The police arrive and stay there with pointed guns. It's laughable. The M.'s bring the workers from the factory in trucks. They [the workers] must be nudged by the *capangas* when the time comes to applaud. . . ."

These are the statements as they were presented. All those 8 or 9 present were in agreement with them. Only with respect to one point there appeared to be a divergence of views. According to some: "During 200 years, the owners oppressed, robbed, beat and killed the farm workers; today they are also beginning to be killed. I believe that they will now retreat and act differently. Therefore I believe that the violence will diminish and end." But others said: "This has no end. Violence begets violence. We will not retreat and the owners will not either. There is no remedy. Now it will go to the bitter end when one or the other wins." [74]

In his book on the Brazilian Northeast, Manoel Correia de Andrade also gives an example of a conflict arising out of the resident workers' demand for the abolition of the feudal free work day and their request to pay rent for their small plot. He notes that on one large sugar plantation "on March 17, 1962 the divergencies between the workers and the guards of the Colonel resulted in a fight in which two *capangas* died by the sickle and the knife; one administrator hurt; one guard disappeared with a bullet in his thigh and two workers were killed by 38 shots." [75]

A private army of strong-arm men is, however, not crucial to enforce discipline on a *latifundio*. The administrator at times may act by himself or he may call upon other workers to mete out the punishment or enforce a decision against a worker. One powerful landlord, an important politician in his country, had the homes of his resident workers burned down and used bulldozers to shut irrigation canals bringing water—without which nothing can be grown—to the workers' garden plots and posted armed guards to impede the workers' opening the ditches at night. This forced the workers to abandon their plots.

Excesses of power are at times picked up by the national or local press of the country. But this overshadows the fact that the daily life of many campesinos is filled with fears of punishment and with actual physical violence. It is not only the actual violence which is conducive to the campesinos' submissive behavior and lack of hope, but the possibility that it can be meted out with little or no possibility of recourse on their part. Their submissiveness has become institutionalized, and at times they carry it over even towards their own leaders and union organizers. Thus the

[74] *Ibid.*, pp. 314f.   [75] *Ibid.*, p. 325; see also p. 243.

society dominated by the estate owners forces the campesinos to become their own enemies.

The Suprastructure of Employment at Subsistence Levels

The analysis of the agriculture of poverty would be incomplete if some reference were not made to some of the institutional arrangements mostly at the higher regional or national level which allow the power elite to effectively oppose rural progress, peasant organizations, and collective bargaining.

The Place of Public Agencies Assisting Farm People in a *Latifundio* Agriculture

Although there is relatively little documentation of the sociopolitical structure of *latifundio* agricultures in Latin America, it is certain that landlords exert a strong influence on the nomination of public officials dealing directly or indirectly with farm people and on the activities they carry out. The political influence under which these officials stand shapes the activities of the agencies to which they belong. The structure, the scope of action, and the budgets of the agencies specifically set up to deal with the problems of farm people are also under the landlords' influence. As a result, the agencies are afraid to act openly in favor of those for whose benefit they have been established. Although few observers of Latin America agriculture ignore the extent of the estate owners' political powers, still fewer have given adequate attention to all their ramifications.[76]

Normally the rural power elite obtains support from the military and police establishments, which can be counted upon to come to the defense of their, rather than the farm peoples', interests. This comes about in a seemingly natural way. In Brazil's Northeast, where conflicts between peasants and landlords have been violent, it is reported, for example, that few appointments of higher military officials take place without the consent of one influential landlord, owner of immense holdings in the sugar plantation region. The alert rural workers who have some experience in matters of politics are of course aware of the opposition they face in the ultimate sources of public power and can be heard to state jokingly that the higher officials of the army in the area consider the residences of the big estate owners as extensions of their own homes. One said that if

---

[76] See, however, CIDA, *op. cit.*, Ecuador, pp. 98ff. for a specification of the political structure of a traditional hacienda agriculture. See also *ibid.*, pp. 107f., for the influence of *hacendados* on national politics.

the army would only help the workers rather than the landlords, they (the workers) would be much better off.[77] They take it for granted, therefore, that landlords will appeal to the local police or the military to settle their difficulties with the workers. Occasionally the requests of the landed elite arouse criticisms. The Brazilian geographer M. Correia de Andrade wrote:

> The Chief of Police of Paraíba, Dr. Silvio Pôrto, expressed himself as follows about [one] conflict: "The appeal to the police for the solution of problems such as that of the *ligas camponesas* is so primitive that it is embarrassing. This practice is defended only by fascist organizations which want to find the solution to all the problems through armed force. Instead of appealing to the police, it ought to be addressed to the National Congress, to the agencies of economic development." And the leader of the government in the State House, Deputy Vital do Rêgo, stated in the name of the government that the crimes in Miriri are due to "a structure which it considers outmoded and whose reform ought to be undertaken urgently."
>
> From these statements one can conclude that the government of Paraíba is aware of the seriousness of the moment in which we live, and understands that this is not a problem for the police to handle; that the social problems must be solved on a national scale.[78]

It must have come as a shock to many of the large estate owners when in 1962–1963 police forces began to adopt a neutral role in landlord-peasant conflicts helping neither the landlords nor the rural workers, but still giving thereby effective indirect aid to the workers' demands for better terms of employment.

But ordinarily the political power structure is clearly "stacked" in favor of the estate owners. This means that the agencies working on behalf of the peasants come under the surveillance of the power elite so that help they give the peasants materializes only in the few cases where it is not openly at the expense of the estate owners. In other words, help normally remains marginal. Thus the role and impact of land reform institutes, government labor offices, and Indian agencies is much weakened by their exposure to the far-reaching influence of landlords felt at the local or national level. A government worker in charge of a regional or local program can be made to feel quickly the support or hostility of estate owners. For example, landlords can be instrumental in having competent directors of land reform programs quickly removed if a "state of estrangement" or lack of confidence exists between the officials and the

[77] CIDA, *op. cit.*, Brazil, p. 317.
[78] *Op. cit.*, p. 251 quoted in CIDA, *op. cit.*, Brazil, p. 325.

latifundistas. It is not unusual for such government officials, bent on carrying out their assignment effectively, to run real risks as far as their professional career, reputation, and tranquility of mind is concerned. Even the open support of the campesinos, then, proves inadequate to prevent these officials' having to give up their assigned jobs. In fact it may aggravate their position, given the existing balance of political power in the rural society. In other words, a national land reform institute may have to sacrifice its personnel in order to appease the hacendados rather than execute the program for which it was set up. This is why peaceful land reforms in Latin America presently face almost insurmountable obstacles.[79]

The political influence of the rural power elite makes itself felt in other ways. If the budgets necessary for the operation of agencies working on behalf of peasants are voted upon by legislative bodies, as they usually are, the influence of landlords and their political supporters in parliament is often strong enough to keep the sums allocated to a bare minimum. It is not uncommon to find that the agencies' resources are barely sufficient to pay salaries and current office expenditures.[80] In addition, the leading officials of the agencies may be themselves members of the rural power elite—either because there is a shortage of other competent and trained administrators or because it makes the supervision of the programs by the power elite so much easier—and their sympathies may not be entirely with the people they are serving.[81] This seems to be a part of the structure of an agriculture dominated by a small elite. This domination has had a well-known impact on colonization programs theoretically designed to allocate land to landless farm people. In Ecuador's coastal settlement project of Santo Domingo de los Colorados, only nine out of thirty-three initial settlers receiving lots in 1959 were farmers or former farm managers. The remainder were ex-employees (7), military personnel including one wife of a military official (7), businessmen (2), chauffeurs (2), an

---

[79] Cf. E. Feder, "Land Reform under the Alliance for Progress," *Journal of Farm Economics,* XLVII, No. 3, (1965), pp. 652ff.

[80] See E. Feder, "When Is Land Reform a Land Reform? The Colombian Case," *American Journal of Economics and Sociology,* XXIV (April, 1965), pp. 131ff.

[81] The conservative London *Economist* stated: "In Peru, ONRA agronomists refuse to ride in rural buses because they are usually packed with Indians" ("More Law than Land for Latins," June 14, 1966). Evaluation of development projects for indigenous communities have stressed the apathy of government employees as an obstacle. See, for example, José Matos Mar, "Cambios Sociales en el altiplano boliviano: El area cultural de Tiahuanaco-Taraco," *Economia y Agricultura* (Lima, Peru), I, No. 2, (1963–1964).

electrician, mechanic, circus artist, dentist, jeweller and telegraph operator. Similarly in 1960, twenty-three more lots were assigned mostly to nonfarmers.[82] This is one of a series of examples throughout the continent where land has been distributed according to political motives—one suspects as political pay-offs—without regard to the many land-hungry peasants whose influence over the scheme is obviously nonexistent. With the existing political framework the rural power elite has little to fear from laws, programs, and agencies designed to further the cause of the peasants because the political control they exert over their operation is very effective.

The defense of the rural workers' rights in the labor courts is also a weak institutional link in farm people's search for greater bargaining power. The lack of bargaining power could be substantially offset by a network of strong and independent labor courts. In some areas a modest beginning has been made in this direction, but it has remained insignificant throughout Latin America for rural labor as a whole. Labor courts exist mainly where industrial labor is abundant and their impact on agriculture is limited to a relatively small geographic zone around the towns where they are situated. In some instances they may have been established in areas where rural conflicts have created significant political pressures. But in the majority of the cases, workers who have demands against their employers lack either courage, time, or money to lodge complaints with the courts directly or through attorneys. It is also significant that in many communities few, if any, lawyers will accept the rural workers' business, as this may threaten their professional reputation, besides not being very remunerative. At times they are accused of being subversives when engaging in the defense of rural workers on a larger scale.[83]

In industrial countries, labor claims for wages and other compensations are normally strictly and promptly enforced. But in Latin America,

[82] See CIDA, *op. cit.*, Ecuador, pp. 355ff. Thirteen of the thirty-three abandoned their parcels, and in the subsequent reassignment only two farmers were selected, the remainder again being mostly former employees and military personnel. After the second allotment, seven gave up their lots and were all replaced by nonfarmers. See also CIDA, *op. cit.*, Brazil, pp. 537f. with reference to the Itaguaí colonization project in Rio de Janeiro.

[83] There are, however, cases where lawyers have devoted their efforts to the defense of rural workers, at times for political reasons. Francisco Julião, the well-known Brazilian politician, began his career in this fashion. For a sympathetic account of his activities, see M. Correia de Andrade, *op. cit.*, pp. 244ff., quoted in CIDA, *op. cit.*, Brazil, pp. 322ff.

courts seem to tend towards long delays in settling cases [84] and to sanction compromises between claims of the workers and low counteroffers of the employers which bear no relation to what they really owe. In Brazil, for example, landlords have apparently made such offers only when the hearings show that claims against them are well grounded. As we know, workers are usually at a disadvantage to prove that they have a claim, no matter how justified it is. Although the voluntary settlement of claims is entirely legal and may shorten the proceedings, it is politically unwise. It shows that in Latin America a precedent for just and thorough enforcement of labor legislation has not yet been established. On the contrary, the provisions of the law relating to farm people are so systematically violated and law enforcement so weak that it may perhaps be generations before the widespread disrespect for the law and the rule of power in agriculture is replaced by the rule of the law.

Collective Action of Estate Owners

Another intriguing aspect of the social mechanism of the traditional agriculture of Latin America is the collective action of landowners in defense of their self-interests and the consequences of this action. Reference here is not to the treatment of farm workers by individual estate owners on their estates but to the overall, quasi-institutionalized political action of the members of the rural power elite to maintain the political, social, and economic status quo.

Concerted action on the part of landowners is not a widely known and documented, or at least not an acknowledged, feature of Latin American agriculture. It is carried out quietly and without propaganda, but this makes it no less effective. It contrasts sharply with the publicity which real or attempted collective action on the part of the campesinos receives in the literature, the press, and in political debates. This publicity is in part sought by the campesinos themselves who need sympathetic public support, but it is also given by landlords to prevent it. As a matter of fact, the exaggerated importance given even minor attempts of farm people to increase their bargaining power seems to be part of the policy of landlords to point out the dangers confronting the nation (that is, themselves) from any concessions made to the campesinos and their reaction, entirely out of proportion with the actual facts, often results (to use the

---

[84] Sometimes the delay may favor the workers, as in the case of resident workers in Brazil, who under the law cannot be removed from their plots until settlement of their judicial claim. But these delays are probably exceptions and require that the workers are already organized.

words of the Brazilian sociologist Carneiro) in the mystification of the issues involved.[85]

Concerted action can be formal through organizations established by and for estate owners, or informal where a community of interests motivates estate owners to adopt common fronts vis-à-vis their opponents. In recent years, landlords have found a fruitful outlet for their energy in obstructing land reform. In Peru, for example, part of the press, to which the rural power elite has easy access, devotes much space to pessimistic, partly incorrect, or misleading reports on the operation and management of the country's land reform institute. Many of the criticisms are focused on the management by the government of a hacienda ("Algolán") which was expropriated in the early 1960's after serious conflicts and invasions of land by Indian communities. A portion of this land has since been turned over to the communities, and according to the best available information, this expropriation has been a real success. However the criticisms serve to discourage further land settlement schemes through expropriation. In fact, practically all land reforms in Latin America have come under systematic attacks by the power elite not only, as one might expect, because their goal is to distribute farm land to farm people at the expense of the large landlords, but also because they encourage the organization of farm people and threaten to increase the workers' bargaining power in traditional farming areas.

Only part of the counterreform, however, is accompanied by publicity. The other (probably no less successful) part is carried on *sub rosa*. Observation reveals that its mechanism is complex and ranges from threats against public officials and landlords' refusals to cooperate with the government as required by law all the way through intimidating peasants to prevent them from taking advantage of the provisions of the law and faking incidents which would deprive them of the benefits of the law.[86] It is not the activities as such which are significant—they might be expected from landlords threatened with losing their holdings—but the fact that they appear to be uniform, systematic, and part of a concerted effort.[87]

[85] CIDA, *op. cit.*, Brazil, p. 233; see also CIDA, *op. cit.*, Chile, pp. 35f. The mystification is the more complete since farm people have little, if any, access to modern means of communication.

[86] Under the Peruvian land reform law of 1964, peasants can be excluded from the benefits of the law if they are found to promote invasions of land or other acts contrary to the interests of the landlords. Such acts can, however, be simulated.

[87] In the United States, too, such concerted action took place during the 1930's and 1940's to prevent farm workers from reaping the benefits of the New Deal labor legislation.

Some of these activities may not be limited to a single country, which suggests some degree of understanding between Latin American estate owners of various nations to resist land reforms and other programs to increase farm people's bargaining power.[88]

Estate owners are organized in various ways. Formally, the most powerful associations appear to be those based on a community of economic interests arising out of the processing or marketing of specific crops and consisting of regional associations combined into national federations. Usually wheat, coffee, cotton, rice, sugar, cacao, or livestock growers' associations exert considerable influence as pressure groups at the national level on pricing, subsidies, market controls, or export and import policies. These groups nearly always represent only the large growers. Their influence spreads, however, beyond purely economic and financial questions and they are known to take strong stands on such matters as farm labor legislation and policies or land reform. In Colombia, for example, sugar and cattle growers' groups have long been active in opposing that country's land reform program. Although the economic interests of the commodity associations may be in conflict, their farm labor policies and their interest in maintaining the existing land tenure systems tie them into a common front.

But there are also purely political associations of estate owners; (the equivalent of the American Farm Bureau) which act in defense of the rural power elite. In Chile the Sociedad Nacional de Agricultura, in Peru the Sociedad Nacional Agraria, in Colombia the Sociedad de Agricultores de Colombia—to name only a few examples—have been active in presenting their views on land reform and other policy issues to the legislators and to the public with considerable success.[89] Usually these groups have their own legislative departments or they hire legal or economic experts to formulate their views or present bills. What is more, there now exists an international landowners' group under the name of Asociaciones Agropecuarias Americanas Amigas (AAAA),[90] with an office reportedly located in Chicago, which holds international conferences where the viewpoints of estate owners are given publicity. It must be assumed that their influence can even be felt in the circles concerned with international technical and financial assistance and with the continent's agricultural

[88] Land reform laws, which have been adopted now by almost every Latin American country, contain identical or similar provisions which make the realization of land reform very difficult.
[89] O. Delgado (ed.), *Reformas agrarias en la América Latina* (Mexico City: Fondo de Cultura Económica, 1965), pp. 301ff.   [90] *Ibid.*, pp. 290ff.

policies, and this influence cannot be negligible, given the enormous material wealth and political power it represents.

Other organized action at the local and regional level may be directed specifically against the campesinos themselves to counteract their organizations, particularly where conflicts have erupted or threaten to erupt, through such methods as armed vigilante groups or the stocking of weapons on estates. Often it is directed against the organizing efforts of the campesinos. Most organizers of farm workers' unions or tenant organizations have learned to face the risks of their occupation, although many have not survived them. The sociologist Semenzato reported from the cacao region in Bahia (Brazil) with respect to the membership drive of one union that

At first groups were formed, or more precisely, two groups, composed of two men which visited the estates, held meetings and at the same time explained to the workers the objectives and goals of the unions which were to be organized. Generally, these groups visited the farms by announcing previously the day and the hour of the meetings by utilizing always the contacts which had been established in advance. *Later the organizers of the movement began to feel the action of the police. They were received by gun fire in one case.* Hence they began visiting the farms without a previous announcement and arrived unannounced to promote these meetings and even penetrated right into the cacao fields. *The reaction of the owners and of the police continued without interruptions;* nonetheless the union succeeded in the beginning in organizing 600 members with a monthly contribution of 5 cruzeiros.[91]

Similarly, in Ecuador, the reaction of most of the hacendados to farm organizations is reported as "always being negative from the very start," beginning with the denial that there exists any union at all, and is almost always violent:

If the encounter between the organizations of the workers and the landlord manifests itself in this continuous hostility, it is no wonder that beyond threats, persecutions, etc. there have been on various occasions attempts against the life of some persons and that the leaders of the syndicates have been eliminated, as well as those individuals who in the eyes of the landlords and the local authorities appear to be dangerous. There is a tradition of violence and it is a tradition to resort to any means whatever to contain the workers. And no one of course is ready to renounce this tradition.[92]

[91] CIDA, *op. cit.,* Brazil, p. 326.
[92] CIDA, *op. cit.,* Ecuador, p. 96. See also *ibid.,* p. 95.

These are typical occurrences in Latin American rural communities and the collective, violent preventions and repressions are the major reason why only a small minority of the farm people are organized and why they often resort to secrecy although the national legislations actually authorize the formation of peasant organization. In cases where the formation of unions or tenant leagues could not be avoided, the hacendados have resorted to methods designed to discourage the workers' participation or the growth of the organizations: blacklists which prevent workers engaged in union activities from finding jobs in the community; subtle attempts to exploit the divided interests or the low level of education of farm people,[93] bribing union officials which makes farm people suspicious even of their own leaders; or making it difficult for the unions to hold meetings.[94]

Thus the road towards the attainment by the peasants of a better life is strewn with many obstacles. The relevant issue, which we attempted to outline, is that these are not individual hurdles which farm people have to overcome: peasants are surrounded by a society hostile to improving their lot, which is to lead a life at the subsistence level, and the various institutions are all linked together and combine to deprive them of the ways and means to improve their status. In a society where farm people have little or practically no voice—except sporadically when, driven by the hopelessness of their suppressed condition, they resort to revolt—there is little expectation that they can improve their status. Hopelessness is characteristic for the peasants in large parts of the Latin America of today because they know, instinctively or by experience, that under present conditions even honest large-scale efforts to improve their lot seem to be bound to failure.

[93] In some cases farm people are made to believe that land reform is "bad" for them.

[94] See, for example, International Labour Office *Plantation Workers; Conditions of Work and Standards of Living* (I.L.O. Studies and Reports No. 69 [Geneva, 1966]), p. 164.

Bibliography on Latin American Peasant Organization

GERRIT HUIZER and
CYNTHIA N. HEWITT *

Latin America (General)

Adams, Richard N. "Freedom and Reform in Rural Latin America," in Fredrick B. Pike (ed.), *Freedom and Reform in Latin America* (Notre Dame, Ind.: University of Notre Dame Press, 1959).

———. "Rural Labor," in John J. Johnson (ed.), *Continuity and Change in Latin America* (Stanford, Calif.: Stanford University Press, 1964).

Blanksten, George I. "Political Groups in Latin America," *American Political Science Review*, LIII, No. 1 (1959).

Brunori, P. G. "El sindicalismo y la reforma agraria," *Economía*, II, No. 4 (1964).

Cámara, Fernando. "Religious and Political Organizations," in Sol Tax (ed.), *Heritage of Conquest* (Glencoe, Ill.: Free Press, 1952).

Chacon, Vamireh. *Cooperativismo e comunitarismo*. Belo Horizonte, Brazil: Universidade de Minas Gerais, 1959.

Cháves, Fernando. "El cooperativismo agrario en América Latina," *Revista del Instituto de Estudios Cooperativos*, XVII–XVIII (July–Dec., 1962).

Delgado, Oscar (ed.). *Reformas agrarias en América Latina: Procesos y perspectivas*. Mexico City: Fondo de Cultura Económica, 1965. Especially ch. 6, part 19: "La política antireformista: El punto de vista de los terratenientes. (A) Las Asociaciones Agropecuarias Americanas Amigas (AAAA); (B) Chile: La Sociedad Nacional de Agricultura; (C) Colombia: La Sociedad de Agricultores y personalidades antirreformistas; (D) Perú: La Sociedad Nacional Agraria."

Erasmus, Charles J. "Upper Limits of Peasantry and Agrarian Reform: Bolivia, Venezuela and Mexico Compared," *Ethnology*, VI (Oct., 1967).

* The authors wish to acknowledge the use of thirty-five entries previously published in *The Political Dimensions of Rural Development in Latin America: A Selected Bibliography (1950–1967)* (Long Beach, Calif., 1968), compiled by Jerry L. Weaver of California State College at Long Beach under a grant from the Center for Rural Development of Cambridge, Massachusetts.

Huizer, Gerrit. "On Peasant Unrest in Latin America." Mimeo. Washington, D.C.: Comité Interamericano de Desarrollo Agrícola, 1967.

——. "Some Preliminary Generalizations on the Role of Peasant Organizations in the Process of Agrarian Reform." Mimeo. Washington, D.C.: Comité Interamericano de Desarrollo Agrícola, 1967.

Lord, Peter P. *The Peasantry as an Emerging Political Factor in Mexico, Bolivia, and Venezuela.* University of Wisconsin Land Tenure Center, Reprint No. 35. Madison: The Center, 1965.

Moreno, Antonio de P. "Grupos y cuasi-grupos sociales de la comunidad rural," *Estudios Sociológicos,* Congreso Nacional de Sociología, I (1955).

Pearson, Neale J. "Latin American Peasant Pressure Groups and the Modernization Process," *Journal of International Affairs,* XX, No. 2 (1966).

Poblete Troncoso, Moisés. *La economía agraria de América Latina y el trabajador campesino.* Santiago, Chile: Ediciones de la Universidad de Chile, 1953.

—— and Ben G. Burnett. *The Rise of the Latin American Labor Movement.* New York: Brookman Associates, 1960.

Quijano, Aníbal. "Contemporary Peasant Movements," in Seymour M. Lipset and Aldo Solari (eds.), *Elites in Latin America* (New York: Oxford University Press, 1967).

Rubio Orbe, Gonzalo. *Promociones indígenas en América.* Quito, Ecuador: Editorial Casa de la Cultura Ecuatoriana, 1957.

Schulman, Sam. "El reconocimiento del papel del campesino en la reforma agraria," *América Latina,* IX (July–Sept., 1966).

Seeburger, Harold M. "The Role of Rural Labor Organizations in Economic Development." Ph.D. thesis, Department of Agricultural Economics, University of Wisconsin, 1966.

Wagley, Charles. "The Peasant," in John J. Johnson (ed.), *Continuity and Change in Latin America* (Stanford, Calif.: Stanford University Press, 1964).

Williams, Edward J. *Latin American Christian Democratic Parties.* Knoxville: University of Tennessee Press, 1967.

Bolivia

Antezana E., Luis. *La lucha entre Cliza y Ucureña.* Pamphlet. Cochabamba, Bolivia. May, 1960.

——. *El movimiento obrero boliviano (1935–1943).* 1966.

——. *Resultados de la reforma agraria en Bolivia.* Cochabamba, Bolivia: Los Amigos del Libro, 1955.

Antezana Villagrán, J. *El indio y la distribución de la tierra en Bolivia.* La Paz, Bolivia: Universidad Interamericana, Instituto de Investigaciones Sociales y Económicas, 1944.

Arnade, Charles W. "Bolivia's Social Revolution, 1952–1959: A Discussion of Sources," *Journal of Inter-American Studies,* I, No. 3 (1959).

Arze Loureiro, Eduardo. "Actitudes sociales relativas a la reforma agraria," *Economía y Ciencias Sociales*, III, Nos. 1–3 (1960–1961).

Balderrama González, Adalid. *Nuestro agro y sus problemas*. Bolivia: Editorial Canata, 1953.

——. *La reforma agraria y la experiencia boliviana*. La Paz, Bolivia: Editorial del Estado, 1960.

Barcelli S., Agustín. *Medio siglo de luchas sindicales revolucionarias en Bolivia*. La Paz, Bolivia, 1956.

Bjornberg, Arne. *Las poblaciones indígenas y el cooperativismo: Observaciones y experiencias del desarrollo del programa andino en Bolivia*. Stockholm: Biblioteca e Instituto de Estudios Iberoamericanos de la Escuela de Ciencias Económicas, 1959.

Bonifaz, Miguel. *Legislación agrario-indigena*. Cochabamba, Bolivia: Imprenta Universitaria, 1953.

Carter, William C. *Aymara Communities and the Bolivian Agrarian Reform*. University of Florida Monographs, Social Sciences, No. 24. Gainesville: The University, 1964.

Caviedes, Homero. "El desarrollo espontáneo de la comunidad indígena de Bolivia," *América Indígena*, XXIV, No. 2 (1964).

Crist, Raymond E. "Los bolivianos emigran al este," *Américas*, XV, No. 5 (1963).

Dandler-Hanhart, Jorge. "Local Group, Community and Nation: A Study of Changing Structure in Ucureña, Bolivia (1935–1952)." M.A. thesis, University of Wisconsin, 1967.

Enríquez, Braulio, Colón Narváez, and Luis Gallegos. *Estudio de Nachoca y Nacoca, Cantón Taraco, Provincia Ingavi*. Lima, Peru: Universidad de San Marcos, Proyecto 208 de la OEA, 1964.

Ferragut, Casto. "La reforma agraria boliviana," *Revista Interamericana de Ciencias Sociales*, II (1963).

Flores, Edmundo. "Un año de reforma agraria en Bolivia," *El Trimestre Económico*, XXIII, No. 2 (1956).

——. "Land Reform in Bolivia," *Land Economics*, XXX, No. 2 (1954).

——. "Taraco: Monografía de un latifundio del altiplano boliviano," *El Trimestre Económico*, XXII, No. 2 (1955).

García, Antonio. "La reforma agraria y el desarrollo social de Bolivia." A series of articles published in the newspaper *La Nación* of La Paz, Bolivia, between September 16, 1964, and October 4, 1964.

García, Raúl Alfonso. *Diez años de reforma agraria en Bolivia*. La Paz, Bolivia: Dirección Nacional de Informaciones, 1963.

Heath, Dwight B. "El cambio social y cultural según la reforma agraria," *Revista del Instituto de Sociología Boliviana*, April, 1960.

——, Charles J. Erasmus, Hans Buechler, and Jorge Dandler. "Land Reform

and Social Revolution in Bolivia." Mimeo. Madison: University of Wisconsin
Land Tenure Center, 1965.

Leonard, Olen. *Bolivia: Land, People, Institutions.* Washington, D.C.: Scarecrow Press, 1952.

Leons, Madeleine Barbara. "Changing Patterns of Social Stratification in an Emergent Bolivian Community." Ph.D. thesis, University of California at Los Angeles, 1966.

McBride, George. *The Agrarian Indian Communities of Highland Bolivia.* New York: Oxford University Press, 1921.

Maldonado, Abraham. *Derecho agrario.* La Paz, Bolivia, 1956.

Matos Mar, José. "Cambios sociales en el altiplano boliviano: El área cultural de Tiahuanaco-Taraco," *Economía y Agricultura,* I, No. 2 (1963–1964).

Moller Pacieri, Edwin A. *El cooperativismo y la revolución.* La Paz, Bolivia: Dirección Nacional de Cooperativas, 1963.

Moncayo, José Flores. *Legislación boliviana del indio: Recopilación 1825–1953.* La Paz, Bolivia: Ministerio de Asuntos Campesinos, 1953.

Morales Condarco, Ramiro. *Zárate, El "Temible" Willka: Historia de la rebelión indígena de 1899.* La Paz, Bolivia: Talleres Gráficos Bolivianos, 1966.

Ostria Gutiérrez, Alberto. *Un pueblo en la cruz.* Santiago, Chile: Editorial del Pacífico, 1956.

Ovando, Jorge. *Sobre el problema nacional y colonial de Bolivia.* Cochabamba, Bolivia: Editorial Canelas, 1961.

Patch, Richard. "Bolivia: U.S. Assistance in a Revolutionary Setting," in Richard Adams *et al., Social Change in Latin America Today* (New York: Harper, 1960).

——. "Peasantry and National Revolution: Bolivia," in Kalman Silvert (ed.), *Expectant Peoples: Nationalism and Development* (New York: Random House, 1963).

——. "Social Implications of the Bolivian Agrarian Reform." Ph.D. thesis, University of Michigan, 1956.

Peñaloza, Luis. *Historia económica de Bolivia.* 2 vols. La Paz, Bolivia, 1953–1954.

——. "Planificación económica de Bolivia," *Revista Industria,* No. 40 (1956).

——. *Política económica oligárquica y política económica de la revolución nacional.* La Paz, Bolivia: Ediciones SPIC, 1958.

Pérez Patón, Roberto. *La reforma agraria en Bolivia.* La Paz, Bolivia: Universidad Mayor de San Andrés, 1961.

Reinaga, Fausto. *Tierra y libertad: La revolución nacional y el indio.* Bolivia: Ediciones Rumbo Sindical, 1952.

Reyes, Celso. *Estudio de Ingavi, Omasuyos y los Andes.* La Paz, Bolivia: Ministerio de Agricultura, 1946.

Rickabaugh, Carey G. "The Politicization Function of Agrarian Interest

Groups: A Case Study of the Bolivian Campesino Sindicatos." Ph.D. thesis, University of Maryland, 1966.
United Nations, International Labour Organization. *Informe de la misión conjunta de las Naciones Unidas y organismos especializados para el estudio de los problemas de las poblaciones andinas.* Geneva: United Nations, 1953.
Urquidi, Arturo. "Antecedentes de la reforma agraria," *Revista Khana*, III, Nos. 5 and 6 (1954).
Vega, Alipio Valencia. *El indio en la independencia.* La Paz, Bolivia: Ministerio de Educación, 1961.

Brazil

Barreto, Lida. *Julião, nordeste, revolução.* Rio de Janeiro: Editôra Civilização Brasileira, 1963.
Benedictis, Michel De. "Problemi economico-agrari de commune brasiliano della zona 'metalurgica' del Minas Gerais: Lagoa Santa," *Rivista di Agricoltura Subtropicale e Tropicale*, (Florence), LVI. Nos. 7–9 (1962).
Borges, F. C. "O movimento camponês no Nordeste," *Estudos Sociais*, IV, No. 15 (1962).
Calazans, Julieta. *Cartilha sindical do trabalhador rural.* Natal, Brazil: Serviço de Assistência Rural, 1961.
——. *Realidade e tendências do sindicalismo brasileiro no campo.* CECO Pamphlet No. 2. Rio de Janeiro: Centro de Educação e Cultura Operária (CECO), 1964.
Callado, Antônio. *Os industriais da sêca e os "Galileus" de Pernambuco.* Rio de Janeiro: Editôra Civilização Brasileira, 1960.
——. "Revolução piloto em Pernambuco." A series of twelve articles in the newspaper *O Jornal do Brasil* of Rio de Janeiro, 1963.
——. *No tempo de Arraes: Padres e comunistas na revolução sem violência.* Rio de Janeiro: José Álvaro, 1964.
Cardoso, Fernando. "Tensões sociais no campo e reforma agrária," *Revista Brasileira de Estudos Políticos*, No. 12 (1960).
Cardoso, Francisco. *Democracia ou servidão rural?* São Paulo, Brazil: Editôra Saraiva, 1953.
——. *Tratado de direito rural brasileiro.* São Paulo, Brazil: Editôra Saraiva, 1953.
Carneiro, Mario Afonso. "Sapé." Manuscript. Rio de Janeiro: Latin American Center for Research in the Social Sciences, 1963.
Carvalho Ribeiro, Augusta. "Aspectos básicos num estudo de reforma sindical," *Arquivos do Instituto de Direito Social*, XIV, No. 2 (1962).
Comité Interamericano de Desarrollo Agrícola (CIDA). *Brazil: Land Tenure Conditions and Socio-economic Development of the Agricultural Sector.* Washington, D.C.: Pan American Union, 1966. Especially ch. 4.

Confederação Rural Brasileira. "Agricultura e associativismo rural no estado da Bahia," *Revista Brasileira dos Municípios*, LIII-LIV (1961).

Correia de Andrade, Manoel. *A terra e o homem no Nordeste*. Rio de Janeiro: Editôra Brasiliense, 1963.

Crespo, Padre Paulo. "Pequeno resumo do movimento sindical rural em Pernambuco." Mimeo. Recife, Brazil: Serviço de Orientação Rural de Pernambuco, 1966.

——. "O problema do camponês no nordeste brasileiro," *Síntese Política, Econômica e Social*, V, No. 17 (1963).

Cunha, Euclides da. *Rebellion in the Backlands*. Chicago, Ill.: University of Chicago Press, 1964.

Dias, Everardo. *Historia das lutas sociais no Brasil*. São Paulo, Brazil: Editôra L. B., 1962.

Diégues Junior, Manoel. *População e propriedade da terra no Brasil*. Washington, D.C.: Pan American Union, 1959.

Duarte de Barros, Wanderbilt. "Previdência social na agricultura," *Síntese Política, Econômica e Social*, No. 16 (1962).

Dumolin, Diana C. "The Rural Labor Movement in Brazil." Mimeo. Madison: University of Wisconsin Land Tenure Center, 1964-1965.

Eckenstein, Christoph. "A Report on Brazil's Northeast," *Swiss Review of World Affairs*, XII, No. 9 (1962) and No. 10 (1963).

"Estrutura agrária e industrial pernambucana," *Desenvolvimento e Conjuntura*, VII, No. 1 (1963).

Faria, Otavio. "Sindicalismo novo," *Síntese Política, Econômica, e Social*, April-June, 1964.

Feitosa Martins, Araguaya. *Alguns aspectos da inquietação trabalhista no campo*. São Paulo, Brazil: Editôra Brasiliense, 1961.

——. "Alguns aspectos da inquietação trabalhista no campo," *Revista Brasiliense*, No. 40 (1962).

Fernandes, Florestan. "Crescimento econômico e instabilidade política no Brasil," *Revista Civilização Brasileira*, I, No. 11 (1966) and No. 12 (1967).

Forman, Shepard. "Disunity and Discontent: A Study of Peasant Political Movements in Brazil." Paper presented at the Colloquium on Crisis, Resistance and Change, University of California, Feb., 1968.

Freitas, Norma Ramos de. "As estruturas agrárias pretéritas e causas da sua modificação no recôncavo açucareiro da Bahia," *Boletim Baiano de Geografia*, II, Nos. 5-6 (1961).

Freitas Marcondes, J. V. "As missões rurais e a sindicalização rural," *Arquivos de Direito Social*, X, No. 1 (1952).

——. *First Brazilian Legislation Relating to Rural Unions*. Gainesville: University of Florida Press, 1962.

——. "Revisão e reforma agrária," *Trabalhos do Instituto dos Advogados de São Paulo*, 1962.

Galjart, Benno. "Class and 'Following' in Rural Brazil," *América Latina*, VII, No. 3 (1964).

Guimaraes, Alberto Passos. "A questão agrária brasileira," *Estudos Sociais*, IV, No. 14 (1962).

Henrique, João. *Organização agrária sem comunismo*. Rio de Janeiro: 1961.

Horowitz, Irving Louis. *Revolución en el Brasil*. Mexico City: Fondo de Cultura Económica, 1966. Ch. 2: "Ideología de la revolución campesina."

Huizer, Gerrit. "Some Notes on Community Development and Rural Social Research," *América Latina*, VII, No. 3 (1965).

Hutchinson, Bertram. "The Patron-Dependent Relationship in Brazil: A Preliminary Examination," *Sociologia Ruralis*, VI, No. 1 (1966).

Ianni, Octavio. "A constituição do proletariado agrícola no Brasil," *Revista Brasileira de Estudos Políticos*, Oct., 1961.

Julião, Francisco. "Brazil: A Christian Country," *Monthly Review*, XIV, No. 5 (1962).

———. *¡Campesinos a mí!* Buenos Aires, Argentina: Cía. Argentina de Editores, 1963.

———. *Escucha campesino*. Montevideo, Uruguay: Ediciones Presente, 1962.

———. *Que são as ligas camponesas?* Rio de Janeiro: Editôra Civilização Brasileira, 1962.

——— et al. "The Declaration of Belo Horizonte," in T. Lynn Smith (ed.), *Agrarian Reform in Latin America* (New York: Knopf, 1965).

Junior, Theotonio. "O movimento operario no Brasil," *Revista Brasiliense*, No. 39 (1962).

Leal, Victor Nunes. *Coronelismo, enxada e voto*. Rio de Janeiro, 1948.

Leeds, Anthony. "Brazil and the Myth of Francisco Julião," in J. Maier and R. W. Weatherhead (eds.), *Politics of Change in Latin America* (New York: Praeger, 1964).

Les ligues paysannes et le réveil du Nord-est. La Documentation Française, Articles et Documents (Paris). (0.1162), 1–10, Oct., 1961.

A Liga. Periodical of the Ligas Camponesas, published from October, 1962, to March, 1964.

Lowy, Michael. "Notas sôbre a questão agrária no Brasil," *Revista Brasiliense*, (Sept.–Oct., 1960).

Martins, Ibiapaba. "Proletariado e inquietação rural," *Revista Brasiliense*, No. 42 (1962).

Martins, Renato Gonçalves. *A questão agrária e o problema do camponês: Fundamentos para uma nova política do campo*. Rio de Janeiro: Casa do Estudante do Brasil, 1955.

Medina, Carlos Alberto. "A estrutura agrária brasileira: Características e tendências," *América Latina*, VII, No. 1 (1964).

———. "Impasse e perspectivas da sociologia rural no Brasil: Estudo de quatro fenômenos sociológicos," *América Latina*, IX, No. 3 (1966).

Melo, Padre Antonio. "Mundo de Deus, mundo de todos." Pamphlet. Recife, Brazil.

———. "Pseudo-solução, derrota, lideranças democráticas na lavoura de Pernambuco." Pamphlet. Recife, Brazil, Sept. 1965.

Nogueira, Oracy. "Os movimentos e partidos políticos em Itapetininga," *Revista Brasileira de Estudos Políticos,* XI (June, 1961).

O problema agrário na zona canavieira de Pernambuco: Conferências e debates no simpósio realizado por iniciativa do Instituto Joaquim Nabuco de Pesquisas Sociais. Recife, Brazil: Imprensa Universitária, 1965.

Pastore, José. "Conflito e mudança social no Brasil rural," *Sociologia,* XXIV, No. 4 (1962).

Paulson, Beldon H. "Local Political Patterns in Northeastern Brazil: A Community Case Study." Mimeo. Madison: University of Wisconsin Land Tenure Center, 1964–1965.

Prado Junior, Caio. "The Agrarian Question in Brazil," *Studies on the Left,* IV, No. 4 (1964).

———. "O estatuto do trabalhador rural," *Revista Brasiliense,* No. 47 (1963).

Price, Robert E. "Rural Unionization in Brazil." Mimeo. Madison: University of Wisconsin Land Tenure Center, 1964.

Primeira Convenção Brasileira de Sindicatos Rurais: Mensagem, Conclusões. Natal, Brazil: The Convenção, July 15–20, 1963.

Pruzensky, William M. "Brazilian Agrarian Reform and Rural Labor." M.A. thesis, American University, 1962.

Rodrigues, J. A. R. "Estrutura sindical brasileira," *Revista de Estudos Sócio-Econômicos,* I, No. 12 (1963).

Sá Leitão Rios, Gilvandro. "Uma experiência de 'Community Development' no sertão do Brasil," *América Latina,* IX, No. 1 (1966).

Saito, Hiroshi. "O cooperativismo na região de Cotia: Estudo de transplantação cultural," *Sociologia,* XVI, No. 3 (1954).

Sampaio, Aluysio. *Comentários ao Estatuto do Trabalhador Rural.* São Paulo, Brazil: Editôra Fulgor, 1964.

Santos de Morais, Clodomir. "Comportamiento ideológico de las clases y capas del campo en el proceso de organización." Mimeo. Santiago, Chile: Instituto de Capacitación e Investigación en Reforma Agraria (ICIRA), 1965.

Schattan, Salomão. "Estrutura econômica da agricultura paulista," *Revista Brasiliense,* No. 37 (1961).

Semenzato, Geraldo. "Itabuna, Bahia." Manuscript prepared for Comité Interamericano de Desarrollo Agrícola, 1966.

Silva, José Fabio Barbosa da. "Organização social de Juazeiro e tensões entre litoral e interior," *Sociologia,* XXIV, No. 3 (1962).

Silva, Manoel. "Congresso dos trabalhadores rurais do Paraná," *Revista Brasiliense,* No. 33 (1961).

"Los sindicatos campesinos del Brasil: Entrevista al Padre Francisco Lage Pessoa," *Comunidad*, I, No. 1 (1966).

Sodré, F. N. *¿Quem é Francisco Julião?* São Paulo, Brazil: Edições pela Redenção Nacional, 1963.

Souza Campos Batalha, Wilson de. "Aspectos do sindicalismo brasileiro," *Arquivos do Instituto de Direito Social*, XIV, No. 2 (1962).

Varela, Pedro Correia. "Situação dos trabalhadores," *Revista Civilização Brasileira*, I, Nos. 9–10 (1966).

Vera, N. "O congresso camponês em Belo Horizonte," *Revista Brasiliense*, No. 39 (1962).

——. "O primeiro encontro camponês de Goiana," *Revista Brasiliense*, No. 50 (1963).

Vinhas, Moisés. "Contribução pelo estudo da estrutura e da organização do proletariado paulista," *Revista Brasiliense*, No. 36 (1961).

Willems, Emilio. "Religious Mass Movements and Social Change in Brazil," in E. N. Backlanoff (ed.), *New Perspectives on Brazil* (Nashville, Tenn.: Vanderbilt Press, 1966).

Willkie, Mary. "A Report on Rural Syndicates in Pernambuco." Mimeo. Rio de Janeiro: Latin American Center for Research in the Social Sciences, 1961

Chile

L'action paysanne au Chili. Documentation Française, Articles et Documents (Paris). (0.1153), Oct. 7–8, 1961.

Barría Serón, Jorge I. *Trayectoria y estructura del movimiento sindical chileno, 1946–1962.* Santiago: Universidad de Chile, Instituto de Organización y Administración, 1963.

Caputto, Orlando. "Las organizaciones campesinas." Thesis, Universidad de Chile, 1965.

Comité Interamericano de Desarrollo Agrícola (CIDA). *Chile: Tenencia de la tierra y desarrollo socio-económico del sector agrícola.* Washington, D.C.: Pan American Union, 1966.

Corvalán L., Luis. *La organización y la lucha de los campesinos impondrán la reforma agraria: Discursos.* Santiago, Chile: Impresora Horizonte, 1966.

Domínguez, Oscar. "Aspiraciones de los inquilinos en la provincia de Santiago." Santiago, Chile: Instituto de Capacitación e Investigación en Reforma Agraria, 1966.

Landsberger, Henry A., and Fernando Canitrot. *Iglesia, clase media, y el movimiento sindical campesino.* Santiago, Chile: Editorial del Pacífico, 1967.

Marshall Silva, Jorge. *La lucha por la reforma agraria.* Santiago, Chile: Imprenta América, 1941.

Menges, Constantine. "The Politics of Agrarian Reform in Chile, 1958–1964: The Role of Parties and Interest Groups." Ph.D. thesis, Department of Public Law and Government, Columbia University, 1966.

Petras, James F. "Chile's Christian Peasant Unions: Notes and Comments on an Interview with Hector Alarcón." University of Wisconsin Land Tenure Center, Newsletter No. 23. Madison: The Center, March–July, 1966.

Revista del MCI. Official publication of the Movimiento Campesino Independiente I, No. 1 (1965).

Revista Nacional de Trabajadores: Número Especial Campesino, I, No. 10 (1965).

Sociedad Chilena de Derecho del Trabajo y de la Seguridad Social. *Manual Campesino.* Santiago, Chile: The Sociedad, 1966.

Sociedad Nacional de Agricultura. Report presented by Luis Larrain Marín, Tomás Voticky I., and Daniel Guell. Santiago, Chile, Oct. 14, 1965.

Thiesenhusen, William C. "Experimental Programmes of Land Reform in Chile." Ph.D. thesis, University of Wisconsin, 1965.

Vera Lamperein, José. "Sindicalización campesina," *Panorama Económico* (Santiago de Chile), XI, No. 117 (1957).

Walker Linares, Francisco. "Sindicalización campesina en Chile," *Revista Internacional del Trabajo* (Geneva) LXVIII, No. 6 (1953).

——. "Sindicalización campesina en Chile," *Revista Mexicana del Trabajo,* I, Nos. 11–12 (1954).

Colombia

Colorado, Eugenio. *El sindicato y la comunidad rural.* United Nations, Serie sobre Organización de la Comunidad, No. 8 (1954). Reprinted in *Colección de Estudios,* No. 19.

Comité Interamericano de Desarrollo Agrícola. *Colombia: Tenencia de la tierra y desarrollo socio-económico del sector agrícola.* Washington, D.C.: Pan American Union, 1966. Especially ch. 4, D.2, "Asociaciones rurales."

"Conozca a FANAL." Mimeographed leaflet. Bogota, Colombia: FANAL, 1966.

Dirigentes Agrarios. Half-yearly periodical of FANAL.

Fearer, Jane. "Social and Political Organization of the Indians of the Sierra Nevada de Santa Marta." Ph.D. thesis, Oxford University, 1967.

Galarza, Ernesto. "La realidad de FANAL y del problema agrario colombiano." Mimeo. Washington, D.C.: National Farmers' Union, 1963.

Gutiérrez, José. *La rebeldía colombiana: Observaciones psicológicas sobre la actualidad política.* Bogota, Colombia: Ediciones Tercer Mundo, 1962.

Guzmán, Germán, Orlando Fals Borda, and Eduardo Umana Luna. *La violencia en Colombia: Estudio de un proceso social,* Vol. I. *Monografías Sociológicas* No. 12. Bogota, Colombia: Universidad Nacional, 1962.

——. *La violencia en Colombia: Estudio de un proceso social,* Vol. II. Bogota, Colombia: Ediciones Tercer Mundo, 1964.

Instituto Interamericano de Ciencias Agrícolas, Centro Interamericano de Reforma Agraria. "Sindicalismo y reforma agraria." Nov., 1965.

Sánchez, A. M. "El cooperativismo en Colombia," *Economía Colombiana*, IV, No. 11 (1955).

Sardo, Joseph. "A Comparative Study of Rural Social Organization in Sicily and El Valle del Cauca, Colombia." Ph.D. thesis, Department of Sociology, University of Florida.

Torres Restrepo, Camilo. "La violencia y los cambios socio-culturales en las áreas rurales colombianas." Bogota, Colombia: Memoria del Primer Congreso Nacional de Sociología, 1963.

Unión de Trabajadores del Valle (UTRAVAL). *Más allá de la huelga: La toma de El Arado*. Cali, Colombia: The Unión, 1966.

Yepes Zuloaga, Horacio. "El movimiento sindical colombiano," *Estudios de Derecho*, XVIII, No. 55 (1959).

El Salvador

Buezo, H. *Sangre de Hermanos*. Panama City, 1937.

Diario de Hoy (San Salvador). Articles of Jan. 5 to Feb. 12, 1967.

Jiménez Barrios, Rodolfo. *La rebelión comunista*. Mexico City, 1937.

Luna, David. "Algunas facetas sociales en la vida de Agustín Farabundo Marti," *Revista Salvadoreña de Ciencias Sociales*, No. 1 (1965).

Machón Vilanova, Francisco. *La ola roja*. Mexico City, 1948.

Méndez, Joaquín. *Los sucesos comunistas en El Salvador*. San Salvador, El Salvador: Imprenta Funes y Ungo, 1932.

Schlesinger, Jorge. *Revolución comunista*. Guatemala City: Unión Tipográfica Castañeda, Ávila y Cía., 1946.

Guatemala

Adams, Richard N. (ed). *Political Changes in Guatemalan Indian Communities: A Symposium*. New Orleans, La.: Tulane University, Middle American Research Institute, 1957.

Bishop, Edwin W. "The Guatemalan Labor Movement, 1944–1959." Ph.D. thesis, University of Wisconsin, 1959.

Bush, Archer C. "Organized Labor in Guatemala, 1944–1949." Colgate University Area Studies, Latin American Seminar Report No. 2 (1950).

Guatemala, Instituto de Investigaciones Económicas y Sociales. *Aspectos jurídicos-laborales de la actividad agropecuaria*. Guatemala City: The Instituto, 1961.

Hoyt, Elizabeth E. "The Indian Laborer on Guatemalan Coffee Fincas," *Inter-American Economic Affairs*, IX, No. 1 (1955).

——. "El trabajador indígena en las fincas de café de Guatemala," *Economía de Guatemala*, Seminario de Integración Guatemalteca No. 6 (1958).

Melgar Rodríguez, Augusto. *El movimiento cooperativo de Guatemala*. Guatemala City: Universidad de San Carlos de Guatemala, Facultad de Ciencias Económicas, 1963.

Newbold, Stokes. "Receptivity to Communist-fomented Agitation in Rural Guatemala," *Economic Development and Cultural Change*, V, No. 4 (1957).

Pearson, Neale J. "The Confederación Nacional Campesina de Guatemala (CNCG) and Peasant Unionism in Guatemala, 1944–1954." M.A. thesis, Georgetown University, 1964.

Rodas Cruz, Manuel. *El cooperativismo: El movimiento cooperativo en Guatemala y su legislación*. Guatemala City: Tipografía Nacional, 1954.

United States Department of State, Public Services Division. *A Case History of Communist Penetration in Guatemala*. Inter-American Series No. 52. Washington, D.C.: The Department, April 1957.

Whetten, Nathan L. *Guatemala: The Land and the People*. New Haven, Conn.: Yale University Press, 1961.

Mexico

Alba, Víctor. *Historia del movimiento obrero en América Latina*. Mexico City: Libreros Mexicanos Unidos, 1964.

Alcántara Ferrer, Sergio. "El proceso de cambio económico-social en Taretan, Michoacán: Un estudio de caso sobre organizaciones campesinas." Mimeo. Mexico City: Centro de Investigaciones Agrarias, 1968. Tesis profesional para la Escuela Nacional de Antropología e Historia.

Araiza, Luis. *Historia de la Casa del Obrero Mundial*. Mexico City, 1963.

Beals, Carleton. *Mexico: An Interpretation*. New York: B. W. Huebsch, 1923.

Brandenburg, Frank. "Mexico: An Experiment in One-Party Democracy." Ph.D. thesis, University of Pennsylvania, 1955.

Cárdenas, Lázaro. *La unificación campesina*. Mexico City: Partido Nacional Revolucionario, Biblioteca de Cultura Social y Política, 1936.

Carrión, Jorge. "Ursulo Galván," *Problemas Agrícolas e Industriales de México*, IV, No. 2 (1952).

Chevalier, François. "Ejido y estabilidad en México," *Ciencias Políticas y Sociales*, XI, No. 42 (1965).

——. "Un factor decisivo de la revolución agraria de México: El levantamiento de Zapata (1911–1919)," *Cuadernos Americanos*, XIX, No. 6 (1960).

Clark, Marjorie Ruth. *Organized Labor in Mexico*. Chapel Hill: University of North Carolina Press, 1934.

Cline, Howard F. *Mexico: Revolution to Evolution, 1940–1960*. New York: Oxford University Press, 1962.

Confederación de Trabajadores de México. *Informe del Comité Nacional, 1936–37*. Mexico City: Consejo Nacional Ordinario, 1937.

Cuadras Caldas, Julio. *El comunismo criollo*. Puebla, Mexico, 1930.

Díaz Soto y Gama, Antonio. *La cuestión agraria en México*. Mexico City: Instituto de Investigaciones Sociales de México, U.N.A.M., 1959.

Dromundo, Baltasar. *Emiliano Zapata: Biografía*. Mexico City: Imprenta Mundial, 1934.

Dunn, H. H. *The Crimson Jester: Zapata of Mexico.* New York: R. M. McBride, 1933.

Durán, Marco Antonio. "El estancamiento en la organización interna de los ejidos," *El Trimestre Económico,* XXXII, No. 3 (1965).

Eckstein, Salomón. *El ejido colectivo en México.* Mexico City: Fondo de Cultura Económica, 1966.

Friedrich, Paul. "Cacique: The Recent History and Present Structure of Politics in a Tarascan Village." Ph.D. thesis, Yale University, 1957.

———. "A Mexican Cacicazgo," *Ethnology,* IV, No. 2 (1965).

Gibb, Bruce L. "A Case Study of Rural Cooperatives," *Public and International Affairs,* II, No. 1 (1963).

Gill, Mario. *Episodios mexicanos.* Mexico City: Editorial Azteca, 1960. Especially ch. 2: "Zapata, su pueblo y sus hijos."

Gómez Jara, Francisco. "Las organizaciones campesinas de México," *Magisterio,* No. 71 (1966).

González Ramírez, Manuel. *La revolución social de México,* Vol. III: *El problema agrario.* Mexico City: Fondo de Cultura Económica, 1966.

Guerra Cepeda, Gilberto. *El ejido colectivizado en la Comarca Lagunera.* Mexico City: Banco Nacional de Crédito Ejidal, 1939.

Hernández, Pedro Félix. "An Analysis of Social Power in Five Mexican Ejidos." Ph.D. thesis, Iowa State University, 1965.

Huizer, Gerrit. "Los movimientos campesinos en México." Translated by Sergio Alcántara Ferrer. Mexico City: Centro de Investigaciones Agrarias, March, 1968.

Kirk, Betty. *Covering the Mexican Front.* Norman: University of Oklahoma Press, 1942.

Landsberger, Henry A., and Cynthia N. Hewitt. "A Pilot Study of Participation in Rural Organizations: 'Political Socialization' in Mexico." Mimeo. Ithaca, N.Y.: New York State School of Industrial and Labor Relations, Cornell University, 1967.

———. "Preliminary Report on a Case Study of Mexican Peasant Organizations." Mimeo. Ithaca, N.Y.: New York State School of Industrial and Labor Relations, Cornell University, 1966.

la Peña, Moisés T. de. *El pueblo y su tierra: Mito y realidad de la reforma agraria en México.* Mexico City: Cuadernos Americanos, 1964.

Liga de Agrónomos Socialistas. *El colectivismo agrario en México: La Comarca Lagunera.* Mexico City: The Liga, 1940.

Liga de Comunidades Agrarias del Estado de Veracruz. *La cuestión agraria y el problema campesino.* Veracruz, Mexico: Jalapa-Enríquez, 1924.

List Arzubide, Germán. *Emiliano Zapata: Exaltación.* Mexico City: Ediciones Conferencia, 1965.

Lombardo Toledano, Vicente. *Teoría y práctica del movimiento sindical mexicano.* Mexico City: Editorial del Magisterio, 1961.

MacLean y Estenós, Roberto. "La revolución de 1910 y el problema agrario de Mexico," *Estudios Sociológicos*, II (IX Congreso Nacional de Sociología, 1958).

Magaña, Gildardo. *Emiliano Zapata y el agrarismo en México*. Mexico City: Editorial Ruto, 1951.

Maples Arce, Manuel. "El movimiento social en Veracruz." Speech, May 1, 1927.

Martínez Múgica, Apolinar. *Primo Tapia: Semblanza de un revolucionario michoacano*. Mexico City, 1946.

Melgarejo, Antonio D. *Los crímenes del Zapatismo*. Mexico City: Editores Rojas, 1913.

México, Departamento Agrario. *Primer Congreso Nacional Revolucionario de Derecho Agrario*. Mexico City: The Departamento, 1946.

Millon, Robert P. *Vicente Lombardo Toledano: Biografía intelectual de un marxista mexicano*. (Translation of a Ph.D. thesis, University of North Carolina, 1963.) Mexico City, 1964.

Morales Jiménez, Alberto. *Zapata*. "La revolución y sus hombres" series, No. 1. Mexico City: Editorial Morelos, 1961.

Munguía, Enrique. "Le problème agraire au Mexique," *Revue Internationale de Travail*, XXXVI, Nos. 1–2 (1937).

Nathan, Paul. "México en la época de Cárdenas," *Problemas Agrícolas e Industriales de México*, VII, No. 3 (1955).

Padgett, L. Vincent. *The Mexican Political System*. Boston: Houghton Mifflin, 1966.

——. "Popular Participation in the Mexican 'One-Party' System." Ph.D. thesis, Northwestern University, 1955.

Palacios, Porfirio. *Emiliano Zapata: Datos biográficos-históricos*. Mexico City: Editores Libro Mex, 1960.

Partido Nacional Revolucionario. *La gira del General Lázaro Cárdenas: Síntesis Ideológica*. Mexico City: The Partido, 1934.

Pavletich, Esteban. *Zapata: Precursor del agrarismo en América*. Lima, Peru: Editorial Tierra Nueva, 1959.

Portes Gil, Emilio. *Quince años de política mexicana*. Mexico City, 1941.

Romanucci Schwartz, Lola. "Morality, Conflict and Violence in a Mexican Mestizo Village." Ph.D. thesis, Indiana University, 1962.

Rouaix, Pastor. "Génesis de los Artículos 27 y 123 de la Constitución Política de 1917," *Biblioteca del Instituto Nacional Estudios Históricos de la Revolución Mexicana*, XVI (1959).

Schmitt, Karl M. *Communism in Mexico: A Study in Political Frustration*. Austin: University of Texas Press, 1965.

Senior, Clarence. *Democracy Comes to a Cotton Kingdom*. Mexico City: Centro de Estudios Pedagógicos e Hispanoamericanos, 1940.

——. "Reforma agraria y democracia en la Comarca Lagunera," *Problemas Agrícolas e Industriales de México*, VIII, No. 2 (1956).

Silva Herzog, Jesús. *El agrarismo mexicano y la reforma agraria*. Mexico City: Fondo de Cultura Económica, 1959.

Simpson, N. Eyler. *The Ejido: Mexico's Way Out*. Chapel Hill: University of North Carolina Press, 1937.

Sotelo Inclán, Jesús. *Raíz y razón de Zapata: Investigación histórica*. Mexico City: Editorial Etnos, 1943.

Tannenbaum, Frank. *The Mexican Agrarian Revolution*. New York: Macmillan, 1929.

——. *Peace by Revolution: Mexico after 1910*. New York: Columbia University Press, 1933; paperback edition, 1966.

Taracena, Alfonso. *La tragedia Zapatista: Historia de la revolución del sur*. Mexico City: Editorial Bolívar, 1932.

Weyl, Nathaniel and Sylvia. *The Reconquest of Mexico: The Years of Lázaro Cárdenas*. London: Oxford University Press, 1939.

Whetten, Nathan. *Rural Mexico*. Chicago, Ill.: University of Chicago Press, 1948.

Wolf, Eric. "Aspects of Group Relations in a Complex Society. Mexico," *American Anthropologist*, LVIII, No. 6 (1956).

Peru

Barnett, Clifford R. "An Analysis of Social Movements on a Peruvian Hacienda." Ph.D. thesis, Cornell University, 1960.

Bourricaud, François. "Sindicalismo y política en el Perú," *Cuadernos*, No. 57 (1962).

Chaplin, David. "Peru's Postponed Revolution," *World Politics*, XX (Spring, 1968).

Comité Interamericano de Desarrollo Agrícola. *Perú: Tenencia de la tierra y desarrollo socio-económico del sector agrícola*. Washington, D.C.: Pan American Union, 1966.

Corduruna, Silvestre. "Las experiencias de la última etapa de las luchas revolucionarias en el Perú," *Vanguardia Revolucionaria* (Lima), 1966.

Cornejo Bouroncle, Jorge. *Pumacahua: La revolución de Cuzco de 1814: Estudio documentado*. Cuzco, Peru: H. G. Rosas, 1956.

Dew, Edward M., Jr. "Peasant Organization in Puno, Peru," Ph.D. thesis, University of California at Los Angeles, 1966.

Díaz Ahumada, J. *Historia de las luchas sindicales en el valle de Chicama*. Trujillo, Peru: Librería y Editorial Bolivariana, n.d.

Dobyns, Henry F. "Peasants, Politics, and Peace in the Andes." Mimeo. Ithaca, N.Y.: Cornell University, Conference on the Development of Highland Communities in Latin America, 1966.

Escobar, Gabriel. *La estructura polítoca-rural del departamento de Puno.* Cuzco, Peru. 1960.

Fonseca Martel, C. "Sindicatos agrarios del valle de Chancay." Tesis de bachiller, Departamento de Antropología, Facultad de Letras, Universidad de San Marcos, Lima, Peru, 1966.

Ford, Thomas R. *Man and Land in Peru.* Gainesville: University of Florida Press, 1955.

Gilly, Adolfo. "Révolution au Pérou: Hugo Blanco et le mouvement paysan," *Partisans* (Paris), No. 13 (1963–1964).

Greaves, Thomas C. "Descent to the Coast: The Labor Supply of Peruvian Coastal Haciendas." Mimeo. Paper read at the 66th Annual Meeting of the American Anthropological Association, Nov. 30–Dec. 3, 1967, Washington, D.C.

Hobsbawm, Eric J. E. "Problèmes agraires à La Convención (Pérou)." Mimeo. Communication présentée au Colloque International C.N.R.S. sur les Problèmes Agraires en Amerique Latine, Paris, Oct. 11–16, 1965.

Letts, Ricardo C. "Breve historia contemporánea de la lucha por la reforma agraria en el Perú," *Economía y Agricultura,* I, No. 2 (1963–1964).

Lewin, Bolislao. *La rebelión de Tupac Amaru.* Buenos Aires, Argentina: Hachette, 1957.

Martínez, Hector. "La hacienda Capana," *Perú Indígena,* X, Nos. 24–25 (1963).

Martínez de la Torre, D. *Apuntes para una interpretación marxista de la historia social del Perú.* 4 vols. Lima, Peru: Editorial Peruana, 1947.

Neira, Hugo. "Le castrisme dans les Andes," *Partisans* (Paris), Nos. 26–27 (1966).

——. *Cuzco: Tierra y muerte.* Lima, Peru: Problemas de Hoy, 1964.

Payne, James L. *Labor and Politics in Peru: The System of Political Bargaining.* New Haven, Conn.: Yale University Press, 1965.

Pumaruna, Américo. "Perú: Revolución, insurrección, guerrillas," *Cuadernos de Ruedo Ibérico* (Paris), VI (April–May, 1966).

Quijano O., Aníbal. "El movimiento campesino del Perú y sus líderes," *América Latina,* VIII, No. 4 (1965).

Valcárcel, Daniel. *La rebelión de Tupac Amaru.* Mexico City: Fondo de Cultura Económica, 1947.

Valcárcel Esparza, Carlos. *Rebeliones indígenas.* Lima, Peru: Editorial PTCM, 1964.

Venezuela

Acosta Saignes, Miguel. *Latifundio.* Caracas, Venezuela: Editorial Popular, 1935.

Federación Campesina de Venezuela. *La cuestión agraria venezolana: tésis política y programa de la Federación Campesina de Venezuela.* Caracas, Venezuela: Tipografía Americana, 1948.

———. "Proyecto de estatutos." Caracas, Venezuela: The Federación, 1967.

Fernández y Fernández, Ramón. *Reforma agraria en Venezuela.* Caracas, Venezuela: Tipografía Vargas, 1948.

González, Armando. "Función de la Federación Campesina de Venezuela en la Reforma Agraria." Report presented at the F.A.O. World Conference on Land Reform, Rome, 1966.

———. *La reforma agraria y el movimiento campesino.* Caracas, Venezuela: Editorial Sucre, 1963.

———. "Reforma agraria y superación nacional," *Política* (Caracas), III, No. 36 (1964).

Mathiason, John R. "El campesino venezolano: Perspectivas de cambio," in Frank Bonilla and José A. Silva Michelena (eds.), *Estudios de la política venezolana: Exploraciones en análisis y síntesis* (Cambridge, Mass.: Center for International Studies of the Massachusetts Institute of Technology, 1966).

Partido Acción Democrática. *Tesis agraria del Partido Acción Democrática.* Caracas, Venezuela: IX Convención Nacional, 1958.

Partido Comunista de Venezuela. *Sobre la cuestión agraria en Venezuela.* Caracas, Venezuela: Editorial Cantaclaro, 1960.

Powell, John D. "The Politics of Agrarian Reform in Venezuela: History, System and Process." Ph.D. thesis, University of Wisconsin, 1966.

———. "Preliminary Report on the Federación Campesina de Venezuela: Origins, Organization, Leadership and Role in the Agrarian Reform Program." University of Wisconsin Land Tenure Center, Research Paper No. 9. Madison: The Center, 1964.

Quijada, Ramón. *Reforma agraria en Venezuela.* Caracas, Venezuela: Editorial Arte, 1963.

Troconis Guerrero, Luis. *La cuestión agraria en la historia nacional.* Caracas, Venezuela: Editorial Arte, 1962.

United Nations, International Labour Organization. *Freedom of Association and Conditions of Work in Venezuela.* Studies and Reports, New Series, No. 21. Geneva: United Nations, 1950.

———. *Freedom of Association and Conditions of Work in Venezuela: Observations of the Government of Venezuela on the Report of the I.L.O. Mission.* Studies and Reports, New Series, No. 21 (A). Geneva: United Nations, 1951.

Vargas Muñoz, Francisco. *Agrarismo, campesinado y reforma agraria.* Caracas, Venezuela: Instituto Agrario Nacional, 1964.

Index of Persons

Index of Subjects

Acción Democrática (Venezuela): "exchange" with peasants, 84-92, 99; land reform and peasant movement, 72-77; peasant leader recruitment, 80-84; rise to power and peasants, 65-70

Agrarian reform, 36; Bolivia, 86-187, 204-205; Brazil, 383-386; Chile, 256; Guatemala, 338, 346; Mexico, 142-169; Peru, 313-314; Venezuela, 66-71, 76

Agricultural labor, see Hired labor, Labor services, and Peasants

Agricultural trade unions, 300-311, 316-321

Agriculture, state of and changes in, 23-28; Bolivia, 180-182; Brazil, 375-383; Chile, 247-251; Guatemala, 323, 333-338, 344-346; Mexico, 112-119; Peru, 282-283, 300-303; Venezuela, 63

Allegado (Peru), see Labor services, Peru

Allies, see Peasant movements, allies

American Federation of Labor, 60

APRA (Peru), 275, 285, 306-310

Arrendire (Peru), see Labor services, Peru

ASICH (Chile), 211-223, 227-247, 256, 261-265

Association of Guatemalan Agriculturalists (AGA), 339

Aymara (Bolivia): culture, 178-179, 184-186; history, 173-178

Banco Agrícola y Pecuária (Venezuela), see BAP

BAP (Venezuela), 71, 76, 86

Black Death, 26, 30

Bolivia, 1952 revolution, 173-176; see also MNR

Bolivian Labor Federation (COB), 193

Bolivian peasant movement (YPS): activities, 188-193; allies and enemies, 199-201; apolitical activities, 193; cooperatives, 191-193; credit unions, 193; economic power, 192; education, 191; goals, 187-188; ideology, 190; land claims, 187-189; leaders, 194-197; legal negotiations, 190-191; means, 186-194; MNR local officials, 197-198; organiza-

Bolivian peasant movement (*continued*) tion, 185-186; political participation, 188-190; suppression by military, 193; violence, 199

Bourgeoisie, see Middle class

Brazilian agriculture: *agreste*, 377-380; *mata*, 380-383; *sertão*, 375-377; see also Agriculture, state of and changes in

Brazilian Communist Party (PCB) and Communist Party of Brazil (PC do B), 374, 384-398; see also Communism and Communist parties

Brazilian peasant movement, 378-398; agitation, 392-394; agrarian reform, 385; alliances, 389-392; Church role in, 379, 385, 388, 393-395; Communist role in, 385-398; divisions in, 390-392; educational program, 392-394; goals, 379, 382-386; leaders, 57-58, 387-389; mass base of, 397-398; means of, 388-394; negotiations, 394-398; obstacles to, 399-450; organization, 388-389; radicalism in, 393; success and failure, 394-398; unification of, 395

Brokers, cultural and political: Bolivia, 195; Chile, 235; Venezuela, 71-79, 84-100

Cambão (Brazil), see Labor services, Brazil

Campesinos, see Peasants

Canadian peasant movement, 45

CCP (Peru), 314-317, 320

Central Unica de Trabajaderos (Chile), see CUT

Chaco War (Bolivia), 30, 45, 173

Chile: Catholicism in, 257-263; changing sociopolitical structure, 265-273; vineyard workers' movement, 210-273

Chilean peasant movement, 28, 43-44, 210-273; allies and enemies, 48, 218, 222-223, 263, 265, 269-272; character-building, 233-237; Church role in, 214, 216, 220-222, 227, 236-237, 257-263, 265-266, 270-272; collective bargaining, 228-235; decision-making, 244; decline of, 240-247; education, 235-237; establishment of, 225-229; finances, 241-242,

471